FROM SOCIOLOGY TO CULTURAL STUDIES

FROM SOCIOLOGY TO CULTURAL STUDIES
New Perspectives

Edited by
ELIZABETH LONG

Copyright © Blackwell Publishers Ltd 1997

First published 1997

2 4 6 8 10 9 7 5 3 1

Blackwell Publishers Inc.
350 Main Street
Malden, Massachusetts 02148
USA

Blackwell Publishers Ltd
108 Cowley Road
Oxford OX4 1JF
UK

Library of Congress Cataloging in Publication Data

From sociology to cultural studies: new perspective / edited by
    Elizabeth Long.
        p.   cm.
    Includes bibliographical references and index.
    ISBN 1–57718–012–7. — ISBN 1–57718–013–5
    1. Culture—Study and teaching.   2. Sociology.   I. Long,
Elizabeth, 1944–   .
HM101.F7737   1997
306'.07—dc21
                                                    97–556
                                                     CIP

British Library Cataloguing in Publication Data

A CIP catalogue record for this book is available from the
British Library.

Typeset in 11 on 13 pt ITC Garamond
by Graphicraft Typesetters Ltd, Hong Kong
Printed and bound in Great Britain by Hartnolls Limited, Bodmin, Cornwall

This book is printed on acid-free paper

Contents

Contributors

Jon D. Cruz is Assistant Professor of Sociology at the University of California, Santa Barbara. He is co-editor, with Justin Lewis, of *Viewing, Reading, Listening: Audiences and Cultural Reception* and author of *Culture on the Margins*.

Andrew Goodwin is Professor of Communication at the University of San Francisco. He is the author of *Dancing in the Distraction Factory: Music, Television and Popular Culture*, and he has co-edited a number of books on music and television, including *Sound and Vision*.

Herman Gray is Professor of Sociology at the University of California, Santa Cruz. He writes about media, popular culture, and black cultural politics. He is the author of *Watching Race: Television and the Struggle for Blackness* and *Producing Jazz*.

Sharon Hays is Assistant Professor of Sociology and Women's Studies at the University of Virginia. She is the author of *The Cultural Contradictions of Motherhood*, and she has published essays on issues of culture and power in *Sociological Theory* and *Media, Culture and Society*.

Richard Johnson is Professor of Cultural Studies at the University of Nottingham Trent, England. He taught social history at Birmingham University from 1966 to 1975, then was appointed to its Centre for Contemporary Cultural Studies, where he served as director from 1980 to 1987. He has published on the theory and pedagogy of cultural studies, popular and working-class cultures, historiography and popular memory, education and social identities. His current interests are in internationalizing cultural analysis, in theories of identity and in sexuality, schooling, and childhood. He has also published poetry and autobiographic commentary.

Michèle Lamont is Associate Professor of Sociology at Princeton University. A former chair of the Culture Section of the American Sociological Association, she is completing a book on racial and class communities in France and the United States with the support of fellowships from the Russell Sage Foundation and the John Simon Guggenheim Foundation. She is the author of *Money, Morals, and Manners: The Culture of the French and the American Upper-Middle Class*, and the co-editor of *Cultivating Differences: Symbolic Boundaries and the Making of Inequality*.

Magali Sarfatti Larson is Professor of Sociology at Temple University. She has worked on South America, on professions, on architecture and is now beginning comparative research on the political culture of "ordinary" citizens. Her most recent book is *Behind the Postmodern Facade: Architectural Change in Late Twentieth Century America*, which was co-winner of the Sociology of Culture Section Book Award in 1995.

Ron Lembo is Assistant Professor of Sociology in the Department of Anthropology and Sociology at Amherst College. He is the author of *Thinking Through Television: Viewing Practices and the Social Limits to Power*.

George Lipsitz is Professor of Ethnic Studies at the University of California, San Diego. Recent publications include *A Life in the Struggle* (1995), *Rainbow at Midnight* (1994), *Dangerous Crossroads* (1994), *The Sidewalks of St. Louis* (1991), and *Time Passages* (1990). His current research centers on the racialization of urban space in the US since the 1970s.

Elizabeth Long is Associate Professor of Sociology at Rice University. A former chair of the Culture Section of the American Sociological Association, she is author of *The American Dream and the Bestselling Novel* and is currently completing work on *Reading Together: Women's Reading Groups and the Making of America*.

George E. Marcus is Professor and Chair of the Department of Anthropology at Rice University. Currently he edits a series of annuals, published by the University of Chicago Press, entitled *Late Editions, Cultural Studies for the End of the Century*. Seven volumes of the series, lasting from 1993 until the year 2000, have been published and are in preparation.

Ellen Messer-Davidow, an Associate Professor at the University of Minnesota, teaches in the Departments of English, Cultural Studies, and Women's Studies. She is co-editor of *Knowledges: Historical and Critical Studies in Disciplinarity* and author of *Disciplining Feminism: Episodes in the Discursive Production of Social Change*.

Chandra Mukerji is Professor of Communication, Science Studies, and Sociology at the University of California, San Diego. She is co-author with

Michael Schudson of *Rethinking Popular Culture* and author of a book on territoriality in gardens and politics entitled *Territorial Ambitions and the Gardens of Versailles.*

Judith Newton is Professor and Director of Women's Studies at UC Davis. Her most recent book is *Starting Over: Feminism and the Politics of Cultural Critique.* She is currently working on the "crisis" in masculinity and the "Promise Keepers," the conservative Christian men's movement.

Tricia Rose is Assistant Professor of Africana Studies and History at New York University. She is the author of *Black Noise: Black Music and Culture in Contemporary America* and co-edited, with Andrew Ross, *Microphone Fiends: Youth Music and Culture in Contemporary America.* Her most recent work centers on black women and the politics of sexuality.

Michael Schudson is Professor of Communication and Adjunct Professor of Sociology at the University of California, San Diego. His works on journalism, politics, and popular culture include *Discovering the News, Advertising, the Uneasy Persuasion, Watergate in American Memory,* and *The Power of News.*

Steven Seidman is Professor of Sociology at the State University of New York at Albany. He is the author of *Contested Knowledge* and *Difference Troubles: Queering Social Theory and Sexual Politics.*

Judith Stacey is the Streisand Professor of Contemporary Gender Studies and Professor of Sociology at the University of Southern California. She is the author of *In the Name of the Family: Rethinking Family Values in the Postmodern Age* and *Brave New Families: Stories of Domestic Upheaval in Late Twentieth Century America,* and has also written widely on issues in feminist knowledge, research, and politics.

Angela Valenzuela is Assistant Professor of Sociology at Rice University. Her most recent published work has focused on extended family orientations and assimilation among Mexican-origin high school adolescents. She is currently completing a book-length manuscript based on her ethnographic study which investigates the assimilationist schooling of Mexican-origin youth attending an inner-city high school in Houston.

Janet Wolff is Professor of Art History/Visual and Cultural Studies at the University of Rochester. She is the author of several books on the sociology of art and on gender and culture, including *The Social Production of Art, Feminine Sentences: Essays on Women and Culture,* and *Resident Alien: Feminist Cultural Criticism.*

Preface

This is the second in a series of occasional volumes published by Blackwell Publishers on behalf of the Sociology of Culture Section of the American Sociological Association. It grew indirectly out of the Culture Section's Program at the 1992 Annual Meeting of the American Sociological Association, a program that I planned as Chair Elect of the Section, with the very able help of John Cruz, Herman Gray, Annette Lareau, Ron Lembo, and JoEllen Shiveley, members of that year's Program Committee. The program was substantively concerned with issues of cultural identity and social inequality, and, in part because these issues have interdisciplinary resonance, with the relationship between the sociology of culture and other branches, schools, or disciplinary traditions of cultural studies. These two concerns have continued to inform the resulting volume, just as the Sociology of Culture Section has continued to provide encouragement during its evolution as a book.

More than many such edited collections, this book represents a genuine conversation between reviewers, contributors, editor, and the broader scholarly community. I would like to thank participants on the American Sociological Association 1994 Panel on "Cultural Studies and Sociology" and the American Studies 1994 Panel entitled "Has American Studies Lost its Sense of Social Structure?" for their contributions to that conversation. I would particularly like to thank members of the Sociology of Culture's Publications Committee, especially Diana Crane, John Hall, and Richard Peterson for help with the editorial process. I am very grateful as well to James J. Dowd, Gary Alan Fine, Chad Gordon, Jonathan Holloway, Nel Noddings, Andrea Press, George Noblit, Barry Schwartz, Olga Vasquez, and Rob Walser for their thoughtful and perceptive reviews. In some cases, contributors also provided helpful comments on each others' work.

I would like to thank Simon Prosser for his enthusiasm about the project in its early stages at Blackwell, and Susan Rabinowitz for all her help in bringing the volume to fruition. A special word of gratitude to Jack Messenger, our copyeditor. Finally, I would like to express appreciation to the Sociology Department and to Rice University for providing funds for editorial expenses, as well as less material support. Thanks also to Diana Strassmann for her editorial and intellectual advice, to Rita Loucks for her masterful organizational skill, and to Joel Riphagen and Felisa Sanchez for helping with all manner of tasks during the editorial process. And for the kind of sustaining presence that makes all such endeavors worthwhile, my loving gratitude to my husband Bill Wallauer and my son David.

Introduction

Engaging Sociology and Cultural Studies: Disciplinarity and Social Change

ELIZABETH LONG

This volume is a contribution to the discussion about how to understand the relationship between culture and society that has so passionately engaged scholars across the humanities and social sciences in the latter decades of this century. The very categories at play here – culture and society – are conceptual expressions of the immense sociocultural changes we think of as "modernity."[1] Change also animates the renewal of interest in cultural/social questions that permeates not only the academy but also the much broader publics debating the nature of "The Western Tradition," multiculturalism and cultural relativism, affirmative action, objectivity and the nature of science, and the effects of commercialized popular culture. Disciplinary encounters between the sociology of culture and other branches of cultural analysis signal change on yet another register. One of the strengths of this volume is that its contributors have minimized territorial bickering and chosen, rather, to engage questions about both change and tradition in work that is complex and generous in spirit, that attends to root issues of responsibility in scholarship, and that is deeply concerned with the relationship between knowledge and democracy.

Sociology's Concerns with Culture

This introduction will discuss some aspects of the two fields in conversation here, while considering some of the issues raised in the volume. Given its more established disciplinary status, as well as what is often considered its marginality to questions of culture (which in the USA are commonly thought of as belonging to the humanities rather than to the social sciences), I shall begin with sociology.

Sociology has been centrally, if ambivalently, concerned with culture from the field's inception. Both responses seem conditioned by the context of sociology's formation in the crucible of "the great transformation" of modernity in the West (Polanyi, 1957). Culture has been crucial in accounting for social change, whether explaining the pull of tradition, or the emergence of new forms of social life and new registers of social experience. In particular, culture offered sociologists a way of discussing social differences with a depth and reach not enabled by models of monadic or rational action – whether such differences were construed as a cause of social problems or a sign of innovative forms of social identity or collective action. Marx's analyses of ideology, consciousness, and commodity fetishism, Weber's concern with the values of traditionalism and the gradual emergence of a more "rational" religious validation of this-worldly asceticism (the Protestant Ethic), and Durkheim's discussions of anomie and collective representations, register the attempts of early social thinkers to grasp various aspects of what we would call culture. These efforts were integral to their overarching project of conceptualizing "the social" as a level of analysis not exhausted by reference to the individual.

Yet culture, especially if defined as symbolic forms, has often seemed the special territory of analysts – whether social philosophers such as Hegel, or cultural historians such as Dilthey – with a commitment to philosophical idealism. In turn, this stance has tended to focus attention away from the more prosaic social or material conditions of life. And it is these conditions and forms of life that have drawn the fullest attention of sociologically oriented thinkers and researchers from Marx onward. Moreover, sociology has always had strong links to science – with its own strong connections to both social reform and social control. From the era of "protosociological" statisticians who gathered data about populations in the early nineteenth century, many social researchers have tended towards quantitative analysis of hard facts about a "world" understood to be well represented by those facts. So, as sociologists fought to establish special disciplinary claims to authority, they have most centrally dealt with culture as subsumed to social institutions (in the nineteenth century, religion most prominently), social processes, social groups and their practices, or social identities and their constitution. Individual cultural artifacts and their meaning or form have similarly garnered less attention from sociologists than the broader contexts of their creation, production, and valuation, or their reception and effects within a wider social world.[2]

The Chicago School and Early American Sociology

Nonetheless, American sociology had a profoundly cultural bent from the start. For example, when American sociology first gained full-fledged disciplinary status as a department at the University of Chicago, two of its framing texts devoted considerable attention to culture, establishing forms of sociocultural analysis that became the hallmarks of important traditions within the field. Both these books focused on urban life, and both were driven by the desire to understand what was changing in both the conditions and the meanings of people's lives. Culture figures mainly as part of their effort to understand both the attitudes and actions of social subjects, and the influences by which collectively held values were transmitted to groups and individuals as part of a "whole way of life."[3]

Least read today, in part because of its length, is W. I. Thomas and Florian Znaniecki's *The Polish Peasant in Europe and America*, published in five volumes between 1918 and 1920. The authors were convinced that understanding social life meant concentrating on social change, and also that the usual lay devices of "ordering and forbidding," or even commonsense or "practical sociology," could give only inadequate control over social change and its attendant social problems. So, they assembled a voluminous and varied set of documents, analyzing them as representing the processes of "social disorganization" and "reorganization" both in Poland and among Polish immigrants in America. Drawing on newspapers, life histories, parish reports, autobiographies, numerous sets of letters, documents from immigrant associations, and case studies from various organizations dealing with economic, familial, and legal problems of immigrants and their children, they attempted to capture the subjective dimension of social change. In over 2,000 pages, they showed the bonds of tradition loosening and – often with great individual and social turmoil – new attitudes and practices (individualism, hedonism, and success seeking, for example) supplanting established ways. In so doing, they gave a remarkably rich and textured portrait of ordinary people in milieux from peasant villages in Poland to the schools and sweatshops, dance halls and juvenile courts of the new world. This massive work only sold 3,000 copies in the first forty years after its publication (Madge, 1962: 52), but it has been remarkably influential. It began a debate about the use of "personal documents" that has continued to inform discussions about the place of qualitative methods and textual analysis in social research. It also presented, in the idea that people act not only in response to objective conditions and pre-existing collectively held values, but also according to their "definition of the situation," one of the first American formulations of meaning-oriented or interpretive sociology (see Volkart, 1951, for Thomas's more theoretical work).

Three years before the initial volume of *The Polish Peasant* went to press, Robert Park's programmatic essay "The City: Suggestions for the Investigation of Human Behavior in the Urban Environment" laid the foundation for a many-faceted investigation of cities as "a laboratory or clinic" of human nature and social processes (Park, 1969 [1915]). Despite this scientific frame, Park's program was built upon a profoundly cultural understanding of the nature of urban life. As he says at the beginning of the essay:

> The city, from the point of view of this paper, is something more than a congeries of individual men and of social conveniences – streets, buildings, electric lights, tramways, and telephones, etc.; something more, also, than a mere constellation of institutions and administrative devices – courts, hospitals, schools, police, and civil functionaries of various sorts. The city is, rather, a state of mind, a body of customs and traditions, and of the organized attitudes and sentiments that inhere in these customs and are transmitted with this tradition. . . . The city has . . . its own culture. (Park, 1969 [1915]: 91)

Park's vision was the inspiration for a department-wide program of researching the neighborhoods, ethnic enclaves, occupational types, and "eccentric and exceptional people" who he felt were a natural part of the ecology of cities. Park had earlier worked as a journalist, so he highlighted the newspaper and other forms of communication such as the radio as critical components in constructing what he and other Chicago School sociologists referred to as the "moral order" of the city and discrete groups within it. His background may have also contributed to his concentration on direct observation as a methodology. He urged his students to:

> Go and sit in the lounges of the luxury hotels and on the doorsteps of the flophouses; sit on the Gold Coast settees and on the slum shakedowns; sit in the Orchestra Hall and in the Star and Garter Burlesk. In short, gentlemen, go get the seats of your pants dirty in real research.

So successful were Park and his colleague Ernest Burgess in implementing their program that dissertations and class papers from their students have remained an important resource for social historians investigating radio listening, musical taste, and consumption patterns in early twentieth-century Chicago (Cohen, 1990: 100–58).

More generally, Chicago School sociologists elaborated several specialties or "genres" within sociology – the study of subcultures and ethnic neighborhoods, of deviant groups and individuals, of socialization into occupations or powerfully marked social statuses (e.g. Becker's 1953 article "Becoming a Marijuana User"), and of "colorful" urban locales or institutions such as hobohemia or the taxi-dance hall – that elicited consideration of cultural differences, if not outright peculiarities (Anderson, 1923; Cressey, 1969 [1932]). Drawing on the theoretical insights of George Herbert Mead and Charles Horton Cooley, as well as those of W. I. Thomas, about the interactively constituted nature of the self and social identities, such work has become known as the school of symbolic interactionism.

Links and Disjunctions Between Early Sociology and Cultural Studies

Whether labeled "the Chicago School" or symbolic interactionism, the influence of this branch of sociology waned after World War II, when European social thought and more rigorous methodology permeated the discipline, but it has continued to stand as a minority tradition in the field. Its emphasis on the complexities of the social construction of identity, on everyday life, on small groups – and their meaning-making and cultural innovation – as well as on culturally and linguistically sensitive field research, shows clear affinities to aspects of work in cultural studies.[4] Indeed, early cultural studies work on subcultures at Birmingham references American work (mainly in the fields of delinquency and deviance) in this school (Hall and Jefferson, 1976).

It is worth pausing here for a moment to consider the ways culture figured in the Chicago School tradition, since its influence has remained important to later students of culture within sociology. Also some of its scholarly hallmarks, such as attention to everyday experience and the importance of meaning, are shared by much contemporary sociological work on culture, even that arising from quite different theoretical and methodological orientations.

To begin with, many early sociologists saw themselves as doing something very similar to anthropologists in their concentration on the entire spectrum of lifeways, customs, and mores of a social group. Park expressed this very clearly, differentiating his work from those of anthropological contemporaries like Boaz only in terms of the object of study. He wanted to see the "patient methods of observation" of the anthropologist brought to bear, not on primitive societies, but on

> the customs, beliefs, social practices and general conception of life pre-valent in Little Italy on the lower North Side in Chicago, or . . . the more sophisticated folkways of the inhabitants of Greenwich Village and the neighborhood of Washington Square, New York. . . . Urban life and culture are more varied, subtle, and complicated, but the fundamental motives are in both instances the same. (Park, 1969 [1915]: 92–3)

This understanding of their work was shared by other prominent early sociologists. For example, when the Lynds' involvement with Christian social reformist foundations brought them the funding to study the religion of a small midwestern city, they rapidly concluded that this required an investigation of "Middletown's" entire range of social institutions and practices. This insight sent them to other social researchers, including anthropologist Clark Wissler, from whom they borrowed the idea that "Whether in an Arunta village in Central Australia or in our own seemingly intricate institutional life . . . human behavior appears to consist in variations upon a few major lines of activity" (Lynd and Lynd, 1929: 4). From this assumption they generated a list of six "main-trunk" human activities that served as the organizational skeleton of their book, from "Getting a Living," to "Using Leisure" and "Engaging in Religious Practices."

Somewhat later, when William F. Whyte earned a grant from Harvard's Society of Fellows to study the slums of Boston's North End, he also turned to anthropologists (among other social researchers) to guide the small-scale participant-observation study of young Italian men that was published in 1943 as *Street Corner Society*. In his words, "I began reading in the social anthropological literature, beginning with Malinowski, and this seemed closer to what I wanted to do even though the researchers were studying primitive tribes and I was in the middle of a great city district" (Whyte, 1993 [1943]: 286).

This kind of perspective had several effects for the study of culture in the works it informed. For instance, the ethnographic, or as it is more commonly known in sociology, the "field work" or "participant observation" method, has often been coupled with a desire to "give voice to the voiceless" in contemporary society. This is quite clear in works like *Street Corner Society*, Elliot Liebow's *Tally's Corner* (1967), or Kai Erikson's *Everything in its Path* (1976). The politics of this stance may be self-contradictory, romantic, pious, or fraught with the reinscription of the scholar's privilege (as is debated in Appendix B and the last pages of Appendix A in *Street Corner Society*'s most recent edition, pp. 359–89), but an appreciation of the politics of knowledge and the social responsibility of the researcher is alive – and often quite self-consciously so – in this tradition.

Other qualities of this approach, however, can work against its political or critical concerns. For instance, although early sociologists accepted, even reveled in, the social differentiation (between ethnic groups, for instance, or occupational "types") that made modern cities unlike small-scale societies, they tended to approach each group or locale they studied as an entity that could be encompassed holistically. This was conditioned in part by a research method geared to ground-level, face-to-face interaction and the study of everyday life. Such researchers were often aware of differences between a particular social sub-group under study and others that were part of the larger-scale environment (Park, for instance, counterposes the Gold Coast and the slum), and sometimes they were aware of obvious cleavages within the group under investigation. The Lynds, for example, divided Middletown into business class and working class; Whyte recognized a division between "corner boys" and "college boys."

But perhaps because of the small-scale focus on the interactional order, less immediately visible forms of power or domination tend not to register in these works. *Middletown*, for instance, does not really deal with either the very poor or the very rich in Muncie, Indiana. The Lynds also explicitly excluded African-Americans from the study, and their research strategy left out other, presumably "marginal" people, such as divorced or childless families and working mothers, thus contributing to, rather than undermining, the dominant normative order. And, taken as a whole, the Chicago School monographs tend to depict a world composed of almost exotic and relatively bounded enclaves and social types. They also tend *not* to deal with issues such as class or institutional forces of domination which could, in other perspectives, be understood as ordering and conditioning life among and between the neighborhoods Park's students studied in such loving detail.[5]

This goes against the grain of much cultural studies work that sees power saturating everything, and often moves very quickly between large registers of social hierarchy (race, class, gender) and the inmost regions of identity. Yet in privileging an interactional order that includes much of import that is not *directly* about power – including voice, differentiation, and social solidarity – the American sociological tradition may also have much to offer cultural studies.

Concentrating on culture as a "whole way of life" of a given group or community also tended to entail its analysis as lived practices or process, rather than as discrete symbolic forms. Certain of the institutions of mass culture (for Park, most prominently the newspaper) as well as institutions whose concerns lay explicitly in the realm of values and beliefs (such as religion) did become part of the domain of sociological study – because of their obvious reach into the lives sociologists were studying, their clear relationship to collective action. But it was precisely the interrelationships between cultural institutions and people's lived experience, especially particular forms of sociality and social action, that sociologists were trying to understand. Thus, the Lynds looked at book clubs as one aspect of business-class women's social distinction, at cars, movies, and other forms of mass leisure in the 1920s as they changed how adolescents lived and thought, and at the complex relationship between religion and optimistic American individualism. Beginning with the "everyday" experience of people can bring cultural processes into focus, and resembles cultural studies' ideal of examining "culture as practice," but it can also remove from notice those cultural forms and processes that are less public, less institutionalized, or less popular than religion, radio, or movies. Or, in the hands of sociologists who are not already sensitive to culture, the turn to "everyday life" can lead to analyses of social practices that downplay their cultural dimension.

Nonetheless, a focus on culture as seen through the prism of everyday life has led to what Mukerji and Schudson call the "leveling" attitude in the sociological study of culture. As they point out, sociologists have from the field's beginning been unembarrassedly interested in popular culture, and have similarly been concerned less with judging the "inherent" value of cultural products or forms than with understanding how they become socially valued or disvalued, by whom and for what purposes, and with what social consequences (Mukerji and Schudson, 1991: 26–37). This orientation towards cultural hierarchies has been carried forward in the work of contemporary sociologists who are more concerned with explicitly artistic institutions and processes (e.g. Becker, 1982; DiMaggio, 1982; Gans, 1974; Lang and Lang, 1990; Long, 1985, 1992; Peterson, 1976, 1994; Tuchman, 1989), or who, like Bourdieu (e.g. 1984), or Lamont or Hays in this volume, are interested in exploring the connections between culture and various aspects of social stratification. Such relativism, perhaps even more than their accompanying desire to study culture for "extrinsic" rather than "intrinsic" reasons, has set sociologists at odds with cultural scholars in the humanities whose work is oriented towards elucidating, defending, and disseminating or preserving high cultural traditions. Yet it may, again, resonate with the anti-canonical bent of much recent cultural studies work.

One could argue in general that the American social-theoretical response to industrialization and urbanization – of which the Chicago School was the dominant exemplar – focused less on the level of large social structures, and more on human agency, than was the case among European social thinkers. This might help to explain the marked shift in the discipline's understanding of culture that occurred in the 1930s and 1940s, when European social thought became more prominent in America – either by way of "translation" and codification, with such books as Talcott Parsons' synthetic *The Structure of Social Action* (1937), or more directly, by way of a generation of immigrant intellectuals. Most influential for the resurgence of interest in both culture and social conflict in the 1960s were scholars associated with or influenced by the Frankfurt Institute of Social Research, but this cohort also included culturally oriented thinkers like Alfred Schutz, Norbert Elias, and Paul Lazarsfeld. The view from Europe tended to comprehend culture both more historically and more structurally – as a pre-existing ontological system (Hartmann, n.d.) and often as a constraint – than did early American sociology.

Whatever its intellectual sources, the view from Europe also accorded very well with a period that seemed, even to Americans, to be in the grip of the constraining or darker aspects of social forces. The Depression sent the Lynds back to Muncie, and the book resulting from that research, *Middletown in Transition* (1937), was much more sensitive to power, conflict, and social inequality.[6] The rise of totalitarianism, World War II, and the importance to both of cultural manipulation, in particular through the mass media, also engendered social scientific concerns not only about the content of mass or popular culture, but also about the intrapsychic sources of people's vulnerability to its suasions.

Ironically, these concerns were not allayed during the period of prosperity and relative social consensus after the war. Many academics feared the unsettling effects of those developments as well. Scholars worried that America had lost its work ethic to the blandishments of a pervasive culture of consumerism, and its commitment to individualism under the onslaught of a massified culture of conformity (Long, 1985). From these concerns came the postwar debate about mass culture and its social effects that engaged scholars in sociology, literature, and communication, and the studies of conformity and authoritarianism that preoccupied many social psychologists for almost a generation (Adorno et al., 1950; Bramson, 1961; Jacobs, 1961; Milgram, 1975; Mukerji and Schudson, 1991: 58, n. 54; Rosenberg and White, 1957, 1971). Yet, paradoxically, this same period saw a marginalization of culture within the disciplinary mainstream of sociology. In part, this had to do with increased specialization and concerns with methodological rigor within the field.

Marginalization of Culture in Mid-century Sociology

Early in the century, American sociologists worked to separate their field from moral or social philosophy and the other branches of social science within the university. At the borders of the academy and beyond, sociologists tended to contrast their efforts with those of social reformers or social workers by invoking special claims to expertise (see the discussion of the Chicago School above), often cast in the name of science. Yet at that time sociology was small (there were less than 1,000 members of the main professional association until 1918) and often precariously situated institutionally. The field was also much less specialized, both internally and at its boundaries, than it is today.[7] Sociologists often did not work in separate departments; joint departments with anthropology were especially common. Moreover, sociologists routinely looked beyond the university (ironically, often to that same broad group of middle-class reformers they were separating themselves from) in search of a nonacademic "public" that could serve as an audience for sociological work and a constituency that would support their endeavors. The model was that of what Buxton and Turner call "edification." Concerns about culture, as part of the social order and its attendant problems, fit easily into several important modes of sociological expression of that period, including journalism and books directed to popular audiences (Buxton and Turner, 1992: 374–6).

During the 1930s, 1940s, and 1950s, the growth of the research university, and of funding sources for the social sciences – mostly private foundations in the interwar years and increasingly the government after World War II – attenuated the relationship of sociology to the general public. More and more, sociologists garnered research funding through a process of review by their professional peers, and wrote for a much narrower audience of professional sociologists, citing work in other fields less and less (Buxton and Turner, 1992: 379–90; Calhoun, 1992b: 143–6; Turner and Turner, 1990: 39–132). Legitimizing the field by claims to "realism" during the period of generous Rockefeller support (1920s into the 1930s), and social control through science later on, practitioners elaborated highly technical quantitative methods and theoretical schemata that were almost as impenetrable to lay readers (Turner and Turner, 1990: 42–8; Wuthnow, 1987: 5).

Culture fared poorly in this climate. Talcott Parsons, a dominant figure in the postwar redefinition of the field and one of the most culturally sensitive, assigned culture to a transcendent place in the structural-functionalist theoretical account that divided human action into the realms of culture, society, and personality. But he effectively removed it from the purviews of the discipline in so doing. True, he himself wrote remarkably trenchant essays about aspects of modern culture, as did fellow structural-functionalist Robert Merton at Columbia. Parsons also institutionalized disciplinary cooperation between anthropologists, sociologists, and psychologists at Harvard's Social Relations Department, helping to form students such as Robert Bellah and Clifford Geertz who later had tremendous influence on the study of culture. Further, the almost baroque complexity of the Parsonian system meant that more modest empirical investigators could insert what were essentially cultural concerns somewhere within its machinery. But Parsons, in cooperation with Samuel Stouffer, and Merton, in relationship with Paul Lazarsfeld, also worked to further survey data collection and analysis that included culture mainly under the rubric of individually held "attitudes." And many sociologists who were not structural-functionalists shared the desire to scientize sociology along similar lines (Buxton and Turner, 1992: 391–9; Calhoun, 1989: 3–5; 1992b: 154–6). Culture thereby either assumed the uneasy position of the most independent and overarching of all variables, or became subjectivized, appearing indirectly within the field of dependent attitudinal variables. This methodological-cum-conceptual apparatus – coupled as it often was with an assumption of American consensus and with relatively formalized and ahistorical modes of analysis – worked quite well to distance culture (especially what Crane (1994) calls "explicit" or "recorded" culture) from sociology, except where it figured in institutional analysis. Religion and mass communication were the most prominent examples of culture-relevant sub-fields, and both stood somewhat apart from the postwar disciplinary core.

Given this history, it makes sense that some of the most compelling postwar sociological discussions of culture have fallen under the rubric of social criticism rather than "pure" or "straight" sociology. Books like David Riesman et al.'s *The Lonely Crowd* (1952), Daniel Bell's *The Cultural Contradictions of Capitalism* (1976), Philip Slater's *The Pursuit of Loneliness* (1970), and Robert Bellah et al.'s *Habits of the Heart* (1985), as well as much of C. Wright Mills' *White Collar* (1951) and *The Power Elite* (1956) all go against the grain of disciplinary specialization and the accompanying stance of value-neutral positivism. Instead, they hark back to the field's earlier explicit concerns with the "moral order" as well as social structure, call American individualism sharply in question, address society and culture holistically (sometimes with the difficulties mentioned above), and direct their arguments to a broad public.

Recent History in the Sociology of Culture

The fragile postwar unity of American sociology as a discipline (fragile because it never achieved the theoretical and methodological consensus of fields like economics) began to fracture during the 1960s, along with the unraveling of the equally fragile American consensus of the early cold war. Sociologists who had predicted a relatively smooth assimilation of racial and ethnic minorities or "the end of ideology" confronted the resurgence of movements demanding social change on many fronts. Race relations, poverty, the Vietnam War, gender, and the environment all surfaced as urgent social problems at the same time that the generational divide itself became a matter of social and cultural conflict. All these factors led to a rapid expansion of the field. The baby boomers arrived in college. Their numerical weight contributed to the postwar, post-Sputnik expansion of higher education that was also driven by an economy increasingly dependent on the link between consumption and sophisticated technology. Unprecedented numbers of undergraduate students – some from minority groups hitherto underrepresented in the discipline, some with agendas shaped by student activism – turned to sociology as a means of understanding a social order that many perceived to be in crisis. That same perception, refracted through the federal government, led to large infusions of government funding as well (Turner and Turner, 1990: 133–57).

Questions about social difference, social conflict, and social change demanded a consideration of both history and culture in ways that unsettled mainstream theory and methods geared to relatively static or universalizing models of social analysis. This opened the door in sociology to theoretical dissension, and the increasing appeal of theories that stressed social conflict and cultural differences. Similarly, the failure of the interventionist social programs of the 1960s and 1970s to solve society's problems seemed to demonstrate the inability of sociologists to fulfill their promise that expert knowledge would bring "control," thus calling the ideals of sociology as a positive science into question.

In the wake of that era, culturally oriented sociology has burgeoned, most commonly among sociologists who see themselves doing "interpretive sociology" rather than science. Cultural sociology has emerged as one of the most prominent sub-fields among many substantive and methodological "sections" of an increasingly fractured discipline, but a sub-field that is, more than many, strongly linked both to many other sub-fields, and to those concerned with social thought in general. The attraction of sociologists to culture signals several developments within the discipline. First, it signals a recognition of the contemporary social importance of both high and mass or popular culture, especially in relation to consumerism, to social identity from the level of the individual to that of the nation and beyond, and to larger processes of social domination and change. Second, it highlights an understanding that almost every substantive field within sociology, from gender and ethnicity to science and the state, must engage culture in order to understand those aspects of the social world that are its particular territory. Third, it demonstrates a desire to find some conceptual rubric that can serve to unify the field, or to permit expression of broad concerns about contemporary society – a yearning, perhaps, for the kind of holism earlier and more culturally informed studies of society unselfconsciously displayed. Fourth, it engages a theoretical imperative to relate subjectivity and social action to structure without impoverishing any of these terms conceptually. Culture certainly plays an important part in thinking through such issues among synthetically inclined theorists as different as Alexander (1989, 1995), Bourdieu (1977, 1984, 1990, 1991), Chodorow (1978), Giddens (1984, 1991, 1992, 1995), Habermas (1971, 1979, 1984–7, 1989), and Smith (1987, 1990a, 1990b). Fifth, the attitude of sociologists towards culture is evidence of a wish to incorporate some of the extra-disciplinary work on culture and society that has proven so useful to sociologists working the ever-more slippery boundaries of their discipline, and so exciting to graduate and undergraduate students in sociology (see, for example, Hall and Neitz, 1993).

The sociology of culture, then, includes a whole constellation of concerns that range from mass, popular, and high culture (especially in relation to their production, evaluation, and reception), the sociology of knowledge (including expert knowledge and science), cultural hegemony, cultural capital, and cultural boundaries (especially in relation to social stratification), and political culture, to questions about the logic of cultural systems, the relative autonomy of culture, and the relationship of culture to everyday interaction. For an excellent overview of the theoretical perspectives at play in the field, see Crane, 1994. As even this partial accounting shows, it is a rich tradition, and one that has had considerable influence beyond its disciplinary boundaries.

This is the recent history that has shaped sociological inquiry about culture into the present, bringing culturally oriented sociologists into engagement with scholars from that interdisciplinary field or movement called cultural studies. So, to raise in a rather different context the question asked over a decade ago by Richard Johnson (who addresses it again in this volume), one might ask, "What is cultural studies anyway?" (Johnson, 1995 [1983]). The next sections will outline different levels of response to this question, highlighting those aspects of cultural studies I think are particularly challenging or useful not simply for sociologists, but for others involved in sociocultural inquiry.

Academic and Political Position of Cultural Studies

First, whatever it is in terms of theory, methods, analytic domain, or objects of study, cultural studies in the United States is also a set of institutional arrangements within higher education. True, the strand of cultural studies that developed at Birmingham originated in the strongly labor-influenced adult education movement in Britain. Moreover, British scholars identified with cultural studies have often worked either in what remains of the adult education and Open Education movements or in various wings of the culture industry in Britain. But America has no alternative education movement cognate with that in Britain, so here cultural studies has developed within established academic institutions. (For insights about Birmingham in relation to American cultural studies, see especially Goodwin and Wolff, Johnson, and Seidman, but also Lembo, Mukerji, and Schudson in this volume.) Americans identified with cultural studies have also occasionally achieved the status of "public intellectuals," but those circuits are less well-developed than, for instance, is the case in France. And, despite the publicity garnered for cultural studies by its most famous practitioners, its status within the university is usually relatively precarious. Cultural studies is generally organized as an interdisciplinary program or center, sometimes as a wing of an existing academic department, and almost always on the edge, both materially and ideologically, of whatever its environing institution defines as central.

This institutional configuration has several consequences. One worth mentioning at the outset is that at any one location, how cultural studies has been institutionalized, and how its neighboring fields are represented, conditions the very possibility of engagement – along the lines of this volume – with the more established disciplines. The vicissitudes of institutionalization may have profounder effects as well. For instance, its integration as a strictly *academic* endeavor in the United States may be reshaping cultural studies as another narrow specialty, detaching it from the broader realm of political relevance and social responsibility. Conversely, the institutional insecurity of cultural studies in the United States may deflect energy towards a politics of survival in a way that impoverishes discussion about the cultural and political issues that were generative of cultural studies as an endeavor in the first place.[8]

Indeed, one of the other levels at which it is possible to define cultural studies has to do with politics. This has meant very different things for the various traditions of scholarship (and activism) making up cultural studies. It continues to be a vexed question for cultural studies in the United States, given the current state of American formal politics, of the collectivities striving for political voice, of the politics of higher education, and of the links and interrelationships among them (in this volume, see especially Messer-Davidow, also Goodwin and Wolff, Gray, Lipsitz, Marcus, Newton and Stacey, Schudson). Overall, however, cultural studies has been identified with progressive or leftist politics, and its theoretical approaches and substantive concerns are conditioned by this identification.

In particular, cultural studies has been in large part a theoretically informed, empirically engaged *critical* commentary on contemporary social and cultural life. Minimally, that means, as Calhoun says in a different context, that cultural studies seeks an "engagement with the social world that starts from the presumption that existing arrangements do not exhaust the range of possibilities. It seeks to explore the ways in which our categories of thought reduce our freedom by occluding recognition of what could be" (Calhoun, 1995: xiv). The tradition of critique in Western philosophy has historical roots almost as deep as that tradition itself. Cultural studies generally draws on its modern or Enlightenment manifestations, either positively – Marx or critical European neo-marxisms often providing authorization – or negatively, as in poststructuralist critiques of humanism and the philosophy of the subject.

This critical tradition demands that thinkers examine – historically, culturally, analytically, and in dialogue with other thinkers – the regnant frameworks, categories, and assumptions about the world. This necessarily includes a critical appraisal of the methods used to grasp that "world" (to gather information or insight, to represent it textually), because of an understanding that both theories and methods are constitutive of the very world we take for granted as a ground for investigation. The "world" to be critically understood also usually includes the sources and conditions of the thinker's own formation and intellectual project. This kind of thoroughgoing reflexivity can be profoundly unsettling to social scientists with a more empiricist or positivist tenor of mind. Especially under conditions of academic isolation, it can lead to a corrosive narcissism or self-doubt, or to a reassertion of universalizing certainty in the guise of its dismantling.

It is worth pointing out that much of sociology has also been motivated by a critical impulse, and that many of its contributions to social knowledge (I think here less of specific findings than of what used to be called "the sociological perspective") resonate, though not always in total harmony, with those of cultural studies. Sociology, for example, has explored the social construction of identity at the psychological, interactional, and institutional levels, and sociologists working in several disciplinary traditions have also shown the ways in which knowledge, including categories of perception, definitions of normalcy, and processes of valuation or hierarchization, is itself socially constituted. (In this volume, see Cruz, Gray, Hays, Lamont, Larson, Lembo, Schudson, and Valenzuela, and, for a discussion of some limitations of sociology, Seidman).

Critical social analysis has also had a long and honorable history outside the scholarly traditions of the academy, expressing – often in forms less scholarly, more "cultural," religious, or utopian – the vantage point of groups denied authoritative voice within systems of domination that truncate their lives in other ways (see Lipsitz in this volume). Perhaps more than has been the case in sociology, important traditions within cultural studies – such as the Birmingham school – have maintained the Marxist idea that a critical knowledge of society and culture must emerge from conversation with such groups so that critique can be integrally engaged with social activism and progressive social change. (See Johnson, this volume, for an appraisal of how Birmingham fared in this project.) Other cultural studies traditions, such as postcolonial discourse, feminism, or queer theory, speak for and about (thus "representing" on several different levels) people who have been underrepresented or misrepresented in mainstream scholarship, sometimes even pre-existing cultural studies orthodoxies. (See Newton and Stacey, and Rose in this volume.)

Cultural studies has in general been more willing than sociology, with its strongly universalizing bent, to grant that knowledge may be inherently perspectival – or to put it differently, may be both limited and enabled by the knower's historical, cultural, and social access to the world, including the world of intellectual traditions – and more eager to explore the links between knowledge and social domination. This urges opening the community of scholars to groups of people who have not had access to it, whether as those who frame the agenda or shape the questions, who produce the scholarship, or to whom, as an audience, the scholarship is directed. Cultural studies has been invigorated by such engagement, however limited. And, like the question of institutionalization, this issue seems crucial to consider in relation to its future prospects as a critical endeavor.

Specifying the Nature and Basis of the "Field" of Cultural Studies

Here it is tempting to characterize cultural studies in one of the established modalities by which intellectual fields are usually classified. One might look, for example, at its objects of study, and claim that cultural studies is "about" popular culture, or "about" the interrelations of race, class, gender, and sexuality. Or one might cite methodologies – such as ethnographically inspired field studies, or the self-reflective essay – that seem especially characteristic of cultural studies scholarship. Or – and this is probably the most common genre – one might map out the traditions at play in the field by constructing genealogies of each tradition's most influential thinkers and the problematics they address. But the development of American cultural studies work shows a complex interchange of disciplinary currents. For example, the critical tradition in cultural anthropology that incorporated insights from poststructuralists about power and positionality to query voice, textual strategies, and audiences in relation to ethnography, has been taken up by scholars from the humanities to authorize ethnographic-like studies of the world outside of texts. Sometimes scholars come to define themselves as "doing cultural studies" only after they have produced work that others see as exemplary cultural studies scholarship. By now the label of "cultural studies" is extremely plastic in the United States. Taking on the perhaps impossible task of defining cultural studies, Nelson, Treichler, and Grossberg proceed thus:

> One may begin by saying that cultural studies is an interdisciplinary, trans-disciplinary, and sometimes counter-disciplinary field that operates in the tension between its tendencies to embrace both a broad, anthropological and a more narrowly humanistic conception of culture. Unlike traditional anthropology, however, it has grown out of analyses of modern industrial societies. It is typically interpretive and evaluative in its methodologies, but unlike traditional humanism it rejects the exclusive equation of culture with high culture and argues that all forms of cultural production need to be studied in relation to other cultural practices and to social and historical structures. Cultural studies is thus committed to the study of the entire

range of a society's arts, beliefs, institutions, and communicative practices. (Grossberg, Nelson, and Treichler, 1992: 4)

Now, cultural studies is clearly both more (if that is possible) and less than this. In fact, Grossberg, Nelson, and Treichler continue their introduction by specifying what they mean – invoking politics, history, the question of intervention and the role of the intellectual, contingency and context in the deployment of theory, etc. But one of the difficulties they, and anyone else attempting a map of cultural studies in the United States, face is that – absent disciplinary policing – cultural studies can and does mean quite different things to different people.

Cultural Studies as a Response to Social Change

Rather than look to objects of study, methods of inquiry, or disciplinary currents, this section will argue (keeping questions about politics and institutionalization in mind) that cultural studies has emerged, with all its complexities and self-contradictions, because of large shifts in the social world that have changed many people's lives. These same social changes, refracted through the academy, have made many scholars – perhaps especially those somewhat on the edges of traditional academic commun- ities, disciplines, or careers – feel quite keenly the distance between their own disciplinary traditions and what seems in need of understanding. A gap always exists between what academics read and the lives they lead or the knowledge they gain outside of books. But at some points in time this gap widens or deepens to such a degree that scholars not only mine their own disciplinary traditions for new directions (see Calhoun, 1995; Lemert, 1995; and Seidman, 1994, in recent sociology) but reach beyond their disciplines for other traditions, other conceptual frames, other ways of gaining knowledge about the world.

The emergence of sociology and the other social sciences, as well as modern forms of national literary studies, provides examples of how new knowledge crystallized along with the multifarious social and cultural changes we call modernity.[9] Standing as we all do in the flux of the present, it is hard to judge how momentous the current upheavals that are registered in contemporary scholarship will prove to have been from some distant future retrospect – whether, for example, we are at the dawn of a new era in global history as some have claimed, or even whether we have adequately comprehended the most far-reaching social shifts of our time. On a more basic level, it is equally hard to know how cultural studies will develop institutionally or what lines of inquiry will prove most fruitful for the cultural studies project of putting knowledge in the service of a more fully realized democracy. What may be possible, however, is to look backwards and outwards from the present moment to see some of what it is about the changing world that people have been trying to understand when they do cultural studies work.

Here I would point first to a constellation of concerns about the new ways social domination operated in a postwar world that was (at least for many in the West) both relatively affluent and at peace. By this time, as well, communism had lost economic, social, and moral legitimacy as an alternative to Western corporate and democratic capitalism. Culture seemed especially important under these conditions, as it had earlier for members of the Frankfurt School who were trying to understand the rise and popularity of Fascism in Germany, in part because economic determinism had not generated a kind of automatic class-based movement of resistance and social transformation, as various traditions rooted in Marxism had predicted. Althusser's theoretical discussion of overdetermination and the relative autonomy of culture can be seen as one – quite limited – attempt to open up Marxism to a more thorough understanding of culture's role in such conditions (Althusser, 1969: 104–20), and other cultural studies thinkers (notably at Birmingham) plucked these ideas out of the terminological thickets of his opus for a similar purpose.

Postwar shifts in the social organization of cultural and communications media also gave popular forms of culture immense social power. This was particularly true of cultural forms and technology developing in and exported from the United States, which was becoming a global force because of television, Coca-Cola, rock and roll, and blue jeans – and later, MTV, the shopping mall, music videos, and theme parks – as well as more traditional forms of economic and military power. This shift, too, required new ways of thinking – ways of thinking that linked culture (as it was linked in the world) more closely to society and politics, especially in relation to critical questions about democracy and equality.

On the one hand, it was clear that culture had become an industry, and one that had close links to other industries harnessing culture in the service of generating consumer demands for mass-marketed commodities and a thoroughly materialistically inflected way of life. Decades before the "culture wars" of the 1990s, culture was also a linchpin of the cold war. Intellectuals in the United States – among them sociologists of communication and countercultural activists of the 1960s – turned to the Frankfurt School to illuminate this aspect of sociocultural reality, including (and here Marcuse was particularly important) the ways in which deep intrapsychic structures played into this process of engineering both needs and consent (Adorno, 1991; Marcuse, 1966, 1974). Others, among them Richard Hoggart in Britain, noted with a sharp sense of loss the ways that American consumer culture broke down traditional working-class communities and cultures, and the sources they might provide for an alternative, and more fully egalitarian, social reality (Hoggart, 1992 [1959]).

The investigation of "mythologies" of popular culture, and other ways language or language-like cultural forms encoded social domination, by structuralist semioticians like Roland Barthes, for example, in France, can be understood as another connected contribution in these terms. It made sense that French scholars would turn to language in their attempts to analyze how culture worked in a changing world. For one thing, they had the tradition of Saussurian linguistics – which analyzed language as a longstanding collective system of arbitrary (thus possibly culturally dependent) discriminations that generated categories for grasping the world. For another, language was a politically sensitive force in France. French elites had identified linguistic culture as the "civilizing" agent justifying colonialism and had institutionalized central policing of language as national culture. So Barthes, for example, analyzed the whole cultural world as – like language itself – a historically sedimented collective system of meanings that retained the traces of prior social relations, and had the capacity in the present to structure people's categories of thinking and thereby obscure or naturalize power (Barthes, 1990 [1972]).

But, on the other hand, even commercialized popular culture also appeared as a democratizing force. To secure mass markets, industries of popular culture had to respond in some fashion, however attenuated or convoluted, to popular desires. Mass media also carried forward, even in transformation, older and more traditional popular cultural forms, and incorporated (again, thanks to the logic of the market) emerging popular voices and visions. Both, at times, challenged the status quo, though usually not in politically "correct" or even explicitly political ways. And, whether because of its sheer economic weight, or because its beat, drive, and utopian desires seduced even the children of the managerial suburbs, commercial popular culture in postwar America unsettled the already-fragile "traditional" cultural hierarchy. So people began to think about culture as an arena for struggles linked to collective interests and political power.

Most influentially, scholars at Birmingham's Centre for Contemporary Cultural Studies adopted a very processual view of Gramsci's ideas about hegemony and resistance in their analyses of popular cultural forms and usages. Subcultures became a particularly interesting object of study for them because they formed collective and often countercultural identities around styles they fashioned from cultural commodities (Willis, 1977; McRobbie, 1984). Appropriations of both Gramsci and Althusser at Birmingham emphasized the contingent nature of ideological formations and their relative autonomy – from class determinism, in particular. This foregrounded history and human activity – which Birmingham scholars often discussed as lived experience or practice – as well as opening up consideration of other forms and sites of domination, such as gender, race, or region (e.g. Bennett et al., 1986; Hall, 1980, 1991). Scholars in the United States pursued similar lines of inquiry. For example, George Lipsitz's *Rainbow at Midnight: Labor and Culture in the 1940s* (1994 [1981]) argues that in the wake of repressive labor laws that silenced political demands by American workers in the late 1940s, popular culture became a significant terrain for struggles over the expression of class- and race-related issues.

If culture was emerging as a crucial site for understanding a double movement of resistance and incorporation within a postwar order that was formally democratic yet clearly riven by new forms of domination, another critical question that emerged at about the same time had to do with the failure of formal politics to address these basic issues. Drawing on the German tradition of critical theory, Habermas's influential response turned towards an analysis of the public sphere – conceived as a "realm" outside of the marketplace and the state, yet not reducible to private life – to answer that question. His formulation was itself profoundly cultural, first, because of its insistence that communication was a crucial aspect of social reality irreducible to economic interests. Further, he discussed the evolution of the public sphere in Europe historically, locating different sites (the coffee house, debating societies) and media (the newspaper, for instance) of communication that enabled a certain kind of discussion – based on reasoned arguments about fundamental assumptions – to take place. In his view, such discussion was necessary for genuine democracy to thrive. His analyses were pessimistic about the prospects for democracy in the present – based on a conviction that the public sphere is being eroded by both state and market – but argued nonetheless for a basic human capacity to engage in the rational discussion it would require (Habermas, 1971, 1979, 1984–7, 1989).

Habermas's work remains at a high level of abstraction. It has filtered into cultural studies mainly as the point of departure for more concrete – and often historical – examinations of "the public sphere" and for critical appraisals of the concept itself (Calhoun, 1992b; Fraser, 1989; Schudson, 1998). Habermas's work also serves as a reminder that the public world and politics matter – both in reality and in sociocultural analysis – and offers a certain kind of public participation as a normative ideal to strive for. But Habermas's opus tends towards a universalizing mode, both because of its invocation of the universal properties of language and by virtue of its historical framing within a schema of universal social evolution. And the social changes that have preoccupied more recent cultural studies scholars have caused many to criticize the search for universal truths or criteria of value. This has proven unsettling not only for sociologists and other social scientists, but for many humanists and natural scientists as well, and has provoked debates that have in their turn, as Messer-Davidow demonstrates so clearly in this volume, contributed to the politically volatile state of cultural studies and – even more broadly – contemporary higher education in the United States.

Cultural Studies in the Contemporary Period

Now we are reaching the very recent past and present, and, as the discussion in this volume and many others show, scholars are sharply debating what needs to be understood as well as how, theoretically and methodologically, we are to understand it. My own provisional reading of the "terrain" at issue would gesture towards the social unrest and social movements that began in the 1960s and 1970s in the United States and Western Europe, at a time when conflicts over economic and national self-determination were also sweeping the developing nations. These movements have continued as local grassroots struggles for equality and political participation within an emerging geopolitical order featuring new constellations of technology and capital and new configurations of collective organization from global alliances of indigenous peoples, cultural and linguistic blocs emerging from former communist nations, and regional religious fundamentalisms, to transnational corporations and political unions.

But what might all this "stuff" mean for the development of cultural studies? To begin close to home, the social movements of the last two or three decades in the United States have raised questions about "identity" that are clearly cultural as well as political. They brought new constituencies into the university as students and scholars who asked – as did movement activists – questions about representation that were "cultural" on several levels. For example, early second-wave feminist writers from Betty Friedan (1965) and Kate Millett (1970) to Sheila Rowbotham (1972) and Nancy Chodorow (1978) looked at dominant forms of knowledge about women, whether popular or scholarly, literary or scientific, to show how women were represented and to offer accounts that more fully explained what they judged from their perspective to be women's experiences.[10] This line of inquiry led, in turn, to important work by scholars who critiqued early feminists' tendency to treat "whiteness" as a taken-for-granted universal category, and who began to study exclusion and normalization both in regard to specific kinds of identity (race or ethnicity, for example) and in general (for example, see Collins, 1990; hooks, 1984; Williams, 1991). Simone de Beauvoir's discussion of woman as "Other" to a dominant group that represents itself as the universal "Subject," or human norm, has been a particularly generative exemplar of this strategy, both within and beyond the field of gender studies (Beauvoir, 1953).

As has been true throughout the development of cultural studies, such questions arose from a lack of fit between people's lived experiences and pervasive and socially influential ways of thinking about the world. This persistent tension has brought forth further questions about the adequacy of foundational conceptual categories in academic knowledge (in relation to gender, for instance, the public/private distinction, or the monadic rational actor of neoclassical economics). It has also generated thinking about the ways social processes give rise to widely accepted hierarchies of cultural value which have great power to structure people's lives, including their "lived experience" or "identity" itself.

Issues like these have found resonance with scholars across a variety of disciplinary boundaries and national traditions in an academic marketplace that is itself suffering the dislocations and dispersals/reconcentrations of power that scholars are attempting to understand in the environing social world. And this situation has brought a bewildering array of discussions into play in the enterprise of cultural studies in the United States. In regard to the questions raised above about social identity, categories of knowledge, and hierarchies of cultural value, for example, a cultural studies scholar might juxtapose explorations of canonization in literary studies and sociology with work on representation and voice among internationally oriented scholars like Said (1978, 1983, 1993) and Spivak (1987, 1990, 1993). Or perhaps one might turn to Pierre Bourdieu's systematic investigation of cultural usages and their links to people's "habitus" and the objective structures of social distinction that help reproduce the status quo. Similar questions, about sexuality and sexual identity, for example, might lead yet another scholar to take up thinking by Foucault that examines how discursive formations linking textual knowledges and institutional developments have worked to structure contemporary sexual subjectivities and their emergence as collectively recognized "identities."

Other lines of inquiry have generated equally complex zones of theoretical and empirical work. Critical urbanists, for example, have noted (like Hoggart in the 1950s) that the communities that provided roots for ethnic or class solidarity have been dispersed by urban renewal, deindustrialization, and other developments effacing an older sense of place in contemporary cities. But since Hoggart's time, gentrification, urban tourism, planned communities, and theme parks have begun to provide other material for thinking through the connections between "community" and identity. So critical geographers have turned to work by Jameson (1991), Lyotard (1984 [1974]), and other postmodernists to understand how these new urban forms might structure people's experiences and possibilities for collective action (Gregory, 1994; Harvey, 1989; Zukin, 1991, 1992).

One thing is clear. Concerns about the new ways both domination and the potential for a more democratic social order are articulated across culture and society have provoked deep-cutting questions about knowledge and tradition in the West. This activity has been inflected differently across traditional disciplines, but has had the general effect of bringing many scholars into the interdisciplinary spaces of cultural studies. For example, if critical literary scholars become self-conscious about the historical roots of national literary studies and the political dimension of canonization, they may begin to analyze a broad range of popular cultural "texts" and their uses in the social world, or examine the institutions (literary criticism, the field of English, the Book-of-the-Month Club) that work to define what we call literature and to assign criteria of literary value. If anthropologists are challenged by geopolitics to rethink the relationship between ethnographer and subject, some will not only begin to share responsibility for ethnographies with erstwhile "subjects," but also begin to search at home as well as among traditional Others for ethnographic opportunities, and recognize affinities between their signature activity and that of tourists or state department officials (see Marcus in this volume).

Some of this questioning and re-invention involves the disappearance of traditional grounds for disciplinary activity. For instance, small-scale low-technology societies are either vanishing or negotiating their induction into global networks of technology, labor, and consumption; high cultural texts no longer have the privileged place they enjoyed in early twentieth-century public education. These developments obviously challenge anthropology and literary studies. Yet similar questions also appear as new disciplinary formations emerge. Social studies of science, for instance, have grown up in tandem with the enormous growth of "big science" in the last few decades, and their critical take on science comes as much from public questions about an endeavor that has brought us nuclear weapons and environmental devastation alongside space flight and the Salk vaccine, as from purely academic developments.

Sociology and Cultural Studies: Tradition and Change

My sense is that all academic knowledge in the human sciences has been unsettled by global developments that challenge Western notions of progress, reason, and objectivity. No longer can Western scholars easily assert, as did Max Weber in what is usually printed as the Introduction to *The Protestant Ethic and the Spirit of Capitalism* (1995 [1904–5]), that "in Western civilization, and in Western civilization only, cultural phenomena have appeared which (as we like to think) lie in a line of development having *universal* significance and value." What in Weber was a parenthetical acknowledgment that he might be writing from a particular perspective has expanded, at the end of this century, into a pervasive unease about

the foundations of all knowledge and all systems of value, an unease signaled by passionate debates in the academy about global periodization
(modernism/postmodernism), humanism, and the Enlightenment. This
unease is not just an academic matter, however, for movements calling for
a return to revealed religious truths, and defenses of Western high cultural
traditions from conservatives and liberals alike, show by their embattled
fervor that many people beyond the university feel their most deeply held
traditions are threatened by contemporary social changes.

What disturbs me most about such discussions of knowledge and tradition in the university is their quasi-theological tone. At a conference on
science, a colleague of mine who studies high-energy physicists found herself asked fervently, "But do you believe in the Enlightenment?" "'Believe'
. . .?" was her response. We in the West are living in and through the
Enlightenment; how can we do otherwise? The Enlightenment is a grand
tradition we are heirs to, and most of us refer to one or another of its
aspects (democracy or equality or science or critique, for instance) for
validation of our scholarship, even as we call into question other parts of
the social or intellectual order we have also inherited from those prior
generations who lived and thought the Enlightenment into existence from
the flux of their own problematic present. It seems to me that one of our
most pressing tasks, in fact, is to use our privileged position as intellectuals to understand which aspects of this tradition we can mobilize in the
present to build a more just and humane social order, and which aspects
will serve us less well.

Some sociologists may find their own disciplinary tradition lacking in
the provision of conceptual and methodological tools for making sense of
culture in the contemporary world. Like others, they are therefore mining
their own disciplinary past, or stretching beyond their accustomed disciplinary boundaries, and like others, they can feel more at ease in the
relatively unbounded spaces of cultural studies. But the very excitement
of interdisciplinarity that has given some sociologists an alternative home
and that has also provided scholars in the social sciences and humanities
with a very broad and very rich array of studies of culture, carries with it
its own unsettling qualities. Questions arise, sometimes dramatically, about
clarity, relevance, and criteria for judgment – questions that are particularly pressing given the insularity of the academy in general. So, it may be
that certain theoretical and methodological conventions that have been
forged within the community of sociology can help in grounding contemporary work on culture, and thus contribute to building traditions of
inquiry that become new resources for scholars both within and at the
boundaries of the disciplines as they are presently constituted.

This volume offers a way of proceeding in this collective endeavor, a
way that promises to build a larger community of mutually critical yet

expansive discourse among scholars – and eventually between the academy and the environing society – rather than enclosing people within the circles of their familiar interlocutors. The authors were chosen with this hope in mind. They represent some of the best among the social "wing" of cultural studies scholars, and among culturally oriented sociologists. Their writings span a continuum from programmatic statements to more specific case studies. Contributions cover a range of substantive concerns from those such as gender, race, and "the popular," which are established areas of inquiry within both fields, to those such as globalization and conservatism, which are of clear contemporary importance. All of them address, whether implicitly or explicitly, the related questions of how to do good scholarship, especially in dialogue across disciplines, and how to make scholarship matter beyond the academy. The latter is, for me, a crucial issue, and one that both cultural studies and sociology must attend to in order to fulfill their promise. As I reflect on these two scholarly traditions, I can see a possible bridge between them – not so much as areas of academic expertise, but as human endeavors – in their fundamental conviction that scholarship can contribute to a more egalitarian and participatory democracy. In the service of this broad social project, questions about turf and tradition take on a new coloration, and issues of teaching, writing, and the relationship of the university to society become salient in practice as well as in theory. This volume speaks primarily to other scholars, but as a scholarly intervention, it raises those wider questions for serious discussion.

NOTES

I wish to gratefully acknowledge all those (including anonymous reviewers as well as Herman Gray, John Hall, Michèle Lamont, Michael Schudson, Janet Wolff, and Sharon Zukin) who commented on the earlier "Rationale" for this volume, and especially those who read and discussed early drafts of the present introduction: Chad Gordon, Herman Gray, Sharon Hays, George Lipsitz, George Marcus, Chandra Mukerji, Michael Schudson, and Katherine Stone.

1 The classic citation here is Raymond Williams's *Keywords* (1976), but see also his discussion on pages 293–355 of *The Long Revolution* (1961).
2 This has been less true of sociologists of art and literature, especially those who concentrate on high culture, or Culture.
3 The move to consider culture as a "whole way of life" has an interesting parallel in writings important to the Birmingham group of cultural studies scholars. See the discussion in chapter two, especially pages 41–4, of Raymond Williams's *The Long Revolution* (1961), for example.

4 Symbolic interactionists have often been very sympathetic to cultural studies. Norman Denzin's work *Symbolic Interactionism and Cultural Studies: The Politics of Interpretation* (1992) and Howard Becker and Michal McCall's collection *Symbolic Interaction and Cultural Studies* (1990) both engage these two traditions.

5 DuBois's concern with race and the immense losses Blacks experienced at the end of Reconstruction make him exceptionally sensitive to power and domination among early American sociologists, but as Cruz points out in this volume, his work was marginalized until the middle of the century.

6 *Middletown in Transition* also reflects Robert Lynd's exposure to European social theory, Marx in particular. The "power elite" of Muncie is one major focus of the book, which can, in fact, be credited with initiating that research tradition among community studies.

7 After the Civil War, bureaus of labor statistics proliferated, and with them surveys about labor issues and problems. Community "social surveys" were also common during the 1905–30 period. They usually dealt with social problems targeted by public movements for municipal reforms and took place largely outside universities. Funded by municipalities or reformers, and staffed by volunteers, they brought socially concerned students into sociology departments, but otherwise remained largely separate from academic sociology. Professors were occupied with teaching and often their research was more theoretically driven, although the field remained oriented to reform publics. There were under 1,000 members of the American Sociological Society until the end of World War I, and at the same period sociology granted only about 20 doctoral degrees per annum (Turner and Turner, 1990: 22–32; Buxton and Turner, 1992: 373).

8 At Birmingham specifically, and – given Thatcher's attack on higher education – in Britain more generally, cultural studies has always labored under conditions of tremendous institutional insecurity. In fact, one might say that this circumstance was generative of its very formation. Why this issue should play out so differently in the United States is a question of some complexity, deserving a more careful analysis than can be accomplished here. But the absence of a strongly institutionalized social democratic labor movement in the United States may be one important factor to consider. Another may be a self-consciously nontraditional organization of graduate study. See Johnson in this volume.

9 See Batsleer et al. (1985), Eagleton (1983, 1984), and Ohmann (1976, 1987) for some discussions of literary studies. Haskell's (1977) discussion of the social sciences remains instructive. Of course, much of Foucault's work deals with the emergence of specifically modern regimes of knowledge and power (Foucault, 1965, 1973a, 1973b, 1977, 1978). Interestingly, many sociologists understood his writings as coming from "the sociological perspective" when they first enountered Foucault, since he wrote about social construction in regard to marginal or deviant subjects much discussed by sociologists. The critical tenor of his thinking about the grounds for knowledge, and about the nature of modernity, have been much less easily assimilated by most sociologists, however.

10 For a discussion of this same line of development at Birmingham, see Long (1991).

REFERENCES

Adorno, Theodor W. et al. 1950: *The Authoritarian Personality*. New York: Harper.

—— 1991: *The Culture Industry: Selected Essays on Mass Culture*. (Edited and with an Introduction by J. M. Bernstein.) London: Routledge.

Alexander, Jeffrey C. 1989: *Structure and Meaning: Relinking Classical Sociology*. New York: Columbia University Press.

—— 1995: *Fin de Siecle Social Theory: Relativism, Reduction, and the Problem of Reason*. London/New York: Verso.

Althusser, Louis 1969: *For Marx*. (Trans. Ben Brewster.) New York: Pantheon Books.

Anderson, Nels 1923: *The Hobo: The Sociology of the Homeless Man*. Chicago: University of Chicago Press.

Barthes, Roland 1990 [1972]: *Mythologies*. (Selected and translated by Annette Lavers.) New York: Noonday Press.

Batsleer, Janet, et al. 1985: *Rewriting English: Cultural Politics of Gender and Class*. London/New York: Methuen.

Beauvoir, Simone de 1953: *The Second Sex*. New York: Knopf.

Becker, Howard S. 1953: Becoming a Marijuana User. *American Journal of Sociology*, 59, 235–42.

—— 1982: *Art Worlds*. Berkeley: University of California Press.

Becker, Howard S. and McCall, Michal (eds) 1990: *Symbolic Interaction and Cultural Studies*. Chicago: University of Chicago Press.

Bell, Daniel 1976: *The Cultural Contradictions of Capitalism*. New York: Basic Books.

Bellah, Robert et al. 1985: *Habits of the Heart: Individualism and Commitment in American Life*. Berkeley: University of California Press.

Bennett, Tony, Mercer, Colin, and Woollacott, Janet (eds) 1986: *Popular Culture and Social Relations*. Milton Keynes, UK/Philadelphia: Open University Press.

Bourdieu, Pierre 1977: *Outline of a Theory of Practice*. (Trans. Richard Nice.) Cambridge, UK/New York: Cambridge University Press.

—— 1984: *Distinction: A Social Critique of the Judgement of Taste*. Cambridge, MA: Harvard University Press.

—— 1990: *The Logic of Practice*. (Trans. Richard Nice.) Cambridge, UK/Oxford UK: Polity Press.

—— 1991: *Language and Symbolic Power*. Cambridge: Polity Press.

Bramson, Leon 1961: *The Political Context of Sociology*. Princeton, NJ: Princeton University Press.

Buxton, William and Turner, Stephen P. 1992: From Education to Expertise: Sociology as "Profession." In Terence C. Halliday and Morris Janowitz (eds), *Sociology and its Publics: The Forms and Fates of Disciplinary Organization*, Chicago/London: The University of Chicago Press, 373–407.

Calhoun, Craig 1989: Introduction: Social Issues in the Study of Culture. In Craig Calhoun (ed.), *Comparative Social Research, A Research Annual: Culture*, Greenwich/London: JAI Press, 1–29.

—— (ed.) 1992a: *Habermas and the Public Sphere*. Cambridge, MA: MIT Press.

—— 1992b: Sociology, Other Disciplines, and the Project of a General Understanding of Social Life. In Terence C. Halliday and Morris Janowitz (eds), *Sociology and its Publics: The Forms and Fates of Disciplinary Organization*, Chicago/London: The University of Chicago Press, 137–95.

—— 1995: *Critical Social Theory: Culture, History, and the Challenge of Difference*. Oxford, UK/Cambridge, MA: Blackwell.

Chodorow, Nancy 1978: *The Reproduction of Mothering: Psychoanalysis and the Sociology of Gender*. Berkeley: University of California Press.

Cohen, Lizabeth 1990: *Making a New Deal: Industrial Workers in Chicago, 1919–1939*. Cambridge/New York/Port Chester/Melbourne/Sydney: Cambridge University Press.

Collins, Patricia Hill 1990: *Black Feminist Thought: Knowledge, Consciousness, and the Politics of Empowerment*. Boston: Unwin Hyman.

Crane, Diana (ed.) 1994: *The Sociology of Culture: Emerging Theoretical Perspectives*. Oxford, UK/Cambridge MA: Blackwell.

Cressey, Paul G. 1969 [1932]: *The Taxi-dance Hall: A Sociological Study in Commercialized Recreation and City Life*. Montclair, NJ: Patterson Smith.

Denzin, Norman 1992: *Symbolic Interactionism and Cultural Studies: The Politics of Interpretation*. Cambridge: Blackwell.

DiMaggio, Paul 1982: Cultural Entrepreneurship in Nineteenth-century Boston: The Creation of an Organizational Base for High Culture in America. *Media, Culture and Society*, 4, 33–50.

Eagleton, Terry 1983: *Literary Theory: An Introduction*. Minneapolis: University of Minnesota Press.

—— 1984: *The Function of Criticism: From The Spectator to Post-structuralism*. London: Verso.

Erikson, Kai T. 1976: *Everything in its Path: Destruction of Community in the Buffalo Creek Flood*. New York: Simon and Schuster.

Foucault, Michel 1965: *Madness and Civilization: A History of Insanity in the Age of Reason*. (Trans. Richard Howard.) New York/Toronto/London: New American Library.

—— 1973a: *The Birth of the Clinic: An Archaeology of Medical Perception*. (Trans. Alan Sheridan.) New York: Pantheon Books.

—— 1973b: *The Order of Things: An Archaeology of the Human Sciences*. New York: Vintage Books.

—— 1977: *Discipline and Punish: The Birth of the Prison*. (Trans. Alan Sheridan.) New York: Pantheon Books.

—— 1978: *History of Sexuality*. New York: Pantheon Books.

Fraser, Nancy 1989: What's Critical about Critical Theory: The Case of Habermas and Gender. In Nancy Fraser, *Unruly Practices: Power, Discourse, and Gender in Contemporary Social Theory*, Minneapolis: University of Minnesota Press, 113–43.

Friedan, Betty 1965: *The Feminine Mystique*. New York: Dell Publishing.

Gans, Herbert J. 1974: *Popular Culture and High Culture*. New York: Basic Books.

Giddens, Anthony 1984: *The Constitution of Society: Outline of the Theory of Structuration*. Berkeley: University of California Press.

—— 1991: *Modernity and Self-identity: Self and Society in the Late Modern Age*. Cambridge: Polity Press.

—— 1992: *The Transformation of Intimacy: Sexuality, Love, and Eroticism in Modern Societies*. Stanford: Stanford University Press.

—— 1995: *Politics, Sociology, and Social Theory: Encounters with Classical and Contemporary Social Thought*. Stanford: Stanford University Press.

Gregory, Derek 1994: *Geographical Imaginations*. Cambridge, MA/Oxford, UK: Blackwell.

Grossberg, Lawrence, Nelson, Cary, and Treichler, Paula (eds) 1992: *Cultural Studies*. New York/London: Routledge.

Habermas, Jürgen 1971: *Knowledge and Human Interests*. Boston: Beacon Press.

—— 1979: *Communication and the Evolution of Society*. Boston: Beacon Press.

—— 1984–7: *Theory of Communicative Action*. Boston: Beacon Press.

—— 1989: *The Structural Transformation of the Public Sphere: An Inquiry into a Category of Bourgeois Society*. Cambridge, MA: MIT Press.

Hall, John R. and Neitz, Mary Jo 1993: *Culture: Sociological Perspectives*. Englewood Cliffs, NJ: Prentice-Hall.

Hall, Stuart 1980: Cultural Studies: Two Paradigms. *Media, Culture and Society*, 2, 57–72.

—— 1991: Signification, Representation, Ideology: Althusser and the Post-structuralist Debates. In Robert K. Avery and David Eason (eds), *Critical Perspectives on Media and Society*, New York/London: The Guilford Press, 88–113.

Hall, Stuart and Jefferson, Tony (eds) 1976: *Resistance Through Rituals*. London: Hutchinson.

Hartmann, Douglas (n.d.): *Culture and Social Theory: Reconstructing the Problematic of "the Cultural"*. Unpublished manuscript.

Harvey, David 1989: *The Condition of Postmodernity*. New York: Blackwell.

Haskell, Thomas L. 1977: *The Emergence of Professional Social Science: The American Social Science Association and the Nineteenth-century Crisis of Authority*. Urbana: University of Illinois Press.

Hoggart, Richard 1992 [1959]: *The Uses of Literacy*. New Brunswick: Transaction.

hooks, bell 1984: *Feminist Theory from Margin to Center*. Boston, MA: South End Press.

Jacobs, Norman (ed.) 1961: *Culture for the Millions?* Princeton, NJ: Van Nostrand.

Jameson, Fredric 1991: *Postmodernism or, the Cultural Logic of Late Capitalism*. Durham, NC: Duke University Press.

Johnson, Richard 1995 [1983]: What is Cultural Studies Anyway?. In Jessica Munns and Gita Rajan, *A Cultural Studies Reader: History, Theory, Practice*, London/New York: Longman, 574–612. (Originally circulated as a CCCS stencilled occasional paper (no. 74) in 1983.)

Lang, Gladys Engel and Lang, Kurt 1990: *Etched in Memory: The Building and Survival of Artistic Reputation*. Chapel Hill/London: University of North Carolina Press.

Lemert, Charles C. 1995: *Sociology After the Crisis*. Boulder: Westview Press.

Liebow, Elliot 1967: *Tally's Corner: A Study of Negro Streetcorner Men*. Boston: Little, Brown.

Lipsitz, George 1994: *Rainbow at Midnight: Labor and Culture in the 1940s*. Urbana/Chicago: University of Illinois Press. (Originally published in 1981 as *Class and Culture in Cold war America: A Rainbow at Midnight*. New York: Praeger.)

Long, Elizabeth 1985: *The American Dream and the Popular Novel*. Boston: Routledge & Kegan Paul.

—— 1991: Feminism and Cultural Studies: Britain and America. In Robert K. Avery and David Eason (eds), *Critical Perspectives on Media and Society*, New York/London: The Guilford Press, 114–25. (Originally published in *Critical Studies in Mass Communication*, December, 1989.)

—— 1992: Textual Interpretation as Collective Action. *Discourse*, 14, 104–30.

Lynd, Robert S. and Lynd, Helen Merrell 1929: *Middletown: A Study in American Culture*. New York: Harcourt, Brace & World.

—— 1937: *Middletown in Transition: A Study in Cultural Conflicts*. New York: Harcourt, Brace and Company.

Lyotard, Jean-François 1984 (1974): *The Postmodern Condition: A Report on Knowledge*. Minneapolis: University of Minnesota Press.

McRobbie, Angela 1984: Dance and Social Fantasy. In Angela McRobbie and Mica Nava (eds), *Gender and Generation*, London: Macmillan, 130–61.

Madge, John 1962: *The Origins of Scientific Sociology*. New York: The Free Press of Glencoe.

Marcuse, Herbert 1966: *One Dimensional Man: Studies in the Ideology of Advanced Industrial Society*. Boston: Beacon Press.

—— 1974: *Eros and Civilization: A Philosophical Inquiry into Freud*. Boston: Beacon Press.

Milgram, Stanley 1975: *Obedience to Authority: An Experimental View*. New York: Harper & Row.

Millett, Kate 1970: *Sexual Politics*. New York: Doubleday.

Mills, Charles Wright 1951: *White Collar: The American Middle Classes*. New York: Oxford University Press.

—— 1956: *The Power Elite*. New York: Oxford University Press.

Mukerji, Chandra and Schudson, Michael (eds) 1991: *Rethinking Popular Culture: Contemporary Perspectives in Cultural Studies*. Berkeley/Los Angeles/Oxford: University of California Press.

Ohmann, Richard 1976: *English in America: A Radical View of the Profession*. New York: Oxford University Press.

—— 1987: *Politics of Letters*. Middletown: Wesleyan University Press.

Park, Robert 1969 [1915]: The City: Suggestions for the Investigation of Human Behavior in the Urban Environment. In Richard Sennett (ed.) *Classic Essays on the Culture of Cities*, New York: Appleton-Century-Crofts, 91–130. (Originally published in *The American Journal of Sociology*, 20, 5, 577–612.)

Parsons, Talcott, 1937: *The Structure of Social Action: A Study in Social Theory with Special Reference to a Group of Recent European Writers*. New York/London: McGraw-Hill.

Peterson, Richard A. (ed.) 1976: *The Production of Culture*. Beverly Hills, California: Sage Publications.

—— 1994: Culture Studies Through the Production Perspective: Progress and Prospects. In Diana Crane (ed.) *The Sociology of Culture: Emerging Theoretical Perspectives*, Oxford, UK/Cambridge, MA: Blackwell, 163–89.

Polanyi, Karl 1957: *The Great Transformation: The Political and Economic Origins of Our Time*. Boston: Beacon Press.

Riesman, David, in collaboration with Nathan Glazer and Reuel Denney 1952: *The Lonely Crowd: A Study of the Changing American Character*. New Haven: Yale University Press.

Rosenberg, Bernard and White, David M. (eds) 1957: *Mass Culture: The Popular Arts in America*. Glencoe, II.: Free Press.

—— 1971: *Mass Culture Revisited*. New York: Van Nostrand Reinhold.

Rowbotham, Sheila 1972: *Women, Resistance, and Revolution: A History of Women and Revolution in the Modern World*. New York: Pantheon Books.

Said, Edward W. 1978: *Orientalism*. New York: Pantheon Books.

—— 1983: *The World, the Text, and the Critic*. Cambridge, MA: Harvard University Press.

—— 1993: *Culture and Imperialism*. New York: Knopf.

Schudson, Michael 1998: *The Good Citizen: A History of US Political Culture and Communication*. New York: Free Press.

Seidman, Steven 1994: *Contested Knowledge: Social Theory in the Postmodern Era*. Oxford, UK/Cambridge, MA: Blackwell.

Slater, Philip Elliot 1970: *The Pursuit of Loneliness: American Culture at the Breaking Point*. Boston: Beacon Press.

Smith, Dorothy E. 1987: *The Everyday World as Problematic: A Feminist Sociology*. Boston: Northeastern University Press.

—— 1990a: *The Conceptual Practices of Power: A Feminist Sociology of Knowledge*. Boston: Northeastern University Press.

—— 1990b: *Texts, Facts, and Femininity: Exploring the Relations of Ruling*. London/New York: Routledge.

Spivak, Gayatri Chakravorty 1987: *In Other Worlds: Essays in Cultural Politics*. New York: Methuen.

—— 1990: *The Post-colonial Critic: Interviews, Strategies and Dialogues*. (Edited by Sarah Harasym.) New York/London: Routledge.

—— 1993: *Outside in the Teaching Machine*. New York: Routledge.

Thomas, William I. and Znaniecki, Florian 1918–20: *The Polish Peasant in Europe and America*. Boston. R. G. Badger.

Tuchman, Gaye 1989: *Edging Women Out: Victorian Novelists, Publishers, and Social Change*. New Haven: Yale University Press.

Turner, Stephen Park, and Turner, Jonathan H. 1990: *The Impossible Science: An Institutional Analysis of American Sociology.* Sage Library of Social Research 181. Newbury Park/London/New Delhi: Sage Publications.

Volkart, Edmund H. (ed.) 1951: *Social Behavior and Personality: Contributions of W. I. Thomas to Theory and Social Research.* New York: Social Science Research Council.

Weber, Max 1995 [1904–5]: *The Protestant Ethic and the Spirit of Capitalism.* (Trans. by Talcott Parsons; Introduction by Randall Collins.) Los Angeles: Roxbury Publishing.

Whyte, William F. 1993 [1943]: *Street Corner Society: The Social Structure of an Italian Slum.* Chicago/London: The University of Chicago Press.

Williams, Patricia J. 1991: *The Alchemy of Race and Rights.* Cambridge, MA: Harvard University Press.

Williams, Raymond 1961: *The Long Revolution.* London: Chatto & Windus.

—— 1976: *Keywords: A Vocabulary of Culture and Society.* New York/Oxford, UK: Oxford University Press.

Willis, Paul E. 1977: *Learning to Labor: How Working Class Kids Get Working Class Jobs.* Farnborough, UK: Saxon House.

Wuthnow, Robert 1987: *Meaning and Moral Order: Explorations in Cultural Analysis.* Berkeley/Los Angeles/London: University of California Press.

Zukin, Sharon 1991: *Landscapes of Power: From Detroit to Disney World.* Berkeley/Los Angeles: University of California Press.

—— 1992: Postmodern Urban Landscapes: Mapping Culture and Power. In Scott Lash and Jonathan Friedman (eds), *Modernity and Identity*, Oxford, UK/Cambridge, MA: Blackwell, 221–47.

PART I

THINKING THROUGH MEMORY
AND TRADITION

Introduction

The essays in Part I all engage with issues of memory and tradition, but in at least two different ways. The pieces that frame the section – Seidman at the beginning and Goodwin and Wolff at the end – deal primarily with questions of disciplinary tradition that emerge when two fields of study – in this case, sociology and cultural studies – encounter each other.

Seidman's essay argues that sociology could become more reflexive by incorporating insights from cultural studies. Despite sociology's claim to a monopoly on systematic analyses of "the social," Seidman views the field as a more local or limited intellectual tradition, and urges that it respond to the challenge of cultural studies in three arenas: the Foucauldian or semiotic "turn" of likening society to a text, psychoanalytic or postmodern concepts of the self, and general approaches to knowledge, including the role of the academic intellectual.

Considering the "textual turn," Seidman argues that, coupled with critical concepts of power, ideology, and conflict, this deeply cultural view of society can illuminate some important aspects of contemporary social life: the new power of the mass media and other innovative information technologies, the commodification of daily life, and the new dynamism of cultural politics. Next, he argues that cultural studies' view that identity is formed by discourses and social practices (in often fragmented and self-contradictory ways) may represent a valuable reprise of classical social theoretical critiques of a presocial, monadic self. Similarly, he thinks that the psychoanalytic theories of the self often deployed in cultural studies are useful because they offer a description of the *social* formation of subjectivity, gender identity, and sexuality.

Seidman explores the different kinds of knowledge claims made by these two approaches to understanding the empirical world. Counterposing the Gramscian image of the "organic intellectual" current in much cultural studies work to that of the objective social scientist commonly held by sociologists, he urges that sociology should modify its Enlightenment heritage enough to acknowledge the moral and political meaning or "interestedness" of its own conceptual categories and strategies.

Seidman argues that cultural studies can enrich sociology; Goodwin and Wolff, on the other hand, argue that sociology can enrich cultural studies. They speak of this as "conserving" cultural studies because at its inception in Britain the cultural studies movement explored "the discursive construction of social relations and institutions, as well as of cultural texts and practices, at the same time as analyzing the grounding of culture in social, economic, and material factors." They also suggest that cultural studies can escape the twin traps of "Grievance Studies" and "Empowerment Studies" by giving up its tendency to focus only on radical, "progressive," or subversive cultural practices. In fact, they argue that a genuinely critical cultural studies must engage with the beneficial aspects of tradition as well as with conservatism as a social and political force. They also make a case for a "conservative" understanding of representation, arguing for the need to understand – not simply deconstruct – the aesthetic dimension of culture. Finally, they propose that cultural studies practitioners return from often privatized readings of texts to engagement with the public realm of social and cultural criticism, as well as active participation in the industries of mainstream and popular culture.

The essays by Magali Sarfatti Larson and Jon Cruz are theoretically informed case studies that deal with questions of memory and tradition that confront the empirical researcher. Larson claims that "reading" architecture and other material objects cannot be easily assimilated to either sociological traditions of analysis like the "production of culture" school, or more semiotic traditions of textual analysis. Rather, she turns to the example of the Holocaust Memorial Museum to show that a full account of this object must build on the specificity of what buildings are ("part of everyday life, a vernacular art") as well as comprehending the complexities of how they came to exist and how they are understood by those who use them. Further, she contends that all these levels of interpretation involve cultural memory.

To begin with, Larson argues that the meaning of buildings appears first at the denotative level – understanding the social functions buildings serve – but that these functions are embodied in buildings as typological codes (this is a house, a subway station) and culturally encoded "scripts" of possible use (windows for seeing, or being seen), both of which are essentially social in nature. The internalization of these codes and repertoires of scripts in a culture is what makes us normally "ignore" architectural objects.

She also claims that buildings embody connotative meanings, often consciously mobilized by architects through formal conventions and stylistic signs. Larson discusses the Holocaust Memorial Museum as a complex example of how architects, in dialogue with other actors, such as the US Holocaust Memorial Council, strove to make a building that would work both as a museum and as a coherent narrative that might "present" the Holocaust. She then attempts to unpack visitors' reception of the Holocaust Memorial Museum. Here, she argues that people's cultural predispositions and more explicit preparation for viewing the museum seemed especially crucial determinants of response, implying that architecture connotes only with great ambiguity. Her analysis not only provides a model for interpreting architectural objects, but also illuminates the dynamics at work in the construction of historical memory itself.

Cruz's essay reframes the scholarly contribution of W. E. B. Du Bois, most often remembered as a founder of ethnic studies and the field of race relations, by representing him as the synthetic culmination of earlier modes of social analysis which are crucial – and often forgotten – precursors of both contemporary social theory *and* cultural studies. He claims that thinkers attempting to grasp the sociohistorical dynamics of modernity from the time of the Romantics to the present have tended to do so through the lens of social subjects – collectivities from uprooted peasants and displaced handloom weavers to the urban underclass. Conceptualizations of such social subjects mark societal crises and present these social groupings as people in need of retrieval, redemption, or other institutionalized kinds of *subject work*.

Cruz identifies three sequential but overlapping intellectual orientations in this long history of social analysis: Romanticism, humanitarian reformism, and social science. He argues that Romanticism inaugurated the search for disappearing subjects (such as peasants), while the more forward-looking reformism of the nineteenth century became preoccupied with social subjects who were present but in some way victimized by modernity (preeminently slaves and women). He contends that social science, with its concern for *new* social subjects (from industrial workers to members of ethnic subcultures), has inherited the questions and concerns behind these earlier, less "scientific" interpretive lenses.

Turning to Du Bois, and especially his work in *The Souls of Black Folk*, Cruz claims him as a conjunctural figure who represents an intellectual continuity between these older lenses and what we would recognize today as the humanistic dimensions within both the sociology of culture and cultural studies. His work, like that of the others in Part I, not only offers us an expanded sense of a usable past, but also a broader appreciation of the long concern with identity that lies at the heart of analyses of social and cultural change.

1

Relativizing Sociology: The Challenge of Cultural Studies

STEVEN SEIDMAN

The relationship between sociology and cultural studies resists a simple or global description, whether it be one of antagonism or kinship. Nevertheless, I wish to emphasize the ways the latter challenges the former. I intend to do this for the purpose of relativizing sociology as a discourse of "the social." Approaching sociology as a local practice, viewing its conceptual strategies and thematic perspectives as indicative of a particular tradition rather than as a universal language of the social, is, I am wagering, useful in that it allows us to become aware of the singular discursive organization of sociology, for example, to have its disciplinary silences and constraints exposed. I aim to induce a certain critical disengagement from the culture of sociology in order to imagine new disciplinary possibilities for social knowledge. Perhaps such a "therapeutic" exercise might permit us to project other ways we might wish to frame "the self" and "the social." If the therapeutic model is to be believed, it is only by making us aware of unconscious compulsions and unnecessary constraints that change is possible.

I intend then to play off "cultural studies" against "sociology," but not to suggest that the former is better in the sense of right or true. I don't believe this. I do believe though that in figuring sociology as a local, not a universal practice, in reading its discursive conventions as a tradition (or multiple traditions), not the very language of the social universe, we gain a critical attitude towards this discipline. I am of the opinion that critique and change are especially pressing at this juncture in sociology's disciplinary history. Much sociology seems to be drifting into a deadening insularity, often unseen and without protest, as many sociologists still march under the triumphant banner of expertise or hold to an indubitable faith in the Enlightenment. Perhaps an engagement with alternative social knowledges such as cultural studies might allow sociology to have its theoretical and political unconscious exposed in ways troubling enough to risk a disciplinary self-examination and reformation.

Admittedly, I've framed this discussion in a suspiciously modernistic and essentializing way. Such suspicions can perhaps be lessened if I insist that terms such as sociology or cultural studies have no right or correct way of being referenced. Their heterogeneity, their instability, and the surplus of meanings they accrue is, I think, inescapable. As I now see such matters, conceptual moves gain whatever legitimacy they manage by virtue of what they allow us to do or say assuming a purpose at hand in a particular conversation at a precise time and place. There is no right or wrong, true or false way of fixing conceptual meaning. There are only different ways, the value or credibility of any specific way being related to the purpose at hand in a particular conversation governed by particular conventions regarding the authorization of knowledge. So, to turn to the conversation at hand, I merely wish to recommend, with no legitimacy claimed beyond this conversation and its purpose, that it might be useful (at least, to those of us who care about the kinds of issues this conversation raises) to think of cultural studies as different in some important ways from at least much of what passes for the central traditions and practices of at least "American sociology."

A word is surely in order regarding my usage of the terms "cultural studies" and "sociology." Is it not foolish or at least contradictory to speak of such a binary? After all, are not many cultural studies practitioners sociologists and do not many sociologists claim to be doing cultural studies? True enough. And yet I still wish to figure an opposition, or at least highlight stress points. How is this possible? Would such a positioning gain plausibility if by cultural studies I intend the work of the Birmingham Centre for Contemporary Cultural Studies, and by sociology I mean the research and discourses produced by American sociologists, work which is largely organized around disciplinary area specialties and which has largely been untouched by a British or European tradition of cultural studies? Additionally, if I note that cultural studies in the past decade has become increasingly uncoupled from sociology, especially in Australia (where academic knowledges are less organized around sharply demarcated disciplines) and in the United States (where cultural studies is housed primarily in the humanities or in new interdisciplinary programs such as "communications"), does the figuring of a critical tension between cultural studies and sociology accrue credibility? Let's continue.

To repeat, I will be using the term cultural studies in a very specific and narrow way. It will refer to the work of the Birmingham Centre for Contemporary Cultural Studies (est. 1964) and to work inspired by the Centre. Initially, I propose to describe certain general features of this tradition of cultural studies. I then turn to the American context, since this is where,

I think it's fair to say, cultural studies in the restricted sense I'm using the term is being elaborated in ways that make for intriguing clashes with dominant disciplinary knowledges.

If we follow what is by now a conventional narrative, British cultural studies "originated" in the writings of Raymond Williams (1958, 1961, 1962) and Richard Hoggart (1957). Their work challenged a dominant tradition in the humanities in postwar England. Culture had been approached as literary and artistic texts and practices to be analyzed in terms of general aesthetic standards. Judged by presumed universal aesthetic values or ideals, popular cultures were viewed as inferior, often interpreted as a sign of the degrading effects of mass communication and commercialization.

Hoggart and Williams made two critical moves. First, they argued that literary-aesthetic culture – the realm of what was considered serious literature, art, and music – is simply one expression of culture.[1] The latter refers to a wide range of meanings and practices that make up social life. "Culture" was said to comprehend the lived experiences of all individuals and groups as manifested in language, everyday mores and behaviors, ideologies, and the spectrum of texts and representations described by the terms literature, art, knowledge, and religion. Thus, in *The Uses of Literacy* Hoggart proposed to trace the changing culture of the English working class. Combining memoir and historical sociology, Hoggart analyzed not only the music or the popular literature of the working class, but everyday linguistic styles, family and neighborhood dynamics, and cognitive frameworks that define "private" and "public" and local and cosmopolitan. Similarly, in *Culture and Society* (1958) Williams not only traced images of "culture and society" in the literary history of modern England; he related aesthetic culture to a broader pattern of cultural meanings. This turn away from a literary-textual approach to a nonreductionist social analysis of culture is developed by Williams in *The Long Revolution* (1961). This text traces the rise of the novel and the theater in modern England as part of the formation of a text-based, literate public sphere. Stuart Hall comments on the significance of this text. "It shifted the whole ground of debate from a literary-moral to an anthropological definition of culture. But it defined the latter now as the 'whole process' by means of which meanings and definitions are socially constructed and historically transformed, with literature and art as only one . . . kind of social communication" (Hall, 1980a: 19).

Enlarging the concept of culture to include the practices and meanings of everyday life was coupled to a second important move by Hoggart and Williams: all cultural expressions were to be analyzed in relation to a social context of institutions, power relations, and history. Thus, in an important programmatic statement on cultural analysis, Williams insisted that "the analysis of culture . . . is the clarification of the meanings and values implicit and explicit in a particular way of life. . . . Such analysis will include . . . the organization of production, the structure of the family, [and] the structure of institutions" (Williams, 1961: 42). Thus, in the *The Long Revolution*, Williams analyzed English literary culture in relation to a "materialist" understanding of broad social changes in education and the mass media. Similarly, in *The Uses of Literacy*, Hoggart situated working-class cultural practices in class-structured social settings, for example, in pubs, clubs, households, and neighborhoods. Hoggart's judgment of the changes in working-class culture was decidedly mixed, and evidenced a nostalgic strain, but he insisted on situating cultural meanings in their actual social setting – a lesson exquisitely made by another major inspiration of cultural studies, E. P. Thompson (1963).

The first generation of British cultural studies made everyday life an object of cultural analysis. Cultural studies could aspire to go beyond aesthetic-literary criticism to become a critical social theory. Nevertheless, Williams and Hoggart were primarily literary critics and their analysis of culture, however brilliant, only pointed towards the articulation of culture and society.

I take it as quite important that the second generation who shaped British cultural studies were not literary critics but chiefly sociologists (e.g. Stuart Hall, David Morley, Dorothy Hobson, Paul Willis, Phil Cohen, Dick Hebdige, Ian Chambers, Angela McRobbie; see the comments by Hall, 1980a: 20–6). They took over the project of the former generation, what Stuart Hall (ibid: 25) once called a "complex Marxism" – Marxist less by any commitment to economism or the reign of class analysis than by a certain aspiration to grasp the formation of contemporary societies, by an insistence that cultural meanings are not free-floating but must be contextualized in relations of power, and by a critical intent to intervene into contemporary public life. Yet the second generation were critical of the humanistic, antitheoretical Marxism of Williams and Thompson. On the one hand, Stuart Hall and his colleagues drew heavily from French structuralism, insisting on a non-intentionalist, semiotic framing of cultural meanings. On the other hand, culture was not to be reduced to texts and representations but to include social practices and institutional structures anchored in history and analyzed in relation to class, gender, racial, or national dynamics. The work of Althusser (1971) and Gramsci (1971), and to a lesser extent Foucault, was in this regard pivotal in broadening the concept of culture while avoiding either an idealist (via structuralism) or materialist (via Marxism) reductionism. Similarly, in the spirit of Althusser and Gramsci, the second generation of cultural social critics aimed to preserve a concept of a social whole while disavowing Hegelian notions of an expressive totality. They advanced the idea of "the social" as a conjunctural articulated order. Culture was seen as part of the daily reproduction of social life, to be analyzed at the level of meaning, social structure, power relations, and history. Much like the Frankfurt School, the second generation of cultural studies sought a theoretical standpoint, roughly Marxist, which transcended the idealism/materialism, agency/structure, and base/superstructure dualisms. This was to be a social perspective which imagined society as articulated in various practices and structures– none of which, in principle, was assumed to be causally determining in the last instance.

Crossing the Atlantic, it is perhaps noteworthy that what we might call a British-inspired movement of American cultural studies has been housed primarily in the humanities. Literary theorists have decisively shaped the transplantation of British cultural studies in the United States. The result is that American cultural studies has been characterized by a strong move towards textualizing the social (e.g. Byars, 1991; Hall, 1992; Murdock, 1989; O'Connor, 1989). However, this textualizing strain has been checked, to some extent, by an ongoing commitment to Marxism. We might situate cultural studies in the United States as the creation of an academic left responding in part to the problematization of Marxism engendered by the end of communism and the disenchantment with Eurosocialism and to the critique of Marxism by the discourses of the new social movements, e.g. feminism, lesbian and gay studies, lesbian-feminism, and anti-racist theorizing. Yet while certain prominent currents of poststructural and postmodern theorizing, which have lately been associated with these new social movements, have effectively abandoned Marxism, most versions of cultural studies have not – though it must be said that the defense of Marxism is often little more than a vague appeal to the importance of the economy or class rather than the deployment of Marxism as a theoretical standpoint (Hall, 1990). The articulation of Marxism and semiotic analysis, as David Morley (1992: 4–5) laments, has been decidedly feeble, often hardly more than a rhetorical gesture. What most versions of British and British-inspired American cultural studies seem to share is an ideal of rethinking Marxism in light of new critical social knowledges such as feminism or poststructuralism.

Let me suggest one final way of positioning cultural studies. In the United States – perhaps less so in Britain or Australia – cultural studies (again, in the narrow way I'm using this term) is, in part, a response to the fracturing of the left in the 1970s and 1980s into quasi-ethnic oppositional communities of feminists, queers, African-Americans, and so on. Cultural studies perhaps formed (in the late 1980s) with the hope that it might serve as something of a common critical approach, uniting into a progressive block a fractured left and a left divided between defenders of a neomarxist socialist politic and advocates of a postmarxist identity-based politic. Claiming a more friendly relation to Marxism than many feminists or queers, or those marching under the banner of postmodernism – while intending to absorb aspects of these left critiques of Marxism – cultural studies seems at times to imagine itself as the heir to the tradition of Western Marxism.

Cultural studies resists – or so its practitioners claim – any definitive description because its form and character is self-consciously conjectural or context-specific. Nevertheless, for those who would benefit from a definition that resonates broadly with my general description, I offer the one provided by the editors of *Cultural Studies.*

> Cultural studies is an interdisciplinary, transdisciplinary, and sometimes counter-disciplinary field that operates in the tensions between its tendencies to embrace both a broad anthropological and a more narrowly humanistic conception of culture. . . . It is typically interpretive and evaluative in its methodologies, but unlike traditional humanism it rejects the exclusive equation of culture with high culture and argues that all forms of cultural production need to be studied in relation to other cultural practices and to social and historical structures. Cultural studies is thus committed to the study of the entire range of a society's arts, beliefs, institutions, and communicative practices. (Grossberg et al., 1992: 4)

Having sketched at least a rough working language in which to speak of cultural studies, I want to briefly and pointedly comment on three ways cultural studies challenges American sociology.

Imagining the Social

To begin, I intend to say something about cultural studies as a way of framing the social that departs in important ways from at least certain prominent conventions in American sociology. I should like, however, to have an initial point at least registered. Sociology has, I think, assumed a monopoly on so-called systematic analyses of society. Sociologists claim to offer the only systematically empirical, analytical, and holistic discourse of "the social." No other discipline can make this claim – not economics, political science, anthropology, or philosophy; nor can the social discourses, which conventionally might be thought of as "political ideology," public commentary, or folk belief, seriously contest sociology's monopolistic claim to furnishing systematic, holistic social understandings. The challenge of cultural studies to sociology, at one level, is that it makes a credible claim of having provided systematic analyses of the social that are empirical and analytical and that offer perspectives on whole societies. Moreover, cultural studies, like American sociology, has its own journals, professional networks, conferences, associations, and at times institutional departments or academic affiliations. Finally, although cultural studies draws from European and American sociological traditions, it figures the social differently in some key ways from American sociology. How so?

In contrast to the dominant intellectual strains in American sociology, cultural studies has made, so to speak, the textual or, better yet, the semiotic turn (cf. Hall, 1980a; Turner, 1992). Social realities are approached as a field of signs, meanings, or, if you will, texts. Whether the object of analysis is television programs, films, romance novels, fashion, or subcultural practices, the social is likened to a text. This suggests a view of the social as deeply cultural or as organized by signs and meanings patterned in relations of identity and difference. Objects and behaviors are viewed as saturated with meanings that are organized by codes whose coherence is to be uncovered through deciphering their symbolic units and operation (e.g. Hall, 1980b; Fiske, 1982; Hartley, 1982).

Textualizing society does not necessarily entail abandoning concerns of power, oppression, resistance, or agency. Texts are said to have multiple and contradictory meanings. They may articulate dominant ideologies that naturalize and normalize inequalities, but the contradictory meanings of texts allow for readers – audiences, spectators, producers and consumers of texts – to resist dominant ideologies or to refashion textual meanings in empowering ways. And, as many cultural analysts have reiterated, readers or interpreters of texts occupy multiple social locations and identities which engender varied, sometimes subversive, ironic readings. Moreover, texts are not approached as universes unto themselves, but are conceptualized as positioned both in relation to other texts – the principle of intertextuality – and in relation to social practices and conflicts – gender-based, class-based, and so on – that produce texts and are affected by them (Dyer, 1982; Hall, 1992; Morley, 1992; Turner, 1992; Williamson, 1978).

Cultural studies makes a strong semiotic turn but retains, if you will, the materialistic and agentic aspects of Marxism. Texts are produced by social practices in particular institutional contexts which have histories and none of these aspects – texts, social practices, institutions, and histories – can or should be abandoned in favor of a false totalization. This is the mistake of structuralism – which totalizes the symbolic code – or of humanism – which totalizes individual choice or will – or of Marxism which totalizes social structure.

American sociology, even today, has not made a semiotic turn. The dominant models of "the social" in specialty areas from demography, criminology, to the sociology of organizations or race, are either variations of humanism in which agents are imagined to willfully construct society, or versions of "structuralism" which installs "social structure" as the organizing social principle or key variable, for example, social class, the market, population, structural location, or network positioning. Even the recent emergence of cultural sociology in American sociology often figures culture as discrete, isolated values, beliefs, attitudes, identities, or ideologies. If American sociologists manage, which is still exceptional, to avoid reducing culture to motivation, intentional action, ideology, or social structure, they rarely articulate a notion of a semiotic order of signs, meanings, and symbolic codes (cf. Lamont and Wuthnow, 1990: 287, 294). There are, of course, exceptions to this disavowal of culture as a symbolic or semiotic order in American sociology (e.g. Alexander, 1989; Berger and Luckmann, 1966; Gottdiener, 1985; Gusfield, 1981; Zerubavel, 1981). Interestingly, sociologists who have made a case for a strong version of cultural sociology have often been situated in a Durkheimian and functionalist tradition which has largely been marginalized in American sociology since the late 1960s (e.g. Lloyd Warner, Talcott Parsons, Edward Shils, Robert Bellah, Jeffrey Alexander). Of course, the Durkheimian and functionalist traditions were a principal source of semiotics and structuralism, as well as the pioneering symbolic anthropology of Victor Turner (1967) and Mary Douglas (1966), both of whom have had little influence in American sociology.

The difference between cultural studies, which has made the semiotic turn, and American sociology, which has not, is evident in research in the area of the media and mass communication. Whereas many American sociologists have focused on content analysis aimed at identifying and quantifying discrete values and beliefs and with tracing media effects on its audiences, British cultural studies has approached television or film as an internal order of signs and meanings organized by codes and conventions. It analyses the process of encoding or the making of meanings, the rules and conventions governing the production of media texts, their ideological role in naturalizing and normalizing the dominant meaning systems and institutions, the multiple ways individuals are positioned and defined in these texts, the multiple audiences and the varied ways media texts are decoded or interpreted and used (e.g. Fiske, 1987; Hall, 1980a: 117–18; Hartley, 1982; Hobson, 1980; Morley, 1980). For example, in an early essay which engaged both the sociological literature in "deviance" and the media, Stuart Hall (1974) analyzed the social production of "political deviance." Specifically, he sketched a perspective emphasizing the role of the media in classifying certain types of behavior, which might very well be viewed as legitimate political dissent or social protest, as deviant or "pathological." Instead of simply analyzing the manifest content of media communications, for example, identifying the frequency of word usage or manifest social values, Hall proposed a "semiological analysis" which approaches media representation as a system of discourse internally organized by "codes" and "logics-in-use" (ibid: 74–5). He identifies the "majority/minority" symbolic opposition, a figure which is inflected by binaries such as normal/abnormal, moral/decadent, mature/immature, or healthy/mentally disturbed, as a chief structuring principle in British media representations at the time. Semiotic analysis, however, is not sufficient. "In the end, these different aspects of the process by which abnormal political events [political deviance] are signified must be returned to the level of the social formation, via the critical concepts of power, ideology, and conflict" (ibid: 86). While deploying the Althusserian and Gramscian ideas of the ideological production of hegemonic consensus or legitimation, Hall insists on the "autonomy" of cultural analysis. The relations between semiotic orders of meanings and structural dynamics of class and state formation are never simply linear, reflective, or superstructural. While structured by power and relations of domination, cultural meanings have their own internal order; signs are always polysemic or exhibit contradictory and surplus meanings; their relations to social structure and power relations is always a matter of empirical conjectural analysis.[2] "These issues can only be clarified by the study of a specific [empirical] conjuncture between the different levels of practice and institution in a historical moment" (ibid). The point to be underlined is that the semiotic turn of cultural studies opened up new fields of social analysis, new ways of analyzing media, audiences, subcultures, the dynamics of ideology, consensus making, domination, resistance, and power which have largely been absent from American sociology.

It's just a conjecture but I suspect a connection between the semiotic turn in cultural studies and its thematic shift from the more conventional social structural concerns of Marxism and American sociology, to a perspective featuring the centrality of symbolic production, knowledges, and cultural conflict in contemporary Western societies. I note something of a parallel with French social theory, especially the early work of Baudrillard (1975, 1981), Lyotard (1984), and Foucault (1979), each of whom broke away from the dominant traditions of Marxism and sociology because, in part, they imagined postwar Europe to be undergoing major changes that rendered less compelling the standard languages and thematic perspectives of social analysis, for example, the language of class conflict or bureaucratization.[3] In this regard, cultural studies seems to parallel French "postmodern" theory in viewing the new role of the mass media, the saturation of daily life by commerce and commodification, the new technologies of information, and the foregrounding of cultural politics as signaling perhaps a second 'great transformation' in post-Renaissance Western societies.

In its recentering of social analysis on symbolic production and politics, cultural studies is effecting a dramatic shift away from American sociology and from the Marxism of the academy which has continued to look to social structure – to social class, economic dynamics, bureaucracy, occupations, status groups, market exchanges, population dynamics, and network structures – as the core categories for understanding Western societies. For example, the Foucauldian turn in British and especially American and Australian cultural studies is virtually absent in American sociology. Like Marx or Durkheim in the last century, Foucault has proposed a new way of thinking about the self, the social, and history (Seidman, 1994). He has elaborated original perspectives on power, knowledge, modernization, politics, and so on. A Foucauldian perspective shifts the ground of social analysis to a focus on the making of bodies, desires, and identities, to power/knowledge regimes and to dynamics of normalization, discipline, and surveillance. A Foucauldian paradigm urges a shift from orthodox Enlightenment models of science and theory to the critical strategies of genealogy and archeology. Foucauldian-inspired social analysis has proven remarkably productive, but almost all of this work has been done outside sociology, e.g. Poster (1990), Haraway (1991), Gane and Johnson (1993), Caputo and Yount (1993), Ball (1990), Messer-Davidow et al. (1993).

I leave this section with questions: why have American sociologists resisted making the semiotic, Foucauldian turn, especially at the very moment when European theorists look to America as the key site for a potentially second great transformation of Western societies? Why have sociologists resisted the symbolic, refused the notion of a semiotic order of signs and meanings? Such questions potentially expose the epistemological and political unconsciousness of sociology, i.e. its boundaries and the defensive reactions that maintain such borders.

Imagining the Self

A second site of difference between cultural studies and American sociology relates to the theorization of the "self" or individual agency. My interest is less the question of whether agency is addressed or whether, for example, action is approached in "instrumental" or "normative" terms, or how agency can be articulated at a "micro" and "macro" level, than in core assumptions about the individual as a subject of knowledge, society, and history.

Put simply and in a very general way, a good deal of American sociology assumes the individual as a foundation of social life and figures the self as an internally coherent, rationally calculating agent. Cultural studies departs from these assumptions by imagining the individual as socially produced; as occupying multiple, contradictory psychic and social positions or identities; and by figuring the self as influenced by unconscious processes.

Classical sociology assumed its shape in part as a critique of the methodological individualism and essentialism of classical political economy and much of early modern liberalism and rationalism. We might recall Marx's critique of the presocially constituted subject in *The German Ideology* and more relentlessly in the *Grundrisse*. Similarly, I remind you of Durkheim's critique of Spencer, the English liberal economists, and the French humanists for anchoring their theories of knowledge and society in a presocial essential self. Durkheim argued that the individual was a social and historical event and seemed to function more as a symbolic or religious idea in Western modernity than as a concrete experiential reality.

As we survey contemporary American sociology, many of its major paradigms such as exchange theory, conflict sociology, rational choice, symbolic interactionism, or network analysis, posit a subject of knowledge and agent of action that is presocially formed – for example, assumed to be self oriented to maximize pleasure and minimize pain; assumed to be a rationally calculating subject; and assumed to be a subject that is naturally sexed as male or female and naturally sexual, indeed naturally and normatively heterosexual. This is a self who is figured as ego-and-present-centered and programmed (seemingly by nature) to be goal-directed, strategically rational, and social, i.e. compelled to interact or engage in social exchange. Propelled by external forces (e.g. class position, market position, the division of labor, or social role), or driven by conscious ego needs or by discrete interests, values, and beliefs, this is a self that dwells and navigates on the social surface. American sociology appears to have forgotten or to have abandoned its original impulse as a critique of the notion of a presocial self and a critique of the idea of "society" as a creation of a conscious rational subject.

In this regard, cultural studies signals a return to the European classical social theorists who aimed to furnish a sociohistorical account of the making-of-the-subject and to expose a social and political unconsciousness in the movement of individuals, societies, and histories. Cultural studies is less a literal return to the European classics than an effort to re-articulate the classical critique by drawing on the contemporary work of Althusser, Gramsci, Barthes, Foucault, feminists and psychoanalysts, especially Lacan.

In both British and American cultural studies, social accounts of the self or subject lean heavily, though by no means exclusively, on either discursive or psychoanalytic narratives. For example, drawing on Althusser's argument that ideology interpellates selves, British media studies have empirically analyzed the ways television, film, advertisements, or fashion, define and position a self. Mass media discourses do not simply influence the attitudes, values, or behaviors of audiences, but construct the self in a normative and normalizing way, for example, as a masculine gendered self or a British national self. The encoding/decoding paradigm of media studies, still perhaps a dominant paradigm despite revisions, is premised on the Althusserian concept of ideology as a social practice and discourse whose force depends on a process of interpellation (Hall, 1980a; Hartley, 1982; Morley, 1992; Williamson, 1980). The self, for example, the consumer or audience, is viewed as a social production, as a subject formed, in part, through the ways he is inscribed in discourses and practices. However, because the self is always interpellated in many discourses and practices, she is said to occupy contradictory psychic and social positions and identities – in principle, making possible opposition to dominant ideologies. Whether the focus is encoding processes in the media, reception studies, or subcultural analyses, the self is assumed to be socially and historically produced and positioned in contradictory ways to structures of dominance and hierarchy.

A striking feature of cultural studies, especially in strains of American cultural studies influenced by feminism and film theory, is its turn to psychoanalytic theory to explain the formation of subjectivity (e.g. Penley, 1992; Radway, 1984; Bhabha, 1992; Curti, 1992). The psychoanalytic turn is particularly impressive if the boundaries between cultural studies and poststructural analysis are blurred (e.g. Butler, 1990; de Lauretis, 1987; Cornell, 1992). I can do no more than briefly remark on this turn to psychoanalysis and perhaps suggest what recommends it for sociology.

Why psychoanalytic theory as a key resource for feminism and cultural studies? At least one answer is that psychoanalytic theory has provided one of the few vocabularies describing the *social formation* of subjectivity. Accordingly, psychoanalytical theory makes possible an explanation of gender identity, male domination, and sexuality which focuses on the interplay between psyche and society and on intrapsychic dynamics. Psychoanalytic theory is a social theory in that at least both object relations (see Chodorow, 1978; Greenberg and Mitchell, 1983) and Lacanian theory (see Grosz, 1990) hold that the key events in the making of subjectivity and selves are "social." Whereas object relations theory revolves around a notion of introjected social relations, Lacanian theory speaks of the introduction of the human infant into the realm of language and the symbolic – a process that elicits the mirror phase, castration fears, and the appropriation or not of the phallus which, for Lacan, are the primary moments in self formation. The power of psychoanalytic theory pivots on the presumption of the unconscious, a concept that in its broadest sense refers not only to repressed wishes and forbidden desires but to primary processes such as identification, introjection, projection, transference, or oedipal conflicts. Indeed, psychoanalysis is largely a theory which intends to expose the logic of the unconscious, to trace its voices as they surface in disguised form in the conscious life of the individual and the group. It is the appeal to an unconscious logic which is its singular contribution, a logic that explains the formation of a subject yet decenters it. Psycho-analytic theory views the self as formed in the matrix of language and communication; it frames a subject who is internally fractured and divided; this is a self driven by unconscious desires, wishes, and fears. Social ana-lysts have drawn on psychoanalytic theory to explain the formation of gender binary concepts and heteronormativity (e.g. Butler, 1990; Chodorow, 1978; de Lauretis, 1994; Coward and Ellis, 1977; Mitchell, 1974; Rose, 1986), to grasp the power of mass culture by interpreting the relation between the self and mass culture as reiterating primary psychological processes relating, for example, to pre-oedipal and oedipal dynamics (e.g. Radway, 1992). Finally, Lacanian psychoanalysis has contested key Western humanistic assumptions regarding a natural, internally unified, ego-and-present-centered subject who rationally produces knowledge, social life, and history (Grosz, 1990).

Psychoanalysis, no less than Marxism or classical sociology, proposes a depth social-theoretical logic for explaining the formation of selves and social life. If Marx can be said to have exposed the unconscious social logic of capital through the labor theory of value, price theory, the theory of surplus value, capital accumulation, the law of profit and its decline – a social logic which proceeds behind the backs of agents – psychoanalysis can be said to have furnished an analogous social logic explaining the intersubjective formation of subjectivity. Instead of the unconscious work-ings of capital, psychoanalysis exposes the operation of primary processes such as oedipal conflicts and castration complexes, shifts from the Real to the Symbolic, the mirror phase, dynamics of multiple identification, regression, narcissism, and so on, to make sense of the formation of sub-jectivity, gender, sexuality, and some of the unconscious psychological and intersubjective aspects of group life. Psychoanalysis offers a language of an intricate, dense, psychic, and intersubjective life, a life of fantasies, wishes, fears, shames, desires, idealizations, identifications, that cannot be comprehended by a vocabulary of interests, means-ends rationality, cost-benefit calculations, need dispositions, or values, or by the surface psychologies of behaviorism, cognitivism, or symbolic interactionism. Only psychoanalytic theory posits an unconscious life that shapes and impels the willfullness of an ego-present-centered self, connecting selves to objects, roles, identities, people, relations, groups, and institutions in ways that we are often unaware of but are yet mighty powerful in their opera-tion and effect.

Psychoanalytic theory has shown its productiveness as a theory of sub-jectivity, as a theory of gender and sexuality, as an account via primary processes of the relation between the mass media and the individual, as a way of imagining multiple identities, and as a challenge to Western humanism. Why have sociologists refused any serious engagement with psychoanalytic theory? Why have American sociologists who purport to aspire to social accounts of the self assumed a presocial subject, or why do they have recourse to minimal, surface concepts of the self – as ego-and-present centered, as driven by discrete needs and interests, and as navigating the world by deploying a strategic means-ends rationality? What is it about sociology that operates to refuse the unconscious? What disciplinary resistances or what defensive reaction formations structure sociological practices?

Imagining Social Knowledge

A third and final point of difference that I wish to underscore between cultural studies and American sociology pertains to general approaches to knowledge and conceptions of the role of the academic intellectual. As these issues have been a topic of much dispute within American sociology in this century, and as we could describe a range of positions cultural studies holds on this issue, my comments will aim to draw out differences by contrasting particular, though prominent, strains within both cultural studies and American sociology.

At the risk of stating the obvious, I want to underscore a point that should not go unsaid: cultural studies aims to speak about the social in a language that is no less empirical and explanatory than sociology. Indeed, in the case of British cultural studies, as I previously mentioned, many of its chief figures have been sociologists who have deliberately and posit-ively drawn on both the European and American traditions of sociology (see Hall, 1980a). Even where cultural studies departs from dominant American sociological conventions of the empirical, for example, in their turn to semiotic and symbolic analysis, such studies are no less empirical, in that they are argued through appeals to documentary evidence or, in the case of ethnographies, lived experience (Willis, 1980). There are, moreover, genres of cultural studies, especially in the United States where such work is often housed in departments of English, film, or commun-ication, which are not empirical in the sense of relying on ethnography, interviews, observation, archival research, statistical analysis, or standard historiography. I am thinking of studies which analyze literary texts or films such as Spike Lee's *Malcolm X* or advertisements for the purpose of uncovering cultural codes, for example, knowledges or symbolic logics that frame bodies in relation to a binary gender order, or that construct racialized identities (e.g. Dyson, 1995), or code identity in a civilizational binary of Orient/Occident (e.g. Said, 1978). These studies proceed on the assumption that the discovery of such "textual" codes renders them sites for "empirical" social analysis, as well as exposing them as social forces in their own right.[4] Such cultural/textual studies are no less empirical than the media studies of British cultural sociologists or the quantiative studies of social structure by American sociologists. They are *differently* empirical, but that does not make social textual analysis any less able to speak "empirically" about gender, sexuality, race, the state, nationalism, and so on.[5]

Cultural studies departs from American sociology not in being nonempirical or nonanalytical. In fact, both discursive formations, especially as practitioners of cultural studies have been trained as, or seriously influenced by, sociologists or historians, share many of the same conventions of the empirical as markers of the real and the true. Perhaps an argument could be made that cultural studies gravitates towards historical, contextualizing, and interpretive styles of empirical social analysis, whereas much of American sociology is structural and quantitative. Even if this claim is credible, these are minor differences in comparison to what I take to be a major difference. Cultural studies, or at least a prominent strain in it, views social knowledge as having value in so far as it contributes to shaping the outcome of public conflicts. Cultural studies abandons the standpoint of value neutrality to legitimate its knowledges. It acknowledges and announces that its concepts and perspectives are deliberately angled to moral and political concerns, and that they gain their warrant less from claims about the progress of science and social enlightenment, than by their practical-moral and political aims. A dominant strain of cultural studies defines the social knowledges it produces as political, as having value by virtue of its intellectual interventions into everyday struggles for social justice.

To the extent that cultural studies aspires to craft academic knowledges in relation to social movements and public conflicts, the positioning of the academic intellectual is somewhat at odds with those sociologists who frame the academic intellectual as an objective, morally and politically detached scientist. We might say, risking a somewhat over-used term, that cultural studies imagines the academic as a public intellectual. Recall that two of the key figures in the founding of British cultural studies, Richard Hoggart and Raymond Williams, taught for most of their careers as adult education tutors for a mostly working-class student body. Unlike some of their successors, they never abandoned a belief that the working class and indeed the Labour Party were the driving force for any progressive change in Britain. Their successors may have had more conventional academic careers, and their faith in the working class is surely less certain, but their work is no less intended to engage current public conflicts. From the numerous studies of popular subcultural and gender resistance inspired by E. P. Thompson's (1963) monumental effort to recover an indigenous and autonomous working-class culture (Chambers, 1985, 1986; Cohen, 1980; Hebdige, 1979; McRobbie and Gardner, 1976), to studies which expose the class, race, and gender structuring and ideological role of the media (e.g. Morley, 1992; Hobson, 1980), to sociologically informed political critique such as Hall's (1988) critical rethinking of Thatcherism as a mode of right-wing politics, to the establishment of the Institute for Social Policy in 1987 at Griffith University in Australia, inspired by the CCCS, cultural studies has aspired to be a politically engaged academic practice.

Stuart Hall (1992) has at times evoked Gramsci's concept of the "organic intellectual" to describe an ideal (p. 281). Such "organic intellectuals," though academic and often lodged in a particular discipline, intend to draw on disciplinary knowledges as a resource to speak to the key public conflicts of the day. Paralleling Foucault's notion of the local intellectual, the organic intellectual aims less to propose grand theories and make weighty pronouncements about the evolution of humanity, than is a type of intellectual who is connected to specific groups, movements, or struggles, and fashions her work as public interventions. The organic intellectual speaks less from the general standpoint of humanity and human justice than from a specific social location addressing events or developments at a particular historical conjuncture. The organic intellectual is always socially and politically situated and it is precisely this embeddedness that motivates public engagement and makes possible an effective public intervention.

American sociology has never spoken with one voice on the matter of knowledge and the role of the academic intellectual. This is a discipline that claims not only Weber and Durkheim and the rhetoric of value neutrality, but Marx and W. E. B. DuBois, Charlotte Perkins Gilman, Robert Lynd, C. Wright Mills, Alvin Gouldner, Robert Bellah, and Dorothy Smith, and that advocates a critical-moral role for sociology. Nevertheless, in contemporary American sociology the friends of scientism continue to speak with authority. To be sure, moral justifications of knowledge have never been far from the surface. Sociologists, from Blau to Collins, have insisted that the value of their work lies in its contribution to public enlightenment or social problems. Sociology is assumed to have a moral, even a political role. Its role is to make available to the public a body of scientific knowledge which might allow citizens to assess the real state of social affairs and make social policy beyond partisan politics and the clash of interests. This moral framing of sociology has not included an acknowledgment of the moral and political meaning of its own conceptual categories and strategies. The politics of knowledge is said to pertain to the uses citizens make of science, not to science itself. Ideally, ideology is to be extrinsic to sociological knowledge. This position, however, has been subject to escalating suspicions – from feminists to poststructuralists and postmodernists, who have exposed the gendered, raced, sexed, eurocentric, class-based character of the human sciences and its entanglement in power relations – from legitimating groups to constructing normative identities and enforcing processes of normalization and surveillance (e.g. Harding, 1986; Foucault, 1980; Said, 1978; Seidman, 1994).

In this regard, cultural studies re-issues the challenge to the project of a scientific sociology. Why have American sociologists refused their own practical-moral intentionality, even as the entanglement of sociology and the human sciences in the politics of the everyday has been repeatedly exposed? Why do many sociologists cling to an objectivism that contradicts the guiding premise of sociology, i.e. that the human is the social and the social is organized by the principle of difference?

Afterword

This essay is not intended to be a brief *for* cultural studies and *against* American sociology. This binary is unstable and perhaps collapses into incoherence if pressed more intently than I did. Moreover, cultural studies, at least its British version and the American rearticulation, have their own problems – for example, a lingering neomarxism that is in tension with its strong culturalism, an abandonment of literary-aesthetic critique, a tendency to lapse into scientism in British cultural studies, a textualist reductionism in some American cultural studies, and a resistance to address in a serious manner its own normative commitments and rationales. More to the point, I believe it is naive and arrogant to judge elaborate, multi-faceted traditions of social inquiry such as "cultural studies" or "American sociology" in a global manner – as if it is possible to somehow rank them as better or worse, inferior or superior. By what possible standards or, better yet, by whose standards, do "we" make such judgments and how do "we" decide whose standards and who is the "we" who decides? In the face of a relentless deconstruction of all such "foundational" efforts, no matter how sincere or inspired by humanitarian goals, to articulate a nonlocal theoretical standpoint, nonlocal standards of judgment, or a noncontextual vocabulary of "the Real," it would seem that the dream of reason to anchor itself in a nonarbitrary, nonlocal, disinterested discursive space ought to remain under permanent suspicion, if not abandoned outright. To be specific, cultural studies does not recommend itself because its language of cultural codes or its models of a layered self are warranted by their mirroring of the social universe. Nor are the quantitatively oriented empirical approaches to the social in American sociology to be recommended because they are closer to the world "as it actually is." There is, as I see such matters, no nonlocal, nonparticular, decontextualized way of deciding between what are simply different ways of mapping the social world, if the pivot of assessment is which language is closer to the real. This does not mean, though, a paralysis of critical will. We can understand traditions of social inquiry in terms of their embedded problematics and social will; we can, moreover, assess them in light of pragmatic considerations. In short, my intent has definitely not been to praise cultural studies or damn American sociology.

My aim, if you wish, has been twofold. First, to relativize sociology, thereby hoping to induce a certain critical reflexivity in a discipline which sometimes fantastically imagines its conventions and languages of the social as providing a privileged access to the social universe. In the name of this scientism it denies its own ethical and political willfulness. Second, to suggest that American sociologists might favorably consider certain conceptual moves in cultural studies, but not because they get us closer to the truth. Rather, it is because they open up new and perhaps productive ways (in terms of the aims and conventions of American sociology) of framing the social and make possible important political interventions.

Why press for relativizing sociology? One reason is that it is perhaps the only way to get sociologists, at least American sociologists, to approach what they do as itself a social construction and political practice. To the extent that sociologists imagine that their conceptual strategies and vocabularies give them privileged access to social reality, they surrender a certain reflexivity about the sociohistorical situatedness and practical-moral aspects of their own social knowledges. Problematizing the scientistic project does not mean abandoning sociology; rather, it suggests approaching sociology as just one tradition of interpreting the social which is itself implicated in the making of the social world. This perspective does not devalue sociology. It assesses its value pragmatically, or in terms of what sociology allows us to say or do about the social and in what ways it is entangled in its making. By sketching "cultural studies" as an alternative discourse of the self and the social, I merely wish to pressure American sociologists to consider the local and practical-moral willfulness of their own practices. To say it differently, relativizing sociology allows us to frame it as a social practice and to reflect upon the social interests that shape its formation and, in turn, shape the formation of the social. Relativizing sociology makes possible a genealogy of this discipline, an inquiry aimed at exposing its social and political unconsciousness. I take this to be a valuable project to the extent that the scientistic self-understanding of sociologists and its supposedly innocent will to truth continues to mask its own social productivity.

As we in the United States and perhaps in Europe increasingly occupy a "postmodern" sociopolitical terrain, we may not be forced to abandon all judgments or normative standpoints, but we may well be pressured to abandon what now appears as a naive, and no longer innocent, hope of warranting social ideas by appeals to the very nature of the social world.

Let us put this hope and project, noble as it is, and humanitarian as its motivations have been, to rest. As we can perhaps see clearer today, difference extends deep into the culture – into our ways of knowing and judging.

Does such an acknowledgment of epistemological difference and plurality entail a surrendering of critique? No. I imagine a "pragmatics of knowledge" in place of a "logic of knowledge." Here I can emphasize my second point. If I recommend certain aspects of "cultural studies" to American sociologists, it is not because I think that they will get us closer to social reality, but because of possible conceptual and social-practical gains. Regarding the former, I merely note that perhaps an argument could be made (though I won't make it here) that at least certain conceptual moves in cultural studies suggest productive ways of handling problems or concerns which are considered important by some American sociologists, e.g. relating social structure and culture, meaning and power, agency and constraint, or articulating a stronger notion of culture. There are, in addition, potential practical-moral or social advantages to cultural studies. For example, to the extent that cultural studies assigns to cultural codes the status of social facts of the first order, "culture" is positioned as a primary site of social structuration and therefore of the politics of domination, resistance, and justice. Cultural studies places struggles over meanings, identities, knowledges, and the control of discursive production and authorization on an equal footing with struggles over the distribution of material resources. Similarly, the psychoanalytical turn in some versions of cultural studies, especially in feminist social theory, suggests similar sorts of disciplinary and practical-moral "gains." A psychoanalytic perspective troubles the rather surface, ego-centered, rationalistic models of self and action that still dominate American sociology. Psychoanalysis opens up new ways of talking about self-formation and the dynamics of group life. From a practical-moral point of view, psychoanalysis contests the extreme voluntarism of much American society and sociology, a world view which undoubtedly expresses a position of social privilege. Psychoanalysis points to a layered concept of the self. It therefore makes possible new ways of imagining self and the social, and a much more layered, complex model of the interpenetration of self and society, and therefore of the dynamics of domination and resistance.

As I said in the beginning, these ideas are part of a larger project of thinking about what social knowledge might look like if we abandon or seriously rethink a modern Enlightenment framework. What happens to sociology if we no longer fetishize the Real as the primary warrant for our knowledges? What happens to the human sciences when our knowledges are viewed as saturated with a social and political willfulness, when their investment in the myth of the Enlightenment, in the grand narrative that

Truth can redeem humanity, is exposed as itself complicit with a social will which has surely, whatever good it has realized, left its mark in a trail of blood and ruined lives? Awakening from this grand stupor may not mean the end of the human sciences, but surely, at least we can hope, the end of their defensive denial of their own social productivity. Relativizing sociology means living with the moral and political responsibility of the productivity – both the good and the bad – of our own will to truth.

NOTES

1   Williams (1961: 41–5) did not abandon a literary-aesthetic approach to analyzing cultural forms. Unlike his successors, he retained the belief that one of the tasks of cultural studies was to identify general or universal aesthetic standards which can serve as norms of cultural judgment. See the comments of Stanley Aronowitz (1993: ch. 3).

2   The parallel between French "postmodern" social theory and British cultural studies which I suggested is somewhat forced and perhaps misguided, to the extent that the latter have been much more friendly to Marxism than the former. Whereas Baudrillard, Lyotard, and Foucault critique Marxism and abandon its productivist, totalizing, class-based, political-economic driven hegomonic model of society, this is not entirely the case with at least much of British cultural studies. As Angela McRobbie (1972: 719) has recently suggested, "it would be wrong to underestimate the extent to which neo-Marxist theory informed a good deal of cultural analysis in the ten-year period between 1975 and 1985" (also see Sherwood et al., 1993). It is impossible to read British subcultural studies (e.g. Cohen, 1980; Hall et al., 1978; Hebdige, 1979; see Brake, 1980), for example, without comprehending the centrality of the Marxist problematic and analytic. Nevertheless, I don't think British cultural studies managed, even then, a satisfactory or comfortable integration of semiotics and Marxism. The late 1980s and 1990s have seen considerable movement within the discourses of cultural studies away from Marxism as a master theory. Marxism is, I think, being positioned as in an equivalent relation to, say, feminism, race-based theory, or postcolonial social criticism (see McRobbie, 1992). For a retrospective view emphasizing stress points or a looser relation between Marxism and British culture studies, see Hall (1992).

3   The slippage, at least ideally, between class, social structure, and culture in much of British cultural studies is commented upon by David Morley: "In short, the relation classes/meaning-systems has to be fundamentally reworked by taking into account the full effectivity of the discursive level. Discursive formations intervene between classes and languages. They intervene in such a way as to prevent or forestall any attempt to read the level of the operation of language back in any simple or reductive way to economic classes. Thus we cannot deduce which discursive frameworks will be mobilized in particular reader/text encounters from the level of the socio-economic position of

the readers. But position in the social structure may be seen to have a structuring and limiting effect on the repertoire of discursive or decoding strategies available to different sectors of an audience. They will have an effect on the pattern of the distribution of discursive repertoires. What is more, the key elements of the social structure which delimit the range of competences in particular audiences may not be referable in any exclusive way to class. . . . The key sites for the distribution of discursive sets and competences are probably . . . the family and the school. . . . Other formations – for example, gender . . . may also have a formative and structuring effect, not only on which specific discourses will be in play in any specific text/reader encounter, but also in defining the range and repertoire of performance codes" (Morley, 1992: 70). This was written in the 1990s and is significant in at least two respects. First, it is in part a reaction to the class-driven Marxism of at least some British cultural studies, despite affirming the autonomy of cultural analysis. In some texts of British cultural studies there has been a tendency to (1) reduce social structure to a political economic concept of class and (2) to read media representations, discourses, and popular culture as an extension or subspecies of class dynamics, or as a displaced articulation of class politics, or as a way to negotiate class hegemony by voluntary or ideological means. Second, this statement shows just how far recent cultural studies, even in Britain, is moving away from Marxism. As the autonomy of sign systems is defended, as gender, race, nationalism, or sexuality is installed as a social structuring principle irreducible to the logic of class or capital, it is perhaps not misguided to describe this conceptual terrain as "post-marxist" (see McRobbie, 1992).

4 To further clarify this point, I am alluding to a body of social analysis, much of it done by professors of English or Film, which often relies heavily on poststructural ideas. Texts, whether literary or popular, official documents (census reports), or aesthetic objects, are approached as organized by cultural codes which are understood as forms of knowledge. That is, these codes are said to structure our perceptions and experiences; they define the universe of objects and their "normal" operation and order. Thus, social analysis involves exposing the knowledges that operate in texts which contribute to the construction of normative and normalizing models of self and institutional life. For example, television programs or popular music might be analyzed with an eye to their construction of feminine/masculine, or hetero/homosexual, or Occidental/Oriental binaries, symbolic figures which are themselves "social forces" no less than, say, law or the control of material resources. For further elaboration of this genre of social analysis, see Seidman (1995).

5 My point, I suppose, is that the category of "the empirical" is hardly one that can or should go uncontested. To say it differently, "the empirical" can never be anything more than "conventional" or in Foucauldian terms implicated in a particular power/knowledge regime. To the extent that "the empirical" serves in some Western societies as a marker of the real and the true, such that to claim a belief has an empirical basis, is to give a "rational" warrant for that belief, and alternatively, to describe a belief as nonempirical is to withhold such a warrant, or is to assume that the belief is held for nonrational considerations, it is important that the category of the empirical be "deconstructed"

or contested by exposing its socially conventional, and hence political, status. This is especially true in the context of a scientific culture which aims to control the conventions of "the empirical" and therefore to control what can count as knowledge and who has the authority to speak knowledgeably. Deconstructing "the empirical," or revealing it as a social artifice entangled in power, does not mean abandoning empirical analysis. We need empirical knowledges to get things done, to map social relations, to criticize social injustices, and to legislate policies, advocate social reforms, and so on. The question is the status of such empirical claims and the role of the empirical in authorizing knowledges. Deconstructing "the empirical" means that we recognize that discursive conflicts, even ones about the social, can never be resolved by appeals to the empirical alone, and that such discourses should acknowledge their own entanglement in power and therefore, at times, when pragmatically useful, bring ethical reflection and political considerations into social discourse.

REFERENCES

Alexander, Jeffrey C. 1989: Durkheimian Sociology and Cultural Studies. In *Structure and Meaning: Relinking Classical Sociology*. New York: Columbia University Press.

Althusser, Louis 1971: On Ideology and Ideological State Apparatuses. In *Lenin and Philosophy and Other Essays*. New York: Monthly Review Press.

Aronowitz, Stanley 1993: *Roll Over Beethoven: The Return of Cultural Strife*. Hanover and London: Wesleyan University Press.

Ball, Stephen 1990: *Foucault and Education: Disciplines and Knowledge*. New York: Routledge.

Baudrillard, Jean 1975: *The Mirror of Production*. St Louis: Telos.

—— 1981: *For a Critique of the Political Economy of the Sign*. St Louis: Telos.

Berger, Peter and Luckmann, Thomas 1996: *The Social Construction of Reality*. Garden City, New York: Doubleday.

Bhabha, Homi 1992: Postcolonial Authority and Postmodern Guilt. In Lawrence Grossberg et al. (eds), *Cultural Studies*, New York: Routledge.

Brake, Mike 1980: *The Sociology of Youth Culture and Youth Subcultures: Sex and Drugs and Rock "n" Roll?* London: Routledge & Kegan Paul.

Butler, Judith 1990: *Gender Trouble: Feminism and the Subversion of Identity*. New York: Routledge.

Byars, J. 1991: *All That Hollywood Allows: Re-reading Gender in 1950s Melodrama*. London: Routledge.

Caputo, John and Yount, Mark 1993: *Foucault and the Critique of Institutions*. University Park, PA: Pennsylvania State University Press.

Chambers, Ian 1985: *Urban Rhythms: Pop Music and Popular Culture*. London MacMillan.

—— 1986: *Popular culture: The Metropolitan Experience*. London: Methuen.

Chodorow, Nancy 1978: *The Reproduction of Mothering: Psychoanalysis and Sociology of Gender*. Berkeley: University of California Press.

Cohen, Phil 1980: Subcultural Conflict and Working-class Community. In Stuart Hall et al. (eds), *Culture, Media, Language*, London: Hutchinson.

Cornell, Drucilla 1992: *Beyond Accommodation*. New York: Routledge.

Coward, Rosiland and Ellis, John 1977: *Language and Materialism*. London: Routledge & Kegan Paul.

Curti, Lidia 1992: What is Real and What is Not: Female Fabulations in Cultural Analysis. In Lawrence Grossberg et al. (eds), *Cultural Studies*, New York: Routledge.

de Lauretis, Teresa 1987: *Technologies of Gender: Essays on Theory, Film, and Fiction*. Bloomington: Indiana University Press.

—— Teresa 1994: *The Practice of Love*. Bloomington: Indiana University Press.

Douglas, Mary 1966: *Purity and Danger*. London: Penguin.

Dyer, Richard 1982: *Stars*. London: BFI.

Dyson, Michael 1995: *Making Malcolm: The Myth and Meaning of Malcolm X*. New York: Oxford University Press.

Fiske, John 1982: *Introduction to Communication Studies*. London: Methuen.

—— 1987: *Television Culture*. London: Methuen.

Foucault, Michel 1979: *Discipline and Punish: The Birth of the Prison*. New York: Vintage.

—— 1980: *Power/Knowledge: Selected Interviews and other Writings*. New York: Pantheon.

Gane, Mike and Johnson, Terry 1993: *Foucault's New Domains*. New York: Routledge.

Gottdiener, Marc 1985: Hegemony and Mass Culture: A Semiotic Approach. *American Journal of Sociology*, 90, 979–1,001.

Gramsci, Antonio 1971: *Selections from the Prison Notebooks*. London: Lawrence and Wishart.

Greenberg, Jay and Mitchell, Stephen 1983: *Object Relations in Psychoanalytic Theory*. Cambridge, MA: Harvard University Press.

Grossberg, Lawrence, Nelson, Cary, and Treichler, Paula (eds) 1992: *Cultural Studies*. New York: Routledge.

Grosz, Elizabeth 1990: *Jacques Lacan: A Feminist Introduction*. New York: Routledge.

Gusfield, Joseph 1981: *The Culture of Public Problems: Drinking-driving and the Symbolic Order*. Chicago: University of Chicago Press.

Hall, Stuart 1974: Deviancy, Politics and the Media. In Paul Rock and Mary McIntosh (eds), *Deviance and Social Control*, London: Tavistock.

—— 1980a: Cultural Studies and the Centre: Some Problematics and Problems. In Stuart Hall et al. (eds), *Culture, Media, Language*, London: Hutchinson.

—— 1980b: Encoding/Decoding. In Stuart Hall et al. (eds), *Culture, Media, Language*, London: Hutchinson.

—— 1988: *The Hard Road to Renewal: Thatcherism and the Crisis of the Left*. London: Verso.

—— 1990: The Emergence of Cultural Studies and the Crisis of the Humanities. *October*, 53, 11–90.

—— 1992: Cultural Studies and its Theoretical Legacies. In Lawrence Grossberg et al. (eds), *Cultural Studies*, New York: Routledge.

Hall, Stuart, Critcher, Chas, Jefferson, Tony, Clarke, John, and Roberts, Brian 1978: *Policing the Crisis: Mugging, the State, and Law and Order.* London: MacMillan.

Haraway, Donna 1991: *Simians, Cyborgs, and Women: The Reinvention of Nature.* New York: Routledge.

Harding, Sandra 1986: *The Science Question in Feminism.* Ithaca, NY: Cornell University Press.

Hartley, John 1982: *Understanding News.* London: Methuen.

Hebdige, Dick 1979: *Subculture: The Meaning of Style.* London: Methuen.

Hobson, Dorothy 1980: Housewives and the Mass Media. In Stuart Hall et al. (eds), *Culture, Media, Language,* London: Hutchinson.

Hoggart, Richard 1957: *The Uses of Literacy.* London: Penguin.

Lamont, Michele and Wuthnow, Robert 1990: Betwixt and Between: Recent Cultural Sociology in Europe and the United States. In George Ritzer (ed.), *Frontiers of Social Theory: The New Synthesis,* New York: Columbia University Press.

Lyotard, Jean-François 1984: *The Postmodern Condition.* Minneapolis: University of Minnesota Press.

McRobbie, Angela 1992: Post-Marxism and Cultural Studies: A Post-script. In Lawrence Grossberg et al. (eds), *Cultural Studies,* New York: Routledge.

McRobbie, Angela and Gardner, Jenny 1976: Girls and Subcultures: An Exploration. In Stuart Hall and Tony Jefferson (eds), *Resistance Through Rituals: Youth Cultures in Post-war Britain,* London: Hutchinson.

Messer-Davidow, Ellen, Shumway, David R., and Sylvan, David J. 1993: *Knowledges: Historical and Critical Studies in Disciplinarity.* Charlottesville, VA: University of Virginia Press.

Mitchell, Juliet 1974: *Psychoanalysis and Feminism.* London: Allen Lane.

Morley, David 1980: *The 'Nationwide' Audience.* London: BFI.

—— 1992: *Television, Audiences and Cultural Studies.* New York: Routledge.

Murdock, George 1989: Cultural Studies: Missing Links. *Critical Studies in Mass Communications,* 6, 436–40.

O'Connor, Alan 1989: The Problem of American Cultural Studies. *Critical Studies in Mass Communications,* 6, 405–13.

Penley, Constance 1992: Feminism, Psychoanalysis, and the Study of Popular Culture. In Lawrence Grossberg et al. (eds), *Cultural Studies,* New York: Routledge.

Poster, Mark 1990: *The Mode of Information: Poststructuralism and Social Context.* Chicago: University of Chicago Press.

Radway, Janice 1984: *Reading the Romance: Women, Patriarchy, and Popular Literature.* Chapel Hill: University of North Carolina Press.

—— 1992: Mail-order Culture and its Critics: The Book-of-the-Month Club, Commodification and Consumption, and the Problem of Cultural Authority. In Lawrence Grossberg et al. (eds), *Cultural Studies,* New York: Routledge.

Rose, Jacqueline 1986: *Sexuality in the Field of Vision.* London: Verso.

Said, Edward 1978: *Orientalism.* New York: Random House.

Seidman, Steven 1994: *Contested Knowledge: Social Theory in a Postmodern Era.* Oxford: Blackwell.

—— 1995: Deconstructing Queer Theory or the Under-Theorization of the Social and the Ethical. In Linda Nicholson and Steven Seidman (eds), *Social Postmodernism: Beyond Identity Politics*, Cambridge: Cambridge University Press.

Sherwood, Steven, Smith, Philip, and Alexander, Jeffrey 1993: The British are Coming . . . Again! The Hidden Agenda of "Cultural Studies." *Contemporary Sociology*, 22, 370–5.

Turner, Graeme 1992: *British Cultural Studies*. New York: Routledge.

Turner, Victor 1967: *The Ritual Process: Structure and Anti-Structure*. Ithaca, NY: Cornell University Press.

Thompson, E. P. 1963: *The Making of the English Working Class*. London: Victor Gollancz.

Williams, Raymond 1958: *Culture and Society 1780–1950*. London: Penguin.

—— 1961: *The Long Revolution*. New York: Columbia University Press.

—— 1962: *Communications*. London: Penguin.

Williamson, Judith 1978: *Decoding Advertisements: Ideology and Meaning in Advertising*. London: Marion Boyars.

Willis, Paul 1978: *Learning to Labor: How Working-class Kids Get Working-class Jobs*. London: Saxon House.

—— 1980: Notes on Method. In Stuart Hall et al. (eds), *Culture, Media, Language*, London: Hutchinson.

Zerubavel, Eviatar 1981: *Hidden Rhythms: Schedules and Calendars in Social Life*. Chicago: University of Chicago Press.

2

Reading Architecture in the Holocaust Memorial Museum: A Method and an Empirical Illustration

MAGALI SARFATTI LARSON

The attention to objects is relatively new for sociologists. Indeed, sociology has never gone as far, nor been as rigorous or exhaustive as anthropology, in the analysis of cultural objects. We have sought to increase precision by concentrating instead on the production of culture, considering the actors who produce and consume cultural artifacts as we would other workers and consumers.[1] The production-of-culture approach has illuminated the particular institutions and organizational settings in which cultural workers produce, and thus clarified the conditions of production. But suppose we want to analyze more rigorously the words written or spoken to us at our request; or suppose we want to move beyond intuition in evaluating shifts that affect different kinds of cultural production, and perhaps be so bold as to attempt an empirical study of the new *zeitgeist*; or suppose, again, that we want to follow the path indicated by Kenneth Dauber in his analysis of differences among artifacts *within* a genre (Dauber, 1992). In all these cases, analysis needs more than repeating in our own words what others say, and more than a clever discursive rendition of our feelings on reception of the object. As sociologists of culture, we need to know what is involved in producing an artifact or a text, but we also need theoretical schemes of the differences inherent in the objects, for these differences logically precede any reception.

Bruno Latour and Madeleine Akrich's analyses of technical objects imply that they differ not by form alone, but most importantly by the *scripts* or, at least, the vague *scenarios* inscribed in them (Akrich, 1987; Latour, 1988). This essay follows their lead. It proposes a theoretical scheme of reception with relation to the built environment, and attempts, in a very preliminary way, to test empirically the scheme's heuristic usefulness. If the method has any merit, it should help us *compare* different objects of the same category or genre. However, because this is just a beginning, I cannot present a comparative series, but only one case study, or a "pilot test." While this limitation leaves a gap between abstract methodology and empirical account, it confirms, I believe, that reception of architecture cannot be easily assimilated to the well-analyzed forms of reception of popular culture products. It is specific and semiotically distinct, even though this one single test highlights the common and primary importance of previous experiences in defining reception.

I have turned for my empirical case to a notable and controversial public building, which has been the object not only of debate but also of much sophisticated critical discussion: the United States Holocaust Memorial Museum, inaugurated on the 50th anniversary of the Warsaw Ghetto insurrection, in April 1993, on the Mall in Washington. The intense and deliberate symbolic function of the building illuminates the relationships between what this artifact, as sign, *denotes* (that is, the referential function that is most concise and closest to univocal), and what it *connotes*, in a halo of polyvalent semantic references which can be tapped by the producers of the object, but neither directed nor easily analyzed. The Holocaust Museum offers us, therefore, a single but rich illustration for the theoretical scheme. James Ingo Freed, its principal designer, has explained its genesis, the use of metaphors, and the problem of intended meanings in precise and moving words. And the attention the building has received in the specialized and general press certainly meets the test of significance: the museum has been hailed by critics, to mention but a few, as "probably the most emotionally powerful architectural event most of us will experience" (Murphy, 1993); "a space of terrible beauty" (McGuigan, 1993); "a pedagogical masterpiece" (Wieseltier, 1993). Moreover, it was awarded an excellence in design award by the American Institute of Architects unanimously in the first round of jury discussions.

A full sociological account of an architectural object requires a social history of how that particular object came to be what it is, a history of the decision to build, and of how the building was commissioned, designed, realized and received.[2] Architecture is a collective undertaking, an economic enterprise, a material intervention with almost inevitable social and political implications – certainly not an autonomously conceived expression of authorship. Arguably, the first meaning of a building is economic: independently of other connotations, a building connotes the complex political economy of construction that gives it birth. Hence, as a form of production, architecture is too complex to afford anything but a limited choice of forms and control over meaning to its producers. The public, official discourse of architects and cognoscenti seldom acknowledges any of this. Yet their emphasis on the evolution of form, on objects for their own sake, indicates at one level that the discourse of specialized producers aspires to relative autonomy, while it tends, here as in other cases, to ignore or conceal its conditions of existence. At another level, it indicates to us sociologists that a theory of cultural production should find ways of taking into account something that so greatly concerns the producers themselves.

Even short of a full historical and economic account, we may want to read in architectural objects the possible responses of different categories of users, forming hypotheses about how different publics would "decode" the meaning of a building. I see the reception of buildings (and of any artifacts or products that viewers must seek out) first, from the standpoint of *access*, with all the triumph over geographic and social distance access implies.[3] Second, I see reception as a particular way of registering the sensorial impact that is inseparable from the first act of understanding and responding to images and sounds, pictures and words, buildings and films. It should be clear that sensorial experience is primordial in the reception of architecture. Furthermore, we shall see that the "reading" of architectural texts is complicated by the immediate usefulness of these objects. The semantic meaning of a building (its "message") must first of all be what it is for, to whom it is open, and subliminally, as I suggested, how costly or cheap it looks. It is obvious that architecture appears always and immediately as a construction, without this implying a "critical" reading (Liebes and Katz, 1990: 100 ff.). Buildings do not deliver a "narrative," although they can be made to suggest one; they conjure up the living purposes which they serve, and they evoke styles of life rich in ideological connotations, but successful evocation depends on knowledge about forms of social life.

In the first part of this essay, I attempt to clarify how architectural objects communicate. Drawing from semiotics and from the sociology of culture and technology, I propose some specific tools for examining the "shared significance embodied" in buildings, following the well-established principle that architectural objects communicate, precisely, through, and against, the stringent constraints to which they are subjected.[4] In the second part, I turn with these tools to my empirical example. I analyze the construction of the National Holocaust Museum by looking, first, at the intentions of the sponsors and the designers, and second, at the translation of the intended meaning into a building program. Finally, I consider how visitors read the building and decode its message. My observations suggest that the reception of *extra-architectural* meanings depends generically on the background, previous experiences, and even immediate circumstances of the viewers (as does the reception of television programs and Harlequin romances). But the reception of *architectural* meanings depends on specific experiences of building and architecture.

The Specificity of Architectural Objects

We cannot regard architectural objects only as sculptures: they are buildings first, meant for use. They are part of everyday life, a vernacular art. We understand the whole building first and above all *by its type*: we classify it as a house, a store, a museum, a prison. Our capacity to read the functions of buildings constitutes our sense of place, and indicates our level of familiarity and ease with the specific environments in which buildings take place. In turn, the clarity (or ambiguity) with which those who design and those who control buildings allow them to be read by specific publics endows buildings with different *images* and degrees of cultural presence for different users. The first meaning that a whole building denotes is the culturally and historically specific social function that it serves. We interpret this function by mobilizing complex *typological* codes that are sociological before being embodied in architectural form. Our appreciation of architecture is inseparable from the sense that its forms are appropriate for the social functions they denote. But the inappropriate, in turn, *means* something.

The utility of architectural objects poses a different challenge to the semioticist, who goes beyond merely classifying them as sociological *gestalten.* Besides association with its social functions (and whatever those evoke in the user), buildings signify as a whole, and as combinations of elements. Here comes the challenge to semiotics, for the components – doors, windows, stairs, roofs and the like – have *no referent*: they do not *mean* anything else than the function they permit. The door is a hole in the wall, which refers primarily to itself as a possibility of passage. Yet, as Umberto Eco notes, we recognize and understand "the *meaning* of 'stair as a possibility of going up' on the basis of a code that [we] can work out . . . even if, in fact, no one is going up that stair at present and even though, in theory, no one might ever go up it again" (Eco, 1973: 134). Therefore, the *denoted* meaning of architectural elements is the possibility of function codified in our culture. *We* (though not a hypothetical primitive) know that stairs as well as elevators are for going up and down and we have internalized the movements required by their use. Indeed, I do intend to suggest that some basic architectural units are more universal and more easily understood than others, *appearing* therefore as "more natural" because they evoke, as do stairs, the stepped ascension of terraced slopes, and vertical motions of the human body in unbuilt habitats.

Bruno Latour's fascinating analysis of "nonhuman actors" applies exactly to what buildings and their units denote: the scripts inscribed in their conventional forms prescribe potential behaviors (Latour, 1988). Function is *encoded* in the nonhuman elements of social life. We can describe it as do instruction manuals. We should not in principle need instructions to understand the primary, utilitarian functions encoded in our buildings. If we find our way *to* them and are allowed *into* them, we can follow automatically the *prescriptions* that their units communicate.[5]

Any building, taken as a sign and an organized system of "nonhuman actors" is a storehouse of "scripts." The internalization of basic types and scripts in a given culture is, I believe, what normally makes us ignore architectural objects. As Walter Benjamin (1968: 241) noted, they are "the prototype of a work of art the reception of which is consummated by a collectivity *in a state of distraction.*" Architects must either take this basic inattentiveness – *take it, in fact, as an indication that the building "works"* – or fight against it. They often attempt both things at the same time. Indeed, while absent-minded reception may seem a challenge for the designer, it is what allows architectural objects to live their useful lives integrated into ours: an architecture of everyday use that would incessantly call attention to itself would be the equivalent of spending one's life with someone who has only him or herself as a subject of ceaseless conversation.

This, I believe, is a paradox inherent in most architectural objects: they are not removed from the mundane contexts of our lives to the rarefied atmosphere of, say, the museum or the concert hall, but inserted into social life, to which they provide shelter, stage, and scenery. Yet the utility of architectural objects ultimately denies them the certainty of being noticed – unless, that is, *they interfere* with common codes and expected scripts.

We have identified and analyzed two different sources of opacity, both of them inherent in the social functions of buildings, which render the architectural object "invisible:" *typological codes* and *behavioral scripts*. It is not only that buildings, while they may be taken as "texts", must satisfy structural conditions based on the laws of gravity and the resistance of materials (semiotics calls these conditions *technical codes*) before they can begin to signify something. In order to denote or connote any meanings, buildings must *also* address and respect the cultural capacity of their users: how the designers (not one author, but a collective which includes the clients) imagine the various publics for the realized design plays a large part in determining reception.[6] Indeed, a public's implicit repertory of appropriate building types drastically limits architectural innovation: an architect who imposes difficult scripts and alien semantic codes on a community of users invites them to either reject or, if they can, subvert the building's design.[7]

In this respect, the reception of architectural objects appears to be generically similar to that of the culture industries' messages: they are actively interpreted in function of what the viewers themselves *are* and what they bring, collectively and individually, to the task.[8] It is not hazardous to presume that designers will feel safer offering novelty at a secondary level – a new twist, a take, a fantastic scenography to decorate the not-for-real, not-for-keeps parts of everyday life. Designers of buildings assume that a potential "public" already knows a large number of utilitarian scripts deeply inscribed in the technological infrastructure (or should we say infraculture?) of our society.

We know well, however, that the primary, utilitarian function of buildings is not all that architectural objects (designed with the intention of being different and being "more than mere building") are meant to convey. Thus, for instance, the program for Philadelphia's late nineteenth-century City Hall brazenly indicated that the doors of public rooms had to be tall and massive enough, and their handles placed high enough, to awe immigrant masses assumed to be short.[9] In Eco's apt expression, an architectural object *denotes a form of inhabitation*, just like a spoon promotes and signifies a form of eating; but it can also *connote* the overall ideology that informed the architect's design, the symbolic differences that architect and client intended to mobilize, either for themselves and other users (as in the example above), or inadvertently, because they ignore what users are capable of decoding.

In sum, the complex cultural codes that a public mobilizes to "read" a specific building depend on how that particular object fits into the public or the publics' tacit repertoires of built forms, which may far exceed their actual experiences with and in buildings. I submit, in fact, that mobilizing *a system of differences* may be the main interest of architects and their clients. Although they obviously must see to fulfilling the primary functions of construction, even typological decoding (and therefore the reading of social functions which I consider primary) is in large part dependent on a repertoire of forms, a system, arranged hierarchically and more or less coherently to reflect social differences. We know that this is a storefront, in part because it is *not* a residence, but then if we are in Harlem we also know it may be a church. We know that the shining BART station must be a station, but it does not quite "fit;" it is, indeed, *different*, a place of departure from tradition, more than a place of return to the home.[10] We know that the Holocaust Memorial Museum is a museum because it is now on the Washington monuments tour (or because our high school takes us there); we may not know much more about it.

Connoted meanings are the secondary function of architectural objects, no less socially significant than the primary uses they *denote*. Responding to a collective intention, architects fill buildings with signs that mobilize systems of difference and convey connoted meanings. Difference can be marked through size, form, ornament, and style (which includes all of the above). By means of formal conventions and stylistic signs, architects proclaim that their product is different from "mere building." Style signifies that something special is happening, both for those who can recognize the conventions and for those who cannot. Style deals in *connoted* meanings. I believe it moves the users *from a form to an ideology* of inhabitation.

The shift in signification depends on a system of differences in which cost obviously plays an important part when we consider the making of a single building. But cost disappears as a determinant of difference when we consider that any new building enters into *immediate relations with its neighbors, and into mediated relations with all the buildings past and present that its users know.* This, perhaps the most distinctive and specific signifying capacity of architectural objects, resides in the *durability* of buildings and in their special relation with cities.

The durability of buildings constitutes a source of opacity and contradiction which the great Austrian novelist Robert Musil particularly applied to monuments. Our scheme can imply that monuments suffer in a particular way from the common paradox of architectural objects. The public's inattentiveness contradicts their difficult mandate, which has to do with embodying or preserving memory, in principle unassisted by historical facts and narrative. Musil wrote:

> There is nothing in the world as invisible as a monument. . . . They are no doubt erected to be seen. . . . But at the same time they are impregnated with something that repels attention. . . . Anything that endures over time sacrifices its ability to make an impression. Anything that constitutes the walls of our life, the backdrop of our consciousness, so to speak, forfeits its capacity to play a role in that consciousness. (Wieseltier, 1993: 19)

Later, we shall see how the Holocaust Memorial Museum knowingly confronts this contradiction.

Buildings *outlive* the inevitable obsolescence of the codes by which we read them. The durability of architectural objects inevitably loads them with historical references: for both learned and lay knowers, the architectural object is full of implicit and explicit comparisons to other objects, past and present. For the architect, every design implicitly or explicitly deals with the history of forms – negating it, alluding to it, analyzing it, invading and remaking it. Inevitably, the durable built environment, formed by accretion, leads owners, architects, direct users, and publics to retrieve and repossess obsolete forms. Some resuscitated forms can be read *philologically*, as Eco says, under the codes pertinent to their birth. Thus, refined users enjoy the performance of medieval or baroque music with the instruments and musical notations of that time. But in capitalist society, the repossessed form-sign (and especially the recycled piece of real-estate) is offered as a commodity, as an object of desire and purchase. Yet, even if it is not commoditized (as public monuments are not), the resurrected form-sign is nonetheless abstracted from its original abode and reinserted in a new context. Eco argues that this recycling of form, which he calls *semantic fission*, enriches the form-signs with new meanings.

The incessant and automatic semantic fission which takes place in cities marks them as the theoretical space where architectural meaning can reveal its fullest and most complex potentials. All buildings, not only those designed to be beautiful or special, constitute by accretion the living fabric of cities; through dense or sparse groupings, through full and void spaces, buildings in the urban tissue make visible not only the obsolescence of old codes, but also the ever-present past of built architectures. In cities, the objects of semantic fission are inevitably *public*, and each of the surviving, resurrected and reinterpreted objects refers us by tacit comparisons to all the other forms and ideologies of inhabitation that we know. Architecture is the most culturally potent in cities because there it becomes the most fully and unavoidably public, the most available for inspection, if not for use. There, architects face the problem of either displacing other objects and their codes of interpretation, or seeking a dialogue with the context, that is, establishing differences within a common code. How users (intended and not) respond to the always rhetorical connotations of architecture depends on who the users are.[11] Yet I am arguing that "reading architecture" may (in fact, should) begin with what the signs themselves convey. In establishing, first, what architectural objects denote, and by what means, we shall ask how well and for whom they denote *their type*, and how well and for whom these objects "work."

I furthermore submit that, as buildings are used, the success or failure of their denotations (which often translates into comfort or discomfort, ease or difficulty of use) is the platform from which connotation takes off. For this reason, we cannot analyze what buildings "mean" to whom, independently of how well they "work." Investigating the relationship of a particular "public" (sometimes hard to define, as in a Washington museum) with a specific building involves finding answers to particular questions. How well does this "public" know the typology of building in its society? How extended is this public's repertory of forms? How flexible is this particular public (and even a generic public, cross-cut by the habitual sociological cleavages of class, age, gender and race, with possibly other qualifications involving indicators of visual and architectural culture) in its interpretations and judgments of architectural propriety? What does it *know* about a specific building and its history? Because people experience architecture in sensorial and kinetic ways that are very hard to put into words, these are only theoretical questions to keep in mind, to translate into more answerable form as we observe how users appropriate a building and enact the scripts it embodies. The same caveats apply, even more forcefully, to the study of what buildings connote.

Clients and their designers can deliberately seek to produce effects or, in other words, to introduce connotation in their building. But a building also (and perhaps more importantly) inadvertently connotes different things for different kinds of publics. If we do not want to confirm our preexisting ideas about reception, only prolonged observation of how a building is used can tap how meaning is constructed by viewers and users. Only in-depth interviewing might (only *might*) allow us, in turn, to check the accuracy of our reading. Because this is a long and difficult method of research, my "case study" illustrates it only by default. The Holocaust Memorial Museum is a powerful example of urban semantic fission and architectural symbolism. My beginning analysis of how the museum achieves its purpose relies most heavily on the architects' interpretation of the clients' program, on the critics' reactions, and on my own brief and preliminary reading of observed behaviors, augmented by a few responses I solicited from willing visitors.

The United States Holocaust Memorial Museum in Washington, DC

Genesis and program

An increasing number of Holocaust memorials have recently been raised in the United States and in Europe, most significantly in Germany.[12] Commemoration is prompted now by the survivors' fear that memory itself will die with them, and by the horror of seeing memory erased by the Holocaust deniers. Commemoration is also politically motivated. In Germany, remembering the victims of Nazi bestiality is a way of signifying that Germany has changed since World War II (Young, 1992). In the United States, also, the idea of a National Holocaust Museum (as the signs in Washington's subway name it) has political implications.

Suggested to President Carter by young Jewish staff members, the project was authorized by Congress in 1980, after the sale of F-15 jets to Saudi Arabia had greatly upset the Jewish community (Lipstadt, 1993: 40). The 1980 Act of Congress charged the US Holocaust Memorial Council (hereafter, "the Council") with the commemoration of the Holocaust in America. Part of its charge was "to plan, construct and oversee the operation of a permanent living memorial museum to the victims of the Holocaust," to be erected on federal land with private donations. The site chosen was 1.7 acres off the Mall, 400 feet from the Washington monument, between the red Victorian Auditor's building on the North side and the enormously long limestone colonnade of the Bureau of Engraving and Printing on the South. Here, in the words of Michael Berenbaum, the project director, started the process of the "Americanization of the Holocaust," including the attempt to connect the Holocaust with the official mythology and idealized self-image of the United States as the world's guarantor of tolerance and freedom (Young, 1993).

Irit Rogoff has noted that traditional forms of commemoration are hard to escape: they involve coherent narratives of the nation, and a homogenization of the image of both perpetrators and victims, who are re-membered (as the contrary of dis-membered) as monolithic symbols of evil and goodness.[13] It was to some extent far-fetched to find a coherent justification of the museum's location. The Council tried, observing that "the Holocaust has special importance for Americans: in act and word the Nazis denied the deepest tenets of the American people" (Young, 1993: 335, 337). Even before the project was built, detractors and supporters alike saw it as the ultimate in semantic fission: a Holocaust Memorial Museum would insert among the nation's sacred shrines the memory of unspeakable evil perpetrated elsewhere, against victims who were not American, by torturers and executioners who were not American either. While the commemoration of ignominy is not infrequent in our century, it is always difficult, and often resisted by public opinion.[14] The fact that Americans had neither committed the horror nor directly suffered it did not make it easy to include into a *coherent* national story.

President Carter had to find "American reasons" for erecting *on the Mall* a memorial to these foreign victims of a foreign power on foreign soil. He could not say, as did some critics, that, in the United States, "the past *is* a foreign country. The collective memory of this country will always include names and dates foreign and far away" (Wieseltier, 1993: 26). So the president had to give reasons that seem contorted, considering the Allies' refusals to aid the Jewish victims of Nazism or to bomb the concentration camps and the railroads leading to them:

> It was American troops who helped liberate many of the death camps and who helped to expose the horrible truth. . . . Also, the United States became a homeland for many of those who were able to survive. Secondly, however, we must share the responsibility for not being willing to acknowledge forty years ago that this horrible event was occurring. Finally, because . . . we feel compelled to study the systematic destruction of the Jews so that we may seek to learn how to prevent such enormities from occurring in the future. (Young, 1993: 335–6)

These reasons did not stop either controversy about the site, or conflict about the design, with both the Council as client and the Fine Arts Commission as Washington's fastidious watchdog. In 1985, after five abortive years of rejecting architect after architect, the firm of Pei Cobb Freed and Partners was selected precisely for how well it had dealt with the Fine Arts Commission during the design of the East Wing of the National Gallery, and James Freed was persuaded to take charge. Yet even then, the Commission rejected his first design. Finally, in 1987, after much wrangling, the basic design that we see today was approved.[15] Once built, Freed's "unquiet" design for that august site off the Mall won nothing but acclaim, despite criticism of *the purpose* of such a memorial.[16] The museum's cost is not officially quoted: estimates go from 90 million (Muschamp, 1993) to 168 million (Gill, 1993); the difference may reside in the inclusion or exclusion of the cost of the exhibits.

For several reasons, this extraordinary building provides a good illustration of how architecture "speaks" in its designers' and in its public's mind. First of all, the Holocaust Memorial Museum is a public building, therefore not in principle shaped by requirements of the commodity form. Furthermore, it is more democratic in its reach than art museums, patronized on the whole by a more educated, more professional, more affluent and somewhat older public than museums in the "history, science, or other" category (Zolberg, 1992: 190). Second, the building is extraordinarily successful. Although the attendance figures publicized by museums cannot be taken at face value, the figures for the Holocaust Museum's first year are remarkable: it has received almost 2 million visitors (62 percent of them non-Jewish); 5,000 visitors *each day* to its permanent exhibits, including an average of 18 school groups; 90,000 school children, of which two-thirds came from public schools (Weinraub, 1994). By comparison, visitors to the Hirschhorn's sculpture museum numbered little over 900,000 and to the Corcoran, 225,000.

The museum's administrators have been quick to interpret these figures as proof that both the building and its contents fully satisfied the Council's difficult and, in fact, contradictory mandate. They attribute the success to the trove of information available in the brilliant, heart-shattering exhibits and in the technologically stunning learning center, as well as to Freed's much acclaimed design. The museum's director, Jeshajahu Weinberg, creator of the story-telling museum of the Diaspora in Israel, attributes this museum's appeal to the coherence of its terrible story; the museum is gripping, he thinks, because it "is built around a plot, like a novel or a movie. . . . You identify with the heroes and resent the villains" (Weinraub, 1994). It is important to note that Freed's design in authoritatively presented as itself embodying the atrocious narrative of the Final Solution, as in Berenbaum's "semi-official" description in the exhibits catalogue:

> The building itself serves as an introduction to the Holocaust's "universe," providing subtle architectural metaphors and reminiscences of historical

experience. Four towers on the north side . . . evoke the watch towers of the death camps. . . . The central atrium-like gathering place of the museum – the Hall of Witness – is defined by its distortions: a skewed and twisted skylight; a glass fissure running the length of the floor. In the idiom of architectural poetry, the building reflects the rupture of civilization that took place during the Holocaust. (Berenbaum, 1993: 234)

In a profound essay, Leon Wieseltier echoes Maurice Halbwachs, for whom history begins when the memory of an event wanes in the consciousness of real subjects. He explains why the museum is "a pedagogical master-piece," which "begins at the beginning and ends at the end:"

One of the achievements of the Holocaust Memorial Museum is that it leads its visitors directly from history to silence. Its exhibition ends in a Hall of Remembrance, a six-sided, classically proportioned chamber of limestone, a chaste vacancy, seventy feet high, unencumbered by iconography, washed in a kind of halting light, in a light that seems anxious about its own appropriateness. There are steps all around the cold marble floor that will most likely serve as seats. The least that you can do, after seeing what you have just seen, is sit down and be still. The Hall of Remembrance is a temple of ineffability. *This, then, is the plot, the historical and spiritual sequence got right of the infernal display on the Mall: memory, stiffened by history, then struck dumb.* (Wieseltier, 1993: 19, 20; my emphasis)

This is then the third reason for choosing this building as illustration: the museum is a magisterial example of deliberate connotation. It was James Freed's decision to fight the Fine Arts Commission and some members of the Council's "unadmitted drive to neutralize, to make it less potent;" it was his desire to make "a building that allows for horror, sadness . . . an architecture of sensibility . . . an architecture that engages viscerally (Freed, 1989: 61).[17]

The President's Commission on the Holocaust had "called for an institution that was at once of 'symbolic and artistic beauty' and which would 'present' the Holocaust" (Sorkin, 1992: 74). Elie Wiesel, who wrote the Presidential Commission's report, said that the building should disturb (Freed, 1989: 61). The task was to make stones speak of the unspeakable, in a context of uncritical nationalism close to the "feel good" sentimentality of kitsch. Freed's daunting task was to let memory speak, yet avoid "theme park" reconstructions, or even allusions that would appear to beautify the memory of Auschwitz. Art was to represent not Auschwitz, but *memory*. The dilemma is that knowledge and expression can conflict, and Freed wanted to achieve both things; in the Hall of Witness, he said, "I wanted to make a scream" (McGuigan, 1993: 51). This was *a shrine*, and as in all shrines, the brief was to make the content sublime.

The Holocaust Memorial Museum is a public building, a museum with a complex program and a paradoxical brief, perceived by many as a purposive semantic fission. The museum shelters a narrative of the event that stands for the perversion of reason in our century. The building itself tells a story. Thousands of visitors to Washington have been exposed to these narratives. To illuminate how the architects went about creating meanings that the crowds might retrieve, I turn now to the architects' story.

Process and resolution

A narrative *of* the Holocaust Museum, as we shall see later, is becoming an integral part of how the narrative *in* the museum is received. The narrative *of* the museum features James Ingo Freed, partner-in-charge of design for the project. In a team that included four partners besides Freed, ten associates and thirty-four other employees of the firm, plus an associate firm in Washington DC, the story gives Freed a role as large and a signature as personal as those of any charismatic genius in architectural tradition. For those who know Freed's previous work, it is almost a narrative of conversion.

James Freed was a student at the Illinois Institute of Technology's School of Architecture, of which he later was to become Dean; there he was able to study and work with Mies van der Rohe, the laconic master of German modernism. The influence, he reported, was profound. Since the mid-1950s, Freed has been associated with I. M. Pei's firm, whose work, says the *New York Times* critic Herbert Muschamp, "has epitomized the corporate acceptance of a once radical style of design. The projects Freed has designed for Pei . . . are late modern classics that achieve visual interest through the minimal manipulation of expressed structure and geometric form" (Muschamp, 1989: 30). Indeed, we were entitled to expect a "black box" container from the man and his firm, but here the other part of the narrative sets in.

Freed is a German Jew who left his native Essen in 1939, at age nine, with his four-year-old sister; his parents fled three years later; most of his relatives died in the ghettos or in the camps. Freed, who defines himself as an atheist (Gill, 1993: 108), remembers the Essen synagogue burning on Kristallnacht. For the first six months of the project, Freed and his team read and looked at films ("until we were blurry eyed"); they studied the buildings Jews inhabited before the Holocaust: images of Jewish life in various parts of Central Europe "had a residual, lingering presence in our minds, and that's partially what our building is about" (Freed, 1989: 62). The memory of the ghettos gave them the image of bridges as markers for the ferocious segregation of the Jews, and the disabling notion of void.

Indeed, after the razing of the Warsaw ghetto only the grid of the streets was left, and silence. Freed told a reporter, "I couldn't get it." So he left in 1986 for Germany and Poland.

From the death camps Freed brought back haunting images: the gates that pretended there was a future ("Arbeit macht frei"); the ubiquitous watchtowers; the blank Killing Wall of Auschwitz; the bricked-in windows, mute; the triangles that sorted prisoners out; fences (they "became an obsessive thing"); and an architect-specific memory of how the camps were built. The brick ovens had to be strapped in steel because overuse created the danger of explosion from internal gases; "the addition of heavy steel to a raw wall became a very important thing for me," says Freed (1989: 62–4). For him, the death camps represented more than an emotional turning point, a demonstration of the terrible incongruity of values: the architectonic truth of which modernists had made a principle may lead to beauty, but it cannot banish evil. Freed reports, movingly: "The memory of the place has to stand in lieu of the event. The silence. Also, when you look at this construction, you see that the sort of modernist attitude towards the showing of structure and the perfection of things is a way of thinking that can also lead to the perfection of a process, but in this case the perfection of a death factory" (Freed, 1989: 63).

We can read in between the lines the words that also resonate throughout Alain Resnais's film *Nuit et brouillard*, another object of terrible beauty: *architects and engineers designed those gates, those towers, the gas chambers like showers, the crematories.* Freed returned from his trip with "a collage of abstracted forms invented and drawn from memory" (Brochure). The camps were systems that dictated the behavior of their inmates, and ultimately abolished life; the shells in which that abolition happened are still there. Out of the recognition that real human beings designed *that*, I believe Freed drew the necessity of an architecture of irresolution and ambiguity. During production, he said: "I go around and take things away from people in the office who are trying to resolve them. I want [this building] to be a little raw still. Not just in the materials but in the conceptualization and even in the actualization" (Freed, 1989: 65, 73). A hard choice to make for an architect of exacting and impeccable craftsmanship, and an impossible objective to achieve: a finished new building is not "unresolved," nor was this particular one left "raw" or undetermined; it is quite evident to knowing critics as well as to naive visitors that this is the meticulous realization of a deeply thought *plan*.[18]

Freed's account is permeated with awareness that he must get the design approved by the client and by the Fine Arts Commission.[19] He repeatedly states the intention of separating the visitor from Washington, yet the building had to "fit," somehow, or it would not be approved. So the building is part brick and part limestone, a dual texture recalling the different materials of which its neighbors are made. "This strategy," the architect says, "tied us to Washington. . . . It allowed us to argue with the Fine Arts Commission for the need to deal differently with the scale of the forms. And it allowed me to form certain critiques of the monumental Washington front" (ibid: 61).

On Fourteenth Street, the facade had to align itself with the monotony of government buildings; the program, on the other hand, called for a big plaza, where buses could unload schoolchildren and visitors could gather. The solution was to make the building visible, next to the interminable linear facade of the Bureau of Engraving, by a curved neoclassical limestone screen which is a pure fake of a facade, with no ceiling: "You pass through the limestone screen to enter a concrete world. We disorient you, shifting and reentering you three times, to separate you emotionally as well as visually from Washington" (ibid: 65). I find the fake facade disturbing: above its rectangular arches are square windows filled in with stone grids; this speaks the pompous official language of the state, but *not quite*, as it leads us uncertainly into that other world that also speaks a language of the state.

A glass cube on the right was meant to take groups directly to orientation classrooms in the lower concourse, but it is closed now;[20] the entrance on the left is "a steel pavilion, angled toward the Mall" (Brochure). What the architects intended as a subtle reference to the Nazis' triage is lost, but not the disorientation: visitors are seen to hesitate between the two protruding entrances. Inside, the semi-circular space is not strongly oriented either, allowing for several possible directions: toward the bookstore, behind the guard's desk and deep to the left of the wall decorated with the flags of the liberating armies, easy to ignore; straight ahead, under a sort of portico, toward the elevators to the permanent exhibits. Going to the right, toward the ticket desk and stairs to the lower concourse, we can turn almost immediately to the left, through a narrow passage, on to the steel platform that overlooks the Hall of Witness. The platform is an extruding hub, separated from the vestibule by glass panes encased in steel, from which it is not easy to go back, although one has the choice to go left to the elevators, right into the temporary exhibition spaces, or straight into the Hall. People stop, however, some for an instant, some longer, sitting down, "reading the script" of the benches, the low overhang, the flat steps. There is a distinct acoustical change in this passage, as Freed desired, and a tactile transition to the Hall of Witness in the platform's raw, stamped-steel plate.

The 7,500-square feet, three-stories high space of the Hall is Freed's "scream." But it works: it serves as the circulation and distribution core, in the same way that the slightly puzzling turns we took, left, right, left, serve to control traffic; in the same way that the five-feet gap between the

floor and the north wall, crossed by small steel bridges, serves to illuminate the Education Center in the basement floor, as does the diagonal
glassblock slit that traverses the granite floor of the Hall of Witness,
exactly mirroring the peak of the skylight's roof, 57 feet above. Here is
how the brochure describes the incision that "[shears] the museum
experience in two: ordinary museum functions (entry/exit, coatroom,
bookstore) on the left and on the right, extraordinary museum content.
The fissure contributes to a general sense of disjunction as it reinforces a
predetermined path of movement toward the west." This is the architect's
art, to make somber poetry out of functional devices.

During my observation, a young guide leaves his post behind the information desk to talk to a young tourist couple. He tells them that the glassblock slit, with its 13-degree angle, points to the Lincoln Memorial at the
end of the Mall: "it says that democracy can prevent the Holocaust from
happening." Later, I ponder about this explanation (also given by the
New York Times' Muschamp): it seems contrived, in a building *without
windows*, where the westward movement of the incision leads *directly* to
the memorable stairs. They stand against a wall of black granite cut by
three rectangular arches at the top, and at the middle, asymmetrically, by
a square window with a steel grate.

The stairway to the second floor is narrower at the top than at the
bottom, flanked by steel railings; it reminds one of a railroad track; it leads
to a bare gray arch in the black granite wall, cut by three open rectangles.
The twin stair to the lower concourse descends along a brick wall, which
is only interrupted by a large grate of steel; this stairway opens on a
stepped landing that is literally torn apart by Richard Serra's vertical sculpture, a 30-ton steel block that forces us to move left, before we can pass
under a square opening and go behind and around the black wall, right
again. The conventional script is that stairway landings give us the option
of moving right or left; here, the interference with that habit is disconcerting.

The Hall that a critic called "the atrium from hell" is hard to describe
(Muschamp, 1993). The only curved lines are the flattened lintels of the
arches in the walls, of the single arch at the top of the stairs, of the
elevator gates; girded in steel, these are not soothing curves. Freed
explained: "We would always use an angle: primary angle construction,
where everything, bracing, bridges, trusswork, is built up of double angles"
(Freed, 1989: 72–3). The windows are blind, shuttered or barred with
steel. The textures are hard, industrial: brick walls, steel railings, steel crossed
bars, glass, except for the shining black granite and its reverse image,
the white marble wall that we only see at the end of the visit. "The brick
is load-bearing, turnbuckles connect tie rods, and structure is exposed.
The tectonic language is used to explore the fateful misperception that
technology is inherently good" (Brochure).

Visitors go up and down the stairs slowly but without any noticeable gravity, although I did not see kids running. Serra's sculpture, however, is more unusual than stairs. It looks as if it has fallen from the sky (from which indeed it was lowered), and abruptly shears the steps of the lower-floor landing. School kids stop and circle it; they laugh in disbelief. I did not see anyone carrying on loudly directly under the skylight, the single most powerful element in the Hall.

The skylight presses down upon the atrium at third-floor height. It "begins with an uneven slope," says the brochure, "and twists on its way to the far end of the Hall. . . . The deformation is dramatized by the shingled glass panels which lift up at the corners as if some great pressure had buckled them out of their aluminum frames." The Holocaust victims, Freed writes, said that "the only thing they had left was the sky" (Freed, 1989: 62). Here we see the sky through the twisted and heavy trusses, but it is not free: it is crossed by a double glass bridge above the skylight at the fourth and third floors; on each side, the brick walls continue into four brooding shapes, reminiscent of the camps' watchtowers; on the bridges, ghost-like silhouettes pass, or hover. When we are inside the Hall, we feel watched.

From the bridges, we look down at the Hall through the distorted sky-light, as through a veil of tears, its long glass wall etched with the names of obliterated communities on the fourth-floor bridge, with first names of victims on the third floor. One can read only a few names; their number is unbearable when you know what they mean. Yet very few people stop: a man shows the names to his child; three schoolgirls on their own saunter by indifferently; old ladies notice that dark clouds have gathered over the dark monitor roof of the skylight; it is raining. Yet the raw power of the distorted skylight form is frightening and riveting; the average viewer, entranced by its abnormal beauty, does not register this as the extraordinary engineering feat it is.

These bridges are part of the "journey through time," which, as the brochure says, "begins with an elevator ride to the fourth floor and descends in rotations around the building to the third and second floors." The steel gates of the unpainted elevator slide heavily, locking some 25 strangers together in a small space for a short but disquieting moment, during which a TV monitor lights up, soldiers crouch, move forward, and an American voice says, "We are not sure what this is . . . a big prison of some sort" and then, he sees: "An American can't imagine. . . ."

On the fourth floor, the exhibit first traces life before the Nazi assault, the rotation ending in the three-story Tower of Faces, a space redesigned by the architects to accommodate the photographs of the people of Eishishok, a *shtetl* in Lithuania: some 900 years of history, 3,500 inhabit-ants, were killed in two days in 1941 by the Einsatzgruppen; there were

29 survivors. One of them spent over 12 years collecting these 1,135 portraits and scenes from 50 years of Jewish life: lining the tower's walls, which narrow at the top, they climb out of sight toward the skylight. We see them and we don't, realizing that these life-loving people, their rich culture, are lost. A man does not understand; he says, unsolicited: "What a way to hang pictures, you can't see them!" He was interested, but discouraged by the unusual display; yet a 13-year-old black kid stops, stays behind his indifferent classmates, leans toward the pictures at his height, looks closely, absorbed. I tell him: "This is what the people who died looked like." He says, "I know" and "I had already seen these ladies before," then runs after his class. A steel bridge forms the floor at this level of the tower; after passing through the infernal third floor, we come back under it, see the rest of the photos, without light, dead.

We descend toward the third-floor exhibit – the Final Solution – by a narrow staircase. We enter "a double-story lounge intended for orientation and composure," in which the artist Ellsworth Kelly has created a white installation and seating. The high school classes sit, their composure not too evident, but they are quiet, on the whole. We enter hell through a wooden bridge. We see part of the Warsaw ghetto wall, and films, objects, pictures, words, relics, authentic artifacts, a car from a transport train. The humble objects speak of everyday life, as in any other history museum. They do not convey the horror, which comes from elsewhere, numbing. After the rotation, the second floor opens with a row of TV sets, projecting the sickening discoveries of the three liberating armies, and "the aftermath." There is place for the rescuers, but the victors' treatment of the survivors, as inconvenient encumbrances, does not bring any relief, any uplift, at the end of the journey. Before the end, next to the replica of a wall made of Jewish tombstones from destroyed cemeteries, the architects have designed a shallow semicircular auditorium; it faces a giant screen, on which survivors appear, tell the tale of the horrors we have seen, often cry. Many visitors congregate and linger here, as if there was a need to know that someone survived, to see people who are alive.

A darkened sloping corridor takes visitors to the opening of the hexagonal Hall of Remembrance, a high, lighted space. This was the only mandated form, and the only allusion that subsists to the six points of the Jewish star or the six million Jewish victims. The Fine Arts Commission, wishing to scale down the assertiveness of Freed's first design, wishing to promote a reading consonant with an idealized version of American democracy, asked for views of the Jefferson and Washington monuments, and forbade the original design of bricked-in windows. Limestone replaced brick, but slits at each corner are the only windows the architects agreed to open. They are visible through triangular cut-outs from the central space, so that the tall chamber appears made by floating tablets.

Most critics think that the Hall of Remembrance is the crowning achievement in this design. It is cold and official. The tempietto-like exterior, detached from the main body of the building, prospects on the Mall from Raoul Wallenberg Place and blends in without "critique" of its official neighbors.

A guard has made the comment that "most people get what the museum means, but the kids are just kids, they run around here like anywhere else in their school visit." Yet in the Hall of Remembrance, I see kids unsupervised but quiet, even as they move around, or look at the altar with its eternal flame. Many of the people I talk to are here *before* seeing the permanent exhibit, which is not what the designers intended.[21] Some of the visitors sit quietly for quite a long time. This Hall was intended for commemoration and meditation; on the whole, it seems to work as a cold, sobering space.

Constructing reception

Contemporary architectural critics are not used to an architecture "of visceral memory," which seems to them perilously close to kitsch. This may be the reason why, as Hélène Lipstadt cleverly notes, the rhetorical power of the narrative has prevented most critics from asking in this case obvious *architectural* questions about form, sources, references (Lipstadt, 1993: 40).[22] What Lipstadt calls an "obsession with the metaphorical" ignores Freed's repeated intention of leaving his "banal" symbolic forms open to multiple readings. Indeed, from the best critics and the sophisticated commentary of the Director of Public Relations for a VIP group, to the young guard I quoted, to the bumbling older guard who "orients" a ninth-grade class from California, the narrative *of* this building consists in fastening to its forms the very personal meanings outlined by Freed in his 1989 article (with a mixture of the requisite official optimism about democratic values). The orientation is interesting: the older guard asks the class if they know what the Holocaust is; they say "yes" (with some mocking "yeeeses" thrown in). His talk goes something like this: "The museum was designed by a man called James Freed. He is from Germany himself, and he went back to Germany [sic] to get ideas for the building. There is more symbolism in this museum than in any other in Washington" [the kids' expressions sink]. He explains that the panels of glass in the skylight are of different sizes and that the bridges "remind you of the Warsaw ghetto bridges that Germans built because they did not want people to have contact with the Jews in the ghetto" [sic]; the brick and the steel "are also to remind you of the concentration camps." He tells them the themes of the exhibit, and tells them to go to the bathroom *before* starting the tour, even though there are bathrooms and fountains also on each floor. "There will be no eating, not even gum and keep your voices down."

The Director of Public Relations, of course, gives exact historical detail; probably because he knows Freed well, he goes beyond the article, matching meaning with form more firmly than does Freed: the Fourteenth Street entrance – the "pure fake" – recalls the deception the Nazis practiced on Jews when they deported them "to be resettled in the East," the steel strapping on the right wall of the Hall of Witness *is* like that of the ovens (in fact, it is *not* strapping) to symbolize that there is explosive knowledge inside that part of the museum, where the Learning Center resides; the glass incision in the floor symbolizes the fracture of civilization. . . . In these narratives, even in those of the critics, the *service* lent by the architectural forms, prominent in the architect's account, is minimized, or disappears. Architecture is reduced to connotation but what it connotes is authoritatively suggested.

Sophisticated viewers respond with perplexity to the fusion of the shrine with its content.[23] Herbert Muschamp asks: "Would we find the design so overwhelming if it served a less urgent moral cause?" But he then concludes: "Mr. Freed defies us to separate esthetics from morality, art from politics, form from content." His "powerful use of references" is far from contemporary pastiches and revivals. To "those architects who have reduced symbolic form to genteel imitation of period styles," but not only to them, Freed "implicitly asks, *You want the past? You want European traditions? Here: take another look*" (Muschamp, 1993; my emphasis). This is perhaps the most devastating of the meanings attached to the Holocaust Museum, were it not weakened by the celebration of democracy, the foremost examples of which were until the bitter end unwilling to stop the catastrophe.[24]

James Freed asked: "Who's going to see this museum?" And he answered himself: "People who don't even know what the Holocaust is. . . . It is not meant to be an architectural walk, or a walk through memory, or an exposition of emotion, but all of this. I want to leave it open as a resonator of emotions" (Freed, 1989: 73). But can this building *create* emotions for those who do not know? Can the stones speak without the exhibits?

In May, the crowds are very large and official Washington is packed full with school buses. In the museum, there is much milling around by visitors who, unable to get into the permanent exhibit, walk around the open temporary exhibits or sit and look. I observe only the Japanese tourists dipping in and out, probably as a stop on the Tour Mobile. On the whole, talk is quiet; few schoolchildren "horse around" when eluding their teachers' eye, but then they are on general "museum behavior." For most people there, the visit to the Holocaust Memorial Museum has become part of a routinized tour.

The first thing to note is that whatever emotions the building awakens cannot easily be put into words, so that talking to visitors is only accessory to observation. For instance, I approach a group waiting in front of the Museum on Fourteenth Street: a very tall, big man in his mid-sixties, sporting polo shirt and baseball cap, with a wife and a thirtyish woman, perhaps his daughter, in shorts and a "tourist hat." What did they think of the building? The younger woman answers pleasantly: "Oh, it's nice, *very* nice." Yes, nods the older man. Nice? I ask. "Well-designed," she adds. The man nods and repeats, "Yes, they did a very good job." They are serious, polite; the inarticulate talking about the ineffable; it seems pedantic to note that the man is, in fact, showing awareness (critical, as the television studies would say) that this building occurred *by design.*

Approached on the spot, similarly unreflective people find more revealing things to say. On the steel platform of the Hall of Witness, a trio of stout ladies in polyester clothes is sitting, one looking to the skylight. When I ask her what she thinks of the building, she says, "I don't like it. It's like a factory." Does she think that might be appropriate? The next one intervenes: "*The outside* is pretty." The first one repeats, "Yes, it's not pretty, the roof looks like a factory." Maybe that is supposed to be the feeling you get? "I don't see why."

Standing next to a railing, in contemplation, a fortyish man from Los Angeles with Latino looks tells me, "I find it *very* moving. I cannot tell why. I did not expect it to be like this, to be moving. It weighs on you. It makes you think. A lot of thought went into this building."

In the Hall of Remembrance, a little group of children stands in the ambulatorium; they look younger than the age of 11, below which kids are not allowed into the permanent exhibits. A young African-American boy sits down not far from me, looking. He is from Rochester; the museum is a stop on his school trip. Is it different from other museums he has seen? "Yes!" Why? "There is nothing in it." What do you mean? "Nothing you can touch, like in other museums." He is going to see the children's exhibit, "Daniel's Story." His teacher hovers around, suspiciously.

I talk with a group of five schoolchildren who sit on the first steps near the entrance. They are no older than 13, from Waltham, Massachussets; they look tired and they are very quiet; they sit, looking, even when their classmates start circulating. One of them becomes the spokesman, while the others pay attention. He tells me they have seen "Daniel's Story;" he urges me to see it. They spent the whole year studying the Holocaust, and they were ready for this visit. They are waiting to see the permanent exhibits next. The kids "from last year" (those who came to the museum last year) told them that there is a stair that makes the same noise as the ramps in the gas chambers, and also a cattle car. He says, "I want to see that very much."

A black family from Texas and I go at the same time through "Daniel's Story." We talk, the women, in deference, letting the one man do the talking. The first thing he says is, "*I want to see more.* I want to know more, definitely. I can relate to this, because I think all the time that we were there too, with our 200 million blacks killed when they brought them over or in slavery [*sic*]." The building? "It gives me goose bumps, I don't know . . . there is something, yes, it makes you feel like you were there." What is it? "Maybe these materials, the iron, the brick."

Back in the Hall of Witness, a couple in their early twenties, obviously college students, whom we already met talking to the young guard about the building, tell me, when I ask them what they think, that they were puzzled, at first; then, she says, "I visited Dachau, so it definitely reminds me of the camps." And he, with a tone of "this explains it all": "I am German. This is not news to me. I understood immediately what it was about. It is clear." Like the man from Texas, this viewer responds in what Liebes and Katz call a *pragmatic* critical mode, aware of how his self is engaged in and by the building (Liebes and Katz, 1990: 115).

A 16 year old sits on the platform, reading a book. He says his classmates are visiting the exhibits; he did not want to go because "I know it." What does he mean? He is Jewish, he says; his grandparents were in concentration camps in Poland; they survived; he had been to Yad Vashem in Israel. I ask him what he thinks of this building. He says, "You are not suppose to like it, I guess." What strikes him most is that "it looks like two buildings."

A Tentative Conclusion

This study of one building shows, first of all, that this approach to the analysis of architectural objects must be developed through comparative study of many buildings of the same and different types. I believe that this empirical illustration lends support to what I sketched in the first part of the essay: the architectural object *denotes its type* (therefore, its social function and some expectations about form and content) globally, gestaltically. It denotes *the services it renders* in practice and by parts, as users enact the scenarios prescribed; it *connotes* globally by departures from the type and its conventions, and it connotes locally, in specific interaction between the denoted functional scenarios and the object's connoted (and logically secondary) signification. The architects can plan this interaction, and like all other artists, propose it to viewers without ever knowing what or how it will mean for them.

Second, because denoted and connoted significations are conveyed interactively by all the components of design (mass, space, openings, light, texture, silence, and more), they are impossible to translate from that silent language into words. The few words I collected, and the observations (in particular of schoolchildren), strongly suggest that what a building shows matters less than the predisposition and preparation of those *to whom* it is shown. Thus, at the Holocaust Memorial Museum, two groups of students from the same college, on the same visit, reacted very differently: the Americans who had attended a semester course on the Holocaust were duly impressed, while the Eastern European visiting students considered it "a Disney horror story." Another instance is the acerbic comments of the Israeli press, comparing the American museum to Yad Vashem in Jerusalem and seeing the former as a usurpation of the Holocaust by American Jews, a marker of their wealth.[25] The reification of memory emphatically depends on the active participation of the viewers.

The importance of the public's predisposition confirms that architecture cannot be deterministic: it connotes with great ambiguity. Hence, the great importance the various narratives acquire in affixing metaphorical meanings to built forms that do not intrinsically have them. Yet the narrative *of* the building cannot be what lasts, for it cannot match the narrative of the exhibits, a story that has become the unquestioned and unquestionable measure of evil in our century. A building is a human achievement, it *cannot* say: "here, only anger and shame are appropriate, sentiment is out of the question; these corpses, these executioners were homo sapiens, *our species,* as were those like us who chose to ignore it all." The objects of everyday life in the ghettos and in the camps cannot say that either. The photographs and films, like ghosts, can.

We do not know if the survivors who consider that the Holocaust Memorial Museum is solemn and appropriate see their building, or their own grief. Yet this building is impressive; it does not jar with the predisposition of those who know, and it exceeds what is required of the museum-type, by means of which most people undoubtedly and immediately read it. It contributes to what Wieseltier calls "a general darkening of outlook." The visitors' uneasiness impeccably confirms the priority of the typological reception of architecture.

It is true, as the critic Michael Sorkin notes, that "the Tour Mobile that stops out front confers a terrible comparability on this place, a stop between the Bureau of Engraving and the Air and Space Museum." It is true that the tourists do not "remove their silly hats at the door" (Sorkin, 1992: 74), and that they think a museum in Washington should be "pretty." They come because the building is on the Washington tour. The informed and the uninformed enter, walk around, and, "in a state of distraction," they decode with exactitude the utilitarian scripts that the building denotes. Where the scripts violate conventional expectations, the majority seem to hesitate. They "do not get it" (like the man in the Tower of Faces, like the schoolchildren circling Serra's sculpture), but this cannot be interpreted as apathy. It is hard to learn empathy with architecture, which does not "tell stories," unless one's mind is seared by those images Freed himself went looking for in Poland. The exhibits sear the mind, and visitors see them in impressive silence, stopping to read the long explanations, and to look at every document, for much longer than the curators had planned. Afterwards, they are quiet.

The Holocaust has become an official story, a state-sponsored act of remembrance, terribly *other* than the slowly vanishing living memory of the Shoah, a moment in the celebration of difference between that state and ours. Yet visitors cannot fail to register, however subliminally, that the brick is raw, the heavy skylight is twisted, something is *wrong.* In the Hall of Witness, they all stop. It is likely that they unconsciously scan their typological repertories, and conclude "it's like a factory, not like a museum." But only the exhibits, even though they, too, are reifications, can teach the history and impress upon anyone that this was a factory of death, that "pretty" would be wrong. Something happens in the combination of name, narrative, and architecture: over all, the experience of this crowded museum is subdued.

In conclusion, we cannot lose sight of the point that architecture *is* an art precisely because it can speak only about that which cannot be said with words. When the architects speak of ambiguous architectural form, they show a precise understanding of how connotation works. *Imposed* meanings become denotation, preestablished content. The imposition of meaning aims at destroying the connotative power of architecture, stunting the viewers' capacity to make their own connections. If the architects had desired to communicate *exact* metaphorical meanings, they would have had to plan for aggressive sharing of their interpretive codes with their public. But this is precisely *not* what James Freed says they intended to create. It does not matter that the people I saw seldom stopped to read the names on the bridges. What matters is the man who says, "I want to know more." The memorial – in fact, the Hall of Witness – has directed him to the history, from which he may come back with memory, neither coherent nor official, mediated, but nonetheless his own.

Designing not a blind container, but a building that "is one with its contents," was a reformulation, a shift from the type's "conventional wisdom." The building effectively conveys this strategy of the designers: the visitors receive it immediately, as a whole, from the first steps taken into this other universe through the Fourteenth Street fake facade. The designers chose to symbolize not the events, but the very process by which they themselves addressed memory that would have been unspeakable if they themselves had lived through it. The architects pursued the fusion of building and content. I believe the public's diverse responses show, on the one hand, that architecture can *impress* even if one does not really have referents that allow the full development of a "semantic" relation to the object. On the other hand, the attitudes of the schoolchildren who had been "prepared," the general response to the exhibits and to the Hall of Remembrance after the visit, suggest that people can learn what is necessary to understand, and perhaps remember, both buildings and history. One reason that the public keeps coming to this building must be, or become, at a certain level, a desire to know.[26]

NOTES

I thank Samuel Ashkenazy of the Holocaust Memorial Museum for my visit to the Museum, at short notice, for two days in May 1994. I am grateful to Susan Stewart for her always acute and sensitive reading, to Michèle Lamont and to two anonymous readers for their comments, and also to Daniel Latouche, Jayne Merkel, and Suzanne Vromen for their enlightening discussion at the workshop "Constructing Remembrance: Visible and Invisible Monuments in Space," organized by Vera Zolberg at the New School for Social Research in December 1994. I thank Vera for this opportunity. My deepest thanks to Charles Larson, for reading, commenting, and making two trips to Washington DC to provide me with pictures I could use and publish.

1   Notable recent exceptions to our avoidance of "object analysis" are Griswold (1987); Akrich (1987) and Latour (1988) of course; Wagner-Pacifici and Schwartz (1991); Dauber (1992), and Brain (1994), though only in passing. For statements on the production-of-culture approach, see Crane (1992) and Peterson's important statement (1979). Two significant examples are Becker (1982) and Crane (1987). See also the various articles in Cantor and Zollars (1993).

   Certainly, in studying the passage of late twentieth-century architecture from a dominant modernist code to postmodern eclecticism, I did no differently: I stayed clear, by deliberate choice, of interpreting the architectural objects themselves (Sarfatti Larson, 1993). Yet, because I relied on the architects' discourse, I had to take form as one of their predominant concerns, even though my account of the postmodern shift concentrated on the social context where it occurred. I admit, in fact, to my repeated frustration and irritation with the relentless insistence on purely formal qualities exhibited by architectural critics, and not a few historians.

2   For a partial attempt in this direction, see Sarfatti Larson (1994). Wagner-Pacifici and Schwartz (1991) provide a convincingly "thick" description of their object's history.

3   This is a first source of difference with the reception of television shows, or of printed material, which have been the concern of the most frequently cited studies of reception (Liebes and Katz, 1990; Press, 1991; Radway, 1984). The choice of the Holocaust Museum, a *public* building, which can be visited

free of charge (although visiting the exhibitions requires advance reservations that are hard to get), controls at least some major problems of access in this preliminary empirical test.

4 I am citing Wendy Griswold's well-known and apt definition of cultural objects as "shared significance embodied in form" (Griswold, 1986: 5).

5 Latour's analysis is based precisely on a breakdown of automatic *subscription*, as he calls our acquiescence to and compliance with the prescribed behaviors encoded in nonhumans.

6 See Ellis and Cuff (1989) for an interesting exploration of how architects see their future "publics."

7 For examples of "subversion," see Wagner-Pacifici and Schwartz (1991) and also the important study by Boudon (1972).

8 Thus, Andrea Press finds that women watching "family television" respond very differently to its messages depending on the generation to which they belong: women who formed their life choices *before* the second feminism wave of the 1970s tend to view women protagonists (even the very sexual action figures of *Charlie's Angels*) with wistful satisfaction, as emblems of opportunities that were not open to them in their formative years. However, the older generation gets less *involved* with, and less angry at the lack of realism of family television. Younger women divide along class lines, although they all focus on the work/family dichotomy that preoccupies them in their own lives (Press, 1991: 152–64). Along the same lines, Liebes and Katz, controlling education, observe that the readings of *Dallas* vary systematically according to the cultural background of their respondents; Russian Jews, Arabs, Moroccan Jews and kibbutzniks in Israel, Americans, and Japanese (Liebes and Katz, 1990).

9 Communication of David Brownlee.

10 I owe this insightful comment to Susan Stewart, who notes that this is how a building can make a profound pun.

11 I implicitly use Schudson's (1989) categories for the analysis of cultural objects.

12 The multiplication of memorials is recent, for in the 1970s projects were resisted, for instance in New York City. The Jewish Museum of New York surveyed these memorials in a 1994 exhibit; see James E. Young, curator of the exhibit (1993), and on Germany (1992).

13 Irit Rogoff, presentation at the Culture and the Arts Workshop, "Constructing Remembrance: Visible and Invisible Monuments in Space." New School for Social Research, December, 1994.

14 For an example, see the controversy surrounding the Vietnam Veterans Memorial in Wagner-Pacifici and Schwartz (1991). See also the articles in Gillis (1994), especially Claudia Koonz, "Between Memory and Oblivion: Concentration Camps in German Memory," and Young (1993).

15 Of the 1986 proposal, the Commission's executive secretary declared that its size and almost brutal aspect made it seem "more a memorial to the perpetrators of the crime, not the victims" (Young, 1993: 340). Freed commented: "they said sandpaper it smooth, get rid of all those quirky things. . . . It's hard to try to keep the things that will tell you that this is not a typical

'good times' building. There was always the conflict between the extrinsic and intrinsic character of the building, and what the city would tolerate" (Freed, 1989: 61).

16   A comment by Daniel Latouche (INRS, Montreal) clarified for me the meaning of Freed's words. Recently, the meaning of the Holocaust Museum – though not the building – was vehemently attacked by the notorious Khalid Muhammad, former minister of the Nation of Islam, in a publicized spring 1994 visit. But, in fact, the museum's presence on the Mall lends opportunity and strength to Muhammad's words about what is silenced in the United States' official narrative, in this instance the "holocaust of black African Americans."

17   Pei Cobb Freed distributes a glossy brochure on the museum which describes the program as follows: "The building is more than a memorial or a museum; it is a living institution dedicated to research, teaching and the performing arts, as well as to contemplation and commemoration. Approximately 25% of its space is devoted to permanent exhibits that document the history of the Holocaust, with another 5% allotted to temporary installations. In addition, the building houses a major research library and archives for scholars, administrative offices, a cinema and a theater, a 10,000 square foot conference center, an interactive computer learning center, classrooms, ceremonial spaces, and areas for impromptu discussion." Among the design challenges, they name "the question of architecture itself: How could stones be made to speak?"

18   The new museum at Buchenwald, housed in the former headquarters of the SS on the plateau that looms above Weimar, has precisely that air of something rapidly built and not well finished, in the middle of a desolate rocky expanse, where smaller, ruined remnants of the camp also arise. I saw it on the 50th anniversary of liberation, on the day of the unveiling of a monument to the Romi victims. The crowd, in which survivors were distinguished by an orange emblem, went from the crematory to the barracks, many of them telling their own stories.

19   To convey how an architect translates meaning into form, I borrow the eloquent descriptions (and the technical terms) used by Freed in his 1989 article and by the unsigned firm's brochure that echoes it. For the sake of order, I intercalate where appropriate my observations of how these devices work.

20   The museum's phenomenal success and the need to limit entry to the permanent exhibits mean that the tickets distributed in advance must be controlled.

21   But then, due to the Museum's enormous success, many people and even many groups do not manage to get into the exhibits.

22   The architect's first formal and typological approach to the design problem of separate volumes/separate functions, interior atrium and bridges, is strikingly similar, she says, to I. M. Pei's East Wing of the National Gallery. She notes, among other references, that the combination of brick and concrete and the flattened arches are identical to the "language" used by Louis Kahn in Dacca.

23   A reader, playing the devil's advocate, asserts "that the Holocaust exhibit would have the same effect if located in Macy's department store as it has

in the Memorial Museum," and adds: "I know I am wrong, but why?" The fusion of container and content, we could say, characterizes "successful" projection of the sacred into built form.

24 The permanent exhibit is unflinching in documenting the Allies' inaction (even after Kristallnacht) in the first period, the paltry number of visas they issued, the refusal to bomb Auschwitz or the railroads near the end, the reconstitution of abysmal camps for the survivors and other displaced persons, even after the pogrom against returning Jews in 1946 in Kielce.

25 I owe both communications to Suzanne Vromen.

26 A survey conducted by the Roper Organization in 1993 reported, it is true, the shocking fact that 22 percent of respondents said it seemed possible the Holocaust never happened, while another 12 percent did not know whether it was possible or not. The ignorance about the numbers murdered and the places where they were killed was staggering (38 percent of adults and 51 percent of high school students did not know the names of Auschwitz, Dachau, or Treblinka). Yet 72 percent of adults and 64 percent of high school students said it was essential or very important for all Americans to know about and understand the Holocaust, even if it had happened fifty years ago (*Philadelphia Inquirer*, April 20, 1993: A13).

REFERENCES

Akrich, Madeleine 1987: Comment décrire les objects techniques. *Technique et Culture*, 5, 49–63.

Baxandall, Michael 1972: *Painting and Experience in Fifteenth Century Italy.* Oxford: Oxford University Press.

—— 1985: *Patterns of Intention: On the Historical Explanation of Pictures.* New Haven: Yale University Press.

Becker, Howard 1982: *Art Worlds.* Berkeley: University of California Press.

Benjamin, Walter 1968: *Illuminations.* New York: Harcourt, Brace & World.

Berenbaum, Michael 1993: *The World Must Know.* Boston: Little, Brown & Co.

Boudon, Philippe 1972: *Lived-in Architecture: Le Corbusier's Pessac Revisited.* Cambridge, Mass.: MIT Press.

Brain, David 1994: Making Sense with Things: The Sociology of Culture and the Art of Artifacts. In Diana Crane (ed.), *The Sociology of Culture.* New York: Blackwell.

Brochure on the United States Holocaust Memorial Museum. Pei Cobb Freed and Partners.

Cantor, Muriel and Zollars, Cheryl (eds) 1993: *Current Research on Occupations and Professions*, vol. 8: *Creators of Culture.* Greenwich, Conn: JAI Press.

Crane, Diana 1987: *The Transformation of the Avant-Garde.* Chicago: University of Chicago Press.

—— 1992: *The Production of Culture: Media and the Urban Arts.* Newbury Park: Sage.

—— (ed.) 1994: *The Sociology of Culture: Emerging Themes and Perspectives.* New York: Blackwell.

Dauber, Kenneth 1992: Object, Genre and Buddhist sculpture. *Theory and Society*, 21, 561–92.

Eco, Umberto 1973: Function and Sign: Semiotics of Architecture. In *Via*, vol. 2, pp. 131–53, Philadelphia: University of Pennsylvania Graduate School of Fine Arts.

Ellis, W. Russell and Cuff, Dana (eds) 1989: *Architects' People*. Oxford: Oxford University Press.

Freed, James Ingo 1989: The Holocaust Memorial Museum. *Assemblage*, 9 (June), 59–79.

Freiman, Ziva 1992: The Sorrow and the Pity. *Progressive Architecture*, February, 75–9.

Gill, Brendan 1993: The Holocaust Museum: An Unquiet Sanctuary. *The New Yorker*, April 19, 107–9.

Gillis, John R. (ed.) 1994: *Commemorations: The Politics of National Identity*. Princeton: Princeton University Press.

Griswold, Wendy 1986: *Renaissance Revivals*. Chicago: University of Chicago Press.

—— 1987: The Fabrication of Literary Meaning. *American Journal of Sociology*, 92, 1,077–117.

Halbwachs, Maurice 1980: *The Collective Memory*, trans. Francis and Vida Ditter. New York: Harper Colophon.

Jameson, Fredric 1987: Postmodernism, or the Cultural Logic of Late Capitalism. *New Left Review*, 146 (July–August), 53–92.

Langer, Suzanne 1953: *Feeling and Form*. New York: Charles Scribner and Sons.

Latour, Bruno (aka Jim Johnson) 1988: Mixing Humans and Nonhumans Together: The Sociology of a Door-Closer. *Social Problems*, 35, 3 (June), 298–310.

Liebes, Tamar and Katz, Elihu 1990: *The Export of Meaning: Cross-cultural Readings of Dallas*. New York and Oxford: Oxford University Press.

Lipstadt, Hélène 1993: The United States Holocaust Memorial Museum and the Critics. *Casabella*, 606 (November), 39–41.

McGuigan, Cathleen 1993: He Built a Space of Terrible Beauty. *Newsweek*, April 26, 51.

Mukerji, Chandra 1994: Toward a Sociology of Material Culture: Science Studies, Cultural Studies and the Meanings of Things. In Diana Crane (ed.), *The Sociology of Culture*, New York: Blackwell.

Murphy, Jim 1993: Memorial to Atrocity. *Progressive Architecture* (February), 60–9.

Muschamp, Herbert 1989: How Buildings Remember. *New Republic*, August 28, 27–33.

—— 1993: Shaping a Monument to Memory. *New York Times*.

Peterson, Richard 1979: Revitalizing the Culture Concept. *Annual Review of Sociology*, 5.

Press, Andrea L. 1991: *Women Watching Television: Gender, Class and Generation in the American Television Experience*. Philadelphia: University of Pennsylvania Press.

—— 1994: The Sociology of Cultural Reception: Notes Toward an Emerging Paradigm. In Diana Crane (ed.), *The Sociology of Culture*, New York: Blackwell.

Radway, Janice 1984: *Reading the Romance: Women, Patriarchy and Popular Literature*. Chapel Hill: University of North Carolina Press.

Sarfatti Larson, Magali 1993: *Behind the Postmodern Facade: Architectural Change in Late Twentieth Century America*. Berkeley: University of California Press.

—— 1994a: Architectural Competitions as Discursive Events. *Theory and Society*, August, 469–504.

—— 1994b: How should we Look at Buildings? *Culture*, vol. 8, 3–4 (spring/summer), 1–4.

Schudson, Michael 1989: How Culture Works: Perspectives from Media Studies on the Efficacy of Symbols. *Theory and Society*, 18, 2, 153–80.

Sorkin, Michael 1992: Between Beauty and Horror. *Progressive Architecture* (February), 74.

Wagner-Pacifici, Robin and Schwartz, Barry 1991: The Vietnam Veterans Memorial: Commemorating a Difficult Past. *American Journal of Sociology*, 97, 2 (September), 376–420.

Weinraub, Judith 1994: The Holocaust Museum: A Year to Remember. *Washington Post*, April 17, G2–3.

Wieseltier, Leon 1993: After Memory. *The New Republic*, May 3, 16–26.

Woodward, Kenneth 1993: We are Witnesses. *Newsweek*, April 26, 48–51.

Young, James E. 1992: The Counter-Monument: Memory against Itself in Germany Today. *Critical Inquiry*, 18 (winter), 267–95.

—— 1993: *The Texture of Memory: Holocaust Memorials and Meaning*. New Haven: Yale University Press.

Zolberg, Vera 1992: Barrier or Leveler? The Case of the Art Museum. In Michèle Lamont and Marcel Fournier (eds), *Cultivating Boundaries*, Chicago: University of Chicago Press.

3

Subject Crises and Subject Work: Repositioning Du Bois

JON D. CRUZ

Sociology and cultural studies have much more in common than is generally thought. But the commonality is not easily appreciated. How they differ has become the subject of debate, especially as the interest in culture has ballooned over the last two decades. These debates often hinge on convictions of how social study and cultural analysis ought to be carried out, and involve conflicting orientations over interpretive license. Some sociologists indict cultural studies for failing to demonstrate familiarity and allegiance to the more established traditions of sociological argumentation and evidence. Canonical disregard signifies an affront to hard-won, institutionally sanctioned vision (Sherwood et al., 1993). Cultural studies practitioners, especially those strongly influenced by post-structuralism, question the envisioning process, the foundations, and presuppositions of social scientific disciplines (Nelson et al., 1992. Cf. also Seidman 1991a, 1991b; Alexander, 1991). Arguments aside, the debates seem to reflect a sense of crowding, or what Durkheim called "moral density," and struggles for distinction in a context where the notion of *culture* has emerged with newly appraised properties. It now functions as a kind of sprawling intellectual real estate that many across the social sciences, as well as the humanities, seek to occupy.

Rather than take sides, I want to probe the presumed divide by shifting the lens away from the debate over the sociology of culture versus cultural studies and refocus upon what I think is a historical problem. This problem has to do with the ways we have come to grasp modernity through how we conceptualize collective subjects. Both sociology and cultural studies, I believe, are part of a deeper and older dialogue over how to grasp the meaning of the immense social changes we call *modernity*.[1] To talk of social subjects is, I argue, unavoidable; it is how we realize what we mean when we invoke the notion of modernity (or "post" modernity for that matter.) Conceptualizing social subjects and modernity are historical – not just methodological or disciplinary – problems, and it is from the historical dimension that we can appreciate how cultural analysis is shaped by interpretive liens that bind the sociology of culture and cultural studies together. This suggestion is not a point readily found within contemporary debates in which many feel reasonably compelled to take sides.

My argument takes two steps. In the first section, I outline the key themes in which social subjects emerge as part of the critical appraisal of modernity, and argue that this history has bequeathed important interpretive forms which we moderns inherit. Central to this dialogue is not only how we conceptualize and talk about social subjects, but also how certain subjects come into fields of critical vision, and why they matter in framing modernity. I argue that the critical view of social subjects was shaped by the way in which romanticism and humanitarian reformism sought to retrieve and redeem subjects as a response to modernity. The second section focuses on W. E. B. Du Bois and argues that this neglected figure actually carried out an important synthesis of the longer and deeper tradition of interpreting social subjects in order to grasp the more nebulous dynamics of modernity. For Du Bois, the salient and grounding thematic is race relations. However, it is against the backdrop of a deeper and broader orientation toward subject crises that allows us a way to reposition the significance of Du Bois. Du Bois is usually seen as a starting point in the American context for many who share interests in the rise of modern studies of race relations and ethnic studies. While this has been a fruitful view, I suggest Du Bois can be seen more broadly as a flowering of the earlier historical responses to modernity. In the attempt to understand how race, modernity, and culture intersect, Du Bois embodied a particular integration of the interpretive liens of romanticism, reformism, and social theory. Grounding the more admittedly abstract and general discussion of subject crisis in a figure such as Du Bois seems timely. Contemporary American cultural sociology tends to operate with a blind spot with regard to the historical liens that bind current sensibilities to older, deeper problems of race and gender which were such defining concerns during the middle of the nineteenth century. One symptom of the historical blind spot today is the notion that race and gender are somewhat new issues in critical social reflection, and discussed as faddish if not renegade inquiries at the borders of sociology proper (where cultural studies tends to work). When taken together, the history of thematizing social subjects as a way of assessing modernity, and the manner in which Du Bois inherited this critical interpretive trajectory and pulled it toward the problem of race, allows us to recapture something bigger than race: how subject crises are woven into the struggle to comprehend an ever-shifting modernity. Such interests form a common current that pulses through the sociology of culture and cultural studies. Revisiting the older modes of interpretation that enabled modernity to be framed through subject crisis enables us to see the missing yet forceful continuities that bind the pursuits of cultural analysis to earlier histories of cultural interpretation.

Modernity through Disappearing, Emergent, and New Social Subjects

The textbook features of modernity with which we are now quite familiar appear as abstractions that tend to make social subjects disappear. Briefly, modernity has come to mean many things: the waning of religious hegemony over the meaning of the cosmos; the rise of science as a technique enabling the discovery of laws and principles leading to experimentation and the endless manipulation and transformation of nature; the constitution of modern polities that rule purportedly in the name of "the people;" the restructuring of rural life and agricultural-centered modes of living into urban and industrial dependency; the shrinking of the world through technological innovation; the emergence of market society and advanced capitalism as worldly powers that reshape local life; and, now, the feel of the world as increasingly fast and fleeting.[2] This litany of modernity's interlocking features constitutes how we see *it* through the lens of social science, and they double as definitions of broad and sweeping social forces. Such abstractions, however, take on meaning only when the fate of fortune of distinct social groups – or what I call *social subjects* – is considered. Ever since the beginning of modernity, attempts to make sense of rapid social change and coinciding human disruptions have involved the critical conceptualization of social subjects – be they uprooted peasants, slaves, women, workers, youth, the poor, the racially and culturally marginalized, subcultures, and so on. Such conceptualizations mark societal crises and they invariably present social subjects as people in need of retrieval and redemption. The urgency behind the contemporary interest in culture – which is not new – is shaped by and thus taps an older and deeper process in which we bring (or fail to bring) collective subjects into the framework of social and cultural inquiry.

When referring to social subjects, I do not mean the individual subject, the person, the self, of the domain of intersubjectivity, all of which are consistent with a phenomenological orientation centering on the coming of the modern self. This tradition concerns the long intellectual heritage rooted in religious and philosophical discourses stretching from Platonism, through Augustine, Descartes, and Locke, and culminates in the modern concerns for autonomy, selfhood, and authenticity (Taylor, 1989). By social subjects I mean *collective subjects* – social groupings that come into view as distinct aggregations. I have in mind collective categories, the social cartography of *types* of people who are known through the framework of socially constructed cultural identities that are imposed upon, imputed to, or ascribed by groups, and these processes are effective at a societal and institutional level. This process, as Michel Foucault has argued, involves the objectification of particular groups which can then be acted upon through a variety of procedures. It also includes self-defined and self-ascribed identities that exemplify the internalization of practices of subjectification resulting in modern notions of identities and the self.[3] Socially generated classifications are thus not of the same social and interpretive order as the phenomenological notion of the individual "subject" and discrete "subjectivity." Indeed, when one pauses to enumerate the wide varieties of how we come to recognize, speak, and live out our social classifications, our sense(s) of social cartography, the wealth of terminology for social distinctions dwarfs the language used to speak of the individual self.[4]

The ways social subjects have been conceptualized has changed historically and somewhat systematically against the backdrop of modernity. I identify three major frameworks in which social subjects come into view as sites of crisis: as *disappearing subjects, emergent subjects,* and *new subjects.* These three forms unfold along three sequential yet overlapping intellectual orientations: *romanticism, humanitarian reformism,* and classical *social theory.* The search for disappearing subjects is inaugurated with romanticism, emergent or exonerated subjects with humanitarian reformism, and new subjects with modern social theory and social science. Furthermore, within these schemas the process of discovering groups in crisis not only marks distinct lives and social change; it also involves defining subjects as worthy of being *rescued* from the ravages of a corrosive or debilitating modernity. Once noticed, subjects in crises are eligible to be salvaged in some manner. We could just as easily say that if social subjects are deemed eligible for redemption, then they can be noticed.[5] The modern language of "rights" coincides with these equally modern sensibilities (e.g. from the generic humanism behind the "Rights of Man" to the theme of "civil rights" and "human rights" so central to the political discourses aimed at, or generated by, distinct groups in the second half of our century). Discovering social subjects thus involves, in the past as well as the present, more than mere observation, and more than sympathetic lament; it involves *working on* subjects – what I call *subject work.* By *subject work* I mean the widespread concern to mobilize in the name of, and to intervene into the lives of, social subjects in crises. Subject work, as I use the term, thus hinges precisely on the spirit of retrieval and redemption against the backdrop of modernity. As noted, this is only one strand of the larger discovery of social subjects, which in Foucauldian terms, marks the evolution of disciplinary strategies and power relations – or "social control" in the parlance of sociology. However, it is from this larger nexus of interventionist discoveries that I want to pull out strands that are symptomatic of the unease with modernity, and which do not rest on theories of fatalistic capitulation to, or blind discursive entrapment and automatic complicity with, modernity. While a distinction can be made between *subject crises* as the attempt to spotlight social subjects in the context of modernity, and *subject work* as involving attempts to salvage and redeem social subjects, the two are nonetheless intertwined and facilitate a complex set of ways to comprehend and confront modernity. I can only briefly sketch these connections with regard to how the legacy of discovering social subjects in crisis and interpreting their societal significance (as did Du Bois in the case of black Americans) represent developments to which our interest in and ways of understanding culture are deeply indebted.

Romanticism and disappearing subjects

It was shortly after the Protestant and Catholic Reformations that intellectuals began to discover "the people," a discovery that was in part a worry about the pace and direction of social change (Burke, 1978). The encroachment of market society, shifting class transformations, status conflicts (cf. Braudel, 1973; Elias, 1978), and the progressive scientific inquiry into questions beyond the domain of religious boundaries, helped foster the important criticisms of traditional cultural and political authority, of the *ancien régime* (Cassirer, 1951; Cobban, 1960; Moore, 1966; Bendix, 1964; Habermas, 1989). Jean-Jacques Rousseau is rightly acknowledged as central to the juncture that generated the concern for modernity and nostalgia. Rousseau's notion of the "noble savage," however, was up to much more than nostalgia. Fueled by a recognition of subjects on the verge of vanishing, it emblematized a new interpretation of how human nature was violated by social custom, as well as by a modernity that was fronted by political power, commercialization, and scientific thought. More importantly, the concept of the noble savage invoked the notion of an oversocialized subject imprisoned and stunted by social conventions. Besides helping to usher in the progressive developments that culminate in *the social* becoming a distinct object of modern inquiry in the nineteenth century, the idea of the noble savage also functioned as a powerful interpretive trope. It thematized the *salvaging* idea of an *authenticity* that was buried beneath the artifice of social norms by juxtaposing social typologies against social systems (a precursor to agency/structure). The opening lines to the first chapter of *The Social Contract* (1762) – "Man was born free, and he is everywhere in chains" – signified the growing critique of what civil society had become: the operative ground for inherited political power, authoritarian prerogative, and despotic rule – in short, *tradition*. And tradition, hitherto taken for granted, could now be thematized as cultural drag. But even the new, counter-traditional forms of science and commercialization contributed to the erosion of an idealized presocial (premodern) notion of authenticity. In this regard, the concept of the noble savage had to perform multiple duties. It mobilized sentiment against the power of a tradition that buried as well as banished subjects, and warned against the power of a modernity that made it difficult to recover subjects being left behind. The quest for an authenticity uncontaminated by the social world simultaneously drew from and fed the idea of subject redemption. What society covered up could also be *discovered, uncovered, recuperated.* (Retrieving and salvaging subjects was not entirely a modern creation; its earlier roots tap deeply into the core precepts of religious redemption, salvation, and perfectibility so central to Christian thought, and it is even prefigured in Platonism.) Rousseau's critique fed a modern politics of social criticism and social salvaging. It was echoed, amplified, and modified by French utopianism and German romanticism, and contributed to the social vision of the English novel, in which authors expressed new class sympathies through lamenting the breakdown of an older world that had been organized hegemonically by an earlier Christian metaphysics (Mazlish, 1989). This larger, nebulous trope of social redemption enabled a philosophical and literary elite culture to attend to the loss of certain modes of life measured by the conceptualization of nature (including human nature) engulfed by change.

As a complex cultural sensibility, romanticism's development during the late eighteenth and early nineteenth century helped chart the crisis of social change through the lens of sentimentalism and nostalgia. Nostalgia, however, is a retrospective lament; it attempts to retrieve social subjects who are already largely disappearing, if not already lost to history. Imagined social subjects who cannot be retrieved in flesh and blood reappear symbolically in romanticism; they provide romanticism with a way to negotiate the pressure to accept and capitulate to modernity while generating a (modern) critique of modernity (Lukács, 1971; Douglas, 1977; Lovejoy, 1941; Fairchild, 1928). As Georg Lukács argued, it was the cultural dynamic of loss and recuperation that engendered the Romantic poets whose "subjectively lyrical attitude toward events" in the form of a "flight from the present" was carried out with a mood of "disillusioned romanticism, an over-intensified, over-determined desire for an ideal life as opposed to the real one, a desperate recognition of the fact that this

desire is doomed to . . . an uneasy conscience and the certainty of defeat"
(Lukács, 1971: 116). Corresponding to this disillusioned romanticism
was a sense of resignation that took the form of an "immoderate elation
of the subject," coupled with "the abandonment of any claim to participation in the shaping of the outside world" (Lukács, 1971: 116–17).[6]

Romanticism thus belies an early modern anguish that stretches from
Rousseau to the English writers and novelists such as George Eliot, Thomas
Carlyle, Elizabeth Gaskell, Benjamin Disraeli, among others, and speaks to
the new conditions of human crisis, and to two conceptual edges, two
warring and unevenly developing sides: the innocence of nature (both
human and nonhuman nature) and the ever-expanding contamination of
social artifice – a grand battle between "purity and danger" (Douglas,
1966). If I may take liberties with Mary Douglas's terms, the crisis is not
so much a problem of "matter out of place" (Douglas's definition of social
pollution as a register for social order). Instead, it hinges on a disenchantment with order, and particularly with regard to social subjects that ought
to matter, not only in terms of their own immediate fate, but in the
interconnection of their fate with the fate of others. It invokes a critical
reflection on subjects who are out of place or unjustifiably placed, and
who are threatened by society's power to resituate, displace, or even
remove them from society. Such subject crises are simultaneously crises of
location, dislocation, and social identity. By the late eighteenth and early
nineteenth centuries, this critical sense of place and displacement of subjects, exemplified by the work of Johann Gottfried Herder, reflected a
deepening concern for groups that were being uprooted by an advancing
political, cultural, and economic modernization. Peasants, artisans, guild
members, and craft laborers were in the process of being eclipsed (the
social theories of Tocqueville, Marx, Durkheim, and Tonnies would later
address this concern). At the broadest level, the crises of dislocation
and disappearance even fueled nationalist discourses. The search for an
aestheticized sovereignty of *identity* based on a reconstructed and unifying notion of a rediscoverable (and even a reinventable) deep culture,
history, and sense of place was exemplified in Herder's romantic notions
of the *volk*, those "moral" and "organic" communities that were being
shouldered aside by progress. Such notions of crises and redemption
reach well into the nineteenth century and were available to the emerging
agendas of reformism as well as social science. Contemporary struggles
over culture and identity are not exempt from these older thematics.

Humanitarian reformism and emergent subjects

Coming on the heels of romanticist orientations to modernity, humanitarian reformism inherited the lament over lost worlds, waning traditions,

and disappearing social subjects. Like romanticism, reformism was caught between critique and capitulation. But unlike the romanticist sensibility, reformism looked forward rather than backward; it planned rather than lamented. And in this manner, reformism expressed new, responsive ties to modernity. The concerns with social subjects and subject work championed by nineteenth-century humanitarian reformists differed in important ways from those of an older romanticism. Reformists focused on *living* social subjects who were *inescapably embedded* in civil society. The social subjects that mattered were no longer the disappearing peasantry, the guild artisans of dying crafts, or other social types rooted in the precapitalist era. Rather, distinct groups of people "mattered" because they were fundamentally present in civil society; and their presence, and more importantly their status as problematic groups, facilitated a sense of social criticism. Of foremost importance were slaves, women, and workers, as well as the poor, the young, and the incarcerated. Corresponding to these groups were the movements to abolish slavery, to address women's rights, to improve the plight of wage laborers, and to ascertain the causes and consequences of pauperism, poverty, delinquency, and crime. While the dominant orientation remained focused upon institutional norms governing aberrant individuals, by the middle of the nineteenth century, slaves, women, and white wage laborers could be understood as aggregate victims of a seemingly intractable set of social and institutional arrangements. Radical reformers came increasingly to view institutions, even the entire society, as in need of serious repair.

Interventionist in spirit and associated with social control, reformers ran the gamut – they could be ameliorative, accommodating, and even exuberant in the desire to streamline institutions with the new forces of modernity; but they could also be critical and antagonistic toward institutions, established forms and norms of power, and market society. At a broad level, reformism accompanied the important discovery of "the people" and aided the emerging political form of representation, the new discourses on "publics," and the principles of plebiscitarianism (Habermas, 1989). In the American context, from which I draw some examples, the politics of recognizing the common (white) man that unfolded in the Jacksonian era of the 1830s was part of this larger process. But reformers' concerns went far beyond formal political representation and the new *laissez-faire* encircled debates on civil society and public and private life. Reformers expanded their recognition of and interest in a much larger number of social subjects, and engaged as well as created new institutions expressly designed to respond to particular social groups. Intervention was certainly deployed for purposes of moral and social control, as in the case of distributing Bibles and religious tracts, prison reform, taming the problems of delinquency, and tracking as well as attempting to free those under the grip of alcohol and other vices. Themes of social control dominate the concerns of reformism, and social scientists for obvious good reason have tended to pursue this much bigger picture (cf. Gusfield, 1966; Rothman, 1971; Levine, 1978; Rorabaugh, 1979; Sutton, 1988). Yet, humanitarian reformism was an uneven and somewhat plastic as well as contradictory enterprise that worked two fronts: to stabilize the status quo, and to reject the institutional matrix of modern life. Of these two constitutive pulls, it is the second that I highlight; for while it illustrates, as do all discussions on reform and social control, the issue of subject crises as social crises, it also frames beyond issues of control the retrievalist, redemptive, and exonerating thematics of subject work.

In the American case, major changes in Protestantism fed into reformism and helped prepare the cultural ground and the retrievalist spirit for subject work. By the early nineteenth century, liberal Protestants had mounted a full challenge to Calvinist notions of human predestination and innate depravity. Of the various post-Calvinist denominations, Congregationalism and Unitarianism had begun to adopt ideas of human perfection (May, 1967). William Ellery Channing and Theodore Parker, both highly influential Unitarian ministers during the 1830s and 1840s, preached the inner goodness of the individual trapped in a society increasingly governed by an emergent industrialism.[7] Unitarianism and its critical–liberal offshoot, Transcendentalism, though "minority planks" in the larger Protestant platform (Howe, 1970; May, 1967), carried perfectionism the farthest, insisting that it implied the transcendence of human or spiritual flaw. Reformism's religious roots may have been concerned initially with perfecting the individual soul, but perfectibility went beyond the self; it applied to the social structure. As a spreading ethos, reformism was carried outward to encompass broader dimensions of civil society. Indeed, if we trace the idea of perfectibility in the nineteenth century as it was extended beyond its initial religious orientation, we begin see how liberal Protestant as well as increasingly secular cultural leaders helped to rationalize the larger historical move from the fate of the individual *soul* to that of the larger *society*. Unitarian minister Orestes Brownson's insistence that "the perfection of the social state" was necessary in order to obtain individual perfection exemplified the new theological shift from soul to society (Hutchinson, 1959: 161). Kindred to German and French utopianism, American liberal theology, tinged by socialism, played a key role in helping *socialize* the notion of perfectibility which retained its application to a crisis of soul and spirit, but was thrown open to a progressive rationalization along secular paths that led to the focius upon entire groups, classes, institutions, and even the whole society. Environments could be changed for the benefit of the individual (cf. Brooks, 1936; Clive, 1960; May, 1991). From this perspective, the reformist impulse that marked Protestantism's *social turn* could just as legitimately start with an engagement of social practices and institutions as it could with the individual (but invariably with the latter in mind). It is also in this juncture that the important socialist and utopian reformers attempted to create new experimental communities.[8]

Of the new emphases on social subjects, the crusade to end slavery and to secure rights for women stand out as the most prominent examples of subject work. They both reflect, in an ideal-typical sense, the spirit of uncovering and redeeming subjects buried by social conventions. While slaves remained politically outside of civil society, their distinction marked the meaning of full-fledged membership in civil society, for the term "slave" was the ultimate counter-concept to the definition of a *man* of freedom, property, and privilege.[9] Thus, contrary to disappearing subjects, slaves appeared everywhere. Materially, they shored up an entire mode of production; politically, they refracted the meaning of freedom and privilege; symbolically, they were central to racial discourses of minstrelsy, the most pervasive form of national–popular culture in the mid nineteenth century (cf. Toll, 1974; Van Deburg, 1984; Wilentz, 1984; Boskin, 1986; Lott, 1993). But for radical abolitionists, slaves were symptomatic of society in crisis, and were to be included in the relatively new definition of *human subjects* and as possessors of "inalienable rights." Such claims to membership in a larger humanity were certainly pressed by many of the early black abolitionists who, in their self-penned slave narratives, challenged the interpretation of the core beliefs of the Christian edifice upon which slavery rested.[10] But only by stripping away the illegitimate layers of the peculiar institution could these new subjects be retrieved and admitted into the broader definition of humanity. The radical humanitarian reformism spearheaded by the antislavery movement thus depended on the principles of recognizing, redefining, intervening, and delivering the shackled, stunted, injured, and overlooked – those that society was quite capable of burying alive. The idea that slaves could be freed and incorporated into civil society exemplifies reformism's most exonerating enterprise.

The most emblematic development of the retrievalist spirit was carried out through the reclassification of the slave as a subject with a soul that could be tracked through religious expression. This development originated when ministers and owners began to provide slaves with religious instruction during the late eighteenth and early nineteenth centuries. Carried out through a mix of moral obligation and concern for social control, religious instruction fostered important assumptions: slaves, too, were eligible for improvement and even perfection. This inaugurated the idea that black souls could be saved like white souls. These working assumptions promoted a very significant turning point in the social system of cultural classifications, for it helped to install an entirely new sensibility toward the *cultural* lives and expressions of slaves (cf. Genovese, 1974; Raboteau,

1978; Sobel, 1988). Central to this cultural turn was the abolitionist-inspired discovery of the Negro spiritual. During the mid-nineteenth century and continuing throughout the Civil War, there emerged a series of protoethnographic ventures into the world of black songmaking in which white abolitionists sought out, transcribed, and published collections of spirituals (Higginson, 1867, 1870; Allen et al., 1867). What began in the 1840s with the serializing of the slave narratives in the early abolitionist papers, culminated in the professional article on subcultural practices published in the new professional publications like the *Journal of American Folk-Lore* (Cruz, 1994).[11] The extension of reform to the racial margins inadvertently launched the protoethnographic "discovery" of the culture of slaves and ex-slaves, and was extended later to American Indians.

The interpretive move from shackled black subjects to white women was not a difficult one to make for radical reformers. Actually, both concerns were forged simultaneously in the process of making transparent the ties between power, subjects, and social conventions. Many radical abolitionists were involved in, or were sympathetic to, the issue of women's equality and forged an early critical American feminism that discussed the issues of patriarchy, gender, race, and power. This sensibility was enmeshed in the confrontation with chattel slavery which helped bring into focus correlative testimonies that illuminated the social, economic, and political deficits that were women's lot within the normative order (Davis, 1981). Reformers applied to women the same principles used to critique slavery. Like slaves, white women could not vote, and thus their capacities for public representation were severely curtailed, and what political rights they had were negligible. Upon marriage, any property a woman possessed passed to their husbands. Women, moreover, were not going to disappear from civil society. As "helpmeets" they had long labored at securing family economies. The livelihood of families, communities, and the larger economy depended on them as they became incorporated into more modernizing forms of labor. In the earliest period of manufacture, women took in piece work by carrying out their labor for an employer in their own homes; later, they joined from the outset the growing ranks of wage laborers in mills and factories. During the last two decades of the eighteenth century, and continuing well into the nineteenth, women were employed in a wide variety of work, especially with the burgeoning shoe manufacturing and textile industries of the northeast, where their presence was undeniably vital (Blewett, 1987). Their functions in domestic and manufacturing economies could be no less ignored than the relationship slaves had to agricultural production in the South. Most of the women involved in the various associations and movements for women's rights were firmly middle and upper middle class, white, educated, and from New England communities. However, it was their gendered collective status as women that marked their precarious political status within both public and private spheres, and within a modernizing process that sanctioned new reflection upon the problems of inequality.

Thus, the movements to redefine, retrieve, and redeem slaves and women (as well as wage workers) refract important negotiations between the notions of subject crises and subject work in the context of modernity. Reformers attributed slaves and women (along with a host of other social groups) with new subjectivities and attempted to map them into new places within society. Though their admission into civil society was piecemeal, conditional, uneven, and limited, the emergence of frameworks that thematized them as social subjects eclipsed by the routines of racial, gender, and class oppression marked an important engagement in the shifting conceptualizations of the meaning of modernity. The abolition of slavery and the extension of the franchise to black men and later to white women were outcomes of humanitarian reformism's retrieval process. These victories, however, were troubled ones, compromised and checked often by much larger social and institutional forces.

During the last decades of the nineteenth century, the themes that had informed the social turn within radical Protestantism were modified by the critical wing of the Social Gospel movement, which mobilized the concern for the downtrodden, sympathized with those who suffered under industrialism, and shared a pronounced hostility to urbanization, all the while fostering a professional interventionist social work (May, 1967: 235; Thomas, 1965: 667; Boyer, 1978). Reformism, however, also took a deracializing path, shifting away from the hitherto urgent problems of Reconstruction and turning toward interventions that targeted white working-class populations. Programs aimed at white ethnic "urban uplift" captured the moral dimension of reformism while merging it with modern social science. The cost born by blacks was abandonment and disenfranchisement coupled with Jim Crow laws that entrenched the politics of racial segregation. Complicating the picture of the new limits on blacks were the losses faced by Native American Indians, Mexicans, and the Chinese immigrants. By the century's end, Indians were sequestered upon reservations after full-scale military intervention; Mexicans in the west and southwest were encircled by political annexation, and the Chinese were banned as undesirable aliens through the Chinese Exclusion Act of 1882. So ended the century with a modern bifurcation between "race" and "ethnicity."

Humanitarian reformism was a reaction to modernity, but it was also more than that. It was a prescient force, functioning as an anticipatory *prescience* of modernity. It operated as a major intellectual forerunner to modern social theory and professional social science and helped bring in the new field of vision.[12] As an antecedent to modern social science, reformism contained many of the seeds that would later germinate into social science's more systematic treatment of reformist ideas. Classical social theory and modern social science inherited (rather than discovered) the crisis of social subjects and the redemptive politics of subject work, and internalized the questions, problems, and concerns behind these interpretive tropes. In the process, social theory rearticulated the dynamics of modernity with an unprecedented systematicity that analyzed modern society's power to make *new* social subjects. Put another way, romanticism and humanitarian reformism helped parent modern social theory.

W. E. B. Du Bois and the Crossroads of Cultural Analysis

The interpretive power of modern social theory lies in its capacity to bring the social into visibility, to render it an object for critical comprehension and debate, and to ascertain (or at least argue the existence of) social laws and forces that shape everyday life. The weakness of classical social theory is that collective human subjects who make these "laws" and "forces" tend to disappear in place of the power of abstractions. The attempt to bring these two issues – subjects and structures – together marks the challenge faced by modern social studies. I turn to a brief discussion of W. E. B. Du Bois to illustrate how the inheritance of early confrontations with modernity were internalized and transformed into a sensibility common to contemporary approaches to the conceptualization of social subjects. I want to argue that there is something to be learned in viewing Du Bois as a junctural figure, one who worked with the inherited interpretive forms of the earlier legacies of romantic and reformist sensibilities, and strove to hold on to the best of earlier critical concerns for disappearing, emergent, and new social subjects. Moreover, I argue that there is in Du Bois an intellectual continuity between the older thematics outlined above and what we, today, would recognize as the humanistic dimensions within the sociology of culture *and* cultural studies. Little of this dimension of Du Bois can be appreciated in the received view, which sees him only as a key founder of black as well as ethnic studies, and as a racially partisan civil rights fighter. His work is ostensibly concerned with black America, but his contributions are more fundamentally rooted in the deeper critical sensibility of subject crisis and subject work, whose threads weave across the study of culture today.

Intellectual historians identify Du Bois as one of the founders of empirical sociology in the United States, a characterization based on *The Philadelphia Negro* (1899), the pioneering study of the largest black urban community in the United States at the end of the nineteenth century. The essays sketched in *The Souls of Black Folk* (1903) display a literary–

humanist bent, but they also point to and prepare the larger thematic field that his magnum opus, *Black Reconstruction in America, 1860–1880* (1935) would explore. *Black Reconstruction* offered the archival studies of the historian, the organizational and institutional critique of the political sociologist, and the interrogation of the social constructs that held together the racial order. Du Bois's feel for the life chances and limits of what surrounded daily life for the masses of black Americans during and after Reconstruction, captured as well something kindred to what French *Annales* historians and British social and cultural historians would later call "everyday life" or the "whole way of life."

But it is *The Souls of Black Folk* rather than the study of *Reconstruction* that I want to single out for discussion. *Souls* is a short work. It lacks the depth of *Reconstruction*. It does not showcase Du Bois's empirical side, nor his rigorous research. Moreover, it is well known that Du Bois modified many of his views in later years; most importantly, he abandoned his open belief in the efficacy of appealing to the better spirits of his white "gentle readers," and he lost his faith in a rational solution to the deeply ossified patterns of racial inequality. *Souls* also appears as a more "literary" rather than "social-scientific" text. So why consider *Souls*? *Souls*, I believe, more than his other works, refracts the intellectual conjuncture between the older interpretive forms associated with romanticism and reformism and the new social-scientific ethos, and integrates all three. It also embraces and synthesizes the longer and deeper legacy of what I have been calling subject crisis and subject work. The essays capture the historical liens of the critique of modernity, subject crisis, and subject work, by speaking to an earlier history and to the concern for culture in ways that point to ensuing issues in cultural analysis, as well as to the resurgent tensions that characterize more recent debates surrounding race, gender, and identity issues today.

Du Bois's emergence as an intellectual trained in the social sciences coincided with the deep toll that the abandonment of Reconstruction was taking on black Americans. In just a decade after having achieved freedom, blacks were being dealt a new social death as reformist idealism was traded for the appeasement of the South's landowning classes. The result was the reentrenchment of free black labor in agricultural debt peonage. Reformism's failure engendered a sense of tragic loss, of justice and opportunity squandered in the deep fissures of old racial norms. Persistent across much of Du Bois's writings are the marks of this juncture and the miscarriage of justice that filled the vacuum created by governmental withdrawal. With the spirit of romanticist critique, *Souls* laments the loss of an inclusion promised by reformism's once passionate rhetoric, and offers an account for the loss through the insights of social-scientific reflection. It is in this juncture that Du Bois draws from the earlier legacies

– from the attitude of crisis and retrieval, the sensibilities that fostered the inward edification of modern subjectivity, and the reformist agendas that hinged on the recognition and redemption of social subjects. In his words,

> The nineteenth was the first century of human sympathy, – the age when half wonderingly we began to descry in others that transfigured spark of divinity which we call Myself; when clodhoppers and peasants, and tramps and thieves, and millionaires and – sometimes – Negroes, became throbbing souls whose warm pulsing life touched us so nearly that we half gasped with surprise, crying, "Thou too! Hast Thou seen sorrow and the dull waters of Hopelessness? Hast Thou known Life?" And then all helplessly we peered into those Other-worlds, and wailed, "O World of Worlds, how shall man make you one?" (Du Bois, 1969 [1903]: 235–6)

These words come toward the end of *Souls*. The passage precedes by just a few years the dark eclipsing lines of disenchantment penned by Weber at the end of *The Protestant Ethic*.[13] But what precedes in the earlier essays are assessments that indict the loss of this sympathy. The sympathy for black Americans (and for Indians and women) had withered under the ascending, rough-riding virtue of the new militaristic masculinity that catapulted the United States into an imperial power with overseas possessions resulting from the defeat of Spain in the war of 1898. Du Bois launched his intellectual career just as the United States was basking in its first overseas military campaign, which culminated in the annexation of the Philippines, Puerto Rico, and Cuba. In the jingoistic climate of military and industrial prowess, modernity and sympathy were engendered anew: modernity was male, sympathy female. Under disrepute, and chastised as effeminate, the broader, more sweeping sympathy of humanitarian reformism was under retreat. Where sympathy remained was in the professionalization of modern social work and the scientized "uplift" projects such as those carried out by Jane Addams. These projects targeted white ethnic working-class families. A cautious, reserved, and conscientiously scientistic version of sympathy survived as well in some of the strains of urban sociology at the University of Chicago (and here in ways that adjudicated the older critical appraisal of modernity and the new pressures to rehabilitate urban immigrant populations in the demanding context of social problems and industrial society). Blacks, however, did not simply experience withdrawal of sympathy; they bore the brunt of the violence that filled the void. Ninety-nine lynchings were recorded in the first year of the new century (Lewis, 1993: 275).

In the opening essay of *Souls of Black Folk* the leadened question drops: "How does it feel to be a problem?" The question is followed by reflection upon a painful childhood memory, as Du Bois recalls the first time he recognized that others saw him racially different, and how this became a weight that had to be carried around. Yet, developing out of the awareness of being "an outcast and a stranger," was the sense of "second sight," of being a black person in an

> American world, – a world which yields him no true consciousness, but only lets him see himself through the revelation of the other world. It is a peculiar sensation, this double-consciousness, this sense of always looking at one's self through the eyes of others, of measuring one's soul by the tape of a world that looks on in amused contempt and pity. (Du Bois, 1969 [1903]: 45)

Only in struggling with this double-consciousness could there emerge a new "self-consciousness, self-realization, [and] self-respect." But the price was high; with some black youth it turned into "tasteless sycophancy" and "silent hatred" (ibid: 49). The mixture of autobiographical reflection (some today would call this "subject-position" or "standpoint" reflexivity) and social-scientific observation (which might be called "objectivism") operated with a sense of critical double-duty, a reciprocity without epistemological antagonism.

On the one hand, *Souls* elaborated the antimodernist lament from a black American perspective rooted in liberal Protestant social critiques. But it was also a major critical appraisal of American modernity and the forces of market society, industrialization, and political expediencies that had pushed aside and excluded the majority of blacks. Du Bois's indictment of American modernity was also fueled by a particularly original blend of cultural and economic sociology. It was undergirded by the romantic sensibility of lost subjects and the reformist and social-scientific perspectives that accounted for devalued as well as newly made lives. Having opened the essay with the idea of the American Negro as a "problem," Du Bois closed it with a conviction consistent with the redemptive spirit of Rousseau in seeking a deeper authenticity that deserved full exoneration:

> There are to-day no truer exponents of the pure human spirit of the Declaration of Independence than the American Negroes; there is no true American music but the wild sweet melodies of the Negro slave; the American fairy tales and folklore are Indian and African; and, all in all, we black men seem the sole oasis of simple faith and reverence in a dusty desert of dollars and smartness. (ibid: 52)

These sentiments echo similar romantic statements written by some of the most ardent white abolitionists, who attributed such authenticity to blacks as a way of grasping the dulling effects of a market society upon people in general. Abolitionist Thomas Wentworth Higginson, who led the first all-black regiment for the Union army during the Civil War, commented on how the soldier's "philosophizing is often the highest form of mysticism" and that they were "all natural Transcendentalists" (Higginson, 1962 [1870]: 71).

Souls is a novel work. But it is also deeply indebted to the historical interpretive traditions that have long championed the enterprise of subject work. It is ostensibly a set of "black studies," but it is also profoundly American, insofar as it refracts what we are obliged to acknowledge – the series of interpretive formations within American cultural and social history, formations organized around the struggle to grasp modernity through the lens of collective subjects. Du Bois's retrievalist aim was to rekindle cultural memory, a politics of remembering, that could be enlisted in the struggle against the larger forces that were sidelining black Americans in every social and institutional sphere. His work was a probe into cultural questions that might contain keys to the new sense of place, work that was requisite to social and political survival. Retrieving historical memory and achieving cultural reflexivity, however, was not a project only for black people. Du Bois also addressed as cultural co-workers the already sensitized (but waning) audience of "gentle readers," professional cultural interpreters who shared traces of an earlier vibrant redemptive pathos. In the seventh essay, "Of the Black Belt," we begin on a train that is speeding from the North. As we travel, Du Bois describes Georgia's racial and political history. And he writes for a white reader: "if you wish to ride with me you must come into the 'Jim Crow Car.'" But the imagined fellow traveler need not worry, for "there will be no objection, – already four other white men, and little white girl with her nurse, are in there. Usually the races are mixed in there; but the white coach is all white" (Du Bois, 1969 [1903]: 142). Du Bois speaks of Creek Indians, Andrew Jackson's military campaigns against them, and their removal, enabling the region to become "the corner-stone of the Cotton Kingdom" (ibid: 143). Families, characters, individuals take shape. When Du Bois renders paraphrased remnants of conversation, it is the sharecropper's voice. A man is asked, "What rent do you pay here?" He answers: "I don't know, – what is it, Sam?" "All we make," answers Sam (ibid: 156). Such men and their families have labored nearly half a century, "beginning with nothing, and still having nothing" (ibid). Situated in debt peonage at the color line, their lives are described as full in ignorance, petty jealousies, violence, and anger.

The mode of writing that Du Bois uses in many of the essays is reminiscent of the popular nineteenth-century travel narrative. Travel narratives have a plasticity that facilitates a wide range of intellectual and emotional dispositions. They run the gamut from popular exoticized tourism, to the natural history studies of Charles Darwin's *Voyage of the*

Beagle, the political, cultural, and comparative institutional observations of Alexis de Tocqueville's *Democracy in America*, and the muckraking and reformist critique of Richard Henry Dana's *Two Years Before the Mast*. Whites also penned travel narratives of the slave states (cf. Bremer, 1853; Olmsted, 1856; Kemble, 1863). But in the American context there was (if I can push the received categories a bit) another kind of travel narrative, one that took the reader into the moral and emotional geography of black domestic existence, and on a tour of the deep psychic pain and wakeful dreams of blacks – the slave narrative. Du Bois writes *between* these black and white forms, the travel narrative and the slave narrative, by revisiting the lives of ex-slaves and their struggling families living in the "black belt." In "The Meaning of Progress" he recalls his first struggle to find a teaching job. His narrative moves from the completion of his high educational training, a rather rare privilege for a black American of his time, to a progressive descent back into the black belt. He tells of the common people that he meets, and singles out a young girl, Josie, who provides him with the tip that results in finding a school in need of his services. Josie is energetic and hopeful; she possesses "a certain fineness, the shadow of an unconscious moral heroism that would willingly give all of life to make life broader, deeper, and fuller for her and hers." Hungry to learn, this "child-woman . . . studied doggedly" (Du Bois, 1969 [1903]: 98–9). She and other young black students were psychically free from the recollection of slavery to cloud their dreams. Yet it is a larger social and institutional fate that Du Bois tries to articulate as "their weak wings beat against the barriers of caste" (ibid: 103).

Du Bois spent two years teaching at the school. It is ten years later that he thus describes his return. Josie has since withered. Her father, accused of stealing wheat from landlord Durban, had to flee for his freedom; her brother Jim was in prison; and Josie's family, fragile in its caste status, had disintegrated. Josie had taken sick, dying young. Du Bois searches for other families of the students. He finds them. But it is not people but dreams and hope that have disappeared. The girls are now with "babies a-plenty," and the young men wait for the chance to leave behind their families and their certain sharecropping fate. Aspirations to learn are also gone, materially erased, for now even the school no longer exists. A foreboding sense of despair structures his visit. He returns home in "the Jim Crow car," pondering "How shall man measure Progress there where the dark-faced Josie lies. How many heartfuls of sorrow shall balance a bushel of wheat. How hard a thing is life to the lowly, . . . is it the twilight of nightfall or the flush of some faint-dawning day?" (ibid: 108). The essay serves as an epilogue to the actual long, downward plunge assured by the abandonment of Reconstruction, and as a preamble to Du Bois's major study on the crisis.

Continuing in the protoethnographic tradition is "Of the Faith of Fathers," an essay that sketches black religious practices and the import- ance of Negro preachers and songmaking. Here is one of the earliest and most insightful though brief treatments of the inner workings of the black church at the turn of the century. The treatment of this institutional forma- tion is contextualized historically, explained in relationship to those Prot- estant sects like the Baptists and Methodists that reached out to blacks in earlier times, and is buttressed by demographic detail. Du Bois also clarifies the role of Africanist cultural traces (or what the anthropologist Melville Herskovits later called "African survivals"), their retention under the "veneer of Christianity," and their eventual absorption into the modern Negro church (ibid: 216). The turn toward culture, particularly in the focus upon religion and songmaking, is important in that it recapitulates the set of earlier discoveries of black voices, especially singing voices fre- quently associated with the Negro spirituals during the Civil War years. Such discoveries were central to the most radical abolitionists, who mined the critical contradiction between politics and religion, between slavery as a politically sanctioned social system and the souls of black Christians (Cruz, 1994).

The last essay of the book amplifies Du Bois's interpretive cultural turn. "Of the Sorrow Songs" concludes with a discussion of the Negro spirituals. This essay reaches back to the forms of cultural revelation written by Frederick Douglass in his account of the "songs of sorrow" (Douglass, 1845) and to the half-romantic, half-reformist writings of white protoethno- graphers like Frances Kemble, William Francis Allen, Charles Pickard Ware, Lucy McKim-Garrison, and Thomas Wentworth Higginson (cf. Douglass, 1845; Allen, et al., 1867; Higginson, 1867, 1870). It also bears traces of the interpretive tropes of the recently professionalized discipline of Folklore which emerged in the late 1880s. The *American Journal of Folk-Lore* had already been in operation for more than a decade with a strong interest in black music, seeking to preserve what its founders believed to be the last rites of a dying culture in the shadow of modernity. Already by cen- tury's end folklorists were publishing interpretations of Negro practices, and furthering interest in black music. Soon to come would be the new wave of cultural sociologists on their way to refining the skills in capturing *subcultures*. In his concerns for historical memory, Du Bois presented a proto-model (indeed, his work has served as a template) of the *recovery* (as well as *discovery*) of racially specific social subjects in ways that pre- figure modern ethnic and racial studies. His major book, *Black Recon- struction in America, 1860–1880* (Du Bois, 1969 [1935]), brought the thematics of racial eclipse sketched in *Souls of Black Folk* into full analytic synthesis. Du Bois was working within the larger tradition of subject retrieval, but also laying the groundwork for a particular kind of modern historical revisionism that came to fruition in the United States only in conjunction with the Civil Rights movement of the 1960s with the *recuperative* cultural work aimed at restoring a sense of place for blacks, women, youth, and other racialized groups.

Souls is thus more than an intellectually pragmatic work, filling in the holes of academic disregard at the beginning of the twentieth century. It can properly be called a *paradigmatically synthetic* work, in that it makes use of a number of analytic modes of inquiry, observation, and interpretation, consolidating them into an intellectual project that maps the irreducible linkages between the hermeneutic and structural, the personal and historical, and the local and national. The issues that Du Bois's collection of essays address thus cannot be reduced to what we would today call identity politics. They are far more complex. Nonetheless, identity politics appear not at all new; they have been the marrow of a long history of social movements in the American context, some big, many small. Further, they matter *sociologically* today as they did yesteryear, and not less because their progenitors and contemporary bearers fail to display the moment's most championed disciplinary protocols. More importantly, contemporary interest in identity embodies (perhaps unwittingly) the historical liens and the interpretive lines of meaning that are shaped by, and thus cannot be separated from, the larger struggle for a *critical grammar of modernity*. As with the critical romantics, reformers, and Du Bois, this is what is at stake in grasping social subjects as sites and as symptoms of our ability (or perhaps our inability) to talk about modernity in the terms of concrete collective groups.

By holding close *his* preferred subjects, Du Bois avoided the abstraction that made social subjects disappear. And through *them* he showed something deeper and more enduring of American society (which he called the "color line"). Du Bois's focus upon black Americans accomplished more than providing a template for the study of the racial and cultural margins, more than a blueprint for American ethnic studies. As I have argued, Du Bois represents not only the coming of the "New Negro," but also – and more importantly – a flowering of an older, long-budding, critical spirit of recognizing social subjects as the terrain upon which modernity is confronted by people. Viewing Du Bois *only* as a new black intellectual and founder of "black studies" is one important way in which he has been read and assimilated into critical American studies. This view clearly has had great intellectual and political payoff; but it also effectively severs Du Bois from the early critical movements, the very legacy I believe gave him some of the grammar that enabled him to speak so forcefully and specifically with regard to black subject crises. Indeed, the lesson of my repositioning Du Bois is that he ought to be viewed as a conjunctural figure. He marks the waning of the earlier critical concern with social subjects, confronts the most advanced eclipse *vis-à-vis* the fate of black Americans, and calls for a retrieval of the critical dialogue between fate and modernity through the lens of race and culture.

Our inherited present

We understand modernity not through abstractions, but through collective life; not through society as a whole, but through the opportunities and limits, the fortune and fate, of particular social subjects. The return of this repressed *recognition* – this modern cognition for social subjects – takes place today through the blended sensibilities of the romantic, reformist, and social-theoretical orientations of the nineteenth century. We are heir to these greater paradigms. Our most socially engaged conceptualizations draw from these historical–interpretive liens. The contemporary concern for social subjects runs a gamut – from the staid, casual, and self-assured paradigms within sociology proper, to the unsettling, sometimes frantic search for subjects as sites of "resistance" in cultural studies. It is the gradations between the two, rather than the presumptive methodological and credentializing divide, that come into view from the historical trajectory sketched above. It is through the work of the older liens that we continue to center the problem of social subjects in ways that make our talk of modernity meaningful. For these reasons, the arguments that map the "sociology of culture" (as established paradigmatic solidarity) and "cultural studies" (as renegade disregard for canonism) deserve a new kind of critical reassessment. Certainly, it is important to acknowledge the tensions generated by the fraying of disciplinary or methodological norms. But we are now compelled to go back to historical reflection in order to move forward.

To talk about social subjects is to talk as well about culture. Certainly, the problem of culture conveys, today as it did in the past, the problem of modernity. Moreover, the linkage of culture with modernity has become a central way in which we confront the interplay between social subjects and modernity. Nebulous as it is, "culture" is correctly recognized as both symptom and register; it is *where* the tensions of social change come to the fore, where ideologies and practices coincide. That the analysis of culture seems just as much caught in the relentlessness of modernity is thus not surprising. Social scientists and humanists pursue culture as if it were the great social symptom of modernity. Perhaps it is. There is the sense that the analysis of culture contains deeply important intellectual stakes. The desire to capture, read, analyze, describe, and bread down culture as taxonomically as possible seems driven in part by the notion that this knowledge will sharpen our ability to map what we sense to be omnipresently real and largely inescapable: that we have to live with and within a modernity whose speed of change continually eludes the forms of institutional knowledge at our disposal. To grasp culture in this manner is to recognize that it is not just another academic domain of shifting paradigmatic proclivities where careers and new lexicons soar or flounder, but rather an urgent social and historical zone where we attempt to come to terms with modernity.

The historical liens I have described reach into our present. As did the romantics before us, we worry about modernity's relentless push forward. Not long ago, Richard Sennett suggested that "the development of personality today is the development of the personality of a refugee" (Sennett, 1976: 260); Neil Postman has warned of the "disappearance of childhood" (Postman, 1982; cf. also Meyrowitz, 1985); Russel Jacoby laments the "last intellectuals" (Jacoby, 1987). Forms of social life and types of livelihood once associated with traditional factories peopled by blue-collar workers organized by unions are no longer common. We speak of unions disappearing. Global forces push people into diaspora. Hitherto small geographic communities take on the feel of strangeness under the proliferation of what Simmel called social forms. Recognizable groups, numerous and distinct, whose experiences within "everyday life" are highly incommensurable, now live in proximity and thus share social space with others, but as social strangers. Loss – romanticized or materialized – makes way for unfamiliarity. Female single heads of households, Hmong extended families, punk rockers, unemployed aerospace executives, gang members of every hue, Jehovah's Witnesses – the list can stretch for pages. Yet the actual face-to-face contact between these socially recognized groupings is most likely limited to the exchange of furtive glances – when we fuel our cars at the local gas station.

On the other end of the spectrum, far removed from local cultures, are the national politicians who dominate the largest reaches of the electronic public spheres, and who are increasingly compelled (political opportunism notwithstanding) to seize some of the cultural flux, to mold it into some modicum of stable meanings and national purpose. Politicians frequently make reference to the culture (or, by extension, the "values") of America. Invoking culture and values has come to signify "common sense," being "in touch" with culture "out there." At the national level culture is not exempt from being deployed instrumentally as a disciplinary discourse. I have in mind here the way that past presidential advisor and two-time presidential aspirant, Patrick Buchanan, has invoked "culture" in national discourse, calling in particularly sharp and strident tones for the nation's need to wage the good "cultural war" against the bad culture of an aberrant and irresponsible liberalism. Beyond moral entrepreneurs on the hunt, even institutions seem on the run, rendering the notion of "settled lives"

(Swidler, 1986) an oxymoron. Corporations once beholden to local communities relocate to other regions of the world to keep pace with the latest convulsions of global capitalism and technology.

Emergent and new social subjects occupy our contemporary attention as well. Consistent with the idea of "the market" as a great metaphysical and worldly power, so appears the explosion of new identities which vie to be born, to be recognized, to be renamed, to achieve new levels of emergent distinction, to stake their place, or to circulate within an increasingly dense milieu of social differentiation. Some of these identities fit the contours of what I have called the hidden, covered up, glossed over, or repressed dimension of social groups, and who now seek exoneration and redemption. The emergence of "race," "gender," and more recently, "ethnic studies," not just as groups but as *institutionalized knowledge formations*, continues as part of the long and deep current of social and cultural retrieval. "Multiculturalism" today is a term used to grasp the rapid production of new identities (Cruz, 1995). These developments have ties as well to the way humanitarian reformism annexed and assimilated romanticism, and created a redemptive intellectual trope that attempted to grasp – and continues to attempt to grasp – the burying as well as birthing forces of modernity. My argument is thus not about the new identities and corresponding forms of knowledge as peculiar moral fictions; it is an argument about how and why these became, and continue to become, possible and operative.

The growing sense of subject crises is both a *means* by which, as well as an *effect* of how, we confront modernity; it is not simply a fringe benefit or a diminishing return of "new" social theory. Consider one of the ironies of poststructuralism. For all of its pretensions to have explained away the problem of the (phenomenological) *subject* as a moral, and worse yet, a political fiction stemming from the epistemological flaws of modernity and Enlightenment, poststructuralism has actually provided the theoretical license for the proliferation of "new" (little, not grand or unitary) social subjects. Moreover, poststructuralism has been appropriated in ways that place a premium on differentiations (or "subject positions"). Poststructuralism may have rendered the subject problematic on a manifest level, but its latent and more significant impact resides in the rather inconvenient fact that is has played a major role in exonerating and unleashing an entirely new round of subjectivization. But this is not that remarkable; for these developments are, in my assessment, quite consistent with the longer historical liens raised earlier. The multiplication of social subjects, the urgency of redemptive struggles, the quick turn to grasping social activity (even the most mundane) as "resistance," the anxieties associated with identity maintenance over the longer haul – these are features of the speed up of social differentiation (*pace* Durkheim) ushered in by even more rapid changes taking place today. These are unintended consequences (*pace* Weber), not of theory, but of the forces of modernization that unfold with hitherto unexperienced rapidity; and they are just as much tied to historical and material transformations, and entwined with economic, political, geographic, social, technological, and cultural forces (*pace* Marx).

The legacy thus operates like a well-endowed cultural investment. We continue to accrue value from the earlier investments of romanticism, reformism, and classical social theory. And as heirs, we draw with ease from the dividends. Yet we seem to remain unfamiliar with the status of its principal – by which I mean the *interpretive principle* of historical indebtedness (e.g. subject crises and subject work). Or if the principle is recognized, it is either embraced uncritically or quickly disavowed as "foundationalist." So deep-seated is this legacy that even the most cultivated attempts to disavow it remain partially captured by it. Consider, for example, how quickly post-Enlightenment and antifoundationalist perspectives respond to the problem of subject crises and subject work with overtures to egalitarianism, radical democracy, and social justice, themes deeply associated with the Enlightenment (Cf. Laclau and Mouffe, 1985; Seidman, 1991b; Flax, 1992). Even out of the politics of internal compression and the search for identities and practices uncontaminated by Enlightenment, there are straining to be born new movements in search of a sense of place. Here, Alain Touraine's argument that "social movements [occupy] a central place and are the basic condition of democratic political life" (Touraine, 1988: 150) – but within a new context in which the classical idea of "society" is rapidly decomposing – seems appropriate in rethinking modernity and collective life.

Thus, to speak of social subjects today is precisely the problem. And it is an unavoidable one. The tensions over what kinds of social subjects matter as socially important – and how, why, when, and through what methods they are to be grasped – underwrites much of the debate surrounding the ostensibly disciplinary tensions within cultural analysis today. Reminiscent of the long historical debates on "the poor" (Piven and Cloward, 1971), we continue a similar confrontation, but over *which* social subjects most (or least) deserve to be admitted into the always seemingly limited intellectual space constituted by the reigning modes of cultural inquiry. How should social subjects come into the purview of cultural analysis? Through which lens? With what lexicon? These questions contain much of the fodder for discipline-based argument. But more important, these questions are not free from historical liens. They come in association with past social transformations, and they inadvertently engage and negotiate the forces of modernity that have shaped the framework as well as the forms in which social subjects are conceptualized.

One thing appears salient: social subjects continue to offer the indispensable framework in which we address social crises and (contradictions notwithstanding) the continual upheavals that come as the norm of modernity. How social subjects are caught in social crises and how they emerge to become the focal point of subject work, are thus key features of our *social talk*, the grammar we use to bring modernity and subjects into visible relations. To grasp the historical liens that shape how we conceptualize social subjects and interpret them in their cultural configuration involves, I believe, some of the most important knowledge stakes inherent in sociology today. These stakes are refracted in, but go beyond, the disciplinary tensions between the sociology of culture and cultural studies.

NOTES

1 The upheavals and transformations ushered in by capitalism have been pushed ever faster and wider in their domestic and global reach (cf. Harvey, 1989; Jameson, 1991; Rose, 1991). Quickened cultural transformations do not in themselves constitute a rupture or distinct break with the forces of modernity which, for Marx and Engels, were inseparable from *capitalism* (Tucker, 1978: 475–6; cf. Berman, 1982). Yet many of the popular treatments of "postmodernism" seem quick to attribute so much autonomy to cultural issues as to dismiss capitalism as an organizing force. For these reasons I reserve prefixing "modernity" with "post," for it is not at all clear that we have fully left behind the capitalist dynamics that mark the core features of modernity.

2 As Raymond Williams has noted, it is for these reasons that the meaning of modernity prior to the nineteenth century was mainly negative. Only in the early twentieth century did modernity come to be more widely embraced by its own self-referencing aestheticization – *modernism* (Williams, 1976: 174).

3 In Foucauldian theory social classifications, by definition, constitutively embody power and social order. Social classifications aid the process of conflict and antagonism, as well as discipline and social control. They also aid in expressing the apprehensions, deep misgivings, and even fear of the developing forms of social power, social order, and social change. My concern is with this latter problem, which I believe is central to how we frame our anxieties about a modernity that we do not control. Social subjects help us to ground the connections between social forces and lives actually lived; they aid in tracing and tracking the operations of modernity upon social groups. Foucault is not wrong about the ties between social classifications and social power (the lesson is actually provided by Durkheim in *The Elementary Forms of the Religious Life*). But the problem is not only of how power is internalized and normalized, and Foucault is silent with regard to how modernity itself is raised as a conscious concern that is accompanied by attempts to bring it into a critical focus.

4   This notion would appear to run counter to the argument put forth by Bellah et al. (1985), that modernity, at least in its American manifestations, is marked by an incapacity for people to speak beyond a narrow grammar of individualism. While I don't discount this, I suspect that most individuals could readily identify a range of significant social groups and their feelings toward them. Individualism may shape the articulation of expressed needs, but individuals probably possess quite elaborate *social maps* which indicate how they make sense of other groups in society. Contemporary political planners and pollsters seem to know this dynamic well – as "wedge issues."

5   The problem I sketch here is of course both more complex as well as subtle. The act of noticing is always a condition of the social context and historically specific formations in which particular groups and distinct sociocultural fractions do the seeing, identifying, and saving. It is not society at large but particular groups that see (an interest in) subjects. Societies do not see. Seeing within society is carried out by collectively coordinated ensembles of people linked constitutively by ideas, ideologies, and interests.

6   For an assessment of how romanticism aided the critique of capitalism and was linked to revolutionary socialism in the thought of Ruskin, Carlyle, and Cobbett, see Williams (1958) and Thompson (1976). Cf. also Raymond Williams' argument of how romanticism absorbs Marx (Williams, 1958: 265–84).

7   While the Quakers were the first Protestant wing to take a strong international stand against slavery (Dillon, 1974: 7–9; Davis, 1992: 27–64), it was the critical wing of Unitarianism that played a key role in bringing white liberal Protestants into the emerging critical imagery of social subjects as well as society in crisis. Theodore Parker's sermons, which might better be called events, often drew several thousand audience members during his peak popularity. William Lloyd Garrison, the leader of the most radical abolitionist group in the antebellum era, was one of an estimated 200 "paying members" of the Twenty-Eighth Congregational Society to which Theodore Parker preached. Another member was Franklin B. Sanborn, who later became the first president of the American Social Science Association that formed in 1865 (Hutchinson, 1959: 183, n. 113). Parker, Sanborn, and Thomas Wentworth Higginson, another ex-Unitarian minister who played a major role in bringing transcribed Negro spirituals to a white audience (Higginson, 1867; 1870), were members of the "Secret Six," who provided financial and political support for the white abolitionist John Brown, who with less than 50 accomplices carried out a raid upon the federal arsenal at Harpers Ferry, Virginia in 1859 (cf. Haskell, 1977: 49; Howe, 1970).

8   On the influence of French utopianism on the New England renaissance, see Brisbane (1843: 34); Parrington (1987: 379); cf. also Easton (1966).

9   Channing was one of the earliest Protestant ministers to liken industrial servitude to slavery, a theme that took hold in a number of important ideological and political struggles. The Transcendentalist Henry David Thoreau rejected market society, in part, for its capacity to reduce workers to slaves; the labor movements that championed white working men dreaded the possibility that they were slipping into "wage slavery;" and the important

Free Soil Party, which resulted in the formation of the Republican Party, used the rallying cries of "free men" and "free labor" to juxtapose the plight of white wage laborers against the unfreedom of slavery (cf. Channing, 1884; Thoreau, 1910; Foner, 1970, 1974; Saxon, 1990; and Roediger, 1991).

10   See, for example, the themes of Christian universalism addressed in the slave narratives of David Walker (1830), Frederick Douglass (1982), and Harriet Jacobs (1861).

11   The interest in the cultural – and especially the racial – margins *vis-à-vis* professional folklore developed increasingly in tandem with a full-scale concern to identify, legitimize, produce, and institutionalize a genuine American high culture (cf. Raleigh, 1961; DiMaggio, 1982; Levine, 1988).

12   On the rise of professionalization within all of the social sciences in the American context, see Haskell (1977) and Ross (1991). Lowenthal (1961), Mazlish (1989), and Lepenies (1988) have made similar arguments with regard to the modern novel as a precursor to modern social theory. Cf. also Marx (1964).

13   Interestingly, a copy of *Souls* was read by Max Weber, who planned to write an introduction to an anticipated German translation (Lewis, 1993: 277).

REFERENCES

Alexander, J. 1991: Sociological Theory and the Claim to Reason: Why the End is Not in Sight. *Sociological Theory* (Fall), 147–53.

Allen, W. F., Ware, C. P., and McKim, L. 1867: *Slave Songs of the United States.* New York: A. Simpson.

Bellah, R., Swidler, A., and Tipton, S. 1985: *Habits of the Heart: Individualism and Commitment in American Life.* Berkeley: University of California Press.

Bendix, R. 1964: *Nation-building and Citizenship.* Berkeley: University of California Press.

Berman, M. 1982: *All That is Solid Melts Into the Air: The Experience of Modernity.* New York: Simon and Schuster.

Blewett, M. H. 1987: The Sexual Division of Labor and the Artisan Tradition in Early Industrial Capitalism: The Case of New England Shoemaking, 1780–1860. In C. Groneman and M. B. Norton (eds), *To Toil the Livelong Day: America's Women at Work, 1780–1980.* Ithaca, NY: Cornell University Press, 35–46.

Boskin, J. 1986: *Sambo: The Rise and Demise of an American Jester.* New York: Oxford University Press.

Boyer, P. 1978: *Urban Masses and Moral Order in America: 1820–1920.* Cambridge, MA: Harvard University Press.

Braudel, F. 1973 [1949]: *The Mediterranean and the Mediterranean World in the Age of Philip II* (2 vols). New York: Harper & Row.

Bremer, F. 1853: *Homes of the New World: Impressions of America.* (Trans. Mary Howitt.) New York: Harper & Brothers.

Brisbane, A. 1843: Spread of the Doctrine of Association. *Phalanx*, 1, 3 (December 5).

Brooks, V. W. 1936: *The Flowering of New England, 1815–1865*. New York: P. Dutton.

Burke, P. 1978: *Popular Culture in Early Modern Europe*. New York: Harper Torchbooks.

Cassirer, E. 1951: *The Philosophy of the Enlightenment*. Princeton: Princeton University Press.

Channing, W. E. 1884: *The Complete Works of William Ellery Channing, D.D.* London: Christian Life Publishing.

Clive, Geoffrey. 1960: *The Romantic Enlightenment*. New York: Meridian.

Cobban, A. 1960: *In Search of Humanity: The Role of the Enlightenment in Modern History*. New York: George Braziller.

Cruz, J. 1994: Testimonies and Artifacts. In Jon Cruz and Justin Lewis (eds), *Viewing, Reading, Listening: Audiences and Cultural Reception*, Boulder: Westview Press, 125–50.

—— 1995: From Farce to Tragedy: Reflections on the Reification of Race at Century's End. In Avery Gordon and Christopher Newfield (eds), *Mapping Multiculturalism*. Minneapolis: University of Minnesota Press, 19–39.

Davis, A. Y. 1981: *Women, Race, and Class*. New York: Vintage Books.

Davis, D. B. 1992: Quaker Ethic and Antislavery International. In Thomas Bender (ed.), *The Antislavery Debate: Capitalism and Abolitionism as a Problem in Historical Interpretation*, Berkeley: University of California Press, 27–64.

Dillon, M. L. 1974: *The Abolitionists: The Growth of a Dissenting Minority*. Dekalb: Northern Illinois University Press.

DiMaggio, P. 1982: Cultural Entrepreneurship in Nineteenth-century Boston: The Creation of an Organizational Base for High Culture in America; Cultural Entrepreneurship in Nineteenth-century Boston, Part II: The Classification and Framing of American Art. *Media, Culture and Society*, 4, 33–50, 303–22.

Douglas, A. 1977: *The Feminization of American Culture*. New York: Alfred A. Knopf.

Douglas, M. 1966: *Purity and Danger: An Analysis of the Concepts of Pollution and Taboo*. Boston: Routledge and Kegan Paul.

Douglass, F. 1982 [1845]: *Narrative of the Life of Frederick Douglass, an American Slave, Written by Himself*. New York: Penguin Books.

Du Bois, W. E. B. 1969 [1903]: *The Souls of Black Folk*. New York: NAL Penguin.

—— 1969 [1935]: *Black Reconstruction in America, 1860–1880*. New York: Atheneum.

—— 1915: *The Elementary Forms of the Religious Life*. (Trans. Joseph Ward Swain.) London: Allen and Unwin.

Durkheim, E. 1984 [1893]: *The Division of Labor in Society*. (Trans. W. D. Halls.) New York: The Free Press.

Easton, Loyd D. 1966: *Hegel's First American Followers*. Athens: Ohio University Press.

Elias, N. 1978: *The Civilizing Process*. New York: Urizen Books.

Fairchild, H. N. 1928: *The Noble Savage: A Study in Romantic Naturalism*. New York: Columbia University Press.

Flax, J. 1992: The End of Innocence. In Judith Butler and Joan W. Scott (eds), *Feminists Theorize the Political*, New York: Routledge, 445–63.

Foner, E. 1970: *Free Soil, Free Labor, Free Men: The Ideology of the Republican Party Before the Civil War*. New York: Oxford University Press.

Foner, P. S. 1974: *Organized Labor and the Black Worker, 1619–1973*. New York: Praeger.

Genovese, E. D. 1974: *Roll, Jordan, Roll: The World the Slaves Made*. New York: Pantheon.

Gordon, A. and Newfield, C. (eds) 1995: *Mapping Multiculturalism*. Minneapolis: University of Minnesota Press.

Gusfield, J. 1966: *Symbolic Crusade: Status Politics and the American Temperance Movement*. Urbana: University of Illinois Press.

Habermas, J. 1989 [1962]: *The Structural Transformation of the Public Sphere*. Cambridge, MA: MIT Press.

Harvey, D. 1989: *The Condition of Postmodernity*. Oxford: Basil Blackwell.

Haskell, T. 1977: *The Emergence of Professional Social Science*. Urbana: University of Illinois Press.

Higginson, T. W. 1867: Negro Spirituals. *Atlantic Monthly*, 19, 684–94.

—— 1962 [1870]: *Army Life in a Black Regiment*. New York: Collier.

Howe, D. W. 1970: *The Unitarian Conscience: Harvard Moral Philosophy, 1805–1861*. Cambridge, MA: Harvard University Press.

Hutchinson, W. R. 1959: *The Transcendentalist Ministers: Church Reform in the New England Renaissance*. New Haven: Yale University Press.

Jacobs, H. (Linda Brent) 1861: *Incidents in the Life of a Slave Girl*. Boston.

Jacoby, R, 1987: *The Last Intellectuals: American Culture in the Age of Academe*. New York: The Noonday Press.

Jameson, F. 1991: *Postmodernism, or, The Cultural Logic of Late Capitalism*. Durham, NC: Duke University Press.

Kemble, F. A. 1863: *Journal of a Residence on a Georgia Plantation in 1838–1839*. New York: Harper and Brothers.

Laclau, E. and Mouffe, C. 1985: *Hegemony and Socialist Strategy: Towards a Radical Democratic Politics*. London: Verso.

Lepenies, W. 1988: *Between Literature and Science: The Rise of Sociology*. (Trans. R. J. Hollingdale.) Cambridge: Cambridge University Press.

Levine, H. G. 1978: The Discovery of Addiction: Changing Conceptions of Habitual Drunkenness in America. *Journal of Studies on Alcohol*, 39, 1, 143–74.

Levine, L. W. 1988: *Highbrow Lowbrow: The Emergence of Cultural Hierarchy in America*. Cambridge, MA: Harvard University Press.

Lewis, D. L. 1993: *W. E. B. Du Bois: Biography of a Race, 1868–1919*. New York: Henry Holt.

Lott, E. 1993: *Love and Theft: Blackface Minstrelsy and the American Working Class*. Oxford: Oxford University Press.

Lovejoy, A. O. 1941: The Meaning of Romanticism for the Historian of Ideas. *Journal of the History of Ideas*, 2, 3.

Lowenthal, L. 1961: *Literature, Popular Culture, and Society.* Palo Alto: Pacific Books.

Lukács, G. 1971 [1920]: *The Theory of the Novel.* (Trans. Anna Bostock.) Cambridge, MA: MIT Press.

Marx, L. 1964: *The Machine in the Garden: Technology and the Pastoral Ideal in America.* Oxford: Oxford University Press.

May, H. F. 1967: *Protestant Churches and Industrial America.* New York: Harper & Row.

—— 1991: *The Divided Heart: Essays on Protestantism and the Enlightenment in America.* New York: Oxford University Press.

Mazlish, B. 1989: *A New Science: The Breakdown of Connections and the Birth of Sociology.* New York: Oxford University Press.

Meyrowitz, J. 1985: *No Sense of Place: The Impact of Electronic Media on Social Behavior.* New York: Oxford University Press.

Moore, B. 1966: *Social Origins of Dictatorship and Democracy: Lord and Peasant in the Making of the Modern World.* Boston: Beacon Press.

Nelson, C., Treichler, P., and Grossberg, L. 1992: Cultural Studies: An Introduction. In Lawrence Grossberg, et al. (eds), *Cultural Studies,* New York: Routledge, 1–22.

Olmsted F. L. 1904 [1856]: *A Journey in the Seaboard Slave States in the Years 1853–1854.* New York: G. P. Putnam's Sons.

Parrington, V. L. 1987 [1927]: *The Romantic Revolution in America, 1800–1860.* Norman: University of Oklahoma Press.

Piven, F. F. and Cloward, R. A. 1971: *Regulating the Poor: The Functions of Social Welfare.* New York: Pantheon.

Postman, N. 1982: *The Disappearance of Childhood.* New York: Dell.

Raboteau, A. J. 1978: *Slave Religion: The "Invisible Institution" in the Antebellum South.* New York: Oxford University Press.

Raleigh, J. H. 1991: *Matthew Arnold and America.* Berkeley: University of California Press.

Roediger, D. R. 1961: *The Wages of Whiteness: Race and the Making of the American Working Class.* London: Verso.

Rorabaugh, J. 1979: *The Alcoholic Republic: An American Tradition.* Oxford: Oxford University Press.

Rose, M. A. 1991: *The Post-modern and the Post-industrial: A Critical Analysis.* Cambridge: Cambridge University Press.

Ross, D. 1991: *The Origins of American Social Science.* Cambridge: Cambridge University Press.

Rothman, D. 1971: *The Discovery of the Asylum: Social Order and Disorder in the New Republic.* Boston: Little Brown.

Saxon, A. 1990: *The Rise and Fall of the White Republic: Class Politics and Mass Culture in Nineteenth-century America.* London: Verso.

Seidman, S. 1990: Substantive Debates: Moral Order and Social Crisis – Perspectives on Modern Culture. In Jeffrey C. Alexander and Steven Seidman (eds), *Culture and Society: Contemporary Debates,* Cambridge: Cambridge University Press, 217–35.

—— 1991a: Postmodern Anxiety: The Politics of Epistemology. *Sociological Theory*, 9, 2 (Fall), 180–94.

—— 1991b: The End of Sociological Theory: The Postmodern Hope. *Sociological Theory* 9, 2 (Fall), 131–46.

Sennett, R. 1976: *The Fall of Public Man*. New York: Knopf.

Sherwood, S. J., Smith, P., and Alexander, J. 1993: The British are Coming . . . Again! The Hidden Agenda of "Cultural Studies." *Contemporary Sociology*, 22, 3 (May).

Sobel, M. 1988 [1979]: *Trabelin' On: The Slave Journey to an Afro-Baptist Faith*. Princeton: Princeton University Press.

Sutton, J. 1988: *Stubborn Children: Controlling Delinquency in the United States, 1640–1981*. Berkeley: University of California Press.

Swidler, A. 1986: Culture in Action. *American Sociological Review*, 51, 2.

Taylor, C. 1989: *Sources of the Self: The Making of the Modern Identity*. Cambridge, MA: Harvard University Press.

Thomas, J. L. 1965: Romantic Reform in America, 1815–1865. *American Quarterly*, 17, 656–81.

Thompson, E. P. 1976: *William Morris, Romantic Revolutionary*. New York: Pantheon Books.

Thoreau, H. D. 1910 [1854]: *Walden*. New York: Longmans, Green, and Co.

Toll, R. 1974: *Blacking Up: The Minstrel Show in Nineteenth-century America*. New York: Oxford University Press.

Touraine, Alain. 1988 [1984]: *Return of the Actor: Social Theory in Postindustrial Society*. Minneapolis: University of Minnesota Press.

Tucker, R. C. 1978: *The Marx–Engels Reader*, (2nd edn). New York: W. W. Norton.

Van Deburg, W. 1984: *Slavery and Race in American Popular Culture*. Madison: University of Wisconsin Press.

Walker, D. 1830: *Appeal in Four Articles, Together with a Preamble to the Colored Citizens of the World, But in Particular, and very Expressly, to those of the United States of America*. Boston.

Weber, M. 1991 [1905]: *The Protestant Ethic and the Spirit of Capitalism*. (Trans. Anthony Giddens.) London: HarperCollins.

Wilentz, S. 1984: *Chants Democratic: New York City and the Rise of the American Working Class, 1788–1850*. New York: Oxford University Press.

Williams, R. 1958: *Culture and Society: 1780–1950*. New York: Columbia University Press.

—— 1961: *The Long Revolution*. New York: Columbia University Press.

—— 1976: *Keywords*. London: Fontana.

4

Conserving Cultural Studies

ANDREW GOODWIN AND JANET WOLFF

Cultural studies, which ought to benefit from its location at the intersection of the humanities and the social sciences, risks falling between the two. In particular, the highly developed professionalization of academic disciplines in the US continues to produce parallel but discrete projects in the study of culture, each weakened by its ignorance of developments in the other. The contrast between sociology and literary studies is especially striking.[1] (Anthropology, interestingly, has been the site of some more productive encounters, resulting in work which explores the complex interrelations between social structure and process on the one hand, and cultural categories and identities on the other.)[2] The "sociology of culture" section of the American Sociological Association goes from strength to strength, matched by growing numbers of publications by sociologists of culture (and by cultural sociologists).[3] Despite the claims of some authors, and the intentions of editors,[4] most work in the sociology of culture retains that positivistic residue which keeps it resolutely indifferent to the insights of critical theory and, especially, theories of representation.[5] Literary versions of cultural studies, on the other hand, have taken poststructuralism in its more radical modes as justification for a textual, nonsociological, approach to cultural texts and practices, both because of the disciplinary bent of its practitioners, and because of the belief that critical theory implies that there is nothing beyond discourse, or that if there is it is unknowable.[6]

There is a certain irony in criticizing American cultural studies for its textual bias, when we recall the academic origins of cultural studies in Britain.[7] The Birmingham Centre for Contemporary Cultural Studies was founded in 1964 as a research grouping within the English Department at the University of Birmingham in the UK. Its first director was Richard Hoggart, Professor of English Literature. Stuart Hall, its second director

(1970–80), was also a literature scholar.[8] As is by now well known, the trajectory of the work of the Centre (always, by the way, a very small unit, with a maximum of three faculty members at any one time) was characterized by the turn from "high" literature to the study of popular culture (inspired initially by Hoggart's 1957 book, *The Uses of Literacy*, amongst other texts), and by the growing recognition of the need to perceive cultural texts, of whatever sort, as immersed in and produced by social practices and institutions. In the process, the members of the Centre turned first to the work of sociologists (Weber and Mannheim, amongst others), then to Marxism (the model which continued to inform much of the work produced by the Centre), and then to the crucial revisions of these approaches engendered by feminism, postcolonial criticism, and structuralist and poststructuralist theories.[9] Out of these developments came the possibility of a way of studying culture which acknowledged (and explored) the discursive construction of social relations and institutions, as well as of cultural texts and practices, at the same time as analysing the grounding of culture in social, economic, and material factors. With the reversion of cultural studies to a disciplinary home in literary studies, and its transformation into what Cary Nelson (1991: 26) has called "recycled semiotics," the once progressive move of "sociologizing" culture now attracts the charge of conservatism from the more radical deconstructors.

In this essay, we want to argue in favor of conservatism in cultural studies. We mean this in a number of senses. First, we comment on the preference by scholars of cultural studies for privileging radical or avant-garde cultural practices (which is not the same thing, of course, as privileging popular culture over high culture – though there has been a tendency to do this, too). Although the whole impetus of cultural studies has been (should be) critical, in the sense that ideologies of "transcendent" art have to be challenged, and the intersections of culture, power, and social privilege explored, this does not mean that only progressive culture is worth analysing. Nor does it mean that the primary objective of cultural analysis is to discover the subversive moment in apparently conservative forms of culture. Second, as we have already implied, we propose returning to a more sociological cultural studies, though, crucially, on the basis of a sociology reconstructed in response to poststructuralist theory.[10] Third, we take up the concerns expressed recently by certain authors, and argue that the critical practice of cultural studies cannot be at the expense of either aesthetics or poetics. Finally (and this may prove to be the most controversial point), we consider the limits and difficulties of interdisciplinary research and, especially, pedagogy, and conclude with a defense of the disciplines.

Actually, conservatism is beginning to get a good name on the left. Anthony Giddens (1994) has recently identified the historical irony by which political conservatism has become "radical" (as opposed to traditional conservatism), and socialist thought has been forced into a position of needing primarily to *conserve*.[11] Politically, socialists confront the task of conserving, or repairing, what has been damaged or threatened – the welfare state, the environment, economic and legal gains for trade unionists, workers, women, and minorities, and so on. As he says, "A radical political programme must recognize that confronting manufactured risk cannot take the form of 'more of the same', an endless exploration of the future at the cost of the protection of the present or past" (Giddens, 1994: 10). For Giddens, a reconstituted radical politics has to draw on "philosophic conservatism." The new conservatism, on the other hand, is no longer committed to the idea of conserving (apart from its empty rhetoric about "family values," which, as historians have amply shown, is not based on any actual historical knowledge of the family in either of the "ideal" periods usually invoked – the Victorian era and the 1950s.)[12] In much the same spirit as Giddens, we want to suggest that a critical cultural studies in the late twentieth century has to engage with aspects of tradition which it seems essential to conserve.

Cultural studies in the United States confronts several difficulties which draw attention to key differences between its work and the project from which it takes its name. While there is a good deal of continuity between cultural studies in the United States and in Britain, their different social contexts have also generated divergent and in some ways incompatible projects. A sociology of cultural studies would concern itself with at least three central shifts, as cultural studies went west, concerning social location, relationship to broader social movements, and object of study.

In the first place, one can hardly overestimate the importance of the fact that cultural studies in Britain did not originate in higher education, but rather was the product of teaching in adult education classes. As Raymond Williams once pointed out (1989b), cultural studies is too often associated with a history of *texts* (the Great Works of the Founding Patriarchs), when in fact it was *teaching* about culture in Workers' Education Association classes and in University Extension courses, as far back as the 1930s and 1940s, which really constituted the genesis of the project. Richard Hoggart makes a similar point in the second volume of his autobiography (1990), when he cites his experience in adult education (and that of Williams and E. P. Thompson) as a catalyst in shifting his work "step by step but inescapably to move out from the study of literature as it is academically defined to work on many other aspects of contemporary culture." For the founding troika of British cultural studies (Hoggart, Thompson, Williams), the analysis of culture came about at least in part because of an engagement with teaching adults. There was little theoretical unity here. Edward

Thompson denied having anything to do with cultural studies and wrote a famously critical review of Williams' book, *The Long Revolution*. Similarly, the approaches of Williams and Hoggart differ even on the question of how "culture" should be defined, as Paul Jones has recently demonstrated (1994)[13] – a difference that was emphasized by Williams' subsequent turn to Marxism. Nevertheless, what is important here is not only a shared commitment to understanding the practices of working-class culture, but also a common link to students, both working class and middle class, who were themselves connected to nonacademic projects and interests. That this teaching did lead to the writing of key "texts" cannot be denied; but its roots in a nonacademic culture (which, for Williams and Hoggart, was also a biographical matter) left this moment of cultural studies less vulnerable to the professionalization and the avant-gardism that came later.

Cultural studies in the United States has not succeeded in forging similar bonds. The explanation lies in part in the second key difference between the two moments: the absence, in the United States, of a common, broad-based social movement with which cultural analysts can identify and engage.[14] In postwar Britain, the labor movement, the New Left, and the British Labour Party provided such a context for intellectual work. (While it is true that the women's movement and other post-1960s social movements have had an important impact on the development of cultural studies, the institutionalization of this work in the university has guaranteed that its primary orientation and *raison d'être* is academic.) Today, the United States lacks such a movement. Indeed, this has been increasingly the case in Britain too, since the early 1980s. One effect of this absence is the tendency for academic radicals to seek out oppositional engagements on-campus, in the form of the adoption of an avant-garde politics of one kind or another, focused on theory, aesthetics, sexuality, and more formal kinds of political identification. We are critical of this trend, though we make our point *sympathetically*. The absence of organic links with blue-collar and other nonacademic constituencies has produced a tendency in American cultural studies to turn to debilitating avant-gardisms of various kinds. This trend is by no means peculiar to American work, but it is noticeable how often sociologists (and others) hostile to cultural studies equate the project with the work of Foucault, Baudrillard, and other poststructuralist writers. For Raymond Williams there was still a connection, the possibility of belonging, of finding community in class and ethnic relations that were also explored in his novels. By the time we reach the students Williams taught, like Terry Eagleton, the strategies have become modernist, and the object is Wittgenstein, not the working class (Eagleton, 1993). The "scholarship boy" (or girl) who makes good and leaves community behind once found a place to connect, and this place (whether it was a trade union, the New Left, the Labour Party, or one of the newer social movements) created the possibility for relations between theory and practice that were not necessarily ironic or modernist. The familiar argument that postmodern cultural studies is symptomatic of changes in real social circumstances[15] illustrates the extent to which strategies of irony and social distance reflect social location every bit as much as political strategy.[16] But if these changes are partly generational, it is also true that they have gone further in the United States than in Britain and have had great consequences for the students we teach as well as the theorists we read.

The extent of this political shift is exemplified by Stanley Fish (1995), who argues that, despite its radicalism and its interdisciplinarity, cultural studies can only ever be a form of professionalized academic practice. While we agree with some parts of this argument (as we say later in this essay), the problem with it is precisely the absence of the sociological frame that accompanied literary studies in the earliest days of cultural studies. Fish is right to argue that aesthetics constitutes an autonomous zone, and that questions of art and form cannot be reduced to issues of politics and sociology, thus leaving the way clear for a defense of criticism as an essentially *aesthetic* activity. This is a valuable contribution to the debate, and a point that we will defend later. But it is at best only a half-truth to suggest that issues of aesthetics and form are unrelated to social power and political influence. Fish's defense of literary studies as text analysis perfectly illustrates the central problem of a good deal of American cultural studies. The "cultural studies" is indistinguishable from the literary theory of F. R. Leavis – except that it is *less* sophisticated than a Leavisism which at least acknowledged correspondences between society and culture. Fish is correct in his assumption that there is nothing necessarily radical or progressive about the new forms of text analysis. His assumption that this kind of work *is* cultural studies is revealing, but flawed. It describes one kind of cultural studies, based in text analysis. For the more sociological approaches to both production and consumption (including through text analysis), the dismissal of such work as irrelevant to policy-making, institutional reform, or actual effects and reading formations is unconvincing. It is achieved, in any case, through a combination of sarcasm, hyperbole, and a shifting of the terms of debate. Fish begins by asserting that the critique (and appreciation) of literary texts is an aesthetic matter that will not generate competences pertinent to changing (or administering) the world. This, clearly, is often true. It echoes the description of cultural studies that critics of the field, such as Nicholas Garnham (1993, 1995), have provided, from a diametrically opposed position – namely, that "lit crit" and cultural studies are both afflicted with a problem that a sociological media studies (or perhaps political economy of culture) has transcended. For where Fish identifies the predicament of cultural and literary studies as an inevitable consequence of disciplinary imperatives, Garnham argues for an interdisciplinary approach to media studies that would foreground issues of practice, policy, and political economy. When Fish goes on to discuss the work of political critics (such as Terry Eagleton) for whom there should be such a dialogue between aesthetics and society, his argument moves into less interesting (and more familiar) territory, by noting that the current powers-that-be pay no attention to discourse theorists when making policy. This begs several questions of some importance, including whether or not this is a desirable situation, and why it might be that administrators of a capitalist culture would choose to ignore theories whose very premise is the abolition of capitalist social relations. That is to say, if at some level cultural studies is still a radical project, then it is hardly any wonder that its critique is marginal during such a hugely conservative period. The Stanley Fish position, provocative and refreshing though it is, is essentially an apology for this state of affairs, rather than an analysis of it.

A third point concerns objects of study. Cultural studies in the US can be criticized for ignoring culture as a practice of everyday life, in favor of textualized analyses of privatized "readings" which overemphasize "anti-hegemonic" elements. Raymond Williams (1989a) argued in favor of an analysis of culture as "ordinary." If a textual, postmodern, American cultural studies has forgotten this, that is no reason to abandon the insights of the earlier paradigm. One effect of this loss is the absence of any serious engagement with conservatism.[17] Academic radicals are too quick to dismiss nonliberal ideas and the resulting distance from ordinary culture is quite damaging. In Britain, some cultural studies scholars have made a real effort to understand the appeal and the effects of political conservatism; this applies particularly to the work of Stuart Hall and analysts in the British Communist Party, publishing in its journal (now defunct), *Marxism Today*.[18] That leftist critics of the new conservatism might reasonably be expected to exert some real influence over public policy (through the labor movement and the Labour Party, or perhaps the Liberal Democrats) helps explain why the discussion of culture and ideology had, in this context, significant nonacademic ramifications.

We are making two related points here about conservatism. In the first place, cultural studies must be prepared to understand conservative cultures and conservative cultural theorists; who now bothers to read T. S. Eliot or Matthew Arnold, beyond the potted cultural studies account of their work? This is essential, not least because the political positions adopted by most people are likely to be far less progressive than those of the liberals and radicals who teach cultural studies, and are in many cases closer to Eliot and Arnold than to Habermas and Derrida. But a second point (and here we should acknowledge a difference between the work of Stuart Hall and some of his more daring collaborators, such as Martin Jacques)[19] concerns the manner in which *Marxism Today*'s analysis of "New Times" led some to conclude that the left could both exert intellectual hegemony by engaging with conservatives, and also actually *learn* from some aspects of the new conservatism, following the defeat of the social democratic policies of the Labour Party in the 1970s.[20] Clearly, the second task is impossible without commitment to the first.

This in its turn suggests the need for a different kind of conservatism, of a more theoretical nature. Nicholas Garnham (1990b) has argued convincingly that the cultural studies emphasis on the concept of ideology has sometimes led to a blindness to material practice – a neglect that we would trace to one of its "founding" texts, Richard Hoggart's *The Uses of Literacy*. This development can be seen in the relative absence of analyses of the point of production of both symbolic and nonsymbolic forms (a problem that originates with Hoggart), where the material basis of ideology is obfuscated in favor of the deconstruction of media texts; and at the point of consumption, where cultural studies "has exaggerated the freedoms of consumption and daily life" (Garnham 1995: 65). This latter point has been developed at greater length by Keith Tester (1994). While we do not accept that political economy and cultural studies are necessarily contradictory approaches, as Garnham sometimes implies, it is clear that there can be no reconciliation between Garnham's historical materialism and a *postmodern* cultural studies. In that regard, we argue that cultural studies should remain closer to the former than to the latter.

One explanation for the postmodern turn taken by some cultural studies scholars in the United States lies in the multicultural nature of American society.[21] Hoggart and Williams were writing about a society that thought of itself, despite the British Empire, as racially homogeneous. Whatever the reasons for this assumption at the time, it is clearly no longer plausible.[22] As cultural studies has made the necessary acknowledgments of difference, with regard to race, gender, and sexuality, it has also become susceptible to the new politics of identity. In relation to this debate, we argue that there are good grounds for maintaining a conservative position. The arguments here are familiar, concerning strategic questions (there can be no hegemony for a progressive politics based entirely on difference), ethical issues (especially as they have been raised by feminists eager to avoid "victimism"), and the extent to which infinitely dividing subjectivities are mobilized as vehicles for consumerism.[23] As James Miller (1993) points out, even the arch poststructuralist Michel Foucault rejected the attempt to turn "deviant" sexuality into a new brand of identity.

However, cultural studies has been an important ally for social groups who have been marginalized or disadvantaged. It has become possible to employ the critical tools of cultural analysis to explore and challenge the discursive and institutional structures of their exclusion, as well as to articulate and mobilize specific group identities. (It should go without saying that the sociology *of* cultural studies would also make it clear that the development of cultural theory has in large part been the *product* of such groups, as Stanley Fish notes. The continuous revision of cultural studies in its 30 years of existence has been very much a response to the particular challenges of the women's movement, ethnic minorities, and non-Western cultures, and of those writing from their perspective.) The negative side of this has been that cultural studies too often seems to be mainly a parade of displeasure and bad temper. Stefan Collini puts this well:

> Texts are interrogated . . . to demonstrate how they distort, occlude . . . or in other ways inadvertently reveal the ideological pressure which shaped them. These pressures are in turn taken to be symptomatic of the way in which power operates in society to the systematic disadvantage of certain marginalized or oppressed groups. One effect of these . . . developments is that cultural studies, particularly as practised in the United States, is in constant danger of turning into "Grievance Studies". (Collini, 1994: 4)

This is a danger worth avoiding, as Michael Schudson shows in this volume, in favor of a critical practice which is not premissed on a hermeneutics of suspicion.

Yet what is even less helpful is the development of Grievance Studies' pathologically upbeat twin, Empowerment Studies. This arm of cultural studies is in many ways a symptom of both its Americanization and the decline of the left. As Judith Williamson observed some years ago (1986), one appeal of cultural analysis is precisely its ability to sustain a radical vision in an ocean of reaction. So we see, in Britain and in the United States, what we might call "empowerment studies," in which disappointment in the radical politics of the New Left is displaced onto the terrain of culture, where, through the magical operation of text analysis, oppositional trends are discerned in almost every area of popular culture. Thus, we are in some agreement with both Michael Schudson, who insists that some areas of culture are more important than others,[24] and Nicholas Garnham, whose related point (1990c) is that text analysis is in itself "banal," since the job of critical theorists should be to comprehend how cultural repertoires operate. But while the insistence on looking at the social terrain of representation on a broad scale is persuasive, this begs the question of how one can ever know about "repertoires," unless one has, at some point, studied texts.

If we believe that cultural studies needs sociology more than sociology needs another "reading" of empowering popular texts, this is not to agree with those who seem to think we can return to a sociology which takes cultural categories for granted. It is not enough, for instance, to engage in sociological analysis which merely leaves categories like "art" unquestioned. Studies of both "high culture" and popular culture make this mistake.[25]

Liberal criticism's tendency to depend on reductive, mimetic theories of representation is never clearer than in public controversies about rap music and pornography (or, indeed, pornographic rap). In both areas, liberal critics repeatedly deploy a kind of literalism that is less often adopted in relation to high-cultural forms, or "politically correct" areas of popular culture, such as "alternative" rock or the art movie. In this respect, sociology continues to repeat its mistake of the last 40 years of cultural analysis: art is left to philosophers and aestheticians, while "mass culture" is analyzed for its "effects." Lyrics in rap music often give offense because they are built around the polysemic nature of language. But "incorrect" terms (like "queer," "nigga," and "bitch") cannot be read as if they have one, uncomplicated, meaning. If rap engenders "hate," then this is partly because it is about anger and frustration. Cultural studies should no more support liberal critics who wish to dictate the "true" meaning of "incorrect" sentiments than it would align itself with those conservatives who have condemned the music of acts such as Ice-T, Dr Dre, and Nine Inch Nails.[26] Similarly, it has taken sympathetic readings which draw on work from cultural studies, psychoanalysis, and film theory to explain what pornography might means to the consumer,[27] in the face of liberal, feminist, and conservative critics who insist that to depict is to advocate.[28] It is not just that sociology must acknowledge the importance of theories of representation; it is also necessary to be *sociological* about the role of fantasy, day-dreams, illusion, and other aspects of the mass-mediated image which defy the reduction to mimesis.

Cultural studies is perhaps re-tracing a history familiar to students of mass communication. Following an initial period in which extraordinary media power was assumed (the "hypodermic needle" model of media effects), there followed an emphasis on "uses and gratifications," which over-reacted to theories of perceived media power by establishing a model of audience power over the mass media. In mass communications theory, when you hear the word "use," you reach for a gratification. Cultural studies has often rendered a too-crudely drawn depiction of other approaches (isn't there anything we can learn from case studies in clinical psychology, for instance?), though this is not a call for a return to that paradigm. Indeed, cultural studies has suggested an answer to two major criticisms of uses and gratifications theory. In the first place, as Justin Lewis (1991) has argued, that approach offers no theory of the subject, bracketing off individual readers from the social forces which construct media texts as if everything but the moment of consumption were socially constructed. Second, uses and gratifications studies are vulnerable to an important critique, hidden inside a footnote in a mass communication textbook: "Empirical research has, to a large degree, failed to investigate gratifications, often assuming that people get the gratification they seek" (McQuail and Windahl, 1981: 78).

Today's optimistic cultural studies school, with its stress on free-floating signifiers and audience empowerment, is in many ways a reaction to the literalism of so much mass communications sociology, every bit as much as it operates as a counterweight to "grievance studies." For these readings (and they are readings of audiences, as well as texts) insist that simplistic "content analysis" of the mass media tells us too little about what images and narratives mean. This elementary point from the earliest stages of cultural studies theory is worth holding onto today. But along-side it we should also remember Stuart Hall's (1980b) insight that polysemy is not pluralism. Cultural studies always insisted upon a model of situated reception, in which actual reading formations were central. We see no reason to abandon this approach. Unfortunately, the concept of polysemy as deployed in text analysis is so unsituated that it all too often leaves space for an endless moving back and forth between "pessimistic" and "optimistic" readings. This recycling of moods has been productive in the political economy of the academy (insuring that while knowledge is never advanced, new papers can always be written), and is now unproductive as a mechanism for telling us anything new about culture, since "gratification" recast as "pleasure" still reveals too little about real use-values or social interests.

What we propose in place of this unhelpful oscillation in cultural analysis is a more conservative, grounded theory which acknowledges the autonomy of representation, both in consumption and in production, without giving way to radical poststructuralist theories of the subject. Roger Silverstone (1993) has explored the possible link between the work of the British psychotherapist D. W. Winnicott, the social theory of Anthony Giddens, and the study of television as the source of "ontological security" in the inner life of the audience. This is relevant for us because of its commitment to understanding, contrary to so much postmodern theory, the issue of the *stability* of the self. Reflecting upon Giddens' work on identity and self in modern societies, Silverstone considers the significance of these ideas for media theory, and argues that the notion of a modern social contract built on a negotiation between psychosocial anxiety and trust needs a psychoanalytic explanation. Silverstone finds this "missing link" in Winnicott's work. "Its significance within psychoanalysis is that it requires consideration of the individual not as a monad, or in isolation from others, but on the contrary, precisely as both the product and producer of symbolic acts of communication" (ibid: 580).

Winnicott's social theory of the individual is predicated on the notion that subjectivity is formed in a third zone, between subject and object, since the first developmental goal of a human being is that of finding a way to be separate from the mother/parent.[29] This task is not achieved unaided, for in the "transitional object" (classically, as on the cover of the Penguin edition of Winnicott's *Playing and Reality*, a teddy-bear) we find the bridge that enables the subject to overcome anxiety in discovering an objective (and not always compliant) reality. Cultural symbols must therefore be understood not only as signifiers of an objective reality, but also as symptoms of an existential need to bridge subject and object. The individual's use of an object is central to Winnicott's theory of development, and may be analyzed in both children and adults. According to Silverstone, Winnicott's work is useful for cultural studies for the following reasons: (1) it begins from a social theory of the individual as a communicating and creative being; (2) Winnicott's ontological theory implies a symbolic sphere, the space between subject and object; (3) this "transitional" space is a place for testing reality, but it is also where we learn "to fantasize, to imagine, to dream and to play" (Silverstone, 1993: 581); (4) thus, Winnicott poses a threat to a reductionist sociology.[30]

Winnicott's challenge is important, and suggests a more conservative understanding of representation than those approaches currently dominant in cultural studies, since it acknowledges the relative autonomy of the symbolic (transitional) zone without collapsing into either a mimetic theory of representation or a radical poststructuralist approach. At the same time, Winnicott's model acknowledges the social construction of subjects (and the plasticity of their "false selves"), without positing a totally "unfixed" social identity. In fact, it is in many ways more amenable to sociological analysis (for instance, of the family and of child development)[31] than are the abstractions of Lacanian theory that have been so influential in cultural studies. What Silverstone sees as a threat to sociology is also an opportunity, for there is no doubt that cultural studies has been cavalier in its dismissal of sociological work. However, the limitations of a strictly sociological understanding of culture are clearly demonstrated in the field of cultural studies. And it is worth noting that a less sophisticated (but nonetheless perfectly valid) articulation of this critique is also present in many conservative commentaries.

It has long been a complaint of the right, and of those unpersuaded by the arguments of critical theory, that cultural studies scholars substitute extrinsic for intrinsic analysis, thereby forfeiting the essentially literary (or musical, or visual) experience of engaging with the text. A letter to the *New York Times*, in response to an article about the new historicism, illustrates this:

The "new historicism" appears to share an old misconception with Marxists, Freudians, New Critics and deconstructionists: the belief that ideas, movements, neuroses, religious conflicts, social upheavals and political crises write books. But this is not so. Only writers write books.

The common reader has known this truth for a long time. It takes experts to overlook it.[32]

An editorial in the *Art Bulletin* reports that students are disillusioned with the discipline of art history, which substitutes "ideological commitments", "abstract, theoretical preoccupations," and "dogmatic historicism which subordinates art objects to the status of unprivileged historical artifacts" for the "direct, personal engagement with works of art"; the author worries about this "deprivation of visual pleasures" (Brilliant, 1993). Critics of the so-called "new musicology" have been especially concerned about such a loss. Alex Ross (1994), in a more or less sympathetic discussion of new (critical, feminist, queer) approaches to the study of classical music, and especially the work of Susan McClary, admits his own anxiety here: "But I worry about the habits of listening that McClary's method encourages. It keeps the music at bay, taking note only of a few extreme surface effects" (ibid: 60)[33] In literary studies, the formation of a new professional society is announced (the Association of Literary Scholars and Critics), its arrival explained by the turn by the Modern Language Association to "questions of race, class and sex," "critical theory," "media studies and popular culture" (Grimes, 1994). The curator of the 1995 Whitney Biennial, Klaus Kertess, sums up his intentions as being "to proclaim the primacy of visual language," quoting in his catalogue essay the words of another critic who states that "the issue of the 90s will be beauty."[34] These laments are matched in the area of popular music, where Martha Bayles (1994) bemoans the state not so much of music criticism, as of music itself, which she sees as in moral and aesthetic decline.

It is important, of course, to distinguish between such critics, and between the rather different arguments deployed. The defense of the aesthetic is most often mounted on the basis of total refusal of critical approaches (the *New York Times* letter-writer, perhaps the *Art Bulletin* editor), in which case it is no defense at all. More complex is the defense of the aesthetic from the point of view of a critical practice concerned about the over-statement of an essentially sound project: the critique of the notion of transcendence in art, and the insistence on the social–historical–ideological coordinates of culture. Stanley Fish is instructive here, with regard to pedagogy, in his insistence on teaching *poetics* as a part of literary criticism. Cultural studies, in removing the aesthetics from the domain of cultural criticism, has arguably done our students a disservice. As Michael Roth (1996) has noted, a pedagogy that is only ever about the critical deconstruction of texts, arguments, and so forth, too easily plays into the politics of a culture of cynicism. Critical thinking is not necessarily progressive; nor is the teaching of aesthetic appreciation necessarily retrograde. Highly persuasive from this point of view is a review by Terrence Rafferty (1995) of a biography of Sam Cooke, the great soul singer.[35] Rafferty's argument is that in his commitment to situating Sam Cooke in the context of contemporary social relations, especially those of race, the author, Daniel Wolff, totally fails to explain the success (the appeal) of the music – indeed, on the contrary, this careful placement renders Sam Cooke typical rather than special. As Rafferty puts it, "Wolff may know plenty about history, but he doesn't appear to know why he loves Sam Cooke" (ibid: 102).

There are several reasons to support the return, or defense, of the aesthetic in culture and in cultural studies. First, as with the rationale for the Whitney Biennial, we may just want to confess a desire for beauty and pleasure.[36] Or, like Rafferty, we may need to make the case that cultural criticism is incomplete if it does not address these questions. Georgina Born has demonstrated that a critical analysis of music cannot afford to bypass or ignore the aesthetic, by which she means "issues of form, meaning, pleasure and displeasure which are specific to a particular medium, which are telling in terms of their relations with an audience, and which cannot ultimately be reduced to a politics of the social or institutional" (Born, 1993: 234).[37] And as Peter Brooks has warned, we risk short-circuiting the aesthetic when we concentrate too enthusiastically on the ideological meaning of a literary text. What is needed, he insists, is "a moment of poetics," in which students "are forced to ask not only *what* the text means but also *how* it means" (Brooks, 1994: 517). The more traditional skills of textual analysis (what he means by "poetics"), not themselves incompatible with critical approaches, are important in this task. So narratology, iconography, musicology, no longer dismissed as inherently conservative by the various "new" approaches (new historicism, new art history, new musicology), reappear as respectable allies in the project of cultural analysis.

A further reason for thinking about the aesthetic concerns the suppressed role that both creativity and cultural production have played in cultural studies. Some years ago, Dick Hebdige, in the course of a lecture on "Yearning," expressed his own "skepticism about the value of negative critique in general," confessing to "a certain weariness with the old language of resistance first and last: resistance as the be all and end all of cultural politics, as the object of fascination in cultural analysis" (Hebdige, 1987). Criticism and production are not necessarily in opposition (and Hebdige does not suggest otherwise), as a reading of either Marxist theories of *praxis* or T. S. Eliot on criticism would teach us. But this longing to abandon "negative critique" is extremely important. Our point is not that ideology-critique should be displaced by Empowerment Studies, but that a more useful shift would involve a commitment not only to aesthetics but also to production. The yearning of Hebdige demonstrates that something went wrong with cultural studies; for it is only after the moment of triumph for High Theory that producing texts disappears from the agenda. Until that moment (and the cultural conservatives deserve some credit for raising this issue) it was assumed that you studied culture because you liked it, or at least cared about it, and not simply in order to engage in ideology-critique.[38]

In this respect, the retreat from creativity and production parallels the left's abandonment of public criticism.[39] For cultural criticism, clearly enough, is also a kind of production, often demanding its own nonacademic use of language. Yet this form of creative social involvement remains at some distance from the concerns of cultural studies. Todd Gitlin (1991) has pointed out that the reasons for the flight from the public sphere that Russell Jacoby and others identified were determined in part by events beyond the left's control. Nonetheless, cultural studies could have done more, and could still do more, to go beyond the seminar room. In theory, many academics agree that cultural studies and communications and media studies should be in the business of producing and validating public intellectuals. Many of us also know from our own different efforts how difficult it is to maintain an academic career and not lose sight of how to communicate with (and listen to) a wider public.

Of course, it helps that these days our faith in theory is somewhat diminished. There is a new interest in the audience, in the popular, in history, and in production, which has led away from more abstract concerns and analyses. Many graduate students are practitioners of some kind, with backgrounds in art practice, theater, video-making, and rock music, as well as social movement activism. Yet we are struck by how irrelevant this knowledge becomes in the context of graduate-level work in cultural studies. Here the British context is once again instructive by comparison. In Britain, Michael Jackson, a graduate of the Media Studies program at the Polytechnic of Central London (now the University of Westminster), went on to become the producer of a BBC arts program (*The Late Show*) which made the new media/cultural studies agenda available to millions of television viewers. Amazingly, his reputation survived this project, and he went on to become the Head of Arts and Music programming for BBC television. It is difficult to identify similar possibilities in the United States in the 1990s.

Cultural studies has taught us this: there are spaces within the mainstream popular media, and this is one place where a "war of position" might be fought. But, as Bourdieu (1984, 1988) reminds us, the avant-gardism of homo academicus has a political price. Why write for the *Village Voice* if you could get a slot in *Entertainment Weekly?* (Answer: how would you explain that at dinner parties, let alone to a tenure committee? Class is still a factor here.) One goal of any radical educational project should thus be to provide students with the skills to produce popular mainstream forms. Cultural studies should be concerned with encouraging students to enter the cultural industries, including at the "popular" end of the axis of cultural capital. It cannot do this if it is not willing to take seriously the aesthetics of the popular (for example, naturalism and realism, rather than modernism), and the techniques which conservative schooling in "communication" routinely teaches.

We began our account of these debates with some thoughts concerning the differences between cultural studies in contemporary America and during its formative years in Britain. There is another cultural difference at work here. Britain, notoriously the playground of the self-satisfied gentleman amateur, developed cultural studies along somewhat in-disciplined lines, partly because the academic game there was less routinized and professionalized than in the United States. There, writers like Dick Hebdige and Simon Frith and Terry Eagleton could move into more poetic modes of expression without hearing complaints about methodology or sample size. Williams wrote novels and made documentaries with the BBC. *Screen* theorist Colin MacCabe went on to produce movies at the British Film Institute. The specific context of such interventions (which clearly reflect a personal "yearning" as much as a political strategy) has something to do with the greater degree of support for public funding of the arts in Britain. But it is also explained by something that Raymond Williams wrote years ago:

> I think many people have now noticed the long-term effects of the specific situation of British intellectuals: a situation which is changing but with certain continuing effects. In humane studies, at least, and with mixed results, British thinkers and writers are continually pulled back towards ordinary language: not only in certain rhythms and in choices of words, but also in a manner of exposition which can be called unsystematic but which also represents an unusual consciousness of an immediate audience: a sharing and equal-standing community, to which it is possible to defer or reach out. (Williams, 1980: 11–12)

Williams goes on to note the negative aspects of this pull, including a tendency to gravitate towards "common sense" and a fierce anti-intellectualism. His comment on "complaints that a man explaining his life's work, in as precise a way as he could, was not instantly comprehensible, in a clubbable way, to someone who had just happened to drop in from his labour or leisure elsewhere" (ibid: 12) is typically dry and to the point. And yet this formation also provided opportunities for shared public debate that cultural studies in the United States still lacks.

Academic professionalism must take its share of the blame for this state of affairs. Yet we also wish to insist on the importance of the disciplines, for precisely the reasons that Williams so wittily identified. If cultural studies has celebrated its commitment to in-discipline for the perfectly valid reason that the disciplines themselves work to inhibit our ability to understand the world and our place in it, we argue that this should not excuse a disregard for the rigors of scholarly work.[40] The critique of the disciplines, with their particular histories and entrenched interests, and the opportunities arising from border crossings (from academic to non-academic, from one discipline to another) are often celebrated in cultural studies. But there are real problems with a practice of in-discipline. This debate was first addressed in Richard Hoggart's founding text, *The Uses of Literacy.* Colin Sparks' (1974) essay, "The abuses of literacy" (ironically enough, the original title for Hoggart's book) offers an important Marxist riposte to Hoggart (and to Raymond Williams), which notes an underlying absence throughout the text – the neglect of relations of production, which are marginalized (indeed, rendered virtually invisible) in an analysis that suggest a free-floating realm of culture. Social history and economics are largely absent from the book. As a consequence, many areas of working-class culture (for example, the "go-slow" in the workplace) are inadequately explained as purely symbolic in nature. It may also be argued that this neglect of the sphere of production leads Hoggart to over-state the role of the emerging mass media in that period.[41] Hoggart himself reports that the Marxist sociologist F. D. Klingender initiated what is now a familiar set of Marxist criticisms, privately, on reading the typescript of the book (Hoggart, 1990: 142). Hoggart's response, that his neglect of this area stemmed from his not wanting to "claim a larger professional knowledge" than he possessed, serves as a reminder that the limitations of individual competence are often the weak link in the chain of cross-disciplinary reasoning. As Fish reminds us (in parallel with Schudson's argument in this volume), to demonstrate the arbitrary and specific nature of a discipline is not the same thing as demonstrating that disciplines are inherently useless.

The problems of interdisciplinarity are different at the level of undergraduate and graduate education, and different again with regard to scholarship and research. For undergraduates enrolled in an interdisciplinary program like cultural studies, one difficulty which presents a particular challenge to the teacher is the likelihood that students come to the class with very varied disciplinary backgrounds.[42] In Britain, this would mean that high-school specialization is less likely than usual to be a grounding for higher education. In North America, it might mean that students select their areas of specialization on the basis of widely differing education in their first couple of years at college; however, this is also common in many disciplines in the North American context, where early specialization, in high school and even college, is rare. It is also the case that what constitutes a cultural studies program, in a context in which such programs are rarely also departments, is very much dependent on which sympathetic faculty colleagues the coordinator can round up across the various disciplinary homes. With few exceptions (that is, actual departments of cultural studies – usually "communication and cultural studies" or "literary and cultural studies"), cultural studies programs come together in a haphazard, though not necessarily unsatisfactory, way. The resulting combinations have produced interestingly varied programs in this area, depending on the particular combination of literary studies, visual studies, media studies, musicology, anthropology, sociology, and gender and ethnic studies.

At the graduate level, there are other issues. In particular, as the first and second generations of cultural studies graduate students get beyond coursework and start work on dissertations, the practical problem of expert advice has come up. The real risk here is the temptation to allow the very legitimate critique of disciplines and their boundary-policing to justify a new dilettantism. A graduate student may decide that he or she wants to undertake a critical study of architecture, as a central or secondary aspect of the research project.[43] But there is an extensive literature on such issues – in architectural history and theory, in urban planning, in urban geography, and in other disciplines. Or the student might take as a topic the relationship between the landscape garden and bourgeois ideologies of property and of the aesthetic in the eighteenth century, in which case the advice of a philosopher and a historian seems essential. A scholarly investigation into the role of visual culture in the Soviet Union in the 1940s clearly necessitates the addition of an expert on Soviet history or sociology. The advisor will often be put in the position of refusing such projects, or, where possible, insisting that the candidate find a suitably qualified advisor to serve on the dissertation committee. The point is that cultural studies projects cannot be based on an arrogant refusal of the expertise (decades of scholarship) which exists within the disciplines. It is true that the lack of self-reflexivity within traditional disciplines renders them subject to critical (historical, ideological, and institutional) analysis – indeed, cultural studies is partly motivated by this project. But there are no short cuts to knowledge, and we do well to continue to work closely with our colleagues within the disciplines, and to benefit from their expertise and learning.

It is also important to argue in defense of the retention of disciplines as a potential arena of engagement and internal critique.[44] In general, it is a little difficult to imagine the future state of cultural studies, if we assume that in another ten or twenty years we will have several generations of scholars working in this area. In particular, are we likely to produce cohorts who specialize in a generic field of "culture"? It seems more likely that cultural studies will continue to develop in engagement with existing areas of study (though many of those are being radically transformed themselves, partly in response to cultural studies – for example, the growing tendency to redefine art history and criticism as "visual studies"). This will mean programs in literary and cultural studies, visual and cultural studies, communication and cultural studies, and so on. Institutionally (and therefore, financially), the situation of such programs has always been precarious, dependent as they are on both the services and time of faculty with primary commitments elsewhere, and the continued existence of courses which departments offer for crosslisting. But perhaps this marginal situation, rather than being characteristic of the early years of cultural studies, is part of the condition of its existence.

Politically speaking, Fish cannot be faulted for deflating the claims made by many radicals who overestimate the currency of intellectual work. Much of what we do is of purely professional interest and will have no purchase off campus. Fish notes the importance of *teaching* as radical practice. Cultural studies in the academy *is* in the "real world," and reaches many thousands of students. That the climate of political opinion is such that this work is unlikely to inform state policy or political platforms is hardly the fault of cultural studies. That the knowledge we produce is often of a specialized professional nature must also be acknowledged. Particularly in the United States, cultural studies has much to be modest about when it comes to praxis. And it is hard to imagine a different relationship between cultural analysis and political action without much more serious attention to matters of political economy. In this respect Michael Schudson, writing from a more academic perspective, echoes Nicholas Garnham's more policy-oriented stance, when he asks that cultural studies think harder about its objects of study. Some objects are more important than others. The notion that *la langue* can be read off from each and every *parole* is one of the conceits of semiotics that we can do without. Cultural studies needs to be more selective abut which texts are considered worthy of study. And it needs to think about the *levels* at which analysis is deployed. Too often the value of individual texts is allowed to stand in for entire "discourses."

We do not mean to suggest that the politics of academic practice is a question that is easily addressed. But there is a politics to the production of knowledge in cultural studies that goes beyond its teaching, and this concerns the relationship between intellectuals and the media professionals who sometimes call on us as "experts." This is a symbiotic relationship, as Garnham (1993) has noted, and it is one that enables savvy academics to speak to a wider audience and help shape and frame public debate. We also agree with Kellner (1993), Tetzlaff (1991), and others who have stressed the need for cultural studies intellectuals to engage in media production, in an effort to widen the audience for these agendas. Once one begins thinking in these terms, it becomes difficult to accept the argument put forward by Stanley Fish concerning the deep and unbridgeable gap between academic and public forms of knowledge. A cultural studies agenda might affect how one organizes a piece of criticism, or a video, or a radio program, but it hardly prevents one from using these forms.

As Anthony Giddens points out, to be "radical" is not necessarily to be progressive. The term is used just as much in the 1990s in connection with the right and with the new conservatism. In cultural criticism, too, what is radical can turn out to be quite conservative. Radical deconstruction and radical styles of semiotic reading have the effect (and, of course, the intention) of undermining conceptions of social structure and, as a result, theories of social inequality and prestige.[45] In addition, commitment to the exploration of the "radical" – avant-garde work, postmodern text, oppositional or transgressive cultural moment – is not in itself either progressive or critical, and nor does it demonstrate the progressive nature of such texts, unless it is based on the careful analysis of these texts in their institutional and social context, especially of reception. Such approaches also tend to alienate nongraduate audiences – a not inconsiderable factor for any popular politics.

It will probably already be apparent that some of our criticisms and proposals sound worryingly like arguments among cultural critics on the right, and particularly the so-called "anti-PC" commentators. The objection to the "wild interpretation" of ungrounded semiotic or psychoanalytic readings has been made (though for different reasons) by many right-wing or mainstream critics who single out the MLA for such attacks, usually by a strategy of citing the most outrageous-sounding papers delivered at its annual conference.[46] Our critique of Grievance Studies risks equation with Robert Hughes' (1993) objections to the "culture of complaint." The proposal that we pay more attention to mainstream culture, and to traditional academic disciplines, seems to parallel the arguments of writers like Harold Bloom and E. D. Hirsch. Gertrude Himmelfarb's (1994) mistaken idea that critical theory inevitably leads to moral relativism (and thus to the immoral) is not entirely remote from our concern about the consequences of ungrounded cultural analysis. Rather than resisting these connections, we see them as potentially valuable. One of the problems of the "anti-PC" campaign of conservative cultural critics has been an unwillingness on the part of those rebutting their arguments to start from an acceptance of what might be *true* in what they say. Writers like d'Souza, Kimball, and Sykes notoriously employ a rhetorical strategy of generalization based on blatant non sequiturs. They find a couple of excessively phrased anti-establishment positions (conference papers, publications, statements, or events), and within a couple of sentences have used these to damn an entire enterprise. If they are successful, it is because their examples manage to shock. The sleight of hand involved in the generalization is rendered invisible. One way of deflecting these critiques would be to make it visible, by accepting the specific charge, and denying the logic of induction. If we are prepared to consider our own criticisms of the distortions of a critical project, including the recognition of what is worth conserving in traditional approaches, we contribute to the rebuttal of such meretricious objections.

A central theme of this essay has been the relationship between cultural studies and sociology. On the one hand, we have been critical of the resistance of sociology to contemporary critical theory, a resistance which continues to prevent the sociology of culture becoming cultural studies. On the other hand, we have been even more concerned to stress the need for cultural studies to be grounded in sociology. The study of culture cannot just be the study of texts, however critically these texts are read. Nor can it be the analysis of texts in relation to social and historical contexts which are themselves entirely "textualized." Cultural studies is concerned with institutions, social relations, and everyday practices, and with the ways in which cultural texts intersect with (are produced by, and produce) these. Scholars of television and popular culture have increasingly realized that the meaning of a text, including its progressive or reactionary ideology, cannot be ascertained by textual analysis, but only by a knowledge of situated audiences and readers – hence, the turn to ethnography in cultural studies recently.[47] As Schudson concedes, "thought-experiments" have their place in cultural studies. Imaginative approaches to the combination of theory and practice also have their place. Wild interpretation may be ingenious. It may even be right. But we cannot know that without some information about actual (or at least potential) situated readers. Sociology acts as a guarantee against the excesses of wild interpretation, and as a perfectly legitimate rationale for the necessary conservatism of cultural studies.

NOTES

1   Lawrence Grossberg (1988) examines the history of this bifurcation, and criticizes it.

2 See, for example, Dominguez (1986) and Marcus and Fischer (1986).

3 Examples of this work include Crane (1994), Becker and McCall (1990), Lamont and Fournier (1992), Alexander and Smith (1993). The term "cultural sociology" is used in the titles of essays by Lyn Spillman and Stephen Hart in the newsletter of the Sociology of Culture Section of the ASA, vol. 9, no. 3 (spring 1995).

4 Becker and McCall (1990: 4–5), in their introduction, explicitly call for a conversation between sociologists involved in symbolic interactionism and those working in the cultural studies tradition of the Birmingham Centre.

5 So, for example, Judith Balfe reproduces another of those models for a sociology of art, in which Artwork, Patron, Critic, Artist, Audience appear as separate nodes, linked by arrows which, despite the fact that they all point in both directions, indicating mutual influence, fail to signify the dependence of those categories themselves on the constitutive effects of language and social interaction (Balfe, 1994: 2). There are, of course, a number of exceptions to this critique of sociology – for example, the essays by Chandra Mukerji and Anne Bowler in Crane (1994), and Nicola Beisel's essay in Lamont and Fournier (1992). And, in contrast to our critique here, Roger Silverstone, discussing the sociology of culture, has pointed to its "capacity, at least in part, to distance itself from the more positivist tradition in American social science" (Silverstone, 1994: 993).

6 Among numerous critiques on these lines are Nelson (1991) and Clarke (1991).

7 It isn't that "British is best," or that we believe that the work of the Birmingham Centre is the only model for cultural studies. But the tradition which developed out of that Centre has been contrasted favorably with American cultural studies by certain American cultural critics, who find themselves dissatisfied with the negative effects of "the linguistic turn" on cultural studies: see Nelson (1991), Grossberg (1989).

8 Other ironies, illustrating the complex disciplinary moves in British cultural studies; cultural studies originated in English Literature; Stuart Hall, on leaving the University of Birmingham, took up a Chair in Sociology at the Open University in England; a decade later, Simon Frith, trained in sociology, and a central figure in British cultural studies since the 1970s, took an appointment as Professor of English at the University of Strathclyde, Scotland. See Frith (1992).

9 Hall (1980a), Hall (1990). See also Turner (1990).

10 There are several signs that this process is under way within the discipline, though to date it is very much a minority enterprise. See, for example, *Theory and Society*, vol. 21, no. 4 (August 1992), special issue: "Forum on postmodernism"; and *Sociological Theory*, vol. 9, no. 2 (Fall 1991), special issue: "Symposium on postmodernism."

11 See also Jenks (1993).

12 See, for example, Stacey (1994), Miller and Nowak (1977), Coontz (1992).

13 An account which places Williams in a similar relation to "left Leavis-ism" and historical materialism is Garnham (1988).

14   Perry Anderson (1976) has explained the transformation of Western Marxism over the past half-century, from a project of political economy to one of cultural critique, in terms of the gradual loss of connection with social movements and political engagement.

15   See, for example, Pfeil (1988).

16   See Moretti (1987).

17   One exception is Grossberg (1992).

18   See Hall (1988).

19   Some of the work associated with *Marxism Today* went beyond Hall's analysis of Thatcherism to suggest a quasi-postmodern analysis of "New Times" as a distinctive political and economic moment.

20   For some criticisms of this strategy, see Sivanandan (1989) and Sparks (1989).

21   Todd Gitlin (1989) cites multiculturalism and the "recombinant" culture of the US as one feature of postmodernism.

22   See Goodwin (1992: xxix).

23   Ross (1993: 51).

24   See his essay in this volume.

25   See Wolff (1993: 105–7).

26   See, for example, Bennett and Tucker (1995).

27   For example, L. Williams (1989).

28   An overview of this debate is provided by Thompson (1994).

29   See Chodorow (1978).

30   In a parallel argument, John Corner notes: "Cultural analysis needs to engage far more closely with questions about the relationship between 'the arts,' self-development and subjectivity. . . . The interplay of use-value and exchange value in aesthetic evaluation, the particular gratificatory economies within which differentiations are made and produced pleasures validated (or perhaps enjoyed as 'outlawed') requires an attention which is able to think subjectivity *sociologically*" (Corner, 1994: 145). For a critical response to Corner, see Jones (1995). For a cogent account of the politics of quality, see Mepham (1990).

31   For a feminist deployment of Winnicott's ideas, see Mahoney and Yngvesson (1992).

32   *New York Times Magazine*, April 18, 1993. On this tendency to dismiss "experts," see Menand (1995).

33   See also Charles Rosen's contention (again, in the context of a sympathetic review of new musicological texts) that "it is not that music is more autonomous, but more ambiguous, slippery: it will not allow itself to be caught and pinned down like a novel or even a poem" (Rosen, 1994: 61). See also Locke (1993).

34   Quoted in Goldberger (1995: 61). This focus, of course, is understood to be a response to the previous Biennial, of 1993, which was widely criticized for being too polemical and crudely political.

35   The book under review is Wolff (1995)

36   See Kaplan (1986); see also *New Formations*, no. 9 (winter 1989), special issue "On Enjoyment."

37 Here Born is taking issue with Tony Bennett's (1990) dismissal of the aesthetic in cultural theory; see also Bennett (1987). On the relative autonomy of the aesthetic, see Wolff (1993).

38 Interestingly enough, David Samuels (1995) uses the terms "yearned for" and "yearning" in his account of recent developments in the discipline of history, to describe the historian's move towards more poetic and expressive ways of writing.

39 See Jacoby (1987).

40 For an excellent defense of this, see Schudson (1992: 205–21).

41 See Goodwin (1992).

42 See Smith (1991: 43).

43 The examples we give here are all actual cases which have come up recently in our experience.

44 See Wolff (1992: 714).

45 See Eagleton (1981, 1986); Norris (1992)

46 For example, Kimball (1990), Sykes (1988), D'Souza (1991).

47 For example, Radway (1988).

REFERENCES

Alexander, Jeffrey C. and Smith, Philip 1993: The Discourse of American Civil Society: A New Proposal for Cultural Studies. *Theory and Society*, 22 (2).

Anderson, Perry 1976: *Considerations on Western Marxism*. New Left Books.

Balfe, Judith Huggins 1994: Sociology of the Arts in Comparative Perspective. *Newsletter* of the Sociology of Culture Section of the American Sociological Association, 8 (1).

Bayles, Martha 1994: *Hole in Our Soul: The Loss of Beauty and Meaning in American Popular Music*. Free Press.

Becker, Howard S. and McCall, Michal M. (eds) 1990: *Symbolic Interaction and Cultural Studies*. University of Chicago Press.

Bennett, Tony 1987: Really Useless "Knowledge": A Political Critique of Aesthetics. *Literature and History*, 14 (1).

—— 1990: *Outside Literature*. Routledge.

Bennett, William and Tucker, C. DeLores 1995: Lyrics from the Gutter. *New York Times*, June 2.

Born, Georgina 1993: Against Negation, For a Politics of Cultural Production: Adorno, Aesthetics, the Social. *Screen*, 34 (3).

Bourdieu, Pierre 1984: *Distinction*. Routledge and Kegan Paul.

—— 1988: *Homo Academicus*. Stanford University Press.

Brilliant, Richard 1993: Editorial: Where's the Poetry? *The Art Bulletin*, LXXV (3).

Brooks, Peter 1994: Aesthetics and Ideology: What Happened to Poetics? *Critical Inquiry*, 20.

Chodorow, Nancy 1978: *The Reproduction of Mothering: Psychoanalysis and the Sociology of Gender*. University of California Press.

Clarke, John 1991: Cultural Studies: A British Inheritance. In *New Times and Old Enemies*. HarperCollins.

Collini, Stefan 1994: Escape from DWEMsville: Is Culture Too Important to be Left to Cultural Studies? *Times Literary Supplement*, May 27.

Coontz, Stephanie 1992: *The Way We Never Were: American Families and the Nostalgia Trap*. Basic Books.

Corner, John 1994: Debating Culture: Quality and Inequality. *Media, Culture & Society*, 16 (1).

Crane, Diana (ed.) 1994: *The Sociology of Culture*. Blackwell.

Dominguez, Virginia R. 1986: *White by Definition: Social Classification in Creole Louisiana*. Rutgers University Press.

D'Souza, Dinesh 1991: *Illiberal Education: The Politics of Race and Sex on Campus*. Free Press.

Eagleton, Terry 1981: Marxism and Deconstruction. In *Walter Benjamin, or Towards a Revolutionary Criticism*, Verso.

—— 1986: The Idealism of American Criticism. In *Against the Grain: Selected Essays*, Verso.

—— 1993: *Wittgenstein: The Terry Eagleton Script/The Dérek Jarman Film*. BFI Publishing.

Fish, Stanley 1995: *Professional Correctness: Literary Studies and Political Change*. Clarendon Press.

Frith, Simon 1992: Literary Studies as Cultural Studies – Whose Literature? Whose Culture? *Critical Quarterly*, 34 (1).

Garnham, Nicholas 1988: Raymond Williams, 1921–1988: A Cultural Analyst, a Distinctive Tradition. *Journal of Communication*, 38 (4).

—— 1990a: *Capitalism and Communication: Global Culture and the Economics of Information*. Sage.

—— 1990b: Film and Media Studies: Reconstructing the Subject. In *Capitalism and Communication*, Sage.

—— 1990c: Media Theory and the Future of Communication. In *Capitalism and Communication*, Sage.

—— 1993: The Media and Narratives of the Intellectual. *Media, Culture & Society*, 17 (3).

—— 1995: Political Economy and Cultural Studies: Reconciliation or Divorce? *Critical Studies in Mass Communication*, 12.

Giddens, Anthony 1994: *Beyond Left and Right: The Future of Radical Politics*. Polity Press.

Gitlin, Todd 1989: Postmodernism: Roots and Politics. *Dissent*, Winter.

—— 1991: The Politics of Communication and the Communication of Politics. In James Curran and Michael Gurevitch (eds), *Mass Media and Society*, Edward Arnold.

Goldberger, Paul 1995: The Art of his Choosing. *New York Times Magazine*, February 26.

Goodwin, Andrew 1992: The Uses and Abuses of In-discipline. Introduction to Richard Hoggart, *The Uses of Literacy*, Transaction Press.

Grimes, William 1994: In the Literary Field, An Upstart Alliance Based on Tradition. *New York Times*, December 7.

Grossberg, Lawrence 1988: *It's a Sin: Postmodernism, Politics and Culture.* Sydney: Power Publications.

—— 1989: Formations of Cultural Studies: An American in Birmingham. *Strategies*, 2.

—— 1992: *We Gotta Get Out of this Place: Popular Conservatism and Postmodern Culture.* Routledge

Hall, Stuart 1980a: Cultural Studies and the Centre: Some Problematics and Problems. In Stuart Hall, Dorothy Hobson, Andrew Lowe, and Paul Willis (eds), *Culture, Media, Language*, Hutchinson.

—— 1980b: Encoding/Decoding. In Hall et al. (eds), *Culture, Media, Language*, Hutchinson.

—— 1988: *The Hard Road to Renewal: Thatcherism and the Crisis of the Left.* Verso.

—— 1990: The Emergence of Cultural Studies and the Crisis of the Humanities. *October*, 53.

Hebdige, Dick 1987: Yearning. In Brophy, Dermody, Hebdige, and Muecke (eds), *Streetwise Flash Art: Is there a Future for Cultural Studies?* Power Institute of Fine Arts Occasional Paper no. 6, Sydney.

Himmelfarb, Gertrude 1994: *On Looking into the Abyss: Untimely Thoughts on Culture and Society.* Alfred A. Knopf.

Hoggart, Richard 1990: *A Sort of Clowning. Life and Times: 1940–1959.* Chatto & Windus.

Hughes, Robert 1993: *Culture of Complaint: A Passionate Look in the Ailing Heart of America.* Warner Books.

Jacoby, Russell 1987: *The Last Intellectuals: American Culture in the Age of Academe.* Basic Books.

Jenks, Chris 1993: The Necessity of Tradition: Sociology or the Postmodern? In Chris Jenks (ed.), *Cultural Reproduction*, Routledge.

Jones, Paul 1994: The Myth of "Raymond Hoggart": On "Founding Fathers" and cultural policy. *Cultural Studies*, 8 (3).

—— 1995: Williams and "Quality": A Response to John Corner. *Media, Culture & Society*, 17 (2).

Kaplan, Cora 1986: Wild Nights: Pleasure/Sexuality/Feminism. in *Sea Changes: Culture and Feminism*, Verso.

Kellner, Douglas 1993: Intellectuals and the New Technologies. *Media, Culture & Society*, 17 (3).

Kimball, Roger 1990: *Tenured Radicals: How Politics has Corrupted our Higher Education.* Harper & Row.

Lamont, Michèle and Fournier, Marcel (eds) 1992: *Cultivating Differences: Symbolic Boundaries and the Making of Inequality.* University of Chicago Press.

Lewis, Justin 1991: *The Ideological Octopus: An Exploration of Television and Its Uses.* Routledge.

Locke, Ralph 1993: Music Lovers, Patrons, and the "Sacralization" of Culture in America. *19th-Century Music*, XVII (2).

McQuail, Denis and Windahl, Sven 1981: *Communication Models*. Longman.

Mahoney, Maureen A. and Yngvesson, Barbara 1992: The Construction of Subjectivity and the Paradox of Resistance: Reintegrating Feminist Anthropology and Psychology. *Signs*, Autumn.

Marcus, George and Fischer, Michael M. J. 1986: *Anthropology as Cultural Critique: An Experimental Moment in the Human Sciences*. University of Chicago Press.

Menand, Louis 1995: The Trashing of Professionalism. *New York Times Magazine*, March 5.

Mepham, John 1990: The Ethics of Quality in Television. In Geoff Mulgan (ed.), *The Question of Quality*, British Film Institute.

Miller, Douglas T. and Nowak, Marion 1977: *The Fifties: The Way We Really Were*. Doubleday.

Miller, James 1993: *The Passion of Michel Foucault*. Simon & Schuster.

Moretti, Franco 1987: The Spell of Indecision. *New Left Review*, 164.

Nelson, Cary 1991: Always Already Cultural Studies: Two Conferences and a Manifesto. *The Journal of the Midwest Modern Language Association*, 24 (1).

Norris, Christopher 1992: *Uncritical Theory: Postmodernism, Intellectuals, and the Gulf War*. Lawrence & Wishart.

Pfeil, Fred 1988: Postmodernism as a "Structure of Feeling." In Cary Nelson and Lawrence Grossberg (eds), *Marxism and the Interpretation of Culture*, Macmillan.

Radway, Janice 1988: Reception Study: Ethnography and the Problems of Dispersed Audiences and Nomadic Subjects. *Cultural Studies*, 2 (3).

Rafferty, Terrence 1995: Soul Man: The Short Life and Long Shadow of Sam Cooke. *The New Yorker*, April 10.

Rosen, Charles 1994: Music à la mode. *The New York Review of Books*, June 23.

Ross, Alex 1994: A Female Deer? Looking for Sex in the Sound of Music. *Lingua Franca*, July/August.

Ross, Andrew 1993: This Bridge called My Pussy. In Lisa Frank and Paul Smith (eds), *Madonnarama: Essays on Sex and Popular Culture*, Cleis Press.

Roth, Michael S. 1996: On the Limits of Critical Thinking. *Tikkun*, 11 (1).

Samuels, David 1995: The Call of Stories. *Lingua Franca*, May/June.

Schudson, Michael 1992: *Watergate in American Memory: How We Remember, Forget and Reconstruct the Past*. Basic Books.

Silverstone, Roger 1993: Television, Ontological Security and the Transitional Object. *Media, Culture & Society*, 15 (4).

—— 1994: The Power of the Ordinary: On Cultural Studies and the Sociology of Culture. *Sociology*, 28 (4).

Sivanandan, A. 1989: All that Melts into Air is Solid: The Hokum of New Times. *Race and Class*, 31 (3).

Smith, Paul 1991: A Course in "Cultural Studies." "Cultural Studies and New Historicism." Special issue of *The Journal of the Midwest Modern Language Association*, 24 (1).

Sparks, Colin 1974 The Abuses of Literacy. *Working Papers in Cultural Studies*, 6. Birmingham.

—— 1989: Experience, Ideology and Articulation: Stuart Hall and the Development of Culture. *Journal of Communication Inquiry*, 13 (2).

Stacey, Judith 1994: Scents, Scholars and Stigma: The Revisionist Campaign for Family Values. *Social Text*, 40, 12 (3).

Sykes, Charles J. 1988: *Profscam: Professors and the Demise of Higher Education.* St Martin's Press.

Tester, Keith 1994: *Media, Culture and Morality.* Routledge.

Tetzlaff, David 1991: Divide and Conquer: Popular Culture and Social Control in Late Capitalism. *Media, Culture & Society*, 13

Thompson, Bill 1994: *Soft Core: Moral Crusades Against Pornography in Britain and America.* Cassell.

Turner, Graeme 1990: *British Cultural Studies: An Introduction.* Unwin Hyman.

Williams, Linda 1989: *Hardcore: Power, Pleasure and the "Frenzy of the Visible."* University of California Press.

Williams, Raymond 1980: Literature and Sociology. In *Problems in Materialism and Culture*, Verso.

—— 1989a [1958]: Culture is Ordinary. In *Resources of Hope*, Verso.

—— 1989b: The Future of Cultural Studies. In *The Politics of Modernism: Against the New Conformists*, Verso.

Williamson, Judith 1986: The Problem of Being Popular. *New Socialist*, September.

Winnicott, D. W. 1971: *Playing and Reality.* Tavistock Publications.

Wolff, Daniel 1995: *You Send Me: The Life and Times of Sam Cooke.* Morrow.

Wolff, Janet 1992: Excess and Inhibition: Interdisciplinarity in the Study of Art. In Lawrence Grossberg, Cary Nelson, and Paula Treichler (eds), *Cultural Studies*, Routledge.

—— 1993 [1983]: *Aesthetics and the Sociology of Art.* University of Michigan Press.

PART II

REFRAMING POPULAR CULTURAL FORMS AND USAGES

Introduction

In contrast to traditional literary studies, both sociology and cultural studies have taken popular culture very seriously, due to its enormous social presence and its centrality for the formation of contemporary individual and collective identities. Each field has been centrally preoccupied by questions about cultural evaluation and the relation of cultural to social hierarchies, and about cultural innovation, especially in relation to social change. Sociology has, perhaps, tended to concentrate on more institutionalized aspects of popular cultural production or the relationship of culture to other institutional spheres, such as that of formal politics. Conversely, cultural studies has been interested in more diffuse cultural collectivities and practices, as well as in Gramscian questions of hegemony and resistance, which may or may not be discussed in relationship to more formal political processes. None of the essays in Part II settles easily into either disciplinary camp, in part because each author is seeking answers to questions that either haunt the margins of both fields, or that cannot be encompassed entirely satisfactorily by either.

Chandra Mukerji argues that sociologists of culture face some severe limitations when they attempt to account for relations between past and present patterns of culture. She turns to cultural studies for aid in analyzing long-standing cultural formations that cannot be easily accounted for by traditional models of how the past enters the present (e.g. historical materialism, collective memory, cultural reproduction), or by accounts of practices that build the present out of the past. Her case study concerns patterns in representations of "the child" in contemporary children's media. Specifically, she examines some Muppet characters in the program *Sesame Street* to see what characteristics of "the child" they express, then locates these particular character types in the history of Western childhood, and explores how they are deployed today as models for children.

Her analysis presents a sophisticated internal reading of Kermit, Oscar the Grouch, Animal, and Miss Piggy, as well as a discussion of how their interrelationships illuminate the broader Muppet "code" of childhood. More generally, she chronicles the conceptions and practices relating children to animals and nature during the past several hundred years of European and American history. Her argument makes the case that the culture of childhood has displayed remarkable historical continuity despite continual reworking, making "childhood an enduring institution that we treat as a natural category." This challenges simple meliorist or apocalyptic views of contemporary childhood, much as it challenges territorial disputes between the two disciplines of cultural studies and sociology.

Rose's contribution, like Mukerji's, engages an issue of cultural representation and boundary drawing. But the issue she takes up – that of black women's sexuality – has been central to public debates about sexual purity and contamination, virtue and vice, normalcy and deviance, that have had profound social and political consequences for all black women, and, one could argue, for the entire discursive structure of gender and race relations as well. Rose outlines interventions black women scholars and writers have made to unseat influential deviance narratives – especially sexual purity defenses and counter-myths like that of the "objectified strong black woman" and "shero" narratives. She shows how difficult it has been for black women to articulate sexual desire and agency "without surrendering the sexual arena through the reclaiming of purity and responsibility on the discursive terms already set."

Rose argues that such cultural efforts must be accompanied by more explicitly political organizing around issues such as reproductive freedom and state-funded social support services. She then examines Leslie Harris's film *Just Another Girl on the IRT* as an important but flawed attempt to articulate black female agency, both sexual and nonsexual, in nonstereotypic ways. Rose analyzes both the cinematic text and its production, dissemination, and reception to give a fine-grained empirical discussion of its achievements, as well as of the forces of silencing and reappropriation at work within the severely polarized discursive context of its creation. This discussion makes it abundantly clear why this one innovative independent filmmaker finds it difficult both to articulate and to be understood (whether by cultural gatekeepers or by a broader audience) *as* articulating – the complexities of a young black woman's sexuality. Rose's empirical and theoretical sophistication also provides a general conceptual exemplar for analyzing the relationship between cultural innovation and sociocultural constraints on representation.

Power relations also figure centrally in Lembo's analysis of television viewing practices. Questioning critical theories of television's power from both the Frankfurt School and cultural studies, he asserts the need to develop an understanding of television's embeddedness in everyday life that more fully conceptualizes its sociality. He draws on his larger empirical study of working people's daily routines to discuss the ritualized nature of many viewers' turn to television as part of their transition from work to leisure. Concentrating specifically on people who watch television simultaneously with other activities, such as preparing meals, reading the newspaper, cleaning the house, or talking to other people, his study shows that this kind of television use is a complicated activity that structures people's interpretive process in fragmentary or dissociated ways that are not easily assimilable to text-based cultural studies analyses. Further, although some people he studied became habituated to relatively mindless television viewing for a period after work (an apparent power effect of television), even the most habituated viewers also used television, and engaged in other activities, in more mindful and self-directed ways. Discussing the distinctive form of sociality that seems to emerge under conditions of simultaneous viewing, Lembo claims that it "cannot be subsumed under the markers of discourse, text, identity, or the interpretive dynamics of power and resistance." Rather, he links it to an increasingly image-based and commodified postmodern corporate culture, and urges that critical theorists of culture and society explore – as Foucault, Rosaldo, Anzaldua, Butler, and Wellman, for example, have begun to do – the possibilities for reflexivity within a social order characterized by discursive disjunctures and more fluid processes of identity formation.

Lipsitz' contribution addresses this same issue by examining grassroots social movements for democracy, social equality, and a livable environment that have emerged around the world in response to the forces of globalization that have transformed the meaning of politics and place. He argues that culture figures largely in grassroots movements, for they often address cultural concerns and make sophisticated cultural interventions by appropriating new media technologies or popular cultural genres. At the same time, an increasingly transnational economy has shifted the terms on which culture is created, circulated, and consumed: the cult of the sneaker and hip hop are now international phenomena, and artists like Michael Jackson belong to video screens and satellite disks around the world rather than claiming a connection to any particular local community. In an effort to illuminate the connections among people, places, and politics both obscured and highlighted by transnational culture, Lipsitz turns to a discussion of innovative artists from aggrieved communities – using Los Angeles as the basis for several of his examples. He shows that these mostly "alternative" filmmakers, poets, musicians, and performance artists are utilizing new cultural circuits to circulate art that offers innovative cultural and political analysis, while helping to build new kinds of social and cultural alliances. Lipsitz calls for similar innovations among intellectuals. He points to the need for scholars to move beyond theoretical paradigms that crystallized in an earlier era, and to "develop forms of academic criticism capable of comprehending the theorizing being done at the grassroots by artists and their audiences, of building bridges between different kinds of theory."

5

Monsters and Muppets: The History of Childhood and Techniques of Cultural Analysis

CHANDRA MUKERJI

In the heritage of Western childhood, there is a long-standing association of children with animals and monsters. It is not just that very old fairy tales often substitute the latter for the former. The world of children is filled with petting zoos, animals and ghoulish characters in children's books and TV shows, images of endangered species on kids' clothes, toy stuffed bears and monsters for play, and a multitude of dinosaurs – the ultimately monstrous animals – to study as well as encode in the childhood imagination. This mobilization of creatures should be no surprise, since the line between humans and nonhumans has been an important part of Western culture, helping to define what makes people distinctive. It should make sense for children, those most human of beings, to be importantly located between the world of people and other-than-human beings. Western art is filled with images of monsters who are half-human and half-animal, who represent inhuman forces or human frailty. Gothic cathedrals have their gargoyles, and paintings by Hieronymus Bosch are populated with comparable godless creatures. The moral structures of the Western world are inscribed through these images. So it does not seem either casual or unimportant that we in America annually dress our children in Halloween costumes with animal or monster heads and human legs. There remains to this day some special cultural affinity between children and animals/ monsters that points toward the "special nature" of childhood.

For sociologists interested in childhood as a social location, an age-grade with its own institutions and culture, the association of children with animals and monsters is an uncomfortable social fact. There is so much evidence of it (in children's songs, school curriculum, library book readings, and weekend entertainments for children), that this cultural constellation has the stubbornness of a social fact. Yet, unfortunately, the relationship of children, monsters, and animals cannot be analyzed with traditional sociological tools. You cannot interview those who run zoos and find out why children belong with animals, and you cannot ask TV producers why kids' shows are filled with rascally rabbits, cheerful mice, or frogs, pigs, ducks, and monsters, because they do not know. Zoo personnel are primed to discuss environmental problems and endangered species with children, but not the traditional significance of monsters. TV producers are prepared to talk about the economic or educational value of their programs, but not their uses of ducks, dogs, and mice as leading characters.

One could do content analysis of TV shows, counting the numbers of times that animals and monsters appear there and see what patterns turn up. If adult shows have few animals or nonhuman monsters (TV writers preferring human monsters in adult programming), while family shows have more pets and wild-animal-friends, and children's shows have the most, then we would have some convincing data linking age-grades to relations to animals. But the study would not show whether or not this was a historical phenomenon.

It might seem possible to turn to the history of childhood to see how children came to inhabit a universe of animals and monsters. There are studies in both sociology and history on childhood and children's play that are very revealing (Zelizer, 1985; Aries, 1962; Pollock, 1983). But child animality is not a normal part of the story. Worse, the past *cannot in principle account for* its movement into the present. Only *the present* has clues about what has been sustained, changed, or lost from the past. As a result, much historical documentation is a surprisingly poor source for addressing directly the kind of historical question posed here.

The most frustrating thing about the dearth of historical methods for this kind of work is that contemporary discussions of children and culture are rife with unexamined historical assertions. Most current work in media analysis, for example, assumes that the media are *changing* the character of childhood. Childhood was fine, once upon a time long ago, but it has been undermined, polluted, or made dangerous by new technological and commercial forces (see, for example, Postman, 1982; Lesser, 1974: sect. I; Engelhardt, 1986; Spigel, 1992: 50–60; Wartella, 1994: 33–43; Chen, 1994, 4: 105–13; Holland, 1992; Seiter, 1993; Kinder, 1991).[1] There is a historical trajectory in such analyses that begs the question of how the history of childhood and media should be told.[2]

It would be nice to say that things were getting definitively better (or even worse) for children, but it actually appears that childhood has been for centuries a mixed, albeit changing, and not-always-wonderful bag (Pollock, 1983). Kids are still abused by parents, teachers, and even priests.

Children run away from home to live on the streets, where they are exploited by adults, and support themselves through stealing, dealing, or prostitution. Children turn out to be not always so wonderful either. Youths in gangs steal, kill, and do drugs. We may describe them as aberrations if we are convinced there has been progress in Western or American childhood, but lots of data suggest that the progress (if existent at all) is limited. Perhaps we thought we had gotten well beyond the Dickensian (Dickens, 1962, 1957) world of poor children begging, stealing, and living lives of exploitation and neglect, but many children still grow up with more violence and fear than love.[3] Failing some convincing data to show that children now live distinctly better or worse lives than their counterparts in the past, we are left to account for the continuities (see, for example, Luker, 1996).[4]

While we may want to emphasize progress or loss in the lives of children, we have many reasons to attend to the continuities (Opie and Opie, 1960). We raise kids using a surprisingly small repertoire of representations of children, and often ones with historical roots even deeper than we imagine. We keep recycling and revisiting many parts of a multi-century heritage of childhood. Through sentimental attachments to the past or perhaps just a lack of imagination about the present, we make childhood an enduring institution – even while we treat it as a natural category. Sociological analyses of children's lives require some way of approaching this long-standing culture of childhood.

Examining the relations between children and animals turns out to be a productive way to do this. For at least 300 years, Westerners have helped naturalize childhood by characterizing children as much like animals. By one (Reformation/Counterreformation) version of this tradition, children are wild, driven by passion, and spiritually suspect – in need of protection and discipline like animals (Aries, 1962: Pt I; Holland, 1992: 18–21; Bettelheim, 1971). Children are associated with a spiritual, mysterious, dangerous, and violent nature, which contains not only animals but monsters or the forces of evil in the world. [For this view of nature, see Merchant, 1980.] The other (Enlightenment) tradition in Western culture considers children as the embodiment of goodness: as the site and source of natural man. Children, by this view, are continuous with the peaceful countryside and are like cooperative, herding, nonpredatory animals. Enlightenment thought suggested that children, if properly educated, could make a utopian world in which human goodness and rationality could reign (Plumb, 1982). The natural virtue in people could be made manifest where children could grow in a protected, nurturing, orderly environment (cf. Cole and Cole, 1989; Holland, 1992: 14–18, 60–76).

In contemporary America, children are often depicted with just these kinds of "natural" characteristics. American kids are presented in the culture as, in some ways, cute, passive, and vulnerable like baby pandas, and in others ways as wild and potentially violent as any predatory cougar. On TV, shining, young, innocent faces of children are shown in ads for family cars just before news stories about gang violence and murders committed by under-age street kids. Proper child management, we are told, can bring out the good in the child and keep the bad qualities in bounds. We are told that children need discipline in the home, or they run wild in the street. They need structure at school, or they cannot learn. The Enlightened child comes from an orderly, disciplined environment where adult supervision keeps the wild child at bay – always lurking in the cultural shadows (or the back of the school room), but not triumphant. Children are at once small and helpless, and also powerful and willful disrupters of adult order. They are like their teddy bears – cuddly little creatures containing the marks of an untamed beast.

J. H. Plumb (1982) provides some clues about why children might be associated with animals from his studies of early modern childhood. Plumb argues that the modern notion of the child was developed at the same time as the modern concept of pets as special "breeds" of animals. Both were invented in the eighteenth century, just when stuffed animals were also gaining currency as children's toys. Children and pets (Plumb argues) seemed to be part of a single cultural constellation of differentiation, domestication, training, and breeding. As both children and animals were domesticated, petlike animals began to stand for children in stories and games. The association of children with animals has been elaborated in some fashion through Western childhood from the eighteenth century into the present day, and seems to be affecting the contemporary world of the American child.

Sociologists are actually confronted with vexing problems when trying to account for these kinds of relations between past and present patterns of culture. If, for some reason, you cannot apply Bourdieu's (1984) conception of cultural reproduction (to explain temporal change and cultural continuity), or you are not able to work with Schudson's (1992) or Schwartz's (1996) writings on collective memory (to account for the proliferation of routes connecting the cultural present to the past), you will find it very difficult to write sociologically about how cultural constellations like this can endure, change, or disappear over time. Weber might seem to provide a model of sociologically good historical explanation, but relations between the Protestant Ethic and the present are problematic.[5] The functioning of belief as a historical force is taken for granted. Sociologists are supposed to locate concrete mechanisms by which the past can enter the present (historical materialism, collective memory, cultural reproduction); the easiest way to do this is to describe the motives and actions of people who are engaged in building the present out of the past

(Berger, 1995; Peterson, 1976; Crane, 1992).[6] But this is not always possible, and it is particularly difficult when studying the culture of childhood, since children have historically been only marginally literate (if at all), and often too powerless to direct their own culture.

While sociologists of culture may not always like the kinds of symbolic historical analyses frequently found in cultural studies, one version provides a systematic, if not scientific, way to study these kinds of long-standing cultural formations. The trick is treating a cultural constellation (in this case, the relations of children to animals/monsters) as a language-like form. If the association of children with animals is like a word in a historical dictionary, we can follow historical manifestations of child–animal relations the way the dictionaries follow word usage. The analyst can pay attention to where this cultural constellation first appeared in Western culture, where it changed radically, and where it split into different sets of meanings. One can look at the animal features of particular characters in books, films, and television as alternative definitions of child/nature/animality. This method allows analysis of a broad expanse of the Western history of childhood without having to *account* for all the historical conditions that gave rise to shifts in the relationship of animals to children. The point is to identify important moments of usage or changes in usage, and then to see how they could be affecting today's culture. Importantly, this approach allows the analyst to study the accretion of culture over time, while avoiding the shaky assumption that the relations of children to animals/monsters today is just a *direct* manifestation of a particular early view of children. This relationship is instead identified as part of a complex, multifaceted culture that has been elaborated and redesigned over the centuries – much as words are elaborated and refashioned over time.

The Muppets and the Animality/Monstrosity of Childhood

To understand this cultural heritage of the animal–child–monster, and through it, to see where and how the history of childhood may affect the present day, I want to look at the Muppets, asking why these beloved icons of American childhood have been primarily monsters or animals. The Muppets that are best known to intellectuals are the ones that appear on the TV program *Sesame Street*. Many others, however, have had a large role, both in a series of full-length motion pictures and two television shows: the cartoon series, *Muppet Babies* and the puppet comedy review, *The Muppet Show*. Wherever they have starred, Muppets have tended to be furry creatures resembling stuffed animals or colorful, stuffed monsters. Some characters like Big Bird are feathered, oversized creatures. Some Muppets, like Bert and Ernie, are more like stuffed dolls than animals. But Kermit, Piggy, Rolph, Gonzo, Animal, Cookie Monster, Grover, Oscar, and many others, are the typical Muppet animal-monsters.

One particular episode of *Muppet Babies*, "The Muppet Family Tree," confronted almost directly what kind of animals the Muppets are supposed to be. It focused on heredity, showing some of the characters climbing a "family" tree to see where they "came from." As the first character, Fozzie, started his ascent it was not clear whether all his relatives had to be of the same species. Could Fozzie-the-Bear be related to some cows or dogs just as long as they told bad jokes? In this episode, the answer was no. His family contained bears who wanted to learn how to be comedians. Species continuity was sustained in his case, along with continuities of character. But another Muppet, a furry monster named Animal, had relatives that were worms. They were only related characterologically, not physiologically. Both Animal and the worms ate everything in sight. The animality of this character, not his species, was reproduced. This episode made clear that the Muppets explored characterological elements of animality, not the character of the animal kingdom.

The Muppet characters turn out to be surprisingly useful objects for studying child animality/monstrosity. Different characters isolate and foreground a range of versions of "the child." As Kermit, Piggy, Gonzo, and Big Bird display some of the innate variations in children, they embody different culturally sanctioned ways of defining "the child." Children watching the Muppets, then, turn out to be viewing some of the options for navigating childhood.

Clearly, children do not simply get born, grow, and learn how to be adults. First they learn to be kids (Cole and Scribner, 1974; Berger, 1971).[7] They may be naturally young, but are not naturally *children* in the way we understand that term. Feral children, who have grown up "naturally" outside of human groups, are never considered "natural children" by development specialists precisely because they have not grown up in a culture. They do not have a language in which to conceive of themselves and their world, and they do not have the social skills to engage in conduct that is supposed to be natural to human beings. They are described as being more like animals than kids (Singh and Zingg, 1966). Being "natural" children within our culture, then, requires some work (some socialization into a culture). This includes finding models of natural child-like behavior in daily life and the media, which children can use as guides in shaping their own behaviors. Animals like Muppet characters or Barney the dinosaur can be particularly compelling sources of information on this subject; as animals, they embody what is "natural" to do.

To see how the Muppets provide exemplars of "natural" childhood to America's TV viewers, I studied in some detail the personal qualities of four Muppet characters.[8] Although analyzing the full array of Muppets would have yielded a more complex picture of the culture of childhood, studying such a large group would not have been feasible for this essay. But some of the characters were so central to the social world of the Muppets or so powerfully "animal" or "monstrous" that they were selected for closer scrutiny. Kermit the Frog was the clear first choice; he was the star of *The Muppet Show, Muppet Babies,* and all the Muppet movies (all major Muppet vehicles except *Sesame Street*), and the purported fictional persona of Jim Henson, the Muppet's major creator. Miss Piggy was the clear second choice because she was the other dominating character (besides Kermit) on these shows, and the only importantly gendered Muppet. A monster, perplexingly called Animal, was the third choice because of his complex relation to animality/monstrosity, and because he was the surprise hero of the first Muppet film. The fourth choice was a monster from *Sesame Street*: Oscar the Grouch, who seemed to have a special place in the hearts of children and parents. As both monster and grouch, he too seemed to embody some important element of animality/monstrosity. These four Muppets, then, were approached as contemporary "usages" of the child/animal/monster cultural constellation.

Why Kermit is a Frog

The Enlightenment view of the child, the one so carefully described by Plumb [1982] as seminal to modern childhood, is embodied in the Muppet universe in the character of Kermit the Frog. He is the leader of the Muppets, not because he is some Donald Trump figure, using willfulness, opportunism, entrepreneurial grit, or even devious manipulativeness to get to the top, but just because he is so naturally good. He is carrier of the natural virtue tradition; he is not just any animal, but the perfect child to natural man. He is not just any leader, but a utopian one, a frog with a mission that is based on the Enlightenment-rooted assumption that group efforts can make a better world. He is from the swamp, the primordial ooze, and emerges from it as a balanced, rational, compassionate, and cooperative young person. He is an American self-made Enlightenment animal–child. He is the father/son to natural man.

The universe of the Muppets revolves around this humble and yet perfect frog. He is indeed a prince inside, and every one of the other characters is drawn to him as their leader. The *Muppet Movie* that tells the story of how the Muppets found each other and became a show-biz group is both an origin myth for the collective and a story of how Kermit made the Muppet universe from his dreams. He goes to Hollywood to use his entertaining nature to make millions of people happy (Crist, 1979).

Importantly for a prince, Kermit pursues commercial success, but he does not make that his goal. He is so good, we can see, that he can use the commercial world for its opportunities and not be corrupted. He is the perfect child of an eighteenth-century commercial world, where idealistic hopes for the future, the opening up of human possibilities through social mobility, and crass commercialism could meet in a hopeful way (McKendrick, Brewer, and Plumb, 1982). J. H. Plumb (1982) argues that the natural child of the eighteenth century was, startlingly enough, a product of this commercial world. Childhood was differentiated from adulthood as a commercial category in that period, setting up a materially based separate world for children, ironically a safe haven from the corruptions of adult life. Children, if different from adults, needed different things: education, books, toys, and special experiences. They needed schools and school rooms where they could retire from the evils of the world. There they could be protected during their vulnerable period of life, encapsulated in a world of specialized architecture, commodities, and activities that would address and cultivate their true natures (Kinder, 1991; Plumb, 1982; Aries, 1962; Pollock, 1983; Lesser, 1974).

In a similar vein in the *Muppet Movie*, corruption might infest the commercial world of adults, but the same commercial world is used by the children/animals to change their world and purify their dreams. In their trip across country, the Muppets visit a dangerous bar, a used-car lot whose owner lies about the cars, a greasy spoon, and many other commercial sites where consumption and corruption meet, but these young creatures are never undermined by these encounters. We can even see why. They look different to all the adult humans; they are qualitatively different *kinds* of creatures who can never wholly fit into the world of adults and commerce. They are encapsulated in their animal skins like most American children are in kids' clothing, schools, and playgrounds. The evils of the world are surprisingly thoroughly explored in this film, but they are never powerful enough to destroy the "animal loyalty" or bonds of affection among the Muppets that make them both childlike and strong.

Being a frog helps make his uncanny virtue more believable. As a frog, Kermit is forced to be mild-mannered; he can't be a big bruiser; he can't manipulate; he can only sing. He is, after all, a peaceable, small, vulnerable, and group-oriented animal. He comes from the kind of bucolic nature where natural virtue was situated culturally in the eighteenth century, so he can carry more of this tradition of childhood (Thacker, 1979; Clifford, 1963; Bermingham, 1986). He may be better than most actual children, but he exemplifies a vision of childhood that remains active to this day.

Kermit has to be an animal to be natural, then, and a rather small and vulnerable one at that, but why couldn't he be a bird like Tweety or a mouse like Mickey? One important reason is that the frog is potentially a prince. The frog is a transformer (a natural one, not a cyborg) – just like the child in a culture that defines children as qualitatively different from adults (Kinder, 1991). Frogs are polliwogs before they become frogs, so they have a distinctive childhood or "toddler" stage before growing up (Cole and Cole, 1989). The frog prince can undergo an even more astounding transformation, going from frog to adult human. Children can easily think of themselves as comparable transformers. The frog prince has the attraction for children, too, of ending up being better than most adults – handsome, kindly, and powerful. There is also something of the "ugly duckling" in this story, but more than that, too.

The prince is born to be a leader, so while he may not look like much as a frog, he always has a virtuous nature that points to his superiority even before he is transformed. He carries the eighteenth-century conviction that people (God's creatures) have natural attributes that are different from one another. The prince is inherently better than other men, and the frog-who-will-be-a-prince displays his possibilities in his character. Kermit is a leader of his animal friends because his fundamental goodness makes him a frog who could become a prince. Kermit holds out a promise to children of reaching a position of power and importance some day through the cultivation of the virtues of the naturally good child: balance, compassion, rationality, uncommon sense, and kindness.

There are other reasons for Kermit to be a frog, less derived from the world of children's literature and child culture, and more from the social history of childhood. As I mentioned earlier, it seems that pets and children developed as cultural types in roughly the same period. Specialized child rearing, animal breeding, and widespread keeping of pets developed together in the eighteenth century – all connected to the idea that creatures, both human and animal, had different natures that were basically genetic (Plumb, 1982). Through preferential breeding and proper training, creatures could realize their natures more perfectly. Just as man had a human nature that came to him through breeding, different breeds of dogs, cats, sheep, and horses also had their natures. The good society of the Enlightenment was meant to recognize and make use of these natural differences, building upon them. This meant breeding sheep and other farm animals for their marketable qualities, breeding and then raising dogs, cats, and other pets to bring out their good natures and useful attributes, and rearing and educating children to bring to life the inherent goodness in the human species (Plumb, 1982; Thomas, 1975; Serres, 1600).[9]

Plumb (1982) contends that a cultural bond was forged between children and animals in this period, although he does not feel prepared to say precisely what it was.

Keith Thomas (1975) may get us closer to it. He suggests that there was an important switch in the relations between animals, plants, and humans in the sixteenth to eighteenth centuries in Europe that resulted from or expressed itself in the development of science. Before this time, creatures, as objects of Creation, had been seen as part of the domain given by God to man. Animals lived closer to humans than they did in the eighteenth century, often sharing residences with peasants and artisans who used their body heat in winter to warm their homes. At the same time, animals could be treated cruelly because they were said to have no soul, and they were so nearby to many people and so invested in the daily routine of human lives that they were easy targets for frustrated owners. By the eighteenth century, when the superiority of the human soul became less an issue, animals and humans developed new relationships that were both more distant and more kind. Most animals were seen as less like humans and more as members of a distinctive and distant species; they were not just less perfect parts of the same Creation. Scientific study revealed qualities in animals that showed their distinctiveness, making it easier to classify them not as soul-less men, but creatures made perfect by God at the moment of Creation. While most wild animals became an "other" to humans in this transformation, some animals (and plants for that matter) took on quasi-human status, and became pets or petted favorites. They were made special by breeding, and they were elevated above the bulk of the creatures through discipline and special training. They were linked to people through bonds of affection and identification, and they stood for a goodness in the natural world that was uncorrupted by human greed and willfulness (Thomas, 1975: 110–21).

In the context of this new culture of nature, children came to be defined as naturally good. They were differentiated from adults and started to receive the proper education to bring out their natural goodness – just like pets. They were tied to their parents through bonds of affection and underwent special training to sustain their distinctive position in the world of people. Children, in this system, were not adults or wild animals, but more like well-fed house cats. They had natures unspoiled by the rigors of life; they were protected from evils in order to keep them "natural" (Perrault, 1967; 1982: 91–2; Elliott, 1992: 162).[10]

The association of the domesticated, cheerful animal faces of the Muppets with the eighteenth-century world of the child, in which Enlightenment hopes for natural man were gaining primacy over images of children as naturally sinful, makes some sense. The Muppets have been used quite explicitly to further utopian hopes about education and human perfectibility in Western culture. The Muppets on *Sesame Street* have been deployed around optimistic principles of child learning and used to reduce some ill-effects of poverty and racism on children (Plumb, 1982; Lesser, 1974; Haraway, 1991: Pt III; Latour, 1993). No wonder such a natural prince as Kermit the Frog would stand as their leader.

Kermit the Frog is both petlike and perfect in his goodness. He is child and pet, the child-as-pet, in its most developed form. He might not have an owner to fawn over like a good dog, or parents to adore like a perfect child, but he has a pet's propensity for service. He is, like most frogs, quite independent and not one to follow owners around on a leash without some difficulty, but he is peaceable and helpful by nature. He could be a pet and clearly would be a good one. He is loyal, responsible, and kind. Most importantly, he has a natural gift for the pet's highest responsibility – entertaining others with charm and enthusiasm (Thomas, 1975). Significantly, in the *Muppet Movie*, Kermit begins the film sitting on a log singing, the model of a natural frog whose peaceful qualities are made audible in his song. It is his ability to sing to others that gets him discovered by an agent from Hollywood who is vacationing in his swampy home. He decides to leave for Hollywood because the agent says he has natural talent/charisma. Seeking this kind of career is the perfect way for him to realize and use his nature-as-pet effectively. Moreover, by avoiding the evils of the adult world while getting to Hollywood and using his natural gift once there, he provides a model for the pet-child of how to get ahead by being naturally good/cute.

The plot of the *Muppet Movie* interestingly makes use of ambiguities in the cultural significance of the frog in American society to show how hard but necessary it is for the pet-child to keep that standing. Once he leaves the swamp, Kermit is pursued by a man who wants to use him in a promotional campaign for selling fried frogs' legs. While Marshall Sahlins argues that Westerners cannot eat those animals they keep as pets, frogs are alternately used as either pets or food (Sahlins, 1991: 278–90). This destabilized classification of frogs undermines Kermit's position as an autonomous creature, who can be assured of his role as a pet. The *mélange* of meanings around frogs is made an issue from almost the start of the film. In the bar scene, a man tells his girlfriend not to touch Kermit because frogs give you warts. Pets, by definition, are creatures that humans like to and can touch; this is the essence of petting. In the same bar, customers are ordering frogs' legs for dinner. Kermit is horrified by this evil practice of turning bodies like his own (petlike) into food, and is even more tortured by the thought of a fast-food, frog-leg chain, which would make this barbaric pattern more widespread. He cannot join the entrepreneur who wants to use frogs' legs to make money because millions of frogs might lose their legs if he did so. Kermit has to stand up for frogs and show their value as pets, and does so by seeking a career in entertainment and the media.

Kermit the Frog, then, simultaneously advocates the life of the pet–entertainer for animals, and provides a model of the good child as petlike. In Kermit the Frog, a model for human rationality and goodness has his residence in the animal kingdom, where true natural virtue can be found. With proper training, animals can make the most of their peaceable traits as loyal and entertaining, just as through proper schooling, kids can turn out OK. Kids can learn from Kermit to be good to their friends, true to their natures, and entertaining to adults. In his world without anger or desire, children can make themselves balanced, thoughtful, cooperative, compassionate, and naturally good creatures – in the image of that frog-prince of the animals: Kermit.

The Building of Child Natures

In the structuralist tradition of literary studies, the Enlightenment figure of Kermit ought to be opposed in the Muppet world by some embodiment of wild nature, that more violent and less contained cultural vision of the natural world. Such symmetries are supposed to be found in culture, so that the binary oppositions of language-based cultural systems can be reproduced. If there is no absolute meaning to cultural categories, then meaning should derive from differences among them and sustaining discourses of difference that keep the categories separate (see, for example, DeGeorge and DeGeorge, 1972; Kurtzweil, 1980; Eagleton, 1983). The problem is that, as Bakhtin (1981) suggests, cultures (like words) have histories as well as structured relations to one another. Layers of significance are built over one another, as the resources of a culture are reappropriated and refashioned to be brought to bear on new historically located problems of human life.

Childhood, then, may have two major streams that define the nature of the child in almost opposite ways, but the two streams are not in clean opposition to one another. They come from a complicated history of cultural refashioning of virtue and vice, nature and culture, childhood and adulthood, that needs some further unpacking. The cultural conceptualization of natural violence, chaos, productivity, and desire came first, and was first projected onto children after being routed through religious imagery.

A wild, chaotic, disruptive view of children had some of its early roots in a premodern conception of the natural world that existed in popular culture well before the eighteenth century that Plumb (1982) describes. This was an erotic, productive, and unpredictable nature, often seen as

Mother Earth, who was both dangerously powerful and the source of human sustenance. Mother Earth was clearly not all bad; she was simply wild and unpredictable, not easily contained and very easily made hostile to human interests (Merchant, 1980; Holland, 1992). This wild, chaotic nature became importantly connected to religious belief, particularly Christian teachings about the Fall, the expulsion of Adam and Eve from the garden of Eden. Nature had been naturally peaceful, the Bible taught, until Eve ate the apple, and then both the human spirit and the natural world went wild. The Christian tradition placed original sin in people, not nature, but the result of the Fall was a dislocation of both. Christians were set up by this story to battle original sin in themselves and the wildness of nature beyond them at the same time (and for the same reason).

The relationship of children to adults was mediated in the sixteenth and seventeenth centuries in Europe through this religious world view. With Reformation and Counterreformation fervor for spiritual reform, the child, who was associated with postlapserian nature, was deemed to need and respond to forms of discipline (like land could respond to tilling), which could transform wildness into goodness. The older "nature," transplanted into the untrained, untamed child, then needed to be battled and broken. This "Mother Nature" in the child needed to be and could be extracted from the youngster to make a true Christian (Aries, 1962; Pollock, 1983; Thomas, 1975: 257–69).

By the eighteenth century, this confrontational predisposition toward children was partially eclipsed, not because children changed, but because of a change in the reigning views of nature. Goodness was once again to be sought and found in nature because it was now evidence of God's hand. Just as God's will had been evident in his Word (the Bible), now it was evident in his works (Creation). The world of the creatures was no longer felt to be tainted by the Fall, but taken as evidence of Creation itself. Science could study God's works for truths, and ordinary Europeans could look for his will in the countryside. Children, who had remained culturally close to nature, took on new stature as creatures who were closer to God's plan. Parents could now find his desires for human perfection in the natural goodness in their children, and were now burdened with trying to keep that spirit alive in their youngsters.

This is a simplified version of a very complicated story, of course, but it suffices to make the point that two "natures" of the child developed, not in a dualistic relation to one another, but from an accretion of hopes and fears about nature that were associated with the child. The location of virtues and vices shifted, as being "natural" gained different meanings. The result, then, was not a culture of childhood made of a singular constellation of meanings and practices, not a world of childhood identified by a clash of conceptual opposites, but a historically layered tradition of age-based difference, organized roughly around poles of natural wildness and natural virtue, but configured differently over time (Carpenter, 1963: 21–56; Pollock, 1983: 143–202). The modern American child derived from this tradition did not develop a Jekyll and Hyde character, swinging between two stable poles of extreme and opposite human "nature." The contemporary child was built from a set of complicated and seemingly contradictory cultural resources historically used to locate the child and negotiate a transformation from childhood to adulthood.

Over time, the combination of dark impulses and natural goodness in children entered the new world of psychology. Freudian psychology began by drawing new attention to and restructuring accounts of the chaotic feelings or wildness in children. This school of thought explained strong and violent impulses in humans by theorizing an "id" that was fundamentally chaotic, violent, and filled with uncontrolled desires. Children were wilder than mature adults because the id was not yet contained in the young. The id was interestingly necessary to the formation of human rationality, a source of energy to be made subservient to the "ego" at the end of the developmental process. The psychology of development later on restored attention to the child as a natural learner. The educational efforts of *Sesame Street* itself were designed to use the natural curiosity of the child to teach not just the ABCs and numbers, but also good behavior. Both these psychological approaches made the child increasingly a psychological rather than a moral category, and the nature of childhood wildness and goodness was deflected away from notions of original sin or natural virtue. By psychological theory, children might be naturally "bad" sometimes (because they could not yet control their feelings), but these moments were either simply passing parts of developmental stages or (in cases of unnatural development) symptoms of psychological damage. (Many Americans continued to believe in original sin in children, but still could use psychological theories to try to build a mature Christian from a sinful child.) Remnants of earlier cultures of childhood were sustained, but placed in a new structure of meaning and action (Seiter, 1993).

Since the Muppet world is informed by, if not entirely built from, the psychology of development, it should come as no surprise that there is no irretrievably sinful Muppet and that the vision of the child-as-learner (from psychology) gives the Enlightenment version of the child's nature precedence (Polsky, 1974). This is not to say that there is no chaotic behavior in the Muppet universe; on the contrary, almost every character has some flaw and creates some narrative opportunities for disaster; most of the segments in *Muppet Babies* end in fighting, falling, or other moments of disorder. It is just that there are no naturally sinful Muppets or even psychologically damaged ones who are as troubled as Kermit is serenely good. The only one who claims evil intentions and seems to delight in creating trouble is Oscar the Grouch. He is proud to be a monster, but he is in fact a poor shadow of the deeply disturbing "troublemakers" who make such frequent appearances on talk shows and news programs – the gang member, the pregnant 12-year old, the runaway prostitute, the 13-year old murderer. He is a psychologically understandable monster: a grouch.

Why Oscar is a Grouch and Not Much of a Monster

Oscar the Grouch may be physically a monster, but really he is just (psychologically) a bad-tempered guy with a lively and playful imagination. He is a trickster without the self-control of a Kermit. He enjoys a mischievous reign over his part of Sesame Street, disregarding the niceties of social etiquette and cultural order. He is, on one level, a homeboy with a heart of gold who talks street smart, and who has more guile and sense of play than anger or an appetite for violence and pain. Oscar is more a prickly personality than a threat to order, holding down a fundamental aspect of childhood. His bad-tempered ways may be grating, and can get him in trouble, but he remains an important part of his community, not a threat to its values and order. His tricks and taunts get him attention while they also protect his freedom. Oscar's personality makes psychological sense for a kid on the street on his own. Oscar has the Muppet body of a monster, and tries to act like one, but he is, in the end, only a Grouch. He is the perfect embodiment of the wild child for *Sesame Street*, where the child's personality, not moral issues or problems of social control, are at stake, but this is just what makes him a less than perfect foil for Kermit. Kermit's personality is not important on *Sesame Street*, where learning is the privileged domain of rationality, but Oscar's personality is essential as a troublesome, but finally reachable, irascible student (Polsky, 1974; Lesser, 1974).[11]

While Kermit makes things happen in the world because of his goodness, Oscar is entertainingly naughty but narratively insignificant. He is stuck in his trash can, unable to move, defining a territory for himself as a grouch. His garbage can may mediate in some symbolic fashion between a strange and surprisingly ample underworld (his home) and the surface of the street, but he is no Satan or emissary from below.[12] If he has a relationship to the religious tradition of the naturally sinful child, he is held fast in a moral purgatory, between the forces of evil and good. He can't go anywhere, and he cannot make much happen around him.[13] In the end, he seems most like a homeboy. He could never be as well respected and understood as he is in his own neighborhood, where everyone knows what is "wrong" (and right, for that matter) with Oscar and accepts him. He doesn't seem likely to outgrow his personality, but he doesn't seem too crippled by it either. He is a person who makes sense on his street.

Oscar can be seen as a stand-in for working-class children who do not leave their communities and do not pursue the American dream [Whyte, 1955]. He makes them seem all right, just another kind of personality manifestation integrated into a social milieu. As a social type, however, he is kept in his social place by his psychological predisposition. Like the "lads" described by Willis in *Learning to Labor* (1981), Oscar sees no real legitimacy in the rules and regulations of adult society, and continually shows contempt for them. The result is that he cannot develop, much less follow, dreams for his future. He has no important role in the longer Muppet narratives in movies and TV shows because he cannot change; he is caught in a cycle of social reproduction by class and personality.

Oscar remains lovable in part because his powers are so limited, and the chaotic nature he contains keeps this part of the child in play among the Muppets. To the extent that he is archetypally wild, he carries a "streak" in the all-American child personality (a preview of Bart Simpson). American kids are not supposed to be too submissive, and they are valued in part as disrupters of social order. They are entertaining when they break social conventions in nonessential ways, or at least do this in short periods during childhood. The monsters on *Sesame Street*, like Oscar, Grover, and Cookie Monster, are there to keep this part of the child intact and amusing. These guys may have funny fur and may break conventions, but they are benign. Cookie monster eats too much; Grover monster is perhaps a bit slow; Oscar has a bad temper; but they all embody easily forgivable weaknesses and express feelings and desires shared by children and adults alike. No wonder we can easily laugh at and with them. If these are the ids of American children, we are reassured, the egos will not have much problem taming them and helping them to maturity.

These characters, then, provide the viewer of Muppet shows with the opportunity to see the "bad" nature of the child as an actually quite attractive and necessary part of the psychology of children. A little wildness is necessary to the freedom of the natural American child.[14] Natural goodness can only be understood in the context of such freedom; only the opportunity to be naturally bad can make it so important to locate what is naturally good. There may not be natural evil in this world of Muppets, but there is a mild form of chaos and wildness that constitutes a kind of not-fatal flaw in the child that, ideally, helps to distinguish them from adults.

From the point of view of children, Oscar the Grouch and Cookie monster give kids permission to be less-than-wholly-good for the duration of childhood. Their benign presence implies there is no evil in it; there is no deep-seated violence or uncontrolled desire in even these monster-children that would begin to injure others. By implication (and psychological theory), all children have the possibility of reaching maturity, no matter what personality quirks they may develop through childhood. They should be left as naturally good and bad as they are. In the Muppet world, natural goodness and rationality will win in the end. In the life of the child, by implication, much the same will prevail. Oscar can have his trash can existence because he is a grouch, but Kermit will shape the future. Oscar may be fun to laugh with, and play vicarious tricks with, but Kermit is the Muppet that children should (and usually do) "naturally" like best in the end. Oscar is not a powerful alternative to Kermit, who can seriously challenge the serene nature of his child identity, but a subversive strain in childhood that might stop some kids from being leaders, but cannot stop the supremacy of the rational man–child–frog in the Muppet world of childhood. The whole premise behind *Sesame Street* is that TV can help children learn and save even poor kids from dismal futures by introducing them to education, the tools of education that were originally designed to create "natural rationality" of the sort embodied by Kermit.

Wild Animal

The modern translation of the monster from the mystical/moral/religious side of Western childhood into safely psychological categories seems to be, oddly enough, worked out in almost an archetypal fashion in the Muppet called Animal. Animal had a character in the early Muppet shows and movies that was replaced in *Muppet Babies*. He was, in his original form, almost an incarnation of wildness itself. He was kept in chains like a zoo animal or prisoner who could never be trusted and would always be unpredictable. Animal seemed like a creature straight from Carolyn Merchant's (1980) world of wild and violent nature; he certainly looked like a godless creature, too. In *Muppet Babies*, however, he was reduced dramatically in cultural significance and effect. He was transformed from a creature with a moral status, who could redeem himself by using his dark forces for good, to a preverbal child from developmental psychology, who was only wild and physically expressive because he could not talk.

Before following his changed status, let us look at the Animal in the *Muppet Movie* and *Muppet Caper*. Unlike Oscar, who is stuck for life on Sesame Street, Animal can and does get out into the world with the major Muppet figures, and can make things happen in their collective narratives. He may not be a world-historical figure, but he does have and use his powers of willfulness and wildness, violence and desire. In the *Muppet Movie* he becomes the hero of the story, who saves Kermit with his frightening, contained violence, when all peaceful solutions to his problems fail. The would-be fast-food frog-leg king has finally hired a killer to do away with Kermit because the young frog has refused to help his commercial venture. Kermit prepares himself for a showdown with the killer, but he is clearly not built for violence. Animal defuses the situation before the showdown starts by frightening away the enemy. He eats a pill that makes him ten times his normal size and he simply roars at the villains until they are terrified and flee.

In this instance, Animal is necessary to the plot because he is the opposite of Kermit. He is more than prepared for violence and unpredictability. These are his powers and attributes. He may not be evil; in fact, he uses his powers to do good. But he is a kind of undisciplined alchemist who illegitimately uses the forces in nature (the pill) to become a "natural" force in himself. He transforms himself, not into a singer or Hollywood star, but a kind of over-scale temper tantrum, used for good ends. He is the guard dog who goes mad when his owner is attacked; he is a bear mother who mauls anyone who gets between her and her cub. His ability to act comes from his nature; his ability to affect the narrative comes from the powers of nature he brings to the world of the child.

Animal, while wild, is (significantly) Kermit's ally, not his enemy or opposite. He may carry other characteristics from nature than Kermit, but Animal puts his powers in the service of the frog. He is not a predator like the villain in the *Muppet Movie* who wants to eat frogs; he wants to protect these helpless creatures and enhance the capacity of Kermit to realize his goals. (As we will see, he eats everything else.) Animal can be a potent narrative force, but not without Kermit. He could not make a story of his own because he has no dreams, just uncontrolled desires. He is an "id" whose power can only be put to use through Kermit's "ego." He may be a force of nature, but not on his own in this psychologically constructed world of Muppets.

The clues to Animal's role as unrestrained desire and will to power are everywhere he is portrayed. When he has nothing else to do, Animal likes to eat everything around him, not for the taste but to destroy it. He is a devouring embodiment of desire. He explores his world with his roaring voice and biting teeth. He is too big to be a baby, but he has some of the same ways of dealing with the world. He has no self-control, but depends on external controls. His way of dealing with bad guys is to roar at them, and blow himself up to giant proportions, like a young child holding his breath during a temper tantrum. He has a raw nature, but it is a contained one because he has his chains and friends to hold them, and because he wants to help Kermit.

The raw potential of Animal that might have made him as capable of creating chaos and nightmares as Kermit is of realizing dreams was perhaps what made Animal undergo such a change when he was brought to *Muppet Babies*. There Animal was normalized by being depicted as a baby, just at the age to crawl and get into trouble, but not yet old enough to have a real voice. Animal kept his voracious appetite for life and the objects in his environment, but he was defanged. His wild nature was made a stage of development rather than a mythic force, and his function in stories changed.

In *Muppet Babies*, Animal is often a source of instability and change in relations. If Kermit is the embodiment of natural balance and rationality, who leads the kids in the nursery on adventures of learning and cooperation, Animal is the wild force that can bring it all to a halt. The other kids build things, and he knocks them down. The other Muppets play together peacefully, and he destroys their projects. If all else is going well, Animal can always be counted on to disappear or break the situation apart. He is a reminder of the chaos in childhood, but he is not a stand-in for the powers of nature in *Muppet Babies*.

This is because Animal was made into a "terrible" two-year-old (or 1½-year-old) in this show, a member of a stage of life, not a really untamable beast-child like the wild, disheveled beast he started to be in the *Muppet Movie* and continued to be in *The Muppet Show*. In that original guise, Animal had too much potential. He could have carried the powers of darkness; he could have shown violence and destruction in the world of kids. He could have pointed to sexual desire as well as the desire to eat, and he could have explored the will to power. In other words, he could have pointed to those parts of childhood excluded from the Muppet universe. He could have been dressed up as a drug-crazed gang member (or a child-beating parent, for that matter), the sort of wild creatures so dear to the culture of television "infotainment." He could have become what was wrong with American society or today's youth that Kermit could have faced down. But that would have required writing on the level of mythology, not psychology, and so Animal was infantilized in *Muppet Babies*. By the time *The Muppets Take Manhattan* appeared, he was all-but-forgotten.

Miss Piggy and the Transvestite Monster of the Muppets

Although Miss Piggy is supposed to be the ultimate (only?) girl of the Muppet universe, and Kermit's partner rather than his opposite, in some ways she is the closest to his nemesis. She is, first of all, supposed to be a girl, but continually undermines her gender identity with her voice, her actions, and her clear play-acting of feminine virtues. There is reason for her gender to be problematic; she is the invention of a male puppeteer. She is the projection of a man through a female puppet: the real s/he. S/he even acts less like a girl and more like a drag queen or transvestite, pretending to be what she is not (by nature). In this sense, s/he is another kind of Muppet monster, who brings to the surface of this universe questions about the differences between the inside and outside of the child. As a "girl," s/he is supposed to be concerned with her appearance, and talks about her beauty and her clothes. S/he wants to be the beautiful heroine, but s/he has none of those personal qualities. S/he is a bad girl, and in that sense perhaps, living up to the epithet, pig (Row, 1995).[15] But Piggy wants most of all to be feminine and refined, not a pig. That is why s/he *earnestly* feigns a kind of goodness that is not in her nature. S/he continually strives to move away from her violent, chaotic nature toward a more docile and kind one. In the end, her "nature" is that of a poser or a posturer. S/he is *fundamentally* unnatural. Her presence among the Muppets not only makes Kermit's natural authority more problematic, but challenges the whole conceptualization of childhood as a natural category.

Even Piggy's skin seems something of a costume. Her inner nature is not visible on her skin the way it is for Kermit. S/he does not pretend to be a girl and then act like a pig. Pigs are supposed to be dirty and lazy; s/he is fastidious and is driven by ambition and desire. Pigs are supposed to be food sources, not charming entertainers or entrepreneurial manipulators, but she is a worldly up-and-coming force in show-biz. It would be hard to argue that s/he acts like a loyal and entertaining pet, even though that is not really expected of pigs in our culture, so s/he is not even a pioneer woman trying to forge a model pet-life for pigs. Most of all, s/he doesn't act like a passive source of bacon; she is a powerhouse. Piggy is some kind of unspeakable creature, pretending to be a pig, pretending to be a girl. She both attracts and detests Gonzo so much that I am often tempted to see her as another kind of alien or at least an embodiment of alienation.

If Piggy is not filled with bacon or the diffuse but pointed hunger of the American pig, what does s/he have inside? Violence, desire, and the will to power. She is Kermit's partner and perhaps his nemesis because s/he can challenge him as no one else can. Even their partnership is her achievement. They are a couple not because Kermit has led them both to this relationship, but because Piggy has willed this relationship into existence and bullied Kermit into accepting it. S/he has made him hers. S/he is the only Muppet character capable of making Kermit do anything against his will. Piggy simply has such powerful desires that s/he is hard to stop, while Kermit only has good sense and leadership potential as his tools for resisting her. If he can get the others to oppose her, Kermit can win in contests of strength between the two, but if he is alone, he cannot hold her back. When Piggy submits to his authority, it is because s/he chooses to do it, and s/he makes the ingenuousness of the submission audible to everyone by declaring her decision in a clearly false singsong voice. If this willfulness can be mapped onto the pig character, then perhaps s/he is not so out of place in her skin. But even in that case, s/he would remain a problematic and in many ways unnatural character.

The relationship to gender in Piggy's character is very complicated. On the one hand, the "inner nature" of Piggy has a great deal in common with the violent, chaotic, seductive, productive nature of Mother Earth. So, maybe she is a girl after all. On the other hand, her willfulness is marked as very masculine. When s/he is about to save her "Kermie" or attack their mutual enemies physically, using her karate skills, her singsong girl voice is supplanted by a husky one that is more masculine and often seems more authentic. (Of course, it *is* more authentic, since the puppeteer making the voice is male.) What the voice may only give away about the puppeteer, the body presents as part of Piggy. S/he is more physically aggressive than Kermit ever is or girls are supposed to be. S/he herself denies this part of her personality in her cultivation of her own femininity, so s/he undermines her own position as a female in the Muppet universe. Piggy seems in many ways like a super hero. No ropes or shackles can stop her. Even Animal can be restrained with chains, but not Piggy. S/he is comfortable with her physicality, and has a will that is marked as masculine as well. Gender is both a problem and yet seems amazingly plastic around Piggy.

Clothing makes the issue of gender all the more flexible and problematic. It is important to note at the outset that most of the Muppets do not cover their bodies with clothing. They do not have genitals to hide or sexual identities to worry about. They are embodiments of unmarked masculinity – male identity that can be assumed rather than shown. Skeeter and Skooter, because they are kids, not monsters or animals, have clothing so they don't look naked. The other animals or monsters have fur coverings and perhaps a signatory piece of clothing. Fozzie has his hat and Rolf has his tie, but they don't need much else. Piggy, on the other hand, needs to cover her body because she harbors and represents sexual desires that come out in her pursuit of Kermit. Moreover, s/he covers her sexuality with a pinkness that is a gender cliché, clearly allied to the identifying world of the Barbie doll. The ruffles on the clothing add to the femininity, and mark her as a child. At the same time, her hair identifies Piggy more as a woman – consistent with her sexual urges. Nonetheless, her face, pudginess, and pinkness still mark her as a pig. None of it looks natural. Either this level of sexuality is unnatural for a child, or Piggy feels unnatural in her gender; or s/he has an unnatural sexual identity. In any case, s/he conveys an unease about gender, sexuality, and identity into the world of children. At the basic level, s/he makes gender both a problem and flexible possibility in the world of kids.

What kinds of lessons is s/he providing for children? Is it that girls can be important narrative forces like Piggy? Or is it that Piggy got ahead because she never really was a girl, but only dressed as one and developed a false voice? Or did s/he develop pretense not because she was naturally false, but to be a seductress and get to her frog? Assuming that children are not concerned with cross-dressing and issues of sexual identity below surface markings, she cannot be taken as an advocate of the life of the transvestite. That is probably too postmodern a thought even for most adults. Perhaps the answer is that she represents some combination of these things, all of which help bring out the unnatural nature of childhood itself. As the ultimate, unnatural child, she makes an interesting foil to Kermit's natural man-child.

More than any other creature in the Muppet universe, Piggy embodies the two sides of childhood (the wild and subdued, violent and orderly) but distributes them as gender attributes through her actions, costuming, and voice. She is an orderly girl and a wild boy.[16] The duality in the childhood that suffuses the Muppet universe may be made most visible and available for meta-commentary in and through Piggy.

The fact that Piggy is dressed up in what looks like doll's clothing allows some thought about the large question raised in this essay: the relationship of children to animals. She is half-child, half-animal – unlike Kermit who is all frog. She is a monster, a creature that is made up of different elements from nature that do not belong together. She spoils the category of pig at the same time that she breaks down the category of child or girl. She is like a stuffed animal dressed up like a doll. Or maybe she is a girl dressed up like a pig. It doesn't really matter. She cannot be reduced to psychological terms because her character stirs *moral* issues about childhood innocence. She embodies the unpredictability of a cultural world when natural categories break down. She poses the question of what "natural" means, and how it might relate to children.

Heroically, Piggy takes her artificiality as a source of strength, not weakness. She embraces it, and shows how to make it serve her will. She demonstrates not how to be naturally a child, but how as a child to work the cultural category and its possibilities. She suggests how to learn rules of childhood, but then refashion them to personal advantage.

Kermit and Piggy, then, are not just a strange and wonderful couple, but divergent models of surviving childhood. Kermit takes the best of the images of childhood from the tradition of natural virtue, and shows how to make it cute and stylish enough for a child-performer. Piggy takes the worst of childhood, the beastly qualities of the self and the enforced markers of sexual identity and decorum, and melds them together in a powerful way to get somewhere. Both can make stories from their lives. Both have visions and means of realizing them. Both can negotiate a route, then, toward adulthood from childhood. But one takes the route worn smooth and elegant by time, while the other (perhaps because as a female she has no precedent for the first) makes a new road for herself through the tangle of contradictory expectations and possibilities in the culture of childhood.

The Child-monster Among Us

The world of childhood in twentieth-century America is organized in the media and in other sites as well around the complex and layered vision of childhood built up for hundreds of years in the West. This childhood constitutes a kind of cultural landscape on which our children must walk and find their ways toward adolescence and finally adulthood. Childhood is not so much what children live through (a stage of life) as a site in the culture where certain ideas have been located, maintained, revised, and elaborated over the centuries. This is what confronts children when they go to school, read books, make friends, watch television, relate to their parents, or try to figure out what they are supposed to do and what they want to do next. As befits any part of culture that has been accreted over a long period and then eroded through use, it is not a simple terrain to navigate and rebuild according to new designs.

Childhood in contemporary America both carries and reworks the problems of order and disorder, natural virtue and natural danger, that are long-standing, variable, and continually enacted in each new "present" – including in the world of the Muppets. Children who watch the Muppets are not only taught by *Sesame Street* to recite their ABCs and count their numbers, but also instructed by Kermit and Piggy about how to make their way through a world of childhood that is both threatening and necessary to adult society. They learn to see themselves as animals and monsters, pets and threats, in a child culture that has spawned a range of strange creatures from the healthy and helpful Little Bear to the Wild Things in Maurice Sendak's imagined world of the child's mind (Sendack, 1963; Minarik, 1960).

Children are naturalized in these works; they are represented as inherently what they are, whether they be orderly or subversive. This naturalness has been translated into many terms. It has been mystical, religious, rationalized, and psychologized, too. This allows children's media to evoke a whole range of visions of children. They can embody utopian natural goodness or a mysterious chaotic quality, sometimes evil, sometimes natural violence and wildness, sometimes an awkward stage of development.

Even in the kind-hearted world of childhood built by the Muppeteers, the separateness of children is emphasized and marked.

To get a sense of the contradictions in contemporary American views of children, listen first to a lecture on child development with all its sympathy for the ways of the child, and then get on an airplane and watch the faces of adults as a mother with small children starts to take a seat near them. Children may be prized as precious resources and life-giving treasures in America, but they are also a threat to order, subversively noisy and willful. Children do not necessarily intend to have this effect, but they can all-too-often pierce the apparently not-too-secure serenity of the adult world with a few well-placed wails or shrieks. The children of poor mothers can even confront powerful politicians who want to cut welfare, but don't know what to do with the children supported by it.

The world of the Muppets, in spite of being more than a little up-beat and extremely pro-child, turns out to be a reasonably good mechanism for introducing children to this complex culture of childhood, because it still holds onto the richness in the Western heritage of childhood. Children can see themselves in these programs as the true "others" of modern American adult life, more problematic than the cyborgs celebrated by Donna Haraway (1991). "Terrible twos" are the monsters who, according to old traditions, combine human and animal attributes; they cultivate multiple natures. The child-monster is a ubiquitous part of the world of American schoolchildren, too. They are visible in the natural faces with unnatural poses that appear in yearbooks; they are in the faceless bodies of Barbie and Power Rangers and the games played with them; they are Dennis the Menace or Cookie Monster, or Bart Simpson and Beavis and Butthead. The monster-children of America get most nightmarish as gang members – young, dangerous, violent, and wild. But they are also visible in the middle-class toddlers having temper tantrums in the supermarket. Order is shattered by those whose natures are meant to reassure us about the moral order and human possibility. They are the counterpart to the well-brushed children of spelling bees, music recitals, and school plays. But all of these kids participate in the complex fears and hopes around childhood, combining chaos and order, possibility and despair. Clearly these "children" carry historical dreams and nightmares of childhood whose origins are often very old indeed.

As does Kermit the Frog, who embodies and helps reproduce the optimism of natural-virtue tradition drawn from Enlightenment belief in natural man. This is the optimism and burden of childhood that children face every day at school. They even play games there in Cartesian spaces, the carefully measured circles and rectangles of playgrounds and basketball courts. In these structured spaces, kids learn to play games which both disrupt and restore rational order through physical effort.

It would be possible to build a sociology of culture and even a sociology of children and childhood without paying attention to these kinds of patterns. But it would impoverish our analyses of child socialization and the problem of generations. Human cultures require work to sustain, but they also have centuries-old roots that are buried deep in unquestioned habits. These patterns are as consequential to social life as they are difficult to identify. Luckily for sociologists, colleagues from the Humanities and cultural studies have been cultivating skills in uncovering these roots and seeing their effects on the present. There is nothing inherent in sociology, particularly the Weberian approach to historical change, that would proscribe borrowing their tools to address fundamental problems of culture that have proved difficult to approach with conventional, contemporary sociological methods. On the contrary, there is much to learn.

NOTES

1   Certainly, there is work done by historians on childhood that argues the opposite. Aries [1962] in particular sees premodern childhood as much more brutal than what followed. The data, however, is much more mixed, suggesting that childhood and notions of childrearing are actually much more historically constant than most people like to suggest (see Pollock, 1983). After reading Pollock, it is harder to know how to interpret Zelizer (1985), because it seems that there was a strong increase in violence against children and legitimations of it in the nineteenth century, that was diminished in the twentieth century. This makes any linear notion of change over the longer haul difficult to sustain.

2   These accounts become particularly suspicious when placed near data on the history of childhood itself. Childhood seems in some ways better and in some ways worse than before (Aries, 1962; Zelizer, 1985). Childhood gained an importance, beginning in the seventeenth century and growing in the eighteenth, that has made the life of many children generally better. From the nineteenth to the twentieth century, there have been improvements in childrearing and the study of child development has purportedly elevated the quality of parenting, and this, too, has supposedly made children in the modern West much better-treated than their historical counterparts. (See Sammond, 1996; this is also implied as a trend in Polsky, 1974.) But these hints of progress are tainted by signs of regress. Children seem to have been treated more kindly by their parents in America *before* the nineteenth century, when even stern Puritan fathers seem to have had soft hearts. The rates of physical abuse and punishment seem to have risen with industrialization – although perhaps declining in the twentieth century.

3   Adult gang members, pimps, and drug dealers still like to get younger kids to do illegal work for them because the laws are more lenient on children, and because their innocent looks can deceive authorities or sell sex (Katz, 1988).

4   Luker (1996) show clearly that we exaggerate change to serve our emotional and political predispositions. While news stories decry the startling increase in teen mothers in America, Luker's data show no real change in rates of pregnancy and childbirth among teens. Again, childhood seems much more stable than we imagined. What has increased are adult *fears* about teen pregnancy and welfare, not the sexual transgressions (or pleasures) leading to new births. The politics of childhood is frought, while the world of childhood remains surprisingly stable.

5   To say culture is epiphenomenal or constructed in local contexts without any constraint is only to deny the problem. Either of these positions may account for cultural changes, but they are not theories of cultural *history* because they do not explain how the cultural past can affect the cultural present (or vice versa). If you keep the time period short enough for a study of culture, you can ignore the problem of history altogether. The old anthropological tradition of envisioning cultural patterns as stable has provided plenty of tools for ahistorical work that sociologists have picked up, elaborated, and domesticated for sociological analysis. If you are clever enough, you can even make history seem like a string of ahistorical moments with their own integrity, and make historical forces and changes seem to be mere constructs themselves. But this requires imagining life to be more like a series of still shots in a movie than like a ballet in which every leap requires a landing and every turn must wind to a stop or evolve into another movement. The film model is a systematic, if not entirely appropriate, way to avoid sociological questions about how the past may require or constrain action in the present. I personally think life is more like ballet – filled with choices, contingencies, and the possibility of agency, but also studded with moments of forced decision-making and action. But whatever your image of history, thinking about how culture can be a historical force is part of the Weberian heritage that raises surprisingly intractable problems of both theory and method.

6   The interest in practice has now migrated to science studies. See, particularly, the essays in Pickering (1992).

7   Cole and Scribner (1974) argue that the central lesson of schooling is how to be a student. This is comparable to the argument that the first lesson of childhood is learning what it is to be a child. Some of the argument can also be derived from Berger (1971), who argued that youth was a learned culture with a long history.

8   I started following the Muppets when my children were young. I, like many other intellectual, middle-class mothers, took note of the departure of this community of puppet characters from *Sesame Street* to enter the world of movies and commercial television. I was interested in how these icons of educational media would be placed in commercial ventures, so I followed the change carefully and surprisingly systematically. I watched and taped all the movies and most of the episodes of *The Muppet Show*. I was particularly skeptical about the Muppets' move into cartoon form, so I made my kids sit with me, watch, and discuss every episode of *Muppet Babies* until Jim Henson died. I taped a sample of 36 reruns of the program, and did shot analyses

of four of them that I found gave particular attention to history, trying to see how the past was used in these programs. At first, I was only interested in the fact that lots of shows used old footage from film and television, inter-cutting it with the cartoons. I wanted to analyze how the history of popular culture was being used in the programs. I thought I might study, too, how George Washington and other textbook figures were depicted as part of American popular culture, but before I finished this work, I started thinking about the animal/monster characters of the Muppets themselves.

9   Interest in animal rearing is already visible in the seventeenth-century estate management tradition exemplified by Olivier de Serres (1600). This interest appears to have been elaborated in eighteenth-century concern for breeds and breeding. (See Thomas, 1975; Plumb, 1982.)

10   The special relationship of children to animals was already starting to be made visible in tales written in the late seventeenth and early eighteenth centuries by Charles Perrault (1967). Comparable stories were in Aesop's fables and illustrated in Perrault's labyrinth at the garden of Versailles, where morals about human life were depicted through animals. This site was used to teach children in the royal family. (See Elliott, 1992: 162. For the use of fables in education in the period, see Michel Conan's "Postface" in Perrault 1982: 91–2).

11   For a discussion of the trickster as a cultural type, see Griswold (1986).

12   Some colleagues have argued that Oscar's garbage can leads to the Middle Kingdom or that Oscar is really a hermit crab. Hermit vs. Kermit? It sounds tempting as an opposition, but I don't see how the Hermit crab image makes sense of Oscar as Kermit's nemesis. The Middle Kingdom is a nice alternative to the underworld, but I don't know what to do with that either.

13   The fact that he lives in a garbage can made me think for a while about spoiled children. He could be seen as a spoiled child caught in the trap of his own willfulness. Maybe he is attractive to middle-class kids because they can identify with this. But he is developed by the writers as a street urchin, who has had to fend for himself. That is the opposite of spoiled.

14   Bennett Berger (1971) pointed out that the "taming" of American children by their parents would not be such an honorable achievement if they had not been seen as so wild.

15   For the use of a Miss Piggy doll as a whore (pig) in a gay man's doll col-lection, see Pearce (1995: 211).

16   In this sense, she is very much like a transvestite who uses costume and voice to work out a dual nature, in the process making the duality in others more apparent.

REFERENCES

Aries, Philippe 1962: *Centuries of Childhood: A Social History of Family Life.* (Trans. R. Baldick.) New York: Vintage Books.

Bakhtin, Mikhail M. 1981: *The Dialogic Imagination: Four Essays*. Austin: University of Texas Press.

Berger, Bennett 1995: *An Essay on Culture*. Berkeley and Los Angeles: University of California Press.

—— 1971: *Looking for America*. Englewood Cliffs, NJ: Prentice-Hall.

Bermingham, Ann 1986: *Landscape and Ideology*. Berkeley: University of California Press.

Bettelheim, Bruno 1971: *Uses of Enchantment*. New York: Vintage.

Bourdieu, Pierre 1984: *Distinction: A Social Critique of the Judgment of Taste*. (Trans. Richard Nice.) Cambridge, MA: Harvard University Press.

Carpenter, Charles 1963: *History of American Schoolbooks*. Philadelphia: University of Pennsylvania Press.

Chen, Milton 1994: Six Myths about Television and Children. *Media Studies Journal*, 4, 105–13.

Clifford, Derek 1963: *A History of Garden Design*. New York: Praeger.

Cole, Michel and Cole, Sheila 1989: *The Development of Children*. New York: Scientific American Books.

Cole, Michael and Scribner, Sylvia 1974: *Culture and Thought*. New York: Wiley.

Conan, Michel 1982: Postface. In Charles Perrault, *Le Labyrinthe de Versailles 1677*. Paris: Editions de Moniteur, 91–2.

Crane, Diana 1992: *The Production of Culture: Media and the Urban Arts*. Newbury Park, CA: Sage Publications.

Crist, Steven. (ed.) 1979: *The Muppet Movie*. New York: Abrahms.

DeGeorge, R. and DeGeorge, F. 1972: *The Structuralists from Marx to Lévi-Strauss*. Garden City, NJ: Doubleday.

Dickens, Charles 1957: *Nicholas Nickleby*. London: Dent.

—— 1962: *The Adventures of Oliver Twist*. New York: Holt, Rinehart, and Winston.

Eagleton, Terry 1983: *Literary Theory*. Minneapolis: University of Minnesota Press.

Elliott, Charles 1992: *Princess of Versailles: The Life of Marie Adelaide of Savoy*. New York: Tricknor and Fields.

Engelhardt, Tom 1986: Children's Television. In Todd Gitlin (ed.), *Watching Television*, New York: Pantheon.

Griswold, Wendy 1986: *Renaissance Revivals*. Chicago: University of Chicago Press.

Haraway, Donna 1991: *Simians, Cyborgs, and Women*. New York: Routledge.

Holland, Paula 1992: *What is a Child? Popular Images of Childhood*. London: Virago Press.

Katz, Jack 1988: *The Seductions of Crime*. New York: Basic Books.

Kinder, Marsha 1991: *Playing with Power in Movies, Television, and Video Games*. Berkeley: University of California Press.

Kurtzweil, Edith 1980: *The Age of Structuralism*. New York: Columbia University Press.

Latour, Bruno 1993: *We Have Never Been Modern*. Cambridge, MA: Harvard University Press.

Lesser, Gerald S. 1974: *Children and Television: Lessons from Sesame Street*. New York: Random House.

Luker, Kristin 1996: *Dubious Conceptions: The Politics of Teenage Pregnancy.* Cambridge, MA: Harvard University Press.

McKendrick, Neil, Brewer, John, and Plumb, J. H. 1982: *The Birth of a Consumer Society: The Commercialization of 18th-century England.* Bloomington: Indiana University Press.

Merchant, Carolyn 1980: *The Death of Nature.* San Francisco: Harper and Row.

Minarik, Elsie 1960: *Little Bear's Friend.* New York: Harper.

Opie, Iona and Opie, Peter 1960: *The Lore and Language of Schoolchildren.* Oxford: Clarendon Press.

Pearce, Susan M. 1995: *On Collecting.* London and New York: Routledge.

Perrault, Charles 1967: *Classic French Fairy Tales.* New York: Meredith Press.

—— 1982: *Le Labyrinthe de Versailles 1677.* Paris: Editions de Moniteur.

Peterson, Richard A. (ed.) 1976: *The Production of Culture.* Beverly Hills: Sage Publications.

Pickering, Andrew (ed.) 1992: *Science as Practice and Culture.* Chicago: University of Chicago Press.

Plumb, J. H. In Neil McKendrick, John Brewer, and J. H. Plumb 1982: The New World of Children. In *The Birth of a Consumer Society: The Commercialization of 18th-century England.* Bloomington: Indiana University Press.

Pollock, Linda 1983: *Forgotten Children.* Cambridge: Cambridge University Press.

Polsky, Richard 1974: *Getting to Sesame Street: Origins of the Children's Television Workshop.* New York: Praeger.

Postman, Neil 1982: *The Disappearance of Childhood.* New York: Dell.

Row, Kathleen 1995: *The Unruly Woman.* Austin: University of Texas Press.

Sahlins, Marshall 1991: La Pensée bourgeoise. In C. Mukerji and M. Schudson (eds), *Rethinking Popular Culture,* Berkeley: University of California Press, 278–90.

Sammond, Nic 1996: Managing Precious Resources: Child-rearing and the Rise of Walt Disney. Unpublished paper.

Schudson, Michael 1992: *Watergate in American Memory: How We Remember, Forget, and Reconstruct the Past.* New York: Basic Books.

Schwartz, Barry 1996: Introduction: The Expanding Past; Rereading the Gettysburg Address: Social Change and Collective Memory. In special issue on "Collective Memory." *Qualitative Sociology,* 19, 275–82, 395–422.

Seiter, Ellen 1993: *Sold Separately: Children and Parents in Consumer Culture.* New Brunswick, NJ: Rutgers University Press.

Sendack, Maurice 1963: *Where the Wild Things Are.* New York: Harper and Row.

Serres, Olivier de 1600: *Le Theatre d'agriculture et mesnage de champs.* Paris: I. Metayer.

Singh, J. A. L. and Zingg, Robert M. 1966: *Wolf-children and Feral Man.* Hamden, CT: Archon Books.

Spigel, Lynn 1992: *Make Room for TV.* Chicago: University of Chicago Press.

Thacker, Christopher 1979: *The History of Gardens.* Berkeley: University of California Press.

Thomas, Keith 1975: *Man and the Natural World.* New York: MacMillan.

Wartella, Ellen 1994: Electronic Childhood. *Media Studies Journal,* 4, 33–43.

Weber, Max 1958: *The Protestant Ethic and the Spirit of Capitalism.* (Trans. T. Parsons.). New York: Scribner.

Whyte, William Foote 1955: *Street Corner Society.* Chicago: University of Chicago Press.

Willis, Paul 1981: *Learning to Labor.* New York: Columbia University Press.

Zelizer, Viviana A. 1985: *Pricing the Priceless Child: The Changing Social Value of Children.* New York: Basic Books.

6

Rewriting the Pleasure/Danger Dialectic: Black Female Teenage Sexuality in the Popular Imagination

TRICIA ROSE

The mainstream cultural history of black women's sexuality is a deeply troubled and bitter terrain. Black women's bodies remain a critical negative point of reference in the racist and sexist battle to define good and evil, normalcy and abnormality, sexual purity and sexual contamination, property and ownership. Not surprisingly, most of the work on black women's sexuality, sexual experiences, and the representation of black women's sexuality, has struggled with the extensive rape legacy of slavery and its especially brutal effect on black women's sexual autonomy. It has struggled as well with the narratives about black women's fundamental sexual deviance that have saturated scientific, sociological, and fictive accounts of black female sexual behavior and desire.

Black women writers, scholars, and others have countered these deviance narratives with black sexual purity defenses, and with counter-myths – especially with that of the strong, yet profoundly victimized, black superwoman, or as Ann duCille recently dubbed her, the "objectified strong black woman" (duCille, 1994; Wallace, 1979). This objectified black woman's epic strength devalues emotional sensitivity, and the capacity for human error, and renders her vulnerable to charges of being too independent, too strong; at the core, it feeds the image of black women as emasculators who wield matriarchy as an agent of family and community destruction (Moynihan, 1965; Rainwater and Yancey, 1967). This "strong black woman's" sexuality is relevant only so far as it destroys or sustains the family and by extension, the race. Primarily a response to slavery-based narratives of black women's impurity and sexual licentiousness, purity narratives defend black women's honor and chastity against this destructive legacy.

For example, as Deborah McDowell has argued, "Many black women novelists responded to these myths of libidinousness by insisting fiercely on their chastity" (McDowell, 1986).

Various critiques of deviance narratives dominate the discussion of black women's sexuality, not only because many black feminists want to expose the way in which racism and sexism have worked intersectionally to oppress black women, but also because these conjunctions continue to be produced and still profoundly shape popular culture, official news, legal decisions, and fictive representations of black women's sexuality and sexual behavior. A quick glance at the framing of the welfare debates, of single motherhood in the black community, of mass-media stories about Tawana Brawley, Desiree Washington, Anita Hill, and Vanessa Williams, of the narrative thrust of films like *Bodyguard, Bommerang, Raw, What's Love Got To Do With It, The Color Purple, Losing Isaiah,* and of numerous television shows and music videos for many musical genres, makes it clear that representation of black women's sexuality remains, for the most part, locked in familiar and problematic patterns of deviant, hyper- and desexualization.

In recent historical and oral histories of sexuality, such as D'Emilo and Freedman's well-received *Intimate Matters* (1988) and *Sex: An Oral History* by Harry Maurer (1994), black women's sexual desires and points of view – when they appear – are problematically figured. As Ann duCille noted in her sustained criticism of *Intimate Matters,* D'Emilio and Freedman claim to incorporate marginal groups' sexualities, but instead re-center and concentrate on white middle-class heterosexual attitudes and "merely append the 'othered' to already existing analytical paradigms rather than fundamentally altering the ideological assumptions" that inform their pluralist methodology. Consequently, she continues, "we learn less about black sexuality than about 'interracial union'; less about the effects of slavery on African-American sexual practice than about the sexual proclivities of the planter class; and far less about the cultural backgrounds and belief systems of Africans than about the normative values of the white EuroAmericans who enslaved them" (duCille, 1990).

Harry Maurer's less academic (and much more widely distributed) and sensitively presented contemporary oral history of sex in America makes a similar mistake, but it does it in more obvious ways. The text is fascinating; the range of white straight and gay experiences are quite a compelling window on the participants' sexual lives and the impact of family life, religious norms, and gender training on sexuality. But, by implicit design, the text appears to "naturally gravitate" toward a white, middle-class American subject. In over 500 pages of oral narratives there are four African-Americans, and even fewer other people of color. By focusing in this way, Maurer pushes many other nonwhite sexual subjectivities to the margins or off the page entirely. *Only two black women are featured: one transsexual and one biological woman.* (There are also only a very few black men featured.) This gross inattention to black women in Maurer's book encourages readings of black female sexuality that attempt to fit these portraits into already existing tropes, rather than drawing on the information to develop more complex understandings. With only two (and two fundamentally different!) sorts of black female identities/experiences, it is difficult to imagine what collective black female experiences and responses might look like. Because there are several white women and men, gay and straight, that terrain has a richness, a fullness that cannot be similarly achieved by these profiles of two black women.

More insidiously racially inscribed, though, are Maurer's introductions to each person's narrative. In the cases of white women, we are told that "her hair is shorter now and dyed a reddish tint," or she is "pretty, buxom, with wavy auburn hair to her shoulders," or "she has the look of a gamine: thin, with close-cropped hair, and big, sad, expressive eyes and mouth." In the case of the black woman who was born a woman, he offers none of the visual details that had been offered for so many others. We learn that Larrice Freeman is a 42-year-old full-figured woman from the South who has a "warm, sassy slang style." We are given no descriptions of her expressions, color, facial features, the length, color, or texture of her hair. Compared to other descriptions, Larrice Freeman is presented without any of the familiar markers associated with female sexuality or sexual desirability which frequently accompany Mauer's descriptions of white women. In fact, the description of Freeman's southern, "warm, sassy slang style" sounds too much like a nostalgic description of a mammy figure (Jewell, 1993). In this way, she is written in (generally) and erased (specifically) at the same time.

These subtle and not so subtle histories of sexuality that marginalize black women and others, the historically entrenched narratives about black women's promiscuity, sexual deviance, and even "shero" narratives about black women's super emotional and physical strength, profoundly shape the terms of back women's articulation of sexual desire and agency. As many black feminist critics have argued, these treacherous narrative waters have rendered public or collective black women's sexual experiences virtually silent. How do you swim in shark-infested waters and not get badly bitten? Some black women writers have survived this terrain by posing as sea algae: Nella Larsen, McDowell argues, frequently camouflaged sexual themes in domestic metaphors. Indeed, retaining one's erotic and spiritual agency by speaking loudly, publicly, and in sexually explicit ways under conditions where such acts are easily reinscribed into oppressive structures of meaning is very difficult and dangerous. Malicious sexual labels, once assigned, seem to remain affixed like superglue. And even women who survive such stigmas, rumors, and media spins, often find themselves censored or with much shorter career ladders than they had previously expected. This mode of policing effectively curtails all women's sexual expression: Maurer noted in his introduction that many of the women with whom he spoke – across ages and backgrounds – expressed worry over being labeled a slut in their lives in general and, more specifically, in relation to participating anonymously in his project.

These factors may partially explain the extraordinary void in black women's self-authored narratives about sex, sexuality, and their role in black women's everyday life. As Spillers (1984) has so vividly characterized it, black women are the "beached whales of the sexual universe, unvoiced, misseen, not doing, awaiting *their* verb." This awaiting has not, of course, prevented verbs and adjectives from being assigned to all black women, but especially to young black women. As explicitly sexualized women in a national atmosphere where young people of color are hypervisible, young black women are highly visible and yet invisible, seen and yet misseen, heard and yet unvoiced. In a cultural moment when black popular culture has been able to center itself in unprecedented ways in American culture, young black women are generally facilitators in young men's efforts to attain status and display burgeoning masculinity. In countless rap, dancehall, and r&b videos, ghetto/gang/drug films, and malt liquor advertisements, young black women are voluptuous, hyper-sexually objectified appendages for young men. Simultaneously, they are "teen mothers," a.k.a., major icons of fiscal waste and moral/sexual depravity in the public policy wars on welfare and AFDC. In both contexts young black women's sexuality is highly visibly exaggerated for the manipulation and consumption of others.

The facility with which young poor black women are negatively associated with sex is substantially motivated by class and race. As historian Nell I. Painter has observed, "sex is the main theme associated with poverty and with blackness. Even where race in not an issue, the presence of the poor introduces the subject of sex." She also points out how this class-based sexuality is inflected with race in the US: "The sexually promiscuous black girl – or more precisely, the yellow girl – represents the mirror image of the white woman on the pedestal. Together, white and black women stand for woman as Madonna and as whore" (Painter, 1992).

In the popular media and political imagination, teen mothers are black teen mothers, and black teen (usually unmarried) mothers are the cause of their own poverty: they are living, breathing examples of black women's wanton sexuality and generally irresponsible behavior. Working-class teenage mothers, whether on welfare or not, are viewed as welfare cheats (actual or potential), their sexual reproductive choices tainted by the implicit and explicit notion that they are participating in fraud and theft by *having* babies to get increases in welfare payments (Luker, 1991). This assault has escalated in recent months, especially with the onslaught from Newt Gingrich and the Republican right. In their agenda to strengthen patriarchal privilege and family control, the Republican right has waged a cultural war on young black women, especially those who are the most economically vulnerable. This assault has been crafted in the language of family values that hinges on the punishment of black and other women who are having sex and the costs of this "morally degenerate" behavior (Ridgeway, 1995). This is not to say that teen motherhood should be encouraged or ignored; these young women are more likely to remain in poverty and to face special parenting difficulties. It is also the case that many teen mothers live in abusive and destructive family environments which directly or indirectly have contributed to their status. However, this serious social problem is manipulated to stigmatize black sexuality and to vilify the poor, rather than support, educate, and protect young women.

The signs "welfare queen" and "teenage mother", and the breadth and scope of their interpolation of poor black mothers, is staggering. But, most relevant for this discussion, are (1) the way they interpret black reproduction and therefore black female sexuality as pathological; and (2) the way in which they empower the state to intervene, materially and discursively, into the sexual lives of black women. The "welfare queen" and the "teenage mother" are now the most prominent "characters" in the drama of the state's multifaceted labeling of black women's sexual behavior as deviant and costly.

The compassion that being a poor, single, and/or young black mother in a racist, patriarchal society might produce in others is tempered by a preponderance of narratives "exposing" cases of moral pathology and negligent motherhood, especially among young black mothers. According to some news reports, these women discard their kids, leave them at home unattended for hours on end, leave children with older relatives while they continue to do drugs, have newly born drug-addicted babies who must stay in the hospital or simply throw them away at birth, leaving the expenses for these costly medical and social-work services to be covered by "us," the taxpayers. This sort of "state-dependent" black mother may or may not be, in fact, receiving welfare, but according to dominant cultural narratives she nonetheless works out of the same sexual and economic ethos as the welfare queen: reckless baby-making and mothering.

In January 1993, the CBS newsmagazine show *48 Hours* presented an hour-long show on this phenomenon, entitled, "Throwaway Kids." Of course, race was not mentioned as a defining characteristic of this rising crisis; instead, six segments were prepared, four of which featured poor black mothers abandoning their infant and preschool children under a variety of circumstances. One other featured an unidentified baby who seemed to be of mixed racial heritage. He was left in a dumpster. The sole segment which featured a white child focused on a *teenage* boy whose mother had thrown him out of the house in Cambridge, Massachusetts. In several of the segments, the cost to the state is prominently discussed, and the seemingly altruistic role of nurses, police, and social workers is highlighted against the backdrop of "delinquent" mothers whose lives are presented so that they begin and end at the point at which the state intervenes. By the end of the program, we have seen over a dozen defenseless black infants discarded, crack addicted or left home alone, and one 16-year-old white teenager living on the streets around Harvard Square.

In the penultimate segment, Cheri, a 17-year-old black girl from Dallas, reports that she heard a baby crying in a wooded area near her apartment. The emergency services are called and the baby is rushed to the hospital. The white middle-class social worker, Jean Michaels, investigates the scene and leaves her telephone number with several neighbors. Michaels learns from Cheri that the baby was grasping some branches when she found her. "If it was my baby," Cheri says, "I'd keep it. It don't make no sense. Why they wanna have a baby if they gonna just drop it somewhere?" Later on that evening Cheri calls the social worker and confesses to being the mother and to having left the baby herself.

This segment is the most arresting for several reasons. Cheri appears to be a young woman who saves a new-born baby but is revealed as an abandoning mother. She is also the only teenage mother, a socially troubling fact which is compounded by her family's apparent poverty, her extreme unpreparedness for the challenges of motherhood, and her capacity to hide the entire term of her pregnancy from her family. Cheri represents, then, a "textbook" example of the narrative intersection of poverty, teen motherhood, negligence, and welfare.

There are a number of strategies for responding to these politically potent conceptions of black women's sexual delinquency. Since these narratives of black female sexual depravity are being used to cut funding for programs that disproportionately aid poor black women and children, outright political protest and organizing (about issues such as reproductive freedoms, domestic violence, rape, federal-funded childcare for the working poor, more family related social support services, and poor women's economic rights) is a crucial mode of counter-response. Another important way to counter-respond to this cultural political war is to continue to craft black women's sexual counternarratives; narratives that affirm black women's sexual rights and freedom, expose the extensive difficulties faced by poor mothers, and refuse the undergirding pathologizing of the political and social arena. While this can be partially accomplished by narratives that deemphasize black women's sexuality, I would like to call for counternarratives that rewrite these sexualized tropes without surrendering the sexual arena through the reclaiming of purity and chastity or relying disproportionately on repressive tropes of sexual responsibility that equate female sexual desire and pleasure with immorality or irresponsibility. We have to collectively reimagine black women's sexuality as well as defend/refashion institutions that police/protect sexual rights. In the case of young black working-class women's coming of age stories, it is especially important that reaching physical sexual maturity is narrated as a point in one's development at which danger – as real as it is – does not overshadow sexual pleasure, will, agency, and a quest for social and sexual equality.[1] Rewriting young black women's sexual narratives is especially important in a mass-media environment where black youth culture wields disproportionate economic clout and is frequently used to support "commonsense" notions of black behavior as deviant.

And yet, rewriting these stories is also especially difficult in a media and cultural environment that limits black women's access to creative resources and capital and renders women's subjectivity "unrecognizable" and "unmarketable." Presenting another version of the demonized figure of the black teen mother, while at the same time retaining black female sexual agency (not "positive image" virgins or sexually degraded "whores"), as well as linking it to other forms of black female agency, is an even more daunting task. In my estimation, Leslie Harris's *Just Another Girl on the IRT* is a flawed but important attempt to do all of the above. In the remainder of this essay, I want to consider *IRT*'s negotiation of this delicate territory and the way cultural perceptions and expectations shaped both production and reception of the film.

"If You Think You Know Her, Think Again"

In some ways, *Just Another Girl on the IRT*, released in April 1993, can be considered a rewriting of segments such as those produced in the *48 Hours* episode on "throwaway kids." In significant ways it is a rewriting that attempts to contest and displace the media's interpretation of young black women's sexuality. The opening sequence of the film is a darkened, littered, and unkempt urban street with a young black man furtively carrying a large black garbage bag toward a small mound of trash in front of an empty lot. Over this, we hear the voice of a young woman:

> Tomorrow, you all might be reading about this in the paper, might even see it on TV. You all might shake your heads, say somebody was real bugged out, say they was on crack or something. Some people hear about my neighborhood and assume some real fucked up things, But I'm gonna tell y'all the real deal.

IRT begins at the point right before "the black baby" is thrown away and works its way backwards. *IRT* is an attempt to retell the story of a young black woman with hopes to leave the ghetto who becomes pregnant and then a young mother, from the narrative perspective of the young woman herself.

Director Leslie Harris's debut independent film is a female, inner-city coming-of-age story that received strong critical praise, including winning Special Jury Prize for Best First Dramatic Feature at the 1993 Sundance Film Festival. Harris's immense personal struggle to see the project to completion and release added punch to the up-from-poverty, self-propelling emphasis of the film's main plot. Articles frequently noted how she edited the film in her tiny apartment, raised all of the small $130,000 budget from not-for-profit agencies and private contributors, and shot the film on a grueling 17-day schedule with a skeleton crew. Ariyan Johnson, who plays Chantel, was responsible for her own wardrobe and had to log her own movements for scene-to-scene continuity.[2]

Harris establishes and then uses Chantel's commentary to challenge a range of presumptions inherent in media narratives and made by other urban dwellers about the young black women who populate urban poor areas. She achieves this by punctuating the story with several direct-camera-address, autobiographical statements by Chantel. The film opens this way, demonstrating Chantel's awareness of the way the media would construct her if they had found out what almost happened. She, though, "is going to tell us the real deal," the story that we would not be told in the tabloid or respectable media. There are many "real deals," many stories about Chantel that we would not be told by popular one-dimensional portrayals of young urban black women, and Chantel tells us about several of them. She explains to us that she is responsible for baby-sitting her two brothers because her parents' work schedules demand it; she tells us how she began pretending to eat more food in the middle of the night to explain her weight gain during her pregnancy; she describes her motivation for going to college, and how she feels about being treated coldly by passengers on the subway because of her working-class black female style and public disposition. In this particular direct address, Chantel says:

> People be buggin'. The other day I was on the number 2 train with my friends just buggin' out, havin' a good time and people just started staring at us like we were some sort of street girls or something with no futures. Yo, when I'm with my friends, I act like it don't matter. Between you and me, that shit pisses me off. What, they think they can judge you by the way you dress?

These direct addresses are frequent and significantly shape our relationship to Chantel. She is telling her own story even as we write our own story for her. She is involving us directly in her version of the events. Her direct statements frame the entire film, making it difficult to observe Chantel without being interrupted by her autobiographical commentary. Harris seems to have intended this effect when she says that

> when I was writing the script,there were a lot of incidents happening in New York involving teenagers like the Central Park Jogger and others. I would ride the subway and I would see people get up and leave when teenagers got on, especially black and Hispanic teenagers. I mean, they were just kids but people didn't know them. That's why I use the device of having Chantel talking directly into the camera in the film, so you have to get to know her, directly. (Petrakis, 1993)

This narrative strategy places the dominant mainstream image of minority teenagers such as Chantel in direct relational conflict with her autobiographical self-narration, producing friction and making more visible the former's problematic ideological content.

IRT is a coming-of-age story. Chantel is a bright, "A" student, with very high aspirations to leave the ghetto behind. A spirited, smart-mouthed, high school girl from Brooklyn, New York, she lives in the projects with her two working-poor parents and two little brothers. We follow her in her daily life at school, work, home, and in pursuit of boys. Chantel is the smartest girl in her class; she especially excels in calculus and chemistry and has aspirations to become a doctor. She speaks frequently of needing to get to college and then medical school so that she can make a better life for herself. She does not want to live, as she notes about her parents, "from paycheck to paycheck." These dreams are cut short by her unwanted pregnancy and the subsequent pressures of young motherhood.

Although Chantel has professional aspirations, seems remarkably self-assured, and displays a strong sense of responsibility, she is far from an unproblematic film heroine. She is an interesting blend of a highly motivated teenager – always doing her homework, making it to school on time, and caring diligently for her two younger brothers – who is yet rebellious and back-talking. She and her best friend Nitette work in a gourmet grocery store on the posh upper-west side of Manhattan, where she gives as good as she gets from wealthy, condescending customers. Chantel's classroom scene is dominated by an angry speech she makes to her history professor about the relevance of the curriculum for the black students in the class, after which she is sent to the school principal who she also answers smartly and treats with contempt. Breaking the good/bad girl narrative opposition, Harris presents Chantel making some strikingly selfish decisions and displaying the kind of courtship cruelty more regularly associated with boys (she publicly dumps a boyfriend because he doesn't have enough money or style and starts dating Ty, the baby's father, partially because he has a nice car and more money). She is boisterous, materialistic, curses freely, talks about taboo subjects on the subways loudly, talks openly with her friends about sex, and is sexually active without apparent anxiety.

To present a black female teenager as protagonist/heroine and at the same time provide sustained references to her sexual thoughts and occasional activity is a dangerous and in a sense "confusing" move for a number of reasons. Most notable is the legacy of the historically constructed binary opposition between women's amoral sexual desire and goodness, and black women's association with the former; and the poweful lure of dominant tropes about how one actually escapes or remains trapped by the ghetto, namely the protagonist as criminal or martyr. By not relying on the familiar plot resolutions for this up-from-poverty narrative and at the same time forcing the viewer to be directly confronted by Chantel's pointed self-presentation, Harris challenges a number of expectations and modes of identification. Relying on our preconceptions, Harris appears to deliberately produce a delicate tension between dispelling and creating disbelief in Chantel's version of her own story. Chantel is a hardworking student with high aspirations, and this makes her seem a reliable witness to her own life; one qualified to bring us the "real deal." And yet she is sexually active, loud, and flirtatious in ways that have historically worked to discredit female character and reputation, especially those of black women. As Kimberle Crenshaw has noted, historical links between race, honesty, and chastity remain part of legal (and therefore, everyday) common sense. Since it is commonly assumed that black women are not chaste (for women, chastity signals honesty and high moral character), they are therefore less trustworthy. As recently as 1971, a judge "admonished jurors not to apply ordinary presumptions of chastity to black women." And since then, a juror noted that "black women are known to exaggerate" (Crenshaw, 1992).

Harris refuses to reduce Chantel to either a "slutty" girl with low expectations for herself, or a good girl with high aspirations who is necessarily without sexual agency and desire. She does this by making Chantel sexually active and by pinning this sexual agency to Chantel's equally compelling commitment to getting to school on time, doing her homework, trying to ease her mom's domestic schedule, and getting good grades. And this already compact drama is complicated by Chantel's "irrational" response to the crisis of her unwanted pregnancy. Chantel descends into deep fear-based denial about her pregnancy. The young, sexually active, sassy-mouthed black woman from the hood is not who we thought we already knew. Harris is clearly playing on this tension; as the film's promotional slogan reads: "If you think you know her, think again."

This may not seen important or difficult at first glance, but the desire to identify with an untarnished or remorseful heroine who overcomes the odds is a powerful cultural convention and consequently an audience desire. Harris does not make it easy to cheer for Chantel, even though she seems to call on the audience to do so. Chantel makes several mistakes, ones we expect her not to make – and has a cruel streak which is not motivated by life's circumstance. In a prescient example, Chantel and friends see a girl who has had a baby and has dropped out of school. While her friends seem sympathetic to her predicament, Chantel displays a great deal of callous disregard for this young mother, saying that the topic of her burden is a "dead issue." Chantel has "more important things to think about," referring to shoes, clothes, and her own social life. What in the moment might be seen as simple cruelty can in retrospect be understood as a way to demonstrate her fear of unwanted pregnancy and foreshadow her response to her own such pregnancy.

Harris's most startling and interesting narrative move is her handling of Chantel's unwanted pregnancy and the unexpected childbirth scene. Midway through the film, Chantel realizes that she might be pregnant. She goes to a clinic, confirms her worst fears, and consults with Paula, a family planning nurse who lays out the reproductive choices for her (although she cannot discuss abortion because of then-current federal regulations). She seems to be considering her options somewhat rationally, not unlike the way she has handled most hurdles up to this point. But in the process of thinking about her predicament, Chantel becomes paralyzed by fear and indecision. She tells none of her friends or family about the pregnancy, hides her expanding stomach with girdles, and buys duplicates of her clothing in bigger sizes to fool her mother. When she tells Ty that she is pregnant, they have a frustrating series of conversations, mostly because he is anxiously prodding her into having an abortion which seems to make Chantel feel manipulated rather than supported by him. At the same time, her ambivalent paralysis leaves him little room to position himself in the decision-making process. Angered by Ty's prodding to have an abortion and dreadfully frightened by her sense of loss of control, she spends $500 he gives her for the procedure on a shopping spree with her best friend.

The second half of the film leading up to the childbirth scene is excruciating. As the weeks in her pregnancy crawl along, we are given no sense of how she will respond. The strong, straight-ahead-in-your-face brightness of the first half of the film dissolves into a more introspective tone, where time passes as it does when one is paralyzed by anxiety: it skips forward, slows down, sometimes appears to stand completely still. Everyday events are charged by our knowledge that Chantel's abortion clock is ticking. For some critics this shift in tempo is unmotivated, inconsistent, and irritating (Canby, 1993; Clark, 1993). It seems to me, though, that this shift is a crucial means by which Harris produces a visceral, indirect emotional tension for audience members – one that mimics the internal roiling Chantel experiences.

In the scene leading up to the film's climax, she goes over to visit Ty and explains to him how scared she is and how that fear powered her shopping spree. They have sex (another bold move: when was the last time you saw a film that suggested or showed a black pregnant woman having sex? Not to mention a black teenage unwed heroine?). Then, while they are asleep, Chantel goes into premature labor. This is a harrowing and long scene; they are totally unprepared for labor and childbirth and Chantel is screaming wildly in pain. Ty wants to take her to the hospital but Chantel adamantly refuses to go. After her instructions to a frantic Ty (to read from a book describing labor) prove useless, she finally calls Paula, who tries to give some advice including calling EMS, but Chantel refuses again. Paula gets the address and goes to help. By the time she has arrived, Chantel has given birth and has screamed at Ty to dispose of the baby. The dialogue leading up to this climax moment is painfully emotionally shrill and chaotic:

> *Chantel:* Take it away. Get rid of it. Let someone find it. Nobody knows I had this baby, except you and Paula. Take it out of here!
> *Ty:* You cannot abandon a baby like that. Somebody might see me with the baby, and we could get arrested.
> *Chantel:* Just take it! [She screams louder] I don't wanna get stuck with this baby, I wanna do things. I wanna have a nice life. I don't wanna end up like my parents. No. No, fuckin' way!

When Paula arrives she finds Chantel alone, no longer pregnant, and inquires anxiously about the baby's whereabouts. Chantel confesses to having made Ty throw it away. She begs Paula not to be angry with her: "I was scared," she pleads. "I told him to take it out in a garbage bag so nobody would know. I want my baby back. Help me find her. She has a right to live." Ty left the baby alone near the trash long enough for a preschooler to hear it crying and for the police to be called. But by the time the police arrive, Ty has taken the baby back to the apartment. Distressed and excited he explains that he couldn't throw the baby away. Paula escorts them to the hospital and the disaster is averted. The next and final scene is a brightly lit coda in which a smiling Chantel is standing outside in front of a large building during a cold, cloudy afternoon. For the last time, she addresses us directly and with aplomb:

Shit, it's been real tough with my mom and dad, two little brothers and the baby at home. I've started going to community college, made new friends, even went on an occasional date with a new fella. Ty's seein' a new girl, though. . . . I don't really be having no time to hang out. Fuck, I mean I'm too busy. The baby's been sick, Ty even sold his jeep to help with Kiana's doctor bills. But we gettin' our shit together.

At this point, Ty enters the frame with his back to the camera; when he turns around he is holding the baby. The film closes on their walking off screen, together.

The way Harris rewrites the trope of the young inner-city heroine brings to the surface the underlying and contradictory expectations many of us have for young women's sexual behavior and the ways these expectations shape our reception of their actions. This tension between Chantel as heroine/survivor of life's winding road and Chantel's life as warning or cautionary tale is dramatically reflected in the divided critical response to the film. While each of the dozen or so major reviews I consulted saw Harris's independent effort as an important breakthrough and cheered her efforts, the reviews demonstrated a clear division around whether or not Chantel is a heroine and the purpose and interpretation of the final scene. Some interpreted the second half of the film and especially her closing statement and up-beat tone as a sobering, tragic sign of the perils of her sexuality, ignorance, race, and class (Rainer, 1993; Sterrit, 1993; McCarthy, 1992). Others found her optimism too pat and cozy, a move that diffuses the cautionary effect and/or muddles the moral statement (Clark, 1993; Canby, 1993). For some film reviewers the ending is consistent with the rest of the film; for them, Chantel is a clear heroine whose "spirit is intact at the end" (Petrakis, 1993) and who "challenges prevailing middle-class assumptions about maternity" (Carr, 1993). For others, Chantel is a vehicle to challenge (white?) audience prejudices, to "cause a sort of racial double-take." As a result, "it takes a while for the audience to realize that Chantel isn't a hero . . . we're so charmed by this flagrant display of moxy and determination that we fail to notice that it's mostly bluff" (Hinson, 1993).

Harris could have concluded the story in a number of different ways, some choices being less disturbing, others less conventional. She chose to take Chantel's profound denial, fear, and isolation to the most painful and difficult conclusion, all the while refusing to take a familiar, identifiable moral stance on teen motherhood. By never really making a clearly identifiable moral statement and suspending Chantel between two comforting shero narratives, *IRT* functions as a sort of Rorschach test in that it offers two equally compelling, interdependent images (e.g. the Rorschach interlocking images of a vase and two faces), either of which can be recognized and favored by a viewer, depending on his/her disposition. Chantel is not an easily popular heroine; she is not easily likable, but she is also very difficult to dislike or dismiss. She is an aggressive young woman who seems at times to fulfill the stereotype of the loud ghetto girl some may have hoped the film would counter, and yet she also has the sort of professional dreams and the aggressive edge needed to beat the odds. She is both remarkably courageous and paralyzed by fear and denial. Those viewers who link her heroic status to her total self-possession and upward-mobility goals might find themselves becoming discomforted or angered by the implications of her fear and paralysis, as well as by the film's conclusion. On the other hand, those viewers who understand the film as a cautionary tale may feel a sense of narrative comfort/affirmation as Chantel begins to play out the "tragic" future of poor teenage mother-hood. Interestingly, in either case, the coda could easily be read, I believe, as a falsely positive ending that attempted to rescue her damaged char-acter, or a sign of her continued refusal to recognize the horror of her circumstances. Following the terms of sympathy or understanding gener-ally manufactured for errors made by the poor and marginal, the subject is required to express remorse, regret, or shame. Therefore, once she had the baby, she somehow should not have been so bubbly and positive in outlook if she was intended to inspire our sympathy and understanding about her unwed motherhood and/or derailed dreams.

If these two familiar tropes are rejected in favor of a third and much less familiar narrative – one which recognizes the heroics in her ability to remain afloat, positive, and to keep moving forward in the face of life's unplanned events and the inevitability of human error – then Chantel's behavior and the emotional tenor of the film's conclusion might be seen as less disturbing, and perhaps even understood as a small victory. The film's coda-like ending scene with Chantel, Ty, and the baby can be read as a sign that she has survived a major crossroads in her life and is taking it in her stride as best as she is able, which is, perhaps, better than many others might do under equally difficult circumstances. In this interpretive frame, Chantel need not be self-chastising; in fact, for her to be so would disable her power as a heroine. Interpreting Chantel in this way encour-ages us to accept her sexuality and understand it as an integral part of life that brings risks, challenges, and joys, rather than see it primarily as a harbinger of danger and self-destruction.

Against Harris's wishes, reviewers have dubbed *IRT* a "girlz in the hood film," referring to John Singleton's ghetto genre film, *Boyz in the Hood*. For critics and Hollywood executives, the similarities between the two films (e.g. they are both set in a hip-hop ghetto, narrate themes of black suffering, achievement, and failure against the odds and feature young black people) outweighed the differences. There are some similarities, but if we look closely at gender and the terms of hero status in each film – especially how sexuality signals one's status – we see some profound differences. While Chantel is not as sexually knowledgable as she would like to think, she is not *pretending* to have already lost her virginity as does *Boyz'* main character and to-be-ghetto-escapee Tray, to impress his friend and father. Chantel really does *have sex.* And she doesn't apologize for it, nor does writer/director Harris make Chantel fall in love to justify her sexual desires.

Chantel does not "make it" out of the "hood" as Tray does; at the end of *Boyz,* Doughboy (played by Ice Cube) is the "bad" kid who gets killed, as we all expect, but Tray goes on to graduate from Moorehouse College. (Even his girlfriend, Brandy, goes off to Spelman College, and their future plans for marriage are strongly implied.) These endings are far more familiar and neat, they provide resolution and a traditional venue for hope and upward mobility. At the end of *IRT,* Chantel is unmarried, caring for an infant baby with medical problems, living at home with her family, and attending community college. In the final scene, we learn that even though she is getting financial support from Ty, he and she are both dating other people – so the "young love surviving against the odds" trope is demolished. Unlike the more traditional ghetto dream films, such as *Boyz, IRT* locates the heroine's innocence and hopefulness in her heart and mind, not in her sexual behavior.

Coda, Too

I have to say that I, too became frustrated with Chantel throughout the second half of the film. I wanted her to "come to her senses" before it was "too late." As her dream future – which was already a stretch – seemed to collapse around her, I began to think about my desires for her and how my needs – my investment in her – shaped my reaction to her behavior. If Chantel remained pregnant and became a teenage mother, then she would, the logic followed, be stuck, failing to become a doctor. But what were her odds without the pressures and difficulties of teenage motherhood? Would she have been able to afford to go on to college? What about the cost of medical school? What other obstacles might she have faced? Would averting this pregnancy "save" her? Then I began to think about how spotty her knowledge about birth control was (she got pregnant because she did not wait the requisite number of weeks before having sex on the pill and thought she could "double" the dosage to compensate for it). Perhaps, I began to wonder, her path to fulfilling her dreams was equally flawed. Maybe her lack of preparedness in matters of birth control was emblematic of the shoddy preparation young people like her are given for life's challenges, thus raising the distinct possibility that even if she did not get pregnant until later in her life, she still might find herself in similar economic and social circumstances after high school (Chambliss, 1973). What really separates Chantel from more privileged 17-year-olds is less related to differences in levels of confidence, sexual values, or behaviors, and much more connected to the relative quality and quantity of one's life options, extra-parental safety nets, resources, and contexts.

It is both easy and comforting to resort to punishing sexuality-based causes for Chantel becoming a teen mother: she wasn't careful enough, she wasn't knowledgable enough, she wasn't properly invested in virginity, etc. But these explanations stigmatize her entire sexuality, reducing its value and significance to the fateful night of conception. Chantel's voice and stance in the film seems to refuse/reject this sort of analysis each step of the way. Similarly, even as the *48 Hours* host tried to make 17-year-old Cheri admit that she was unfit to be a mother, she seemed to have a kind of honest self-possession that did not easily submit to the chastising discourse that surrounded her. What, I wondered, was her childbirth like? Was she alone? What kinds of pleasures might have been coupled with the fears we were made privy to? By not allowing us to see the pleasures and agency that might have preceded and, it is to be hoped, will follow Cheri's fearful pregnancy, *48 Hours* constructs her as a victim of her own sexuality, someone who "just gets pregnant," rather than a proactively sexual person whose pregnancy is one manifestation of her sexuality.

IRT, while clearly flawed in some important ways, is nonetheless a significant and gutsy attempt to rewrite the black urban teen mother – to normalize her sexual desires and fears and draw our attention away from "up-from-poverty dreams" and female sexual punishment stories to a wider range of contexts and expressions that define Chantel's life and her sexuality. *IRT* works self-consciously within/against the larger discourses about poverty, black female sexual promiscuity, and cultural difference that frames Chantel, and through her, *IRT* challenges the discourses that frame many young black women in urban centers around the country. It also challenges our ways of seeing adolescent black female sexuality and each other.

NOTES

1 Locating these sorts of black women's self-authored texts about sex and sexuality is difficult, but not impossible. Probably the richest site is black women's musical production. The tradition of black women singer's sexual self-narration features many artists, such as Millie Jackson, Bessie Smith, Dinah Washington, and Koko Taylor, who have staked out explicit and significant

black female sexual territory. More recently, many young female rappers and R&B singers have been tackling similar issues. Roxanne Shante, Queen Latifah, Salt, Pepa, Monie Love, Sparky D, TLC, SWV, and others have developed reputations by singing songs and raps that heavily critique sexism, claim ownership of their sexual desires, and make demands for sexual satisfaction. In music, explicit sexual expressions – exploitative and resistant – have always been more accessible and permissable, even as they are policed.

2   Nationally distributed feature-length films by black American women are still quite rare. The nationwide release of *IRT* in April 1993 makes Harris the third African-American woman to have a film nationally released in the history of cinema. Julie Dash's *Daughters of the Dust* and Ruby Oliver's *Love Your Mama* preceded the release of Harris's film by one year and one month respectively. Darnel Martin's *I Like It Like That* was released the following year. Important film and video works by Zeinabu Davis, Ngozi Nwarah, Aiyoka Chinzera, and Sharon Larkin are available through independent outlets, but have not been nationally released.

REFERENCES

Canby, Vincent 1993: Just Another Girl on the IRT. *New York Times*, March 19, C12.

Carr, Jay 1993: "Just Another Girl" Isn't Just Another Movie. *Boston Globe*, April 9, 46.

Chambliss, William J. 1973: The Saints and the Roughnecks. *Society*, 11, 24–31.

Clark, Mike 1993: "Just Another Girl" is on Right Track. *USA Today*, March 23, D12.

Crenshaw, Kimberle 1992: "Whose Story is it Anyway?" Feminist and Antiracist Appropriations of Anita Hill. In Toni Morrison (ed.), *Race-ing Justice, Engendering Power: Essays on Anita Hill, Clarence Thomas and the Construction of Social Reality*, New York: Pantheon, 402–36.

duCille, Ann 1990: "Othered" Matters: Reconceptualizing Dominance and Difference in the History of Sexuality in America. *Journal of the History of Sexuality*, 1, 102–27.

—— 1994: Occult of True Black Womanhood: Critical Demeanor and Black Feminist Studies. *Calaloo*, 19, 591–629.

D'Emilio, John and Freedman, Estelle 1988: *Intimate Matters: A History of Sexuality in America*. New York: Harper and Row.

Frazier, E. Franklin 1948: *The Negro Family in the United States*. Chicago: University of Chicago Press.

Hinson, Hal 1993: "IRT": Express Line to the Inner City. *Washington Post*, April 2, D1.

Jewell, K. Sue 1993: *From Mammy to Miss America and Beyond: Cultural Images and the Shaping of US Social Policy*. New York: Routledge.

Lubiano, Wahneema 1992: Black Ladies, Welfare Queens and State Minstrels. In Toni Morrison (ed.), *Race-ing Justice, Engendering Power: Essays on Anita*

Hill, Clarence Thomas and the Construction of Social Reality, New York: Pantheon, 323–63.

Luker, Kristen 1991: Dubious Conceptions: The Controversy over Teen Pregnancy. *The American Prospect*, 5, 73–83.

McCarthy, Todd 1992: Just Another Girl on the IRT. *Variety*, September 21.

McDowell, Deborah E. (ed.) 1986: "Introduction." In Nella Larsen, *Quicksand and Passing*, New Brunswick: Rutgers, ix–xxxv.

Mauer, Harry 1994: *Sex: An Oral History*. New York: Random House.

Moynihan, Daniel P. 1965: *The Negro Family: The Case for Nation*. Washington, DC: Department of Labor, Office of Policy, Planning and Research.

Painter, Nell I. 1992: Hill, Thomas and the Use of Racial Stereotype. In Toni Morrison (ed.), *Race-ing Justice, Engendering Power: Essays on Anita Hill, Clarence Thomas and the Construction of Social Reality*, New York: Pantheon, 200–14.

Petrakis, John 1993: Just Another Succcess: How Young Film Director Leslie Harris Beat the Odds. *Chicago Tribune*, April 4, sect. 13, 10.

Rainer, Peter 1993: "Just Another Girl on the IRT" Moving in the Right Direction. *Los Angeles Times*, April 2, F4.

Rainwater, Lee and Yancey, W. L. 1967: *The Moynihan Report and the Politics of Controversy: A Trans-action Social Science and Public Policy Report*. Cambridge, MA: MIT Press.

Ridgeway, James 1995: Father Knows Best: Patriarchy is Back and Badder than Ever. *Village Voice*, January 17, 15–18.

Schaefer, Stephen 1993: Newcomer Ariyan Johnson Rides "IRT" to Fame. *USA Today*, March 23, D12.

Spillers, Hortense 1984: Intersticies: A Small Drama of Words. In Carol S. Vance (ed.), *Pleasure and Danger: Exploring Female Sexuality*, New York: Routledge, 73–100.

Sterritt, David 1993: A Movie that Harnesses a Teen's Energy. *Christian Science Monitor*, March 15, 14.

Wallace, Michelle 1979: *Black Macho and the Myth of the Superwoman*. New York: Basil Blackwell.

Wechsler, Pat 1993: The Focused Filmmaker: For "Just Another Girl" Director Leslie Harris, Reality Leaves Plenty of Room to Dream. *Washington Post*, April 2, D1.

Willis, Andre C. 1997: A Womanist Turn on the Hip Hop Theme: Leslie Harris's Just Another Girl on the IRT. In Joseph K. Adjaye and Adrianne R. Andrews (eds), *Language, Rhythm, and Sound: Black Popular Cultures into the 21st Century*, Pittsburgh: University of Pittsburgh Press.

7

Situating Television in Everyday Life: Reformulating a Cultural Studies Approach to the Study of Television Use

RON LEMBO

In my studies of television, I want nothing less than to get inside people's heads to determine the mindfulness that emerges from their use of the medium, and further, to understand its ritual significance within the culture of television use. In doing so, I want to gain a better understanding of the role of the structural features of television – and the broader, meaningful context of people's lives – in giving shape or form to this mindfulness. I want to know how it is that television viewing actually becomes a ritual practice for people. I want to know what participation in *this* ritual (as opposed to others) means for people over the long run in their everyday lives. Among other things, this means gaining a solid understanding of the fate of people's ability to think for themselves and to act on their own terms in a culture that is dominated by large corporations. These corporations increasingly control the production and distribution of what we see and hear, not only on television, but on radio, in films, newspapers, and magazines, and popular music, too.

In this essay, I discuss a ritual of use that is quite common among people who use television: what I refer to as "turning to television simultaneously with other activities." I lead up to this discussion by first explaining the methodology, research design, and strategies that I employed in my study of the viewing culture and in my documentation of this particular way of watching television. Following the discussion of simultaneous viewing, I conclude the essay by considering briefly some of the implications that this way of watching television carries with regard to living everyday life in the image-worlds of corporate culture.

Conceptualizing and Investigating the Viewing Culture

The social experience of people who watch television has not been conceptualized or documented adequately by social theorists, social scientists, or more recently, by cultural studies analysts. In contrast to earlier sociological views, cultural studies does, in fact, accord television watching a legitimate place in its account of power, but it fails to adequately theorize the context of television watching as a new and distinctive cultural form. Cultural studies tends to examine texts as exemplars of ideology or discursive power, understanding them in terms of the social and historical conditions under which they are produced. I argue that unless critical analysts generate categories of reception, of use, that can document the social function of television, the emphasis on textual reading among audience members remains incomplete, and perhaps misses what is arguably most important about television use.

I use the construct of *sociality* to incorporate and move beyond ideas about discourse and textuality, and to systematically explore how television is used in ways that allows me to focus on more than just the dynamics of power and resistance, at least as they have typically been formulated in cultural studies' accounts. My strategy is to work through ideas about power by grounding them empirically in reconstructions of the practical uses that people make of television on a day-to-day basis.

The social world of television use is no doubt a complicated one. It's complexities – the differences in mindfulness that emerge there, the variety of ways that people construct social relations with others, as well as the ways that television fits with everything else that people do in their everyday lives – are certainly understandable as power effects, but not *only* as power effects. The language that we use to analyze and account for the complexities of this world must be able to say, with clarity and precision, what *else*, besides power and resistance, they are about. If analysts believe that they can do so with discursive constructs, fine; the point is, to account for the complexities. If discursive or textual constructs fall short in this regard, then I think it is incumbent upon critical analysts to think through the limitations of these constructs to arrive at a more adequate conceptual grounding for documenting the workings of television's power in the social experience of people who watch it. It may be worthwhile to keep in mind the cautioning that Bakhtin extended to his readers in *The Dialogic Imagination* – not to confuse the world *of* the text with the world *outside* the text; the two, he said, are not the same (Bakhtin, 1981).

Research strategy and methods

Generally speaking, conceptualizing television use involves reconstructing the practical ways in which people who watch television situate themselves with the medium on a day-in, day-out basis. Contrary to appearances, television use is a multifaceted activity, one that is much more complicated than it seems. Assessing its meaning for people and the significance it carries in their lives involves nothing short of the analytical reconstruction of it as a distinctive kind of culture. I have referred to this elsewhere as "the viewing culture" (Lembo, 1994).

My strategy of empirical research, beginning in 1987, was to reconstruct people's social experience with television across the different, yet interrelated, phases of the viewing culture: the turn to television, interaction with television imagery, and leaving television and fitting it back into daily life. I used a variety of different methods to do this. The bulk of my empirical documentation came from 60 two-hour interviews with wage and salaried workers. I also spent considerable time watching television with people (participant observation), and in addition, I asked a smaller number of people to fill out viewer diaries.

In carrying out my field research and in conducting depth interviews, it was my intention from the very start to account for the social relations that were a part of people's television use. Virtually all research perspectives acknowledge (even if they don't focus on it) that *what people do with one another* can mediate the power of television in important ways, in some cases amplifying it and in other cases deflecting and qualifying it. I documented the social interactions and the group life that often shaped what happened in the home, but I also focused on capturing *individual* thoughts and feelings that emerged both when people watched with others and when they were *alone*. A good deal of the mindful encounters that people have with objects in their world, such as with television and with other people, can be *socially constituted*, without it ever having to find outer expression, either in words or actions. In fact, as a social activity, television use is typically constituted as a relation, but one in which the people who use it have a certain separateness, or distinctiveness, with regard to the object, television, and to the other people that use it with them. At the same time, they remain connected to the television and to other people who may be using it with them. It is this simultaneous separateness and connection that makes it possible for there to be an inside, a mindfulness, to people's use of television or, for that matter, for there to be an inside or a mindfulness to any of the activities that comprise social life.

To speak about a sociality of television use is to acknowledge that the inner mindfulness that people have when they are engaged with the medium is just as important as the more conventionally understood, outward indicators of social life when it comes to providing cultural form to their experience. This is particularly true, I think, when we are dealing with a technology that is as private as television. Typically, it is this inner mindfulness, this inner world of emotional experience, that is often ignored in scholarly explorations of the viewing culture, and it is this inner world that I sought to document empirically across the different phases of the viewing culture.

At this point, I want to focus on the first phase – the turn to television – and describe how I went about reconstructing the empirical patterns that constitute people's use of the medium in this particular phase. This will then be followed with an account of one particular pattern that emerged in this phase of participation in the viewing culture: turning to television simultaneously with other activities.

Reconstructing the turn to television

In turning to television, people provide an opportunity for the discourses of power that are inscribed in the medium to enter their homes and become a part – in some cases, a very important part – of the social world that they create, inhabit, and sustain there. Practically speaking, everyone who watches television is aware of the regularity (or irregularity) with which they turn to the medium, and because of this, if they are given the opportunity, they can indeed reconstruct a good deal of what they think and do to bring television into their lives on a regular basis. It is this sense of typicality in people's turn to television that served as my starting point in reconstructing what people do with television.

Typically, the first opportunity working people have for turning to television comes after work, when they make the transition to their home life. A significant portion of my interview schedule focused on the reconstruction of this transition from work to home life. I was especially interested in understanding how people typically structure this transition time with regard to their use of television. But in order to understand what it meant for them to turn to television, I needed to reconstruct the *place* of television in their everyday lives during this transition time. This meant that in the interviews, I had to account for how they typically oriented themselves to (thought about) television and other activities. I also had to account for what they watched, how they watched, as well as what they usually did besides watching television at this time, including how they typically did those other things. Furthermore, I had to do all of this *without* presupposing that television occupied any special, or privileged, position for these people.

In addition to identifying what their activities were and who was included in them, I found it was important to be explicit in documenting the *mindfulness* with which they went about their activities. As I said earlier, one of my major concerns was to treat this inner social world as carefully as most analysts have treated the outer one. In the real time of the viewing culture, people do not ordinarily make distinctions between the phases of their activities. They are not generally in the business of analyzing their own television use, or their own participation in any other activity, for that matter. People pass through mindful phases during their activities. They orient themselves mentally to what they are about to do, based on whatever it is they are presently doing, and then, once they have actually turned to a particular activity, they enter a new phase, one in which they become mindfully engaged in the activity itself. In passing through these phases of any activity, people are mindful – they think – and their mindfulness undergoes changes and transformations. This mindfulness, then, constitutes a most important *interior* dimension to social actions and activities. Through prior field research, use of viewer diaries, the completion of preliminary, open-ended interviews, and more informal conversations with people who watch television, particularly working people, I found that it made sense to distinguish between the mindfulness with which people *turned to* activities, including television, and the mindfulness of the activities themselves. That is, *how people think in orienting themselves* to activities is not necessarily the same as *where it is they end up while engaged in the activities*, mindfully speaking.

In order to systematically investigate the mindfulness in the turn to television (and to other activities) I asked working people in my interviews to provide an account of the typical course of their after-work routines. I approached this investigation using the idea of a *continuum of mindfulness*. Points along this continuum that I established are:

- *habitual*, the least mindful way of approaching activities, where people are acting out of habit or in effect, orienting themselves to doing things in an unthinking way;
- a slightly more mindful approach to things is *escapist*, where people typically have at least some awareness of a desire to be freed, mentally, emotionally, physically, or socially, from their present situation (not acting simply out of habit);
- a *playful* orientation to activities is where people are getting away from not only what they were previously doing or feeling but also, more importantly, where they are thinking in terms of separating themselves from what they were doing, and by virtue of this separation, turning to something else in a creative or imaginative frame of mind;
- finally, a *reflective* turn to activities, the most mindful of the qualities, is when people monitor and evaluate their present thoughts and

feelings, trying to anticipate how they might think or feel if they were to choose one activity over another, and in general, trying to be conscious of where and how the activity might fit into the larger context of their free-time activities.

In describing how they typically went about doing things, I thought that my interviewees could, in a discussion that focused their attention on this range of mindfulness, provide reliable indications regarding how they typically oriented themselves to what they did after work and then to what they did later in the evening. Of course, I was well aware that some people, either after work or in the evening, might orient themselves to different activities in different ways, or to the same activity in different ways, with all of this, in their eyes, defining what was typical for them. For this reason, I discouraged them from making forced choices between mindful orientations, and instead asked them to indicate *all* orientations that might typically apply to their situations.

When it came to documenting the mindfulness of people's actual involvement in activities (as opposed to the act of turning to them), I identified four dimensions of social action that would be applicable to a wide variety of activities, and at the same time, allow meaningful comparisons to be made between them. In the first place, I wanted to know whether people participated in a more active or passive way in the activities that they chose. Second, I thought it important to know whether or not people typically had control over the pace with which their activities proceeded. Third, I wanted to determine whether people become engaged in activities in such a way that one occurrence was connected to and built upon the last, so that over time, the activity could be understood by them to have a developmental course to it. Fourth, I was interested in knowing the possibility for insight that various activities held for people; that is, whether or not, and to what extent, their participation in activities provided them with insight about themselves, about others in their world, or about the broader environment in which their lives were situated.

As you might expect, the mindfulness of people's involvement in activities varies greatly. Determining this mindfulness is a difficult analytical task, in part because mindful participation depends on so many things, including, obviously, interviewees' backgrounds, the kinds of work they do, the situations they typically find themselves in after work, the way they think and feel in those situations, their living situations, the kinds of responsibilities they have there, the activities that are available to them, and so on.

By asking working people to provide an account of the typical course of their after-work routines I was able to reconstruct the broader context of their television use, including the activities that preceded, followed, and occurred simultaneously with it. By asking them to recall something of the mindful way in which they typically went about these activities, I was able to understand something of their inner process of mind as well. With these constructs of mindfulness in place, I was able to determine whether or not working people turned to television with a particular frame (or frames) of mind that recurred from one occasion of use to the next. I was also able to determine whether they approached other activities in the same way; and if they didn't, I was in a position to know how they did approach other activities, mindfully speaking, and I attempted to determine why this was the case. Perhaps most importantly, this kind of documentation enabled me to compare people's mindfulness in turning to television with their mindfulness in turning to other activities. Similarly, I was also able to compare where it is, mindfully speaking, that people ended up as a result of having turned to television, as opposed to their having turned to other activities on a routine basis. As a result, it was possible for me to move beyond an understanding of television use as something isolated, and see it instead as something thoroughly situated. Taken together, these interview accounts, along with my field research of watching television with people and watching them watch television, provided me with an empirical reference point, a kind of evidence, really, for thinking through ideas about television's power in this particular phase of their participation in the viewing culture. Power was no longer simply an abstraction (albeit a useful one) but, rather, something concrete. Against the documentation provided by empirical research, I have been able to interrogate notions of standardization, normalization, and discursive structuring by examining the ways in which this power works to shape working people's everyday experiences. By virtue of these interviews I was put in the position of understanding something of the extent to which these people were able to direct and control what they did with television, and hence the extent to which they could call into question, circumvent, or simply ignore its power.

Turning to Television Simultaneously with Other Activities

The documentation of use

Approximately 25 of the 60 working people that I interviewed did not typically separate their turn to television from their turn to other activities. Instead, they said that they turned to television and other activities *at the same time*. This way of watching television represented one of the most significant, and unanticipated, findings that emerged from my research. I have come to refer to this particular use of television as viewing while simultaneously participating in other activities, or more simply, simultaneous viewing.

Of the 25 people in this category of simultaneous viewers, 14 said that they almost always turned simultaneously to television and other activities after work, and doing other things unrelated to television was for them, at this particular time, very much the exception rather than the rule. Of course, on occasion, they came home from work and did things without the television on; or, alternatively, they visited friends or family, or went shopping. These things happened sometimes. But typically, they said, they came home from work, and if the television wasn't already on, they turned it on and kept it on while they, and perhaps other members of their household, proceeded to do a variety of other things that had become part of their after-work routine. So, for example, Toni, a senior editorial supervisor at a publishing house, turned the television on as soon as she came home, and watched the local and national news as she went about preparing dinner and taking care of things around the house. Diana, a laboratory technician, said that she had the time to shop for herself after work and sometimes thought about doing so, but usually she didn't. Similarly, she thought about reading instead of watching television when she came home, but usually she didn't do this either. It may be that reporting that they considered (but didn't actually engage in) other activities was a way for these people to rationalize, to me, the interviewer, their seemingly mindless use of television: they could do other things if they wanted, but they chose not to. Ten of the 14 made no mention of these other possibilities for mindful involvement.

For these particular people, turning to television in this way had become a habit; they just did it automatically, without thinking, when they came home from work. Furthermore, in establishing this particular pattern of television use, they excluded other, discrete activities from their daily routine. As a result, there was no mindful counterweight, in the form of other, ongoing activities, to the role that television played in their lives at this time.

The other 11 of these 25 people said that they, too, turned simultaneously to television and other activities after work, but with one notable difference compared to the fourteen just discussed: these eleven also turned, with some regularity, to other activities besides television during this time. They did this, they said, in the same mindful way that they turned to simultaneous viewing, which meant that, at the outset, they didn't ordinarily envision their involvement with television differently than they did these other activities. For example, Terry, a telephone operator at a publishing house, ordinarily had the television on while she prepared dinner and tidied up around the house, but she also sometimes took walks, or read the newspaper or magazines instead. Nancy, a machine operator, usually watched television with her boyfriend as they relaxed and prepared dinner together, but sometimes she visited with friends or went shopping instead. For Kirk, who worked on a loading dock, simultaneous viewing was his "routine of choice" after work, but he also became involved in one or another of his ongoing household projects with some regularity. Similar accounts were offered by other people as well. The particular activities differed from person to person, but the fact that each of them turned to other activities, besides simultaneous viewing, was a constant across all their interview accounts. Even though these people, too, watched television while simultaneously doing other things, this kind of viewing did not occupy the same prominent and constant position in their lives as it did in the lives of the 14 people who always viewed simultaneously after work. In contrast to the 14, these 11 regularly became involved in activities that did not revolve around the world of television or become broken up by it on an ongoing basis.

For all 25 of these people (a little less than half of the people I interviewed), this way of spending time after work had become automatic for them. There were numerous activities that typically took place in conjunction with television use, and this varied from person to person, depending, for the most part, on whether or not they lived alone or with other people. For those who lived alone, interaction with others was not typically a part of their simultaneous viewing routine, unless, of course, they talked on the phone with family or friends, which was for some people a common occurrence. For the most part, the people who lived alone enjoyed a greater freedom in structuring their daily routines. Living with family or roommates often complicated people's simultaneous viewing routine, because at the very least, every activity was now, at least potentially, a socially interactive one. In general, though, the hustle and bustle of household life was considerably greater when family members or housemates were present, which meant that a person's involvement in any particular activity was more likely to be interrupted, which, in turn, meant that people were more likely to experience shifts in mindfulness as they moved back and forth between various levels and types of activities.

Virtually all of these people said that they typically took care of the more mundane household chores or responsibilities they felt needed to be done. These included preparing dinner or a snack, washing clothes, straightening up the house, vacuuming, taking out the garbage, sorting through the mail, paying bills, and working on various small "fix-it" jobs around the house. (Many, if not most, of the women I interviewed felt a greater sense of responsibility, if not of need, for attending to the day-to-day work that kept the household functioning smoothly. Whether by design or by choice, it was they, more often than the men, who cooked, cleaned, washed clothes, etc. In contrast, the men spoke of doing yardwork, or working on projects of various sorts around the house, things such as woodworking, replacing tiles, and painting, that were a step removed from what had to be done everyday. This is not to say that many of the men did not also assume responsibility for cooking, cleaning, or doing house-work, because they often did. These kinds of gender-defined household roles are evident in many of the interview accounts.)

Next on the list of most frequently occurring activities was casual con-versation with family members or housemates (and this included, for some people, talking on the phone). People said that they typically moved in and out of casual conversations, and sometimes these casual conversa-tions might deepen into more serious discussions having to do with such topics as work, their children's school activities, their housemates' social lives, paying bills, the pros and cons of making a major household pur-chase, or other issues pertaining to family or household relations. Occa-sionally, some of them said, time was set aside for more structured kinds of discussions or social interactions, such as helping their children with homework, or talking through a more immediate issue or problem which might have come up with a family member or housemate and that needed to be dealt with right away. In addition to conversation and social inter-action, some people (though fewer in number) also used at least some por-tion of this transition time after work to read the newspaper or look through magazines, sometimes doing so while they sat and watched television.

With regard to the actual use of the television during simultaneous viewing, people reported watching and listening to news (both local and national), game shows, syndicated reruns of prime-time network pro-grams, and to a lesser extent, talk shows and previously recorded pro-gramming (usually soap operas). The segmented formats of news and game shows, in particular, were quite compatible with the demands of simultaneous viewing. Compared to typical television drama or situation comedy formats, the news typically presented short and, for the most part, unrelated news items that viewers either followed or ignored as they saw fit. Although the structure of game shows resembles the traditional narrat-ive structure, game shows are segmented into a succession of puzzles, or games within a game, and people reported that they could pick and choose what they wanted to watch here as well. The fact that the rules of the game are relatively simple and known in advance by those who watch meant that they could follow the dialogue and interaction of the parti-cipants in these shows with less attention than, say, a soap opera or a drama. This was true, too, although perhaps not to the same degree, for the reruns of prime-time programming that some people watched after work. Taken together, news, game shows, and prime-time reruns constituted 85 percent of the programming that people tuned into when they became involved in simultaneous viewing after work.

Simultaneous viewing typically lasted anywhere from an hour and a half to two, or sometimes two and a half hours, as people moved back and forth, continually, between watching or listening to something on television and doing any, or all, of these other things. Cooking, cleaning, talking, reading, and so on – all of this went on, from their point of view, at the *same* time. Most people said that they held to this routine until just after dinner time, when they, and usually others in their family or household, faced a decision, of sorts, as to what to do with the rest of their evening. None of them did exactly the same things, in the same way, every day. No doubt there were variations in their routines. In fact, in the interviews, they sometimes found it difficult to reconstruct what typically transpired from moment to moment in any single situation of simultaneous viewing, or, for that matter, in one situation as opposed to another. The time that people typically spent in one or another activity, how particular activities succeeded one another in time, how, when, and why people shifted their attention from one activity to another, how their mindful involvement varied from one activity to another, how and when they brought their participation in any of these activities to a close – all of this was, for them, generally unpredictable.

Although it was difficult, if not impossible, to define a single, mindful pattern that constituted simultaneous viewing, there were, nevertheless, regularities evident in this kind of television use. After careful consideration of all the interview accounts of people's turn to television, as well as a systematic review of field notes pertaining to my observation of and participation in the viewing culture, I found that the regularities comprising simultaneous viewing were perhaps best described as occurring along a continuum of use. The continuum ranged from intermittent viewing to focused, interpretive viewing.

At one end of this continuum, television played more of a background role for people as they carried on with any number of the things that I have mentioned – cooking, cleaning, eating, talking, reading, and so on. People followed what was on television, but in an intermittent manner. Often, they listened more than they actually watched. On occasion, a particular news story, or an exciting moment in a game show or a sit-com rerun, caught their attention, and they stopped what else they were doing and focused on what was on television. At moments such as these, they were drawn into the representational world that television provided for them, and they did so in a way that approximated the kind of mindful involvement that they typically exhibited when they watched television in a more careful and focused way, which was usually later in the evening. These were interpretive moments, and sometimes they found things plausible, sometimes not. In either case, at this end of the simultaneous viewing continuum, the more focused, interpretive moments passed rather quickly, because people's attention usually shifted back to their involvement in another activity, whether it was cooking, cleaning, snacking, talking, or something else. After all, people who were using television in this way were not that intent on sustaining these kinds of interpretive moments to begin with. Even so, most people indicated that even after they turned their attention back to doing other things, they continued to keep an eye, or ear, open to what was on television, so as not to miss anything exciting or important that might have come up. At this end of the continuum of simultaneous viewing, the actual time spent watching or listening to television was clearly outweighed by people's involvement in other activities. But because the television stayed on, programming could always be heard, if not watched, and this alone made it possible for their involvement in the other activities to be interrupted at any time. Consequently, people could, also at any time, immediately be *there*, in the image-worlds of television, with all the power that these image worlds carried for organizing their meaningful experience.

This kind of simultaneous viewing was exemplified in the daily routine that Paula, a secretary, maintained for herself and her family after work. Married, with a son, Paula said that "the TV is already on when I come home, because my son is watching." After settling into things, she said that she usually proceeded to cook and clean and her son continued to watch cartoons or *Sesame Street*. At some point, she said, her son began his homework, and she helped him with some of it while she continued cooking and attending to her other household responsibilities. Amidst all of this, she usually switched the television to the local news, since her son was now occupied with other things. "Having the TV on," she said, "helps me to relax." Paula said that she liked the local news and soap operas because, as she put it, "I can follow [them] without having to pay much attention to what's on. Things are simple enough that I can understand what happens [without paying much attention]. I can miss parts of shows and it won't bother me." Usually, she watched the news, but if she remembered to tape *One Life To Live*, her favorite soap that was on earlier in the day, she put it in the VCR and had that on instead of the news. Typically, Paula moved in and out of paying attention to what was on television, as she continued cooking, cleaning, and talking with her son, and later with her husband when he came home from work. Sometimes, she said, "if I get a break from my housework, I'll sit down and read the newspaper." It was not a problem for her to "follow the TV and read the newspaper"; "I can do both," she said. By the time her husband came home, she had usually finished with her soap opera, and the television was switched back to the news, since that was what he preferred to watch. This routine went on from 4:30 or so until around 7:30 or 8:00. In Paula's house, the television typically stayed on through the later after-noon and into the evening, although this simultaneous viewing gave way to a more focused kind of viewing, as she and her husband (and some-times her son, too) settled down to watch prime-time programs for the rest of the night.

At the other end of the simultaneous viewing continuum, watching television seemed to be the primary concern, and preparing dinner, fixing things to eat, taking care of things around the house, or talking to other people were all activities that fit around television viewing. As a result, the time that people spent watching outweighed, by a considerable margin, the time and energy they devoted to the other activities that were a part of their after-work routine. Typically, people said that they sat and watched for considerable stretches of time, perhaps paying attention to an entire portion of the news, such as the sports or weather, or following a game show or sit-com segment through to its completion. During the commer-cial breaks they got up and attended to one or another thing that also occupied their attention (typically, cooking or eating), or they stayed put in front of the television but turned their attention to other things, such as looking through the newspaper, or talking to people in a more extended way. This pattern of alternating attention between television and other activities continued, maybe for an hour or two, and people simply picked up where they left off, either with what was on television, or with what-ever else they were doing, as they went back and forth between these things. Some people said that even though their television set was in the living room, or the family room, it was situated in such a way that they could see what was on from the kitchen, or from the doorway leading to the kitchen, and this enabled them to continue watching while they pre-pared dinner, fixed something to eat, talked, or did other things. Others had smaller television sets in the kitchen, making it possible for them to simply shift their gaze to catch what was on the screen while they stayed involved in what else they were doing. When people watched in either of these ways, their viewing pattern shifted in such a way that shorter but more frequent periods of attention to the television were interspersed with continued involvement in these other activities, as opposed to when they sat and watched shows, or portions of shows, right through. But watch-ing television was still the most mindfully engaging activity they were participating in.

Richie, a security officer, usually came home, turned on the television, sat or lied on the couch, and "relaxed for a while by watching television." His wife usually took care of most of the cooking and the other house-work that needed to be done, and this, coupled with the fact that they didn't have any children, freed Richie to watch television in a focused way for longer stretches of time than most people in the category were used to doing at this particular time. Typically, Richie watched local and national news and ESPN, switching back and forth, depending on the stories being presented and whatever sports programming happened to be on at the time. Because he enjoyed sports, he usually watched the sports segment of the local news all the way through, often doing the same with the weather, too. He preferred to watch baseball, golf, and tennis, and if any of these sports were on ESPN, he stayed with them for a while. Richie usually picked up the newspaper and read through it while he watched television, and it was also common for him to carry on conversations with his wife, who was either in the kitchen, or moving about the house. From time to time, he got up and went into the kitchen, either to talk with his wife or to help her with one or another aspect of the evening's dinner preparations, and then he went back to sit and watch television, and perhaps read the paper again.

This kind of movement back and forth, between these somewhat sustained periods of attentiveness to television and reading, talking, and helping out in the kitchen, continued for about an hour and a half, until 6:30 or so, when they sat down to eat dinner. The television stayed on through dinner, and between eating and talking, both of them would catch bits and pieces of what was on. When dinner was over, Richie said that he usually helped his wife clean up for a while, and then he went back to the living room, lay down on the couch, and watched *Wheel of Fortune* and *Jeopardy*, two of his favorite game shows. Sometimes his wife joined him and they would watch these shows together for a while, until she tired of television and got up to do other things. Richie then either continued watching right on through for the rest of the evening, or he got up to work on one of his cars or other projects in the garage. Eventually, though, he came back into the house and took up watching television again, and his wife usually joined him at some point. Typically, they spent the rest of the evening together, watching television and talking.

Other viewers fall somewhere between these two ends of the simultaneous viewing continuum. Sometimes, as with Richie, they engaged in periods of sustained attention to what was on television, at which time whatever else was going on in their lives was clearly backgrounded to their viewing. At other times, they devoted their energies more wholeheartedly to other activities, as Paula did, and it was television imagery that seemed to slip into the background. This was evident, for example, in the daily routine of Susan, a statistical clerk in a quality control department. When she arrived home from work, the television was usually already on, because either her husband, or one of her two sons, had turned it on when they came in. Susan set to work in the kitchen, preparing dinner for her family, and for about an hour or so, the television was, for her, merely a background to her cooking and cleaning up. Earlier on, her sons usually watched sit-com reruns, and she was less inclined to follow what went on, although she would listen and from time to time notice particularly funny lines or become aware of exciting situations. At some point, either she or her husband switched to the news, and even though she was still primarily in the kitchen, Susan said that she was more inclined to follow particular stories, and on some occasions, she came into the living room and watched what was on. Around 6:00 or 6:30, the family sat down and ate, and amidst family talk at the dinner table, they watched *Magnum P. I.* reruns. After dinner, *Wheel of Fortune* and *Jeopardy* were on, and at this time, with her cooking and cleaning out of the way, Susan said that she usually sat down and watched these shows with her husband and their two sons. Conversation continued, and sometimes, she, like Richie, picked up the paper and read through it while she watched and spent time with her family. But compared to late afternoon, when she listened to television largely from the kitchen, the early evening was a time for more focused viewing: even though she read and talked, she, along with everyone else in her family, followed what the contestants did. When these shows were over, Susan attended to her children's needs, perhaps helping them with homework or talking to them about their day, and at that point, she, like many of the people I interviewed, faced a decision as to what they would do with the rest of their evening. Since she was very involved in the PTA and local school politics, Susan often attended meetings that took her out of the house for the rest of the evening. At other times she sewed, but after a while she came back to television and, with her husband, watched some of their favorite shows together. Generally speaking, though, if she didn't have a meeting, or she was too tired to take up one of her sewing projects, Susan sat and watched television, using it to continue spending time with her husband.

Analyzing power relations in simultaneous viewing

For these 25 people, this simultaneous turn to television and other activities, including the relatively mindless way that they oriented themselves to it, was their primary after-work routine. It was what they did first, or most of the time, as they made the transition from work to home life day after day. Watching television while simultaneously becoming and staying involved with other things is actually a very complicated activity, more complicated, really, than most other kinds of television use. Because simultaneous viewing is such a complicated activity, it poses distinctive problems for the study of power. In simultaneous viewing, television's power works in different ways at the same time and not always in the manner that cultural studies' accounts have led us to believe.

Structuring the interpretive process   For cultural studies analysts, more often than not, it is television's power to structure people's interpretive process that occupies center stage in their accounts. Certainly, this kind of power was operative in simultaneous viewing, since, as my earlier account indicates, people who watched in this way continued to make interpretations of what they saw and heard. This meant, among other things, that the discourses of programming provided them with normative frameworks for making meaningful connections to the larger culture. But in simultaneous viewing, as opposed to more focused and exclusive ways of watching, this structuring of interpretations occurred in a more frag- mented manner. The meanings that emerged were very often dissociated from one another, since people were usually moving back and forth between television and other activities, and their attentiveness to the dis- courses of programming was intermittent, at best. In simultaneous view- ing, the movements of a story line, the interrelations between different story lines, the integration of characters' actions within story lines, and especially, the way that these representational forms come together to constitute the narrative significance of the show as a whole – all of the things that elaborate the deeper meaning of social action in programming – are much less likely to serve as a centering presence for people's mind- ful experience. It is not so much these deeper, more elaborated levels of meaning that this group of interviewees became mindfully involved with in simultaneous viewing. Rather, it was the more clearly delineated, easily recognizable, and repetitive meanings that the image flow and segmented programming structure elevate to a potentially more prominent position in people's minds. Thus, it was shorter, more discrete segments of a show, or the hyperritualized scenes of social action taking place inside these segments, or various combinations or juxtapositions of such segments and scenes, sometimes drawn from different shows over a period of time, that this group of people paid attention to. When this happened, the continu- ity and developmental quality of social action, two features of sociality that are crucial in allowing discourse to anchor and stabilize people's mindful experience, were diminished, if they mattered at all.

In simultaneous viewing, the mindfulness exhibited by people does not have to be consistent or integrated from one moment to the next, or, for that matter, over the broader course of the viewing experience. As a result, people don't necessarily come away from television with discurs- ively coherent or stable ideas about social life, about the world "out there," or about their own life in relation to what was depicted in these image-worlds, as they might have done if they watched a particular show from beginning to end. This is what I mean when I say that, in simultaneous viewing, television shapes people's interpretive process in a fragmented manner; that it dissociates meaning while at the same time enabling meaning to emerge. To the extent that critical analysts attribute television's power in structuring people's interpretive process to the regularities of discourse, they may inadvertently underestimate the medium's role in bringing about the dissociated kind of social experience that is typical of simultaneous viewing. This more distracted way of watching requires that the analyst look further inside the workings of television's discourses in order to better illuminate the distinctive sociality of their use.

Habituation For those people who turned to television simultaneously with other activities, television could also be understood to have "leveled" their thinking, and over time, habituated them to a relatively mindless way of doing things. As a form of power, this is really very similar to the standardizing effect that figured so importantly in the work of the Frankfurt School. It derives from the fact that for those who engaged in simultaneous viewing, there was no distinction, mindfully speaking, between turning to television and turning to other activities. Rather, this power effect was constituted by their linking, over time, of a certain unthinking way of approaching television and other activities in combination. In the interview accounts, I could not distinguish people's mindful and emotional expectations regarding television from their expectations regarding any number of other activities as they made the transition from work to their home lives. This was true both for the handful of people who didn't become engaged in simultaneous viewing and for all the rest who did. As with watching television, these other activities (cooking, cleaning, and casual conversation being the most frequent) had become routine for the people I interviewed: they were not the kinds of things that people looked upon as particularly noteworthy to begin with. Despite, or perhaps because of, this apparent indistinguishability in the mindfulness of their approach to television and other activities, the accounts indicate that the majority of these 25 people had become habituated to this relatively mindless way of watching television. Of all the people that I interviewed who turned to television after work, those who turned simultaneously to television and other activities were more likely than any of the others to do so in an unthinking way – that is, out of habit. In fact, the more exclusively that people turned to simultaneous viewing, the more likely they were to act out of habit in the after-work period. The 14 people who said that they usually used television *only* in this way acted out of habit 90 percent of the time in making their transition from work to home, as opposed to acting in more mindful or self-directive ways. Furthermore, among 10 of the 14, their relatively mindless orientation to things showed no change when they described themselves as feeling relaxed (as opposed to stressed) after work – a situation that would otherwise seem to enable people to act more mindfully. It was in the after-work routines of these 10 people that I found the clearest association between television use and relatively mindless behavior; an association that was repeated day-in and day-out, with little else occurring in that time period to counteract or qualify this apparent power effect.

Limits to habituation   In following the reports of mindfulness of this same group of 14, who did little else but use television in a simultaneous way as they moved into the evening, the next morning (the next available period of free time for those who worked evenings), or the weekend, it quickly became clear that even these people, as habituated as they might have been to television after work, acted in more mindful and self-directive ways at other times. Eight of the 14 who almost always viewed simultaneously after work either continued to watch television into the evening or, if they worked evenings, regularly turned to television in the morning and early afternoon before they went to work. Interestingly enough, almost all of them indicated that their orientation to television was more mindful at these times. They were looking for something stimu-lating or fun to watch, they said, something that would allow them to become imaginatively engaged and focus their attention for a while, unlike what they did while engaged in simultaneous viewing after work. They all had favorite shows that they watched every week, which enabled them to establish continuities in their television use – again, something that was absent in simultaneous viewing. Furthermore, all of the 14 people became involved in various activities at times other than after work. For example, Paul sometimes read detective stories at night, and played golf, or under-took small projects around the house on the weekends; Elizabeth read romance novels; George read and wrote poetry; Diana read historical novels and sewed in the evening, and on the weekends, she did yardwork and small "home improvement" projects; Susan went to school board and PTA meetings or went shopping; Terry went for walks, read autobio-graphies, or wrote letters in the evening, and on the weekends she worked in the garden; Kirk worked on household projects, read the paper, or cleaned his guns. I mention all of this to point out that even though these people repeatedly turned to television out of habit after work, they continued to act in more mindful and self-directive ways, both with and without the television, at other times throughout their daily and weekly routines. Even for these 14 people who were the most thoroughly en-sconced in a pattern of relatively mindless viewing, habituation was for them a process, not a state of mind.

There were other people who were less exclusively oriented to simultaneous viewing after work, and because of that, they were more distanced from the medium's habituating effects. Those people who turned to simultaneous viewing but who also turned, with some regularity, to other discrete activities, acted out of habit 53 percent of the time, a significant drop from the 90 percent reported by those who turned exclusively to simultaneous viewing. And unlike the exclusive simultaneous viewers, when these people described themselves as feeling relaxed as opposed to tired or stressed, after work, their orientation to things was significantly more mindful: at these more relaxed times they reported acting out of habit only 38 percent of the time. Continuing with this comparison, those who turned to television and other activities in the same way (with the same degree of mindfulness), but not at the same time (they didn't engage in simultaneous viewing), acted out of habit only 28.5 percent of the time, with this figure dropping even further, to 22 percent, when they described themselves as feeling relaxed after work. People in both of these groupings, then, continued to watch television after work, most of them simultaneously, yet their approach to things at this time was significantly more mindful than those who became involved in simultaneous viewing alone. Here, the very fact that there were variations in mindfulness means that a more complex sociality was taking shape as well.

For both of these groupings of people – those who participated in simultaneous viewing after work and those who did this at times but also turned to other discrete activities regularly – individually oriented and socially mediated activities were a routine part of what else they did, in addition to watching television, after work. They read books – science fiction, romance novels, and non fiction – as well as newspapers and magazines, and all of it provided them with an opportunity to think inside the social worlds represented there, sometimes reflecting on what they read, and perhaps drawing parallels to their own lives, or the lives of people that they knew. In a less self-conscious way, reading enabled them to try out imagined roles, or more simply, to sense what it may be like to live in some other time or place. Furthermore, book reading in particular is an activity that typically develops from one occasion to the next, providing the reader with a kind of mindful continuity that is for the most part absent in simultaneous viewing.

The same is true of conversation, another activity that was typical of the after-work routine for these groups. Sometimes, their conversations centered on run-of-the-mill kinds of things, such as what they wanted for dinner, what to buy, what to wear, and plans for visiting family or friends later in the week. These kinds of things surfaced somewhat randomly and they usually passed quickly from people's minds. At other times, the talk and interaction in the home was reported to be deeper and more meaningful.

For example, it was not uncommon for some people to say they became engaged in conversations about work, co-workers or supervisors, the progress of their children's schooling, and so on; and when that happened, it provided them with at least some insight, however momentary it might have been, about themselves, others, or their world. For example, Nancy, a packer, usually sat and talked with her co-workers at the end of their work day. In addition to the more obvious development of friendships that occurred in this activity, some if not most of the time these casual conversations provided her and her co-workers with some insight into the situations that they confronted at work, including the power relations intrinsic to the work process. They sometimes discussed such things as which of their supervisors was more responsive to problems with their machines, how supportive other workers (and supervisors) were when they complained or when they had ideas about correcting problems with a machine, and the pace of line production on particular shifts. But whether conversation was superficial or deep, like book reading, it afforded people opportunities for *developing* their relations with one another, and enabled them to experience meaningful continuities in their lives. This was true, I think, even when conflicts and tensions surfaced, because they, too, developed over time, and were integral to the ongoing nature of people's sense of themselves.

Besides reading and talking, there was a variety of other things that people did, too. They took walks (alone or with others), worked in the garden, made phone calls to family and friends, had drinks with co-workers, played with their children, went to meetings, played softball games, repaired cars, ate out, or went shopping. In all of this, they were active participants who controlled the pace of what they did, unlike what typically happened in simultaneous viewing. Conversation was often an integral part of these activities, and this alone allowed people to develop their relations with others and experience a continuous sense of themselves, as they did when they read or simply talked at home. But even as solitary activities, they were often highly mindful, because they exhibited continuity and a developmental course as people connected, in their minds, one occasion of their participation to the next. People had the opportunity to monitor and evaluate what they were doing as they did it; they also created a mindful space in which they could think about other things, unrelated to their participation in the activities themselves, and in this way gain insight about themselves or their world. Along these lines, Kim, a designer at a publishing company, said that painting and drawing, as opposed to simultaneous viewing, provided her with a means for creative expression in the after-work period, because when she paints or draws, she said, she is engaged in a continual process of translating ideas to paper (or canvas), testing them out, evaluating their outcome, and then redirecting her efforts accordingly. Similarly, Susan, a secretary, said that she routinely played with her baby daughter when she came home, and that for her this involved noticing the developments of her daughter's muscular coordination and her use of words. Beyond that, she said that the shared intimacy of this mother–daughter relation made it mindfully and emotionally fulfilling.

Compared to simultaneous viewing, all of these activities were, to different degrees of course, more mindful: people participated in them more actively than they did in simultaneous viewing; they were more likely to control the pace of their involvement, something that they didn't do with television at this time; they were also more likely to carry with them a sense of development as their discrete instances of involvement often built upon one another over time. People were able to gain insight about themselves and their world to a greater degree in these activities than in simultaneous viewing. Even though these people had become habituated to watching television in a relatively mindless way, they continued to act in more mindful and self-directive ways in other activities after work, sometimes choosing to do so rather than simply falling into the habit of watching television. And like those who were more exclusively oriented to simultaneous viewing, these people who pursued other activities thought about and became involved with television in a more mindful manner in the evening. So, here again, I am led to see habituation as a process, rather than a state of mind.

The functional use of television after work

By using television while simultaneously doing other things, people have in effect created a new activity, one in which the continual movements back and forth between watching or listening and doing other things allows them to not only shift the focus of their attention, but also to shift ground, mindfully speaking, between an activity (television viewing) which is generally receptive in nature, with no control over the pace, to other activities (cooking, cleaning, conversation, reading, etc.) that tend to require more active participation and allow for control over the pace. When they alternated their attention between different activities for any length of time, or when they became involved in different activities at the same time, it was no longer possible for them to maintain the kind of continuity that they might have had if they were focusing their attention on a single activity. When it came to activities that typically accompanied their simultaneous television use, people were active participants, and they usually controlled the pace of their involvement in these activities. In contrast, watching television almost always involves a more receptive form of participation, where the pace is not under the viewer's control. Of course, when a person switches between stations or watches recorded programs, there is control, to some extent, of the pace of involvement, even if the actual moments of watching are still basically receptive in nature. But for most people in my interviews, most of the time, the television was simply left on during simultaneous viewing, and they either followed what came on or ignored it as they saw fit. Active participation and the control over pace is continually interrupted and then reversed. It is this interruption and reversal of their mindful involvement that, in a peculiar sort of way, comes to define the continuity of simultaneous viewing.

Simultaneous viewing carries with it, then, a distinctive sociality, one that seems well suited to assisting people as they make the transition from work, where their minds usually have had to be focused on particular things outside themselves, to home life, where they have the opportunity to reorient their mindful and emotional experience back to themselves or their relationships with family and housemates. Although it sounds like a relatively simple adjustment to make, in actuality, shifting one's gears between work and home requires a certain space and time in which people's mindful and emotional experience can find a new and different grounding, one that enables them to reestablish control in their own lives. This kind of adjustment is further complicated by the fact that, if those I interviewed are representative, most people continue to be faced with work responsibilities of one sort or another (usually cooking and cleaning) when they arrive home from work. By providing people with a ready-made but constantly changing imaginary space that they can move in and out of at will, television in some sense frees people from these continued responsibilities, and more generally, from having to sustain a more focused kind of mindful involvement in any particular activity. All of this leads me to understand the sociality of simultaneous viewing less as habituation than as a *functional* use that people make of television in order to ease this transition from work to their home life, especially when it involves the continuation of work in one way or another. In using television for this purpose, people seem to be calling into question the need, so prevalent in our culture, to remain constantly productive by using their time efficiently, with clear goals or outcomes in mind. What is functional for them, at this time, is to disrupt the normalcy of productive activity.

This particular way of understanding simultaneous viewing is supported by the fact that the simultaneous viewers I interviewed in my study made certain choices in order to set up situations in which they did not need to maintain a high degree of mindful attention toward any one object that they became involved with after work. Furthermore, they expressed an awareness of their own (and others') motivations for becoming involved in this kind of television use in the first place. The language of their interview accounts indicated this. When they said such things as "television is just easier than doing anything else," or "with television, I don't have to think too much about anything," or "television gives me something to fall back on when I'm tired after work," or "with television, I don't have to think about *one* thing," they are seeing television, not as something that has become inscribed in their experience out of habit; rather, they see it as an object, as something separate from themselves. Furthermore, they recognize that other people, too, see television in this more distanced way. In doing so, they become mindful of a ritual significance of their own and others' simultaneous television use. Indeed, they become aware of simultaneous viewing as a distinctive form of their own cultural practice. Even though simultaneous viewing has become "habit" for people, and even though, over time, they have become "habituated" to it, this does not mean that they do not at the same time operate with an awareness of it *as* a habit, and in doing so, maintain, however much it is in the background, a knowledge of their own habituation to television as something socially constructed and therefore *changeable.*

This is not to say that this functional use of television is without unintended consequences. One of the most significant of these has to do with the effect that this kind of viewing has on the continuity and developmental course of people's involvement in other activities. Although this was not an issue when it came to preparing dinner or taking care of household responsibilities, it did become significant for some people when their intermittent attention to television interrupted, or displaced, the progressively interactive potential of conversation and social interaction with family members or housemates and, to a lesser extent, the continuity and developmental course of their reading, sewing, or other household projects and hobbies. When it comes to this issue, the interview accounts indicate that people had mixed feelings, and that they often held onto contradictory thoughts and feelings about television's role in their lives. On the one hand, conversation or social interaction in the after-work period was looked upon as just another activity, like preparing dinner or taking care of household responsibilities. In this sense, those I talked to didn't really want to become too mindfully engaged in talk and interaction. They often felt mindfully and emotionally drained by the demands of their work day, and they simply didn't have the energy for attentive participation in any activity, let alone conversation and meaningful interaction. At times like these, television came into play by taking their minds off such talk and interaction and substituting in its place the possibility for a more disengaged kind of involvement in its image-worlds. On the other hand, many of these same people who used television in this functional way also said that they sometimes felt guilty about not being able to be more attentive and focused when they were talking and interacting with one another around the house. They were quite open in acknowledging that if the television were not on as much as it was at this time, then they would probably have had more time – more "quality" time at that – for such talk and interaction with others. But practically in the same breath, they would go on to say that, in the past, they have been unwilling to alter their routine and give talk and interaction without television, or alternatively solitary activities, a more prominent place in their lives after work. Thoughts about the virtues of more and better communication are one thing; the reality of having to live everyday life, and meet the demands and responsibilities that it places upon people, is another. Some people even commented, jokingly of course, that they were not so sure that actually having more time to talk and interact would be a good thing. Better to leave well enough alone, they seemed to be saying. All joking aside, it appears that people wish to be able to remain somewhat disengaged from the demands of more mindful involvement at this time of transition.

Conclusion

People who regularly engage in simultaneous viewing also, at other times, become involved with television, other media, and other activities in more focused and normatively consistent ways. This should be clear from my earlier account, but I make the point again to dispel the impression that simultaneous viewing simply engulfs the time that these people spend away from work. In fact, in both simultaneous viewing and in the range of other activities that occur during their free time, people can and do cultivate a directive sense of self; they can and do experience the normalizing power of discourse that is exerted through storytelling conventions; and they can and do have moments, less in simultaneous viewing, when they *identify* themselves with the characters and the characters' actions depicted on television.

But beyond all of this, in simultaneous viewing there is a less clearly definable world of viewers' practical encounters with television, in which neither the discourses of programming, nor the identities that people have established in other areas of life, can provide them with the kind of consistency and coherence that has proven to be the hallmark of the productive individual who is believed to use television in a more discrete way.

In contrast to what cultural studies analysts understand as the dynamics of power and resistance, in simultaneous viewing people more often than not use their capabilities of self, *not* their identities, to *disengage* themselves from the storytelling conventions of programming. Even though they do not always "identify" with, or live inside, various discourses, or with various socially constructed determinations of themselves, they continue to make social claims over the time and space of their cultural world. And what is crucially important, because these social claims emerge from repeated encounters with image-worlds that are as fragmentary as they are discursively consistent, such claims cannot always take a cohesive, coherent, or integrated form. In fact, in simultaneous viewing people do not necessarily strive for consistency or coherence in what they do, at least not in ways that have typified our understanding of what television viewing, personhood, and cultural practice are about. While lacking cohesiveness, coherence, or direction in a conventional sense, these fleeting, constantly changing, and seemingly trivial relations that people have with programming in simultaneous use – relations that shape, in a similar way, their involvement in other activities, too – are indicative of a kind of practical knowledge that many people come to have as they attempt to meet work, family, and household responsibilities, as well as to negotiate the transitions that must routinely be made between these different aspects of their everyday lives. As a disengaged kind of sociality, simultaneous viewing is indicative of an emergent cultural form; one that enables people not to be implicated in the workings of television's discursive power. I have found that the distinctiveness and importance of this sociality cannot be subsumed under the markers of discourse, text, identity, or the interpretive dynamics of power and resistance.

As a quite common viewing practice, simultaneous viewing is also indicative of our entry, as a society, into a new historical era, one marked increasingly by the corporate production of goods, ideas, and imagery of all kinds – not just television imagery. The proliferation of corporately produced and distributed image-worlds is not only responsible for increasing fragmentation and the declining significance of community. Perhaps more importantly, it actually creates the conditions in which time-honored assumptions about the intersubjective basis of meaning, self, and identity-formation no longer apply, and people accept the fact that, in certain respects, they live in a culture that is not always, or only, normatively based.

As I see it, this is not simply another cycle or stage of modern dilemmas regarding individual identity and community formation. It is, instead, a distinctively postmodern condition. This proliferation of image-worlds generates disjunctures, a time and space of split-off experiences, in which continuity doesn't occur, meanings don't add up to anything, people no longer construct a developmental course to things, and unified experience is no longer a given. It also generates flows and interruptions of desire on a *social* level that is analogous to what, in the psychoanalytic literature, is theorized as an individual experience of unconscious processes. As a result, establishing boundaries of self becomes increasingly problematic, as does the very formation of a stable and coherent self – with its various identities – as a normatively based reference point for social action. And because this social field of unconscious processes is corporately produced, the formation of self and culture – whether we think of them as integrated or not – becomes a political concern that must be addressed.

None of this is really cause for celebration. Some writers, theorists, and critics have attempted to explore this postmodern condition in ways that point to patterns of identity-formation and cultural practice that are distinctive to it. In volume three of *The History of Sexuality*, for example, Foucault (1986) discusses the ability that people have to make judgments regarding the images of themselves that they confront in daily life. This reflexivity provides a line of escape from the discursive construction of subjectivity. Deleuze and Guattari (1983) theorize the "deterritorializations" and the "lines of flight" from ordered discourse – again, as a way of highlighting what is emergent in cultural practice. Rosaldo (1989) uses the construct of "borders" to illuminate how subjects move, create, or play with the disjunctures of discourses. In this way, he says, they disrupt the normalizing power of discourse, and emphasize its processual, and hence, changeable qualities. Anzaldua (1987) uses the construct of the mestiza to articulate how movements and shifts across and between discursive determinations make for a more fluid process of identity formation, one that recognizes and validates simultaneity and cultural difference. Butler (1990, 1995) proceeds with the idea in mind that the repetitions of discourse generate instabilities, gaps, and disjunctures in the workings of power, providing a space for transgressions of power to emerge. And Wellman (1993) speaks of blacks and Latinos in Los Angeles beginning to forge new, hybrid identities out of the disjunctures provided by their neighborhood borders.

Like these writers, theorists, and critics, I want to explore the kinds of social maneuvering and practical knowledge that emerge from the image-worlds of corporate culture. My documentation of the viewing culture, and in this essay my presentation of simultaneous viewing, represents a first step in this direction. In simultaneous viewing, people cultivated an *indifference* to much of what was held out in the storytelling conventions as normatively appropriate for them. They routinely distanced themselves from the normative reference points inscribed in the discourses of programming, and from their own identity positions, too. Theirs was a *disengaged* sociality. I document it in the viewing culture, but it is increasingly characteristic of how people *live* in an image-based culture. To be disengaged is to be situated outside the logic of social action depicted in images, but not outside the logic of images themselves. That is, mindfully speaking, people can place themselves outside the perspective of an "other" that requires a reflexive response from them. In doing so, they can continue to look at the people or characters who are located in the social action depicted in images, and observe from a distance what it is that they do. By suspending the more conventional dynamics of role-taking in this way, they can then see others, not as intersubjectively-based social actors, but *as images*. This image-based sociality can then be extended beyond their involvement in the image-worlds per se, to any variety of settings in which people routinely encounter one another, only now their relations are constructed through the projection of an image rather than by taking on more conventional interactionally based identities. People see others as the images they project, and in turn they expect to be seen by others as an image themselves. They become objects to each other and consequently, objects to themselves. They are, as T. J. Clark has said in discussing spectacle, "a separate something to be looked at" (Clark, 1984: 63).

This is not to say that the more conventional avenues of reading, listening, watching, buying, and interacting are not still important in the postmodern condition. They are. Nor is this to say that people do not have serious problems in trying to use conventional markers of self, meaning, and culture to craft themselves, and their lives, in normatively consistent ways. They do. Nevertheless, disengaged forms of sociality like simultaneous viewing exist and are probably on the rise, given the prevalence of corporately controlled image-worlds and their growing presence in people's everyday lives. As such, they are indicative of the challenges that sociologists face in explaining how people live everyday life *in* corporate culture, not outside of it.

REFERENCES

Adorno, Theodor 1945: A Social Critique of Radio Music. *Kenyon Review*, 7, 2.

—— 1957: How to Look at Television. In B. Rosenberg and D. White (eds), *Mass Culture: The Popular Arts in America*, New York: The Free Press.

—— 1974: The Stars Down to Earth. *Telos*, 19.

—— 1976: *Introduction to the Sociology of Music.* New York: Seabury.

Adorno, Theodor, and Horkheimer, Max 1972: *Dialectic of Enlightenment.* New York: Seabury.

Allen, Robert (ed.) 1987: *Channels of Discourse.* Chapel-Hill: University of North Carolina

Ang, Ien 1985: *Watching Dallas: Soap Opera and the Melodramatic Imagination.* London: Methuen.

Anzaldua, Gloria 1987: *Borderlands.* San Francisco: Spinsters/Aunt Lute.

Aronowitz, Stanley 1992: *False Promises.* Durham, NC: Duke University Press.

—— 1993: *Roll Over Beethoven.* Hanover, NH: Wesleyan University Press.

—— 1993: *Toward A Philosophy of the Act.* Austin: University of Texas.

Bakhtin, M. M. 1981: *The Dialogic Imagination*. Austin: University of Texas.

Barnet, Richard and Cavanagh, John 1994: *Global Dreams: Imperial Corporations and the New World Order*. New York: Simon and Schuster.

Barnouw, Erik 1975: *Tube of Plenty*. New York: Oxford University Press.

—— 1978: *The Sponsor: Notes on a Modern Potentate*. New York: Oxford University Press.

Barthes, Roland 1968: *Elements of Semiology*. New York: Schoken.

—— 1972: *Mythologies*. New York: Hill and Wang.

Baudrillard, Jean 1981: *For a Critique of the Political Economy of the Sign*. St Louis: Telos Press.

—— 1983: *Simulations*. New York: Semiotexte.

Bauman, Zygmunt, 1973: *Culture as Praxis*. London: Routledge and Kegan Paul.

Blumer, Herbert 1936: Social Attitudes and Non-symbolic Interaction. *Journal of Educational Sociology*, 9.

—— 1962: Society as Symbolic Interaction. In Arnold Rose (ed.), *Human Behavior and Social Processes*, Boston: Houghton Mifflin.

—— 1969: *Symbolic Interactionism*. New York: University of California.

Bourdieu, Pierre 1977: *Outline of a Theory of Practice*. Cambridge: Cambridge University Press.

Butler, Judith 1990: *Gender Trouble: Feminism and the Subversion of Identity*. New York: Routledge.

—— 1995: *Bodies That Matter*. New York: Routledge.

Carey, James 1988: *Media, Myths, and Narratives*. Beverly Hills: Sage.

—— 1989: *Communication as Culture*. Boston: Unwin Hyman.

Clark, T. J. 1984: *The Painting of Modern Life*. Princeton: Princeton University Press.

de Certeau, Michel 1984: *The Practice of Everyday Life*. Berkeley: University of California.

Delueze, Gilles and Parnet, Claire 1987: *Dialogues*. New York: Columbia.

Deleuze, Gilles and Guattari, Felix 1983: *Anti-Oedipus: Capitalism and Schizophrenia*. Minneapolis: University of Minnesota.

Denzin, Norman 1992: *Symbolic Interactionism and Cultural Studies*. Cambridge, MA: Blackwell.

Dewey, John 1934: *Art as Experience*. New York: Capricorn.

Eco, Umberto 1976: *A Theory of Semiotics*. Bloomington: University of Indiana Press.

—— 1972: Towards a Semiotic Inquiry into the Television Message. *Working Papers in Cultural Studies*, 3.

Fiske, John 1986a: Television: Polysemy and Popularity. *Critical Studies in Mass Communication* 3(4).

—— 1986b: British Cultural Studies and Television. In Richard Allen (ed.), *Channels of Discourse: Television and Contemporary Criticism*, Chapel Hill: University of North Carolina.

—— 1987: *Television Culture*. London: Methuen.

Fiske, John and Hartley, John 1978: *Reading Television*. New York: Methuen.

Foucault, Michel 1980: *The History of Sexuality, Volume I*. New York: Vintage.

—— 1985: *The Use of Pleasure: The History of Sexuality, Volume II.* New York: Vintage.

—— 1986: *The Care of the Self: History of Sexuality, Volume III.* New York: Vintage.

Gergen, Kenneth 1991: *The Saturated Self.* New York: Basic Books.

Gitlin, Todd 1978: Media Sociology. *Theory and Society,* 6(2), 205–54.

—— 1979: Prime-time Ideology: The Hegemonic Process in Television Entertainment. *Social Problems,* 26(3), 251–66.

—— 1983: *Inside Prime Time.* New York: Pantheon.

—— (ed.) 1986: *Watching Television.* New York: Pantheon.

Goffman, Erving 1959: *The Presentation of Self in Everyday Life.* Garden City, NJ: Doubleday.

—— 1979: *Gender Advertisements.* New York: Harper.

Grossberg, Lawrence 1987: The In-Difference of Television. *Screen* 28, 28–45.

—— 1988: It's a Sin: Postmodernity, Popular Empowerment and Hegemonic Popular. Paper presented at Rice University Conference on the Sociology of Television, Houston, TX.

Grossberg, Lawrence, Nelson, Cary, and Treichler, Paula (eds) 1992: *Cultural Studies.* New York: Routledge.

Hall, Stuart 1975: Television as a Medium and its Relation to Culture. Stencilled Occasional Paper, Centre for Contemporary Cultural Studies. Birmingham, UK.

—— 1980: Cultural Studies: Two Paradigms. *Media, Culture, and Society,* 2, 57–72.

Hall, Stuart, Jefferson, Tony (eds) 1976: *Resistance Through Rituals: Youth Subcultures in Post-war Britain.* London: Hutchinson.

Hall, Stuart, Connell, Ian, and Curti, Lydia (eds) 1976: The Unity of Current Affairs Television. *Working Papers in Cultural Studies,* 9.

Hall, Stuart, Hobson, Dorothy, Lowe, Andrew, and Willis, Paul (eds) 1980: *Culture, Media, Language.* London: Hutchinson.

Harvey, David 1989: *The Condition of Postmodernity.* Oxford: Basil Blackwell.

Hawkes, Terrence 1977: *Structuralism and Semiotics.* Berkeley: University of California Press.

Hewitt, John 1989: *Dilemmas of the American Self.* Philadelphia: Temple University Press.

Hoggart, Richard 1966: *The uses of Literacy.* Boston: Beacon.

Jacobs, Norman (ed.) 1961: *Culture for the Millions? Mass Media and Society.* Princeton: Van Nostrand Press.

Jameson, Fredric 1983: Postmodernism and Consumer Society. In Hal Foster (ed.), *The Anti-aesthetic: Essays on Postmodern Culture.* Port Townsend, WA: Bay Press.

—— 1991: *Postmodernism, or The Cultural Logic of Late Capitalism.* Durham, NC: Duke University Press.

Jenkins, Henry 1992: *Textual Poachers: Television Fans and Participatory Culture.* New York: Routledge.

Langer, Suzanne 1957: *Philosophy in a New Key.* Cambridge, MA: Harvard University Press.

Lazarsfeld, Paul, Berelson, Bernard, and Gaudet, Hazel 1948: *The People's Choice*. New York: Columbia University Press.

—— and Merton, R. 1977: Mass Communication, Popular Taste, and Organized Social Action. In W. Schramm and D. Roberts (eds), *The Process and Effects of Mass Communication*, Chicago: University of Illinois Press.

Lembo, Ron 1994: Is There Culture After Cultural Studies? In Jon Cruz and Justin Lewis (eds), *Reconceptualizing Audiences*, Denver: Westview.

Lembo, Ron and Tucker, Ken 1990: Culture, Television, and Opposition: Rethinking Cultural Studies. *Critical Studies in Mass Communication*, 7, 97–116.

Lewis, Justin 1991: *The Ideological Octopus*. New York: Routledge.

Long, Elizabeth 1990: Reading Groups and the Postmodern Crisis of Cultural Authority. *Cultural Studies*, 1, 30, 306–27.

Lull, James 1980: Family Communication Patterns and the Social Uses of Television. *Human Communications Research*, 7(3), 319–34.

—— 1990: *Inside Family Viewing: Ethnographic Research on Television's Audiences*. New York: Routledge.

Lynd, Robert and Lynd, Helen 1929: *Middletown: A Study in American Culture*. New York: Harcourt Brace.

Mead, G. H. 1932: *The Philosophy of the Present*. Chicago: University of Chicago Press.

—— 1934: *Mind, Self and Society*. Chicago: University of Chicago Press.

—— 1938: *The Philosophy of the Act*. Chicago: University of Chicago Press.

Merton, Robert 1968: *Social Theory and Social Structure*. New York: The Free Press.

Morley, David 1980: *The Nationwide Audience*. London: British Film Institute.

—— 1986: *Family, Television and Domestic Leisure*. London: Comedia.

—— 1994: *Television, Audiences, and Cultural Studies*. New York: Routledge.

Newcomb, Horace 1974: *TV: The Most Popular Art*. New York: Doubleday.

—— 1982: Television: *The Critical View*. New York: Oxford.

Poster, Mark 1990: *The Mode of Information*. Chicago: University of Chicago Press.

—— 1995: *The Second Media Age*. Cambridge: Polity Press.

Postman, Neil 1985: *Amusing Ourselves to Death: Public Discourse in an Age of Show Business*. New York: Viking.

Press, Andrea 1992: *Women Watching Television*. Philadelphia: University of Pennsylvania Press.

Radway, Janice 1984: *Reading the Romance*. Chapel Hill: University of North Carolina Press.

Rosaldo, Renato 1989: *Culture and Truth*. Boston: Beacon Press.

Rosenberg, Bernard and White, D. (eds) 1957: *Mass Culture: The Popular Arts in America*. New York: The Free Press.

Saussure, Ferdinand 1966: *Course in General Linguistics*. New York: McGraw-Hill.

Schudson, Michael 1984: *Advertising: The Uneasy Persuasion*. New York: Basic Books.

Seldes, Gilbert 1957: *The 7 Lively Arts*. New York: Sagamore Press.

Silverstone, Roger 1995: *Television and Everyday Life*. New York: Routledge.

Simpson, Philip 1987: *Parents Talking Television*. London: Comedia.

Spigel, Lynn 1992: *Make Room for TV: Television and the Family Ideal in Postwar America*. Chicago: University of Chicago Press.

Streeter, Thomas 1984: An Alternative Approach to Television Research: Developments in British Cultural Studies at Birmingham. In Donald Rowland and Bruce Watkins (eds), *Interpreting Television: Current Research Perspectives*. Beverly Hills: Sage.

Swanson, Guy E. 1965: On Explanations of Social Interaction. *Sociometry*, 28:2 101–23.

—— 1970: Toward Corporate Action: A Reconstruction of Elementary Collective Processes. In Tamotsu Shibutani (ed.), *Human Nature and Collective Behavior*, Englewood Cliffs, NJ: Prentice-Hall.

—— 1971: Frameworks for Comparative Research: Structural Anthropology and the Theory of Action. In Ivan Vallier (ed.), *Comparative Methods in Sociology*, Berkeley: University of California Press.

—— 1974: Family Structure and the Reflective Intelligence of Children. *Sociometry*, 37:4, 459–90.

—— 1978: Travels through Inner Space: Family Structure and Openness to Absorbing Experiences. *American Journal of Sociology*, 83:4, 890–919.

Tichi, Cecilia 1991: *Electronic Hearth: Creating an American Television Culture*. New York: Oxford University Press.

Wellman, David 1993: Honorary Homeys, Class Brothers, and White Negroes: Mixing Cultural Codes and Constructing Multicultural Identities on America's Social Borderlands. Paper presented at the American Sociological Association Annual Meetings, Miami Beach, Florida.

Williams, Raymond 1974: *Television, Technology, and Cultural Form*. London: Fontana.

—— 1982: *The Sociology of Culture*. New York: Schocken.

—— 1983: *Culture and Society*. New York: Columbia University.

Willis, Paul 1977a: *Learning to Labor*. London: Saxon House.

—— 1977b: The Man in the Iron Cage: Notes on Method. *Working Papers in Cultural Studies*, 9.

—— 1978: *Profane Culture*. London: Routledge, Kegan, Paul.

Winnicott, D. W. 1965: *The Maturation Processes and the Facilitating Environment*. Madison, WI: International Universities Press.

—— 1971: *Playing and Reality*. New York: Tavistock.

8

Facing Up to What's Killing Us: Artistic Practice and Grassroots Social Theory

GEORGE LIPSITZ

In Toni Cade Bambara's story *The Organizer's Wife*, members of a radical commune compress their beliefs into a simple slogan emblazoned across the front of a mural – "Face Up to What's Killing You" (Bambara, 1982: 16). The indecent social order of our own day renders the urgent anxiety encapsulated in that slogan relevant to grassroots cultural creation all across the globe. Performance artists and poets, graffiti writers and rappers, photographers and filmmakers, car customizers and computer hackers, create sights and sounds, poetry, prose, and performance art that turns talking back into an art form and enables their audiences to confront new conditions that are killing them.

The rise of satellite, computer-chip, and fiber-optic technologies, coupled with 20 years of neoconservative "structural adjustment policies," has created new economic, social, and cultural realities all over the world. The rapid movement of capital, commodities, and culture across the globe has transformed the meaning of politics and place. Since the start of the industrial era, the "old social movements" exemplified by social democratic and socialist political movements have based their strategies for social change on struggles over space, in efforts to control the neighborhood or the nation by trapping capital in one place in order to wrest concessions from it. But the mobility of capital has rendered those strategies incomplete. Today, municipalities, trade unions, and even nation-states compete to offer ever greater concessions to capital in the false hope that benefits will trickle down to the majority of the population. These arrangements inevitably fail, producing only a downward spiral of lower wages, wretched working conditions, and unmet social needs.

"New social movements" – community-based coalitions that emphasize democratic participation and address issues of culture, identity, and the environment – have great potential for linking local concerns with global realities, but while they have emerged everywhere in the world over the past two decades, they remain embryonic in form and largely untested in their capacity to meaningfully interrupt, much less reverse, the unprecedented power of transnational corporations and their agents like the International Monetary Fund and the World Bank (Fisher, 1993: 5–7).

The new social movements often address common cultural concerns and frequently make sophisticated strategic interventions on the terrain of culture, appropriating media technologies, forms of address, and channels of discourse for their own purposes. Yet the new social movements are also a product of cultural change. The reach and scope of mass media and their role in producing the prestige hierarchies of consumer culture have undermined the authority of cultural arbiters connected to traditional institutions – universities, conservatories, art museums, and publishing houses. At the same time, global marketing, grassroots cultural creation, and mass migration have produced new axes of affinity and identification that undermine old social movements and the social world that gave them determinate shape. As Robert Dunn argues in work that makes productive use of the insights of Anthony Giddens and Zygmunt Bauman, contemporary cultural expressions emerge out of profound dislocations in social relationships, out of a perception of the compression of time and space, out of the ways in which abstract meaning systems augment social relations and push them beyond local experiences, and out of the ways in which new social relations make it quite difficult for most people to see the structures that shape their lives or to comprehend how they belong to something called "society" in any meaningful way (Dunn, 1997).

New social movements shape and are shaped by culture in particularly profound ways. Similarly, the transformation of the spatial basis for politics and economics in the present (reflected in the emergence of new social movements) holds profound consequences for the creation, consumption, and circulation of culture in the future. During the industrial era, for example, Peetie Wheatstraw sang the blues to black workers in taverns along Biddle Street in St Louis. Reflecting the harsh realities that his listeners faced every day from racism and class subjugation. Wheatstraw billed himself as "the high sheriff from hell" and "the devil's son-in-law." In today's postindustrial world, Michael Jackson makes music and images that entertain young people on every continent, not as the "high sheriff from hell" or "the devil's son-in-law," but as the "king of pop" who is Elvis's son-in law. Wheatstraw lived a life very much like those of his listeners, and his nicknames reflected an understanding of how tough they had to be to survive economic exploitation and racial oppression. Industrial production created the preconditions for Wheatstraw's career, bringing rural blacks to the cities, paying them with the wages that sustained taverns and nightclubs, and providing them with their shared indignities and alienations that Wheatstraw's songs addressed. Michael Jackson, on the other hand, has been a celebrity since he was a child, entering different stages of his listeners' lives as a media icon with a new image each time. Postindustrial society has created a global market in need of commodities that can transcend the limits of immediate experiences and local conditions; Jackson's skills as a singer and dancer, his superb sense of style and fashion, and his fascination with other celebrities, plays to the needs and preoccupations of mass media in the postindustrial era. His home town of Gary, Indiana has much in common with Wheatstraw's depression-era St Louis, but Jackson's real homes are the video screens and the compact disc players that make him part of people's lives all around the world.

Something more than matters of biography and personal idiosyncrasy divide Peetie Wheatstraw and Michael Jackson. Their different trajectories represent different systems of cultural production. The industrial communities, nation-states, social movements, and civic institutions that supported and subsidized cultural production in the industrial era have lost power and influence in the postindustrial age. Transnational corporate marketeers and "philanthropic" foundations increasingly determine the nature, reach, and scope of the most available forms of art, music, drama, poetry, and prose (Canclini, 1992: 33). Traditions of cultural contestation based upon the creation of free spaces or liberated zones independent of commercial culture – for example, efforts to preserve preindustrial folklore and folkways, to fashion "oppositional" cultures out of common experiences of race, ethnicity, and gender, or to invent an avant-garde art capable of contesting the categories of commercial culture – now seem decidedly obsolete. Instead, even artists from the most aggrieved communities seem inescapably drawn to the networks, circuits, and sites of cultural production generated by the new transnational economy (Harvey, 1989; Jameson, 1991; Lipsitz, 1994).

Cultural production today takes place in circumstances where one-third of the world's private sector productive assets are owned by transnational corporations. "Structural adjustment policies" favored by neoconservative governments and global financiers have imposed trade liberalization, privatization of public enterprises, higher interest rates, lower wages, currency devaluation, and drastic reductions in social spending on transportation, housing, and healthcare. Thus, the growing wealth of transnational corporations has been made possible by the growing misery of millions of people. Nearly 30 percent of the world workforce (820 million people) work at less than subsistence wages or are unemployed. The richest fifth of the world's population receives 150 times as much income as the poorest fifth. During the 1980s alone in Asia, Africa, and Latin America, the gap between rich and poor doubled (Gallin, 1994: 106; Wright, 1995: H1; Budhoo, 1994: 22).

Cultural commodities play a crucial role in the transnational economy. Media monopolies seek the economies of scale attendant to global marketing, creating transnational status symbols and hierarchies of prestige in the process. Yet the very forces of production and consumption most responsible for bringing the world together through common signs and symbols also generate and expose grotesque inequities that divide people as much as ever. The young women in Indonesia who make the "Air Jordan" athletic shoes receive around $1.35 per day in factories and workshops subcontracted by the Nike Corporation. Nike spends about $5.60 on materials and labor for each pair of shoes produced, but sells them for $45–80 per pair. The women workers in Indonesia would need 320 hours' wages to purchase one moderately priced pair of the shoes that they make.

At the same time, Nike pays basketball star Michael Jordan $20 million every year to endorse their brand. Jordan's fame is more lucrative than his work; he receives five times as much money for simply endorsing Nike shoes than he gets for actually playing basketball for the Chicago Bulls. His fame is also more valuable than the labor of the workers who make the shoes that carry his name. The fee paid to Jordan for this endorsement exceeds the total wages that Nike pays to its combined workforce in all six of the factories under contract to produce the company's shoes (Barnet and Cavenagh, 1994: 325–9).

The athletic shoes that bring extraordinary wealth to Michael Jordan (and even more to those who employ him) hold a variety of different meanings for different populations. The low-wage women workers in Indonesia who produce the shoes face exploitation, austerity, repressive surveillance, and unsafe working conditions that are completely hidden from consumers by a brand name, a celebrity endorsement, and technologies that allow for the separation of management, production, advertising, and consumption. At the same time, the popularity of Nike shoes with affluent consumers rests on another association, on their reputation as the preferred fashion among impoverished inner-city African-American youth. Along with graffiti writing, break dancing, and rap music, "street" styles based on athletic wear contain important symbolic meanings, functioning as expressions of "prestige from below" emblematizing the sense of style, self-assertion, and even rebellion associated with African-American inner-city culture. Thus, part of their popularity stems from their significance as part of a symbolic rebellion against the very global urban austerity economy that makes their production possible.

Yet these athletic shoes also enjoy enormous popularity among genuinely dispossessed and aggrieved young people from oppressed communities of color in countries around the globe, paradoxically as both icons of inclusion into the global consumer economy *and* as symbols of a global pan-ethnic anti-racist youth culture. Maghreb and French youths in the inter-racial hip-hop group IAM in Marseilles, the Surinam/Dutch rapper Def Rhymes from Amsterdam, and the Maori hip-hop activists from

Wellington, New Zealand calling themselves the Upper Hutt Posse all belong to what MC Solaar, the African/French rapper from Paris, calls "the cult of the sneaker" (Lipsitz, 1994: 63, 123; van Elteren, 1994: 200).

Of course, in some cases, much is lost in transnational translation. The Osdorp Posse in the Netherlands attempted to appropriate African-American slang to the Dutch language when they told their audiences "Beneden met vrede," signifying that they were "down" with peace, that they approved of it. But taking them literally, audiences thought the group was saying "down with peace" and booed them lustily (van Elteren, 1994: 200). On other occasions, however, transnational communication augments rather than diminishes understanding. Explaining the interest in hip hop among Maoris in New Zealand, journalist Kerry Buchanan argues:

> With our links to the land broken, our alienation from the mode of production complete, our culture objectified, we have become marginalized and lost. This is not to say beaten. And this is what we have in common with Black America. When Maori hip-hop activists Upper Hutt Posse visited America recently, these political, social and racial links were brought into perspective. Upper Hutt Posse were welcomed as people involved in a common struggle, linked symbolically through hip-hop culture. (Buchanan, 1993: 27)

The idea that Maoris from New Zealand would express their unique and particular grievances through the language of black nationalists in the African-American inner city seems a quintessentially contemporary development, a connection made possible only by the transnational reach and scope of mass media. But it would be more accurate to say that some of the most creative uses of contemporary media come from cultures with long histories of dispossession and diaspora who see families of resemblance between their circumstances and those of people far away. Sometimes, the family ties turn out to be more direct than they know. For example, when the members of Upper Hutt Posse appropriate lyrics, music, and political stances from African-American rap groups associated with the Nation of Islam, including Poor Righteous Teachers, Big Daddy Kane, and Brand Nubian, they may feel a powerful but largely symbolic connection. Yet the nation of Islam actually does have some Maori roots. The man known as W. D. Fard, the prophet saluted by Elijah Muhammed as the key force behind the forming of the Nation of Islam in the 1930s, appeared to be an Arab to some acquaintances and a "dark complected Mexican" to others. But in actuality, W. D. Fard was Wallace Dodds Ford, born in Hawaii in 1891 to a white British father, Zared Ford, and a New Zealand Maori mother, Beatrice Ford (Evanzz, 1992: 142). This is not to claim any "race memory" or secret Maori symbols sedimented within hip hop, but it is to suggest that the same decentered experience with race

that made Wallace Ford one of the founders of an important black nationalist group may well have made the messages of North American black
nationalism credible and convincing to Upper Hutt Posse. The Nation of
Islam and other black nationalist groups have drawn some of their appeal
to inner-city North American blacks precisely by preaching an international connection among people of color, by describing American
blacks as not only African, but Asiatic. As Lisa Lowe argues, transnational
encounters produce contradictory subjects with finely honed capacities
for what might seem to others like unlikely coalitions (Lowe, 1996).

The "cult of the sneaker," rap music, and subaltern struggles for municipal services in cities around the world, have complex and complicated
points of conjuncture and contradiction. It is difficult to know if the global
popularity of hip hop represents the ultimate triumph of commodity capitalism or the sophisticated subversion of new communications technologies; the final consolidation of a global market or the first stirrings of
social movements as mobile and flexible as transnational capital itself.
Low-wage women laborers in Asia and oppressed inner-city African-
American youths play crucial roles in creating products that circle the
globe while they remain confined to dead-end jobs and dangerous neighborhoods. Transnational culture both highlights and obscures new connections among people, places, and politics. In that context, efforts by
innovative artists from aggrieved communities to turn the terms and tor-
ments of urban life into art take on special meaning.

Contemporary Los Angeles conceptual, performance, and spoken-word
artists Harry Gamboa, Jr, Luis Alfaro, and Marisela Norte demonstrate the
complexities and contradictions of cultural production in the postindustrial
city. Firmly grounded in the history, politics, and aesthetics of Chicano life
in Los Angeles, their art engages with commodities and commercialized
leisure, with the instability of identities, and with the ways in which new
communication technologies and social relations erase old affiliations while
generating new ones. They create an art that moves, that rides the circuits
of commodity circulation and turns them into a new public sphere, into
a discursive space that has no fixed physical home.

As one of the "world" cities created by deindustrialization, economic
restructuring, and globalization, Los Angeles has felt the full impact of
urban austerity. Some 40,000 young people (nearly 20 percent of the city's
16- to 19-year-olds) have no jobs and are not in school (Waters, 1992: 26–
7). In poverty-stricken areas of the city, 22 out of every 1,000 babies die
in infancy, a figure far worse than that of many impoverished "Third
World" countries (Hamilton, 1992: 20). Close to 500,000 full-time workers
in the city earn less than $10,000 per year, and one out of every four Los
Angeles city residents has no health insurance of any kind (Mann, 1991:
7). The State of California has tripled its prison population over the past

decade; the state now spends more on corrections than on colleges. Los Angeles police officers arrested more than 50,000 young people during their well-publicized Operation Hammer, designed to identify and harass suspected gang members, although nearly every reliable study shows nowhere near that many gang members in the city. The ultimate effect of this action was not to reduce gang activity, but to tag as many inner-city youths as possible with "criminal" records to be used against them in the future, to disqualify them from employment opportunities, and to disenfranchise them politically (Cooper, 1992: 15).

Mass migration from around the world has made Los Angeles the second largest Mexican, Filipino, Armenian, Salvadoran, and Guatemalan city in the world, the third largest Canadian city, and a metropolis with more Samoans than American Samoa itself (Naficy, 1994). A center of global culture with highly concentrated film, music, and television industries, Los Angeles is also the home of innovative artists whose creations stem directly from the contradictions between local conditions and global realities. By facing up to the things that are killing them and their communities, they have a great deal to teach us about the world that is emerging all around us.

Harry Gamboa, Jr grew up in a monolingual Spanish-speaking family in East Los Angeles in the 1950s and 1960s. During his first day at school, the teacher ordered him to use scissors, construction paper, and glue to make a "dunce" cap for himself. But instead of writing the word "dunce," Gamboa was instructed to write "Spanish" on the cap and forced to wear it in front of the entire class until he learned to speak English. Looking back on the incident years later, he muses that ever since that day he has been engaged in a crusade to undermine the reliability of the English language (Gamboa, 1993). Toward that end, his art features irony, puns, and double entendres that undermine the stability of words, and he inserts his work into existing circuits and networks of public relations and mass media like community newspapers or evening news reports to introduce contingency and chance into what seem like reliable narratives about civic life.

An accomplished painter, filmmaker, and performance artist, Gamboa prefers to make art that intervenes subtly in already existing channels and conduits of information. For example, he takes pictures of strangers, gives them invented names, and writes fictional stories about them – portraying them receiving an award from the King of Sweden, retiring from a distinguished career in the military, or giving a forthcoming speech before a service club. He then sends his stories off to small community newspapers as "press releases." The papers often publish these stories in unedited form because of their perpetual need for copy. Another project entails making videos of real and staged street scenes, and then sending copies to the first 20 people listed under the name "Rodriguez" in the telephone book. Some years ago, Gamboa pioneered the concept of "No Movies," staging scenes to make city streets look like sites of gang shootings or suicides in hopes of enticing local television news crews into covering events that had not happened, but also responding to a shortage of equipment and supplies by finding a way to make "movies" without cameras and film (ibid). On occasion, his staged events have appeared on the evening news as purported "gang" shootings. By placing his "art" in community newspapers, home video screens, or broadcast news, Gamboa feels that he is intervening in the circuits that make meaning for people. If people discover his fabrications, he feels that it makes them question their standard sources of information. But even when his authorship remains completely undetected, Gamboa feels that he is injecting art within zones created solely for the convenience of commerce.

Gamboa tries to make his art as mobile and as ephemeral as the everyday life experiences of the postindustrial city. He carries a video camera with him at all times and tries to record moments of danger, anger, and fear. When family members or friends start arguing he asks them to extend those emotions by improvising on scenarios that he presents to them. These scenes often involve people negotiating the most desperate precincts of the inner city and attempting to fend off disaster in their personal lives as their support structures crumble around them.

Why would a recognized artist whose works have been exhibited in museums and lauded by distinguished critics choose to work covertly and anonymously in sites that no one associates with art? Part of Gamboa's motivation stems from resentment at the pervasive power of publicity and public relations, at the ways in which powerful communications media are used to obscure rather than illuminate the lives people lead. "Horrible tragedies don't seem to be tragedies" once the media has processed them, he asserts. At the same time, the things that are held up to be desirable "are either things you would never want to do, or things that are completely unattainable anyway" (ibid). By luring newspapers and television stations into lies of his own making, Gamboa attempts to insulate himself and his audience from the lying that goes on every day under the guises of news, information, and entertainment. By creating sporadic but independent channels of production and reception, he hopes to dramatize how dependent people are on sources, circuits, and sites controlled by others.

Gamboa's art engages directly with the logic of time and space in the postindustrial city. He prefers photography, print, performance, and video art to painting, plays, and film because the former entail very short "turnaround" times: they emerge as finished products almost immediately. He chooses to emphasize transitory moments rather than monumental artifacts because he senses that he lives in a world where there is only the present. "Everyone feels they're in the line of fire," he explains. "There is no such thing as a long view, everything is a short take." Driving Los Angeles freeways, Gamboa may encounter as many as one million people, but he rarely sees anyone he recognizes. "I've lived here since I was born in 1951, but some times I feel that maybe everyone I know is gone" (ibid). His art emphasizes the immediacy of the moment rather than any sustained sense of project, reflecting the sense of dizzying and debilitating change engendered by fast capital.

At one time, Gamboa seemed to be an artist firmly connected to a place and to a community. He grew up in East Los Angeles, in a Mexican-American community with distinct artistic practices displayed everywhere – in calendars distributed by local businesses, in graffiti and murals, in low rider cars, in the paint used to decorate homes and advertise businesses. He participated in the Chicano movement as a student activist and as an editor and contributor to the community journal *Regeneracion*. But today, the neighborhood centers and youth clubs that taught him about art are closed due to the fiscal crisis imposed on the state by 20 years of neo-conservative cuts in taxes and social services. Transportation to museums is more expensive, travel through inner-city neighborhoods more danger-ous, and the museums themselves more costly to enter. Some 600,000 Spanish-speaking migrants from Central America have changed what it means to be Chicano in Los Angeles, and the Latino population has spread far beyond East Los Angeles to what is known as "South Central," as well as to industrial suburbs in the southeast corridor where they experience new kinds of coalition and conflict with African-Americans, Asian-Americans, Pacific Islanders, and Anglos. Rather than retreating back into the physical space of East Los Angeles and the art that it spawned 20 years ago, Gamboa carries East Los Angeles with him, fashioning a fugitive art that is at home everywhere precisely because it has no home, because it deals directly with displacement, circulation, and speed.

Just as Harry Gamboa, Jr draws artistic inspiration from changes that have come too quickly, Luis Alfaro devises performance pieces that point to the changes that have not come quickly enough – the happiness that has never happened despite all the promises made by popular culture and political leaders (Alfaro, 1994). Alfaro's stories proceed from personal memories – about his aunt dying of cancer, about traveling to Delano as a child to march with Cesar Chavez and the United Farm Workers, about decorative objects in his childhood home, about the Los Angeles rebellion of 1992. He contrasts and correlates sentimental songs, popular television shows, and advertising slogans with the material and political depriva-tions of aggrieved communities. Alfaro puts on performances that address other performances – both the popular-culture stories that have been per-formed for us in romance novels, on television, and in the movies, as well as the multiple social "roles" that we "perform" every day.

From his perspective as a gay Chicano, Alfaro explores the intersections of nationality, sexuality, and class in the postindustrial city. His ethnicity inflects his identity as a gay man, while his homosexuality shapes the ways he experiences being Chicano. Sexual and racial identities intersect in his art, not so much as twin oppressions as much as complicated sources of empathy and insight. Alfaro shows how social forces shape sexual and racial identities, moving deftly among a broad range of institutions and images including the Catholic Church, commercial television, household objects, and political struggles.

One of Alfaro's most popular and moving pieces concerns *The Huggy Boy Show*, a televised rock'n'roll dance party hosted by Dick Hugg, a popular Los Angeles disc jockey. As a pioneer of rock'n'roll radio in Los Angeles during the 1950s who hosted live shows in El Monte, Pomona, and other cities with large Chicano populations, Huggy Boy holds special meaning for Mexican-Americans throughout southern California. Alfaro turns Hugg's stage name into an unintentional pun by recalling a teenage crush on one of the males who appeared regularly on *The Huggy Boy Show*. By wanting to hug a boy from *The Huggy Boy Show*, Alfaro brings a Chicano accent to an articulation of gay desire while revealing the sexual heterogeneity of the mostly Chicano audience for the program.

Alfaro conflates popular culture, Chicano identity, and gay experience in another piece based on memories of watching televised roller derby matches as a child. Alfaro roller skates on stage (and often through the crowd) while wearing a dress and talking about his memories of watching Ralph Valladares, a macho Chicano roller derby star of the 1950s and 1960s. By identifying himself with one of the few Chicano roller derby stars (and one of the few Chicanos visible on television at all in those years), Alfaro taps both popular culture and ethnic memories, yet interrogates them at the same time from the perspective of gender roles and sexual preference.

In one of his most poignant pieces, Alfaro dons a dress and speaks in thickly accented English to present himself as "Lupe," a woman out for a good time on a Saturday night, someone whose self-affirmation and sense of style masks a desperate desire to block out the day-to-day realities of her life as a woman, as an ethnic "minority," and as a low-wage worker. Alfaro shows how dressing up and dancing and looking for love help people to stay alive, to stay human, to endure the indignities of daily life and still hope for something better in the future.

By working his way back through memories of roller derby, *The Huggy Boy Show*, and women claiming space for themselves on the dance floor of a neighborhood club, Alfaro situates himself as someone whose important artistic and public spaces have come from his identities as a popular culture consumer, as part of an ethnic community, and as a member of a sexual minority with a long and particular history of performance and spectatorship in dance and athletics. His recollections are not nostalgic hymns of praise to a lost community, but rather a conjuring up of lost possibilities, a reworking of spaces in which he never felt comfortable into scenes that can be used to discover the things that unite us as well as the things that divide us in the present.

By demonstrating the conjunctural, composite, and intersectional nature of identities in his own past, Alfaro offers a constructive and instructive example of how to deal with anxieties about the multiple identities that postindustrial society demands from us. He shows how to make creative use of contradictions and conflicts, to use anxieties about identities to augment rather than diminish our capacity to connect to a wider world. Yet his performances offer no simple celebration of difference; on the contrary, they bring to the surface some of the differences that make a difference, such as homophobia, racism, and class oppression. Through his performances, Alfaro brings to the surface the often suppressed struggles about identity that characterize much of postindustrial society. Lisa Lowe (1991) has theorized these struggles brilliantly in relation to ethnicity by focusing on categories that also hold great relevance to the lessons we can learn from Luis Alfaro's art – heterogeneity, hybridity, and multiplicity. His performances expose the heterogeneity of all the groups that might claim his allegiance; they show that gays, Chicanos, the working class, or popular-culture consumers are not monolithic or homogeneous groups, but rather coalitions of heterogeneous elements. His performances demonstrate the hybridity of his culture, memories that have attachments to commerical television as well as the Teatro Campesino, to displays of gay "camp" as well as to demonstrations about civil rights, peace, and gay rights. Most of all, his art displays the multiplicity of roles open to any one individual, building investment and engagement with audiences by showing how the different identities that define us coexist uneasily with one another.

Like Alfaro and Gamboa, spoken-word artist Marisela Norte draws both the form and content of her work from the conflicts and communities she finds in the postindustrial city. In a city designed for automobile transportation, Norte has no driver's license and rides the bus to work downtown every day from her East Los Angeles home. For many years, she let the length of her trip on the bus determine the length of her poems: when she reached her stop, the poem ended. Of course, Los Angeles's public transportation system is so bad that she probably had time to write an epic on most trips. But by taking a moving bus as a source and site for artistic practice, Norte incorporates movement and circulation into the process of her poetry as well as into the final product.

Norte populates her poems with the people she meets on the bus and sees through its windows, blending their experiences together with images from popular songs, imaginary headlines from tabloid newspapers ("Bored Housewife Falls in Love With Jesus"), and advertising signs. In one of the world's great fashion centers and retail shopping cities, Norte goes to second-hand discount stores to document *las vidas de ellas*, the lives of the women of Los Angeles, especially the Latinas who compensate for the low-wage labor and sexual harassment in their lives by constructing "looks" for themselves with make-up, attitude, and clothes that they purchase at discount stores (Norte, 1991). She describes the clothes that her characters wear as items that have the label cut out, referring to the practice of discount stores to remove labels so they can sell brand-name items for less than the suggested retail price. But she makes a pun on that practice in describing her own aversion to being "labeled" simply as a woman, or as a Chicana, or as a worker, explaining "I'm the one who cut the label out."

In spoken-word performances replete with Spanish, English, and interlingual puns, Norte details the dangers that await women in the city. Inadequate public transportation and street harassment make getting to work unpleasant, and render going out for pleasure practically impossible. Patriarchal attitudes in the Chicano community provoke her protests. "My father put bars on my bedroom before I was born" she asserts in one poem, referring to the "burglar bars" that people in poor neighborhoods use to protect their homes from criminals, but also to the psychic and emotional barriers to sexual pleasure that Norte experienced within her own culture. In one poem, suppression of information about family planning and birth control lead to an unwanted pregnancy and an anguished abortion, the effects of which Norte's narrator describes eloquently in an interlingual rhyme "Estoy destroyed" ("I am destroyed"). Norte learned English from the mass media, comic books, and public school classes because her Spanish-speaking father banned the use of English in their home. Her reminiscences about conversations with her Mexican cousins emphasize her discomfort with both Mexico and the US, and her wonder at the misconceptions and mistranslations that binational identity engenders. Norte makes especially effective use of her off-centered reception of some English phrases, as in the poem where her narrator talks about a frosty dinner with hostile prospective in-laws who serve her "punch" and "cold cuts" (Habell-Pallan, 1995: 11, 15).

Although she has participated in Chicano art groups in East Los Angeles for more than 20 years, Norte's art has been completely neglected by the cultural institutions of her city. She has never received support from the city's main artistic and cultural institutions, although she recently received her first grant to make art from the Rapid Transit District. She has never had her work published in a poetry journal or anthology, and has secured no visiting appointments as artist-in-residence at local colleges or universities. She does, however, have a devoted, indeed a fanatical, following among young women who purchase compact discs and cassettes of her spoken-word art released on New Alliance Records at underground raves and her own readings. Her art reaches its listeners through conduits every bit as circuitous as the Los Angeles city bus routes that inspired it in the first place. Norte's devoted female fans, who see much of their own story registered for the first time in her spoken-word art, regularly secure invitations for her to read her work before community and school groups, and her work is assigned often in college classrooms. But the poet who produces it makes her living as an office worker and museum ticket-taker, unconnected to the ongoing work of educators and arts institutions.

Like Alfaro and Gamboa, Marisela Norte fills her work with references to popular culture – to Mexican and US motion pictures, television programs, and popular music – using the unstable dialogue between national cultures and the peculiar preoccupations within each to bring to the surface all the inequalities, injustices, and private anxieties glossed over by both transnational and national cultures. Harry Gamboa, Jr, Luis Alfaro, and Marisela Norte address issues of identity and culture of tremendous importance to the contemporary urban environment of Los Angeles. They proudly proclaim their Chicano identities, but refuse to be reduced to them, staking out roles for themselves as citizens, gendered subjects, and sexual beings as well as members of one ethnic group. They demonstrate knowledge about the past and display respect for it, but their art emerges out of present concerns and conditions. None of them work within mainstream commercial culture or within the avant-garde art forms favored by cultural institutions, but they repeatedly engage popular culture products and canonized art works in the decisions they make about their art. They use the city itself as a site for art, as a source of inspiration, and ultimately, as what is at stake in art and in politics, i.e. what kinds of communities we live in.

Twenty years ago, artists with the commitments and interests of Gamboa, Alfaro, or Norte might well have thought of themselves as representatives of a discrete, homogeneous, identifiable Chicano community. But two decades of plant closings, economic restructuring, migration from Central America and Asia, declines in real wages, and defunding of community institutions have changed what it means to be Chicano. At the same time, the rise of feminism, gay and lesbian organizations, environmental coalitions, and interracial youth subcultures organized around punk rock and hip hop have created new axes of identification. Gamboa, Alfaro, and

Norte work within widely recognized traditions of Chicano art, but their creations are also acclaimed and claimed as their own by women, gays and lesbians, youth, and urban social activists.

The political implications of the art created by Gamboa, Alfaro, and Norte extend beyond the internal content of their work to the social networks and matrices in which they are located. Community-based cultural production in Los Angeles draws upon a broad range of participants who represent a diverse group of institutions. In February 1995, for example, students from the California State University at Northridge Chapter of MEChA (Moviemiento Estudantil Chicano/a de Aztlan) staged a "happening." It featured Chicano rappers, comedians, musicians, and the theater group Teatro Por La Gente ("theatre for the people/community") performing "social/political/cultural Edu-drama-dies." Proceeds helped to fund a suit against the University of California regents by a prominent Chicano Studies professor. The same weekend, Chicano singers, artists, poets, and Japanese taiko drummers joined Mexican "rock en espanol" groups and the African-American poets/rappers The Watts Prophets at a warehouse loft owned by Chicano heavy metal musician Zack De La Rocha of Rage Against The Machine. The event was in support of the LA Chapter of the National Commission for Democracy in Mexico, which used the proceeds to fund supplies to the EZLN rebels fighting against the Mexican government in Chiapas. A journalist writing in the hip-hop magazine *Urb* described the weekend's events as "a new culture with roots in the old and appreciation for the art of people who need to be heard whether anyone likes it or not" (Meraz, 1995: 69).

De La Rocha and Rage Against the Machine embody many of the most important features of contemporary cultural politics. De La Rocha was born in Lincoln Heights in East Los Angeles, the center of the Chicano community in Los Angeles since the 1930s, but he soon moved to a suburban and largely Anglo neighborhood in Irvine when his parents divorced. His music mixes together aspects of inner city *barrio* culture with the hardcore punk rock popular among white suburban youths to form a hybrid that creates a new synthesis among hip hop, heavy metal, and hardcore. In the 1960s, De La Rocha's father, mural artist Roberto de la Rocha (*sic*), worked with Harry Gamboa, Jr to help found a Chicano artists' collective, Los Four, and the vision of that group remains an inspiration for Rage Against the Machine. As the younger De La Rocha explains,

> During that time period, there seemed to be an incredible push for Chicanos to become a self-determined people. We wanted to identify ourselves, that was the thing. Los Four intended on making sure that throughout their artwork they could make our experiences tangible and also to reestablish

a part of our culture that had been lost, pointing out that we were originally an indigenous people. Pointing out that we aren't a disposable community. (Arenas, 1996: 60)

As a participant in the hardcore scene, De La Rocha embraced music as an alternative world, as a way of avoiding the alienating low-wage work increasingly characteristic of the postindustrial economy. "The root of our fear in the hardcore scene," he relates, "was always the question of how we could live and keep this lifestyle. That was the fundamental rally cry in our hearts, you know?" "We're not going to be wage slaves! We're not going to work nine-to-five!" But sometimes that comfort takes away so much of what made this music vital and what made what we were doing so important" (ibid: 62).

Confronted with the limits that even an "alternative" subculture imposes, De La Rocha rediscovered politics. He went to Mexico to meet with representatives of the Zapatista National Liberation Front, and began to work with the National Commission for Democracy in Mexico on behalf of the EZLN and against the free-trade agreement and the disastrous conditions it imposed on the indigenous people of southern Mexico. De La Rocha views the situation in Chiapas as a harbinger of what might happen in the US, of the destruction caused by people who "envision progress through cash-flow reports" (ibid: 61). He uses his celebrity status to promote intercultural fundraising events at his loft in Los Angeles, but also to use the conduits of commercial culture to call attention to social conditions. "Even getting a mention of the Zapatistas in a paper, that in itself can end all of this," he argues, referring to the US role in suppressing and oppressing the people of Mexico (ibid). At the same time, he has been active in supporting Regeneracion, a Chicano cultural center in Highland Park. The center takes its name from a Chicano magazine of the 1960s that in turn took its name from the official journal of the Mexican Liberal Party published by the Magon brothers during their exile in the US in the last years of the Diaz dictatorship. "The only way that Rage Against the Machine could see a substantial change in our lifetime is to ensure that our resources and ideas are integrated into the community," De La Rocha contends.

I have to make sure that this band doesn't become a removed entity from the grassroots. The center here is to provide a space for dialogue. When a person's sense of political action rests solely on pulling a ballot box every four years, there's going to be a sense of desperation because its been proven to fail in bringing about changes that the working poor need. Especially in a community like this one. (Ibid)

The other members of Rage Against the Machine share De La Rocha's politics, but not his exact social location. Thomas Morello was born in

Harlem, where his father was a Kenyan delegate to the United Nations and his mother a civil rights activist. After his parents divorced he grew up in a predominately white suburb of Chicago. He majored in social studies and graduated from Harvard in 1986, and moved to Los Angeles to play music. Frustrated by the music industry, he became scheduling secretary for Alan Cranston, one of California's United States senators. "That was sort of a last-gasp effort to work within the system," Morello relates.

> Cranston was probably as far left of a Senator as you're going to get, but it didn't really matter. Despite the fact that he had progressive views on the environment or immigration, he spent all day on the phone calling the wealthy and the powerful, exchanging favors for campaign money. I realized that once he was elected, who would he owe? Would he owe single mothers of the homeless and the guy working at Kentucky Fried Chicken, or would he owe ITT, GE, and other savings and loan tycoons? (Ibid: 58)

Morello and De La Rocha work in areas of commercial culture more mainstream and more influential than those accessible to Harry Gamboa, Jr, Luis Alfaro, and Marisela Norte. But they share with them a desire for social connection and a determination to use new methods to accomplish old ends. In a city where low-wage labor, mass migration, racism, sexism, and homophobia compound the alienations and indignities of everyday life for millions of people, Gamboa, Alvaro, and Norte face up to the things that are killing them and their communities. They are not alone in their endeavors. The work they do is shared, not just by artists with access to the powerful publicity outlets surrounding commercial culture, but by visual and conceptual artists in other communities as well. For example, San Diego artists David Avalos, Louis Hock, and Deb Small produced a particularly creative and provocative means of using art to expose the hidden realities behind the emerging transnational economy in their "Art Rebate." Avalos, Hock, and Small secured federal funding for a project where they drew designs on dollar bills and handed them out to undocumented Mexican immigrant workers in San Diego. They used the normal processes of commerce to spread their art around, to get their work into the hands of "respectable citizens" and teach them that part of their incomes came from the exploitation of much-despised low-wage immigrant laborers. When neoconservatives in government attacked the federal arts agency that supported Art Rebate, Avalos, Hock, and Small used local media coverage as an opportunity to work hostile reaction from parts of the public into the piece, since their goal all along had been to challenge the invisibility of undocumented workers and California's reliance on them.

In a previous project, Avalos and Hock collaborated with Elizabeth Sisco to produce posters displayed on the back of city buses in San Diego. They created a parody of the local tourist promotion agency slogan describing San Diego as "America's Finest City" by displaying the words "Welcome to America's Finest Tourist Plantation" over photographs of "brown working hands" – pointing to a sign that reads "Maid Service Please," scraping food off a plate, and being placed in handcuffs by an officer from the Border Patrol. Asserting that no real public space existed in San Diego, the artists aimed to create "a public forum within conceptual space" using the circuits of advertising to attack other kinds of advertising and public relations. Securing their space on the buses at a time when San Diego hosted the Super Bowl, the bus poster project provoked extensive media coverage – most of it hostile – but then worked that coverage into the art by making a video, a book, and a traveling exhibit incorporating attacks on their posters into the art project itself (Chavoya, 1996: 208–14, 216).

These Los Angeles and San Diego artists have generally displayed an oblique engagement with commercial popular culture. But in some places in the world, artists thoroughly immersed in the most sophisticated conduits of commercial culture have made significant political interventions. The Senegalese musician Baaba Maal, one of the star's of "world beat" music, included a song called "Njilou" on his last album. "Njilou" uses the circuits of transnational capital and culture to protest against the effects of structural adjustment policies in Africa, especially currency devaluation. As Maal explained in a recent interview, his purpose was to start discussion about what Africans can do about the transnational economy.

> Poor people are becoming poorer. Even if you are sick, you can't afford to go to the hospital. It's not new in Africa. With colonialism, slavery – every time something bad happens to Africa, it's not the sons of Africa, but outsiders. But I say, in life, you must have hope. In Fouta, for example, the devaluation is all around, but you don't see it. The people live by their own experiences, their own community, helping each other, working together. African people must not shake their heads waiting for something to come from outside. This is the new face of Africa, these people of Fouta. (Eyre, 1995: 35)

As the nature of cultural production and consumption changes, as global austerity, deindustrialization, and economic restructuring continue to foment changes in grassroots community-based art making and art-based community making, scholars will need to develop new and better methods of cultural criticism. Artists are not just saying new things with their art; rather, they are calling into question the nature of art itself. Because validation in the university flows from within, scholars tend to be conservative, to repeat what has been done before and secure validation from the people who did it. But the dire emergency facing people around the world no longer allows us the luxury of this traditionalism, of scholarship that (to paraphrase Ulf Hannerz) is like Scandinavian cooking – something "passed down from generation to generation for no apparent reason" (Hannerz, 1992: 42).

Yet those of us who work and teach and study as "traditional intellectuals" in institutions of higher learning have an important role to play in analyzing and interpreting the changes that are taking place around us. We need to develop forms of academic criticism capable of comprehending the theorizing being done at the grassroots by artists and their audiences, of building bridges between different kinds of theory. This kind of work is already in existence, even if in embryonic form. An exemplary body of scholarship on culture by sociologists in recent years has illumined complex connections linking cultural expressions with their social causes and consequences. For example, research on the American Dream and popular novels by Elizabeth Long, on the evolution of romantic love by Steven Seidman, and on the emergence of new gendered identities during the 1950s by Wini Breines, all show how culture functions as a social force as well as the ways in which transformations in social relations call forth new forms of culture. Line Grenier's analyses of how the structure of the music industry in Quebec encouraged the emergence of the *chanson* as the emblematic icon of Quebecois nationalism, and Herman Gray's splendid discussions about how the music recorded by small record companies stems as much from the industrial and commercial imperatives of their niche in the market as from aesthetic choices, serve to render relations between cultural structures and social structures in all of their proper complexity.

Sophisticated work by these sociologists complements nicely the new interest in social structure among humanities scholars of culture. Feminist musicology shows how aesthetic choices often are actually social choices in disguise, because musical compositions build affect, engagement, and investment among audiences through complex codes and metaphors that connote social roles, including gendered identities, individualism, heroism, and danger (McClary, 1991). Cinema studies scholars have developed stunningly successful schematizations of the race–gender hierarchies in romantic relations in Hollywood films of the 1950s by demonstrating the connections between the emergence of the US as a global military and economic power after World War II and representations of Asians in films including *Sayonara* and *Teahouse of the August Moon* (Browne, 1992) Within Asian-American studies, exemplary efforts include an important study of D. W. Griffith explaining the difference between that filmmaker's overt anti-black racism in *The Birth of a Nation* and his paternalism toward Chinese people in *Broken Blossoms* by showing how the two films sought very different market niches (Tchen, 1992).

Arjun Appadurai, Luis Guarnizo, Chandra Talpede Mohanty, Roger Rouse, and Michael Peter Smith, among others, have shown how the new cultural realities of the global economy create the possibility for what Smith calls "transnational grassroots politics" (Smith, 1994: 15). Displaced Andean Indians in Peruvian cities produce new social movements organized at a local level to secure city services at the same time that they create new cultural categories through artistic expressions like chicha music. (Bullen, 1993: 229–33; Rowe and Schelling, 1991: 121–2). The banda music that so effectively forges a new cultural identity for Mexican migrants to Los Angeles serves as the subtext and unifying cultural icon for social struggles including the 1992 strike by immigrant Drywall Workers and the efforts by immigrant high school students to challenge California's anti-immigrant Proposition 187 (Puig, 1994: 24; Hayes-Bautista and Rodriguez, 1994: 10–11; Flagg, 1992: 3; Stokes, 1994: B4). The new social movements emerge from and within a cultural context that needs to be recognized, understood, and analyzed by cultural workers, scholars, and movement activists alike.

Social scientists and humanists have made important strides in theorizing the relations between cultural production and social life in recent years, but our work still speaks more to paradigms established during the industrial era than to the emerging realities and changing nature of the relations among culture, politics, and place in the postindustrial world. In this respect, we have much to learn from artists who are facing up to the things that are killing them and their communities. Important social theory is being generated by cultural creators. Engaged in the hard work of fashioning cultural and political coalitions based on cultural affinities and shared suffering, they have been forced to think clearly about cultural production in contemporary society. For example, Australian *Yolngu* tribal musician, school principal, and internationally popular recording artist Mandawuy Yunupingu argues that some of his community's oldest traditions prepare them to face up to the peril and promise of postindustrial society. When devising a *Yolngu* curriculum for the Yirrkala Community School, an elder in his tribe advised Yunupingu to think about the process of *ngathu* – the gathering of nuts to make bread. The nuts that grow in the rugged landscape of Arnhem Land contain a kind of cyanide, but by collecting, sorting, and cleaning them in the right way the *Yolngu* people wash away the poison and make a bread that can feed many people. Yunupingu asserts that the *ngathu* process can serve as a model for disputes about school curricula or relations between social groups. "Remembering the preparation of *ngathu* reminds us that there are right and wrong ways," Yunupingu claims. "Hurry, and the poison will remain in the bread," but "there are ways of proceeding that, structurally, ensure that the interests of all are recognized and respected" (Yunupingu, 1994: 117, 118).

Yunupingu, whose musical group named itself Yothu Yindi, a name that connotes the harmony and balance that indigenous Australians work to create, explains that the *Yolngu* concept of *ganma* also offers a model for social relations. *Ganma* describes the brackish places where fresh water and salt water mix together. Nonaboriginal people "wrinkle up their noses" at this water because they find it distasteful, but "for us, the sight and smell of brackish water expresses a profound foundation of useful knowledge-balance" (ibid: 118). *Yolngu* people know that brackish water contains a complex and dynamic balance that can serve as a way of thinking about relations between black and white Australians, and about other kinds of balance that need to be achieved in the world. "*Ganma* is a metaphor," Yunupingu explains. "We are talking about natural processes but meaning at another level. *Ganma* is social theory. It is our traditional, profound, and detailed model of how what Europeans call 'society' works" (ibid: 117).

According to Yunupingu, *ganma* allows us "to see European-type knowledge as just one sort of knowledge among many," to theorize the synthesis of seemingly incompatible cultures and forces, and to see that the knowledge needed to comprehend the world that is emerging is already here if we know how to find it. The cultural work that his theory has generated has been singularly effective in that regard: Yothu Yindi's song "Treaty" gained national and international attention, securing a power in the market that helped spark a successful struggle to force the Australian government to negotiate a new treaty between that continent's original inhabitants and the descendants of European settlers. In addition, on recent world tours, members of Yothu Yindi have met with Native Americans in Los Angeles and hip-hop activists in Marcus Garvey Park in Harlem to discuss "common" concerns among these disparate communities of color (Castles, 1992: 31; Breen, 1992: 150; Neuenfeldt, 1993: 1, 2, 4, 7 11).

Artistic production plays a central role in Yunipingu's vision. "When you talk about the revolutionary things that have happened in the world, it's always been connected with art and I think the Aboriginal people are in that process now. Our art is a mechanism for change" (Yunipingu[e], 1990: 103). Yunupingu is not alone in theorizing about transnational culture from the grassroots, in facing up to the things that are killing him and his community. Singer and composer Jocelyne Beroad of the West Indian zouk band Kassav offers metaphors parallel to Yunupingu's in her story about how her group chose its name. Before the emergence of the band Kassav, musicians from Guadeloupe and Martinique rarely played music from their own communities, seeking commercial success with formulas that had been devised elsewhere. The success of Kassav in local and world markets with *zouk* music generated enormous local pride and helped build greater unity between the two islands. Kassav is the name of a cake made from cassava, also known as manioc, an edible root. But unlike African cassava, the kind that grows in Martinique and Guadeloupe cannot be eaten directly because it has a poison in it. As Beroad explains,

"You've got to know how to extract this poison before you can eat it. It's a traditional family thing. So because they had to extract what was poisoning Martiniquian and Guadeloupian music, they called it Kassav" (Eyre, 1994: 15). Beroad and her group knew about the presence of poison and the possibility of succumbing to it. But they used local knowledge and grassroots theorizing to "take the poison out" and play an unexpected role in transnational culture and economics.

All around the world, new social movements are forging unexpected and improbable coalitions. Trade unionists organizing mostly Latino workers at the New Otani Hotel in Los Angeles confront an employer (Japan's Kajima Corporation) advantaged by its global reach and scope. Yet the very power of their adversary enabled the New Otani workers to ally with Korean nationals and Korean American groups who also had grievances against Kajima dating back to the company's role in the occupation of Korea by Japanese forces. At the same time, the San Diego Maquiladora Workers Support Committee has successfully mobilized feminist activists from the US to support the self-activity of young women workers in Tijuana organizing against low wages, unsafe working conditions, sexual harassment, and environmental hazards on the Mexican side of the border. Asian Immigrant Women's Advocates waged a successful boycott against Jessica McClintock dresses by building a cross-class interracial coalition among women of color. The Haiti National Network has connected US human rights advocates with Haitian exiles in providing material aid and political support for social activists working on agrarian reform issues in that Caribbean country. In each of these endeavors, campaigns against injustice drew strength from the power of cultural expressions and ideas to forge alliances among people with distinctly different social roles and status. Intellectuals have played an important role in each of these coalitions, in part because they have skills as attorneys, researchers, and writers that social movements need, but also because the writing and teaching of traditional intellectuals functions as a node in a network of oppositional discourse along with the cultural expressions and practices of organic intellectuals and community groups.

New cultural practices require scholars to develop new ways of studying and analyzing culture. As Nestor Garcia Canclini argues in *Hybrid Cultures*, we are ill-served in the present by traditional categories that relegate the "traditional" and the "modern" to totally separate realms of experience, and, similarly, it is imperative that we move beyond paradigms that present "the cultured, the popular, and the mass-based" forms of culture as atomized and mutually exclusive endeavors. He advises that "we need nomad social sciences, capable of circulating through the staircases that connect those floors – or better yet, social sciences that redesign the floor plans and horizontally connect the levels" (Canclini, 1995: 2).

The global disaster created by structural adjustment policies and transnational capital and culture may well be irreversible. But if change were to come, it would most likely emanate from people whose political and cultural practice flows from exploiting the contradictions in the new world order, whose theories about culture mix old and new insights for the purposes of popular democracy, and who look at the world without succumbing to either cynicism or sentiment: in short, from people who face up to the things that are killing them, and us.

REFERENCES

Alfaro, Luis 1994: "La Virgen," "HuggyBoy," "Roller Derby." Performance, August 8, American Sociological Association meetings, Los Angeles.

Appadurai, Arjun 1991: Global Ethnoscapes: Notes and Queries for a Transnational Anthropology. In R. G. Fox (ed.), *Recapturing Anthropology: Working in the Present*, Santa Fe: School of American Research Press.

Arenas, Norm 1996: Rage Against the Machine: Doing is the Best Way of Saying, *AP: Alternative Press*, 96, July.

Bambara, Toni Cade 1982: *The Sea Birds are Still Alive*, New York: Vintage Books.

Barnet, Richard J. and Cavenagh John 1994: *Global Dreams: Imperial Corporations and the New Word Order*, New York: Simon and Schuster.

Breen, Marcus 1992: Desert Dreams, Media, and Interventions in Reality: Australian Aboriginal Music. In Reebee Garofalo (ed.), *Rockin' the Boat*, Boston: South End.

Breines, Wini 1992: *Young, White, and Miserable*, Boston: Beacon Books.

Browne, Nick 1992: Race: The Political Unconscious of American Film, *East-West Journal*, 6, 1, 5–16.

Buchanan, Kerry 1993: Ain't Nothing But a G Thing, *Midwest*, 3.

Budhoo, Davison 1994: The IMF/World Bank Wreak Havoc on the Third World. In Kevin Danaher (ed.), *50 Years is Enough: The Case Against the World Bank and the International Monetary Fund*, Boston: South End.

Bullen, Margaret 1993: Chicha in the Shanty Towns of Arequipa, Peru, *Popular Music*, 12, 3.

Canclini, Nestor Garcia 1995: *Hybrid Cultures: Strategies for Entering and Leaving Modernity*. Minneapolis: University of Minnesota Press.

Canclini, Nestor Garcia 1992: Cultural Reconversion. In George Yudice, Jean Franco, and Juan Flores (eds), *On Edge: The Crisis of Contemporary Latin American Culture*, Minneapolis: University of Minnesota Press.

Castles, John 1992: Tjungaringanyi: Aboriginal Rock. In Philip Hayward (ed.), *From Pop to Punk to Postmodernism: Popular Music and Australian Culture from the 1960s to the 1990s*, North Sydney: Allen & Unwin.

Chavoya, C. Ondine 1996: Collaborative Public Art and Multimedia Installation: David Avalos, Louis Hock, and Elizabeth Sisco's "Welcome to America's Finest Tourist Plantation" (1988). In Chon A. Noriega and Ana M. Lopez (eds), *The*

Ethnic Eye: Latino Media Arts, Minneapolis: University of Minnesota Press, 208–27.

Cooper, Marc 1992: L. A.'s State of Siege. In Don Hazen, *Inside the L. A. Riots*, New York: Institute for Alternative Journalism.

Dunn, Robert 1997: *Identity Crises*, Minneapolis: University of Minnesota Press.

Evanzz, Karl 1992: *The Judas Factor: The Plot to Kill Malcolm X*. New York: Thunder's Mouth Press.

Eyre, Banning 1994: Kassav, *Rhythm Music Magazine*, 3, 3.

—— 1995: Africa Fete, *Rhythm Music Magazine*, 4, 6.

Fisher, Robert 1993: Grass-roots Organizing Worldwide: Common Ground, Historical Roots, and the Tension Between Democracy and the State. In Robert Fisher and Joseph Kling (eds), *Mobilizing the Community: Local Politics in the Era of the Global City* Newbury Park: Sage.

Flagg, Michael 1992: Unions Get a Wakeup Call as Drywallers Achieve an Unlikely Victory, *Los Angeles Times*, November 8.

Gallin, Dan 1994: Inside the New World Order, *New Politics*, summer.

Gamboa, Harry 1993: Interview with Author, Los Angeles, California, August 12.

Gray, Herman 1988: *Producing Jazz*, Philadelphia: Temple University Press.

Grenier, Line 1993: The Aftermath of a Crisis: Quebec Music Industries in the 1980s, *Popular Music*, 12, 3, 209–28.

Guarnizo. L. E. 1994: Los Domincanyork: the Making of a Binational Society, *Annals of the American Academy of Political and Social Science*, 534, May.

Habell-Pallan, Michelle 1995: No Cultural Icon. Unpublished manuscript.

Hamilton, Cynthia 1992: The Making of an American Bantustan. In Don Hazen (ed.), *Inside the L. A. Riots*, New York: Institute for Alternative Journalism.

Hannerz, Ulf 1992: *Cultural Complexity: Studies in the Social Organization of Meaning*, New York: Columbia University Press.

Harvey, David 1989: *The Condition of Postmodernity*, Cambridge, MA: Basil Blackwell.

Hayes-Bautista, David and Rodriguez, Gregory 1994: Technobanda, *New Republic*, April 11.

Jameson, Fredric 1991: *Postmodernism, or the Cultural Logic of Late Capitalism*, Durham, NC: Duke University Press.

Lipsitz, George 1994: *Dangerous Crossroads: Popular Music, Postmodernism and the Poetics of Place*, London: Verso.

Long, Elizabeth 1985: *The American Dream and the Popular Novel*, Boston and London: Routledge, Kegan Paul.

Lowe, Lisa 1991: Heterogeneity, Hybridity, Multiplicity: Marking Asian American Differences, *Diaspora*, 1, 1.

—— 1996: Decolonization, Displacement, Disidentification: Asian American "Novels" and the Question of History. In D. Lynch and William Warner (eds), *Cultural Institutions of the Novel*, Durham, NC: Duke University Press.

McClary, Susan 1991: *Feminine Endings*, Minneapolis: University of Minnesota Press.

Mann, Eric 1991: *L. A.'s Lethal Air: New Strategies for Policy, Organizing, and Action*, Los Angles: Labor/Community Strategy Center.

Naficy, Hamid 1994: *The Making of Exile Culture*, Minneapolis: University of Minnesota Press.

Neuenfeldt, Karl W. M. 1993: Yothu Yindi and Ganma: The Cultural Transposition of Aboriginal Agenda through Metaphor and Music, *Journal of Australian Studies*, 38, September.

Meraz, Gerry 1995: Culture for the Cause, *Urb*, 42, May, 69.

Norte, Marisela 1991: *NORTE/word*, Los Angeles: New Alliance Records.

Puig, Claudia 1994: Banda, *Los Angeles Times Magazine*, June 12.

Rouse, Roger 1991: Mexican Migration and the Space of Postmodernism, *Diaspora*, 1, 1.

Rowe, William and Schelling Vivian 1991: *Memory and Modernity: Popular Culture in Latin America*, New York and London: Verso.

Seidman, Steven 1991: *Romantic Longings*, New York: Routledge.

Smith, Michael Peter 1994: Can You Imagine? Transnational Migration and the Globalization of Grass Roots Politics, *Social Text*, 39, summer.

Stokes, Sandy 1994: INS Picking on Drywallers, Leader Claims, *Riverside Press-Enterprise* March 22, B4.

Tchen, John Kuo Wei 1992: Modernizing White Patriarchy: Reviewing D. W. Griffith's *Broken Blossoms*. In Russell Leong (ed.), *Moving the Image*, Los Angeles: UCLA Asian American Studies Center, 133–43.

Van Elteren, Mel 1994: *Imagining America: Dutch Youth and its Sense of Place*, Tilburgh, Netherlands: Tilburg University Press.

Waters, Maxine 1992: Testimony Before Senate Banking Committee. In Don Hazen (ed.), *Inside the L. A. Riots*, New York: Institute for Alternative Journalism.

Wright, Robin 1995: A Revolution at Work, *Los Angeles Times*, March 7.

Yunupingu, Mandawuy 1994: Yothu Yindi: Finding Balance, *Race and Class*, 35, 4.

Yunupingu[e], Mandawuy, 1990: Yothu Yindi Band. In Liz Thompson (ed.), *Aboriginal Voices: Contemporary Aboriginal Artists, Writers and Performers*, New York: Simon and Schuster.

PART III

RELATING CULTURAL PROCESSES AND SOCIAL INEQUALITY

Introduction

Part III takes as its explicit concern a preoccupation that is implicit in almost every contribution to this book and central to the two fields of study it engages. All of the contributions happen to be by sociologists. Part III therefore represents various sociological "takes" on how to relate culture to social inequality, some more and some less engaged with the concepts and orientations of cultural studies.

For example, Michèle Lamont speaks from within the sociological tradition in her discussion of moral and symbolic boundaries between racial groups, although this issue is certainly alive in cultural studies. Lamont's chapter concerns the alternative frames of meaning that African-American working men mobilize to describe their differences from Euro-Americans. Based on findings from in-depth interviews with 60 stable blue-collar workers, 30 African-Americans and 30 Euro-Americans, Lamont argues that black workers are often more concerned with the ways they resemble white workers than with the differences between them. However, she also argues that morality figures importantly in what both groups most value, and that white and black workers stress very different dimensions of morality. Black workers place high value on solidarity and generosity, in general expressing a more collectivist view of morality than their white peers. Whites reveal a more individualistic world view, emphasizing the work ethic and personal responsibility. While black workers also value the work ethic and individual responsibility, their primary commitment is to the virtues of solidarity and they often ascribe moral virtue to that commitment, claiming moral superiority over whites because of what they see as white people's egotism, sneakiness, detachment from family and community, and domineering or superior attitudes. Lamont argues that such boundary-drawing processes among blacks and whites, though similar in nature, have unequal social impact. Whites are much more successful at legitimizing their definition of morality in the public sphere than are blacks. This reinforces racism, thereby contributing to the growing inequality in the two groups' access to resources. Finally, Lamont argues that her approach might enrich our understanding of identity politics by focusing on how ordinary people (rather than cultural producers or influential texts) define social hierarchies, and by documenting the salience of various dimensions of identity across populations, the degree of cultural distance between dominant and subordinated groups, and the processes by which different groups are able to circulate their representations of the "other" in mainstream culture.

By contrast, Sharon Hays analyzes the implicit cultural assumptions in bestselling books by Dr Spock, T. Berry Brazelton, and Penelope Leach, the most influential "gurus" of contemporary childrearing. She argues that these texts all elaborate a culturally dominant model of parenting as "child-centered, expert-guided, emotionally absorbing, labor intensive, and financially expensive" – and also primarily the responsibility of the individual mother. Pointing up the paradoxical disjunction between this model and the competitive, gain-driven ethos of the public world, as well as the contradictory demands it places on women, Hays seeks to understand its pervasiveness and power. Drawing on theoretical models current in both sociology and cultural studies, she analyzes the ideology of intensive mothering as in part a consequence of women's powerlessness *vis-à-vis* the state, capitalism, and men; as an attempt by the white middle class to construct class and race boundaries to valorize their own social position; and as a result of women's efforts to claim status as women and mothers. Moving beyond the logic of self-interest, Hays also argues that because it embraces a view of the child as sacred and the unselfishness of child nurture as morally exemplary, this world view actively opposes the dominant ideology of competitive individualism in childrearing books that are also "hesitant moral treatises." Yet the ideology of intensive mothering also places an unjust burden on women, and obscures the subordination of the ethos of nurture to that of the market and that of women to men. So, Hays contends, to really address the moral concerns raised by the ideology of intensive mothering, we need to reconfigure the beliefs and social relations – both public and domestic – that have contributed to its hold.

Angela Valenzuela also addresses issues of "caring," exploring a pattern of divergent understandings of what it means to "care about school" held by students and school personnel at a predominantly Latino inner-city school. Drawing on the work of educational theorists who developed the discussion of caring from their concern for the alienating effects of large, bureaucratic schools, she differentiates between *aesthetic* caring, which is an abstract commitment to ideas or practices that ostensibly lead to achievement, and *authentic* caring, which gives emphasis to reciprocal relations between teachers and the youth they serve. Valenzuela argues that her field work at Seguin High shows that most teachers there emphasize aesthetic caring, while most students desire to be cared *for* before they care *about.* She also expands the theoretical discussions of caring at school by incorporating cultural studies' discussions of cultural difference, ethnicity, and power to demonstrate that in this school, the mutual alienation different definitions of caring engender is exacerbated by social and cultural distance between teachers and students, and by the nonneutral demands of an assimilationist curriculum. Exploring the school culture that discourages most teachers from caring about their students, as well as the urban hip-hop style teachers see as evidence of the "uncaring student," Valenzuela discusses *not* caring as student resistance, as well as the remarkable results that occur when teachers do genuinely care for those they teach. Finally, she proposes a new educational trajectory that might enable schools to be truly responsive to the needs of Mexican-origin youth.

Gray's contribution links the contemporary "politics" of jazz to the broader framework of contemporary black oppositional cultural politics in general through an examination of Wynton Marsalis – installed in 1991 as the first director of Lincoln Center's Jazz Program – as an exemplar and spokesperson of a very effective canonical project to legitimize jazz. Gray discusses Marsalis's vision of jazz as a modernist and anticommercial artistic form and the cultural politics that underwrite it, which combine racial nationalism and a strong belief in American democracy. Describing Marsalis's success as an "institutional revolutionary" at Lincoln Center – as well as some of the developments within the music industry that have affected jazz – Gray elucidates the complexly conservative nature of this kind of institutionalization. He counterposes to it a view of jazz rooted metaphorically and historically in musicians' experiences on "the road and the street," which directed their attention outward into local audiences and towards other popular musical forms. Both trajectories, he argues, express an oppositional black cultural politics, though each contains different limits and possibilities. Analytically, Gray argues that the sociology of culture, with its tendency to focus on cultural institutions and the production of culture, can best illuminate projects like that of Marsalis, while cultural studies, with its attention to diffuse everyday (and marginalized) cultural practices, is necessary for keeping sites such as "the street" and the cultural politics it represents in view.

9

Colliding Moralities Between Black and White Workers

MICHÈLE LAMONT

In recent years, analysts of contemporary culture have become increasingly concerned with the demonization of African-Americans in the press and the mass media. For instance, in her influential book *Black Feminist Thought*, Patricia Hill Collins (1991) argues that popular representations of black females oscillate between several negative stereotypes such as the mammy, the welfare queen, and the Jezebel. Similarly, the literature on the Anita Hill–Clarence Thomas affair is largely concerned with the pernicious effects that the widely publicized senate hearing had on already massively negative representations of African-Americans in public opinion (Chrisman and Alan, 1991; Morrison, 1992). Most often at stake in these writings is the portrayal of African-Americans as morally lacking in areas such as sexual restraint, traditional morality, responsibility, a work ethic, and so forth. Echoing this moral concern, social scientists suggest that a new form of racism is increasingly prevalent in American society, a symbolic racism embodied in widespread Euro-Americans' perceptions that African-Americans are violating mainstream American moral values.[1] This rhetoric of superiority suggests that the Euro-American majority perceives African-American culture as very differentiated from their own culture, which is congruous with observations that poor African-Americans are now more culturally distinct from "mainstream America" than they were 30 years ago (Anderson, 1990).[2] It is important to analyze this rhetoric of moral superiority because, as we will see, capturing race differences in moral status signals might also help us better understand cultural mechanisms of reproduction of inequality.

This essay is concerned with the alternative frames of meaning that African-American workers mobilize to define their differences in relation to Euro-Americans. I show that both groups value morality highly, but emphasize different moral status signals that they mobilize in the boundary work they produce against one another.[3] African-American workers often perceive Euro-Americans as immoral on the basis of status signals that are peripheral to the world view of the Euro-Americans I talked to, namely solidarity and generosity. Conversely, Euro-American workers often criticize African-Americans for not valuing as much as they themselves do other dimensions of morality, namely work ethic and responsibility. In conclusion, I shall draw the implications of my research for understanding how the ability to legitimize specific representations of one's identity and that of others can contribute to the reproduction of racial inequality. Also, taking this specific piece of research as a point of departure, I shall point at ways in which the boundary approach can enrich work on identity politics conducted from the perspective of cultural studies.

Very little scholarly work has been done on the extent to which African-American culture is differentiated from Euro-American culture in the contemporary United States.[4] Social scientists have had difficulty addressing these issues in part because talk of cultural differences was, until very recently, always viewed as a way to "blame the victim."[5] It is only in the last few years that American sociologists have again conceptualized culture as institutionalized repertoires that have as powerful an effect on the structuration of everyday life as do economic forces.[6] These repertoires are studied here by drawing on in-depth interviews with members of an important symbolic community of American society, that of the *working man*.[7] I study how white and black blue-collar workers draw boundaries against each other, viewing these boundaries as institutionalized cultural repertoires, that is, as publicly available categorization systems that are prevalent within their symbolic community.[8] Instead of focusing on the much-studied black "underclass," I look at African-American working-class men because they represent a significant proportion of their racial group, yet remain largely understudied.[9]

In this essay I focus primarily on moral boundaries and on the boundary work of blacks, and refer to racial differences exclusively to elucidate the cultural specificity of African-American workers. At times, I discuss class differences, comparing the blue-collar men I talked to with white male college-educated professionals and managers I interviewed for an earlier study of the American upper-middle class.[10] I draw on in-depth interviews to reconstruct the symbolic boundaries or mental maps through which individuals define *us* and *them*, simultaneously identifying the most salient principles of classification and identification that are operating behind these definitions, including race and class. I asked the men to describe their friends and foes, role models and heroes, and likes and dislikes.[11] In so doing, I tapped the criteria that are the basis of their evaluations and self-identity and reveal the natural order through which they hierarchalize others when, for example, they declare that, of course, it is more

important to be honest than refined, or that money is not a good indicator
of a person's value. The result is both a multifaceted theory of status that
centers on the relationship between various standards of evaluation across
populations, and a comparative sociology of models of inclusion/exclusion,
that is, of the relative salience of various bases of societal segmentations
across classes, races, and eventually, nations.[12]

For this study, I talked for approximately two hours with 60 stable blue-
collar workers who have a high school degree but not a college degree[13]
– 30 self-identified African-Americans and 30 self-identified Euro-Americans
who were, when possible, matched in terms of occupation and age.[14] They
were randomly selected from phone books of working-class towns located in the New York suburbs, such as Elizabeth, Rahway, and Linden, in
New Jersey, and Hampstead and Uniondale on Long Island. This random
selection and the relatively large number of respondents aimed not at
building a representative sample, but at tapping a wide range of perspectives within a community of workers, thereby going beyond the unavoidable limitations of site-specific research.[15] Although produced in specifically
structured interactional contexts, interviews can get at relatively stable
and powerful aspects of identity by documenting what respondents take
for granted in their responses.

While the growing presence of women and immigrants has dramatically
altered the character of the American working class,[16] the latter remains a
highly gendered – masculine – cultural construct. I talked to nonimmigrant
men only in order to minimize cultural variations unrelated to occupation
and race/ethnicity – this choice is justified because the larger study within
which this particular project takes place is concerned with cultural differentiation between college and non-college educated men, and not with
the character of the American working class *per se*; the gendered nature
of working-class discourse will be discused elsewhere. My interviewees
include plumbers, electricians, truck drivers, letter carriers, plant workers,
painters, and other blue-collar workers.[17] Each in-depth interview lasted
approximately two hours – long enough for me to develop a complex
view of the ways in which these men understood the similarities and
differences between themselves and others. I conducted all the interviews
myself at a place these men chose.[18] Future research will compare the
trends that emerged from the interviews with national survey data and
other secondary sources.

Boundary Work Among White and Black Workers

The African-American men I talked to are often more concerned with the
similarities between themselves and Euro-Americans than they are with

the differences. In the view of Brian Washington, a textile worker, both groups "want a decent paying job, a few credit cards, a car that's decent, and a nice place to live. I think people in a certain age, certain income bracket, their thinking is just about equal or the same." Similarly, John Patterson, a plumber, believes that blacks and whites both want "good education for the kids, an environment that you could come to and have nice things and not have them destroyed or vandalized, or threatened in any way, and have a lawn to cut." Nevertheless, discussions of the differences between both groups are omnipresent in the interviews. Blacks alternatively describe whites as power-mongers and as morally flawed because they are inhumane and sneaky. I analyze these aspects of African-American working-class discourse on Euro-Americans in turn, after discussing the dimensions of morality that both groups value most. If I focus on differences between groups herein, I plan to explore intra-group differences elsewhere.

Collectivist definitions of morality among black respondents: solidarity and generosity

When defining what they value, the white and black workers I interviewed emphasized moral criteria more than socioeconomic or cultural criteria. They value moral criteria even more than the upper-middle-class men I talked to. Moral criteria are most salient when individuals discuss the values they hope to pass on to their children,[19] the qualities they like and dislike in others,[20] and the meaning they attach to success.[21] This itself is less striking than the fact that African-Americans and Euro-Americans stress very different dimensions of morality. In general, African-American workers have a more collectivist view of morality that accentuates solidarity and generosity. Whites have a more individualistic view that emphasizes the work ethic and responsibility. These traits are also valued by blacks, but they are less central in black understandings of morality than they are in white understandings, maybe in part because blacks also value solidarity.

The importance that black workers put on solidarity is evidenced by the fact that when asked to choose from a list a quality that they value highly, more than a third of them, as compared to only a fifth of whites, choose "shows solidarity" as an important quality – the same proportions apply to the choice of "generous" as an important quality. Beyond these simple percentages, the content of the interviews themselves – which can only be painted in broad strokes here – reveal that the themes of solidarity and generosity penetrate deeply into African-American discussions of moral character. Solidarity toward the black race outweighs discussions of solidarity toward other workers or toward the human race.

The premium put on racial solidarity is exemplified by Jimmy Light, a phone technician, who defines the whole black race as his kin.[22] He says he would like to have enough money to help people: "They don't have to be our relatives, just be black and need it." Using the kinship metaphor, Tyrone Smith, a chemical operator, also states that his goal in life is "helping my brothers. If somebody needs help and we can help them, we put our arm up to help them. Help anybody as much we could without putting myself in danger." Another phone technician also describes his goals in life by stating: "I'm more interested in things that are going to help minorities. I've always been for the underdog because of my upbringing when you're discriminated against."

The promotion of solidarity among blacks means fighting daily for social justice as well as helping "the brothers." Concretely, this requires standing up against people who make racial slurs at the workplace and "getting on the case" of those who "feel through the thing of being slaves and things like that, they're supposed to be superior to you."[23] When asked to name their hero, several mentioned Martin Luther King, expressing their commitment to the peaceful fight for social justice.

The emphasis that black workers put on solidarity is expressed in their greater reluctance to describe themselves as feeling superior or inferior to others: when asked what kinds of people they feel inferior and superior to, more than twice as many African-Americans say that they never feel superior to people than do whites. Generally, they justify this reluctance by wishing that "people [would] realize that we have one creator, and not many creators, and . . . there are many different colors of birds, and trees, and fishes, and everything that crosses this globe." Their egalitarianism goes hand in hand with their emphasis on solidarity, generosity, and other such qualities.

Finally, the centrality of solidarity for these men also manifests itself in the way they discuss their friendships and the strength of their community. Taking the time to talk with people is something they value highly.[24] They say that they like to relate to people, to have a strong bond with others. Like many interviewees, Jimmy Light, the phone technician, explains that "I have my networks of friends, where we still have [a strong community.] We look out for each other, we 'diss' each other, we know each other's families." Like white workers, they often define happiness in terms of being able to relate, and to have good, warm relationships with friends and family.

Generosity is one of the moral traits highly valued by the black men I talked to. When discussing the types of people they do not like, they often point to people who took advantage of their generosity – black or white. They criticize individuals who do not reciprocate when expected and who break the implicit social contract that unifies people, thereby violating the integrity of the person who helps. Concretely, this means borrowing money and not returning it, taking advantage, free-loading, or even manipulating to get certain benefits from a relationship. For instance, when asked to describe the types of people he does not like, Jerry Bloom, a machinist, mentions "people that sponge, that try to use you or con you. . . . Just people that try to get over on you. . . . People that use you and be your friend and tell you anything in the world as long as you have money." Answering the same question, Art Armstrong, a newspaper worker, points to people "who want to hurt other people and try to control other people to get them to do things for their benefit; so these people that are doing it don't get anything out of it." For his part, John Robinson, a union representative who works in a large automobile plant, says that he dislikes people who are "lookin' for somethin for nothin' . . . try to chisel you, play games with you. Some people have a way of, you know, makin' themselves look good and then do it at my expense." This widespread dislike for people who "use" others is expressed succinctly by Lou Johnson, a maintenance worker, who says:

> There's a thing you just don't do. You don't take a person's kindness for weakness or play him for a fool. You don't do that. . . . If I'm sitting here and eating and I have enough for myself and you sittin' there, . . . I give it to you, and then once you get yours, it's like, the hell with you. You don't take a person's kindness for weakness' cause they're giving from here, you know, they feeling sorry for you and giving it from here [pointing to his heart].

Studies show that blacks are in general more supportive of public redistributive measures than whites, which is added evidence of the premium they put on generosity.[25] As Anderson (1990: 61) and others have shown, they are particularly critical toward upwardly mobile blacks who do not "put back" in the community.[26] Finally, only one of the 30 black men I talked to said that he feels inferior to people in general on moral grounds, compared to one fifth of white blue-collar workers. Clearly, the black Americans I talked to often view themselves as very moral and are not about to yield to the notion that they are less so than white people.

Black workers set limits to racial solidarity when they discuss the "no-good niggers" who "have no morals, no respect, no plans, no hopes, no outlook" (quality inspector, paper plant) and who "don't want to go out there and get a job, or when you do get a job, you don't keep a job. You'd rather be out there with your friends, hanging out in the street, not having a purpose or a direction" (security agent).[27] If they respect work ethics and mainstream definitions of success, stressing how they have or have not been able to get "a nice home, a nice private yard, whatever"

(fumigation technician), they often make room for alternative, more personal definitions of success: they recognize the limits that racial discrimination puts on their ability to achieve success and often have a somewhat
sociological understanding of the dynamics of closed opportunities. This
does not mean that their emphasis on generosity and solidarity is only a
self-interested form of resistance to dominant culture – it can also find
meaning in itself.

Individualist definitions of morality among white respondents: work ethic and responsibility

Like black interviewees, the white men I talked to valued being helpful
and friendly, for instance, stopping to assist people who have problems
with their cars, giving a hand when they can, and so forth. They also like
to point out that "everybody's born and everybody's gonna die" and that
there is no use to try to show your superiority. Like black workers, they
also put a premium on sincerity, integrity, and "speaking one's mind."
However, white workers have a more individualistic concept of morality
than do blacks. This was already suggested by figures presented above
concerning black/white differences in the importance each group gives to
solidarity and generosity. In addition, when asked to choose a quality that
they value highly, whites emphasize slightly more traits pertaining to the
Protestant ethic: more whites than blacks chose "hardworking" (18 compared to 12) and "responsible" (21 compared to 17). While none of the
African-Americans put work at the center of their definition of success, a
fifth of the whites did. In the interviews themselves, white workers were
very critical of people who do nothing to improve their lot and take no
pride in their work.[28]

Another racial difference in definitions of morality is that white workers
were more likely to label "dishonest" people who do not respect traditional morality, who cheat on or physically abuse their wives, and who lie
and steal. They say that they like strong morals because they are "worried
about the country, the state of affairs we're in . . . [the] groups that are
trying to break our morality. . . . like the rainbow coalition that pushes the
rainbow curriculum" (train conductor). However, like blacks, whites are
very sensitive to drugs, alcohol, and violence as sources of problems in
their environment. These were rarely mentioned by the upper-middle-
class men I talked to.

In short, the black and white workers I interviewed value morality
highly. While blacks value responsibility and work ethics slightly less than
whites, they put a much stronger emphasis on solidarity and generosity
than whites do.[29] As we shall see, the descriptions that blacks produce of

the differences between themselves and white people point again to major contrasts in definitions of morality.

The moral flaws of white people

In the eyes of most of the black men I talked to, moral differences between whites and blacks are abundant. African-Americans often describe white people as essentially sneaky and not to be trusted. They often believe blacks to be superior to whites because blacks are more communal and intimate. Jimmy Bloom, a machinist who lives in Elizabeth, New Jersey, said that black people are more humane than white people: "Black people are sensitive toward human needs because we are concerned humans, whereas the white people that I have met in my life seem detached from the human thing." An assistant cable splicer, John Patterson, echoes this perspective when he says that blacks "have a strong sense of family, a strong sense of togetherness." Illustrating his cultural distance from white culture, he adds:

> Black people, actually black women for one, they hold together much more. White people they don't take as much time with their families as we do. . . . How they let their kids be so much more on their own. Blacks seem to take more time with their children. Whites, I've noticed they have a tendency to always have someone else there. Like their kids will go maybe to school away from home and might come home one weekend a year. . . . And then when they're there, the parents are always going somewhere and they have a babysitter, then they have a nanny. That's to me, that's a big difference and to me a lot of the black family compared to the white family. It's a big difference. I mean, I don't know if it makes the kid eventually better. But it's just, as far as the closeness and stuff, it's different.

The egotism, sneakiness, and essentially unfair nature of white people is a theme that came back repeatedly during the interviews. It is expressed by Larry Black, a plumber, who says:

> White people . . . probably 95 percent of the time they're going to . . . screw me over, and probably 35 percent of the time, I think that blacks are going to do that. So when I meet a white person, [the probability is] three to four times more greater that I'm scared they're going to do something really sneaky and nasty . . . screw you over, trying to set you up, being nosy, trying to get you fired from your job, trying to trick you to go to certain places and do something wrong, have you set up and frame you, everything you think that a person can do that's no good. . . . Sell you things that are no good, get you hooked on drugs, alcohol. Yeah, I believe in that. A

matter of fact I think black peoples do think white peoples as that, yeah. Honestly, I think 95 percent do believe that.

He adds:

I'm scared of white people too 'cause I say to myself, this guy's gonna fuck me somehow or another. He's gonna fuck me, I've gotta watch him. I don't know how he's gonna do it, but I gotta watch him, until feel comfortable and I see that he's not gonna charge more . . . and see that maybe I can trust him.

This view is echoed by Steve Simpson, a worker in a recycling plant, who describes his co-workers, who are predominantly white, as sneaky. He says:

They try to basically figure, get into your personality, [see] what you think about certain things, and why. My black friends would never ask me a question [like that] while 99.9 percent of the white people constantly ask you. . . . How you spend your money, what you do with your money, what kind of girlfriend you deal with, do you deal with Hispanic women, do you deal with white women. . . . A black person couldn't care less. . . . I guess it's competitive, I guess [whites] probably get an idea of do black men think their womens is the choice of the female over black race or Hispanic race, or their politician is the choice over a black politician.

On the other hand, Tony Clark, who works for a medical supply company on Long Island, perceives whites as too rigid. He says that what characterizes blacks is

To believe in God, to believe in hope, believe in heaven and hell. To believe that if you live a good life, and you are a good person, generally, good will come from it. Those kinds of things I feel are there as opposed to like when I relate to a white person as far as that same kind of situation, they seem to have a more structured aspects of it. . . . They say you can't go [to church in blue jeans and sneakers] because that wouldn't be polite. That's not right. . . . They have a hard time understanding concepts. . . . They live in certain boxes. They live in more boxes. Some have more corners cut off. There are things they can't relate to.

For many of these black men, white people are too concerned with status when deciding who they will interact with. Like Larry Black, the plumber, many also view whites as having inherent domineering tendencies. He says, talking about blacks:

We didn't create the bombs, we didn't play with gunpowder, we didn't do this. . . . The interest of white America was always to build and be better and be competitive, and in doin' that, that's more reading and sitting and studying and being more manipulative, and more deceiving, and more, you know, whereas we weren't.

Larry implicitly suggests that the exercise of power implies moral deception and corruption, as if moral purity and socioeconomic success were mutually exclusive. The domineering tendencies of whites are also emphasized by John Smith, a letter carrier concerned with white cultural imperialism. He explains:

> I see [whites] as being, or as wanting to be, the dominant force in everything. I see them as being intolerant of other lifestyles and other thoughts from other people what other people think. Especially American whites. . . . They think everybody, I mean other people from other countries or other races, should bend and do things their way. If their clothes are not like their, they're funny. If you can't speak English, you're inferior. And the people in other countries, it looks like they feel an obligation to learn to speak English to satisfy the Americans. . . . They want to impose their philosophy or thoughts on other people.

Similar examples abound: a phone technician explains that blacks dislike whites for their "superior attitude. They think they are above you, you know." In the view of a bindery worker, white people "try to be more domineering. Some of them have a more superior attitude if you allow them to get away with it." Along the same lines, a truck driver contrasts the domineering tendencies of whites to the playfulness of blacks when he says that "white people always lookin' for a way to beat you. . . . Everything is how to keep somebody else, how to beat you at the game. . . . [Blacks] enjoy havin' a good time, hangin' out in the park, playin' sports, stuff like that. I think they enjoy that a lot more."

Other black interviewees stress that there are good white people and bad white people, just like there are good blacks and bad blacks. At times, they appeal to the Bible to justify their claim that we are all equal because we are all the children of God. Others appeal to biological argument to ground equality in the fact that we have all spent nine months in our mother's womb, and have similar anatomies. While these religious/biological *qua* universalist statements are relatively widespread, they are often voiced simultaneously with denunciation of the domineering tendencies of whites (Lamont, 1996a).

Partly influenced by the mass media depiction of society as an overwhelmingly (white) middle-class world,[30] the black men I talked to easily move from drawing boundaries against whites to drawing boundaries against the middle class, at times confounding both categories and using similar rhetorics to describe both, equally exploitative, groups. In particular, Jerry Smith, the machinist, says that "most (workers) believe that management [who is white] is trying to squeeze them like a grape and get more, more, more." Art Armstrong, the newspaper worker, says about his bosses that "they don't really care about anyone anyway. . . . It's like sometimes they will do things that will remind you 'Well, you're a commodity to us, and if we feel we're not getting anything out of you anymore, or we feel we can get more out of that person, you're out.'" These comments all reveal a view of the higher social echelons as morally bankrupt, selfish, and exploitative. The class struggle takes a distinctively moral tone for these men. At the same time, black workers define the scale of evaluation such that they can put themselves above the middle class and white people in general, rejecting and resisting the principles of evaluation that would attribute them a lowly place.[31]

The explanation for these instances of boundaries that African-Americans draw against whites has to be found in the relationship between both groups. Indeed, the very frequent racial *qua* moral boundary work that whites produce against blacks certainly sustains for blacks a view of whites as unfriendly villains. Furthermore, the boundary work of blacks is steeped in categories borrowed from cultural repertoires of discrimination that Americans have produced over the last three centuries. For instance, that a young plumber like Larry Black – who grew up on Long Island – presumes that white people will try to trick him into getting into trouble brings up images of overt pre-desegregation racial persecution. Along these lines, Mia Bay (1994), in her study of slave narratives, found that like contemporary African-Americans, slaves associated whites with power and domination yet stressed that both the white race and the black race include good and bad people. The use that interviewees make of these historically constituted cultural repertoires remains to be explored in the context of their particular experience and life conditions.[32]

Social implications of the research

What does this analysis tell us about the cultural mechanisms of reproduction of inequality? If black and white workers are equally concerned with morality, differences in the emphasis that each racial group gives to specific dimensions of morality allow them to locate themselves above the other group, demonizing it in the process. However, whites are much more successful at giving their own definition of morality legitimacy in the workplace, as suggested by the research of Kirschenman and Neckerman (1990), who show that white employers discriminate against black employees based on preconceptions concerning their work ethics. Whites are also more successful at legitimizing their definition of morality in the public sphere at large – witness the popularity of Rush Limbaugh and other producers of hate speech in contemporary America. Public criticisms of egotistic whites rarely reach the intensity and frequency of condemnations of the always-implicitly black welfare queens, deadbeat dads, and teenage mothers. The support that Congress gave to the Personal Responsibility Act is only one measure of the cultural resilience of these representations. It is this context that gives the findings presented here their significance. The asymmetry in the ability of both groups to diffuse a demonized view of the other is key to understanding how representations of reality play a crucial role in the reproduction of inequality in American society. The definitions of morality that are documented here are not only different: they also have very unequal impact on American mainstream culture and reinforce racism, which contributes to the growing inequality in the resources that whites and nonwhites have access to.[33]

The extent to which whites are ignorant of the complexities of black culture, and vice versa, should not be underestimated. That John Patterson, the assistant cable splicer, describes white people as typically having nannies is evidence of this gap, as is the dismay of the medical supply worker, Tony Clark, when he finds that his white colleagues think that he resembles Arsenio Hall although he himself is fat and short. Although talk of racism is pervasive in American public discourse, it is easy to forget how few contacts blacks and whites have with one another due to segregation in housing and employment. With the increase in the level of education of African-Americans, many are now closer to white culture than they were 20 years ago.[34] However, the percentage of blacks who have a college degree still hovers around 10 percent. The vast majority live in communities that are exclusively black and many enter in contact with white culture primarily through the mass media.[35] The relative isolation of blacks from whites and whites from blacks plays a key role in sustaining ignorance, an impoverishment of understanding of the culture of the other, and racial stereotypes in both groups. The spatial distance reinforces a social and cultural distance that remains largely understudied. Mainstream black American culture, in particular, deserves much more attention.

While influential scholars including Bellah, MacIntyre, Taylor, and Bloom have decried the decline of morality in American society, the men I talked to expressed very important moral concerns. Despite the success of Hernstein and Murray's (1994) *The Bell Curve*, the naturalization of racial inferiority via genetics remains unacceptable in many circles, at least at the level of public discourse. As suggested by theories of symbolic racism, moral themes have come to occupy the central stage in talks about racial differences, in part because they better accommodate universalistic rhetorics than do biological differences.[36] We need to explore further the place of biological, traditional, religious, legalistic, humanitarian, or market-oriented arguments in the rhetorics that the men I talked to deploy to describe others. More work is also needed in understanding the salience of various dimensions of identity – here primarily morality and race, but also class, gender, culture, religion, and nationality – in boundary work. This is key to gaining a richer understanding of the mechanisms that allow racism to remain so alive and well in America today. If moral arguments are particularly central in racist discourse, it is undoubtedly in part because they sustain individual explanations of failure that are more compatible with the American Dream than more structural explanations.

Implications for cultural studies

This essay deals with issues that have been at the center of the cultural studies agenda: it analyzes alternative moralities as grounds for classification struggles. It also speaks to the process through which evaluation and identification, combined with spatial distance, leads to the naturalization of differences and to inequality. To conclude, I want to highlight the ways in which the study of boundary work can contribute to cultural studies.

Contrary to important currents in cultural studies, I resist adopting key aspects of poststructuralism, for instance, the fascination with intertextuality. I reject as empirically implausible the popular theoretical position, inspired by structuralism and deconstruction, that, by definition, texts take their meaning relationally within a global universe of interacting texts.[37] Instead, as illustrated here with morality, I trace empirically in relation to whom people define themselves with and against, and how different interpretations of reality meet one another (see also, for example, Schudson, 1993). In line with Lacan, Freud, Taylor, and others, who agree that identity is defined by contrast with the other,[38] I hope to document the salience and meanings of various categories through which the men I talked to define their identity. I accomplish this by getting them to describe their definitions of "us" and "them" through a set of questions aimed at tapping concrete and abstract descriptions of people they consider to be similar to and different from them, better and worse, higher and lower – focusing here on black/white relationships only, because of space limitations. In the larger project, I thereby document the salience of the category "whites" and its meanings for a large group of black workers, instead of positing that the meaning of race is "generally" relationally defined.

This approach does not privilege bounded or diffused identities, nor ascribed or achieved characteristics, as does some of the recent work on identity that focuses on the "race, class, and gender" triad. Also, contrary to Bourdieu's (1984) writings on symbolic boundaries and to studies of symbolic racism,[39] this approach is resolutely inductive in that it does not predefine categories of evaluation/identification. Contrary to a large portion of the literature on identity politics, it draws on systematically gathered empirical data, bracketing or giving a backstage role to issues of self-reflexivity, while being critical of unreflective positivism.[40] And contrary to poststructuralist critiques of essentialism, it aims at documenting the full range of universalistic arguments that people make to describe differences (including biological, moral, civic, religious, political, and cultural arguments), instead of asserting the inadequacy of natural, ahistorical, or other universalistic arguments, prior to demonstrating empirically their relative salience (for an illustration, see Lamont, 1996a and 1996b).[41] Finally, instead of positing that identities are unstable or fragmented as do postmodern theorists, this approach can, with the appropriate data, establish empirically the extent to which specific identities are fluid across a variety of contexts, and identify factors that might explain variation (cf. Stinchcombe, 1995; Lamont, 1992: ch. 5). For instance, in the present project, I find that the men I talked to often provide fairly consistent definitions of symbolic boundaries and that their identities appear to be relatively stable, in part because their social networks are largely family-based and their rate of professional or geographic mobility relatively low.

If the theoretical goal of cultural studies is truly to go further in our understanding of the intermingling of meaning and inequality, it would benefit from infusion from this approach, which can be more pointed and can open new roads in the study of naturalization of differences. Indeed, studying identity politics should mean more than deconstructing categories, showing that they are related to one another, that something is nonuniversal about them, that power is discursively constructed, that politics is about contestation over meaning, or that agency is expressed through micropractices. Our understanding of identity politics might be richer if we were to document the salience of various dimensions of identity across populations, the degree of cultural distance between dominant and dominated groups, and the process by which various groups are able to diffuse their representation of the other in mainstream culture. Again, instead of denouncing universalism and providing an epistemological critique thereof, we need to identify which types of universalistic logics people – not academics – use in their definitions of the other and how beliefs about these universalisms are distributed in the population. In other words, instead of deconstructing hierarchies in scholarly or popular culture texts, we need to focus on how people – more than cultural producers – define hierarchies. Confronting the power/culture/inequality nexus surely means refocusing our attention away from ourselves – being less egocentric and more absorbed in other realities.

NOTES

My research was supported by a fellowship from the German Marshall Fund of the United States and grants from the National Science Foundation (SES 92–13363) and the University Committee for Research in the Humanities and the Social Sciences, Princeton University. I gratefully acknowledge comments from Jason Duell, John Hall, Elizabeth Long, Kathryn Newman, Angela Tsay, and Maureen Waller.

1   Symbolic racism "represents a form of resistance to change in the racial status quo based on moral feelings that blacks violate such traditional American values as individualism and self-reliance, the work ethic, obedience and discipline" (Kinder and Sears, 1981: 416). This theory suggests, for instance, that "resistance to busing may be as intense as it is in part because it conjures up images throughout the white population of innocent white children being sent far from their safe white neighborhoods into schools jammed with academically unmotivated, disorderly, dangerous blacks" (ibid: 429). Symbolic racists do not necessarily view any black individual as immoral, but they draw broad conclusions about blacks as a group and their lack of morality. McConahay and Hough (1976) identify several dimensions of symbolic racism: blacks are viewed as too pushy and as not playing by the rules applied to earlier generations of a deprived minority. They violate the sense of propriety and do not deserve further advance: "Welfare, black anger and militancy, black mayors, riots in the streets, affirmative action programs, public officials sensitive to black demands, fair housing laws – all symbolize the unfair advance or demands of blacks at the expense of the values that made this nation great" (ibid: 38).

2   Massey and Denton (1993) showed that in 1980 the average black person in the ten largest US cities lived in a neighborhood that was at least 80 percent black and that the vast majority reside in areas that are 100 percent black (ibid: 160). Spatial isolation leads to social isolation which means that blacks are less likely than members of any other groups to report friendship with anyone else but members of their own group. There is a genuine lack of social connection with mainstream society that translates into growing cultural autonomization.

3   By boundary work, I refer to the process by which individuals define who they are by opposition to others, and to traits associated with others. This use of the term differs from that of Gieryn (1983), who refer to "boundary work" to describe how scientific disciplines compete for resources at the organizational level by increasing their sphere of competence.

4   In their study of a Washington DC black high school, Fordham and Ogbu (1986) argue that blacks "develop a sense of collective identity and a sense of peoplehood in opposition to the social identity of white Americans because of the way white Americans treat them in economic, political, social, and psychological domains." They found that the students they studied identify as distinctively white, behaviors such as speaking standard English, listening to white music and white radio stations, going to opera and ballet,

spending a lot of time in the library studying, working hard to get good grades in school, getting good grades in school, going to the Smithsonian, going to a Rolling Stones concert at the Capital Center, doing volunteer work, camping, hiking, or mountain climbing, having cocktails or a cocktail party, having a party with no music, listening to classical music, being on time, reading and writing poetry, and putting on airs. Besides this study, few social scientists have addressed black definitions of white culture. But from a historical perspective, see Bay (1989).

5 Waller (1995) critiques this reluctance to study the cultural dimension in research concerning poor single parents.

6 See Durkheim (1965). On cultural repertoires, see Geertz (1973), Swidler (1986), Wuthnow (1988). For more recent work using this approach, see Emirbayer and Mische (1995), Hall (1992), Lamont (1992), Sewell (1992).

7 The blue-collar workers studied by David Halle (1984) in his excellent ethnography of a New Jersey chemical plant use the term "working man" to describe themselves. By symbolic communities, I refer to groups of individuals that are socially defined as showing a certain symbolic cohesion and as having at their disposal similar categorization systems to differentiate between insiders and outsiders, as well as common vocabularies and symbols through which they create a shared identity. On this concept, see Gusfield (1975).

8 For a cognate perspective on identity and cultural repertoire, see Somers (1994), White (1992), Tilly (1994, 1995). These authors are variously concerned with the use of repertoires in the construction of identity and with the ways in which this use is shaped by contexts or relational settings defined more or less broadly as "institutions, public narratives, and social practices," including social networks (Somers, 1994: 626).

9 While African-American blue-collar workers comprise 2.3 percent of the total US population, they represent 32 percent of the African-American labor force and 36 percent of the employed African-Americans. In contrast, Euro-American blue-collar workers make up 16 percent of the population. They represent 27 percent of the total US labor force and 29 percent of the employed white labor force (Bureau of Labor Statistic, 1989).

10 The 40 white upper-middle-class men interviewed for this earlier project also reside in the New York suburbs. They were randomly sampled form the phone books of towns such as Madison, Summit, and New Providence, New Jersey, and Massapequa and Merrick, Long Island. For more details, see Lamont (1992).

11 As was the case in the upper-middle-class study, respondents were asked to concretely and abstractly describe people with whom they prefer not to associate, those in relation to whom they feel superior and inferior, and those who evoke hostility, indifference, and sympathy. They were also asked to describe negative and positive traits in their co-workers and acquaintances, as well as their childrearing values. The criteria of evaluation behind their responses were systematically compared to recreate a template of their mental map of their grammar of evaluation.

12 This is part of a larger project based on 150 interviews with low-status white-collar workers and blue-collar workers and on 80 interviews with professionals and managers residing in the Paris and New York suburbs. The goal of this study is to analyze the relative salience of dimensions of identity in France and the United States, comparing white and blue-collar workers, lower-middle-class and upper-middle-class workers, North African immigrants and *français de souche*, as well as African-American and Euro-American workers.

13 These workers have been working full-time and steadily for at least five years. They do not supervise more than ten workers.

14 Hundreds of letters were sent to potential respondents living in working-class suburbs in the New York area. In a follow-up phone interview, these men were asked to self-identify themselves racially and we chose interviewees who categorized themselves as black and whites and who meet other criteria of selection pertaining to occupation, age, nationality, and level of education. I take the terms "black" and "white" to be categories that are the object of some intersubjective negotiation, but analyze black and white subpopulations at a specific point in time. I focus on the relationship between blacks and whites because both groups occupy polarized positions in American society, symbolically as well as economically. However, while both groups often define themselves in opposition to one another, they often take into consideration other racial and ethnic groups in so doing.

15 By using in-depth interviews instead of ethnographic observation, I sacrifice depth to breadth. However, by choosing respondents in 12 different communities, I maximize the likelihood of tapping internal differences within both populations. Furthermore, while interviews cannot tap class consciousness "in action," they can tap broader cultural frameworks that are transportable from one context of action to another.

16 Space limitations prevent me from dealing with the complexity of the changing social, occupational, and economic characteristics of the working class. On these issues, see Stacey (1989), Dudley (1994), and Rubin (1994).

17 The black and white samples are somewhat comparable in terms of level of education and household income, although the African-Americans I talked to generally fare less well than white respondents. Some 63 percent of the Euro-Americans have completed a high school degree or a GED. This is the case for only 40 percent of the African-Americans. However, while 30 percent of the Euro-Americans have completed some college, it is the case for 50 percent of the African-Americans – only one respondent in each group has less than a high school degree. Some 36 percent of the African-American households make $39,000 or less a year, compared to 22 percent of the Euro-American households; 39 percent of the African-American households have incomes between $40,000 and $59,000 a year, compared to 36 percent of the Euro-American households. Finally, 10 percent of the African-American households have incomes above $60,000, compared to 40 percent of the Euro-American households. Half of both the white and black households are two-income households and 60 percent of the interviewees are married or cohabiting. African-Americans have more children; 33 percent

of them have four or more children, compared to only 10 percent of the Euro-American sample.

18   I have no privileged relationship with workers, black or white. Cultural stud-ies proponents are increasingly sympathetic to "alloidentified" studies pro-duced by non-group members, and encourage, for instance, studies of blacks by whites or of female cultures by males. The effect of my own identity on the interviews was to some extent mitigated by my attempt to present myself with a blurred national and professional identity, for instance, as a foreigner to the culture I studied. On this topic, see Lamont (1992).

19   Among the men I talked to, 76 percent of the Euro-Americans and 67 per-cent of the African-Americans stress morality in their discussion of child-rearing values. In contrast, only 1 percent of the Euro-Americans and 7 percent of the African-Americans stress socioeconomic achievement, while respect-ively 12 percent and 22 percent stress cultural values.

20   Some 78 percent of the Euro-Americans and 75 percent of the African-Americans put a premium on moral values in the qualities they appreciate. Less than 10 percent of both samples put a premium on cultural and socio-economic values together. Similarly, 75 percent of the Euro-Americans and 65 percent of the African-Americans stress moral values when discussing the traits they dislike in others; less than 10 percent of both groups value cultural and socioeconomic traits.

21   When asked to define success, 49 percent of whites and 43 percent of blacks use moral references of one type or another. In contrast, 38 percent in both groups stress socioeconomic achievement; 8 percent of the whites and 11 percent of the blacks use cultural criteria, such as being educated, to define success.

22   Social scientists have stressed the importance of solidarity for blacks by dis-cussing fictive kinship and loyalty. Fordham and Ogbu (1986: 185) describe fictive kinship as "not only a symbol of social identity for blacks, it is also a medium of boundary maintenance *vis-à-vis* white Americans."

23   This description is evocative of the traditional African-American figure of "the race man" described by St-Clair and Clayton (1962).

24   In a descriptive ethnography of a predominantly black community located in a large industrial metropolitan city of the Northern United States, Jacqueline Mithun (1973) found that cooperative networks were predominant in the lives of the people she studied. She argues that family and church continue to emphasize cooperative behaviors and that greater time and consideration are taken for human interaction and polite inquiry than in mainstream cul-ture. "Blacks invest as much interest in human relations as in the business at hand if not more."

25   Lomax Cook (1979: 106–9) compared the willingness of African-Americans and Euro-Americans to support social services for a variety of potentially needy groups. She found that blacks are more likely than whites to support an overall increase in service for each of these groups. Blacks show a slight tendency to prefer to help poor persons and persons of working age, whereas whites would give more support to the disabled and elderly, suggesting that whites put more emphasis on responsibility when judging deserve. Further-

more, Sigelman and Welch (1991: 143) show that blacks are in general more supportive of increased welfare spending and government action.

26 A few interviewees deplore the lack of solidarity among blacks. A chemical operator says, "One thing with black Americans [is that] when we do make it we don't pull our brothers and sisters up that don't have at all." Similarly, a recycling plant worker says that "white people would rather hang out with their own. Blacks would rather hang out with probably anybody. I don't think, black people got that close ties amongst their race."

27 Based on an ethnography of a black community located in Corona (Queens) that focuses on the effect of home ownership on boundaries, Steven Gregory (1992) found that home owners try to protect their community and quality of life against poor blacks, and that the segmentation of the black "community" is in part the product of the integration of middle-class blacks in mainstream politics.

28 For a discussion of how white workers deal with the problem of worth, partly in relation to moral values, see Sennett and Cobb (1972).

29 The point here is not that African-Americans have no work ethic, but that the black men I talked to value it slightly less than their white counterparts. It is also possible that they define work ethic differently, focusing more on the effort that individuals provide than on other aspects of the work ethic. On the commitment that poor African-Americans have to work ethic, see Anderson (1979). For a discussion of the importance of responsibility and honesty for black working-class men, see Duneier (1992).

30 Richard Butsch (1991) shows that between 1956 and 1990, more than two thirds of the families depicted on television were middle class.

31 Commitment to community, individual work ethic, and responsibility play somewhat opposite roles in the moral rhetoric of white and black workers. On this topic, see Gans (1988).

32 Lamont (1995) argued that evaluative frameworks valued by symbolic communities can be viewed as illustrative of aspects of national cultural repertoires that exist to a certain extent (to be assessed empirically from group to group) above specific contexts because they are transportable from one situation to the next (although enacted in context). These symbolic boundaries are determined over time by both the supply side of culture (the macrocultural repertoires that are made available to people) and the factors that make individuals more likely to draw on some dimensions of these repertoires rather than others (these factors include the broad characteristics of the society in which they live and the structural characteristic of their own social position as well).

33 On the widening inequality of wealth between whites and nonwhites between 1983 and 1990, see Wolfe (1995).

34 Collins (1979) and Davis (1982) argue that the college-educated population continues to show a high degree of similarity in its cultural practices and attitudes over a wide range of areas.

35 On this point, see note 2. Only 11 percent of African-Americans had a college degree in 1990, compared to 22 percent of the Euro-Americans (Department of Commerce, 1990: 151–4).

36   On the properties of moralist rhetoric, see Jasper (1992). Lamont (1996b) analyzes how respondents draw on universalistic and particularistic principles when justifying their evaluations of others, but I will not address this subject here. Particularly useful on this topic is the work of Boltanski and Thèvenot (1991).

37   One of the reasons for rejecting the poststructuralist position is that the universe of texts used to define meaning being infinite, the analyst is bound to focus on idiosyncratically chosen relationships in analyzing the production of meaning. For an elaboration of this point, applied to the use of literary evidence in historical studies, see Peter Laslett (1976). This criticism has often been addressed to structuralism, reflection theory, psychoanalysis, and even to Bourdieu's field theory. For a critique of structuralism in this regard, see Mark Schneider (1993: ch. 4).

38   For a perspective from cultural anthropology on the self and the other, see Renato Rosaldo's (1989: 28) discussion of the importance of shifting attention to human differences and of studying boundaries between groups.

39   Using Lickert scales, theorists of symbolic racism measure how strongly people believe in certain statements representative of symbolic racism. They predefine the moral shortcomings that whites attribute to blacks (e.g. their pushiness) instead of analyzing inductively the exact content of this boundary work. One of the contributions of this essay is to expand the theory of symbolic racism by spelling out how whites and blacks perceive each other in moral terms.

40   For a discussion of the issue of self-positioning, see Chicago Cultural Studies Group (1994: 120). On the issue of bracketing, see Griswold (1990).

41   Drawing on Rorty's antifoundational pragmatism and on Derrida's understanding of signification as unstable and shifting, cultural studies is concerned with the fixity/fluidity of dimensions of identity and the extent to which they presume fondational artifice that allows dominant groups to make universal statements. On this point, see Lash (1992: 14.) A research program on "Symbolic Boundaries and Modes of Justification in Comparative Perspective" has been jointly proposed by myself and Laurent Thèvenot to develop a collective agenda focusing on the forms of evaluation that are used in France and the United States to assess people, events, and situation. This project pays special attention to the place of the various types of rhetoric discussed above and brings together researchers from the Ecole des Hautes Etudes en Sciences Sociales and from the Department of Sociology, Princeton University.

REFERENCES

Anderson, Elijah 1979: *A Place at the Corner.* Chicago: University of Chicago Press.
—— 1990: *Streetwise: Race, Class, and Change in an Urban Community.* Chicago: University of Chicago Press.

Bay, Mia 1989: *White Images in the Black Mind: African-American Ideas about White People 1930–1925.* Unpublished dissertation, Department of History, Yale University.

—— 1994: "Us is Human Flesh:" The Racial Thought of American Slaves. Paper presented in the work-in-progress series, Program in African-American Studies, Princeton University.

Boltanski, Luc and Thévenot, Laurent 1991: *De la justification: les économies de la grandeur.* Paris: Gallimard.

Bourdieu, Pierre 1984: *Distinction: A Social Critique of the Judgment of Taste.* Cambridge, MA: Harvard University Press.

Bureau of Labor Statistics 1989: *Handbook of Labor Statistics,* Bulletin 2340. Washington, DC: US Department of Labor.

Butsch, Richard 1991: Class and Gender in Four Decades of TV Families: Plus Ça Change. Unpublished manuscript, Department of Sociology, Rider College.

Chicago Cultural Studies Group 1994: Critical Multiculturalism. In David Theo Goldberg (ed.), *Multiculturalism: A Critical Reader.* New York: Blackwell, 114–40.

Chrisman, Robert and Alan, Robert (eds) 1991: *Court of Appeal: The Black Community Speaks Out on the Racial and Sexual Politics of Thomas Vs. Hill.* New York: Ballantine.

Collins, Patricia Hill 1991: *Black Feminist Thought: Knowledge, Consciousness, and the Politics of Empowerment.* New York: Routledge.

Collins, Randall 1979: *The Credential Society.* New York: Academic Press.

Davis, James 1982: Achievement Variables and Class Cultures: Family, Schooling, Jobs and Forty-nine Dependent Variables in the Cumulative GSS. *American Sociological Review,* 47, 569–86.

Department of Commerce, Bureau of the Census 1990: *Statistical Abstract of the United States, 1990.* Washington DC: Government Printing Office.

Dudley, Kathryn Marie 1994: *The End of the Line: Lost Jobs, New Lives in Postindustrial America.* Chicago: University of Chicago Press.

Duneier, Mitchell 1992: *Slim's Table: Race, Respectability, and Masculinity.* Chicago: University of Chicago Press.

Durkheim, Emile 1965: *The Elementary Forms of Religious Life.* New York: Free Press.

Emirbayer, Mustapha and Mische, Ann 1995: What is Agency? Working Paper Series, Center for Studies of Social Change, New School for Social Research.

Fordham, Signithia and Ogbu, John 1986: Black Students' School Success: Coping with the "Burden of Acting White." *Urban Review,* 18 (3), 176–206.

Gans, Herbert 1988: *Middle Class Individualism: The Future of Liberal Democracy.* New York: Free Press.

Geertz, Clifford 1973: *The Interpretation of Culture.* New York: Basic Books.

Gieryn, Tom 1983: Boundary Work and the Demarcation of Science from Nonscience: Strains and Interests in Professional Ideologies of Scientists. *American Sociological Review,* 48, 781–95.

Gregory, Steven 1992: The Changing Significance of Race and Class in an African-American Community. *American Ethnologist,* 19 (2), 255–75.

Griswold, Wendy 1990: Provisional, Provincial Positivism: Reply to Denzin. *American Journal of Sociology*, 95 (6), 1,580–83.

Gusfield, Joseph 1975: *Communities*. Chicago: University of Chicago Press.

Hall, John R. 1992: The Capital(s) of Cultures: A Non Holistic Approach to Status Situations, Class, Gender, and Ethnicity. In Michèle Lamont and Marcel Fournier (eds), *Cultivating Differences: Symbolic Boundaries and the Making of Inequality*, Chicago: University of Chicago Press, 257–88.

Halle, David 1984: *America's Working Man: Work, Home, and Politics among Blue-collar Property Owners*. Chicago: University of Chicago Press.

Hernstein, Richard J. and Murray, Charles 1994: *The Bell Curve: Intelligence and Class Structure in American Life*. New York: Free Press.

Jasper, James M. 1992: The Politics of Abstractions: Instrumental and Moralist Rhetorics in Public Debates. *Social Research*, 59 (2), 315–44.

Kinder, Donald and Sears, David O. 1981: Prejudice and Politics: Symbolic Racism Versus Racial Threats to the Good Life. *Journal of Personality and Social Psychology*, 40 (3), 414–31.

Kirschenman, Joleen and Neckerman, Kathryn M. 1990: We'd Love to Hire Them, But . . . : The Meaning of Race for Employers. In Christopher Jencks and Paul E. Peterson (eds), *The Urban Underclass*, Washington, DC: Brookings Institute.

Lamont, Michèle 1992: *Money, Morals, and Manners: The Culture of the French and the American Upper-middle Class*. Chicago: University of Chicago Press.

—— 1995: National Identity and National Boundary Patterns. *French Historical Studies*, 19 (2), 349–65.

—— 1996a: The Rhetoric of Racism and Anti-racism in France and the United States. Paper presented at the meetings of the American Sociological Association, August, New York.

—— 1996b: North-African Immigrants Respond to French Racism: Demonstrating Equivalence Through Universalism. Paper presented at the conference on "Universalizing from Particulars: Islamic View of the Human and the UN Declaration of Human Rights in Comparative Perspective," May, Princeton University.

Lash, Scott 1992: *Sociology of Postmodernism*. London: Routledge.

Laslett, Peter 1976: The Wrong Way through the Telescope: A Note on Literary Evidence in Sociology and in Historical Sociology. *British Journal of Sociology*, 27 (3), 319–42.

Lomax Cook, Fay 1979: *Who Should be Helped? Public Support for Social Services*. Beverly Hills, CA: Sage Publications.

McConahay, John B. and Hough, Joseph C. Jr, 1976: Symbolic Racism. *Journal of Social Issues*, 32 (2), 23–45.

Massey, Douglas and Denton, Nancy A. 1993: *American Apartheid: Segregation and the Making of the Underclass*. Cambridge: Cambridge University Press.

Mithun, Jacqueline 1973: Cooperation and Solidarity as Survival Necessities in a Black Urban Community. *Urban Anthropology*, 2 (1).

Morrison, Toni (ed.) 1992: *Race-ing Justice, En-gendering Power: Essays on Anita Hill, Clarence Thomas, and the Construction of Social Reality*. New York: Pantheon.

Rosaldo, Renato 1989: *Culture and Truth: The Remaking of Social Analysis*. Boston: Beacon Books.

Rubin, Lilian B. 1994: *Families on the Faultline: America's Working Class Speaks about the Family, the Economy, Race, and Ethnicity*. New York: Harper Collins Publishers.

St-Clair, Drake and Cayton, Horace 1962: *Black Metropolis: A Study of Negro Life in a Northern City*. New York: Harper and Row.

Schneider, Mark 1993: *Culture and Enchantment*. Chicago: University of Chicago Press.

Schudson, Michael 1993: *Watergate in American Memory: How we Remember, Forget, and Reconstruct the Past*. New York: Basic Books.

Sennett, Richard and Cobb, Jonathan 1972: *The Hidden Injuries of Class*. New York: Vintage.

Sewell, William Jr 1992: The Theory of Structure: Duality, Agency, and Transformation. *American Journal of Sociology*, 98 (1), 1–29.

Sigelman, Lee and Welch, Susan 1991: *Black Americans' Views of Racial Inequality: A Dream Differed*. Cambridge: Cambridge University Press.

Somers, Margaret R. 1994: The Narrative Constitution of Identity: A Relational and Network Approach. *Theory and Society*, 23, 605–49.

Stacey, Judith 1989: *Brave New Families: Stories of Domestic Upheaval in Late Twentieth Century America*. New York: Basic Books.

Stinchcombe, Arthur 1995: *Sugar Island Slavery in the Age of Enlightenment: The Political Economy of the Caribbean World*. Princeton: Princeton University Press.

Swidler, Ann 1986: Culture in Action: Symbols and Strategies. *American Sociological Review*, 51, 273–86.

Tilly, Charles 1994: Citizenship, Identity, and Social History. Working Paper Series, Center for Studies of Social Change, New School for Social Research.

—— 1995: Social Movements and (All Sorts of) Other Political Interactions – Local, National, and International – Including Identities: Several Divagations from a Common Path, Beginning with British Struggles over Catholic Emancipation, 1780–1829, and Ending with Contemporary Nationalism. Working Paper Series, Center for Studies of Social Change, New School for Social Research.

Waller, Maureen 1995: Claiming Fatherhood: Paternity, Culture, and Public Policy. Paper presented at the annual meetings of the Eastern Sociological Society, Philadelphia.

White, Harrison 1992: *Identity and Control: A Structural Theory of Social Action*. Princeton: Princeton University Press.

Wolff, Edward N. 1995: *Top Heavy: A Study of the Increasing Inequality of Wealth in America*. New York: Twentieth Century Fund Press.

Wuthnow, Robert 1988: *Meaning and Moral Order: Explorations in Cultural Analysis*. Berkeley and Los Angeles: University of California Press.

10

The Ideology of Intensive Mothering: A Cultural Analysis of the Bestselling "Gurus" of Appropriate Childrearing

SHARON HAYS

According to a 1981 study, 97 percent of American mothers read at least one childrearing manual and nearly 75 percent consult two or more for advice on how to rear their young (Geboy, 1981). Exemplifying this, Dr Spock's *Baby and Child Care* (1992) has outsold all other books in the history of publishing with the single exception of the Bible – to date, it has sold 40 million copies in its six editions (At S & S . . . , 1992; Hackett, 1967). Two of Spock's major contemporary competitors are T. Berry Brazelton (whose *Toddlers and Parents* has sold 400,000 copies; his *Infants and Mothers*, 315,000) and Penelope Leach (whose most popular book, *Your Baby and Child*, has sold 1.5 million copies) (Lodge, 1993). Together, these three bestselling authors have been named as the central "gurus" of appropriate childrearing (Allison, 1990; Chira, 1994; Lawson, 1991). Given the ubiquity of these advice books, an examination of their contents is surely in order.

What follows is an analysis of these childrearing manuals in the traditions of cultural studies and the sociology of knowledge. Many people, including many scholars, would simply argue that the methods of parenting presented in these manuals follow from some combination of the inherent needs of children, the natural propensities of parents, and the scientifically discovered "truth" about what children require for proper development. But I understand these books as symbolic products that represent cultural realities rather than natural ones. The methods of childrearing that Spock, Brazelton, and Leach recommend, and the view of mothers and children they convey, did not arise spontaneously in the minds of these authors, did not spring from nature, and are not a measure of some absolute or timeless truth. Instead, the argument presented in these books is tied to a larger cultural model of appropriate childrearing – a model that was socially constructed, over time, under specifiable and complex circumstances. My approach, therefore, will be to unpack, decode, and deconstruct the implicit rules for social behavior and the underlying images of social life that are found in these particular symbolic products. Rather than look to any genetic, instinctual, biological or otherwise immutable basis for this bestselling advice, I will look to its social basis, considering the relationship between ideas and interests, culture and power, and meaning systems and political and economic systems. Ultimately, I will argue that an understanding of the foundations of this model of socially appropriate childrearing requires the use of a number of distinct, and even conflicting, theoretical approaches that have been central in the development of cultural studies and the sociology of culture.

In other words, my primary purpose here is to tease out the logic of the materials presented in these advice books and to speculate on its social basis and social significance. But first, let me make it clear that I recognize that there are very real limitations in using childrearing manuals to learn about childrearing ideologies. There is, of course, no direct correspondence between what these manuals advise, and what mothers and parents actually think, say, and do. As many scholars of culture have pointed out, different people make use of and interpret cultural materials in different ways.[1] Mothers interpret what they read in childrearing manuals and alter its meaning through the lens of their own circumstances, needs, and desires. Furthermore, many mothers get their childrearing ideas not from books, but from their friends, their family, other media sources, and their own upbringing – and this information, like the information found in books, is filtered through their pre-existing beliefs and their present social position. Much of my own research, in fact, is dedicated to uncovering the ideology of motherhood as it is expressed by mothers themselves. The following analysis is only a small part of a much larger project for which I analyzed the historical development of childrearing ideas and conducted depth interviews with women of varying class backgrounds and varying employment situations (Hays, 1996). All this research figures into my understanding of these childrearing manuals, and all this research is necessary to fully grasp the nature and significance of the ideology these manuals espouse.[2]

Nonetheless, these bestselling advice books remain an important source of information in and of themselves. The popularity of these particular manuals, rather than others, indicates they struck a chord with readers, and evidently supply what many parents perceive as the necessary and appropriate information and guidance. At the same time they thus (imperfectly) reflect the prevailing views of many parents, the wide distribution of these books and the regular appearance of their authors in the national media also mean that the ideology they espouse potentially affects the ideas and practices of contemporary parents. Though the following interpretation can only be suggestive, we can nonetheless understand the material presented by these child-rearing manuals as a rough *approxima-tion* of the dominant cultural model of appropriate childraising.

The model elaborated in these contemporary manuals takes the form of what I call "the ideology of intensive mothering." There are three connected, yet distinct, components to this ideology. First, these manuals clearly understand children as outside of market valuation. Children are treated as "priceless" in Zelizer's (1985) terms: they are not economic assets, they are not little workers in a family economy, nor are they seen as a future source of financial gain. Instead, children are sacred, innocent, and pure, their value immeasurable, and decisions regarding their rearing completely distinct from questions of efficiency or profitability. Second, the methods of good childrearing that these manuals recommend require an intensive commitment on the part of the caregiver. It is assumed that the parent will experience a deep and positive emotional response to the child; that response will lead the parent to focus all their attention on the child's needs and desires; and that attention will, in turn, lead the parent to seek out expert knowledge of childhood development, to engage in the unselfish nurturing of the child, and to expend a great deal of time and financial resources to insure that the child's wants and needs are met and that the "proper" development of the child is fostered. In short, for these advisors the appropriate methods of childrearing are child-centered, expert guided, emotionally absorbing, labor intensive, and finan-cially expensive.

These first two elements provide a model of intensive parenting. But there is a third central element to this ideology. The final assumption of these authors is that childcare is primarily the responsibility of the indi-vidual mother. Although fathers, day care workers, family members, and friends may help out, in the end it is the mother who is held responsible, not only for the physical well-being of the child and for the way in which the child is raised, but also for the type of adult that child becomes.

This model of intensive mothering seems paradoxical in the context of contemporary society for two connected reasons. First, in a society where the individualistic, calculating, competitive pursuit of personal gain dom-inates the larger "public" world of formal economic and political life, the ideology of intensive mothering, requiring a moral commitment to unre-munerated relationships based in affection and mutual obligations, seems clearly out of place.[3] Second, connected to this tension in the culture as a whole is a tension that runs through the lives of individual women – especially now that the paid employment of mothers has become the norm. In a social context where 58.3 percent of mothers with children under the age of six and 66.6 percent of mothers with children under the age of three are working for pay (US Bureau of the Census, 1994; Hayge and Bianchi, 1994), the superhuman effort recommended by the ideology of intensive mothering places a tremendous burden on every mother who wants or needs a paying job. Draining away time, money, and energy, this ideology clearly interferes with a mother's pursuit of financial gain. And by placing many women on a real or imagined "mommy track" (Schwartz, 1989) at the same time it implicitly urges all mothers to cut back or to cut out their paid working hours, this ideology not only diminishes a mother's potential for financial success, but also for social status in the context of a larger world that measures one's worth by the size of one's paycheck.

Given the contradictions faced by individual women, and the fact that intensive mothering seems in tension with the ethos of modern society as a whole, one might well wonder why it persists at all. Yet a look at contemporary bestselling childrearing manuals substantiates the intensive character of present-day advice on mothering. And such an examination, I argue, can also provide some important clues as to the social basis of this ideology.

At first glance, these three childrearing advisors and their manuals appear quite distinct. Spock is a pediatrician whose *Baby and Child Care* (1985) is something of an encyclopedia on childcare, providing answers to every question that parents could conceivably ask their pediatricians (or their own mothers, fathers, or best friends) – and more. Over half the book is dedicated to practical advice for parents on such topics as the supplies needed for the newborn, the pros and cons of breast feeding, the elements of a good diet for infants, the symptoms of illness, and instructions on first aid. The rest of the book provides step-by-step advice on how to understand and respond to the child's behavior at each stage of its development.

Brazelton, on the other hand, provides anecdotes. Most of his books are centered around four or five particular families, telling the stories of their childrearing practices and problems, and demonstrating how their pediatrician, Dr Brazelton, helps them cope (e.g. Brazelton, 1989, 1987, 1983a, 1983b). While this format means that no single one of his books is a comprehensive guide to childraising and that each book contains less advice than it might if it treated parenting in more general terms, Brazelton is quite prolific, and if all the reader's concerns are not covered, he or she can simply buy another Brazelton book (or read Brazelton's syndicated newspaper column, or watch one of his widely distributed videos, or tune in on an episode of the numerous television series he produces and in which he stars).

Leach, a British social psychologist, explicitly and self-consciously writes her books from the child's point of view. She supplies detailed information on the infant and child's physical make-up, behavioral habits, psychological states, and cognitive abilities at every developmental stage up to age five. Given this emphasis, Leach is able to provide the reader with more specific information than the other two authors on what she considers the (scientifically discovered) facts of child development. Leach suggests that any given parent, thus armed with the knowledge of what children in general tend to want and need, can make more informed decisions regarding their own unique children.

Although the format and the focus of these books vary, I will demonstrate that all three have in common a specific set of assumptions about the elements of good childraising, and that these assumptions ultimately add up to a demand for intensive mothering. Let me also make it clear, however, that in reporting this cultural model of appropriate childrearing from a social constructionist position, I am not attempting to degrade or dismiss it. Neither is it my intent to endorse it. While a dispassionate (or childless) outsider may be tempted to attack the prescriptions of Spock, Brazelton, and Leach as over-zealous or overly demanding, the insider (or parent) is likely to understand the recommendations of these authors as following from knowledge and concern for what is best for children. I want to avoid taking either of those positions. As I have stated, the central aim of the following analysis is to clarify the logic of childrearing ideas outlined in these manuals and to thereby make explicit a set of beliefs that, while in apparent contradiction with the ethos of the larger society and the practical needs of paid working mothers, is nonetheless quite powerful. In the end, it will be my argument that the ideology of intensive mothering presented in these childrearing manuals is extremely significant, not only because of its impact on women and mothers, but also because it is reflective of a number of less obvious yet nonetheless central and important trends in modern society as a whole.

The Mother is Primarily Responsible

Each of these authors in their earlier days assumed absolutely that mothers would raise the children; their original manuals referred to mothers almost exclusively. However, the most recent editions of the childrearing manuals by Spock, Brazelton, and Leach are addressed in an egalitarian fashion to "parents." They tend to be conscientious in their use of pronouns: Leach claims to use "she" to refer to the caregiver and "he" to refer to the child *only* for the sake of convenience and consistency, while Spock and Brazelton try to switch back and forth between "he" and "she" when speaking of parents and children. And all these authors, at one time or another, proclaim the mother's equal "right" to paid work. How, then, can I claim that their books are directed primarily at mothers and that they assume the individual mother is the primary caregiver?

First, these authors and their publishers are well aware of the fact that it is primarily mothers who buy their books. They are also aware that over half of mothers with small children now have paid jobs. Combined, this knowledge may well account for their attempts to use gender-neutral language and their underlying assumption that the primary childraisers will be mothers.

Second, all these authors argue that consistent nurture by a *single primary caregiver* is crucial; while day-care centers, preschools, spouses, and babysitters may help out, the child needs to bond with an *individual* adult (e.g. Brazelton, 1983b: 56; Leach, 1989: 196; Spock, 1985: 45). In demonstrating who they believe this individual caregiver will be, one must read beyond these authors' proclamations of gender neutrality.

Spock, for instance, seems to undermine his use of gender-neutral pronouns when he suggests that the "parent" buy "a new dress" or go to the "beauty parlor" if childrearing is giving (him or) her the blues (1985: 32). Further, when Spock writes, "The mother (as if she didn't have enough to do already!) has to remember to pay some attention to her husband" (1985: 33), yet finds no reason to make an equivalent comment about fathers, he clearly informs the reader who is expected to do the childrearing, and who is actually responsible for the emotional well-being of all family members. Spock also participates in gender stereotyping. Just as he implies that women like to go to beauty parlors and buy new dresses, he also makes it clear that men are "virile," that the father is the "head of the family," and that husbands are interested in sports, fishing, camping, ball games, and reading the newspaper after a hard day at the office (e.g. 1985: 31, 34, 389–90). Implicit in such characterizations, of course, is the additional stereotype of women as nurturers and, by extension, those best suited for raising a child.

Similarly, Brazelton did not bother to change the title of one of his most widely read books in its 1983 revised edition: it continues to be called *Infants and Mothers*. Brazelton further contradicts his self-conscious attempt to promote egalitarian parenting when he makes such statements as, "Mothering is too complex and instinctive to teach" (1983a: 42). And in his treatment of the social pressure for women to seek paid careers, Brazelton reinforces this assumption of maternal instinct. He writes:

> We may be ignoring . . . a *deep-seated drive* in women – a strong feeling that their primary responsibility is to nurture their children and their spouse. It may be unfair to expect a woman to be the fulcrum of her family; but it has always been so, and women feel it *instinctively*. (1983b: xviii, my emphasis)

Instincts and drives, of course, are immutable. Women, Brazelton thus suggests, *inevitably* take primary responsibility for the well-being of their children.

As for Leach, even more telling than her use of gendered pronouns are her constant and explicit references to what mothers should do: the "mother meets and anticipates [the child's] needs," the "mother gets up cheerfully in the night to feed her baby," the "mother wants to help father avoid a rough and tumble game," "mothers have to learn to interpret their infants' cries," and "mothers spend a good deal of time . . . expanding their children's telegraphese into sentences" (Leach, 1989: xx, 62, 383). Yet Leach never seems to feel the need to tell us what fathers should do. And when Leach writes, "Few fathers are in a position to receive their baby's first attachment because mundane matters like jobs prevent them from being that ever-present, always-responsive person" (1986: 122), she manages to simultaneously valorize motherhood, assert its intensive nature, and inform us who is expected to stay at home with the children. Leach further underlines this belief when she writes, "In an ideal world no woman would ever have a baby unless she really knew that she wanted to spend two or three years being somebody else's other-half" (1989: 196). There is no doubt that Leach assumes full-time mother care.

Not surprisingly, then, Leach never treats at any length the issue of mothers who work in the paid labor force.[4] Spock and Brazelton, however, have both made additions to their earlier works that consider the position of paid working mothers. While these additions are meant to encourage father participation, the more general advice of these authors tends to leave mothers the primary childrearers, while fathers are understood as additional "help." Often, the assumption is that fathers can be of help only *after* they come home from work. Spock, for instance, writes "the father *may* be home in time to give the bath before the 6 pm or 10 pm feeding" (1985: 203, emphasis mine). In this same vein Brazelton tells us, "even when a father can *fill in* for just a few hours, the baby will have more sense of belonging and an opportunity to know him, and the mother will be less stretched" (1983a: xxvii, emphasis mine). And further suggesting that the mother–child bond is far more crucial than that between fathers and children, Brazelton claims that "whenever a mother returns to work, her baby will likely regress," and elsewhere adds that such a mother "feels so torn and grieved at losing part of her baby's day that she feels less than adequate" (1983a: 61; 1983b: 83). At the same time this portrait might lead one to wonder how Brazelton would account for all those mothers who seem eager to return to their paying jobs, this rendition could also lead one to ask why the father's "return" to paid work doesn't seem to lead to the child's regression or to the father's experience of grief and inadequacy.[5]

Clearly, these authors have not escaped the assumption that individual mothers are primarily responsible for raising children. While one may be tempted to excuse them since, after all, they are living in a world in which mothers *do* generally take primary responsibility, this is not the point. It is not a question of whether Spock, Brazelton, and Leach are responsible for creating this state of affairs; the fact is that they participate (intentionally or unintentionally) in reproducing it.

Intensive Methods

Not only do these manuals reflect the belief that individual mothers should take primary responsibility for raising children, they also reflect the belief that appropriate childrearing requires intensive methods – methods that demand a deep emotional commitment on the part of the individual mother and that oblige her to expend a tremendous amount of time, energy, and money in attempting to meet the needs and desires of her progeny.

First, the authors portray good childraising as emotionally absorbing. Affectionate nurture is considered the absolutely essential foundation for the proper rearing of a child. Leach believes that "the most important thing one can give a child is genuinely unconditional love" (in Lawson, 1991); Spock argues that children need loving nurture "just as much as [they] need vitamins and calories" (1985: 3), and Brazelton claims that children who are not allowed to experience full emotional attachment to an adult in the early stages of infancy may later be unable to establish human relationships at all (1983b: 56).

For these writers, maternal love and affection are not only vital, they also come "naturally." Leach writes, "Whatever your mind and the deeply entrenched habits of your previous life may be telling you, your body is ready and waiting for him. Your skin thrills to his. His small frame fits perfectly against your belly, breast, and shoulder" (1986: 34). For Leach, then, a mother is naturally "thrilled" to cuddle her child, even if her "mind" seems to tell her otherwise. Spock also consistently refers to parental "instincts" toward loving nurture. And Brazelton claims that parents are "programmed with a whole set of 'reflex' responses" which leave them "geared to lavish affection on the child" (1983a: 2, 11).

The methods of childrearing suggested by these authors are also clearly child centered. They are child centered not only in the sense that the beloved child is considered as extremely important and the center of familial attention, but also, and more crucially in this context, the child is understood as the person who *guides* the process of childraising. The mother's day-to-day job is, above all, to *respond* to the child's needs and wants. This logic is the basis for childrearing methods that have come to be known as "permissive." And Spock, of course, is considered the central proponent of this permissive ideology in his recommendation that parents should "follow [the] baby's lead" (1985: 200). But his bestselling successors actually have even more pronounced views in this regard. Brazelton highlights the notion that "every baby knows what is needed" and will show "a sensitive parent" just what to do (1987: 3). Good parenting, he argues, follows directly from attention to the child's cues and requests. And while Spock actually warns that "the more parents submit to their babies' orders, the more demanding the children become" (1985: 249), for Leach (1986) submitting to the child's orders is the only logical approach, since she believes there is a "natural harmony of interests" between mother and child. According to Leach, if you give the child what the child wants and needs, the child will be happy and you will be happy; if you don't give the child what the child wants, the child will simply keep asking for more and more, and both of you will be frustrated and upset. Mothers must therefore "anticipate wishes which [the baby] can barely recognize let alone formulate" (1989: xvii). Such parenting requires extreme sensitivity, since children in general are not always very articulate about what (they know) is needed.

In order to properly decipher and appropriately respond to a child's needs, a mother must take action on a number of fronts, all of which make for childrearing that is labor intensive. The first task is to acquire knowledge of what the experts know to be the changing requirements of children as they pass through the stages of development. For these thinkers, there is a multitude of developmental stages. Brazelton (1983a), for instance, breaks down the stages of infanthood month by month, while Leach's (1986) most popular manual uses the stages of 0–6 months, 6 months to 1 year, 1 to $2\frac{1}{2}$ years, and $2\frac{1}{2}$ to 5 years. Each of these age-graded stages must be further subdivided in terms of physical, psychological, and cognitive development. And knowledge of all these stages and their subdivisions is considered absolutely essential to good parenting.

But such knowledge alone is not considered sufficient to fully prepare the mother to correctly respond to her *own* child's needs and desires. The mother must also learn how to interpret the particular behavior and peculiar needs of her child, moment by moment. General childrearing advice is therefore insufficient, and mothers must constantly worry if they are properly reading their own child's behavior and using the specific techniques appropriate to it in light of the advice given. Often, this requires finding just the right balance. For instance, Brazelton (speaking of the first week of the child's life) warns the reader that "overstimulation can be very demanding" while the lack of stimulation can be "devastating" (1983a: 32). Elsewhere, he adds, "Without the advantage of a stimulating, individualized environment in infancy, a child's future development will be impaired" (1983a: xxvii). The only way to determine precisely the *correct* amount of stimulation is to watch the baby at every moment, interpret its behavior, and analyze its requirements at that particular time. Another example of the kind of fragile balance mothers must attend to is provided by Leach. She argues that it is essential for good mothers to simultaneously provide the toddler with just enough protection and just enough autonomy:

> If you surround your toddler with too much close care and protection, the need for independence will break out in anger and frustration. If you give too much personal autonomy, too much responsibility for self-care, the need to be close and protected will break out in separation anxiety. Keeping the balance between the two is the essence of your job as parent. (Leach, 1986: 318)

As before, the only way to know if the proper techniques are being used is to conscientiously attend to the child's responses at every moment.

Leach also brings out the necessity of particularized responses and careful attention to the child's cues in her emphasis on the importance of learning to "read" the baby's cry. Babies, she writes, can cry for a number of reasons: it may be from fear, an encounter with the unexpected, a sense of helplessness, anger, or frustration. The mother must conscientiously "decode" the cry, determine its specific cause, and provide an appropriate solution (1986: 235). Of course, anyone who has ever listened to a wailing child recognizes that one would do anything to stop it. But the point here is that these authors imply that good mothers, to do their job properly, must be gathering and analyzing data constantly.

Further, good parenting requires the connected understanding that all children are "unique individuals." Spock is always careful to remind the reader that "every baby's pattern of development is different" (1985: 4). Brazelton points out differences among children and categorizes their expected needs and wants by their character as active, quiet, or average children, as well as their position as first-born, middle, or youngest children. At the same time, he stresses that such categories are only the first step toward understanding the more complex differences among individual children. And it is these individual differences among children that lead Leach to suggest that a mother should raise her child not "by the book," but "by the baby " (1986: 16).

The parent is thus provided with a complex map of children's needs, all of which must be attended to carefully and consistently. First, there are the age-graded developmental stages. Second, there are the subdivisions within these stages of physical, psychological, and cognitive development. Third, there are the different circumstances that impact children's developmental stages and therefore require different parental responses. Fourth, there are the general distinctions among "types" of children. Finally, there are the characteristics unique to each child. All these elements must be kept in mind by the good mother who ("naturally") wants to provide the appropriate response to her child. In practical terms, this means that the conscientious mother should not only spend a great deal of time educating herself as to the latest expert knowledge on childhood development, but should also spend even more time (and money) on a day-to-day basis attempting to appropriately apply that knowledge to her individual child.

Further indicating the labor-intensive character of present-day child-rearing advice are the recommended methods of child discipline. In line with the emphasis on responding to children's needs rather than enforcing parental desires, all these authors recommend the careful molding of the child's self-discipline, as opposed to demands for compliance to an absolute set of rules or the use of physical punishment. Like the childrearing advisors of the nineteenth century, Leach refers to this process as the development of the child's "conscience" (1986: 434).

For all these authors, the use of physical punishment is a mistake. Brazelton makes it clear that "physical punishment should be the very last resort" (1987: 63). Spock feels that such punishment is completely unnecessary, adding that the "American tradition of spanking may be one cause of the fact that there is much more violence in our country than in any other comparable nation" (1985: 408). Leach seems to concur. "There is nothing good to be said of physical punishments," she writes, since a "gradual and gentle exposing of the child to the results of his own ill-advised actions is the only ultimate sanction you need. Any other kind of punishment is revenge and power-mongering" (1986: 440).

By and large, discipline is to be accomplished by "setting limits" for the child, providing a good example in one's own behavior, and giving the child the love that will make her want to internalize those limits and those examples as her own (e.g. Spock, 1985: 249; Brazelton, 1983b: 168; 1987: 64; Leach, 1986: 434). As Spock puts it, since children have an "intense desire to be as much like their parents as possible," the "main source of good discipline is growing up in a loving family" (1985: 406).

Although Spock makes this sound simple, it is not. If the parents' example is crucial, then such parents must constantly monitor their own actions – never exhibiting any type of inappropriate behavior lest the child make it his or her own. And even if the parents' example is (miraculously) perfect, the child might still pick up bad behavior elsewhere. Leach suggests that in this case the parent should "expose the child to the results of his own ill-advised actions," adding that this process should be "gentle and gradual" (1986: 440). But one should recognize that, in practical terms, this means that the primary caregiver must expend much energy to ensure that this exposure process goes smoothly, must put up with a great deal of frustration (and fear) as the child experiences the consequences of his or her actions, and must, above all, suffer patiently through the child's (temporary?) bad behavior.

In addition, the good parent will set limits. As Brazelton puts it (in a curious turn of phrase that nonetheless captures the logic of instilling self-discipline), "the most critical thing we can do for a child is to let her learn her own limits by setting them and helping her to live up to them" (1987: 54). Of course, the full elaboration of such limits generally requires a verbal child, which leaves a couple of years of the child's life during which the parent is potentially without recourse beyond the command of "no!" More importantly, since physical punishment is taboo, it cannot serve as a sanction when the command of no proves inadequate or when more verbally competent children overstep their limits. According to the logic implied by all these authors, love is the *sole* foundation of good discipline. It is the bond of love that leads children to want to make their parent's limits their own limits. It is the carefully managed temporary withdrawal of loving attention, then, that serves as the central form of punishment. And this means that proper discipline techniques are emotionally absorbing as well as labor intensive.

Finally, it is suggested that setting limits for the verbal child requires "reasoning" with the child. Leach elaborates on this process. First, the mother should recognize that it "is an insult to your child's intelligence to tell him to do something without telling him why." And "telling him why" is not enough; you should also consistently "let your child join in the decision-making process." This means that you must give the child a chance to provide "reasonable arguments" and should always be willing to allow your mind to be changed by such arguments (1986: 435, 442–3). Anyone who has ever tried to "negotiate" with a three-year-old in this fashion knows that it requires a tremendous amount of time and effort. There is no question that demanding absolute obedience to a strict set of rules and backing up these demands with the threat (and reality) of physical punishment would make the parent's job much easier.[6]

A further example of the intensive character of appropriate childraising that is particularly illuminating is these authors' treatment of nonparental childcare. Given mothers' increasing participation in the paid labor force and the widespread use of day-care facilities, these advisors all spend some time considering the issue of childcare arrangements. While Spock, Brazelton, and Leach all argue that it is critical for the primary parental caregiver to stay at home with the child for at least the first several months (up to the first three years), they recognize that at some point both parents may be working outside the home and alternate care will be discussed.

Spock prefers, however, that both parents cut down to less than full-time jobs or "dovetail" their work schedules so that one parent can be with the child at all times (1985: 49). And Leach believes that day-care facilities established to serve full-time paid working parents are in *all* cases bad for kids; for Leach, the only form of nonmother care that should ever be considered is a part-time preschool (and this only when the child is "ready") (1986: 392).

All these authors recognize, however, that in *some* cases nonparental childcare will be necessary. But even in this situation, the list of appropriate concerns is virtually endless. First, all three authors recommend a child-to-caregiver ratio that the average mother would have tremendous difficulty finding, let alone affording: for Spock, there should be "not more than four children under age five, nor more than two under age two" (1985: 49); for Brazelton, more than three babies to one adult is a problem, and four toddlers to one adult is the "upper limit" (1983b: 90, 120); for Leach, even three babies to one caregiver is "unmanageable" (in Lawson, 1991). And the mother must, of course, make sure that the "basics" of safety, cleanliness, and proper nutrition are attended to. But this is just the beginning. For Brazelton, mothers must also find day-care arrangements where the children are treated as "individuals," where stimulating experiences are provided, where the staff are ready and willing to adjust to differences between children, and where the caregivers are well paid (1983b: 119). Leach additionally urges mothers to seek programs where the children are "happy and busy," "talk freely," are given a "choice of activities," and where the caregivers "really like small children" (1986: 395). Spock believes it is better to have someone come into the home or to place the child in a home setting rather than use a commercial center. He also feels it is essential to find childcare providers who are "affectionate, understanding, comfortable, sensible, self-confident," and provide the "responsiveness to the child's questions and achievements that good parents naturally give" (1985: 48–51). Certainly, such advice makes the search for appropriate day-care long, hard, and expensive.

Once proper alternative care is found, the mother's job is not over. Spock tells us that it is critically important for mothers to "take great care in observing the way a prospective caregiver or family day care parent takes care of their children and other children over a period of several weeks" (Spock, 1985: 50); Brazelton suggests that the good parent will work with the caregiver to plan the child's day each and every morning (1983b: 174). Additionally, the mother should never be late in picking up the child, should always watch for signs of the child's unhappiness, should consistently talk to the child about the events that took place while she was away, and should occasionally "spy" on the day-care provider to make sure things are going well. If the parent should find the day-care situation less than perfect, the long, hard, and expensive search for proper childcare begins anew.

Of course, there are many good reasons to be concerned about the quality of childcare arrangements today. And my research suggests that most mothers would agree, in principle, with most of the recommendations these authors offer in this regard. But there is also no question that this long list of appropriate concerns contributes to the demanding character of childrearing advice and the anxiety many mothers experience.

Throughout such discussions of child nurture, childhood development, proper discipline, day-care, and other related matters, these authors also make it clear that expert guidance is crucial. This expert advice is, of course, provided by the books themselves. Spock and Brazelton additionally urge parents to see their child's doctor, child guidance clinics, child psychologists, and social workers whenever necessary (e.g. Brazelton, 1987: 38, 264; Spock, 1985: 83, 493–4).[7] Leach dedicates a separate book, *Babyhood* (1989), to providing the expert-informed theoretical background for her more widely read instructions.

Finally, it should be clear that these recommended methods of childrearing are financially taxing. Although these authors rarely refer to the expense of childrearing, it is clearly implied in much of what they say. Attending to the basics of providing for the child's general health, safety, and physical comfort is just the beginning. Since a child's desires can be quite far-reaching, "following the child's lead" and attending to all his or her needs and wants can be extremely costly. And the importance of ensuring proper cognitive and psychological development means that parents are implicitly urged to buy the right toys, provide the right learning experiences, take the child on the right outings, and offer the child swimming and dancing and judo and piano lessons. When extra expert advice is needed, parents must also incur the expense of child psychiatrists, child development specialists, and child guidance clinics. One must also take into account the lost wages of the parent who stays at home with the young child, and the financial drain on parents who must cut back their paid work hours in order to "dovetail" their schedules and make sure that they have the maximum amount of time to spend with their progeny. And, of course, when both parents are working for pay, the childcare arrangements they use must be "the best," their ratios low, and their workers well paid. All of this seems to require a bottomless pocketbook.

In sum, the methods of mothering which these authors recommend are extremely intensive, as is demonstrated in their attention to every detail and their concern for every consequence. What these methods add up to is an extraordinarily demanding vision of appropriate childrearing that requires a mother to focus all her time, money, emotion, and intellect on the child and the child alone.

Understanding Intensive Methods and the Mother's Responsibility

To many mothers, the value and truth of these methods seem self-evident. Many scholars also treat these methods as a form of truth or, at least, a measure of what is "correct" or a reflection of what is "traditional" (e.g. DeMause, 1974; Held, 1983, 1990; Hewlett, 1987, 1991; Ruddick, 1982). But it is important to recognize that this particular approach to childrearing is, in fact, historically and cross-culturally peculiar. While all cultures have a set of explicit or implicit rules and rituals for proper childrearing, those rules and rituals are quite varied. And practices that would make a mother's job easier, or at least more clearly profitable, are quite common in other times and places. In most cultures, for instance, the mother shares the task of childraising with other women and the child's older siblings. Further, far from being a net financial drain on their parents, in most cultures children are primarily economic assets – at very young ages they are taught to work, and in later years it is expected that children will help to support their families of origin.[8]

Such arrangements also held true for much of Western history. The ideology of intensive childrearing only began to develop in the United States in the late eighteenth and early nineteenth century with the discovery of childhood and the valorization of nurturing motherhood.[9] Since then, various elements have been added to the cultural model of appropriate childrearing and, in each case, these elements have made mothering *more* intensive than it was before (Hays, 1996). While we might be tempted to argue that these intensive methods are a measure of progress in caring for the young, it should be recognized that claims to progress are developed from a particular perspective and, in this case, would imply (among other things) that the methods of other cultures are obviously and inherently inferior. Attempts to sidestep this ethnocentrism by claiming that, while intensive methods may not be superior in any absolute sense, they are nonetheless fitting for contemporary Western societies, neglect not only the question of why women rather than men must serve as the primary caregivers, but also neglect debates regarding what methods are actually best for preparing children to live in the modern world (e.g. Ariès, 1962; Berger, 1981a, 1981b; Kagan, 1986; Moore, 1958; Sennett, 1970).

If the model of appropriate childrearing laid out in the manuals of Spock, Brazelton, and Leach is not natural, normal, or absolutely necessary, one might well wonder why these manuals have found such a wide audience in a society that is guided by the ethos of the market and a society where the participation of mothers in the paid laborforce has become the norm. Why wouldn't the socially constructed model of childrearing be reconstructed to one more in line with the logic of instrumental calcula-tion and profit-maximization so pervasive in modern societies? And why wouldn't childraising be further reconstructed in such a way as to be simpler for the majority of mothers who are now working for pay?

A number of ways to explain the apparently paradoxical persistence of the ideology of intensive mothering can be extrapolated from the work of scholars who have analyzed the social bases of the modern family through the lens of culture. All these analyses follow from what have, at one time or another, been important theoretical positions in cultural studies. Though they are distinct and at times appear conflicting, none of these approaches, if taken alone, is sufficient or wholly satisfying. I will demonstrate that a complex interpretation and synthesis of these analyses, however, can ultimately go a long way towards making sense of many elements of the first two components of the ideology of intensive mothering.

First, models of childrearing and mothering have been understood as the consequences of women's relative powerlessness. Following a long tradition in studies of culture, these arguments place the ideology of mothering in the context of larger cultural, economic, and political sys-tems and understand it as the result of unequal power relations within those systems. In this case, the ideology of intensive mothering is under-stood as the consequence of the fact that women are powerless in the face of a patriarchal cultural system, a capitalist economic system, and a rationalized political system. The model laid out by Spock, Brazelton, and Leach is thus implicitly or explicitly interpreted as a hegemonic vision that is imposed on mothers in the service of the powerful.[10]

For instance, extrapolating from and extending the work of Donzelot (1979), one might argue that the ideology of intensive mothering is part of a larger model of family life that serves state interests. By urging women to fulfill an elaborate set of instructions for training the young, childrearing advisors are effective proponents of parenting ideas that help to spare state authorities from having to pay for or oversee the job themselves. The emphasis on teaching children to internalize discipline, in particular, saves the state from future dependents, guards against potential insurrec-tion, and provides the state with relatively compliant, tax-paying citizens. Women, as social subordinates, are those the state finds best suited to carry out this important yet uncompensated task.

Many scholars have also argued that women's commitment to child-rearing serves capitalism. Not only does women's unpaid work of main-taining the home and raising the children help capitalists to sustain and reproduce labor power at a relatively low cost, the methods women use to rear those children also help to produce obedient young workers for the future (e.g. Acker, 1988; Bentson, 1984; Hartmann, 1981). Further, by disseminating the ideology that a woman's central responsibility is as the keeper of home and hearth, these manuals contribute to the maintenance of women as a relatively cheap and expendable pool of paid laborers (who should be willing to take lower status and lower-paying jobs since what they earn is, after all, only "pin money") (e.g. Kessler-Harris, 1982; Weiner, 1985). In addition, the permissive, child-centered nature of intensive mothering also helps to create little consumers. Trained in having all their desires met, these children grow up hungry to buy every new commodity that capitalism produces (e.g. Ehrenreich, 1989; Ehrenreich and English, 1978; Slater, 1976; Zuckerman, 1975).

Another central and related line of analysis emphasizes that the ideology of intensive mothering serves men. First, as Polatnick (1983) argues, men are thus freed from the tedious tasks of changing diapers, cleaning up infant spittle, and talking baby talk. Second, as many other feminist scholars have made clear, women's responsibility for childrearing is part of a larger cultural system that makes women responsible for all household chores – thus supplying men with personal servants and at the same time sparing men from any serious threat arising from women's competition in the labor market (e.g. Delphy, 1984; Hartmann, 1981; Mainardi, 1970). Third, and in a connected way, women's commitment to this socially devalued task helps to maintain their subordinate position in society as a whole.

In all these arguments emphasizing unequal power relations, the ideology espoused in the bestselling childrearing manuals can be interpreted as one that operates to *convince* women that they must commit themselves to a task that, in actual fact, ultimately serves men, capitalists, and the state. One need not imagine a self-conscious conspiracy of politicians, CEOs, and patriarchs to recognize that the ideology of intensive mothering is nonetheless quite "functional" in a male-dominated, rationalized market society. In the same terms, we need not picture advisors like Spock, Brazelton, and Leach as mere dupes operating on behalf of capitalists, state administrators, and men to recognize that they respond, as do their readers, to the particular cultural models that are the products of the specific power arrangements of the society in which they are enmeshed. There is, in other words, little doubt that the ideology of intensive mothering, in part, serves the interests of the powerful.

These arguments regarding hegemonic imposition are thus useful, but they are also incomplete. While they provide a portrait of how the ideology of intensive mothering might operate on behalf of capitalism, the state, and patriarchy, one still has to wonder what the interests of other social groups might be, and how the actions of these groups might impact the social construction of childrearing ideologies. A connected yet distinct line of analysis in scholarship on culture helps to fill this gap, leading us to examine unequal power relations not just at the level of overarching economic, political, and cultural systems, but also to consider more carefully the historical and contemporary part played by people seeking to mark and sustain class and race boundaries (e.g. Bourdieu, 1984; Collins, 1991; DiMaggio, 1982; Hall, 1992; Lamont, 1992; West, 1993).

Following this line of reasoning, one might extrapolate explanations for the ideology of intensive mothering from historical analyses demonstrating white middle-class attempts to construct class and race boundaries that would ultimately valorize their own social position. A number of cultural historians have shown that earlier versions of intensive mothering were deployed by the native-born middle class in its struggle to claim superiority to the superficial and frivolous rich, the uneducated and promiscuous poor, and the improper and "deviant" immigrant, colonized, and enslaved populations (e.g. McGlone, 1971; Ryan, 1981; Stansell, 1987). Ryan (1981), for instance, argues that nineteenth-century childrearing ideas were directly connected to the creation of the class-consciousness of the (then almost exclusively white) American middle class. Central to the establishment of itself as a class was the focus on childraising methods that included both a stress on internalized self-discipline and a long, relatively protected, and carefully monitored preparation for adult life. Ehrenreich (1989) implicitly supports this analysis with her demonstration of the persistence of similar forms of middle-class ideology in the present day, and many others have underlined the race-based nature of current cultural models of appropriate childrearing (e.g. Chang, 1994; Segura, 1994; Solinger, 1994; Wong, 1994). In these terms, contemporary childrearing advisors, as white middle-class members themselves, not only understand white middle-class methods as the "best" methods, they also manage to valorize their own position and that of their white middle-class readers by implicitly degrading those mothers who are unable or unwilling to live up to such standards.

This addition of race and class boundary-maintaining processes gives us a clearer picture, but the portrait of the social basis of the ideology of intensive mothering is still incomplete. One of the central problems with all the aforementioned analyses is their implicit or explicit rendition of social subordinates as relatively inconsequential groups whose behavior and beliefs seem to have little impact. Another central theoretical model in cultural studies would suggest that this problem might be remedied by recognizing that subordinate groups are active participants in cultural formation and are, in fact, quite capable of resisting hegemonic ideologies or transforming existing ideologies to suit their own purposes (e.g. Hebdige, 1979; Piess, 1986; Thompson, 1967; Willis, 1977).

With reference to childrearing ideologies, the most powerful examples of the cultural power of social subordinates are provided by those who demonstrate that women have actively shaped the ideology of mothering as part of their historical and contemporary attempts to gain and retain status for themselves as women and mothers. Urban middle-class women were some of the central proponents in the early valorization of mothering in the United States, and it is important to recognize that they did so during the time of early industrialization, when the move from family farms to city dwellings left them with an uncertain social role and a particularly precarious position in the marriage market. To replace their contributions as working members of the family economy, these urban middle-class women sought to claim social status by elaborating their special contributions as mothers (e.g. Collins, 1971; Degler, 1980; Kerber, 1986; Matthaei, 1982; Ryan, 1981). By the same logic, the more intensive childrearing becomes, the more mothers are able to claim that theirs is a highly-skilled job that requires the analytical, interpretive, and independent decision-making capacities of a professional.[11] In this way, it could be argued, mothers have continued to contend that their job is a demanding and crucial one, and therefore deserving of social recognition. Childrearing advisors, by specifying a model of complex and difficult childrearing, may help to ensure the selling of their books by aiding women in such efforts.

An analyst of the culture of mothering might be tempted to ally with just one of these perspectives, but I would argue that all the above arguments must be taken into account in order to begin to provide a fully contextualized account of the social and historical basis of the ideology found in contemporary childrearing manuals. While these cultural analyses are distinct, what they have in common is a logic that understands the social construction of childrearing ideas as an expression of the self-seeking strategies of various social groups in the context of a system of structured social inequalities. To the extent that the ideas of childrearing advisors mesh with the combined interests of men seeking power, capitalists seeking a well-nourished and consumption-hungry workforce, state leaders seeking an obedient citizenry, white middle-class members seeking to claim superiority by marking the cultural boundaries of their race and class position, and mothers hoping to name their job as highly skilled and therefore socially worthy, such advisors serve their own interests as well – by gaining the status and the remuneration due to "experts." In other words, taken together, these arguments provide an implicit vision of society as one guided by the logic of self-interest, with various social groups trying their best to see to it that their own interests win out over others. Those with the greatest social power are those who are most likely to be heard, but less powerful groups also participate in the conversation and shape its outcomes.

This reasoning goes a long way towards making sense of why it is that childrearing advice books tell us that mothers are primarily responsible for childcare, why the methods the books recommend are so labor intensive, why they are expert-guided, and perhaps even why they are financially expensive. But there is something more in the ideology of intensive mothering. And that something more is also reflected in the bestselling contemporary childrearing manuals.

The Ideology of the Sacred Child

Not only do these childrearing manuals reflect the belief that mothers are primarily responsible and that the appropriate methods of childraising are intensive, they also reflect the belief that children are sacred and should be cherished for their innocence, purity, and inherently loving and trusting nature. These authors participate, in other words, in what Zelizer (1985) has called the "sacralization" of the economically "worthless" but morally and emotionally "priceless" child. At the same time these authors thus valorize the innocence of children, they also valorize the work of mothering, treating it as a special and highly virtuous task – particularly with reference to its unselfish qualities. In both cases, these childrearing advice books not only implicitly deny the logic of self-interested market relations, but explicitly *reject* that logic.

There is a paradox here. If the logic of self-interest is so pervasive in modern society, why is it that children are said to reside in a sphere that is outside that logic? If mothers, like capitalists, state leaders, men, whites, and middle-class members, are focused on pursuing their interests in money, status, and power, why would these manuals portray their mothering as operating according to an opposing logic, especially in a social context in which they would seem to have so much more to gain by pursuing their paid work rather than their mothering? This, of course, is the very same set of cultural contradictions I alluded to earlier. In the face of these contradictions, there is no question that these childrearing manuals treat "good" mothers as devoid of self-interested motives. In fact, the authors treat mothers' rejection of self-interested logic as the *basis* for all the labor-intensive practices in which mothers engage. Mothers' unselfish love, their "natural" urge to give freely of themselves on behalf of others is portrayed as the underlying motivation for all the work they do to foster the well-being of their children. The overall logic of socially appropriate childrearing, in other words, stands quite apart from any form of profit-oriented, efficiency-maximizing, cost-benefit analysis.

From a historical and cross-cultural point of view, it is important to begin with the fact that the children described in these books are certainly not treated as productive household laborers. Even the future wage-earning capacity of these children is never mentioned. Although any parent pursuing self-interested gain would, theoretically, want some tangible return on their investment, according to the ideology of intensive mothering, the child is emphatically *not* to be valued for the financial profits he or she might bring. What is to be valued is the child's "goodness." And the child's goodness is derived from its purity and innocence. This, in turn, is a marker of the child's distance from the "corrupt" modern world. "Naturally friendly" children who "mean well" and should be welcomed with "unconditional love" are not the individualistic competitors one encounters in the world of paid work; they are affectionate and caring others who can be trusted without question.

Not only do these advisors treat children as outside of market logic, they also portray childrearing as a practice that stands in opposition to the self-interested, competitive pursuit of personal gain. In other words, just as the "nature" of children stands in contrast to the outside world, so the methods of childrearing contradict the practices of corporate enterprises and the centralized state. In childrearing, love is the foundation. One must "lavish affection" on the child, "anticipate" the child's every desire, and be constantly attentive to the child's unique characteristics and special needs. Yet love is certainly not the essential ingredient in the average business transaction. And any bureaucrat attending to the "unique" characteristics of the individual with whom he dealt would soon find himself without a job. But in childrearing, giving freely of one's love, one's labor, and one's resources is the appropriate code of behavior; any self-serving concern for efficiency or profitability is condemned.

Most critically, it is important to remember that from a market perspective, time is money, efficiency is the watchword, and financial profit is the goal. Adults are simply more productive than children: their time is more valuable, and their labor more efficient and manageable. From this point of view, asking parents to pump copious amounts of time, energy, and money into children, without a thought to the efficiency of the methods or the profitability of the enterprise, is surely bizarre. But not one of the bestselling authors of contemporary childrearing manuals considers such facts. The very *absence* of discussions of profitability or efficiency in these manuals speaks volumes on the special value placed on the child.

The authors of these manuals are quite explicit in articulating their belief that appropriate childrearing is in opposition to the behavior that is appropriate in the outside world. While emotional distance and efficiency are appropriate in the workplace, Brazelton writes, "an efficient woman could be the worst kind of mother for her children"; at home with her child, "a woman must be flexible, warm, and concerned" (1983b: xix). Mothers who work in the paid labor force must therefore learn to "switch gears" when they come home from their paid jobs, since the values that are applicable outside the home are destructive inside it. Spock similarly worries about the "focus on money and position" that prevails in our "industrialized society," concerned that it tends to "foster rivalry" between people as they strive to acquire more money and more status than others. This, he argues, is clearly inappropriate in childrearing. According to Spock, the value of money and position cannot and should not compete with what he calls "the warm glow that comes from working cooperatively" (1985: 40).

In fact, I would call these childrearing manuals hesitant moral treatises. All these authors' prescriptions for appropriate childrearing contain an underlying moral condemnation of impersonal, competitive, market relations and a celebration of the importance of caring for others. And appropriate childrearing, they imply, in its fostering of unselfish love, caring, and sharing, is not only important for the creation of the home as a haven in a heartless world, but may ultimately lead to a positive transformation of society as a whole.

Leach makes it clear that childrearing is a morally grounded undertaking: "Unrealistic though this view of dedicated parenthood may seem, I make no apology for it . . . there is a moral obligation to choose carefully whether or not to have a child. There is then a moral obligation to rear the children we do choose to have as well as we can (1989: xix)." And that moral obligation, as we know, involves selflessly giving much of one's time and attention to the unspoiled and unspoilable child. Leach also implies that the mother's moral obligation includes the creation of a "haven" against the potentially cold and cruel outside world. As the child grows up, she writes, he will always find security in this: "Because he has you; because you care and he knows that you care, his sadness need never be solitary; his despair need never be desolation. Whatever the world must do to him, he has a safe haven with you (1986: 444)."

The value of home as a protected haven against the impersonal pecuniary relations that dominate outside it also comes out in the authors' treatment of day-care. Spock stresses the importance of choosing childcare arrangements that are "home like" and condemns "the common [day-care] situation in which a person takes in many babies and small children with the idea of making as much money as possible, and with no idea of what children's needs are" (1985: 50). Leach disapproves of childcare centers established to serve paid working parents (as opposed to those established to serve child development), implying that the message sent by such parents – paid work is more important than the child – rubs off on the workers, so that "your child's happiness may not be of as much concern to them. . . . It will be assumed that he is there because he has got to be there rather than because you expect them to derive positive enjoyment" (1986: 393). In these ways the authors remind us that it is absolutely inappropriate to mix the pursuit of self-interested gain with the rearing of a child.

Appropriate childrearing, these advisors suggest, may also have larger implications for the good of society as a whole. For instance, Brazelton tells us that "the 'ME' generation is a blot on our society" (1983b: 182) and lets us know just what is at stake when he writes, "Our society may need a serious reevaluation – we are raising children to be highly individual-istic, intellectually clever, and self-motivated – to the exclusion of caring about others around them" (ibid: 129). Raising children using proper methods and proper values, it is implied, may transform society by cre-ating kind and sharing adults rather than selfish market competitors. Spock expresses like sentiments. "The child-centered, psychological approach," he writes, "can leave parents in a lurch unless it is backed up by a moral sense." And the moral sense Spock recommends becomes clear when he tempers his pessimism regarding today's "disenchanted world" with an optimism about the "only realistic hope" he finds: "to bring up our chil-dren with a feeling that they are in this world not for their own satisfaction but primarily to serve others" (1985: 19).

Even the "natural" quality of children and childrearing speaks to its car-ing and cooperative rather than impersonal and competitive character. It is implied that there is something "false," unnatural, and therefore bad about life in the outside world, while that which is natural is good. The natural innocence of the child is one side of this, the parents' natural love for their progeny completes the portrait. What is natural and good is the purity of love, caring, and sharing, untouched by the corruption of the larger world outside the home. Not only is this made clear in Spock's criticism of the rivalry that comes from struggles for money and position, Leach's stress on the creation of a "haven," and Brazelton's condemnation of the "ME" generation, but both Spock and Brazelton also express this in their nostalgia for societies where the market is not the central feature of social life. Brazelton speaks of Mayan Indians in southern Mexico, Spock speaks of "simpler" societies, and both focus on the natural quality of the extended and sustained contact these societies allow between mother and child, as well as the "natural" system of mutual support they provide between nuclear and extended families. In such societies, it is implied, warm and supportive relationships between people take precedence over competition and the pursuit of individual gain. And this is the appropriate value system.

Childrearing is surely envisioned here as a moral enterprise. But unlike their predecessors in the eighteenth and nineteenth centuries, these child-rearing advisors often hesitate to explicitly state the goals of this enter-prise, in part because they do not want to claim an absolute *shared* morality. Of the three, Spock is the most willing to clearly articulate his larger vision of the common good: throughout his book, he explicitly condemns injustice, urges the creation of caring and sharing children with a greater sense of social responsibility, and speaks out against the problems of violence, of war, of racism against blacks, and of the massacre of the American Indians. Brazelton, as we have seen, is equally concerned to create a more caring world, but he also expresses a certain reluctance to elaborate on this concern beyond his particular area of expertise. This is evidenced in the following statement:

> Parents today search for values for their children. . . . Nuclear warfare, misuse of our resources, the breakdown of the family – all contribute to a kind of emptiness for parents. They are missing a set of sturdy values with which to indoctrinate their children. We [childrearing advisors] know a great deal about child development, but *we don't yet know how to direct parents in their search for meaningful values* for their children. . . . What parents need instead is a respect for the importance of the the child's personality and self-esteem, as well as a sense that they have values to impart. (Brazelton, 1983b: 143, my emphasis)

While Brazelton is *sure* that fostering the child's self-esteem is a positive goal, in this instance he finds himself unable to name the other meaningful shared values that all parents should want to impart. But it is Leach who is the most hesitant of the three to make any claim as to the larger moral goals that are being served by the proper raising of a child. The only goal she is willing to explicitly state (and this she does throughout the volume) is the "happiness" of mother and child.

Individual "happiness" becomes that elusive "good" upon which we can all agree. In fact, the permissive era has been identified with the trend toward what Wolfenstein (1955) calls "fun morality," where the central goal and prescription for both parent and child is to enjoy themselves. But fun and happiness are slippery concepts. As Varenne (1977) points out, although happiness is an individualistic notion, one experiences it in the context of relationships with others. Varenne therefore suggests that the concept of happiness "form[s] a bridge between the two poles of American culture" by emphasizing the importance of both individualism and community (ibid: 185). In the case of these childrearing advisors, happiness seems to be a code word for the sense of security, continuity, trust, and love that the mother–child relationship engenders. While this happiness is understood as a property of the individual participants, to the extent that it is also connected to notions of caring and sharing that are in opposition to the self-interested rivalry that dominates many other relationships, it takes on a larger significance.

Overall, each of these authors is quite certain that raising a child is one of the most important things one can do for society. Brazelton writes, "My bias is that a woman's most important role is being at home to mother her small children" (1983a: 173). Leach, in the context of a discussion of moral obligations, informs us that raising a child is "more worthwhile than any other job" (1989: xviii). For Spock, money and position are "meager substitutes" for the "joy" of childrearing, and "pride in our worldly accomplishments is usually weak in comparison" to the satisfaction that comes from raising our children to be "fine people" (1985: 40, 23). These authors here imply that childrearing is more worthwhile than paid work, and thereby risk incurring the wrath of all those readers who are also paid career women. They take this risk, however, in order to bring out the special nonmarket value of the child and the parent–child relationship.

At the same time, while one might expect these authors to recognize the need to prepare children for their future roles and therefore advise that children be simultaneously trained in the appropriate behavior for home *and* workplace, Spock, Brazelton, and Leach *never* advise parents to teach their children to be competitive, efficient seekers of financial success. Implicit in this omission (particularly for Spock and Brazelton) is the belief that if we raise our children to be nurturing, caring, and sharing they can one day help to make the world a better place. In short, these authors clearly suggest that the reason childrearing is so important is that it is meant to create both a protected space of security, trust, and close human connection, and people who are nurturing and generous rather than individualistic and competitive.

The Cultural Contradictions

In all this, the three most widely read childrearing authors have fully elaborated an ideology of intensive mothering. First, despite their reluctance to claim shared moral values, they are not at all hesitant to portray childrearing as completely distinct from the self-interested pursuit of pecuniary gain, and children as completely immune to market valuation. Second, the unremunerated task of childrearing, they claim, is appropriately child centered, expert guided, emotionally absorbing, labor intensive, and financially expensive. Finally, the task of childrearing is considered primarily the responsibility of the individual mother.

To the extent that the logic presented in these manuals is indicative of the dominant cultural model of appropriate childrearing, the paradoxical nature of the ideology of intensive mothering is brought into sharp relief. In no previous historical period has the distinction between what is considered appropriate behavior in relation to mothering and what is considered appropriate behavior in the outside world been at greater odds. The sacred character of the child is fully elaborated and articulated: nowhere does the language of impersonality, efficiency, and the pursuit of profit enter in. Also fully codified is the logic of unselfish and nurturing motherhood: good mothers, we are told, will dedicate themselves to the well-being of others without a thought to the financial returns or status rewards of their efforts. Further, according to the logic elaborated in these childrearing manuals, the central foundation for the time, energy, and money that a mother expends is the mother's love and the child's innocence, and these forms of love and innocence, in turn, are treated as morally superior to selfish individualism and competitive materialism and are placed squarely above any concern for personal wealth, status, or power. All this is true at a time when the outside world seems to be impacting the world of the mother and child to an increasing extent – not only in terms of commercial childcare centers, surrogate contracts, frozen dinners, and diaper services, but also in the form of mothers who spend much of their lives in a paid workforce where time is money, efficiency the watchword, and personal profit the goal.

A cultural analysis of the social basis of the ideology of intensive mothering requires a highly complex and multifaceted approach. As I have suggested, one might be tempted to begin and end with an argument about patriarchy, for instance, but this would leave much of the ideology of intensive mothering unexplained. The ideology of intensive mothering is, in part, a hegemonic vision constructed to serve the powerful, but it is not solely that. The ideology of intensive mothering is, in part, a method used by whites and middle-class members to enhance their social status by marking the boundaries of their positions, but it is not merely that. The ideology of intensive mothering is, in part, a cultural model deployed by women in an attempt to resist their subordinate status, but it is not only that. If one examines closely the content of the ideology of intensive mothering, it becomes clear that no simple argument about the pursuit of self-interest in the context of a male-dominated, racially stratified, rationalized market society will suffice. If the logic of bureaucratization, capitalism, and patriarchy, and the selfish interests of women, whites, and middle-class members were *all* that was at stake here, the ideology of socially appropriate childrearing might just as well include a vision of 24-hour day-care centers operating efficiently and at a profit for their owners, sorting the children according to their class, race, and gender positions, training the nonwhite, working-class future laborers in hard work and obedience while training the white, middle-class future managers in delayed gratification and self-discipline, and leaving both their mothers and their fathers free to enhance their own (race, class, and gender-bounded) status by more effectively engaging in the business of producing commodities and building the nation's wealth, unaffected by the "silly" impediments of love of obligation.

But the story is far more complex. The ideology represented in these bestselling childrearing manuals includes an explicit rejection of a society based on the impersonal, competitive pursuit of self-interested gain. This rejection, and the cultural opposition it highlights, is of no small social significance. And this cultural paradox is also no accident, no mere slip of the pen, and no mere strategy of manipulation.[12] It would, in other words, require a long theoretical stretch to somehow simply explain away the oppositional logic contained in these manuals as solely a legitimation of selfish interests or as purely a disguise for a system of unequal power relations. When one imagines the model of mothering laid out in these manuals as a method used by men, capitalists, and state leaders to convince women that they should dedicate themselves to home and family, one has to ask why this *particular* model is so convincing. By the same token, when one considers attempts by women and white middle-class members to use versions of this model to define their social positions both historically and in the present day, one should recognize that part of the reason this ideology has promised to confer status is that many nonmothers as well as mothers have found its oppositional logic appealing. It is on this level that it becomes clear that the ideology of intensive mothering is not simply about children, or mothers, or even the family, but is instead an ideology that speaks to a more prevalent set of social and moral concerns. To the extent that the childrearing manuals of Spock, Brazelton, and Leach have found a wide and receptive audience, then, modern society is not completely dominated by the individualistic, impersonal, competitive pursuit of self-interested gain, and people are not simply "rational actors" whose sole aim is to maximize efficiency in a struggle for money and position.

But my argument about the oppositional logic contained in these manuals does not supersede or nullify my arguments about the way these books contribute to the power, wealth, efficiency, and status-seeking efforts of men, state leaders, capitalists, whites, the middle class, and women. I think that there is no question that the ideology of intensive mothering helps to assure the reproduction of gender hierarchy, the reproduction of white middle-class status advantages, the reproduction of labor power and commodity fetishism, and the reproduction of obedient, tax-paying citizens who understand their social position as purely a result of their own individual choices and abilities and who are therefore reluctant to blame "the system." My point is that the ideology articulated in these manuals illuminates *both* the existence of such competitions for power and the existence of forms of opposition to the logic that informs those competitions.[13]

It is also important to recognize that this model of childrearing is not an entirely satisfactory solution to the moral concerns that inform portions of its reasoning. While it does highlight the significance of *gemeinschaft* relations of unremunerated commitment in the context of a cold-hearted *gesellschaft* world, it does so by assigning one gender, namely women, as the group responsible for the maintenance of those unremunerated commitments. It thus suggests that all of the troubles of the world can be solved by the individual efforts of superhuman women. This is an impossibly tall order. It is also an order that shapes and is shaped by the fact that, just as the ethos of the nurturant mother is subordinated to the ethos of the competitive businessman, so women are subordinated to men. These inequalities are ultimately masked by the sentimentalized portrait that Spock, Brazelton, and Leach paint – of a nurturing home where a mother's love leads her to cheerfully minister to the needs of others, where hearts are warmed by children's innocence and purity, and where dad is revived and redeemed when he comes home from the office to help out with the baby's 6 p.m. feeding. This vision not only serves to disguise the subordination of women, but also obscures the less-than-blissful reality of family violence, widespread divorce, and the growing numbers of women and children living in poverty.

The ideology of intensive mothering, in other words, while it may contain a logic that many find alluring, also places a tremendous and unjust burden on women. This burden becomes increasingly difficult to maintain as more and more mothers go out to work for pay. But the continued importance of the cultural opposition underlying this burden is clearly indicated in the persistent popularity of Spock, Brazelton, and Leach. And, I would suggest, any solution to the complex problems that underlie the nature and consequences of this ideology would require not only the advent of shared parenting, but also a reconfiguration of the social beliefs and social circumstances that have made the ideology of intensive mothering as popular and as deeply entrenched as it is.

NOTES

I gratefully acknowledge Yale University Press for permission to reprint portions of my book, *The Cultural Contradictions of Motherhood* (1996) for use in this essay. Special thanks are also due to Elizabeth Long, Jeff Weintraub, Laura Miller, and Sarah M. Corse for helping me to think through the issues presented here.

1   For arguments regarding the variable use and interpretation of elements of culture, see, for instance, Berger (1981a), Griswold (1987), Long (1986, 1987), Press (1991, 1994), Radway (1984), and Swidler (1986). For analyses of the problems involved in using childrearing manuals to understand childrearing practices, see Mechling (1975) and Zuckerman (1975).

2   Although I cannot document it here, there is, in fact, a very close match between the advice found in these manuals and both the historical construction of American childrearing ideas and the model of appropriate childrearing espoused by mothers themselves (see Hays, 1996). This is not say that the authors of these books or their predecessors are responsible for creating this model, or that mothers unequivocally embrace the advice found in these manuals. Rather, such advice books are just one element in a larger social process. And while childrearing advisors are participants in this process and they therefore affect its course, their ideas are mainly a reflection of it. This is perhaps most powerfully indicated by the fact that mothers' own rendition of appropriate mothering tends to be more complex and elaborate than that of these authors.

3   Indications of the fact that the instrumentally rational pursuit of self-interested gain dominates political and economic life are so pervasive in the sociological literature that I hardly feel the need to cite them here. Such analyses began, of course, with the classical works of Marx, Weber, and Tönnies. More recently, it has been argued (implicitly or explicitly) that the ethos of *homo economicus* increasingly dominates in *all* spheres of life, including the family. See, for instance, Bellah et al. (1985), Donzelot (1979), Hartmann (1981), Lasch (1977), Polanyi (1944), Rapp et al. (1979), Rothman (1989), and Sahlins (1976). And, of course, the "rational actor" model of social life assumes that the logic of self-interest not only dominates, but is the sole logic in operation within the family, as elsewhere (see especially Becker, 1981; Coleman, 1993).

4   Leach does not even mention the possibility of paid work for the parental caregiver until the child begins to attend preschool (from age three to five, depending upon when "he" is "ready"). At this point, Leach realizes that the mother may begin to wonder what to do with her "free time" but argues that "a demanding part-time job is risky" since the child is likely to get sick while attending preschool and the mother will need to be available to stay at home with him (1986: 396).

5   These equivocating renditions of women's paid labor force participation clearly ignore the reality of the one in five US households that are now single-parent households (Sorrentino, 1990). Certainly, those families that are headed by fathers are implicitly treated as inadequate. As to the 85 to 90 percent that are headed by women, one has to wonder how these authors expect such women to balance this demanding childrearing advice against their family's financial needs, and why these advisors do not seem to be vocal advocates for expanded federal welfare programs. Though Brazelton and Spock both give the nod to single parenting and recognize that such parents will likely have to work for pay, in the context of the rest of their advice on the crucial importance of intensive maternal care it is doubtful that most single parents would be reassured by the cursory treatment of their circumstances that these authors provide.

6   The emotionally absorbing and labor-intensive aspects of these authors' recommendations regarding discipline are connected to a larger historical trend in Western societies toward the increasing importance of training the

child to internalize social (and parental) limits and thus to achieve *self-discipline*. This concern began to be explicitly articulated in American childrearing advice in the nineteenth century, with the focus on the development of the child's "conscience" (e.g. Ryan, 1981, 1985). But the logic of training in self-discipline was fully elaborated only in the permissive era and since then, I would argue, has been put into practice by an increasing number of mothers. This historical trend toward an increasing emphasis on self-discipline is highly significant and has been linked, for instance, to the increasing division of labor and the rise of individualism, to the process of rationalizing economic and political life, to the spread of the ideology of "civilization," and to particularly harsh forms of cruelty to the individual psyche (e.g. Collins, 1974; Durkheim, 1978; Donzelot, 1979; Elias, 1978; Freud, 1961; Foucault, 1979, 1978; Weber, 1958; Weinstein and Platt, 1969). While Riesman (1961) and Lasch (1977) have claimed that the focus on internalized self-discipline is diminished or eliminated with the twentieth-century rise of a bureaucratized, consumption-oriented society, the story is actually more complex. It might be argued that what Riesman and Lasch actually point to is the tension inherent in childrearing methods meant to instill self-discipline: that is, the very same constant loving attention that is meant to serve as the foundation for the development of conscience might also breed narcissistic or other-directed personality types.

7   Brazelton, for instance, suggests that if your child is "listless," you should have her "checked over by an expert" (1987: 38).

8   For a sampling of the anthropological literature documenting such facts, see, for instance, Margolis (1984), Mead (1962), Mead and Wolfenstein (1955), Rogoff et al. (1976), Scheper-Hughes (1987, 1992) Weisner and Gallimore (1977), Whiting and Edwards (1988).

9   This is made explicit by some scholars, and is implicit in the data of many others. See, for instance, Cott (1977), Kerber (1986), Matthaei (1982), and Ryan (1985, 1981). For class and regional differences in the development of childrearing methods, see also Gordon (1988), Greven (1983), Jones (1985), McGlone (1971), Stansell (1987), Zelizer (1985). For the earlier "discovery of childhood" in Western Europe, see, for instance, Ariès (1962), Gottlieb (1993), and Stone (1977).

10   See Gitlin (1980), Gramsci (1971), and Horkheimer and Adorno (1989) for some of the cultural studies models for this interpretation.

11   Ehrenreich (1989) and Margolis (1984), for instance, imply this argument with reference to modern-day mothers.

12   One might also be tempted to argue that this paradox is simply an illusion based on a reading of a small and select group of childrearing advisors. After all, mothers are also listening to other advisors. Books such as James Dobson's *Dare To Discipline* (1970) and the mass-market bestseller *Tough Love* are far from permissive ("Childcare Bestsellers" 1991). In fact, many popular books have satirized today's childrearing techniques, including two of the 25 non-fiction top-sellers of the 1980s: Bill Cosby's *Fatherhood* and Erma Bombeck's *Motherhood* ("The Top 25 . . ." 1990). Nonetheless, the other most popular childrearing guides (including the widely read *What to Expect . . .*

series), as well as most popular parenting magazines (*Parents, Parenting, Child* [Brown, 1993; Lodge, 1993]), include much the same advice as is found in the works of Spock, Brazelton, and Leach. And, I would argue, popular satirizations and attacks on the methods of intensive mothering are themselves best understood as measures of the power and wider social significance of the ideology they attack and satirize.

13   For similar arguments about such contradictory trends and cultural ambivalence in modern society, see, for instance, Ariès (1962), Bellah et al. (1985), Berger et al. (1974), Polanyi (1944), Sahlins (1976), Watt (1957), and Wolfe (1989).

REFERENCES

Acker, Joan 1988: Class, Gender, and the Relations of Distribution. *Signs,* 1, 473–97.

Allison, John 1990: Parenting Books for a New Generation. *American Bookseller,* 13 (12), 129.

Ariès, Phillipe 1962: *Centuries of Childhood: A Social History of Family Life.* New York: Vintage Books.

At S & S, Spate of Bestsellers Onto Audio Tape 1992: *Publishers Weekly.* November 2, 28.

Becker, Gary S. 1981: *A Treatise on the Family.* Cambridge, MA: Harvard University Press.

Bellah, Robert, Madsen, Richard, Sullivan, William M., Swidler, Ann, and Tipton, Steven M. 1985: *Habits of the Heart: Individualism and Commitment in American Life.* Berkeley: University of California Press.

Bentson, Margaret 1984: The Political Economy of Women's Liberation. In Alison M. Jaggar and Paula S. Rothenberg (eds), *Feminist Frameworks: Alternative Theoretical Accounts of the Relations Between Women and Men,* New York: McGraw-Hill, 239–47.

Berger, Bennett M. 1981a: *Survival of a Counterculture.* Berkeley: University of California Press.

—— 1981b: Liberating Child Sexuality: Commune Experiences. In Larry L. Constantine and Floyd M. Martinson (eds), *Children and Sex.* Boston: Little, Brown and Company, 247–54.

Berger, Peter, Berger, Brigitte, and Kellner, Hansfried 1974: *The Homeless Mind: Modernization and Consciousness.* New York: Vintage Books.

Bourdieu, Pierre 1984: *Distinction: A Social Critique of the Judgement of Taste.* (Translated by Richard Nice.) Cambridge, MA: Harvard University Press.

Brazelton, T. Berry 1983a: *Infants and Mothers.* New York: Delacorte Press.

—— 1983b: *Working and Caring.* Reading, MA: Addison-Wesley Publishing.

—— 1987: *What Every Baby Knows.* New York: Ballantine Books.

—— 1989: *Families: Crisis and Caring.* New York: Ballantine Books.

Brown, Patricia Leigh 1993: Magazines Remake Family, or Vice Versa. *New York Times,* August 19.

Chang, Grace 1994: Undocumented Latinas: The New "Employable Mothers." In Evelyn Nakano Glenn, Grace Chang, and Linda Rennie Forcey, *Mothering: Ideology, Experience, and Agency*, New York: Routledge, 259–86.

"Childcare Bestsellers" 1991: *Publishers Weekly*, June 14, 64.

Chira, Susan 1994: Still Guilty After All These Years: A Bouquet of Advice Books for the Working Mom. *New York Times Book Review*, May 8, 11.

Coleman, James S. 1993: The Rational Reconstruction of Society. *American Sociological Review*, 58, 1–15.

Collins, Patricia Hill 1991: *Black Feminist Thought*. New York: Routledge.

Collins, Randall 1971: A Conflict Theory of Sexual Stratification. *Social Problems*, 19, 3–21.

—— 1974: Three Faces of Cruelty: Towards a Comparative Sociology of Violence. *Theory and Society*, 1, 415–40.

Cott, Nancy F. 1977: *The Bonds of Womanhood: "Woman's Sphere" in New England, 1780–1835*. New Haven: Yale University Press.

Degler, Carl N. 1980: *At Odds: Women and the Family in America from the Revolution to the Present*. Oxford: Oxford University Press.

Delphy, Christine 1984: *Close to Home: A Materialist Analysis of Women's Oppression*. (Translated and edited by Diana Leonard.) Amherst: University of Massachusetts Press.

DeMause, Lloyd 1974: The Evolution of Childhood. *History of Childhood Quarterly*, 1, 503–75.

DiMaggio, Paul 1982: Cultural Entrepreneurship in Nineteenth-century Boston. *Media, Culture, and Society*, 4, 33–50.

Dobson, James 1970: *Dare to Discipline*. Wheaton, IL: Tyndale House Publishers.

Donzelot, Jacques 1979: *The Policing of Families*. New York: Pantheon Books.

Durkheim, Emile 1978: Two Laws of Penal Evolution. In Mark Traugott (ed.), *Emile Durkheim on Institutional Analysis*. Chicago: University of Chicago Press, 153–80.

Ehrenreich, Barbara 1989: *Fear of Falling: The Inner Life of the Middle Class*. New York: HarperCollins Publishers.

Ehrenreich, Barbara and English, Deirdre 1978: *For Her Own Good: Fifty Years of Experts' Advice to Women*. New York: Doubleday.

Eisenberg, Arlene, Murkoff, Heidi, and Hathaway, Sandee 1989: *What to Expect the First Year*. New York: Workman.

Elias, Norbert 1978: *The History of Manners*. New York: Pantheon Books.

Faber, Adele and Mazlish, Elaine 1982: *How to Talk So Kids Will Listen and Listen So Kids Will Talk*. New York: Avon.

Foucault, Michel 1978: *The History of Sexuality, Volume 1, An Introduction*. New York: Vintage Books.

—— 1979: *Discipline and Punish*. New York: Vintage Books.

Freud, Sigmund 1961: *Civilization and Its Discontents*. New York: W. W. Norton.

Geboy, Michael 1981: Who is Listening to the "Experts"? The Use of Child Care Materials By Parents. *Family Relations*, 30, 205–10.

Gitlin, Todd 1980: *The Whole World is Watching: Mass Media in the Making and Unmaking of the New Left*. Berkeley: University of Californa Press.

Gordon, Linda 1988: *Heroes of Their Own Lives: The Politics and History of Family Violence.* New York: Penguin Books.

Gottlieb, Beatrice 1993: *The Family in the Western World.* New York: Oxford University Press.

Gramsci, Antonio 1971: *Selections from the Prison Notebooks.* New York: International Press.

Greven, Philip J. 1983: Patterns from the Past. In Michael Gordon (ed.), *The American Family in Social-Historical Perspective.* New York: St Martin's Press, 38–53.

Griswold, Wendy 1987: The Fabrication of Meaning: Literary Interpretation in the United States, Great Britain, and the West Indies. *American Journal of Sociology*, 92, 1,077–117.

Hackett, Alice Payne 1967: *Seventy Years of Best Sellers, 1895–1965.* New York: R. R. Bowker.

Hall, John R. 1992: The Capital(s) of Culturals: A Nonholistic Approach to Status Situations, Class, Gender, and Ethnicity. In Michèle Lamont and Marcel Fournier (eds), *Cultivating Differences: Symbolic Boundaries and the Making of Inequality,* Chicago: University of Chicago Press, 257–85.

Hartmann, Heidi 1981: The Unhappy Marriage of Marxism and Feminism: Towards a More Progressive Union. In Lydia Sargent (ed.), *Women and Revolution: A Discussion of the Unhappy Marriage of Marxism and Feminism,* Boston: South End Press, 1–41.

Hayghe, Howard V. and Bianchi, Suzanne M. 1994: Married Mothers' Work Patterns: The Job–Family Compromise. *Monthly Labor Review*, 117 (6), 24–30.

Hays, Sharon 1996: *The Cultural Contradictions of Motherhood.* New Haven: Yale University Press.

Hebdige, Dick 1979: *Subculture: The Meaning of Style.* London: Methuen.

Held, Virginia 1983: The Obligations of Mothers and Fathers. In Joyce Trebilcot (ed.), *Mothering: Essays in Feminist Theory,* Savage, MD: Rowman and Littlefield, 7–20.

—— 1990: Mothering Versus Contract. In Jane J. Mansbridge (ed.), *Beyond Self-interest,* Chicago: University of Chicago Press, 287–304.

Hewlett, Sylvia Ann 1987: *A Lesser Life: The Myth of Women's Liberation in America.* New York: Warner Books.

—— 1991: *When the Bough Breaks: The Cost of Neglecting our Children.* New York: Basic Books.

Horkheimer, Max and Adorno, Theodor W. 1989: *Dialectic of Enlightenment.* New York: Continuum.

Jones, Jacqueline 1985: *Labor of Love, Labor of Sorrow: Black Women, Work, and the Family from Slavery to the Present.* New York: Basic Books.

Kagan, Jerome 1986: The Psychological Requirements of Human Development. In Arlene S. Skolnick and Jerome H. Skolnick (eds), *Family in Transition,* Boston: Little, Brown, 373–83.

Kerber, Linda K. 1986: *Women of the Republic: Intellect and Ideology in Revolutionary America.* London: W. W. Norton.

Kessler-Harris, Alice 1982: *Out to Work: A History of Wage-earning Women in the United States.* Oxford: Oxford University Press.

Lamont, Michèle 1992: *Money, Morals, and Manners*. Chicago: University of Chicago Press.

Lasch, Christopher 1977: *Haven in a Heartless World*. New York: Basic Books.

Lawson, Carol 1991: Advice on Child Care From, of All People, a Mother and a Doctor. *New York Times*, June 13, B1.

Leach, Penelope 1986: *Your Baby and Child: From Birth to Age 5*. New York: Penguin Books.

—— 1989: *Babyhood*. New York: Alfred A. Knopf.

—— 1994a: *Your Baby and Child: From Birth to Age 5*, revised and expanded. New York: Penguin Books.

—— 1994b: *Children First: What Our Society Must Do – And is Not Doing – For Our Children Today*. New York: Alfred A. Knopf.

Lodge, Sally 1993: Raising Today's Kids by the Book. *Publisher's Weekly*, October 18, 36–41.

Long, Elizabeth 1986: Women, Reading, and Cultural Authority: Some Implications of the Audience Perspective in Cultural Studies. *American Quarterly*, 38, 591–612.

—— 1987: Reading Groups and the Postmodern Crisis of Cultural Authority. *Cultural Studies*, 1, 306–27.

McGlone, Robert Elno 1971: *Suffer the Children: The Emergence of Modern Middle-class Family Life in America, 1820–1870*. Doctoral dissertation, University of California at Los Angeles.

Mainardi, Pat 1970: The Politics of Housework. In Robin Morgan (ed.), *Sisterhood is Powerful*. New York: Vintage, 447–54.

Margolis, Maxine 1984: *Mothers and Such: Views of American Women and Why They Changed*. Berkeley: University of California Press.

Matthaei, Julie A. 1982: *An Economic History of Women in America*. New York: Schocken Books.

Mead, Margaret 1962: A Cultural Anthropologist's Approach to Maternal Deprivation. In Mary D. Ainsworth, R. B. Andry, Robert G. Harlow, S. Lebovici, Margaret Mead, Dane G. Prugh, and Barbara Wootton (eds), *Deprivation of Maternal Care: A Reassessment of its Effects*, Geneva: World Health Organization, 45–62.

Mead, Margaret and Wolfenstein, Martha 1955: *Childhood in Contemporary Cultures*. Chicago: University of Chicago Press.

Mechling, Jay E. 1975: Advice to Historians on Advice to Mothers. *Journal of Social History*, 9, 44–63.

Moore, Barrington, Jr 1958: *Political Power and Social Theory: Six Studies*. Cambridge, MA: Harvard University Press.

Piess, Kathy 1986: *Cheap Amusements*. Philadelphia: Temple University Press.

Polanyi, Karl 1944: *The Great Transformation*. Boston: Beacon Press.

Polatnick, M. 1983: Why Men Don't Rear Children: A Power Analysis. In Joyce Trebilcot (ed.), *Mothering: Essays in Feminist Theory*, Savage, MD: Rowman and Littlefield, 21–40.

Press, Andrea L. 1991: *Women Watching Television: Gender, Class, and Generation in the American Television Experience*. Philadelphia: University of Pennsylvania Press.

—— 1994: The Sociology of Cultural Reception: Notes Toward an Emerging Paradigm. In Diana Crane (ed.), *The Sociology of Culture: Emerging Theoretical Perspectives*, Cambridge, MA: Blackwell, 221–46.

Radway, Janice 1984: *Reading the Romance: Women, Patriarchy, and Popular Literature*. Chapel Hill: University of North Carolina Press.

Rapp, Rayna, Ross, Ellen, and Bridenthal, Renate 1979: Examining Family History. *Feminist Studies*, 5 (1), 174–200.

Riesman, David 1961: *The Lonely Crowd: A Study of the Changing American Character*. New Haven: Yale University Press.

Rogoff, Barbara, Sellers, Martha Julia, Pirrotta, Sergio, Fox, Nathan, and White, Sheldon H. 1976: Age of Assignment of Roles and Responsibilities to Children: A Cross-cultural Survey. In Arlene Skolnick (ed.), *Rethinking Childhood: Perspectives on Development and Society*, Boston: Little, Brown, 249–68.

Rothman, Barbara Katz 1989: *Recreating Motherhood: Ideology and Technology in a Patriarchal Society*. New York: W. W. Norton.

Ruddick, Sara 1982: Maternal Thinking. In Barrie Thorne and Marilyn Yalom (eds), *Rethinking the Family: Some Feminist Questions*, New York: Longman, 76–94.

Ryan, Mary P. 1981: *Cradle of the Middle Class: The Family in Oneida County*. Cambridge: Cambridge University Press.

—— 1985: *The Empire of the Mother: American Writing About Domesticity 1830–1860*. New York: Harrington Park Press.

Sahlins, Marshall 1976: *Culture and Practical Reason*. Chicago: University of Chicago Press.

Scheper-Hughes, Nancy (ed.) 1987: *Child Survival: Anthropological Perspectives on the Treatment and Maltreatment of Children*. Boston: D. Reidel Publishing.

—— 1992: *Death Without Weeping: The Violence of Everyday Life in Brazil*. Berkeley: University of California Press.

Schwartz, Felice 1989: Management Women and the New Facts of Life. *Harvard Business Review*, 67 (1), 65–77.

Segura, Denise A. 1994: Working at Motherhood: Chicana and Mexican Immigrant Mothers and Employment. In Evelyn Nakano Glenn, Grace Chang, and Linda Rennie Forcey (eds), *Mothering: Ideology, Experience, and Agency*, New York: Routledge, 211–36.

Sennett, Richard 1970: *Families Against the City: Middle Class Homes of Industrial Chicago, 1872–1890*. Cambridge, MA: Harvard University Press.

Slater, Philip 1976: *The Pursuit of Loneliness: American Culture at the Breaking Point*. Boston: Beacon Press.

Solinger, Rickie 1994: Race and "Value": Black and White Illegitimate Babies, 1945–1965. In Evelyn Nakano Glenn, Grace Chang, and Linda Rennie Forcey (eds), *Mothering: Ideology, Experience, and Agency*, New York: Routledge, 287–310.

Sorrentino, Constance 1990: The Changing Family in International Perspective. *Monthly Labor Review*, 113 (3), 41–56.

Spock, Benjamin M. 1985: *Dr. Spock's Baby and Child Care*. New York: Pocket Books.

Spock, Benjamin M. and Rothenberg, Michael B. 1992: *Dr. Spock's Baby and Child Care*. Sixth edn, revised and updated. New York: Pocket Books.

Stansell, Christine 1987: *City Of Women: Sex and Class in New York 1789–1860*. Chicago: University of Illinois Press.

Stone, Lawrence 1977: *The Family, Sex and Marriage in England 1500–1800*. New York: Harper and Row.

Swidler, Ann 1986: Culture in Action. *American Sociological Review*, 51, 273–86.

"The Top 25 of the '80s: Nonfiction Bestsellers" 1990: *Publishers Weekly*, January 5, 5.

Thompson, E. P. 1967: *The Making of the English Working Class*. New York: Pantheon Books.

US Bureau of the Census 1994: *Statistical Abstract of the United States*. Washington, DC: US Government Printing Office.

Varenne, Herve 1977: *Americans Together: Structured Diversity in a Midwestern Town*. New York: Teachers College Press.

Watt, Ian 1957: *The Rise of the Novel*. Berkeley: University of California Press.

Weber, Max 1958: *The Protestant Ethic and the Spirit of Capitalism*. New York: Charles Scribner's Sons.

Weiner, Lynn Y. 1985: *From Working Girl to Working Mother: The Female Labor Force in the United States, 1820–1980*. Chapel Hill: University of North Carolina Press.

Weinstein, Fred and Platt, Gerald M. 1969: *The Wish to be Free: Society, Psyche, and Value Change*. Berkeley: University of California Press.

Weisner, Thomas and Gallimore, Ronald 1977: My Brother's Keeper: Child and Sibling Caretaking. *Current Anthropology*, 18, 169–89.

West, Cornel 1993: The New Cultural Politics of Difference. In Simon During (ed.), *The Cultural Studies Reader*, London: Routledge, 203–17.

Whiting, Beatrice Blyth and Edwards, Carolyn Pope 1988: *Children of Different Worlds*. Cambridge, MA: Harvard University Press.

Willis, Paul E. 1977: *Learning to Labor: How Working Class Kids Get Working Class Jobs*. New York: Columbia University Press.

Wolfe, Alan 1989: *Whose Keeper? Social Science and Moral Obligation*. Berkeley: University of California Press.

Wolfenstein, Martha 1955: Fun Morality: An Analysis of Recent American Child-training Literature. In Margaret Mead and Martha Wolfenstein (eds), *Childhood in Contemporary Cultures*, Chicago: University of Chicago Press, 168–78.

Wong, Sau-ling C. 1994: Diverted Mothering: Representations of Caregivers of Color in the Age of "Multiculturalism." In Evelyn Nakano Glenn, Grace Chang, and Linda Rennie Forcey (eds), *Mothering: Ideology, Experience, and Agency*, New York: Routledge, 67–91.

Zelizer, Viviana A. 1985: *Pricing the Priceless Child*. New York: Basic Books.

Zuckerman, Michael 1975: Dr. Spock: The Confidence Man. In Charles E. Rosenberg (ed.), *The Family in History*, Philadelphia: University of Philadelphia Press, 179–207.

11

Mexican-American Youth and
the Politics of Caring

ANGELA VALENZUELA

· I'm not here to babysit and I'm certainly not their parent. . . . I finally told them, "Listen, you don't have to be here if you don't want to be here. No one's forcing you."

Seguín algebra teacher

The teachers . . . they're not bad. It's just that they're not good.

Seguín ninth grade, male student

I almost feel I gotta' get in trouble again so someone will notice me and push me to do good in school. It's that kick in the *nalgas* [butt] I need from someone who cares for me.

Seguín ninth grade, female student

Introduction

The manifest purpose of schooling is the creation of a fully acculturated and well-informed citizenry. According to this ideal (or ideology) schools enable students to master a universalistic and color-blind curriculum. In turn, this allows them to assimilate into the mainstream of the American meritocracy contingent on their levels of ability and effort. But rather than functioning as the conduit for the attainment of the American Dream, large, crowded, and underfunded urban schools like Seguín High in Houston, Texas, reproduce the Mexican as a monolingual, English-speaking, ethnic minority, neither identified with Mexico nor equipped to function competently in America's mainstream. So schools in fact serve a more insidious, latent function for Mexican-origin youth: their reconstitution both as members of a quasi-Anglo working class and as members of a culturally and linguistically fractured national origin group – a class of people divided against itself.[1]

Nationwide data and small-scale ethnographic studies support this dual imagery of truncated mobility and cultural de-identification for Mexican Americans.[2] Cross-generational research evidence on educational attainment points to an "invisible ceiling" of blocked opportunity for Mexican-origin people.[3] Similarly, a survey administered to all youth at Seguín in November 1992, showed that first-generation students, both males and females – who are largely Spanish dominant – significantly outperform their English-dominant, second-, third-, and fourth-generation peers.[4] Findings of immigrant achievement and US-born underachievement not only challenge the notion of schools as channels for upward mobility, they also point to an experience of marginality for US-born youth.

The larger study from which this essay is drawn examines this general problem via an in-depth quantitative and qualitative investigation of a predominantly Latino inner-city school in Houston, Texas.[5] With a focus on relationships between school personnel and US-born, Mexican-origin youth, this essay draws from the ethnographic component of the larger study to investigate the pattern of mutual alienation and distrust between teachers and students at Seguín that is one of the major reasons schools like Seguín so dramatically fail Mexican-American youth. Although urban schools, generally, are burdened with an array of problems which vary in magnitude, positive teacher–student relationships can offset the disadvantages that typically accompany resource-poor schooling situations (Meier, 1995; Ladsen-Billings, 1994). Conversely, the history of Seguín High shows how poor teacher–student relations mitigate the effectiveness of bureaucratic responses to students' academic problems (Valenzuela, 1995).

This essay illuminates a pattern of divergent understandings between students and school personnel of what it means to "care about school." From the vantage point of the students, this divergence leads either to leaving school altogether or "dropping out" mentally as students withdraw, or "tune out" from school and classroom engagement to form oppositional peer-group cultures that reinforce teacher misperceptions. On the teacher's side, their conviction that students do *not* care leads to stereotypic views of their students and rationalization of the school's failure by either blaming individual students or their culture and community for their "bad" behavior.

The structure of blocked opportunity is thus implicated in the divergence of views of caring between students and adults at Houston's inner-city Seguín High School. Teachers expect students to demonstrate caring for schooling with an abstract, or *aesthetic*, commitment to ideas or practices that ostensibly lead to achievement. Students, on the other hand, are committed to an *authentic* form of caring that gives emphasis to reciprocal relations between adults and the youth they serve. These divergent perspectives reflect social and cultural distance and contribute to opposing perceptions that undermine achievement opportunities. Teachers often conclude on the basis of so many urban youths' attire and off-putting behavior that youth do not care about schooling and fail to pursue effective reciprocal relationships with students. This response leads youth to further devalue a schooling process they see as impersonal, irrelevant, and lifeless. They advance a critique of schooling as characterized by a scarcity of caring relationships, pointing to a lack of reciprocity between themselves and their teachers.

The thesis developed herein is that misunderstandings of caring subtract resources from youth by impeding the development of authentic caring and by obliging youth into a non-neutral, power-evasive position of aesthetic caring. Schooling at Seguín High is thus a form of cultural politics which necessitates a deconstruction of students' subjectivities and difference (Giroux, 1992). To this end, this study examines student disaffection and resistance that results from their marginal location in the school's formal and extracurricular program, as well as from their unrewarding and detached relations from teachers. I argue that when Mexican-American youth reject schooling, they do so because their teachers do not fully apprehend their ethnic, social-class, and peer-group realities, including their culture of caring. I suggest that the problem of caring has contributed significantly to the school's record of underachievement and high dropout rate.

Caring and Education

The caring literature developed out of a concern for the alienating consequences of large, bureaucratic schools (Noddings, 1984, 1992). This literature critiques technical rationality and its failings by arguing that trusting relationships facilitate and maximize opportunities for learning, growth, and the development of full human potential. A focus on relationships further provides a tangible, real-life sense of what goes on in schools and how these relationships mediate large-scale social structures like educational institutions. Educational theorists developed an analysis of the problematics of caring to better understand why well-intentioned people (both teachers and students) so often find themselves at odds. I turned to this literature because in the context of my field work, the word "caring" emerged as an emic construct utilized by students and adults at school to help them explain the conditions of schooling, with both saying that the other does not care. Upon closer examination, I found that though students and adults use the same terminology, they hold different meanings.

Moreover, these meanings correspond to definitions of caring found in the caring literature. With a qualification discussed below, students' definition of caring further corresponds more closely to theorists' definition of caring than that provided by their teachers.

Noddings (1984, 1992) and others (Gilligan, 1982; Prillaman and Eaker, 1994; Courtney and Noblit, 1994) contend, and this study confirms, that schools are structured around *aesthetic,* or superficial, caring. Noddings (1984) argues that attention to things and ideas is the essence of aesthetic caring. Rather than moving toward another human being to grasp their subjective reality, the overriding concern is with form and nonpersonal content. Mathematicians, for instance, speak of "falling in love" with the elegance of a theorem. Such caring can be a profoundly moving experience. Yet undue attention to ideas, objects, and rules often occurs in schools at the expense of human beings who are there to learn.

In a similar vein, Prillaman and Eaker (1994) critique the privileging of the *technical* over the *expressive* in discourse on education. Technical discourse refers to the impersonal and objective language used in decisions made by one group for another that includes such terms as goals, strategies, and standardized curricula. Expressive discourse entails "a broad and loosely defined ethic [of caring] that molds itself in situations and has proper regard for human affections, weaknesses, and anxieties" (Noddings, 1984: 25). Caring theorists propose the alternative educational model expressed by the students themselves in this study – that is, a more humane and compassionate pedagogy premised on reciprocal relationships.

From a cultural production perspective that examines "lived culture" (see Levinson and Holland, 1996) a focus on caring interrogates what it means to be educated from the standpoints of both school and student. This question provides an enhanced understanding of conflicts that develop when schooling contexts are not mindful of competing definitions, or even when one group attempts to impose its definition on another group. As this study will show, conflictual teacher–student relations represent a key site of contestation over the process and content of schooling constituted around issues of class (e.g. Willis, 1977), ethnicity (e.g. Solomon, 1992), and an ideological divide between students and their teachers (e.g. Bourdieu and Passeron, 1977). These variables mediate definitions of caring even as they reflect asymmetrical relations of power.

How teachers and students are oriented to each other is central to Noddings' (1984) framework on caring. In her view, the caring teacher's role is to initiate relation, with engrossment in the student's welfare and emotional displacement following from this search for connection. A teacher's attitudinal predisposition is essential to caring, for it overtly conveys acceptance and confirmation to the cared-for student. When the cared-for responds by demonstrating an unselfconscious revealing of self, the reciprocal relation is complete. In nonteaching situations, the status differential becomes blurred with teacher and student experiencing friendship. The benefit of relatedness for the student is competence and mastery of worldly tasks. In the absence of such apprehension, students who experience distance from teachers not only are made to feel like objects, they may also forego opportunities to achieve mastery in schooling.

Noddings (1984) and others (see especially Danin, 1994) persuasively argue that care-giving is driven by a desire to apprehend the other's reality, yet "otherness" remains insufficiently problematized in the literature. At Seguín and similar schools, teachers' and school officials' limitations at understanding their students' cultural world and structural position limit caring.[6]

Cultural studies' concern for cultural difference, ethnicity, and power relations (Levinson and Holland, 1996) alongside the multiculturalist critique of subtractive assimilation, or culture eradication (Bartolomé, 1994; Gibson, 1993), and Coleman's (1988, 1990) concern in the sociological literature with resource-rich networks – expressed as "social capital" – combine to amplify the extant literature on caring. An obvious limit to caring exists when teachers ask students to *care about* school while students ask to be *cared for* before they *care about*. With students and school officials talking past each other, a mutual sense of alienation evolves. This dynamic is well documented in thinking about caring and education. Less obvious to caring theorists is the implicit threat to ethnic identity that accompanies the demand at places like Seguín that youth *care about* school. This demand asks students to embrace a curriculum that either dismisses or derogates their ethnicity and to respond caringly to school officials who hold their culture and community in contempt. Conceptualizations of educational "caring," in other words, must more explicitly challenge the notion that assimilation is a neutral process.

Rather than building on students' cultural and linguistic knowledge and heritage to create biculturally and bilingually competent youth in an additive fashion, schools subtract these identifications from youth to their social and academic detriment.[7] Teachers who are disconnected from their students' lived experiences as members of a subordinate group generally fail to acknowledge or appreciate the subtractive quality of the curriculum and its consequences for most Mexican-origin youth schooled in US public institutions.

An additive model would, among other things, take into account Mexican-American students' definition of education, or *educación* (Mejía, 1983). *Educación* has cultural roots that help explain why authentic caring is particularly important for Mexican-origin youth. *Educación* is a conceptually broader term than its English-language cognate. It refers to the family's role of inculcating in children a sense of moral, social, and personal responsibility and serves as the foundation for all other learning. Though inclusive of formal academic training, *educación* additionally refers to competence in the social world wherein one observes the dignity and individuality of others. This person- (as opposed to object-) orientation further suggests the futility of academic knowledge and skills when individuals do not know how to live in the world as caring, responsible, well-mannered, and respectful human beings. Non-Latino teachers' characteristic lack of knowledge of the Spanish language and broader Mexican culture divorces them from this cultural definition of *educación*.

An additive model would also militate against the creation of divisions among youth along linguistic, social, and generational status lines that develop within a subtractive framework. Subtractive contexts promote divisions through an "Americanization" project that marginalizes or derogates Mexican culture, as well as through a key organizational feature, namely, the separation of the Spanish from English-speaking students through the English as a second language program. This separation encourages and legitimates, on the one hand, a status hierarchy which relegates immigrant youth to the bottom. On the other, it nurtures distinct and distorted identities that coexist uneasily with, and often in stark opposition to, each other.[8] The key academic consequence at Seguín is the loss of an achievement-oriented ethos among many US-born youth. The divisions fostered by a subtractive schooling model make it difficult though not impossible for constructive social ties or "social capital" to develop between immigrant and US-born youth.[9]

From a practical standpoint, the misunderstandings of caring obvious at Seguín subtract resources from youth by impeding the development of authentic caring and by obliging youth into a non-neutral position of aesthetic caring which compromises their cultural integrity. That is, for school success, students must not only *care about* without expecting to be *cared for*, they must also embrace a paternalistic curriculum divorced from the needs and interests of the larger collectivity. The theoretical implication is that when the schooling of historically oppressed groups is circumscribed by an ethic of aesthetic caring that asks them to care about school, youth are not simply being asked to focus their attention on an abstract set of ideas and practices. They are also subjected and socialized into a power-evasive, culturally chauvinistic framework that individualizes their difficulties with schooling while larger structural issues like the school's subtractive curriculum go unnoticed.

In sum, de-identification from Mexico, Mexican culture, and things Mexican, alongside a school culture of aesthetic caring, engender the special category of student appearing in the pages that follow. Resource-poor social networks encourage US-born youth to elaborate peer group identities which make them appear in opposition to achievement. This situation "produces" the type of student who walks the halls vacillating between displays of aggressiveness and indifference. Such students either underachieve or psychically and emotionally withdraw from the academic mainstream. While this representation of self is fueled, on the one hand, by its compatibility with being in style under conditions of poverty, it also constitutes a basis for teachers' and administrators' negative appraisals and attention. Rather than seeing urban youths' bodies as the site of agency, critical thinking, and resistance to their lack of connectedness to schooling, school officials see hapless, disengaged individuals acting in defiance with their strut-and-swagger attitude toward school rules. Yet, beneath this facade, are youth who seek unconditional acceptance and caring relationships as the fundament of the teacher–learning exchange.

Teacher Caring

The view that students lack caring stems from several sources, including social and cultural distance in student–adult relationships and the school culture itself. The majority of teachers at Seguín are non-Latino.[10] Except for a literal handful, they neither live nor participate in the predominantly Mexican-origin community. They are doubtful and even defensive about the suggestion that more Latino teachers would make any difference in school climate. In fact, teachers rationalize the cultural and language differences of students by dismissing the potential curricular relevance of Mexican culture since "the school is already 'all-Mexican,'" as the teachers' union leader put it to me.

Seguín's low teacher–student ratio with 3,000-plus students also exacerbates distance and perhaps even the development of an explicit ethic of caring. In contrast to Danin's (1994) ethnography of an elementary school which had consciously articulated an ethic of authentic caring, no such culture has existed at Seguín High. Except for a minority of teachers for whom aesthetic and authentic caring are not mutually exclusive, a more general pattern of aesthetic caring prevails among faculty responsible for the "middle majority" of general track youth.

Mainstream teachers are biased toward Seguín students in several ways. Their more privileged backgrounds inevitably set them up for disappointment in youth whose life circumstances are so radically different from their own when they were the same age. A sense of a golden, mythic past leads teachers to enforce conformity to their dated image of schooling, making it hard for them to see the students in an appreciative, culture-affirming way. In the teacher's lounge, they openly express their contempt toward many students with clichéd phrases that reveal their distance. "My father was poor and he worked hard for everything he earned. . . ."

"Where I grew up, if you raised your voice. . . ." Committed teachers who invest their time in students are often derided with the all too common expression that working hard is not worth the effort "since these kids aren't going anywhere anyway." Devoted teachers consciously avoid the teachers' lounge, fearing the disabling potential of negativity.

The following situation shows how objectifying students and opposition to a nurturing view of education go hand in hand. An algebra teacher with serious discipline problems in her classroom notes that many youth are not in school to learn. She complained to me one day, "I'm not here to babysit and I'm certainly not their parent. . . . I finally told them, 'Listen, you don't have to be here if you don't want to be here. No one's forcing you.'" Teachers often give youth an option of remaining or leaving the classroom, and tend to justify their actions by saying that they are inculcating in youth a sense of adult responsibility. At issue here is the means by which youth acquire a sense of adult responsibility. When uttered in the absence of authentic caring, such language objectifies students as dispensable, nonessential parts of the school machinery.

Because of several changes in its administration within the past six years, leadership in these areas has been a serious problem at Seguín. Assistant Principal Ana Luera, who by her third year at Seguín became significantly involved in working toward changing the culture of the school, maintains that changing counselors' and teachers' practices is a long and patient process that can only occur if their respect and trust is earned:

> You can't do anything with them [teachers and counselors] your first couple of years because you have to gain their trust. They're just like kids. You have to show you love them. . . . Now, by the third year . . . you don't know *how many* teachers I called in to tell them to show more respect to the students, to not do certain things. Now that I got their trust, I can tell them. Sometimes they deny what they do or they admit it and say that they won't do it again. I respect them and I give them due process. You have to do that. . . . This year, we're going to do some cultural sensitivity training. . . . Students' schedules were also fixed this time at the end of the school year . . . you just can't do anything as a new principal the first couple of years.

Assistant Principal Ana Luera reveals the need for teachers to feel cared for. As Noblit (1994) similarly found in his case study of a caring principal in a school, principals can assert their leadership by authentically caring for teachers and also by promoting honest dialogue on how to authentically care for students. The brief tenures of principals – a widespread problem in the Houston Independent School District due to burnout as well as to an accountability scheme which makes their position contingent on raising students' test scores on a statewide exam within a three-year time period – appear to produce the unintended consequence of reinforcing counselors' and teachers' sense of autonomy in a system where they must continually be "won over."

Because of the intransigency of teacher and counselor culture at Seguín, parents, PTA members, and community advocates have, on numerous occasions, been forced to circumvent the school to make their appeals known to the District Superintendent or the school board. According to one PTA leader, the highly predictable surplus of students enrolling each semester relative to spaces available is tolerated, "knowing that the students will drop out anyway by the fifth or sixth week of classes." Enrollments of between 3,000 and 3,400 each semester in a school capable of housing no more than 2,600 students lend credence to this claim. And not surprisingly, the numbers do substantially trim down within five or six weeks.

Teachers can be seen to occupy an uncomfortable middle ground. They are victimized by a system which structurally neglects Latino youth at the same time that their propensity toward aesthetic caring alienates scores of marginalized students, blocking any possibility of alliance with them, or even of making their work personally rewarding. Large class sizes overflowing with overaged, at-risk, and underachieving youth often combine with other pressures to privilege efficiency and the "hard line" over humanistic concerns.

This very preoccupation is evident in one teacher's self-proclaimed role as student advocate. Mr Johnson, an English teacher, is openly critical of the counselors and administration for their incompetent handling of students' course schedules, a common occurrence at Seguín. Although Mr Johnson undoubtedly rescues some students from bureaucratic harm, his good deeds get nullified by his abrasive and overbearing behavior in the classroom. Ironically, the possibility of reciprocal caring relationships gets destroyed, in this case, by the very individual who seeks to help. As the following classroom situation shows, his apparent need to feel and be powerful blinds him to his cardinal contradiction.

One sunny day in April in a ninth-grade, English classroom, I hear Mr Johnson say to his class – yet somehow for my benefit – in a loud, deep southern drawl, "The main problem with these kids is their attitude. They're immature and they challenge authority. Look at them, they're not going anywhere. I can tell you right now, a full quarter of these students will drop out of school come May." One of the girls sitting right in front of the teacher smiles awkwardly and rolls her eyes in apparent disgust. Most students pretend not to hear him, though a few glance at me and chuckle cathartically. The teacher sounds like he is joking but the students do not find him funny. "See what I mean?" Mr Johnson says. "They think they can get by in life without having to take orders from anyone." Another student slumped in his chair with his chin and arms on his desk peers up, then lifts his head, responding in a mumbling tone, "Aw, Mr Johnson, you don't . . . you're just. . . ." Mr Johnson interrupts, "Joel, stop thinking, you know it might hurt you, cause you some damage upstairs." Joel smiles wryly and sinks back into his chair. Later, Joel tells me how much he dislikes the teacher, "Johnson's full of shit . . . he's always got an attitude."

As extreme as Mr Johnson's behavior may seem, teachers at Seguín often engage in such abuse of their students. He communicates – perhaps more vividly than most – a sentiment shared by teachers and other school personnel, namely that Mexican students are immature, unambitious, and defiant of authority, and that teachers have no power to change the situation, since it is the students' fault. Much to my chagrin, he patronized the students still further by emphatically introducing me to the entire class as a doctor from Rice University – "something y'all could be if you just stopped your foolishness and grew up." I am sure I gave students the same disappointed and humiliated look that they were giving me.

During this entire interaction, students were passively sitting in their seats instead of working on the *Romeo and Juliet* writing assignment scribbled boldly on the chalkboard. So Mr Johnson was accurate in one respect: they were challenging his ability to make them learn under abusive conditions. However, Mr Johnson and other teachers conveniently overlook the fact that he does have some sway in the classroom. In this case, for instance, no one showed outright anger despite the tension in the air. Students were clearly deferring to authority in this sense, thus demonstrating in an ironic way the fallacy in the teacher's view. More importantly, they demonstrate extraordinary self-control, calling into question common perceptions among teachers that students are simply immature and defiant. This was particularly evident to me when Joel later expressed the depth of his anger.

Skewed, blanket judgments for Latino underachievement provide simplistic explanations for complex problems. They also signify a larger framework that often defines Latino underachievement as a problem with defective values, reflected, to some extent, in students' dress, demeanor, and friendship choices. This tendency of placing the onus of students' underachievement on the students themselves has been observed in other ethnographic research among youth in urban schools (Peshkin, 1991; Fine, 1991). Larger structural issues that subtract resources from youth – such as the school's poor performance record, curricular tracking, limited resources, a predominantly non-Latino staff, the absence of a culture of caring, etc. – are not weighed against individual students' proclivities to provide a more fair portrayal of their academic predicament. Moreover, the absence of a self-critical discourse inadvertently promotes the problematic view that students simply do not care about school.

The "Uncaring Student" Prototype

US-born Seguín ninth-graders are especially preoccupied with looking and acting in ways that make them seem cool. Though males are more involved in subcultural stylistics, many females share these same preoccupations. They wear tennis shoes, long t-shirts, and baggy pants with crotches that often reach the knees. Also popular are *pecheras* (overalls), with the top flap folded over the stomach, dickies, khaki pants, and sometimes tattoos on their hands and arms – many of which are self-inflicted – and earrings. Among boys, and some girls, ostentatious "fades" or partially shaved hair styles are very popular. Golden chains, crucifixes, and name-pendants often dangle from their necks. The stylistic tastes of these urban youth closely resemble those of Latino Angelino youth studied in an ethnography of a Los Angeles high school (Patthey-Chavez, 1993).

The mainstream values of the school and its organizations tend to ensure that high achievers and students involved in school activities will be under-represented in the ranks of the "uncaring-student" prototype. Average and low-achieving ninth-graders concentrated in the school's regular track, on the other hand, are likely to fit the type. Under these conditions, greater amounts of garb signal greater trouble in the minds of teachers and school officials, who readily associate their clothing with gang apparel though the majority do not belong to gangs. Any parent of these youths will tell you that their manner of dress is an important part of "fitting in."

Though the school disapproves of urban, hip-hop styles, and views the more exaggerated manifestations as a problem to fix, the school ironically cultivates this taste in attire through its Channel 1 television programming, accessible to students in virtually every school space where students congregate. Students huddled around rap exhibitions on TV in the cafeteria or in a homeroom classroom are a familiar sight. Not all youth, of course, prefer rap or "hip-hop," but the vast majority of US-born youth appreciate it. These "hip" urban youth strut lethargically in a stiff, rhythmic, slightly forward-bouncing fashion and act like they do not care much about anything. In groups, such posturing helps mark group boundaries and communicate solidarity.

Students who are marginal to the mainstream values of the school overwhelmingly conform to the "uncaring student" prototype. They engage in such deviant behaviors as skipping class and hanging out – for example, in the cafeteria through all three lunch periods. A visit to any of the four vice-principals' offices on any day of the week reveals a great deal of homogeneity in this segment of the student population. They tend to be ninth-grade males, though girls are increasingly represented. According to one school cop whose opinion is widely shared by staff,

"More and more . . . the girls are no different from the guys." My observations during my many visits to the assistant principals' offices reveal a ratio of one girl for every three boys that gets processed. Despite increasing similarities between males and females with respect to overtly deviant acts, the extreme levels of alienation among many US-born females manifest themselves as passivity and quietness in classroom situations. Females thus probably deviate less in a visible way because they respond to the same stimulus of an uncaring environment in a gender-appropriate manner.

The over-representation of ninth-graders in this "uncaring student" category is due to three factors. First, many of these students are still in the popular middle-school mode, carrying on with tough, gangster-type personas and a clothing style to match. The social pressure to continue in this mode is abetted by the fact that more than half of the school population is comprised of freshmen, due to the school's high dropout and failure rates. With respect to the failure rate, a full quarter repeat the ninth grade for at least a second time. School officials refer to many of these students as "career ninth-graders." Second, because many of the ninth-graders were members of middle-school "gangs," loosely defined, they are subjected to intense scrutiny by an aggressive, discipline-focused, "zero-tolerance" administration that tends to deal with disciplinary problems in a reactive and punitive fashion. "Withdrawing students for inattendance," for example, is a customary way of handling students like these with high absentee rates. In this context, even the appearance of gang membership often results in unwelcome attention from school officials.

Third, upperclassmen tone down their appearance. Tenth- but especially eleventh- and twelfth-grade students even distinguish themselves from the freshmen by dressing differently. Whereas baggy jeans or khakis may still be worn around the hips, they may be pressed and only somewhat baggy. One student I interviewed spoke of how he was a "punk," too, when he was a freshman. Now that he was a football player and working part-time, he had to grow up.

Students' discussions of their orientations toward schooling and achievement makes teachers' judgments difficult to endorse. What appears to be students' lack of caring about school is really their manifestation of powerlessness against large doses of alienating mental labor. Indeed, if all the so-called "uncaring students" decided to care about school today according to their teachers' definition, limited opportunity would still prevail. An intact compensatory framework that makes for a watered-down, lackluster, and regimented curriculum would continue to place limits on their prospects for mobility. If higher-achieving students in the school's academic track face difficulties getting into four-year colleges and universities because of the inferior quality of their education, the fate of their lower-track counterparts is that much more circumscribed.

Carla, a track runner, affords an opportunity to look more closely at the fragile nature of much teacher caring. Her case vividly demonstrates that a change in dress and friendship choices makes her an object of extraordinary scrutiny from her coaches despite a seemingly close relationship with them. Carla is a student who lives with her 60-year-old grandmother in a neighborhood where many gang members reside. Having been abandoned by her mother, who did not want to raise her or her younger brother, she has experienced her fair share of suffering. Family life at home is stressful because she lives under the constant threat of losing her grandmother to emphysema and her younger brother to middle-school gangs. The family is on welfare and they barely manage to survive in their one-bedroom house from one month to the next.

Although her background makes her an unlikely candidate for school success, Carla is well connected to the school through its athletic program and her honors classes. Her precarious life in the *barrio*, however, places her at great risk. A key support is her relationship to track team members. It is a small, tightly-knit group which includes her coaches, who treat the girls like family, providing various kinds of help – like money, rides home, or someone to talk to with a problem. Her lower jaw stiffens and her large, brown eyes squint as she speaks, exposing teeth-gritting strength and the embittering effects of poverty, abandonment, and an intense sense of responsibility for both her grandmother and her younger brother's well-being. Expressing determination to conquer her circumstances, she confidently states, "I plan to get an athletic scholarship and go to college."

Her coaches fear that her recent friendships with "gangster-looking" types at school and her shift toward gang-like attire may jeopardize her dreams. In response to a question about why she dresses as she does, Carla flatly states that she has to be able to "fit in" her neighborhood. She indicates to me that she is not trying to make a statement. Rather, she is doing what she can to *not* stand out in her neighborhood. She also holds a different interpretation of her friendships from that of her coaches. She is merely spending more time with people that she has known all of her life.

Carla vividly conveyed the relation between "fitting in" and survival, necessities that high-achieving, low-income, African-American youth express in other urban research (Fordham and Ogbu, 1986). The irony here is that in the context of the school, she calls unwanted attention to herself, whereas in her neighborhood, she blends perfectly into the scenery. I further noticed that Carla strikes a middle ground which her coaches may not notice or acknowledge. Although her pants are baggy, they are not falling off her body and her clothes are neatly pressed. Nor does she smoke or display any tattoos. Beyond the protective mask is a savvy young woman negotiating two conflicting identities.

The clear risk here is that she will not be seen by adults at school in her own terms, but rather as someone separating herself from the scholarship identity her coaches would prefer she sustain. Ironically, such an assessment could impede Carla from getting the guidance she needs at the time that she needs it most. Of further import in this account is a breakdown in the process of authentic caring.

Carla's coaches initiate caring but fail to achieve the state of engrossment and emotional displacement discussed by Noddings (1984). Such a state would have revealed greater understanding for Carla's need to be an insider in her own community. Instead, her coaches fall prey to aesthetic caring when they interpret Carla's changes in attire and friendship choices as failure to reciprocate their caring. Her coaches are correct to be taking notice of changes in Carla. The problem lies in their too ready portrayal of her as oppositional when she continues to care deeply about her future in the very terms they value.

In the absence of complete information, teachers must rely on students' self-representations, or changes therein, for signals about their predispositions. Contextual–ideological factors, however, may preclude consideration that meaning may be severed from representation. The preexisting ideological frame is comprised of the following: a disparaging view toward the underachieving student; a narrow definition of the way that "good" students are supposed to appear and behave; and a culture of pedagogy which demands that students must first care about school and commit to its ideas and procedures before teachers will care about them. Moreover, students' lack of power to insert their definition of education – as optimally premissed on caring relationships – exacerbates problems of disparagement, bias, and ineffectual pedagogy. Finally, an absence of authentic caring heavily influences the propensity to negatively label and sanction subtractively schooled, US-born youth whose having become *Americanizados* (or assimilated) all but enhances their public appeal.

Not Caring as Student Resistance

The preceding discussion shows that looking like one does not care about school is really the look of powerlessness and alienation. As will be demonstrated, students' weak power position politicizes some into deliberately conveying an uncaring attitude as a form of resistance not to education, but to schooling – that is, the irrelevant, uncaring, and controlling aspects of schooling (LeCompte and Dworkin, 1991; Callahan, 1962).

Rodrigo is a convincing example of "not caring" as resistance. Though capable of excelling in honors classes, he chooses to remain in the regular curriculum to which he had automatically been assigned after transferring in from a specialized academic program in another area school. Besides being an avid reader, Rodrigo has been writing poetry and prose for much of his young life. Wellsprings of inner strength emanate, in great part, from his family's protracted struggle with his mother's comatose condition of many years. "The last time I saw my mother was in kindergarten," he reminisces, referring to the last time he saw her as a whole person. After seeing him off to school, she went to the hospital for a routine hysterectomy. The operation went awry when human error resulted in oxygen loss to her brain, causing extensive brain damage. Despite a decent monetary settlement, neither his father, nor his three older sisters and brother, have quite recovered from this mishap.

Rodrigo's speech is laced with his poetic voice, interspersing lines of poetry from various works, including his own. A memorable verse from one of his poems entitled "Woman" brought tears to my eyes as it flowed sweetly from his mouth: "I have touched Mexican women, but not as much as they have touched me." Personal tragedy, coupled with his intellectual expeditions through literature, have made him the feminist that he is today.

Rodrigo's breadth of knowledge of Chicana and Chicano literature easily rivals that of any college graduate specializing in this field. Not only does he have detailed knowledge of poets and authors of poems and books, he also knows which publishers are more progressive than others on questions of multiculturalism. He has an expansive portfolio of written works, parts of which he takes to high schools and community gatherings where he has been invited to read. Gifts of books from publishers, professors, and donors alongside those he purchases occupy a large space her refers to as his "library" in his backyard garage.

His project at the time of our first encounter involved preparations to teach a multicultural literature class after school to at least ten fellow students who had already expressed an interest. Though successfully securing permission from the principal to teach the class, his efforts were to no avail. He was extremely disappointed in the principal's inability to come up with the funds to cover the cost of the text he wished to use. This process also brought him into contact with teachers who wondered where this remarkable young man had come from and who also thought he might be half white because of the lightness of his complexion. He felt insulted by the implication that a Mexican could not be so gifted or accomplished. One of his aims through this course was to combat the negative images held by teachers toward his less prosperous age-mates:

> They have this image of kids, that we are just messed up in the head. That's not really true because many students here, I think, their intellectual ability is just too high for them to be in regular classes, but they don't enter honors

classes. There are people out there who just think that we are into sex and drugs. That's not true. I can't say that I'm just one exception because there are many exceptions. At this school, there are many students, but some teachers at this school . . . I'll start saying this because it's true. Certain teachers say, "No, let's not read this. This is too hard for these kids. No, let's not read John Keats. No, Shakespeare's *Hamlet.* Let's show the movie or let's not learn about Excalibur. Let's not read it, but let's watch the film." That's something that I see, always some other kind of source that they turn to that is some kind of a secondary source, something that is not on level, but a little bit more basic.

Rodrigo's decision to remain in the regular track at Seguín was influenced by his disappointment with the magnet program in which he was previously enrolled. "There they paid more attention to the grades rather than to your thinking ability," he said. A key consequence is that "kids have good arguments, but they have absolutely no argument skills. The only argument they have is probably to curse. Say the F-word and that's it." He added that if it were not for his independent study, he could not realize the wrongs that exist in the schools. He further speculated that his independent-mindedness also made school tolerable, keeping him from dropping out. He attributed blame for widespread academic failure to the administration and teachers, not to the students. Schooling was thus an obstacle to Rodrigo's education and his devaluation of scholastic achievement represented his silent rebellion against uninspiring curricula, misplaced priorities, and teachers' lowered expectations. Health was the class he valued the most at Seguín. In a pragmatic tone, he remarked, "Health is important to keep your body maintained."

After experiencing rejection from Rice University and the University of Houston because of his low grades and SAT scores which belie his vast and creative intellect, Rodrigo is now an undergraduate student at a prestigious, Midwestern liberal arts college. He found out about the school by rescuing an information brochure out of the trash bin in the counselor's office. Unlike the two universities that rejected him on the basis of "objective" data, the Midwestern college saw his merits. Rodrigo becomes angry when he thinks about the earlier rejection he experienced:

> U of H told me that I needed to apply through special admissions. I told them, "No! Look at my portfolio. This is who I am and what I can do. If I didn't do well in school, it's because I didn't care about school. It wasn't challenging. Accept me for who I am, not for some number or letter on a piece of paper."

Rodrigo's words and experiences summarize students' experiences, generally, of profound alienation from, and hostility toward, uncaring bureaucracies. By blindly demanding evidence of student conformity to the school curriculum, however degrading or punishing, universities can represent yet another blockage to opportunity. Under such circumstances, how much greater is the sense of alienation and hostility among students whose academic trajectories are significantly more restricted? How much greater are students' needs for the authentic caring that develops through relationships?

When Teachers Initiate Relationships

Some of the most compelling evidence for students acting like they do not care about learning when in fact they do, is the great number of students who skip class chronically but who will attend one class that is meaningful to them. For example, Terry, a young man who attends his other classes erratically, never misses his mechanics class. Auto-mechanics, taught by Mr Lundgren, is the only class where he feels he really learns something. Mr Lundgren indicates to me that he comes across many students like Terry. He tells me that they are not really convinced that all of the other classes they are taking are really that important since they have so little relevance to their lives. "Mechanics is more closely connected to their sense of the future than their academic classes." Mr Lundgren is certain that were it not for the vocational courses provided by the school's Career and Technology Education (CTE) program, many more students would find school meaningless and drop out. His sentiments are unanimously shared by all other CTE teachers at Seguín.

My extensive observations of Seguín's CTE program lead me to conclude that the acquisition of work skills is compatible with students' college-going aspirations because it reinforces the academic curriculum. CTE teachers nonetheless feel misunderstood by their peers, who tend to judge the program negatively on the mistaken grounds that it is not sufficiently academic. Several CTE teachers told me that they suspected their disrepute was also partially motivated by teachers and administrators who envy their higher pay, smaller class sizes, and their ability to select their students in the upper-level courses.

Mr Lundgren models well the view of a positive interface between the academic and the CTE program. He notes that he preoccupies himself with students' writing. The example he gave was a descriptive paper all his students must write on internal combustion. Since the majority find the subject interesting, he says that he feels comfortable holding the high expectation that his students produce a well-written paper. He says that he grades it and gives students a chance to rewrite it if they wish for a higher grade. Because he provides a detailed evaluation of their paper, most students take advantage of the opportunity and few ever attain a poor grade on the assignment. Mr Lundgren has also given his Spanish-dominant students the opportunity to write the paper in Spanish. He mentioned, for instance, a female student who was forced to do so because of her poor English-language skills. "She struggles a little bit but she does read a little bit in English." For the most part, language is not a barrier for Mr Lundgren because he understands some Spanish, but also because he makes use of other students in his class. "The ones who don't understand [English], I know who they are and they're sitting next to a friend of theirs who translates to them and tells them what I expect," he says. While I found his capacity and willingness to reach out to students extraordinary, Mr Lundgren could not have been more unassuming: "My goal is to get them to write and what language they write in makes no difference to me."

Alice is another student who attends none of her classes except the one with the teacher who unconditionally accepts her. Alice got off to a bad start her freshman year. It took a month to get her schedule in order, which put her behind in three classes. Frequent visits and lengthy daily waits in the counselors' office made her despondent. Alice was also pegged as a troublemaker by her teachers after she was put on three-day suspension for fighting a girl who, according to Alice, had been picking on her. All her teachers were subsequently annoyed with her except for Mrs Donnely, a history teacher who took Alice under her wing:

Alice: I go to Mrs Donnely's class because she wasn't like everybody else who just thought the fight was my fault or thought that I was an idiot for fighting. It was that bitch's fault. She gave me lip one too many times and I told her to stop that fuckin' shit. She gave me lip and pushed me so I hit her and then the cops broke it up. Except for Mrs Donnely, everyone else just saw me and said "oh-oh, here comes Alice again." One teacher wouldn't even accept my homework because I turned it in late. Another teacher didn't even tell me what the homework was. I decided just to go to Donnely's class even though I know I failed the semester.

AV: She's a good teacher, huh?

Alice: I appreciate her because she never told me I was stupid for fighting. . . . She treated me better than my mother who screamed at me and called me stupid. It *was* dumb to fight but I knew that already. And Mrs Donnely didn't throw it in my face. She's my teacher, but she's also my friend. I can also say now that I like history.

Mrs. Donnely told me that although Alice certainly has some growing up to do, she should not be judged too harshly. "If she had been in her right classes the first day of school, who knows? Maybe none of this would have happened. I do blame her for fighting, but not for being frustrated with school." Although Alice had earned only one credit by the time the second semester had begun, her hard-earned "A" in history made her hopeful that she could do well in her other subjects. I managed to run into Alice the following spring, and it occurred to me to ask her how she was doing in her classes.

> Hmmm, I don't know. Except for math, the classes seem too easy to me. None of my teachers push me and so I still don't try hard even though they're easier. Just joking but . . . I almost feel I gotta' get in trouble again so someone will notice me and push me to do good in school. It's that kick in the *nalgas* [butt] I need from someone who cares for me. *El golpe avisa* [The punch warns you], my Mom tells me.

Noddings' (1992) prescription for continuity (in place, people, and curriculum) and trusting relationships assumes great importance in the case of Alice, whose alienation from schooling overrode some hard-won gains from the previous semester. Alice's story clearly reveals that learning and appreciating school subjects can follow from caring relationships, while simultaneously revealing that low motivation and underachievement are connected to an absence of relationships combined with low teacher expectations. Since positive relationships with teachers promote optimum results when the curriculum is also challenging, Alice's story reveals the continuing relevance of relationships with teachers even in those instances when the subject matter is "easier."

When Teachers Do Not Initiate Relationships

Despite students' desire for reciprocal relationships with adults at school, experience teaches them not to expect such relationships. Moreover, as stated in Noddings (1984), their weak power position relative to school personnel makes it incumbent that adults do the initiating. An average-achieving, ninth-grade male student named Marcos, expresses why he performs in school far below his potential:

> *Marcos:* It's cool to look like you don't care 'bout nuthin' 'cause then you're bad. Maybe some students act that way to get at the teachers, I don't know. I do it just to be cool, I guess, though I don't really think about it.
> *AV:* But underneath, you really care about school, huh?
> *Marcos:* [pausing] Yeah, I guess so.

AV:	You had to think about that.
Marcos:	I know like school is good for me, but there's lots of things I don't like about it.
AV:	Like what?
Marcos:	I don't know, I can't explain.
AV:	Like your classes?
Marcos:	The teachers . . . they're not bad. It's just that they're not good.

Further discussion revealed that Marcos had some basis for his assessment. He said that he attended a Catholic private school during his eighth-grade year because his parents were concerned about his declining grades and the rowdy set of boys he had befriended. He said that he decided to go along with his parents because he was not learning much in his middle school anyway.

Each passing phrase removed his thin layers of aloofness and defensiveness, exposing an impish personality. I detected an up-coming "punch line." He said that he really enjoyed his one-year stay in the school and would have continued except that his parents could not afford the tuition after his father had lost his job as the manager of a small business. He spoke of a Sister Mary Agnes who took an interest in him. This relationship allowed him to discover his knack for world geography. "I can name you the capital of almost any country in the world," he said, smiling. "What's the capital of Ireland?" I asked. "Dublin." "Zaire?" "Kinshasa." "Honduras?" "Tegucigalpa." "Excellent!" I said, simultaneously realizing that his unusual talent was the impending revelation. "I don't know why, it just comes to me," he said, snapping his fingers as the ends of his lips turned downwardly with pride. "I know all the states and capitals in the US and Mexico, too." His radiant face starkly contradicted his earlier nonchalant demeanor.

"She took me just like I was, you know, like I don't want to be pushed to do things, like I need time to think about it," he said. Most importantly, she let him use her computer with the world atlas software on it. "I liked it so much it'd be just me 'n' her after school sometimes," he said. Marcos has been a map collector ever since. In a summer trip to and from Mexico, he also got to apply his interest by assuming primary responsibility as the family navigator. To encourage his interest, Marcos' parents promised to buy him a world atlas for his birthday.

He regretted losing touch with his former teacher, saying how she was "*really, really* cool," with all her students. "No one here is like the Sister," he said softly. "She liked you no matter how you were or how you looked." I asked Marcos whether he had a map for his life. He said that he would like something to do with maps or travel. "The Sister said that I could be a plane pilot and I liked that," he said, smiling. "So you'll need to go to college first," I suggested. "Yeah, she talked to me about that, too." Based on the first part of our conversation, I had no inkling that my parting comment would be to tell him to keep reaching for the sky.

Most informative was Marcos's definition of caring that surfaced. Sister Mary Agnes's capacity to accept her students unconditionally had a profound impact on Marcos's life. This acceptance lured him into her sphere, where she apprehended his need at that time to work alone and at his own pace. This enabled Marcos to receive a vision of his teacher's reality, as well as master geographical knowledge. Particularly noteworthy is the quiet and subtle form engrossment and emotional displacement took. Clearly, Sister Mary Agnes's authentically caring attitude was evident to Marcos, who experienced freedom to unconsciously reveal himself to the point of discovering and developing a hidden talent.

Marcos seemed pleased with himself for being able to strike up such an unusual friendship. It made him feel extra special. It remains to be seen whether Marcos will experience similar fortune at Seguín. His thin facade and his newfound talent provide some hope that another perceptive teacher will continue where the Sister left off. Until this happens, Marcos's peer group will occupy the more salient position in his life.

Because schools concentrate more on what students learn than on the kinds of meaningful experiences that will allow learning to naturally follow, important opportunities for growth are missed (Smith, 1995). As schooling is currently structured at Seguín, alienation and tension between students and school personnel are inescapable and the possibility of creating the necessary collective contexts which facilitate the transmission of knowledge, skills, and resources get subverted.

Conclusion

The extant literature on caring is properly based on the notion that individuals need to be whole. Being understood, appreciated, and respected are basic needs all people share. In a strange twist of fate, however, acculturated, US-born, Mexican-American youth at Seguín implicitly – and at times explicitly – demand the very pedagogy they are least likely to receive. Their culturally assimilated status amplifies their vexed institutional relationship wherein they are deemed as in continuing need of socialization and reparation.

This study finds that American urban youth culture, filtered through a Mexican-American ethnic-minority experience, is at odds generationally with adults' tastes and preferences in dress and self-representation. This generational divide combines with a subtractive schooling experience among youth to heighten their sense of disconnectedness from school and also to remind them of their lack of power, expressed in occasional acts of defiance, but mostly through psychic and emotional withdrawal. Rodrigo conveys students' lack of power in his view that "Kids have good arguments, but they have absolutely no argument skills." Those who do, like Rodrigo, articulate resistance not to education, but to schooling.

By examining misunderstandings of caring, this study sheds light on a fundamental source of students' alienation. Schools like Seguín not only fail to validate their students' culture, they also subtract resources from youth; first, by impeding the development of authentic caring and, second, by obliging youth into a non-neutral, power-evasive position of aesthetic caring.

Yet, however necessary, authentic caring as currently described in the literature is not sufficient. Students' cultural world and structural position must also be fully apprehended, with adults in school bringing issues of race, difference, and power into central focus. This move necessitates abandoning the notion of a color-blind curriculum and a neutral assimilation process. A more profound and involved understanding of the socioeconomic, linguistic, sociocultural, and structural barriers that obstruct the mobility of Mexican-origin youth needs to inform all caring relationships (Phelan et al., 1993; Stanton-Salazar, 1996). Authentic caring cannot be said to exist unless it is imbued with, and motivated by, such political clarity (Bartolomé, 1994).

A finding of opposition to schooling rather than education expands current explanations for oppositional or reactive subcultures that characterize many urban US-born youth in inner-city schools. Rather than signifying an anti-achievement ethos, oppositional elements constitute a response to a Eurocentric, middle-class "culture of power" (see Delpit, 1994, for a similar argument with respect to African-American underachievement). This culture of power individualizes the problem of underachievement through its adherence to a power-neutral or power-evasive conception of the world (Twine, 1996; Frankenberg, 1993). Its discourse further stresses the technical over the expressive (Prillaman and Eaker, 1994).

Noddings (1992) rightly argues that the current crisis of meaning, direction, and purpose among youth in public schools derives from a poor ordering of priorities, wherein the current emphases on both achievement and the standard subjects may actually lead youth to conclude that adults do not care for them. Noddings further acknowledges that her call for a reordering of priorities to promote dedication to full human growth necessarily means that not all youth should be given exactly the same kind of education.

To be truly liberatory and responsive to the needs of Mexican-origin youth, an entirely new trajectory must be pursued. This trajectory would interrogate the context of education for Mexican-origin youth in its fullest sense. This re-investigation would reveal the damage to self and community that subtractive schooling contexts promote.

In conclusion, youth are correct in saying that adults at school do not care for them. Their complaint suggests a fundamental criticism with schooling, namely, that their deficient relationships are an impediment to learning. Students resist rules they see as arbitrary and a curriculum they see as irrelevant. They seek respect and acceptance for who they are as individuals and they demand that trusting relations constitute the basis for learning. Indeed, the teacher of the year is referred to by his students as their friend. Caring about school is not an *a priori* disposition. Mexican-origin youth are telling us that they will learn from people who know them, respect them as individuals, and attend to their needs.

NOTES

This research was funded by grants from Union Texas Petroleum, the Center of Education, Price Waterhouse, Towers Perrin, Fulbright and Jaworski, and Andrews and Kurth. I wish to acknowledge Elizabeth Long, George W. Noblit, Nel Noddings, Ricardo Stanton-Salazar, Olga Vasquez, and Emilio Zamora for assisting me with the essay in its various stages. Special thanks to the students and school personnel who made this work possible.

1 All names used herein are pseudonyms. US-born Mexican youth are the focus of this analysis because of a scarcity of ground-level ethnographic research on this population. They are referred to as "Mexican," "Mexican-American," and "Chicana/o" throughout. The term "Latino" is used when referring to the aggregate Latin American-origin group.

2 Pertinent national-level data include Kao and Tienda (1995), Portes and Rumbaut (1990), Portes and Zhou (1993), and Zsembik and Llanes (1996). Small-scale studies arriving at similar findings include Matute-Bianchi (1991), Buriel and Cardoza (1988), and Buriel (1984). This literature refers to the marginality of much Mexican-American youth, who by the second or third generation identify weakly with both Mexican and Anglo-American culture. Also see Ogbu (1991) for a related discussion on oppositional identities that develop with time in the US.

3 Looking specifically at educational attainment levels among Mexican-origin adults, Bean et al. (1994) observe a curvilinear trend – that is, a sharp increase between the first and second generation, with the third falling below the second (also see Chapa, 1988, 1991; Gans, 1992). In Chapa (1988) the most substantive gains among Mexican-origin adults occurred between the first and second generation.

4 Data available upon request from the author. Based on a sample of 2,281 students, numerous regression analyses also support this pattern of immigrant

achievement, compared to later-generation youth. Differences among second, third, and fourth-generation students are not statistically significant. Although the achievement variable is based on students' self-report, administering the survey the day after their student report cards were issued makes it sufficiently reliable (see also Kao and Tienda, 1995).

5   The school has been one of the lower-performing schools in the Houston Independent School District. Between 1,200 and 1,500 students enter the ninth grade each year and only 400 or 500 students graduate in any given year. In 1995–6, 415 seniors graduated; 151 students, mostly seniors, took the SAT. Their combined verbal and math scores averaged 674. More than half of the school population is comprised of freshmen due to the school's high dropout and failure rates. The principal at Seguín during the time I administered the survey in Fall, 1992, conveyed to me on several occasions in logistical, procedural terms his "concern" for dropouts. In one conversation, he worried over scheduling the student body photograph in time, "just before the sixth-week grades get handed out because the school then experiences a peak period in dropouts."

6   Fisher and Tronto (1990) move in this direction in their discussion of how racism can factor into caring relationships. Noblit (1993) explores "otherness" in his ethnographic study of an African-American teacher in a multicultural, elementary classroom. He suggests that the racial and cultural background of the African-American teacher informs the teaching process. Rather than departing from an individualistic framework, the teacher promoted a strong sense of the collectivity. Her power was used "to confirm, not disconfirm, the other" (ibid: 35).

7   In contrast to Gibson's (1993) concept of subtractive assimilation, I prefer the term "subtractive schooling." The concept of subtractive schooling shifts the focus from individuals' attributes to the school site and allows me to challenge the pejorative imagery in the extant literature of a generational achievement "decline." In this literature (Matute-Bianchi, 1991; Buriel and Cardoza, 1988; Buriel 1984), the virtues of immigrant youth are unwittingly extolled at the expense of their "deficient" later-generation counterparts. US-born youth are depicted as lacking in the drive and enthusiasm manifested by immigrants. Rather than signaling a deficiency, this difference is better read as a product of a larger schooling context which deprives youth of resources. The theoretical question that emerges is not whether achievement declines generationally, but rather *how schooling subtracts resources from youth*.

8   An additive model would help both Spanish and English-speaking youth to maintain and improve their literacy development in both languages. The curriculum would also address centrally the students' history, cultural backgrounds, and experiences. Lucas, Henze, and Donato (1995) provide evidence that schools that enjoy higher success with predominantly Latino youth are additive in philosophy and practice.

9   Social capital refers to scholastic support networks that consist of two or more (frequently more) students who share school-related information, material resources, and knowledge. These groups may or may not continue over

time, or they may shift in composition from one semester to the next. Though uncommon, as underscored in this study on student–teacher relations, these groups may also include school personnel. In contrast to other forms of capital (e.g. human and physical), social capital is not a single entity, but is defined by its function. Inhering within family and social relations, social capital helps individuals attain such goals as human capital (that is, education and skills). In scholastic support groups, trust, norms, and expectations develop among youth who come to share a similar goal-orientation toward schooling. Exchanges of various kinds – like having access to another's homework or belonging to a study group – enable youth embedded in such networks to adapt positively toward schooling. Appropriate to this study is Coleman's (1988, 1990) caution that ideology and social structure can either destroy or work against the formation and maintenance of social capital.

10 Between 1992–3 and 1993–4, when much of the data for this study were collected, the following distribution held true: out of between 149 and 155 teachers in 1992–3 and 1993–4, respectively, approximately 55 percent were white, 27 percent were African-American, and 16 percent were Latino. The remaining faculty were either Asian or Native American.

REFERENCES

Bartolomé, Lilia I. 1994: Beyond the Methods Fetish: Toward a Humanizing Pedagogy. *Harvard Educational Review*, 64, 173–94.

Bean, Frank D. and Tienda, Marta 1987: *The Hispanic Population of the United States*. New York: Sage.

Bean, Frank D., Chapa, Jorge, Berg, Ruth, and Sowards, Katherine 1994: Educational and Sociodemographic Incorporation among Hispanic Immigrants to the United States. In Barry Edmonston and Jeffrey S. Passel (eds), *Immigration and Ethnicity: The Integration of America's Newest Arrivals*, Washington, DC: Urban Institute Press, 73–100.

Bourdieu, Pierre and Passeron, Jean-Claude 1977: *Reproduction in Education, Society and Culture*. Beverly Hills: Sage.

Boykin, A. Wade 1986: The Triple Quandary and the Schooling of Afro-American Children. In Ulric Neisser (ed.), *The School Achievement of Minority Children: New Perspectives*, Hillsdale, NJ: Lawrence Erlbaum Associates.

Buriel, Raymond 1984: Integration with Traditional Mexican-American Culture and Sociocultural Adjustment. In J. L. Martinez, Jr and R. H. Mendoza (eds), *Chicano Psychology*, 2nd edn, Orlando, FL: Academic Press.

Buriel, Raymond and Cardoza, Desdemona 1988: Sociocultural Correlates of Achievement among Three Generations of Mexican American High School Seniors. *American Educational Research Journal*, 25, 177–92.

Callahan, Raymond E. 1962: *Education and the Cult of Efficiency*. Chicago: University of Chicago Press.

Chapa, Jorge 1988: The Question of American Assimilation: Socioeconomic Parity or Underclass Formation? *Public Affairs Comment*, 35, 1–14.

—— 1991: Special Focus: Hispanic Demographic and Educational Trends. Ninth Annual Status Report, *Minorities in Higher Education.* American Council on Education, Office of Minorities in Higher Education, January 11–18.

—— 1995: Personal communication.

Chapa, Jorge and Valencia, Richard R. 1993: Latino Population Growth, Demographic Characteristics, and Education, Stagnation: An Examination of Recent Trends. *Hispanic Journal of Behavioral Sciences,* 15, 165–87.

Coleman, James S. 1988: Social Capital in the Creation of Human Capital. *American Journal of Sociology,* 94, 95–120.

—— 1990: *Foundations of Social Theory.* Cambridge, MA: Harvard University Press.

Courtney, Michael and Noblit, George W. 1994: The Principal as Caregiver. In A. Renee Prillaman, Deborah J. Eaker and Doris M. Kendrick (eds), *The Tapestry of Caring: Education as Nurturance.* Norwood, NJ: Ablex Publishing, 67–85.

Danin, Susan 1994: Contradictions and Conflicts in Caring. In A. Renee Prillaman, Deborah J. Eaker, and Doris M. Kendrick (eds), *The Tapestry of Caring: Education as Nurturance,* Norwood, NJ: Ablex Publishing, 51–66.

Darder, Antonia 1991: *Culture and Power in the Classroom: A Critical Foundation for Bicultural Education.* New York: Bergin and Garvey.

Delpit, Lisa 1995: *Other People's Children: Cultural Conflict in the Classroom.* New York: New Press.

Fine, Michelle 1991: *Framing Dropouts: Notes on the Politics of an Urban Public High School.* New York: State University of New York Press.

Fisher, Bernice and Tronto, Joan 1990: Toward a Feminist Theory of Caring. In Emily K. Able and Margaret K. Nelson (eds), *Circles of Care: Work and Identity in Women's Lives,* New York: State University of New York Press, 35–62.

Fordham, Sygnithia and Ogbu, John U. 1986: Black Students' School Success: Coping with the "Burden of Acting White." *Urban Review,* 18, 176–206.

Frankenberg, Ruth 1993: *White Women, Race Matters: The Social Construction of Whiteness.* Minneapolis: University of Minnesota Press.

Freire, Paolo 1985: *The Politics of Education.* South Hadley: Bergin and Garvey.

Gans, Herbert, J. 1992: Second-generation Decline: Scenarios for the Economic and Ethnic Furtures of Post-1965 Immigrants. *Ethnic and Racial Studies,* 15, 173–92.

Gibson, Margaret A. 1993: The School Performance of Immigrant Minorities: A Comparative View. In Evelyn Jacob and Cathie Jordan (eds), *Minority Education: Anthropological Perspectives,* New Jersey: Ablex Publishing.

Gilligan, Carol 1982: *In a Different Voice.* Cambridge, MA: Harvard University Press.

Giroux, Henry A. 1992: Resisting Difference: Cultural Studies and the Discourse of Critical Pedagogy. In Lawrence Grossberg, Cary Nelson, and Paula A. Treichler (eds), *Cultural Studies,* New York: Routledge.

Gordon, Milton M. 1964: *Assimilation and American Life: The Role of Race, Religion and National Origins.* New York: Oxford University Press.

Hayes-Bautista, David E., Schink, Werner O., and Chapa, Jorge 1988: *The Burden of Support: Young Latinos in an Aging Society.* Stanford, CA: Stanford University Press.

Houston Independent School District 1994: *District and School Profiles, 1993–94.*

Kao, Grace and Tienda, Marta 1995: Optimism and Achievement: The Educational Performance of Immigrant Youth. *Social Science Quarterly*, 76, 1–19.

Keefe, Susan E. and Padilla, Amado M. 1987: *Chicano Ethnicity.* Albuquerque: University of New Mexico Press.

Ladsen-Billings, Gloria 1994: *The Dreamkeepers: Successful Teachers of African American Children.* San Francisco: Jossey-Bass Publishers.

Lareau, Annette 1989: *Home Advantage: Social Class and Parental Intervention in Elementary Education.* New York: The Falmer Press.

LeCompte, Margaret D. and Dworkin, Anthony Gary 1991: *Giving Up on School: Student Dropouts and Teacher Burnouts.* Newbury Park, CA: Corwin Press.

Levinson, Bradley A. and Holland, Dorothy C. 1996: The Cultural Production of the Educated Person: An Introduction. In Bradley A. Levinson, Douglas E. Foley, and Dorothy C. Holland (eds), *The Cultural Production of the Educated Person: Critical Ethnographies of Schooling and Local Practice*, New York: State University of New York Press.

Lucas, Tamara, Henze, Rosemary, and Donato, Ruben 1995: Promoting the Success of Latino Language-minority Students: An Explanatory Study of Six High Schools. *Harvard Educational Review*, 60, 315–40.

Matute-Bianchi, María E. 1991: Situational Ethnicity and Patterns of School Performance among Immigrant and Nonimmigrant Mexican-descent Students. In Margaret A. Gibson and John U. Ogbu (eds), *Minority Status and Schooling: A Comparative Study of Immigrant and Involuntary Minorities*, New York: Garland Publishing, 205–47.

McLaren, Peter 1995: *Critical Pedagogy and Predatory Culture.* New York: Routledge.

Mehan, Hugh, Hubbard, Lea, and Villanueva, Irene 1994: Forming Academic Identities: Accommodation without Assimilation among Involuntary Minorities. *Anthropology and Education Quarterly*, 25, 91–117.

Meier, Deborah 1995: *The Power of their Ideas: Lessons for America From a Small School in Harlem.* Boston: Beacon Press.

Mejía, Daniel 1983: The Development of Mexican American Children. In Gloria Johnson Powell (ed.), *The Psychosocial Development of Minority Group Children*, New York: Brunner/Mazel.

Noblit, George W. 1993: Power and Caring. *American Educational Research Journal*, 30, 23–38.

Noddings, Nel 1984: *Caring: A Feminine Approach to Ethics and Moral Education.* Berkeley: University of California Press.

—— 1992: *The Challenge to Care in Schools: An Alternative Approach to Education.* New York: Teachers College Press.

Ogbu, John 1991: Immigrant and Involuntary Minorities in Comparative Perspective. In Margaret A. Gibson and John U. Ogbu (eds), *Minority Status and Schooling: A Comparative Study of Immigrant and Involuntary Minorities.* New York: Garland Publishing, 3–33.

—— 1993: Variability in Minority School Performance: A Problem in Search of an Explanation. In Evelyn Jacob and Cathie Jordan (eds), *Minority Education: Anthropological Perspectives*, New Jersey: Ablex Publishing, 83–111.

Patthey-Chavez, G. Genevieve 1993: High School as an Arena for Cultural Conflict and Acculturation for Angelinos. *Anthropology and Education Quarterly*, 24, 33–60.

Pedraza-Bailey, Silvia 1985: *Political and Economic Migrants in America: Cubans and Mexicans*. Austin: University of Texas Press.

Peshkin, Alan 1991: *The Color of Strangers The Color of Friends: The Play of Ethnicity in School and Community*. Chicago: University of Chicago Press.

Phelan, P., Davidson, A. L., and Cao Yu, Hahn 1993: Students' Multiple Worlds: Navigating the Borders of Family, Peer, and School Cultures. In P. Pheland and A. L. Davidson (eds), *Renegotiating Cultural Diversity in American Schools*, New York: Teachers College Press.

Population Reference Bureau 1989: *America in the 21st Century: Human Resource Development*. Washington, DC: Population Reference Bureau.

Portes, Alejandro and Rumbaut, Rubén G. 1990: *Immigrant America: A Portrait*. Berkeley: University of California Press.

Portes, Alejandro and Zhou, Min 1993: The New Second Generation: Segmented Assimilation and its Variants. *Annals of the American Academy of Political and Social Sciences*, 530, 74–96.

Prillaman, A. Renee and Eaker, Deborah J. 1994: The Weave and the Weaver: A Tapestry Begun. In A. Renee Prillaman, Deborah J. Eaker, and Doris M. Kendrick (eds), *The Tapestry of Caring: Education as Nurturance*, New Jersey: Ablex Publishing.

Putnam, Robert D. 1993: The Prosperous Community: Social Capital and Public Life. *The American Prospect*, 13, 35–42.

—— 1995: Bowling Alone: America's Declining Social Capital. *Journal of Democracy*, 6, 65–78.

Romo, Harriett 1985: The Mexican Origin Population's Differing Perceptions of their Children's Schooling. In Rodolfo de la Garza (ed.), *The Mexican-American Experience: An Interdisciplinary Anthology*, Austin: University of Texas Press.

Rumbaut, Ruben G. 1994: The Crucible Within: Ethnic Identity, Self-esteem, and Segmented Assimilation among Children of Immigrants. *International Migration Review*, 28, 748–94.

Smith, Frank 1995: Let's Declare Education a Disaster and Get On With Our Lives. *Phi Delta Kappan*, 76, 584–90.

Solomon, R. Patrick 1992: *Black Resistance in High School: Forging a Separatist Culture*. New York: State University of New York Press.

Stanton-Salazar, Ricardo 1996: A Social Capital Framework for Understanding the Socialization of Ethnic Minority Children and Youths. Paper presented at the annual meeting of the American Educational Research Association.

Suarez-Orozco, Marcelo M. 1991: Immigrant Adaptation to Schooling: A Hispanic Case. In Margaret A. Gibson and John U. Ogbu (eds), *Minority Status and Schooling: A Comparative Study of Immigrant and Involuntary Minorities*. New York: Garland Publishing, 37–61.

Twine, France Winddance 1996: Brown-skinned White Girls: Class, Culture and the Construction of White Identity in Suburban Communities. *Gender, Place and Culture: A Journal of Feminist Geography*, 3, 2 (July), 205–24.

US Census Bureau 1989: *Current Population Reports*, Series P-20.

Valdivieso, Rafael 1986: *Must They Wait Another Generation? Hispanics and Secondary School Reform.* Washington, DC: Hispanic Policy Development Project.

Valenzuela, Angela 1995: Mexican Origin High School Adolescents and "The Problem of Discipline." American Sociological Association Annual Conference, Washington, DC.

—— and Dornbusch, Sanford M. 1994: Familism and Social Capital in the Academic Achievement of Mexican-origin and Anglo High School Adolescents. *Social Science Quarterly*, 75, 18–36.

Willis, Paul 1977: *Learning to Labor: How Working Class Kids Get Working Class Jobs.* New York: Columbia University Press.

Zsembik, Barbara A. and Llanes, Daniel 1996: Generational Differences in Educational Attainment among Mexican Americans. *Social Science Quarterly*, 77, 363–74.

12

Jazz Tradition, Institutional Formation, and Cultural Practice: The Canon and the Street as Frameworks for Oppositional Black Cultural Politics

HERMAN GRAY

In a historic move, in 1991 the Lincoln Center for the Performing Arts in New York city inaugurated its Jazz Program and installed its first Artistic Director, trumpet virtuoso Wynton Marsalis. This event – an important programmatic and financial commitment by a major American cultural institution – signaled the emergence of a new period of visibility and legitimacy for jazz in the national culture. The Lincoln Center's announcement provides me with an occasion to explore the operation of cultural politics – including issues of aesthetics, race, and institutional formation – within a dominant cultural organization (Gendron, 1995; Elworth, 1995; Walser, 1993). Moreover, it is also an opportunity for reflecting on the sometimes tenuous and often misunderstood relationship between the sociology of culture and cultural studies as analytic strategies for making sense of contemporary culture.

Marsalis's centrality here is by no means accidental or coincidental. Indeed, given his leadership of the generation of jazz musicians often referred to in the jazz press as "the young lions," his musical formation in New Orleans, his formal training at Tanglewood and the Julliard School of Music, and his unparalleled recognition and achievements (e.g. Grammy Awards in jazz and classical music), Marsalis's role is perhaps singularly significant. I mean, then, to highlight the media's representation of Marsalis, as well as his own use of media and Lincoln Center as platforms, in order to make sense of his discursive impact as a musician and cultural advocate. In other words, it is in the discursive context of the media representations, debates, and polemics surrounding Marsalis and the legitimation and recognition of jazz by a major cultural institution like Lincoln Center that I examine the tactical moves, social conditions, and cultural politics of the renewed attention to jazz as a cultural practice.

While I develop the cultural politics of Marsalis and his work at Lincoln Center more thoroughly, I also gesture toward an alternative cultural approach to the practice of jazz. The set of productive practices and aesthetic approaches associated with Marsalis and Lincoln Center I shall refer to as a "canonical project." The alternative, a view of aesthetics and productive practices which I locate in the metaphor of the "road and the street," approaches the jazz tradition as a site for expansion and re-invention. I explicitly mark the social, cultural, and political boundaries of these practices, since they draw on distinct (though sometimes shared) technical vocabularies, cultural assumptions, aesthetic conceptions, and social investments in African-American music traditions.

At the level of cultural and aesthetic politics, these distinctive approaches and practices enact different but important oppositional possibilities. Thus, while I place these practices in dialogue with each other, I also want to suggest that, in the end, they involve different ways of seeing the music in particular and (African-American) cultural politics in general. I deliberately set into analytic (and political) tension, then, these cultural projects and the cultural politics – aesthetic and institutional – that they enact.

The growing media attention and public interest in jazz – the critical debate over its direction; the installation of the Lincoln Center Jazz Program; the proliferation of philanthropic, public, and corporate financial support; and the growth of research and training opportunities in conservatories, institutes, and universities – signal a significant advance in the institutional recognition and legitimation of jazz (*New York Times Magazine*, 1995; Santoro, 1996; Watrous, 1994; Williams, 1986). This recognition and legitimation is especially striking when seen from the analytic perspective of the sociology of culture, which foregrounds the organizational, structural, and social relationships within which and through which such recognition is achieved. In short, I view the activities and debates surrounding Marsalis and his canonical project at Lincoln Center as an effective (and largely successful) struggle for institutional space and recognition within contemporary culture. This effective struggle for institutional recognition and legitimacy is all the more significant when considered from the long view of the historic relationship between jazz and a dominant cultural institution like Lincoln Center. As the *Los Angeles Times* described it, Lincoln Center is an "institution that has looked down its nose at jazz for decades" (*Los Angeles Times*, 1992: 6). Similarly, cultural studies helps to clarify the cultural politics involved by alerting us to the racial, aesthetic, and discursive constructions and struggles which also lie at the center of this process.

Wynton Marsalis and his supporters are absolutely central to under-standing this move toward institutional recognition and legitimation. In his varied roles as media personality, recording artist, cultural advocate, arts administrator, composer, and performer, one can tease out elements of his aesthetic and cultural project, as well as the institutional strategies for realizing them. Marsalis's vision and the cultural politics that under-write it are pivotal for grasping the significance of the cultural struggles surrounding jazz in the last 15 years. His effective, though no doubt polemical, directorship of the Lincoln Center Program is a useful entrée to this instance of contemporary cultural struggle.

Wynton Marsalis is simply one of the most accomplished, celebrated, and rewarded musicians of his generation (Anderson, 1994; Guilliat, 1995; *New York Times Magazine*, 1995; Santoro, 1993; Williams, 1986). He has won Grammy Awards in both classical and jazz music; indeed, so prolific and celebrated is Marsalis that there have even been the inevitable com-parisons in the press to Leonard Bernstein (Ross, 1995). Marsalis works in a variety of venues (e.g. jazz clubs, concerts, festivals), media and edu-cational settings (e.g. workshops, universities, radio, television), and per-formance contexts (e.g. modern dance, ballet, opera, quintet, big band, orchestra). His collaborations in related art fields include work with cellist YoYo Ma, choreographers Garth Fegan, Peter Martins, and Twyla Tharpe, as well as opera diva Kathleen Battle. His Grammy Awards, lucrative recording contracts, television and radio series, and directorship at Lin-coln Center ensure a busy and demanding schedule.

It is not just Marsalis's public visibility, commercial success, and profes-sional achievements that I want to highlight here, but rather how the "figure" of Marsalis, in the discursive sense, in critical and popular dis-course, may be read as an example of an oppositional cultural strategy by African-Americans engaged in struggles for institutional legitimacy and recognition.[1] Marsalis himself has, in fact, used the social space of cultural performance and the institutional space of Lincoln Center as platforms from which to issue certain pronouncements about his vision of the music, culture, and tradition. Anchored by a modernist vision of aesthetics, a purist suspicion of the dangers of commercialism, and a deep commit-ment to racial pride, his is a cultural project – a canonical project to be more exact – which aims for institutional recognition, codification, and legitimation.

From his highly visible and influential public platform Marsalis articu-lates a cultural, social, and aesthetic vision which aims to canonize jazz and to ensure it a significant place of cultural recognition and legitimacy for his and future generations (Conroy, 1995; Marsalis, 1988, 1994). Part race man, aesthetic modernist, and institutional revolutionary, Marsalis's cultural project is a complex mixture of racial nationalism, anti-commercialism, and elitism (Santoro, 1993; Ross, 1995; Williams, 1986). In order to more fully apprcciate the complex way that each of these elements fit into Marsalis's cultural vision and is in turn mobilized into a cultural project, I want to examine each one in considerable detail.

Aesthetic Modernism and Anti-commercialism

One of Marsalis's most impressive qualities is his ability to clearly and forcefully articulate his aesthetic approach to jazz. Tony Scherman (1995) observes that "Many disagree with him but few musicians or critics have what Marsalis can claim: a thought-out unified view, a cosmology, and aesthetic." Marsalis's aesthetic approach to jazz involves a complex understanding of the music's contemporary cultural context, its historical formation and tradition, its technical elements, and the significance of its key innovators.

Socially, Marsalis's aesthetic is founded on what he calls jazz's essence:

> Some of the essential traits of jazz are things that have nothing to do with music. . . . First comes the concept of playing. You take a theme, an idea, and you play with it. Just like you play with a ball . . . so you have the spirit of playing. Next is the desire to play with other people. That means learning to respect individuality . . . playing jazz means learning how to reconcile differences, even when they're opposites. . . . Jazz teaches you how to have a dialogue with integrity. . . . Good manners are important and spirituality. . . . The soul of the music comes out of that. You have to want to make somebody feel good with what you play. Many so-called cutting edge forms assault the listener. But that's not the identity of jazz. The identity of jazz is to present itself with some soul to people. (Scherman, 1995: 66ff)

These social characteristics form one part of Marsalis's view of jazz as a modern form. This social understanding is very much organized around his conception of the American character and his belief in the possibilities of American democracy. For Marsalis, jazz expresses a modern impulse. It "means a group of people coming together and playing without prepared music. It means negotiating your personality against the personality or with the personality of another musician with no controls over what the other musician is going to play. That's modern to me. That never existed before the twentieth century" (ibid).

Musically, Marsalis stresses conventional elements that characterize and hence distinguish jazz. These include blues, swing, collective improvisation, syncopation, call and response, and vocal effects. So central are these constitutive elements to Marsalis's particular musical approach to jazz that it is worth quoting him directly and at length on each element:

Blues: Blues gives the jazz musician an unsentimental view of the world. Blues is adult secular music, the first adult secular music America produced. It has optimism that's not naive. You accept tragedy and move forward. . . . Blues is down home sophistication. . . . Blues is such a fundamental form that it's loaded with complex information. It has a sexual meaning, the ebb and flow of sexual passion; disappointment, happiness, joy, and sorrow. It has a whole religious connotation, too, that joy and lift. . . . And blues gives you a way to combine dissonance and consonance.

Swing: Swing means constant coordination, but in an environment that's difficult enough to challenge your equilibrium. In jazz somebody's playing on every beat. . . . That's what makes swinging in jazz a challenge. On every beat there's the possibility of the rhythm falling apart. You have the constant danger of not swinging. Swing isn't rigid. Somebody might take the swing in a new direction, and you have to be ready to go that way. You're constantly trying to coordinate with something that's shifting and changing. . . . A lot of what Afro-Americans did in music was refine things that already existed. Afro-Americans didn't invent it, but they refined it to another level and put another type of American twist to it.

Collective improvisation: People getting together and making up music as a group.

Syncopation: A syncopated approach to rhythm means you're always prepared to do the unexpected, always ready to find your equilibrium. . . . In jazz you're improvising within a form. You challenge that form with rhythms and harmonies. . . . It's all connected to the notion of playing. You set parameters and then you mess with them.

Call and response: Statement, then counter-statement and confirmation. . . . In jazz, the call and response is spontaneous. You invent it. Players call and respond freely, all the time. You have two types of call and response in jazz. The first is concurrent. . . . That's the most fascinating call and response, the simultaneous type. That's true collective improvisation. . . . The big bands made call and response sequential – that's the second type – and orchestrated it. In big band music, the soloist played and then the ensemble responded with an arranged phrase.

Vocal effects: There's achieving vocal effects on instruments, vocal effects that come, for the most part, from the Negro tradition, down home tradition. Southern shouts and moans, those slides and growls and cries and screams.

Worldliness: There is a spirit of worldliness in jazz. You can hear how jazz is connected to other musics from around the world. Folk musics specifically, but also classical tradition. . . . Ellington is the prime example. . . . He was trying to apply the sound of jazz, not by imitating other people's music but by understanding how its elements fit jazz, jazz music is not provincial. (Scherman, 1995: 66ff)

For Marsalis then, jazz is the expression of the highest ideals of the black cultural (as opposed to racial) imagination. Jazz emerged out of a traceable past, structured by a formal set of elements, and practiced by a recognizable group of composers and performers. In other words, jazz is characterized by a complex set of social values, a sophisticated tradition of recognizable texts and practitioners, and a systematic means of reproduction. Recognizing these qualities means that, for Marsalis, jazz must be formally studied, systematically codified, and practiced through performance, education, institutional recognition. It must be supported as well through an informed and critical public discourse.

Marsalis's aesthetic approach to jazz forms the basis upon which he identifies a particular corpus of styles, players, compositions, and standards by which the music is measured and judged. Within the jazz formation, he draws a rather sharp distinction between what he calls jazz and the avant-garde, particularly with respect to the seminal contributions of artists like Cecil Taylor and Ornette Coleman. Marsalis is especially forceful about this distinction: "I've talked to Ornette about his notion of free jazz. I think it's chaos. Maybe it's not, but that's what I think it is. Chaos is always out there; it's something you can get from any fifty kids in a band room" (Scherman, 1995: 66ff). While he is quick to note that the family of players loosely known as the avant-garde do not call their music jazz, his view applies particularly to post-Coltrane stylistic developments in jazz; for example, the work of the World Saxophone Quartet and the Art Ensemble of Chicago.

> I've listened to it [the avant-garde], I've played with the musicians, I was at the first concert the World Saxophone Quartet gave. I played on bills with the Art Ensemble of Chicago. It's not interesting to me to play like that. If I've rejected it, it's not out of ignorance of it. I don't know any people who like it. It doesn't resonate with anything I've experienced in the world. No food I've eaten, no sports I've played, no women I've known. I don't even like Coltrane's later stuff, to be honest. I don't listen to it like I do "A Love Supreme." It was with the type of things that that late period Coltrane did that *jazz destroyed its relationship to the public. That avant-garde conception of music, that's loud and self-absorbed – nobody's interested in hearing that on a regular basis.* I don't care how much publicity it gets. The public is not going to want to hear people play like that. (Scherman, 1995: 66ff, my emphasis)

Since, for Marsalis, jazz must be supported by a critical and informed discourse, in addition to decrying avant-garde musicians and composers, Marsalis directs some of his most unforgiving criticism towards critics, journalists, and music-industry personnel who in his estimation profoundly misunderstand and misrepresent the music:

Jazz commentary is too often shaped by a rebellion against what is considered the limitations of the middle class. The commentators mistakenly
believe that by willfully sliding down the intellectual, spiritual, economic, or
social ladder, they will find freedom down where the jazz musicians (i.e.
"real" people) lie. Jazz musicians, however, are searching for freedom of
ascendance. This is why they practice. Musicians . . . are rebelling against
the idea that they should be excluded from choosing what they want to do
or think, against being forced into someone else's mold, whether it be the
social agendas of the conservative establishment or the new fake liberal-
establishment of which many well meaning jazz observers are part. (Marsalis,
1988: 24)

Along these same lines, Marsalis has more recently observed that

in jazz it is always necessary to be able to swing consistently and at different
tempos. You cannot develop jazz by not playing it, not swinging or playing
the blues. Today's jazz criticism celebrates as innovation forms of music that
don't address the fundamentals of the music. But no one will create a new
style of jazz by evading its inherent difficulties. (Marsalis, 1994: 141)

It is in the deployment of his aesthetic vision against critical excesses and
misrepresentations that one begins to get a glimmer of Marsalis's cultural
politics. As early as 1988 in the editorial pages of the *New York Times*
(Marsalis, 1988) and more recently in his own volume, *Sweet Swing Blues
on the Road* (Marsalis, 1994), Marsalis intervenes directly in the public
discourse about jazz. These interventions are key, for in them Marsalis
offers a corrective to what he sees as a misrepresentation of jazz. The
objective for Marsalis is, of course, to restore to musicians the authority of
judgments and representation of the music and thus reestablish levels of
competence, musicianship, and artistic integrity. This is how Marsalis puts
the matter:

right now we're trying to get back to people playing at a competent level
of musicianship. Another battle is for musicians to be recognized as authorities on music. That's never happened in jazz. And we're battling for the
recognition of the ritual aspects of jazz, of the fact that jazz music is not like
European classical music. (Scherman, 1995: 66ff)

Marsalis's attempt to distinguish jazz from what he regards as excessive
(and damaging) confusion between European classical music and the jazz
avant-garde is perhaps matched only by his contempt – aesthetic and
technical – for the corrosive effects of commercialism on jazz. He has
consistently distanced and distinguished jazz from commercial forms like
pop, rock and hip-hop. His aesthetic modernism is complemented, then,

by contempt for commercial contamination that threatens the purity, nobility, and integrity of jazz through confusion and mimicry. "Jazz is not entertainment" Marsalis once quipped early in his career (Williams, 1986: 1). This sentiment captures Marsalis's contempt for the corrupting influences of commercialism on jazz. And he does not mince words to express his feelings about contemporary popular music: "*Popular tunes are sad pieces of one chord shit. Today's pop tunes are sad.* Turn on the radio and try to find a pop tune to play with your band. You can't do it. The melodies are static, the chord changes are just the same senseless stuff repeated over and over again" (Liska, 1994: 42ff, my emphasis).

Jazz needs to be "protected," as it were, from these leveling influences because in a culture driven by profit and record sales, confusion, misrepresentation, and worse, for Marsalis, misuse of the term "jazz," can easily result. Again, Marsalis puts the matter forcefully and directly:

> Anything is jazz; everything is jazz. Quincy Jones' shit is jazz, David Sanborn . . . that's not to cut down Quincy or David. I love funk, it's hip. No problem to it. *The thing is, if it'll sell records to call that stuff jazz, they'll call it jazz.* They call Miles' stuff jazz. That stuff is not jazz, man. Just because someone played jazz at one time, that doesn't mean they're still playing it. (Ibid, my emphasis)

In a rather ironic twist Marsalis suggests that while commercialism contributes to the social diminution and loss of cultural respect and legitimacy for the music (in the eyes of some), popular music benefits, aesthetically and culturally, from its association with jazz. This is how Marsalis explains it in his 1988 *New York Times* editorial, "I recently completed a tour of jazz festivals in Europe in which only two out of ten bands were jazz bands. The promoters of these festivals readily admit most of the music isn't jazz, but refuse to rename these events . . . seeking the aesthetic elevation that jazz offers" (Marsalis, 1988: 21). In the same editorial he observes,

> To many people, any kind of popular music can now be lumped with jazz. As a result audiences too often come to jazz with generalized misconceptions about what it is and what it is supposed to be. *Too often, what is represented as jazz isn't jazz at all. Despite attempts by writers and record companies and promoters and educators and even musicians to blur the lines for commercial purposes, rock isn't jazz and new age isn't jazz and neither are pop or third stream.* There may be much that is good in all of them, but they ain't jazz (Ibid, my emphasis)

Such confusions and misrepresentations, when combined with the relentless commercial imperatives to sell records and at all costs to turn out hits, is, for Marsalis, at the heart of the matter. It is this situation which generates misconceptions, misunderstandings, and appropriations of jazz that seem to trouble Marsalis most.

Racial Nationalism and American Democracy

A similar kind of protectionist stance defines Marsalis's conception of the role of African-Americans in relationship to jazz. While certainly not limited to it, this conception begins with and is, perhaps, most evident in his defense of both jazz and African-Americans against persistent and destructive racial myths, which still permeate many of the critical and popular conceptions about jazz and its practitioners. Marsalis confronts this myth directly in the editorial pages of the *New York Times*. The myth of the noble savage in jazz, he asserts, "which was born early and stubbornly refuses to die, despite all the evidence to the contrary, regards jazz merely as a product of noble savages – *music produced by untutored, unbuttoned semiliterates – for whom history does not exist*" (ibid, my emphasis). Again, for Marsalis, jazz critics and the misinformed critical commentary they produce are partly responsible for the perpetration of this myth:

> This myth was invented by early jazz writers who, in attempting to escape their American prejudice, turned out a whole world of new clichés based on the myth of the innate ability of early jazz musicians. Because of these writers' lack of understanding of the mechanics of music, they thought there weren't any mechanics. It is the "they all can sing, they all have rhythm syndrome. (Ibid)

In contrast to the "semiliterate unbuttoned" image of the music which the myth of the noble savage presents, Linda Williams, writing in the *Wall Street Journal*, describes Marsalis as "a show business rarity: a black performer who has built up a big mass-market audience while taking a black nationalist approach to his art (Williams, 1986: 1). Williams suggests that for Marsalis, "jazz is much more than entertainment: *It is an important expression of the 20th century Black experience in America. Jazz is, he recently wrote, 'the nobility of the race put into sound; the sensuousness of romance in our dialect; it is the picture of the people in all their glory'*" (ibid, my emphasis).

Given the history, social climate, and deep cultural roots of the myths that Marsalis has taken on, one can begin to see the crucial role of racial (and for some, black nationalist) politics within his larger cultural and aesthetic project. Indeed, as counterdiscourse, Marsalis attacks this poisonous cultural assault on black people and jazz from a position carefully crafted from his own cultural formation in the black South, his intellectual mentoring by Stanley Crouch and Albert Murray, and his considerable command of musical history, aesthetics, and mechanics:

> My generation finds itself wedged between two opposing traditions. One is the tradition we know in such wonderful detail from the enormous recorded legacy that tells anyone who will listen that jazz broke the rules of European conventions and created rules of its own that were so specific, so thorough and so demanding that a great art resulted. This art has had such universal appeal and application that it has changed the conventions of American music as well as those of the world at large. (Marsalis, 1988: 21)

As with his conception of aesthetics and his position on the commercial corruptions threatening jazz, Marsalis's racial politics are the source of considerable controversy. He has publicly debated with jazz critic James Lincoln Collier on jazz criticism (especially Collier's writing about Duke Ellington). He has attracted bitter and often heated criticism from neo-conservative, liberal, even progressive cultural critics like Terry Treachout, Peter Watrous, and Gene Santoro. Neoconservative critic Terry Treachout has even charged Marsalis with reverse racism, owing to Marsalis's hiring practices, booking policies, and his choices of repertory and commissions in the Jazz Program at Lincoln Center. While Treachout uses Marsalis's directorship of the program at Lincoln Center to attack Marsalis's intellectual mentors – Stanley Crouch and Albert Murray – by far his most vehement criticism are directly toward Marsalis.[2] And while criticisms of Marsalis's choices in programming, orchestra personnel, and musical styles have come from musicians and critics alike, Treachout's is some of the most venomous in its disdain for the way that race underwrites Marsalis's tenure as Director so far. This criticism of Marsalis stems from Treachout's view of jazz as a politically neutral, colorblind space of cultural and social practice, a space where, in his estimation, race should not, indeed cannot, matter. Treachout suggests for example that,

> so far as can be determined, jazz was "invented" around the turn of the 20th century by New Orleans blacks of widely varying musical education and ethnic background. . . . *But whites were playing jazz within a decade of its initial appearance, and began making important contributions to its stylistic development shortly thereafter. Until fairly recently, most musicians and scholars agreed that jazz long ago ceased to be a uniquely black idiom and became multi-cultural in the truest, least politicized sense of the word.* (Treachout, 1995: 50ff, my emphasis)

Having established his view of jazz's historic multiculturalism, Treachout singles out Marsalis's Lincoln Center Program for its race-based hiring policies and commissions. "Under Marsalis and Crouch," Treachout writes,

Jazz at Lincoln Center presents only programs about black musicians; whites are allowed to play with the Lincoln Center Jazz Orchestra, but the historic contributions of earlier white players, composers, and arrangers are systematically ignored, and contemporary white composers are not commissioned to write original pieces for the full orchestra. This policy is so egregiously race-conscious that it has even been attacked by admirers of Wynton Marsalis. (Ibid)[3]

Treachout's essay is peppered throughout with direct attacks not just on Marsalis's guidance of the Lincoln Center Jazz Program, but Marsalis's character, politics, and musicianship. Here is a sampling:

Marsalis is unapologetic about such matters [his controversial leadership at Lincoln Center] and apparently he can afford to be. At thirty-three, in addition to having performed and recorded much of the classical trumpet literature, he is the most famous jazz musician in America. . . . *Interestingly, not all of these achievements hold equally well under scrutiny.* Technically speaking, Marsalis is a virtuoso by any conceivable standard . . . but *his jazz playing is felt by many to be cold and ironically enough derivative.* (Ibid, my emphasis)

And:

Marsalis takes seriously, his job as an *unappointed spokesman for Albert Murray's and Stanley Crouch's version of the jazz tradition.* . . . He has been quick to criticize other musicians, notably, Miles Davis and Sonny Rollins, for "selling out" to commercial music. And he is *adamant in defending his conduct as artistic director of Jazz at Lincoln Center.* (Ibid, my emphasis)

And finally:

Although he uses white players both in the Lincoln Center Jazz Orchestra and in his own group, *it is widely believed that he harbors a general disdain for white musicians,* and the belief seems to be borne out by the facts. (Ibid, my emphasis)

With passing digs at the generation of so-called "young lions" spawned by the success of Marsalis, Treachout details how racial politics in jazz operates – how privileging blackness in jazz works to the advantage of black players – in recording contracts, bookings, and appearances; how it contributes to the misrepresentation of social relations in the music (colorblind multiculturalism); and, perhaps most important, how it disadvantages white players. In the end, for Treachout, Marsalis is the most visible, successful, and hence egregious demonstration of the presence of reverse racism in jazz. He notes, quite bitterly, that

> one can easily multiply such examples to show how *reverse racism has become, if not universal, then potentially legitimate in jazz and indeed, how it has insinuated itself throughout the jazz community*. . . . The new reverse racism in jazz is not, of course, an isolated phenomenon. It has arisen at a time when such government policies as quota-based affirmative action have made race-consciousness a pervasive feature of American society. In the absence of these policies . . . it is unlikely that public institutions like Lincoln Center and the Smithsonian Institution would lend the prestige of their names to artistic enterprises run on racialist lines, or submit meekly to cynical politicians playing the race card. . . . But that is just what makes the current epidemic in the jazz world so disturbing, and its implication so far-reaching. (Ibid, my emphasis)

Marsalis's aesthetic and racial politics makes for some strange bedfellows indeed. White neoconservative idealists who celebrate the colorblind, multicultural aspects of jazz, mainstream critics, and in some cases black radical avant-garde players have, for different reasons, challenged Marsalis's heady pronouncements and his leadership of the Lincoln Center Program. On the other hand, Marsalis has also brought together neoconservative African-American cultural critics and intellectuals, young black performers, and largely liberal middle-class (white) audiences under a banner of a challenging but accessible middle-brow music, racial pride, and affirmation of American democracy and culture.

Marsalis's racial politics aim to establish the centrality of black presence and contributions to the American experience. Where Treachout sees (and aspires to) colorbindness, Marsalis sees (and rejects) racial and cultural invisibility which is sustained by the continuing salience of racism in all aspects of American life and culture. Consider this 1994 exchange between Marsalis and an interviewer:

Q: How closely is jazz bound up with the experience of African Americans?

Marsalis: *It is inseparable – in its inception. They created it.* But why has who created it become more important than what was created? It has transcended its inception . . .

Q: One wonders if there will ever be a jazz innovator, someone on the level of Ellington, who is white?

Marsalis: There might not, but it's not important. It doesn't make a difference. It is of no significance . . . why is it even an issue? That's the thing you have to examine.

Q: OK, why is it?

Marsalis: *Because in our time racism still carries more weight than*
          musical fact. Duke Ellington didn't have enough white
          in him? He's an American. He's from Washington DC.

Q: People probably assume that it's important to you to say
          that all great innovators in jazz have been black.

Marsalis: I don't have to say it. I just say Louis Armstrong. I don't
          say black Louis Armstrong. I mean "what about pride in
          humanity?" Ellington's achievement is his achievement.
          It's a human achievement. Because, remember, the Afro-
          American experience is American experience. *Whenever*
          the Negro is successful at something, there has to be an
          excuse made up for the why. The best way to do this is to
          make his achievement seem like something only he can
          do, for some racially derived reason – which removes the
          direct competition and exchange that actually exists.

                              (Scherman, 1995: 66ff, my emphasis)

And in the more controlled context of his own book – *Sweet Swing Blues
on the Road* – Marsalis put the matter (i.e. the relationship between jazz
and black folk) this way:

> As Crouch says, "They invented it." People who invent something are
> always best at doing it, at least until other folk figure out what it is. If you
> celebrate less accomplished musicians because you share a superficial bond,
> you cheat yourself. Anyway if you ask most black Americans today who is
> their favorite jazz musician, they will name some instrumental pop musi-
> cian. So much for race. The younger musicians of any racial group today
> swing in spite of their race, not because of it. (Marsalis, 1994: 142–3)

Regardless of the venue or the occasion, in the final analysis Marsalis's
view of the relationship between race and jazz is a complex amalgama-
tion of deep belief in the possibility of American democracy, a celebration
of African-American contributions to American culture, and a critique
of racism. An individualist ethic drives both his creative spirit and his
sense of possibility for realizing his project in the institutional space of
Lincoln Center.

Institutional Revolutionary

If nothing else, Marsalis has certainly used his position as Artistic Director
of the Lincoln Center Jazz Program as a platform to bring together and

realize a broader cultural project, i.e. to establish a jazz canon and create a space for its institutional legitimacy within a premier cultural institution. The conflicts over the realization of that project are as much generational as aesthetic and political. Peter Watrous, jazz critic with the *New York Times*, characterizes the conflicts this way:

> In many ways the fight is over not only the direction of jazz at Lincoln Center, which has been an exceptional advocate of younger musicians, but also the direction of jazz: Who has the right to represent it? What will its future be? How will its history be written? And despite the critics' pre-scriptive sound and fury, it's a fight that is over. The musicians, who commanded the bandstand, have won. (Watrous, 1994: C11)

If one accepts Watrous's critical appraisal, and I am strongly inclined to do so on the broader issue of cultural politics, then it is necessary to turn once again to Marsalis. Most critical observers agree he is *the* pivotal figure around which important institutional spaces have been opened and significant legitimation of and interest in the music realized. How Marsalis initially sought to realize this vision was set out in his 1988 *New York Times* editorial (well before his directorship of the Lincoln Center Program was announced). At the time he wrote,

> We designed a Classical Jazz Series this year that deals with the music of Duke Ellington, Tadd Dameron, and Max Roach, as well as evenings given over to singers and instrumentalists interpreting standard songs. This series focuses on two things: *the compositions of major writers and the quality of improvisation.* . . . While enjoyment and entertainment are paramount mat-ters in the Classical Jazz Series, it should be clear that we also see a need to *help promote understandings of what happens in jazz.* An important part of the series, therefore, are program notes by Stanley Crouch, which seeks *to explain the intent of the musicians as well as the meaning of the art.* . . . We feel that the proper presentation of notes, song titles and even small discographies will help audiences better understand the essential elements of the music and thereby enjoy the music even more. . . . Classical Jazz at Lincoln Center – whether celebrating the work of individual artists or using improvisational talents of masters . . . is intent on helping to give jazz, its artists and its products their deserved place in American culture. I also feel that the Classical Jazz Series gives Lincoln Center additional reason to regard itself as a center of world culture. (Marsalis, 1988: 24, my emphasis)

Since 1988, through the Classical Series, commissioned works, collab-orations, media and education, performance, and critical engagement with the discourse on jazz, Marsalis has used the institutional space and international reputation of Lincoln Center quite effectively – namely, to increase the visibility and legitimacy of jazz (Santoro, 1996: 34; Ross, 1995: J3; Watrous, 1994). For Marsalis, the recognition of a jazz canon by cultural institutions like Lincoln Center not only ensures the music's survival and legitimation in the society's dominant cultural institutions, but also provides him with a prominent public forum from which to engage in political struggles over culture.

The effectiveness of Marsalis's cultural project cannot be ascribed solely to him in isolation from the social, economic, and cultural transformations that have occurred in jazz in the last 15 years. Quite apart from his effective intervention in the discursive debates about jazz, there have been notable developments in the political economy of the recording industry, corporate sponsorship of jazz festivals and performance venues, media coverage, education and training, and research on jazz. Many of the performance venues – notably the small independent jazz clubs – have been replaced by corporate sponsorship, national franchises, mega-festivals, and multi-city tours (Santoro, 1996; Watrous, 1995). Local independent venues that remain have to regularly book "name" talent for their marquee value in order to attract audiences that are large and affluent enough to make their operations profitable. Although clubs and local performance venues long associated with jazz continue to turn over at a rapid pace, new forms of public cultural and financial support for the music have appeared in the form of foundation support, juried competitions, degree programs, research programs, and repertory programs at colleges and universities. Programs like those at Lincoln Center, the Kennedy Center, and Carnegie Hall are complemented by performance competitions like the Theolonious Monk Institute and research archives like the Institute for Jazz Studies at Rutgers University, the Center for Black Music Research in Chicago, the Smithsonian Institute, and the American Research Center (Santoro, 1996).

As for recorded music, the compact disk has replaced the vinyl LP as the standard format in which recorded music is presented. Through various distribution arrangements and marketing strategies between record companies and major corporations, jazz is effectively reaching new markets. Notable examples are arrangements between Blue Note Records and Starbucks Coffee, as well as those between cigarette manufacturers and liquor companies and jazz festivals (Santoro, 1996). Music video, television commercials, and special campaigns (e.g. the US Postal Service commemorative stamp series on jazz legends) have also become an important means through which the music gains exposure. And, of course, public television and more recently cable television (e.g. Bravo, Black Entertainment Television) have become important media outlets for showcasing jazz. For the most part, public radio and college radio remain the primary outlets for jazz, particularly since commercial outlets in major urban areas like New York, Los Angeles, and the San Francisco Bay area no longer exist.

Audiences for jazz, both those who purchase the music on compact disk and those who attend concerts and clubs, are increasingly educated, affluent, young, and very often white (Williams, 1986). To be sure, Marsalis and his "young lion" associates have also helped stimulate interests in jazz on the part of black middle-class youth, some of whom, ironically, are also drawn to those commercial forms which Marsalis fears most for their insidious effects on the music – rap, acid jazz, house, jungle music, dance hall, and reggae. These styles have brought young people to jazz by way of a search for new stylistic possibilities, as well as a familiarity with earlier players and styles within the jazz tradition (Lipsitz, 1994; Santoro, 1996).

The popular and critical coverage of jazz, much of which is aimed at young affluent consumers, is limited to a small but energetic jazz press, including publications like *Downbeat, Jazz Times,* and *Jazz Is.* In the press, popular coverage of the music is limited largely to major metropolitan dailies like the *New York Times* and the *Los Angeles Times.* A growing body of independent films (e.g. *A Great Day in Harlem*), biographies, and scholarly monographs have begun to emerge as well (Gabbard, 1995; Santoro, 1996).

I want to propose that Marsalis's canonical project at Lincoln Center, while an expression of one form of resistant black culture, is also fundamentally conservative. Musicians and critics alike view this as a project which constructs a classical canon by formalizing it into static texts and confining it to museums, conservatories, and cultural institutions (Mackey, 1995; Santoro, 1993; Watrous, 1994). In fact, drawing on the insights of Amiri Baraka and African-American literature, Nathaniel Mackey (1995) argues that such projects move jazz from a "verb" to a "noun." In its high modernist tone and aesthetic assumptions, Marsalis's pronouncements on the aesthetic dangers and commercial corruptions of popular music join longstanding cultural debates about the relationship of high culture to popular culture and the contaminating effects of the latter on the former (Brantlinger, 1983; Horkheimer and Adorno, 1972). In Marsalis's cultural universe, the move to locate the corrosive effects of the popular arts on the jazz canon is, no doubt, a powerful political move.

In a climate of neoconservative assault on the arts and culture, Marsalis's cultural project is especially appealing precisely because it is built on crucial assumptions about the value of "culture" (and morality) in the still-unrealized potential of American democracy. Politically, this scheme accepts a (traditional) view of the erosion of culture and values (which are under assault) and links it to powerful agencies of legitimation and recognition which aim to fix the limits of culture and protect it from the corrupting forces of the market, commerce, and untutored tastes. I find this position and the aesthetics on which it is built culturally and politically conventional and elitist in much the same way as traditionalists (both radical and conservative) have always been on the question of popular culture. This vision relies on discourses and institutions of legitimation and power, a discerning and informed public, a critical community of judgment and evaluation, and powerful institutions to value and signal as important the conventions, technical rules, literatures, practitioners, and tradition on which a canon is constructed (Santoro, 1996; Williams, 1986; Walser, 1993).

Conservative or not, I do recognize, even applaud, the strategic and effective interventions of Marsalis. I do so not so much as a capitulation to Marsalis's aesthetic and the cultural politics on which it is built, but to acknowledge the sheer complexity of the position and the effective results which Marsalis has staked out and enacted at Lincoln Center.

Where Marsalis mobilizes his rhetorical positions and institutional tactics around the need to canonize jazz to ensure it institutional legitimacy in the broader American cultural landscape, when examined from within the politics of African-American music, a different set of cultural practices and political possibilities emerge. There *is* another approach to the jazz tradition. Indeed, when one considers the tradition itself and the productive practices and social conditions that shaped it, one finds many of the social and cultural elements and corruptions which Marsalis and his intellectual mentors fear most for their baneful effects on the music – popularity, dance, mass-marketing, and the influence of popular styles.

While I can only gesture toward this other approach to the tradition – an approach which I characterize as the sensibility of the "road and the street" – I do so in order to make a larger point about the study of cultural practices and to foreground the cultural politics at work in a different approach to jazz as a site of cultural struggle. By indicating an alternative to what I have called a "canonization project," I do not mean to suggest that the sensibilities and practices of a "road or street" aesthetic do not exist in Marsalis's own project. In fact, in *Sweet Swing Blues on the Road* Marsalis writes quite robustly about the centrality of the road to his own formation and continuing practice as a jazz musician. I do, however, mean to underscore the fact that the locations and conditions of production where jazz maintains its *motion and movement, innovation and expansion* continue, to a considerable degree, to remain in those cultural spaces and practices located outside of and beyond formal canonical discourses and institutional legitimation.

I take the metaphor of the "street" and the "road" from the great territory bands of the 1930s and 1940s. The road (as opposed, for instance, to the "tour") was an expression used by musicians to describe life on the road – the nomadic experience of traveling from community to community, town to town, city to city, to perform. The music, social relations, and cultural styles which defined urban black communities in the 1940s and 1950s especially, were, as cultural historian Robin D. G. Kelley (1994) brilliantly details, the basis for the formation among many working-class blacks of political consciousness and cultural understanding of blackness. Kelley argues that it was black popular forms and cultural styles found in the streets and clubs of black urban America which gave shape and expression to the cultural and political consciousness of blacks.

On the road, musicians perfected their skills, discovered new musical influences and players, made friends, and constructed communities which extended beyond the immediate confines of geography. Encounters on the road allowed musicians and bands to sharpen their acts, pick up new talent, modify their books, and gauge the response to their music. The literal road and the street, then, were places where musicians borrowed and mixed styles and experimented with new possibilities. In the process, they created music that was dynamic, dialogic, and fashioned out of the experiences and needs of everyday life. While I have no desire to recreate this literal "road and street," I do want to shift the discussion from this literal and historical road and street to a metaphorical one.

Although very much rooted in a jazz tradition, the metaphorical street and road of jazz as a cultural practice depends on a different conception of and relationship to the tradition: one rooted in constant change and transformation, where tradition is not simply abstracted, codified, and preserved in critical judgments, cultural institutions, and repertory performance. In this image of jazz as a cultural practice the music lives and breathes, as it were, in the active creations and experiences of changing performance and encounters with contemporary ideas, styles, influences, and performance possibilities, including those in popular and commercial culture. This difference in conception and approach represents far more than a semantic disagreement or conceptual dispute over how the music is represented. The point of the tradition in this view of jazz practice (including its canonical manifestations) is to change it, to reinvent it, to emphasize its "verbal" character, as Mackey (1995) puts it.

In contrast to the aim of building a canonical tradition in order to ensure a place of legitimacy and recognition by dominant cultural institutions, an entire cohort of Marsalis's contemporaries – Don Byron, Gerri Allen, Steve Coleman, Cassandra Wilson, Graham Haynes, Courtney Pine, Kenny Garrett, and Branford Marsalis – continually draw from a range of stylistic influences which challenge and stretch the tradition. These musicians, like many of their predecessors, keep jazz moving through its engagement with popular forms, new technologies, and commercial routes of circulation. Instead of protecting the jazz tradition from the corrupting influences of popular and commercial forms like reggae, rap, rhythm'n' blues, dance-hall (as well as Native American, South Asian, and African forms), these contemporary musicians expand the jazz tradition by reworking it through metaphorical encounters in the literal street. With an emphatic stress on the verbal rather than nominal dimension of the music, as Mackey puts it, these musicians are engaged in a dynamic reinvention and dialogic rewriting of the tradition.

Let me conclude, then, by highlighting the analytic and political implications of these two distinct, but related, cultural practices. These two kinds of practices operate simultaneously, very often existing side by side, within the same social, economic, and discursive space. And yet I think it is fair to say that, culturally, the distinct political effects and possibilities of each are quite different. Those practices that gain a measure of institutional recognition and legitimacy are privileged in terms of visibility, funding, and reproduction. I believe that this very move also results in the marginalization and displacement of practices (and musicians) which do not enjoy a similar recognition and legitimacy. In different ways they point to different modalities and registers, different aesthetic possibilities, and cultural strategies which challenge, even rearrange, dominant conceptions and judgments of the music.

Marsalis and his supporters have effectively consolidated and institutionalized a very specific conception of jazz within a dominant cultural institution like Lincoln Center for the Performing Arts. Popular and critical discourses, as well as significant financial support and interest, have congealed around Marsalis's notion of jazz, its key texts, and exemplars. Culturally, this has resulted in the creation of a significant social and cultural space for jazz in popular discourse, the marketplace, and cultural institutions. In the context of ongoing wars over culture, values, and art, this is surely a significant accomplishment culturally and politically. And as the polemic surrounding Marsalis's tenure at Lincoln Center indicates, the continuing political struggles over how jazz is constructed, represented, and positioned do matter.

What does any of this have to do with sociology, cultural studies, and the study of cultural practices? In my estimation, everything. My analysis of Marsalis in relationship to cultural approaches which I call "the road" might even be seen as an allegory of the relationship between sociology of culture and cultural studies. Sociology of culture has largely taken as its site of study dominant cultural institutions and organizations like art museums, conservatories, symphony orchestras, and opera companies.

The art produced by these institutions, the cultural practices that structure them, and the critical systems of judgment which evaluate them have benefited from the field's identification of them as worthy of study. In this respect, my analysis of Marsalis and the cultural politics surrounding the Program at Lincoln Center has benefited from this sociological tradition and, therefore, can be read discursively, as rooted in this tradition. Although I have tried to draw on the sociology of culture to illuminate and understand the situation at Lincoln Center, I also feel limited by an analysis which centers largely on the social context, institutional rules, and competing constructions about Marsalis and his aesthetic choices. If it remained at this analytic level, my analysis would fail to appreciate the more complex social relations and practices which structure and shape these institutional machinations, including, especially, race, aesthetics, technology, generations, and so on.

But the analysis would also be limited and incomplete in yet another sense. For insofar as it does not focus on alternative practices that may be less institutionally recognized because they are dispersed, diffuse, threatening, even invisible, to dominant academic and critical discourse, the sociology of culture necessarily remains complicitious in the reproduction of institutional domination and legitimation. Hence, my gesture toward the marginalized cultural practices of the street and the road.

For me, then, cultural studies is instrumental, indeed necessary, for making visible these alternative practices. By proceeding from the assumption that cultural practices, like analytic frameworks for analyzing culture, are dynamic, dialogic, and social and political phenomena, I have had to remain alert to the ways that cultural practices and cultural analysis move inside and outside of institutions and discourses of power. The cultural politics surrounding jazz and the corpus of issues and debates swirling around the trope of Wynton Marsalis represent fertile ground for cultural analysis which extends beyond the immediate activities at Lincoln Center. It is here that the sociology of culture and cultural studies meet, each contesting and displacing, extending and complementing the other in terms of foci, data, method, perspectives, theory, and social context.

As the practices developed on the metaphorical road and in the metaphorical streets indicate, different kinds of cultural possibilities and social alliances are being formed all the time. These new alliances and explorations have the political possibility for creating new social and cultural spaces which can and often do challenge dominant aesthetic sensibilities and the institutions on which they are erected and consolidated. New developments in cultural studies can help make such developments visible and consequential. As institutions like Lincoln Center continue to recognize and legitimate canonical traditions like those advocated by

Marsalis, the sociology of culture can help to illuminate the social and organizational mechanisms by which power operates and is challenged within dominant cultural institutions. In a contemporary moment, where cultural products, practices, discourses, and artists circulate across all kinds of boundaries and compete for recognition and legitimacy, the crucial analytic and political question is no longer which kind of analysis or practice is more powerful or salient, but under what conditions each can answer and illuminate the salient questions, relationships, and processes.

NOTES

My thanks to the following friends, colleagues, and students who generously encouraged, read, and commented on various drafts of this chapter: Rosa Linda Fregoso, Leonard Brown, Bill Lowe, Tommy Lott, Saidiya Hartman, Richard Yarborough, Ronald Redano, David Scott, Robert Thompson, Lisa Guererro, Elizabeth Long, Russell Ellis, Sterling Stuckey, David Wellman, Deborah Woo, Robin D. G. Kelley, Janet Francendese, Dwight Andrews, Stephen Feld, and Lisa Thompson. Special thanks also to my research assistant, Cindy Lui, who helped me track down press accounts of Marsalis and the Lincoln Center Program.

1 Other notable examples of the effective use of similar strategies in important cultural sites include theater, film, and African-American Studies.
2 Stanley Crouch is an essayist and jazz critic and Albert Murray is a novelist, biographer and jazz writer.
3 Crouch serves as artistic advisor to Marsalis in the Jazz at Lincoln Center Program.

REFERENCES

Anderson, Jervis 1994: Medium Cool. *New Yorker*, December 12, 69–83.

Baker, Dave 1994: Strictly Jazz. *Oakland Tribune*, December 15, 1, 5.

Brantlinger, Patrick 1983: *Bread and Circuses: Theories of Mass Culture as Social Decay*. Ithaca: Cornell University Press.

Calmore, John O. 1995: Critical Race Theory, Archie Shepp, and Fire Music: Securing an Authentic Intellectual Life in a Multicultural World. In Kimberle' Crenshaw, Neil Gotanda, Gary Peller, and Kendall Thomas (eds), *Critical Race Theory: The Key Writings That Formed The Movement*, New York: New Press, 315–29.

Conroy, Frank 1995: Stop Nit Picking a Genius. *New York Times Magazine*, June 25, 28–31, 48, 54, 70.

Crouch, Stanley 1995: *The All American Skin Game or, The Decoy of Race*. New York: Pantheon.

Davis, Miles and Troupe, Quincy 1989: *Miles Davis: The Autobiography*. New York: Simon and Schuster.

Ellington, Duke 1973: *Music Is My Mistress*. New York: De Capo.

Elworth, Steven B. 1995: Jazz in Crisis, 1948–1958: Ideology and Representation. In Krin Gabbard (ed.), *Jazz Among the Discourse*, Durham, NC: Duke University Press, 57–76.

Gabbard, Krin (ed.) 1995: *Jazz Among the Discourse*. Durham, NC: Duke University Press.

Gendron, Bernard 1995: Moldy Figs and Modernists: Jazz at War (1942–46). In Krin Gabbard (ed.), *Jazz Among the Discourse*. Durham, NC: Duke University Press, 31–57.

Guilliatt, Richard 1995: Eminence Jazz. *San Jose Mercury News*, June 11, 19–20.

Hinton, Milt 1982: *Bass Lines*. Philadelphia: Temple University Press.

Horkheimer, Max and Adorno, Theodor 1972: The Culture Industry: Enlightenment as Mass Deception. In Max Horkheimer and Theodor Adorno (eds), *Dialectic of Enlightenment*, New York: Seabury Press.

Kelley, Robin D. G. 1994: The Riddle of the Zoot Suit: Malcolm Little and Black Cultural Politics during World War II. In *Race Rebels: Culture, Politics, and the Black Working Class*, New York: The Free Press, 161–83.

Lipsitz, George 1994: *Dangerous Crossroads: Popular Music, Postmodernism, and the Poetics of Place*. London: Verso.

Liska, A. James 1994: Wynton and Branford: A Common Understanding. *Downbeat*, February, 42–4.

Los Angeles Times 1992: The Young Lions Roar. *Los Angeles Times*, Calendar Section, 56–7.

Lott, Eric 1995: Double V, Double-Time: Bebop's Politics of Style. In Krin Gabbard (ed.), *Jazz Among the Discourse*, Durham, NC: Duke University Press, 243–56.

Mackey, Nathaniel 1995: Other: From Noun to Verb. In Krin Gabbard (ed.), *Jazz Among the Discourse*, Durham, NC: Duke University Press, 76–100.

Marsalis, Wynton 1988: What Jazz Is – And Isn't. *New York Times*, July 31, 21, 24.

—— 1994: *Sweet Swing Blues on The Road*. New York: W. W. Norton.

Murray, Albert 1976: *Stomping the Blues*. New York: McGraw-Hill.

—— 1996: *The Blue Devils of Nada: A Contemporary American Approach to Aesthetic Statement*. New York: Pantheon.

New York Times Magazine 1995: Jazz: A Special Section. *New York Times Magazine*, June 25, 29–40.

Radano, Ronald 1993: *New Musical Figurations: Anthony Braxton's Cultural Critique*. Chicago: University of Chicago Press.

Ross, Alex 1995: Asking Some Good, Hard Truths about Music. *New York Times*, November 12, 35.

Santoro, Gene 1993: Young Man with a Horn. *The Nation*, March 1, 280–4.

—— 1996: All that Jazz. *The Nation*, January 8/15, 34–6.

Scherman, Tony 1995: What is Jazz? *American Heritage*, 46, 66–86.

Smith, Joan 1994: Wynton Blows his Horn for Jazz. *San Francisco Examiner*, December 18, C17.

Treachout, Terry 1995: The Color of Jazz. *Commentary*, September, 50–4.

Walser, Robert 1993: *Running with the Devil: Power, Gender and Madness in Heavy Metal Music*. Hanover: Wesleyan University Press.

Watrous, Peter 1994: Old Jazz is Out, New Jazz is Older. *New York Times*, March 31, C11–12.

—— 1995: Is there a Mid-life Crisis at the JVC Festival? *New York Times*, July 8, Arts and Leisure Section, 13.

Williams, Linda 1986: A Young Musician Trumpets a Revival of Traditional Jazz. *Wall Street Journal*, September 24, 1, 29.

Zabor, Rafi and Garbarini, Vic 1985: Wynton vs. Herbie: The Purist and the Crossbreeder Duke it Out. *Musician*, March, 52–64.

PART IV

ENGAGING DISCIPLINARITY AND OTHER POLITICS OF KNOWLEDGE

Introduction

The essays in Part IV all address – empirically or more programmatically – questions about the social organization of knowledge, in relation to both academic structures and the social collectivities and political projects of the contemporary social order. All the authors are concerned with how to make knowledge more adequate and thus more useful for the general project of a self-reflective understanding of the social world. In that sense, all are engaged in coupling critical analysis with endeavors of retrieving and reworking the past and influencing the course of the future.

For example, Schudson describes a slippage from the sociological view that emphasizes the *social* construction of reality, to a view which he ascribes to much cultural studies work, that examines the *cultural* construction of reality as if it lay largely outside the social. He claims that this has tended to truncate inquiry by leading analysts to jump too quickly from "reading" a cultural object or text, to assuming they know which abstract relations of power (race, class, patriarchy, capitalism) it embodies. To concretize his concerns, he turns to Donna Haraway's influential essay "Teddy Bear Patriarchy."

Schudson argues that Haraway fails to adequately connect the exhibits in the American Museum of Natural History she so brilliantly describes to the "tale of the commerce of power and knowledge in white and male supremacist monopoly capitalism" she contends that they tell: she overlooks the level of social organization and conflict among the individuals and groups who were active in founding the museum and planning its exhibits. This, he contends, is a common problem in much cultural studies work because of unexamined assumptions that the governing discourses of the social world are the constructions of a system of monopoly capitalism and white male patriarchy. Given such assumptions, the task of cultural interpretation is reduced to illuminating the strategies employed in a process whose ontology is already easily understood. Schudson argues that such oversimplifications can have profound consequences for the "culture of cultural studies," since they lead to the effacement of traditions – such as liberalism – which may be of great value, both intellectually and politically, in the present.

Marcus also expresses some criticisms of recent "postmodernist" or "cultural studies" scholarship, urging that critical academics recognize themselves as having affinities with "Other" academics and with nonacademic "Others" powerful in their institutional governing functions. To that end, he suggests that critical cultural studies both identify and engage with arenas of knowledge it has traditionally defined itself in opposition to. He examines different possible strategies of critical engagement through discussion of the new journal *Feminist Economics*. He suggests that possibilities for dialogue with the mainstream could be discovered through an ethnographic-like investigation of the cracks and fissures that might express self-doubt or potential for self-criticism within the mainstream. Marcus again draws on anthropology to suggest another strategy of *oblique critique* that would proceed by mapping out the cultural field where economics exerts influence, and critiquing it as a derived mode of thought in these other locations and spheres, thereby eroding the prestige of the academic mainstream and rendering it more amenable to transformation.

Marcus next proposes a project of critical and ethnographically sensitive translation across arenas of power/knowledge that appear to be worlds apart. Such a task, accomplished by discovering converging or intersecting genealogies of shared concepts and concerns, might promote dialogues across estranged boundaries of discourse between academics and other experts. This, in turn, could bring critical anthropology, sociology, or cultural studies into conversation with policy studies and operations. Marcus exemplifies this proposal by examining affinities between postmodern academic critique and nuclear diplomacy of the 1980s.

Newton and Stacey also speak out of the desire to build new alliances in order to broaden the base of critical academic work, but they discuss alliances within the academy, and the ways those alliances challenge truisms that have developed in relative isolation. Specifically, they critically survey the trajectory of their own involvement in the largely female circles of feminist scholarship, and then report on findings from interviews with white, leftwing, academic men about the place of feminism in their scholarly and domestic lives. They discover that for many of these men, encounters with the women's movement were much less transformative than encounters with the civil rights and antiwar movements. Yet the men they interviewed have come to regard gender critique as their legitimate and necessary scholarly terrain, despite a not always friendly reception from feminist women. The authors' discussion is a thoughtful example of the difficult self-critical conceptual work required to instantiate the common call for building bridges between groups, be they within or beyond the university.

Richard Johnson argues that, in its "best" version, cultural studies is a critical process that works across disciplinary boundaries to qualify the academy, and on the relations between the academy and other political sites. In making his case for renewal of cultural studies, he recalls certain salient aspects of the CCCS at Birmingham, such as their derivation from adult working-class education and, later, their close connection to the student movement. Within the academy, this led to a commitment to participatory ways of working, to "collective work" in small groups that could include people outside the university, and to a thorough-going collaboration between teachers and students. Johnson describes in some detail the organizational and pedagogical practices of the CCCS, pointing out that transforming academic routines in the direction of democracy, of openness to socially marginalized groups and their perspectives, and of recognition of power and difference in the classroom can reduce the tension between "the academic and useful political–intellectual activity." He defends some aspects of both the semiotic turn and the small scale of many cultural studies investigations. Nonetheless, Johnson feels that real marginalizations and exclusions in the social world may prioritize a focus on issues of political agency and human practice. Alongside post-structuralist understandings of culture and subjectivity, he urges the incor-poration of insights from such fields as political economy and economic geography, which have themselves been reshaped by feminist and global perspectives. Further, he argues that political work also includes "the making of links with other political sites and their critical activists." He discusses difficulties cultural studies scholars have faced in what he calls the "cycle of return" of ideas outward from the academy. Here he considers both public policy and formal political parties (the classic sites), but finds more hopeful the prospects of forging links to counter-educational activity, informal community organizations, and local–global campaigns and social movements.

Messer-Davidow's essay is a sustained theoretical analysis of the ways academic practices – whether traditional disciplines or more innovative cross- or interdisciplinary programs – are grounded in the social universe of extra-academic constituencies, institutions, funding sources, and dis-courses. She links theory to a detailed case study of the contemporary threat posed by conservatives – innovatively organized and discursively sophisticated – to the traditional university, and most explicitly to the humanities and social sciences. Her analysis makes a strong case that this threat must be fully understood both theoretically and empirically, so that progressive academics can begin to address it both by enlarging the scope of academic discourses and undertaking other forms of social action available to us both as academics and as citizens.

13

Cultural Studies and the Social Construction of "Social Construction": Notes on "Teddy Bear Patriarchy"

MICHAEL SCHUDSON

It can be an unsettling experience for a sociologist to browse a university bookstore these days. It is easy enough to find the women's studies or gender studies section, African-American studies or cultural studies, but not so easy to locate sociology. These areas collectively, and sometimes individually, dwarf sociology, increasingly a residual category. This is especially unnerving when each of the other sections is full of books that look a lot like what sociology was supposed to be. Perhaps this is a sociological victory, proof of what journalist Richard Rovere wrote two generations ago, that "Those of us who have been educated in the twentieth century habitually think in sociological terms, whether or not we have had any training in sociology" (Rovere, 1959: 265). But somehow it does not feel like a victory. Something is missing. As something called "cultural studies" has grown, the sociology of culture seems to have been shouldered aside.

"Cultural studies," struggling to assert itself in departments of literature, media studies, and communication, and making its presence felt in anthropology, history, and elsewhere, refuses to be defined or to define itself. Still, some of its features can be discerned. It is something like the extension of literary studies to texts outside a conventional canon – including science fiction, pornography, rock music, MTV, television generally, popular culture at large. So cultural studies moves toward a relativization of the objects of study. It tends to embrace an anthropological understanding of culture as a whole way of life, rather than culture as a set of privileged aesthetic objects. But if cultural studies recognizes culture as comprising the universe of social practices, it also redefines social practices as an ensemble of cultural texts. "A whole way of life" is itself reconceived as a set of discourses susceptible to literary or rhetorical interpretation or deconstruction. The impulse of cultural studies seems to promise a sociologically enriched analysis of cultural objects; that is, one that locates the objects in relation to the social context in which people produce them and use them. But instead, I shall suggest, the result is too often a sociologically impoverished view of politics and social action.

If cultural studies tends to be shy about defining its boundaries, it is often bold in proclaiming its politics. No conservatives need apply. "Cultural studies," Lawrence Grossberg has recently observed, "may have been (and I would hope still is) opposed to capitalism, its structures of inequality and exploitation" (1995: 76). As a field, perspective, or tendency arising as a rebellion within established university departments or finding a home base in politically precarious programs like women's studies, cultural studies is not surprisingly characterized by forms of address that testify to shared political principles. Since many scholars who identify with cultural studies are self-conscious advocates for women, gays, and lesbians, or people of color in higher education, it is easy to see why the fashioning of a distinctive intellectual vision becomes identified with political virtue. While political like-mindedness is a familiar basis of human solidarity, it is a dubious groundwork for a whole field of study. In contemporary sociology and many other social sciences, in contrast, it is taken for granted that conservatives, liberals, and Marxists can and should coexist (though not too many conservatives and not too many Marxists). In cultural studies, for all of its variations and fierce internal debates, there seems to be an unwritten loyalty oath to uphold the trinity of class, race, and gender as the three fundamental dimensions on which difference is inscribed in human experience. On the American scene, in practice, class regularly drops out of view. Actual work in cultural studies focuses on race, gender, and sexual preference. Not only does class recede, but so do other major social bases of discrimination, conflict, and differential power. That a sociologist could write a book called *Culture Wars* (Hunter, 1991) that takes the most basic division in American life today to be one separating religious orientations would not make sense or attract much interest in cultural studies (but see Harding, 1994).

Whatever the shortcomings of "class, race, and gender" as a description of the basic dimensions of domination in contemporary societies, it certainly has a sociological ring to it. Equally sociological is the view that the privileged texts of literary or art historical study should be forced to rub elbows with rock lyrics, science fiction, talk radio, nursery rhymes, and appellate court opinions. Quintessentially sociological is the notion, in which cultural studies is deeply invested, that apparently "natural" categories are in fact socially constructed. Indeed, the whole cultural studies enterprise, as David Chaney suggests, might well be regarded as a subdivision of the sociology of knowledge, which has long taught that "traditions insti-tutionalise ideologies and privilege" (Chaney, 1994: 42). Even so, cultural studies of the sort I want to criticize here is remarkably innocent of soci-ological insight. Sociology can learn from cultural studies, but cultural stud-ies is more in need of sociology than the other way around.

Of course, cultural studies ranges so widely across popular cultural forms and draws from so many diverse and difficult theoretical works, I claim no comprehensive view. Nonetheless, I hope to express some gen-eral doubts about it by centering my remarks around one much-admired, practically canonical work in the field, Donna Haraway's "Teddy Bear Patriarchy".

Social Construction of Reality

In the move from the sociology of culture to cultural studies, I am particu-larly concerned with the slippage from a view that emphasizes the *social* construction of reality to a view that examines the *cultural* or *symbolic* construction of reality as if it lay largely outside the social. In cultural studies there is much talk of social construction, but the work tends to be about something different – cultural or symbolic construction.

The analytical distinction between the social and the cultural is not always kept in mind, nor is it always easy to keep straight, but it seems to me fundamental. It goes like this: the "social" is people interacting and the "cultural" refers to the perceptual frames, symbolic structures, and narrative conventions framing, guiding, or governing how they do so. This is a distinction between culture – the scripts in people's heads – and behavior or action – what people do with respect to one another as they use these cultural scripts. This is the distinction between words and things or between consciousness and social existence.

For instance, "murder" is a cultural label that refers to one person's taking another person's life without legal warrant. "Murder is wrong" is a cultural injunction inscribed in dominant religious and legal texts and available as cognitive schema in people's heads. It is discourse, revisable and contestable. A given act of killing may or may not fit the legal and moral category "murder," but killing takes place regardless. It is social rather than cultural, behavior rather than consciousness. It makes a living person a dead one. While discourse affects the fate of the perpetrator (first or second degree murder? premeditated or not? mitigating or aggravating circumstances? justifiable homicide?), no words and no social constructions resuscitate the victim. Of course, we experience the world through culture. Different societies, and people differently situated in a single society, may see death, or aging, or kinship in very different ways accordingly, but no person and no society can escape addressing, through culture, death and aging and kinship.

Now, there are several cultural studies traditions and my criticism is not apposite for all. One tradition grows out of the British effort to write of the relationship of culture and society in a way that keeps ever-present the "lived experience" of people who make use of culture. This is the tradition established in the work of Richard Hoggart, Raymond Williams, and E. P. Thompson. While that tradition takes pride in its express social-ist political commitments, its intellectual orientation or methodological precepts are not essentially foreign to conventional sociological approaches to culture and popular culture. Of course, Williams and Stuart Hall and others of this tradition insist strenuously, against what I claim here, that it is dangerous and misleading to distinguish the "social" and the "cultural." For them, the cultural, linguistic, and symbolic are "indissoluble elements of the material social process itself" (Williams, 1977: 99). The old distinc-tion between "base" and "superstructure," they argue, has to be jettisoned altogether. What seems to me a risky blurring works well enough in British cultural studies, which has as strong an identification with soci-ology as with literary studies, where a doggedly empirical style of work keeps the study of culture anchored, and where the leading lights of the tradition have insisted on the centrality of "lived social experience." So long as lived social experience remains an anchor, the danger that the social will collapse into the cultural is averted.

But in the United States, borrowing from French more than British intellectual culture, a different tradition has grown out of literary studies. Here, where the social barely operates at all, a notion of "lived experi-ence" figures only marginally; the primary concern has been to rethink the literary text itself. One of the messages of this multistranded line of work has been to demonstrate that knowledge and discourse arise in historic-ally preconstituted discursive structures and that each individual human "subject" is created by discursive formations that exist prior to and set the conditions of possibility for that individual's consciousness. No know-ledge can be unattached to prevailing organizations of knowledge, and if knowledge is not directly subversive, it is by definition reinforcing of the existing relations of power. We are urged to examine closely the cultural context, not just the social context, within which cultural work gets done, talk comes to have meaning, and images come to make sense.

What follows from this is important: if knowledge (and culture) arise in a historically preconstituted discursive setting, all knowledge is necessar-ily in the service of power, whether the subjects intend it or not. Know-ledge is inevitably knowledge "for." This is the common kernel of cultural studies and the sociology of knowledge. But if this insight becomes the end, rather than the opening, of inquiry, then trouble begins. "Knowledge for" is also "knowledge of," to adapt a distinction of Clifford Geertz (1973: 93). This does not presume that "science" or any other human representations are accurate recording devices of a real world. But nor should we assume that knowledge is *only* ideology or only the projection of the "positionality" of the observer onto some object in the world. Neither the one extreme (that the object itself dictates how people will know it and represent it) nor the other (that the object does not exist for human knowledge except as humans project themselves onto it) is defensible. Nor is either extreme position very interesting. The first denies human agency; the second denies the world. Both deny the problem. The problem is to comprehend the *relationship* between human knowledge and the world we seek to know.

A Case in Point: Teddy Bear Patriarchy

Let me bring these general remarks down to earth by looking more closely at one much-admired paper in cultural studies, Donna Haraway's "Teddy Bear Patriarchy: Taxidermy in the Garden of Eden, New York City, 1908– 1936." This paper was first published in *Social Text* in 1984, was incorporated as chapter three into Haraway's 1989 book, *Primate Visions*, was singled out in one review of the book as a "stellar" chapter, was hailed in a 1991 collection of essays on "the poetics and politics of museum display" as "the most compelling analysis to date," and was reprinted in 1994 as an "exemplary" piece in a reader on social theory.[1] The paper is a reading of "African Hall" in the American Museum of Natural History (AMNH) that takes the museum to be instrumental in the politics of cultural reproduction. It treats a museum exhibit as a readable text, one that purports to offer from the viewpoint of "science" a window on the world of nature. Haraway, however, intends to reveal African Hall to be little more than the reproduction and naturalization, through the cultural form of the diorama, of the master narrative of race, class, and gender in a capitalist society.

The meaning of the hall cannot be read off from a quick pass through it but from its genesis – in this case, its origins in the collection of specimens in African safaris: "I want to show the reader how the experience of the diorama grew from the safari in specific times and places, how the camera and the gun together are the conduits for the spiritual commerce of man and nature, how biography is woven into and from a social and political tissue" (Haraway, 1994: 59). Incorporated in *Primate Visions*, the essay becomes part of a sprawling, multifaceted, ambitious attempt to describe Euro-American primate studies as a story Western science tells itself in ways that reproduce social inequalities embedded in its own presuppositions. Taken on its own, the essay looks at the life of Carl Akeley, the taxidermist who designed African Hall (even though it did not open until ten years after his death), to show that the museum exhibits display, not Africa, but "a history of race, sex, and class in New York City." What is revealed in the hall is not Africa but America, "a tale of the commerce of power and knowledge in white and male supremacist monopoly capitalism" (ibid: 50).

At this point, a skeptical reader should be on guard – the leap from the specifics of reading a museum exhibit to these wooden and formulaic abstractions is risky, especially when the abstractions presume that "America" can be fully represented by a set of universal categories (white, male, capitalist) whose distinctively American inflection is nowhere broached. Let alone what might be distinctively New Yorkish; Haraway's claim that the exhibit displays the history of race, sex, and class "in New York City" is the first and last suggestion that anything about New York itself, as opposed perhaps to Boston or Chicago with their distinctive cultural formations, can be read in the exhibit.

Still, the essay operates from what appears a sound sociological premise that, as Cesar Grana wrote, "Museums . . . have ideologies" (1971: 97). So, on guard or not, readers move on to a few engaging pages where Haraway takes them into the museum through its great Central Park West facade, past the gift shop (stopping to read a photobiography of Teddy Roosevelt) and into African Hall. Haraway is a perceptive guide; some of her observations on the dioramas are striking, especially her remark that in each diorama "at least one animal . . . catches the viewer's gaze and holds it in communion." This is an informative tour, though it is not clear what justifies Haraway's pronouncement that "the central moral truth" of the museum is "the effective truth of manhood" which is "conferred" on the visitor who "passes through the trial of the museum" (Haraway, 1994: 52). Apparently deriving this claim from some of Teddy Roosevelt's words on the walls just inside the main building, Haraway concludes that any visitor to the museum becomes "necessarily a boy in moral state" (ibid), or, as revised for the book, "necessarily a white boy in moral state."

How this grand theme of what the museum means to visitors is connected to Carl Akeley's intention, as Haraway understands it, to use "the hygiene of nature" to "cure the sick vision of civilized man" (ibid: 54) is nowhere clarified. How a ritual that symbolically brings "boys" through "the trial of the museum" (ibid: 52) into manhood is equally a curative rite to repair decadent civilization is a neat trick never explained. Are the boys sick and decadent too? Or does the curative trip to the museum inoculate innocents against a decadence that has not yet affected them? Either of Haraway's suggestions separately might be defended; both of them together create incoherence.

The use of "nature" as a cure for the ills wrought by civilization is indeed a theme in American attitudes toward nature, well marked in *Walden* and extending back at least to the agrarianism of Thomas Jefferson, but it does not necessarily entail the pessimism and sense of decline Haraway rightly sees in the views of some AMNH trustees. It is possible to seek solace, even salvation, in nature without being pessimistic. One of the most popular novelists of the 1910s and 1920s was Gene Stratton-Porter, who saw in nature "a source of beauty and contentment" but also "moral and religious truth." Her sense of the redemptive quality of nature could not have been more different from what Haraway implies for the AMNH leaders – "Second only to nature in Porter's scale of values was cheerfulness." Readers who felt lost or displaced in the onrushing, urbanizing society of the 1920s may have found solace in her pastoral ethic, but Stratton-Porter herself seems to have shared none of the anxiety of the AMNH trustees (Nash, 1970: 137–8). If they also visited the AMNH, they were exposed to two very different world views.

So some people fretted about that "sick vision" of civilized society a good deal more than others. Haraway's writing is simply too vague to specify where anxiety about civilization was located and how it was channeled. She suggests that Carl Akeley and the trustees believed civilization to be sick and encounter with nature to be a possible cure. In fact, the trustees may have worried more about socializing the *not-yet-civilized* than about redeeming the civilized. They understood the educative functions of the museum to be a form of social control of New York's immigrants more than self-therapy for its civilized elites. Museum Director Henry Fairfield Osborn held, "Nature teaches law and order and respect for property. If these people cannot go to the country, then the Museum must bring nature to the city" (Kennedy, 1968: 169).

"Moral boys" and "sick civilization" may be just a bit of rhetorical excess as Haraway warms to her theme, but it keeps her from ever addressing the question of what message real visitors to the museum might take from the exhibit. Haraway knows that different people will experience a museum in different ways. But, then, what exactly are readers to understand by her insistence that African Hall encodes a single narrative about white male patriarchy and that it situates every visitor to the museum as a "boy in moral state"?

What I take to be going on here is a kind of experiment in interpretation. That it ultimately fails, as I will try to suggest, is no crime; that the essay is cited reverently rather than answered critically, however, should give pause about the culture of cultural studies. This is not to deny the achievement of "Teddy Bear Patriarchy" as an original attempt to direct attention to museums as cultural constructions. My objection is not to the aim of the essay, as I understand it, but to the superficiality of its sociology and its oddly ahistorical history, about which I will say more in a moment. My objection, further, is to its celebrity. The wide use of the essay and deference to its semicanonical standing seems to signal an interpretive community that shares with it four central assumptions:

1   that the important thing to know about the cultural world is that the discourses that govern it and through which its inhabitants work are the constructions of a system of monopoly capitalism and white male patriarchy;
2   that it is an act of political virtue and intellectual courage to convincingly demonstrate the constructedness of these discourses or of the cultural artifacts to which they give rise;
3   that such demonstrations override any need to inquire about whether, how, or to what degree some aspect of what we can only term "reality" nonetheless constrains the discourse and its degrees of freedom; and
4   that the task of interpretation is reduced to illuminating the strategies and stratagems employed in a process whose ontology is already easily understood.

I leave aside now the question of how real people read museums, for "Teddy Bear Patriarchy" falls fully into the trap of leaving the lived social experience of audiences to the side. No more need be said on this. The essay teaches us nothing about what meaning actual visitors take from African Hall or from the museum generally. But is the approach Haraway adopts to interpretation convincing in its own terms?

The essay works by a linked chain of synecdochic conversions, a part standing for a whole, each of which has to be convincing for the analysis to succeed. That is, the reader must be won to the view that, first, the Theodore Roosevelt Memorial entry and especially African Hall stand adequately for the AMNH. No other part of the museum ever speaks in this essay, no dinosaurs, no Margaret Mead Hall of Pacific Peoples, no Stephen Jay Gould columns in *Natural History*. For that matter, Haraway's insistence that the gorilla dioramas are the heart of African Hall is itself a dubious substitution of part for the whole, especially for a hall that Director Osborn originally proposed as "Elephant Hall," collaborating in the proposal with Akeley, who had an "inexplicable fascination with elephants" since boyhood and believed that the hall should center on – as it does – a group of elephants (Kennedy, 1968: 104).

The second synecdochic link is that the meaning of African Hall lies in the original plans for it and the collecting, by gun and photograph, of the materials that were to go into its dioramas. This link makes a powerful claim of authorship on behalf of safari leader, taxidermist, and great white hunter Carl Akeley, biographical material about whom dominates the essay.

The fact that African Hall did not open until ten years after Akeley's death is mentioned, but no mention is made of how Akeley's original plans were affected by the passage of a decade; indeed, no mention is made of just how extensive or complete his conception of African Hall was at any point.

Speaking of American art museums, sociologist Vera Zolberg writes that they are "complex, multipurpose organizations" responding to various pressures within and without, emphasizing now one goal, now another. While founded to serve the status and taste of the trustees, the reign of the trustees over time came to be contested: "Curators seek autonomy from their boards to pursue research and acquire works that they themselves consider important; dealers and collectors try to influence aesthetic choices; artists seek entry for their works; public groups demand a say in policy decisions; national museum organizations criticize the stodginess of trustees" (Zolberg, 1986: 186). This is no less true of natural history museums. Haraway's analysis of the American Museum of Natural History skips over all such organizational complexities; she does not take the museum seriously as a social organization competing in a sometimes hostile environment for public notice, private donation, and academic approval. In her account there is only a broad cultural discourse represented by the museum's trustees, the museum's director, Henry Fairfield Osborn, and the mastermind of African Hall, Carl Akeley. This discourse goes into the museum machinery at one end and out the other end come the African Hall exhibits. In between, a void: no social organization, no social conflict, no contention.

And no passage of time. The third synecdoche is that African Hall in 1921 (the year of a key collecting safari, and the year, Haraway reveals as if uncovering the deep secret core, in which AMNH hosted the Second International Eugenics Conference) or perhaps in 1926 (the year of Akeley's death) or at least in 1936 (the year of the hall's opening) represents the unaltered meaning of African Hall at the time of Haraway's essay in the 1980s. As white male patriarchal monopoly capitalism is a transhistorical structure, so apparently are its expressions and representations. That the meaning of a cultural object can change over time does not stir Haraway's interest. We know, from Lawrence Levine's work, that Shakespeare was popular melodrama in America in 1850 and classical high culture by 1920. We know, from John Higham's work, that even the meanings of cultural objects more fixed than a dramatic text – at least as fixed in time as a diorama – change radically in their meanings. The Statue of Liberty, Higham shows, was in the 1880s meant to be and taken to be a symbol of how American republican government, established with the aid of France in the Revolution, served as a beacon to the world. By the 1920s and fully by 1940 it came to have a meaning never dreamt of by any of the individuals or groups responsible for its development and installation in New York harbor. It came to mean "Welcome to America!" an inspirational greeting to new immigrants, a meaning the immigrants themselves conferred on the statue (Higham, 1984: 71–80). But Haraway presumes without argument that the African Hall dioramas are preserved in historic amber, untouchable by the shifting interactions of text and context.

Each of Haraway's synecdochic links stretches her materials to the breaking point. If we tried to walk a similar interpretive path with different materials, her sleight of hand might be more visible. For instance, let me propose that the essence of New York University is represented in its imposing Elmer Holmes Bobst Library, completed in 1973 as part of a major redesign and development of the Washington Square campus. Further, let me argue that the meaning of the library is biographically located in its architect, the modern master Philip Johnson. Johnson, into the late 1930s, was attracted to the Nazis. He was a vocal Fascist sympathizer, and, like others who spoke the language of eugenics, he was anxious about "race suicide" of the white race (Schultze, 1994). If I am of a mind to see Fascism as the dark truth of capitalism, I can proceed to argue with a logic parallel to Haraway's in "Teddy Bear Patriarchy" that the truth of New York University is Fascism. I do not need to know what NYU students or faculty read or write, any more than Haraway needs to know what visitors to the AMNH experience; I do not need to complicate the story with the plural or changing meanings of NYU to be assured that I have reached the central moral truth of the institution. If NYU is its library, the library its architect, and its architect a Fascist, NYU is Fascist.

If I made such an argument, would it be seriously entertained? Would people judge my work "stellar," "compelling," and "exemplary?" I do not think so. Why, then, has Haraway's essay escaped close scrutiny? Why has an argument stretched so thin seemed so attractive to so many? Her argument's logic is just the same: AMNH is its African Hall, African Hall is Akeley's and Osborn's visions, their visions were rankly racist and sexist, so the AMNH is Teddy Bear Patriarchy.

About that Second International Eugenics Congress that the AMNH hosted in 1921: Haraway is onto something here. AMNH leaders were indeed important figures in an effort mounted on behalf of scientific racism. The trouble is her sense of inevitability about it. The eugenics movement, after all, lost the battle for the hearts and minds of the American elite, and a former AMNH employee, Franz Boas, the most politically influential and very likely the most intellectually important American anthropologist ever, won it. He won it so well that I think it is probably fair to say that the museum is today more identified with one of his students, Margaret Mead, than it is with Teddy Roosevelt or the publicly unknown Carl Akeley.

So why does Haraway highlight the 1921 conference as especially indicative of the moral truth of AMNH? Why not the fact that the next international conference, in 1932, also in New York, attracted less than 100 people? (Kevles, 1985: 169). Why this fact and not the fact that later in AMNH history a hall would be dedicated to Margaret Mead? Why 1921 and not 1927, when Mead was first hired as an assistant curator? Why this fact about 1921 and not the fact that Boas would be far more successful in developing the "culture" concept in American social science than AMNH leaders were in legitimating scientific racism? Haraway reports correctly that eugenics was a significant movement in 1921, coloring the views of museum trustees and officials, but she fails to mention that it was essentially dead by the time African Hall opened.[2] She urges upon readers that the eugenics conference of 1921 is the tell-tale detail, weighted with meaning, but does not mention Robert Lowie's public lectures at the museum in 1917, where he insisted so powerfully on the autonomy of culture in human affairs, following his teacher Boas, and argued that biology or race had to be completely rejected as explanation for the differences in behavior of different groups of humans. There was, Lowie explained, an unbridgeable disjunction between the study of nature and the study of human beings (Degler, 1991: 100–2).

If description were important, if historical accuracy were important here, the *de rigueur* connection of the subject, AMNH in this case, to race, class, and gender would have been contextualized so readers could actually understand it. Haraway fails to do this. Implicit in today's coding of "class, gender, race" is that "race" refers to a distinction between white and nonwhite rather than, as was the case among Protestant elites in the 1920s, between Nordic and non-Nordic. Certainly, racism toward African-Americans was part of the preconception of New York Protestant elites in the 1920s. Nineteenth-century Americans were taught in the schools about different races, with Caucasians invariably deemed the highest and Negroes the lowest. But the language of race shifted at the turn of the century and the racial divide elites worried most about was between people of north European heritage and the immigrants from southern and eastern Europe, particularly the Jews (Elson, 1964: 65–9).

Haraway observes that the notorious popularizer of scientific racism, Madison Grant, an AMNH trustee, was worried about "the importation of non-white (which included Jewish and southern European) working classes." This is false. The immigrants he worried about did not simply "include Jewish and southern Europeans" – this was the primary group that troubled and threatened him. In his key racist tract, *The Passing of the Great Race* (1916), a work that identifies the author as trustee of the AMNH and whose preface is written by Henry Fairfield Osborn, Grant makes this abundantly clear. He devotes the book to showing the differences among "the three main European races" – the Nordic, Alpine, and Mediterranean races, and the point of the book is to demonstrate the superiority of the Nordic to the others. Grant mentions but in no way dwells on "Negroids" and "Mongoloids." His primary objection is to what was called "the new immigration" that contained, as he wrote, "a large and increasing number of the weak, the broken, and the mentally crippled of all races drawn from the lowest stratum of the Mediterranean basin and the Balkans, together with hordes of the wretched, submerged populations of the Polish Ghettos." He objected to the "pathetic and fatuous belief in the efficacy of American institutions and environment to reverse or obliterate immemorial hereditary tendencies" that had led to welcoming these newcomers. The result of the new immigration, he believed, was utterly disastrous:

> The man of the old stock is being crowded out of many country districts by these foreigners, just as he is to-day being literally driven off the streets of New York City by the swarms of Polish Jews. These immigrants adopt the language of the native American; they wear his clothes; they steal his name; and they are beginning to take his women, but they seldom adopt his religion or understand his ideals, and while he is being elbowed out of his own home the American looks calmly abroad and urges on others the suicidal ethics which are exterminating his own race. (Grant, 1916: 80–1)

By 1920 Jewish enrollment at Columbia was 40 percent and at NYU's Washington Square campus 93 percent, with more than 80 percent Jewish enrollment at City College and Hunter (Feingold, 1992: 15). That is what the AMNH trustees had in mind. (The two Jewish members of the House Committee on Immigration and Naturalization recognized this very well. They alone on the committee opposed the Immigration Restriction Act of 1924, one of them complaining, "If you had been a member of that committee, you could not help but understand that they did not want anybody else in this country except the Nordics" (Ludmerer, 1972: 106)).

Haraway, writing decades after Hitler and the concentration camps had finally reduced the respectability of antisemitism, fails to acknowledge that Jews were not so long ago a leading "other" in American culture. She chose not to tell her readers that the passion behind the eugenics movement aimed to protect, not "whites," but "Nordics."[3] Of course, racism directed against African-Americans runs more deeply, more centrally, and more enduringly in American history than prejudice against Jews and southern and eastern Europeans. But this is not what was at stake in the AMNH story.

The problem here is not only imprecision about what "race" meant in the origins of African Hall. It is a failure to recognize how badly racism was reeling by the 1930s, how genuine was the Boasian victory. Indeed, that victory had something to do with Jewish immigration, and not only in that Boas himself was a Jewish immigrant. Unimaginable in America before the 1920s, Jewish intellectuals and scientists entered the mainstream of academic life and literary life – not without resistance, to be sure, but ultimately with extraordinary success in reshaping that life. A new and powerful intelligentsia committed to a cosmopolitan vision of the world transcending race and ethnicity emerged and came to dominate intellectual life from 1930 into the 1960s, as historian David Hollinger has argued. A powerful liberal consensus developed, cutting right across the lines that the Madison Grants of the world had wanted to keep strictly separate (Hollinger, 1985: 56–73).

That liberal consensus has been sharply challenged in the past generation. Still, it remains very much alive, battered, bruised, and re-equipped with prosthetic devices as it may be. It is a tradition, some of whose representatives from the 1920s and 1930s, the likes of Walter Lippmann or Franz Boas or John Dewey, are still read and argued about, while Madison Grant is at most a historical footnote. By what screwball logic, then, does Haraway land on Grant as the animating spirit of the white male patriarchal capitalist vision that dominates American society?

"Teddy Bear Patriarchy" is ungainly in organization, immodest in its claims, and choppy in its logic. Haraway seeks to establish her authority by displaying a dizzying array of historical and biographical details meant to be telling but, in fact, largely extraneous. It was not news in 1984 that wives of famous men often deserve more credit than they get from historians or from their husbands. Haraway shows that this was true for the Akeleys, and adds the nice twist that Carl Akeley's second wife and literary executor edited out key contributions of wife number one. Interesting? Yes. But Haraway does not show what this absence signifies for the exhibits in African Hall – or that it signifies anything at all for how to read African Hall or how to understand the social construction of scientific knowledge. Yes, Akeley's treatment of his African assistants on safari seems shockingly paternalistic, possessive, and condescending, but Haraway never shows that these facts mark the exhibits. For those who lead the strenuous life close to nature today by jogging or backpacking rather than by shooting big game, the very fact that Akeley hunted at all may be discrediting enough. But is it? This paper professes to be showing social construction, but instead it seems dedicated to distancing the reader from any human sympathy with its primary human subject. The effort is not to see – that is too passive a metaphor for this intellectual style; it is to *see through*. Not vision but the x-ray is the reigning mode of perception.

Why does it matter if Haraway got the history wrong, just so long as her main point – that science is socially constructed in the service of power – remains correct?

If the past is dead and should be dead, as Haraway seems to believe, then it really doesn't matter a whit. But if, as Faulkner put it, "the past is not dead, it's not even past," then it makes a very big difference that Haraway translated the 1920s "Nordic" into the 1980s "white" and blended in her postmodern cuisinart the liberalism of Boas with the racism of Grant. If it is worth knowing what achievements in our past we can draw on for strength and inspiration and if it is worth distinguishing them from the shortcomings and sins we want to avoid repeating, then the errors here are serious, and it is shocking that in the ten reviews of *Primate Visions* I have read and the dozen references to the work I have come upon, not once has any of this been noted.

Liberalism is one of several powerful traditions of political thought in American history. Another tradition is ethnocultural nativism, one of whose expressions was the eugenics movement. But, obviously, nativism has never had full sway and, I hope, never will (see Smith, 1988). Its strongest enemy, past and present, has been liberalism and the Enlightenment ideal of human equality. It is not only historically defensible but politically desirable to try to find in the American tradition resources for promoting equality, liberty, and justice, rather than painting over the past as if it spoke in one voice, or as if the only voices that could be heard spoke in unison while dissenting voices were stilled or devalued. It is just not so.

Haraway did not set herself an easy task, especially methodologically. She wants to claim both that Akeley's biography matters and, simultaneously, that it does not – both that the details of Akeley the taxidermist are of peculiar interest and importance and that the suffusion of American elite culture with reprehensible values has been so complete that individuals within it have barely a chance to resist. Her knowledge of the particularities of Akeley's life gives her essay authority, but then she undercuts that authority by proposing that the details are irrelevant and that Akeley is no more than the mortal vessel through which a cultural logic for the reproduction and naturalization of hierarchies and exclusions works. So she gets caught up in asserting that Akeley *had to be* some things (like a businessman) that he was not ("no Yankee boy could miss the connection of life's purpose with business" – but she later acknowledges that he did not make money at his craft and that he subordinated business to a larger missionary purpose); that he was a bad scientist in romanticizing nature (when what he sought to be was in part a good artist); and that his was "a literal science dedicated to the prevention of decadence, of biological decay" when he could just as easily be portrayed, in his conservation interests and his campaign against trophy hunting, as a relatively optimistic manager of nature, rather than a zealot of antidecadence.

In the end, it is not Haraway's essay so much as the absence of serious published criticism of it that disturbs me. Cultural studies, especially in its postmodernist or poststructuralist vein, has features of a social movement and some of the edgy self-confidence of prior academic movements – psychoanalysis comes to mind. It develops its own critical terminology, it offers an epistemology that runs counter to standard scientific practices, it promises emancipation through critique, and it takes on a messianic cast. It also introduced new methods and new frameworks for understanding human behavior that many people, even those who remain dubious about the project as a whole, have found valuable. Postmodern cultural studies may be following suit. I hope it does not repeat psychoanalysis in constructing defense mechanisms. Psychoanalysis is famous for having perfected a method of discounting criticism by treating it as a symptom – "if you disagree, you are resisting." I see signs that cultural studies is succumbing to that sort of solipsism. It needs not only to generate criticism, which it does, within its own set of political assumptions, but to respond to criticism that calls those assumptions into question.

Conclusion

Cultural studies correctly emphasizes that no knowledge is innocent. But this must include the fervent belief that "no knowledge is innocent." That claim serves ends just as the claim of scientists or journalists to objectivity does. Most obviously, it is a rationalization for expanding and making relevant the fading place of literary studies in our culture. It also protects political presuppositions from critical examination because it takes for granted that political and moral presuppositions are beyond rational debate. They are discourse in the service of power.

This short-changes everybody. It cocoons the left from having to deal with the right – and at a time when the rhetorical force of the left seems to be evaporating in the culture at large. Oddly enough, it also diminishes culture. If culture is only the discursive shaping and serving of power, there is no place for the radical assertion of some (like Geertz, 1980) that power is designed and valued to serve culture. Or the assertion in a work like Mukerji's *From Graven Images* (1983) that the industrial revolution served to justify a fashion for calicos, not that a fashion for calicos served to enrich the emerging industrial bourgeoisie. Culture is if anything more important, not less important, than the theoretical presuppositions of "cultural studies" acknowledge. The tendency to reduce culture to emanations of preconstituted power positions trivializes culture and fails to recognize politics. To improve upon this with the claim, grown vacuous by repetition, that culture is "contested terrain," is no solution. Yes, culture is contested terrain. And, yes – thanks in part to cultural studies – we can now say "of course" it is. But then we are at the beginning, not the end, of analysis.

Cultural studies has something to teach sociology. Cultural studies certainly seems to have connected with and responded to a thirst, at least among graduate students, for a way of scholarship that is also a self-conscious moral mission and that validates rather than attacks the students' attachments to popular culture, sense of social marginality, and unfocused but strongly felt sense that something is rotten in these not so united states of America. Some of what attracted students to sociology a generation ago, when Daniel Bell, Nathan Glazer, C. Wright Mills, David Riesman, and others wrote sociology as cultural critique, fuels the warm student reception for cultural studies. Cultural studies can sometimes respond to these students in a way that arms them with critical skills and interpretive facility at a time when sociology, in contrast, is unsure of its methods.

Cultural studies also has something to teach sociology about texts. It forces social scientists to recognize a simple truth too long resisted by too many: that one of the things we do when we "commit a social science," as W. H. Auden caustically put it, is to write, and that writing is a socially and culturally constructed act within a cultural field. It is not, as people still like to believe, a transparent record of data or observations. If cultural studies sometimes produces too much reflexivity, it is certainly true that conventional sociology has produced too little. Cultural studies helps remind us that sociology is itself a construction, a writerly construction, and that, as Geertz concluded for anthropology, "Attention to how it gets its effects and what those are, to anthropology on the page, is no longer a side issue, dwarfed by problems of method and issues of theory. It . . . is rather close to the heart of the matter" (Geertz, 1988: 149). This is a part of cultural studies that should make a sociologist productively rather than dyspeptically nervous.

The nervousness is on both sides, of course. There is a skittish, stuttering quality in much cultural studies writing, as if all that can now be said is that nothing definitive can be said or that, in saying something presumably definitive or "foundational" or "essentialist," one necessarily is taking sides with the powers-that-be who, it goes with and without saying, are repressive.

The "sociology of culture" by its very name professes to be *one* approach to the study of *one* sort of human domain. "Cultural studies," despite protestations about the undecidability of knowledge and the blurring of boundaries and so forth, often lays claim to being "the" approach to the study of just about *everything*. It cannot make such a claim without rejecting everything else that people have thought. So another reason sociologists may resist the semiotic turn is that, in its postmodernist modes, it does not claim to add a dimension to prior work so much as to invalidate prior ways of seeing altogether. It is less a turn than an overturn and it has something of the spirit of a millenarian movement. At that level, it seems to me, it requires a lot better warrant than it has, and needs a lot more to show for itself.

What I claim to be the superiority in conventional sociology's (and conventional history's) attention to lived social experience is then a claim for a modest sociology. With the fall not only of Marx but of Freud and Weber and Durkheim, with the fall of "grand narrative analysis," what may best endure of sociology and restock its bookstore shelves are its more modest forays or its ambitions to what Robert Merton famously called "theories of the middle range." Tocqueville looks better and better. Demography and epidemiological studies provide, with all their faults, real and useful information about what people there are in the world, how often they are born, how they die, when and where and why they move from one place to another. Ethnographies provide, with all their faults, some lasting insight into what it may have been like to live in Muncie in the 1920s or Newburyport in the 1940s. And sociology also contributes the general insight, at once obvious and deeply unsettling, that culture, knowledge, and values are social constructions. Sociology has certainly not accepted that its greatest claims to public attention may be among the works least celebrated by the profession of sociology itself, those closer to the descriptive than to the explanatory, those nearer the particular, local, and discrete than the grand and transcendent. But I think this may be the case. I suspect the same may be true, one day, of cultural studies as well, and that the works of cultural studies that last will be the sort that follow Williams and Hoggart and Thompson, in close attention to lived experience – which is, of course, both socially constructed and culturally constructed and, for all that, really felt, fought, and fraught.

NOTES

I am very grateful to many readers and critics of drafts of this essay, some of whom disagreed sharply with my views and tried to save me from the error of my ways. Whether in agreement or disagreement, I have been greatly helped by Susan Davis, Andrew Goodwin, David Hollinger, Elizabeth Long, Tanya Luhrmann, Ryan Moore, Janice Radway, Vicente Rafael, Steven Seidman, and Karin Swann.
1 "Stellar" is the judgment of Margaret Rossiter (1990: 712); "compelling" the adjective of Steven D. Lavine and Ivan Karp (1991: 3); and "exemplary" is the term of Nicholas Dirks, Geoff Eley, and Sherry Ortner (1994: 10). Some of the ten reviews of the book I read were quite critical, but criticism tended to focus on Haraway's sprawling and jargon-ridden style and the difficulty of making sense of a work that almost seems to taunt readers to find a coherent thread of argument. Even the favorable reviews, that ranged from admiring to

gushing, regretted the style. But none of the ten academic reviews I read challenged the historiography of the "Teddy Bear Patriarchy" chapter. The most instructive of the reviews I have read, and the one that comes closest to taking Haraway on substantively, is by Matt Cartmill (1991).

For other recent critical work on museums, see Daniel J. Sherman and Irit Rogoff (1994) – where, again, Haraway is cited and not criticized, in the editors' introduction (p. xvii).

2   "The most significant development in eugenics after 1930 was its rapid decline in popularity and prestige" (Haller, 1952: 179). Or see "Repudiation of Eugenics" in Ludmerer (1972: 121–34), a work Haraway cites. Or see the standard work on American nativism, John Higham's *Strangers in the Land* (1974), which points to a "slackening of nativist impulses after 1924" in the intellectual world. After the mid-1920s "interest in eugenics declined steadily, and the movement shrank to the status of a dedicated but ineffectual cult" (ibid: 327). While Haraway does not cite this work, she does cite another book of Higham's that covers some of the same territory, failing to note its conclusion: "As early as the late 1920's, a decline of racism in intellectual circles set in. The eugenics movement waned; the Nordic cult lost its vogue. The change reflected the emancipation of American thought from biological determinism" (Higham, 1974; 1984: 58).

The information I point to here is available in works Haraway cites and in other standard works available at the time she wrote. More recent works do not substantially alter the picture. In *In Search of Human Nature* (1991), Carl Degler writes that geneticists in the 1920s sounded "the death knell" for eugenics (p. 150). He notes that the prominent biologist, Raymond Pearl, denounced eugenics in the *American Mercury* in 1927 and his colleague, Herbert S. Jennings, condemned the elitism and racism of eugenics. In the 1933 *Encyclopedia of the Social Sciences*, he wrote that "racial arrogance and the desire to justify present social systems find a congenial field in eugenic propaganda" (p. 150). "By the 1930s the popularity of eugenics declined precipitously, not only among social scientists and biologists but among the public" (p. 151). The work of Daniel Kevles, *In the Name of Eugenics*, appeared in 1985, and Haraway cites it in the somewhat revised version of "Teddy Bear Patriarchy" that appeared in her book. Kevles takes the position that by the 1930s mainline eugenics was indeed dead but that another brand he calls "reform eugenics" lived on. Kevles notes that psychologist Carl Brigham in 1930 referred to some of his own earlier work on racial differences in mental abilities as "without foundation." (Kevles, 1985: 134). In the early 1930s, books and articles on eugenics declined. In a word, "the mainline movement collapsed" (ibid: 170). The "reform" version that survived was not necessarily socially conservative, as the mainline movement had been; particularly in its British version, it included antiracist conservatives, social radicals, and representatives of the Marxist left. Indeed, Kevles sums up the reform position as holding that "valuable characteristics were to be found in most social groups, and that the best in human variation was to be encouraged" (ibid: 175).

3   As for the presumed connection of this racism to "monopoly capitalism," that cannot be taken for granted. Monopoly capital, one would presume, other things equal, seeks a labor supply as cheap and mobile as possible and would, therefore, oppose the sorts of restrictions on immigration the scientific racists recommended. Generally, they did exactly that, while organized labor came to the aid of the racists (Solomon, 1956: 203; Haller, 1952: 153).

REFERENCES

Cartmill, Matt 1991: Review of Donna Haraway, *Primate Visions. International Journal of Primatology*, 12, 67–75.

Chaney, David 1994: *The Cultural Turn*. London: Routledge.

Degler, Carl 1991: *In Search of Human Nature*. New York: Oxford University Press.

Dirks, Nicholas B., Eley, Geoff, and Ortner, Sherry B. (eds) 1994: *Culture/Power/ History*. Ann Arbor: University of Michigan Press.

Elson, Ruth Miller 1964: *Guardians of Tradition* Lincoln: University of Nebraska Press.

Feingold, Henry L. 1992: *A Time for Searching*, vol. 4 of *The Jewish People in America*. Baltimore: Johns Hopkins University Press.

Geertz, C. 1973: *The Interpretation of Cultures*. New York: Basic Books.

—— 1980: *Negara*. Princeton: Princeton University Press.

—— 1988: *Works and Lives: The Anthropologist as Author*. Stanford: Stanford University Press.

Grana, Cesar 1971: *Fact and Symbol*. New York: Oxford University Press.

Grant, Madison 1916: *The Passing of the Great Race*. New York: Charles Scribner's.

Grossberg, Lawrence 1995: Cultural Studies vs. Political Economy: Is Anybody Else Bored with this Debate? *Critical Studies in Mass Communication*, 12/ 72–81.

Haller, Mark H. 1952: *Eugenics: Hereditarian Attitudes in American Thought*. New Bruswick: Rutgers University Press.

Haraway, Donna 1989: *Primate Visions: Gender, Race, and Nature in the World of Modern Science*. New York: Routledge.

—— 1994: "Teddy Bear Patriarchy: Taxidermy in the Garden of Eden, New York City, 1908–1936." In Nicholas B. Dirks, Geoff Eley, and Sherry B. Ortner (eds), *Culture/Power/History*, Ann Arbor: University of Michigan Press, 49–95.

Harding, Sandra 1994: The Born-again Telescandals. In Dirks et al. (eds), *Culture/ Power/History*, Ann Arbor: University of Michigan Press, 539–58.

Higham, John 1974: *Strangers in the Land*. New York: Atheneum.

—— 1984: *Send These to Me*. Baltimore: Johns Hopkins University Press.

Hollinger, David 1985: *In the American Province*, Baltimore: Johns Hopkins University Press. (Material under discussion in this essay originally appeared in 1975, in *American Quarterly*, 27, 133–51.)

Hunter, James 1991: *Culture Wars*. New York: Basic Books.

Kennedy, John M. 1968: Philanthropy and Science in New York City: The American Museum of Natural History, 1868–1968. Ph.D. dissertation, Yale University.

Kevles, Daniel J. 1985: *In the Name of Eugenics*. Berkeley: University of California Press.

Lavine, Steven and Karp, Ivan 1991: Introduction. In Ivan Karp and Steven D. Lavine (eds), *Exhibiting Cultures: The Poetics and Politics of Museum Display*, Washington, DC: Smithsonian Institution Press.

Levine, Lawrence 1984: William Shakespeare and the American People. *American Historical Review*, 89, 34–66.

Ludmerer, Kenneth M. 1972: *Genetics and American Society: A Historical Appraisal*. Baltimore: Johns Hopkins University Press.

Mukerji, Chandra 1983: *From Graven Images*. New York: Columbia University Press.

Nash, R. 1970: *The Nervous Generation: American Thought, 1917–1930*. Chicago: Rand McNally.

Rossiter, Margaret 1990: Review of Donna Haraway, *Primate Visions*. *Journal of American History*, 77, September, 712.

Rovere, Richard 1959: *Senator Joe McCarthy*. New York: Harcourt, Brace.

Schultze, Franz 1994: *Philip Johnson: Life and Work*. New York: Alfred A. Knopf.

Sherman, Daniel and Rogoff, Irit (eds), 1994: *Museum Culture*. Minneapolis: University of Minnesota Press.

Smith, Rogers 1988: The "American Creed" and American Identity: The Limits of Liberal Citizenship in the United States. *Western Political Quarterly*, 41, 225–51.

Solomon, Barbara Miller 1956: *Ancestors and Immigrants*. Chicago: University of Chicago Press.

Williams, Raymond 1977: *Marxism and Literature*. Oxford: Oxford University Press.

Zolberg, Vera 1986: Tensions of Mission in American Art Museums. In Paul J. DiMaggio (ed.), *Nonprofit Enterprise in the Arts*, New York: Oxford University Press.

14

Critical Cultural Studies as One Power/Knowledge Like, Among, and In Engagement With Others

GEORGE E. MARCUS

In October, 1994, I convened a seminar at the School of American Research in Santa Fe, ten years after the seminar that led to the well-known collection, *Writing Culture: The Poetics and Politics of Ethnography* (Clifford and Marcus, 1986). Including some of the same participants in that earlier seminar, this one was intended to consider broadly the current prospects of an anthropology that had become deeply embedded in the intellectual movements of which the *Writing Culture* seminar was both a reflection and a shaper (see Marcus, n.d.). During the intervening decade there have been deep challenges to the founding assumptions of most of the disciplines that constitute the human sciences in the USA. Under the label first of "postmodernism" and then "cultural studies," many scholars in the social sciences and humanities subjected themselves to a bracing critical self-examination of their habits of thought and work. This involved reconsiderations of the nature of representation, description, subjectivity, objectivity, even of the notions of "society" and "culture" themselves, as well as of how scholars materialized objects of study and data about them to constitute the "real" to which their work has been addressed. Personally transformative for some, excessively skeptical for others, this trend was conducted in the name of "theory" and "critique," and in the US, was largely diffused through literary studies, which was trying to remake itself into a more interdisciplinary cultural studies.

We are now at a critical moment of intense interest in how to deploy this intellectual capital in projects of long-term research, as well as in interventions in contemporary debates about politics, policies, and national problems – how to communicate and use in inquiry what was essentially a reformation of thought among scholars. Especially in disciplines that consider themselves empiricist, such as anthropology, there is interest in how the ideas and concepts of the past decade can be used to reformulate traditional protocols of research.

At the same time, I have noted a pervasive nervousness about the legacy of past self-critical ferment, a lack of confidence about the relevance of all the theory, a sense that maybe the so-called crisis of representation has only been an intellectual crisis, offering very little possibility of effective theoretical or analytic engagement with those outside academia. This sort of pessimism is easy to spot in conferences, publications, and corridor talk at present.

It is undoubtedly the case that the discussions that developed the intellectual capital of the past decade ideologically and theoretically for academics were hermetic, but the precise legacy of this capital is now being determined in the kinds of research projects that it has inspired. The 1994 Santa Fe seminar consequently took up two urgent tasks, mainly with the effects of the 1980s crisis of representation on anthropology in mind. One was to address the changing research process itself in anthropology. We wanted to demonstrate that the fate of the so-called postmodernist critiques of anthropology lay not in further discussions of postmodernism, but in the enactments of new kinds of research projects in anthropology, differently problematized and conducted (for a personal assessment of these changes in method, see Marcus, 1995).

The other task, and the one I want to elaborate upon in this essay, was to address squarely, by a kind of experiment in the ethnography of knowledge, the creeping lack of confidence regarding the integrity, worth, and relevance of the stock of critical ideas that had been introduced to American academics over the past decade and more. Indeed, we thought that this was the more urgent task of the seminar. We wanted to test (and, frankly, undermine if warranted) the sense that critical reflexivity has been an insular activity simply involuting upon abstractions and self-importance. Our idea was to affirm that social scientists, such as anthropologists, participate in a regime of power/knowledge (a term, derived from Michel Foucault, to designate formal institutions of modernity that exercise power through the creation and management of knowledge) such that self-critical trends in academia would be similar to trends in other power/knowledges, particularly those more directly concerned with the performance of instrumental functions in society: the professions, corporations, publishing, the military, finance, politics, public policy, science and technology. Because any self-critical trend is unlikely to take the same form of discourse, consciousness, practices, or contexts of activity across such disparate sites of power/knowledge, this task is eminently suitable for ethnographic research, deeply familiar as it is with subjects' views in the contexts within which it situates itself, and oriented to translating across them in a comparative way.

By recruiting a combination of practitioners within a range of institutions, and scholars who had conducted ethnographies within them, we hoped to provide a discussion about how widespread and relevant the crisis of representation had been. At the same time, we wished to assert an affinity between bureaucrats, officials, professionals, and left-liberal scholars, perhaps disturbing to the latter, but one that they would have to take self-consciously into account in pursuing future projects. Our experiment was thus to have been an exploration in ethnographic terms of Bourdieu's provocative designation of academics and intellectuals as the "dominated fraction of the dominant."

The relativization of academics along such a dimension of overlapping power/knowledges, often ignored or only superficially acknowledged by them in their own self-identifications, would be an important by-product of addressing the fear among scholars that they are only projecting their own problems or habits of thought upon the world. It would be very interesting to know whether similar crises of representation have appeared in domains of power/knowledge far from the self-identifications or sympathies of left-liberal scholars.

In the realm of social theory, the task that I have in mind has been discussed in terms of "reflexive modernization" (see Bauman, 1991; Lash, 1993; Beck, Giddens, and Lash, 1994). The construct of reflexive modernization specifies and gives a theoretical context for the the task of cultural critique that I want to pursue here. It is indisputable that reflexivity as self-monitoring is pervasive in modern rationalist organizations and institutions. Rather, as Beck, Giddens, and Lash's (1994) critique of reflexive modernization suggests, the question worth addressing, both for the continued relevance of critical intellectual movements that have arisen in the academy over the past two decades and for the possibility of a future conversation of critical substance between the human sciences and the policy sciences, is the following. How postmodern (how critically reflexive, how hermeneutically open in rationalist cognition) are the conditions of reflexivity within the operations of various institutions and formal organizations of American life?

I argue that this is an urgent and eminently empirical question, requiring the sensibility of ethnographers, since the reflexivity of the sort I am interested in assaying is not likely to announce itself doctrinally, or say, in the planning departments and functions of organizations. Rather, it must be read as cracks, fissures, and shifts in cases and processes of dealing with phenomena, clients, and situations that don't fit operative traditional categories and resist easy fixes. In other words, the indications of reflexive modernization of the critical hermeneutic sort are likely to be registered not seismically, but in terms of tremors and cracks. At least this is my orienting supposition.

Clearly, I am not interested in the cultural studies cliché of "resistance" by often sentimentalized "Others," but in critiques relying upon affinities between critical academics and either "Other" academics or "Others" powerful in their institutional governing functions. Indeed, the future of critical ethnography itself depends on an understanding of its relationships and affinities to critical sensibilities within other power/knowledges. Far from taking the traditionally distanced perspective on the "Other," ethnographers involved in such new locations are altogether differently positioned. The fact of affinity with these powerful "Others" becomes "useful" knowledge for exploring this new terrain and modifying standard field-work assumptions and settings.

As a contribution to this task, I want to devote the remainder of this essay to the presentation of two occasional exercises of my own that probe techniques and possibilities for bringing critical cultural studies into a perhaps uneasy relationship of both identification and engagement with arenas of knowledge that it has had great distance from, or even actively opposed. The first brief exercise deals with the possibility of success or efficacy of different strategies of critical engagement. It confronts the daunting task of actually pursuing such dialogues. On the occasion of commenting on the inaugural issues of a new journal of *Feminist Economics*, I survey the various senses in which an engagement with mainstream economics by (mainly feminist) economists, deeply affected by the intellectual capital of diverse critical theories over the past decade, might be possible. In this case, the sense of developing engagements across power/knowledges happens to remain within the academy, though it does move beyond it to assess the vulnerabilities of the prestige of economics in its diffuse and derived practices in society, when the prospects of an engaged or dialogic critique of the discipline's academic mainstream appear bleak.

The second exercise deals with technique. It suggests how converging or intersecting genealogies of shared concepts and concerns might be established through a sort of ethnographically sensitive translation between "worlds apart" power/knowledge arenas, such that mutually relevant discussions might occur between scholars and experts who might never have thought they had much in common. Once convincing linking genealogies are established, then the agenda of critical anthropology is defined for the present in trying to exploit or explore them in further dialogues across very strange, and estranged, boundaries of academic/expert discourse. What is at stake is the movement of critical anthropology into conversation with policy studies and operations. Here the task of translation consists in making visible and conscious across domains the intertwined histories of conceptual frameworks that powerfully orient cognitions, practices, and senses of problems. The case developed in the second exercise, concerning cold war nuclear diplomacy, moves this project of critique outside a strictly academic frame, and in so doing also demonstrates how implicated the academy has been in forms of power/knowledge relating to high-level politics within and between states.

Exercise 1: The Case of the Journal of *Feminist Economics*: Strategies of Critical Work and their Potential Efficacy

The recent founding of the journal of *Feminist Economics* presents an interesting opportunity to assess the prospects for the effective internal critique of a discipline, which in its methods and ethos seems to be the very antithesis of styles of analysis and discourse in critical cultural and/ or feminist studies. The opening editorial of the journal gives a flavor of its intent (Strassman, 1995: 2–3):

> At issue is not merely the merits of one theory over another, but the relative merits of entire research agendas and disciplinary identities. Economists have rarely acknowledged the multifaceted character of research priorities or the consequences of socially constructed preferences in diminishing women's voices in economic conversations . . . feminists have begun to shed light on policy concerns integral to women's lives and conceptual flaws in the mechanisms by which economists have claimed the superiority of some ideas over others . . . feminists are exploring the historical construction of disciplinary categories in relation to the composition and other features of communities of economic practice.

Correspondingly, the articles in the first issues of this new journal exhibit work that ranges from the use of standard economic tools to address gender issues, to theoretical and methodological critiques of economics, empirical studies using nonstandard methods or theories, and contributions by non-economists.

For example, in the first issue of the journal, Sandra Harding, a prominent feminist critic of discourse and practice in science, addresses parallel issues in the critique of economics (Harding, 1995). In reading the responses to Sandra Harding's article, a line in the piece by Don McCloskey, who earlier pioneered the critique of economics based on its rhetoric, especially caught my eye (McCloskey, 1995): "My question is, is this or that argument by Harding going to persuade the kind of person I once was [presumably, a mainstream economist]? What *would* convince such a person?" It keys the question of what sorts of efficacy and transformative potential the authors of the various recent projects of cultural critique might desire. I especially have in mind those projects that seek to alter mainstream habits of thought and practices of work in paradigms of knowledge production, such as science, diplomacy, law, and for *Feminist Economics*, economics, all of which have great prestige as the intellectual engines of modern rationality with embedded institutional functions related to governance and social order.

So, is there any hope of "convincing" practitioners and scholars working within the mainstreams of such culturally prestigious formations of knowledge production? If so, then by what strategies of critique? Further, if there is not much hope, then what alternative, or rather supplementary, strategies of critique are available?

Of course, one could claim a much more limited purpose for feminist economics: merely to secure a domain for alternative work on its own merits. Engaged dialogue with the mainstream would not be sought as much as, at most, a legitimate, if marginal, space to operate alternatively within the discipline.[1] The real constituency for such a vibrant alternative economics is located within the contemporary interdisciplinary realm of critical literary/cultural studies, broadly conceived, from which it has importantly derived its intellectual capital. The work of an alternative feminist economics (among other critical social sciences) is the kind of complementary social science that cultural studies scholars, who are its inspiration, need in order to ground empirically their own more broadly based interdisciplinary endeavor. Satisfying by its own standards and supported by interdisciplinary alliances, a feminist economics can thus thrive in structural opposition to mainstream economics without any effort to engage with it on its own terms, or to transform it. It would then become, with viable institutional support, another "tribe" within economics.

Yet, to me, having worked with the signature ethnographic method of cultural anthropology and having attempted to practice cultural critique derived from it, this limited purpose is insufficient. However difficult, to find an engaged constituency within the disciplinary mainstream that might even be "convinced" (in McCloskey's terms) is irresistible for me. It also figures for me as the most important index of the power of a particular project of critique.[2]

The strategy of engagement with the disciplinary mainstream that I have in mind rests on finding and intellectually probing effective oppositional space within mainstream discourses. This means finding where the "fissures" are – that is, finding those concepts, methods, ideas, practices, and life experiences within the culture of the mainstream, about which there is self-doubt and uncertainty among mainstream economists themselves. This in turn means understanding these potentially self-critical cultural formations within mainstream economics, *ethnographically*, in their own terms and expressions.

To proceed ethnographically, one would address such questions as: what are the anxiety and rationalization structures supporting the maintenance of conservative modes of thought in economics? How are such anxieties and rationalizations expressed, in what cultural idioms, and to whom? (Perhaps, for example, they are not directed to the overt critics of mainstream economics, but rather to those who expect most from it in government and business.) What arguments could be developed to establish a sustained connection with embedded self-critical tendencies in mainstream economics? What are the perhaps buried intellectual affinities between these discovered and elicited self-critical tendencies within the mainstream and the manifest forms of critique which oppose it?

According to this strategy, the measure of the power of critique is involved response from within that mainstream. But this strategy does not argue against the mainstream with a counterdiscourse more powerful than its own, because it does not have one that is more powerful. Rather, this strategy depends on mapping the cracks, inconsistencies, and hesitations of mainstream discourse, such that if the critic pointed these out, the mainstream would become upset and moved to respond because it would recognize the critique *in its own internal idiom*. The test of such critique is that the mainstream would neither be indifferent to nor dismissive of what the critic says, but would at least partially recognize itself in such critique.

Now, what I am proposing may seem like "psyching out" mainstream economics in order to convert (or convince) it, but as I indicated, I prefer to understand this strategy in terms analogous to the practice of cross-cultural ethnographic research in anthropology. Based on recent critical discussions of this enterprise (Clifford and Marcus, 1986, and the decade-long stream of discussion that it has initiated), the creation of ethnographic knowledge is inseparable from its contexts of collaborative productions with specific others as informants (in the older terminology), consultants, associates, or simply interlocutors in the field. Indeed, its very form, substance, and purposes are entwined within the self–other negotiations so central to the formulation of translations and interpretations in anthropology.

I am suggesting analogously that any critique of mainstream economics seeking engaged response would proceed approximately like ethnographic practice. This requires working dialogically within the mainstream. In other words, this means being oppositional, without a clear "outside" bounded space of opposition. Certainly, the open-ended possibilities of the pursuit of ethnographic knowledge through dialogically working on the "inside" of another culture makes the idea of "converting" or "convincing" the other side far too simple and inappropriate a metaphor to describe this sort of critique. To be effective, one must put one's own position at risk in opposing and critiquing an "other's." There is no other way to be effectively oppositional from within.

The ideal measure of the success of such a strategy of critique – that those critiqued be motivated to respond and engage with the critique – derives from a parallel "ethos" of success or achievement in ethnographic practice, relating to central issues of cultural translation. Even though anthropologists have always produced interpretations and descriptions primarily for their own academic, largely Western community, they have always had a deep sense that the knowledge that they produce should be accountable to the "natives." In fact, anthropological knowledge has been rarely tested in this way, away from sites of fieldwork, but it is increasingly the case that as objects of study and world conditions change, the nature of the realms of reception of anthropological scholarship are both broadening and diversifying.

The simplest and ethically least implicated form of this concern is often expressed as a wondering whether the discourse that the anthropologist has produced would be meaningful at all to natives, and whether the latter would even be able to comment at all on what the anthropologist says (writes?) about them. The worry of the anthropologist is less that the native would be dismissive than that she would be indifferent to what the former produces as "knowledge." "Getting it right," about which ethnographers argue endlessly, is more about being meaningful to an "other" than being accurate about a particular detail.

The imaginary of such successful ethnographic engagement has been a very strong guide and self-critical measure in anthropological work, and would operate analogously in the strategy of engaged critique "from within" mainstream economics that I am proposing. At the level even of an imaginary, the requirement of accountable engagement serves to keep ethnography, and presumably would keep the critique of economics, honest, by not hardening the lines of its own inevitable self-promotions and morale-building endeavors.

However, practical as well as imaginary success is also at stake in most projects of critique. And there may be some mainstreams or dominant discourses for which the strategy of engaged critique will just not succeed in any way that satisfies the critic. Even if such connection is made, exchange might be endlessly frustrating or contentious. Or pure acts of institutional power, prerogative, and arrogance might summarily end overtures to engaged critique, even when such critique skillfully strikes the right nerve. Indeed, there may be some discourse domains in which, however good the strategy of engaged critique may sound, there is simply no "talking to it." Mainstream defenses (as well as those on the side of critique) may be too great: sufficient, minimal good faith may not exist. Such, for example, may be true for mainstream economics.

So, let's suppose, then, that such a project of critique by transformative engagement with reasonable openness as to the results is finally insupportable – not because the idea is naive, but because it will prove to be just too wearing on the positive spirit which powers a project of critique. To persist, engaged critique needs interlocutors "on the other side," for whom there is some possibility for movement and development in debate. This leads me, then, to the final suggestion of a critical strategy inspired by the project of feminist economics.

I shall call this strategy "oblique critique." The strategy that I have just described for probing mainstream economics suggested by the experience of ethnographic research in anthropology – that of developing engaged critique through finding affinities with the "other" critiqued by dint of the equivalent of ethnographic knowledge, itself derived through dialogue – remains the same. What changes is the field in which it is exercised.

The use of the concepts and modes of economic thinking are widely diffused beyond the activities of academics who centrally define the discipline of economics itself. The economics of the Wall Street broker, the judge, or even the middle-class investor are of course not the same as those of the economics professor, but they are related in complex ways and patterns of influence that have not yet been studied. Like literature and history, most college undergraduates at least pass through economics. Because of the general cultural prestige of economics as a specific expression of reason and rationality, its ideas and models permeate many other specializations and technical spheres of knowledge production. For example, in Exercise 2, I study the interesting career of "the prisoner's dilemma" from game theory (which itself has complex associations to economics) as an artifact of the epitome of the application of rationality, complexly distributed over time and space in recent American cultural history. Indeed, it was my effort to see the "postmodern" in this seminal formalist puzzle of strict rationality and its particular ramifications in the formation of cold war nuclear weapons strategies that led me to both clarify what I mean by a strategy of engaged critique and to see its most potentially successful applications. Those applications confront the practices, not of the ur-disciplines of rationality, such as economics, but obliquely, of those fields into which the ideas of economics have migrated as dominant, prestigious models of operation.

Thus, in establishing such an oblique and extended field of critique of economics, the point is to conceive of this branch of technical knowledge on a broadly cultural map. The prestige of economics is certainly based on its complex spread and genealogies of influence in different locations of American life as well as internationally. And it is the prestige of economics as a discipline at the core of this broad cultural field that most protects its mainstream practitioners from more direct critiques. So, if the path of directly engaged critique of the disciplinary mainstream is necessary to try, but fraught with difficulty, then the critique of economics as a derived mode of thought in locations and spheres to which it has migrated is perhaps a more promising, if supplementary project of feminist economics. If done systematically, the project of oblique critique could have, over time, a profound effect on the configurations of prestige which give the mainstream in academic economics the power to ignore or downplay either the challenges of marginalized sectors within its own disciplinary boundaries (i.e. Marxists, feminists, postmodernists), or its own very masked tendencies toward self-critique.

Finally, would it in fact be easier to "translate" through engaged critique the economic models and practices at work in the broader cultural field of oblique critique than to connect with self-critical hesitations in the thought of mainstream economists? Of course, this is very much an empirical question, but merely the effort to do so would shift feminist economics from being the critique of a discipline to being a powerful and broad form of cultural critique in the name of economics (and, of course, feminism). From the domains of application of the prisoner's dilemma, to those of rational choice theory, to the way that the contemporary middle classes manage their finances and plan for the education of children, the oblique critique of economics by those trained within its sanctum is likely to produce an immense amount of intellectual capital through which the frameworks of mainstream economics might be eventually transformed.

Exercise 2: The Affinity between Postmodernist Critique of the 1980s and Nuclear Diplomacy by Way of a Modernist Avant-garde Link to the "Prisoner's Dilemma"

This exercise is one of critical translation in a world of family resemblances of overlapping power/knowledges – moving beyond the critical field of discourses that have emerged in the human sciences to the discovery of affinities, parallels, and differences within other power/knowledges for which these critical discourses have meant little or nothing. If, indeed, overt styles of critical postmodern thought have cogently gestured toward conditions "out there," then through a kind of ethnographic translation, a similar de facto postmodernism "in its own terms," however subtly marked and even resisted, should be found in other power/knowledges. Such an exercise would at least indicate with great specificity what are useful and less useful ideas in the central trends of academic postmodernism of the past decade. It would also map with equal specificity a much needed and perhaps provocative expansion in the range of discourses of scholarship, technical thought, and expertise with which critical postmodernism and cultural studies might engage, other than in their distancing and clichéd "oppositional" stance to all that is "dominant" and "hegemonic."

This form of critique looks for affinities between postmodern academic thought and other power/knowledges precisely where they are *not* obvious, where they emerge in the latter as unintended consequences of trying to deal instrumentally with the contemporary world. For example, at what points is a power/knowledge that has comfortably dealt with constructs of integral selves and individuals, faced suddenly with multiple subjectivities (a key artifact of postmodern/feminist/cultural studies thought) in the course of its problem-solving? It is precisely at such points that two-way translations and engagement might be strategized. The fact that these affinities are discovered/negotiated within the "enemy" territory of the dominant/hegemonic, rather than imposed by the power of postmodern thought in brilliant applications, marks the difference between the project suggested here and the existing domains (reservations?) of postmodern critique.

I want to work through an example of this critical project focused on the power/knowledge of high-level cold war diplomacy at its twilight. I have decided to give my example at least a short historic perspective. I have selected nuclear/arms control diplomacy of the 1980s as the target "other" power/knowledge to try to discover affinities with moves and constructs of so-called postmodern critique within the academy for two reasons. First, nuclear diplomacy is clearly distant from postmodern critiques of academic disciplines. Second, it was at the very vortex of the most dramatic structural and cognitive real-world changes of that decade, including the shift in leadership in the USSR and the latter's eventual dismantling. My question is whether there are any affinities between the radical shifts of framework and representation practices suggested by postmodern critiques in the academy of the 1980s and the discourse of diplomacy of the same period, which, albeit insular, was having to navigate radically changed conditions and new assumptions.

At the Institute for Advanced Study, 1982–3: storylines

I was invited to be a visiting member at the Institute for Advanced Study during 1982–3, primarily because of Clifford Geertz's interest in the paper that I published (with Dick Cushman) in the 1982 *Annual Review of*

Anthropology – "Ethnographies as Texts." It was also during my time at the Institute that I planned the Santa Fe SAR "Writing Culture" seminar with Jim Clifford, and drafted (in partnership with Mike Fischer) the arguments for *Anthropology as Cultural Critique*. Clifford visited me at the Institute during this year, and met Geertz for the first time. There was clear mutual respect between them as writers, although at the time Geertz was attracted to, but also wary of, the coming "literary" turn – even though before the days of "theory" he himself had been associated with a literary influence on anthropology. The concerns with textuality, disciplinary history, critical modes of reflexivity, and the critique of realist practices of representation that informed my (and to a far lesser extent, Geertz's) thinking was just a local case of what was then happening in many disciplines. This was one clear "storyline" in the atmosphere of the Institute during my year that was to become a major story of the decade and beyond.

Amid the diverse other projects that were in play at the Institute that year, there were three other salient storylines being pursued, two of which figure into the exercise that I have designed for this paper. One of the other storylines (not directly relevant here) was the focused attention given to cognitive science that year.

Another of the storylines derives from the work that Charles Sabel was doing as a visiting member of the Institute during 1982–3. He was working on the manuscript that was to become *The Second Industrial Divide* (Piore and Sabel, 1984). This was to be one of the first major statements about the changing conditions of capitalist political economy in the West. In addition, in 1982–3, the middle of Reagan's first term, analysts were noting adverse changes for the US economy in a rapidly changing world of competitive capitalism. The rapid changes in markets, production processes, and consumer choices were very apparent to the "person on the street" in the early 1980s. These realities, I would argue, played a crucial off-stage role in giving postmodernist critiques a sense of their own possibility. Indeed, this new work on emerging political economy was frequently referenced in works of cultural critique.[3]

This brings me to the final storyline, which circumstantially happened to be quite salient at the Institute during the 1982–3 year, and which I found perhaps the most fascinating of all. It dealt with the seemingly Spenglerian moment that the Reagan administration had begun to create with its departure from detente and its more agressive stance toward the Soviet Union. This was the moment of the invocation of the "evil empire" and of debates about the feasibility of direct military intervention in Central America. I recall public debates between Richard Ullman (professor at the Woodrow Wilson School and visitor at the Institute that year) and Bill Luers (former ambassador to Venezuela, then visitor at the Institute, nervously awaiting reassignment) about the dangers of Soviet footholds in Central America. Most memorably, I participated in a weekly series of informal lunches at the Institute dining hall, that brought together a diverse group of international relations scholars from the Woodrow Wilson School, some weapons scientists, occasional persons who had moved between academia and government or diplomatic service, and always George Kennan, who had for many years been a member of the School of Historical Studies at the Institute.

In terms of sharp, edgy discussion about something that clearly mattered, about "events of the day," these lunches were for me the most stimulating events at the Institute that year, and have stood out for me since then. The discussions were dominated by young, very bright scholars of international relations arguing point-counterpoint over US strategy in competition with the Soviets, with a narrow focus on nuclear arms policy. I was captivated by the elegance and intricacy of this very reductionist game, while finding the game itself obtuse.

Others on the sidelines at the lunches made commentaries or more philosophical glosses on the tight tension of US–Soviet competition at the time. The strategic threat of revolutions in Central America and the background to US policy there often came up. For Charles Sabel, the interesting developments in IR at that time concerned the evolution of a new international regime which was reorganizing world economies, but the group's main focus was on the narrow game/discourse of US–Soviet nuclear strategy totally insulated from immense changes in political economy, thereby maintaining a surreal, but also very locally real, centering to the cold war order.

The major counterweight at these lunches was the quiet, but large presence of George Kennan, whose comments persistently undermined the assumptions of the revitalized neorealist game being pursued by the younger men. I later learned that Kennan was well known for his distaff view about the Soviet threat that powered cold war competition, but he was very involved at the time in rearticulating this view as the Reagan administration was heating up the cold war. Not long after his crucial early cold war articulation of containment strategy, Kennan had begun to argue for a complex and nondemonized view of the Soviets as "others" in the great game that would have precluded, for example, Reagan's returns to a nuclear brinksmanship strategy. Kennan was thus once again the colossal rallying point for left-liberal opinion against what looked like a return to the old cold war in the early 1980s.

As we know from the 1990s, this early 1980s cold war strategizing discourse was to go through dramatic changes after Gorbachev came to power in 1985, moving from the challenge of the Spenglerian specter of the "decline of the West" at the beginning of the decade to a jingoist, but still not fully confident, heralding of the "triumph of the West" at the end, as in Francis Fukuyama's *The End of History*. Now in the 1990s, I want to juxtapose and mutually engage this power/knowledge of high-level diplomacy during the 1980s to that of postmodernist critical thought of the same period that was related to it only distantly (if at all), but was certainly spurred on and stimulated (through the off-stage real effect mentioned above) by the spectacle of the dramatic changes in post-World War II order that were centered in the terms of "the great game" of Soviet–US relations. Was there any parallel sense of postmodernist moods deep within the distant power/knowledge of nuclear diplomacy?

The avant-garde (post) modernist fascination with simultaneity and the prisoner's dilemma

Working into the 1980s power/knowledge discourse of nuclear diplomacy in practice, starting from within "postmodernist" critical thought of the same period, requires the construction of intersecting critical genealogies between two domains apparently "worlds apart." I can only offer a sketch here of such an analysis of an opening, posited affinity. The specific locations I would like to probe are the long-term fascination with simultaneity in the discourse of avant-garde modernisms and postmodernisms, and an identifiable similar fascination with simultaneity in the construction of the key problematic of game theory – the prisoner's dilemma. In turn, the development of game theory (the prisoner's dilemma in particular) in the US is intimately related to the formulation of early cold war stategies of nuclear diplomacy. Nuclear diplomacy was not in the hands of game theoreticians, nor is it clear that game theory was prominent in the thinking of the main actors of Soviet–US relations, but game theory was certainly a powerful intellectual expression on the inside of the actual "great game" (if "game" is the correct metaphor) of nuclear arms competition and control. Thus, I am wagering that making the connection between a problematic of simultaneity in postmodernism and game theory will create a vehicle to probe the power/knowledge of nuclear diplomacy in practice for its parallel to critical postmodernism's evoked projections of immense change upon the contemporaneous world.

The fascination with simultaneity among avant-gardes

Techniques of juxtaposition have been at the center of avant-garde practices throughout modernism and postmodernism. Montage, collage, assemblage – these have been avant-garde critique's forms of representation or anti-representation, with sharp, implied challenges to construction of discourses of the real in conventional genres.

One of the most important moves in the so-called postmodernist trend in the academy has been the adoption in both spirit and practice of these avant-garde techniques of (anti-?) representation in humanities/social science writing as a means of challenging the academy's mode of realism: analytic reason. The power of this form of reason for scholarly practices remains overwhelming. Even when writing against it, one is writing in its terms, or least in reference to it. Thus, "reality"-testing lurks as a criterion even for the most distanced, theoretical uses of strategies of critique by juxtaposition. The key empirical question embedded in the practice of juxtaposition concerns the state and experience – the phenomenology – of simultaneity. This is the condition that the discourse of analytic reason might acknowledge, but must evade, and which postmodernist critique wants to address squarely, but for which it might not have a substitute discourse that would by any means satisfy analytic reason.

Analytic discourse about the real employs linear representation, and sequence, making possible statements about causation, if not rigorously articulated, then implied. It allows for systematic theorization and description of social and cultural life. Its basic representational mode depends on the taken-for-granted capacity to articulate *relationships* (of people, parts, distinctions, things, etc.) as the most basic object of study. A relationship, however complex and multilevelled, entails linearity and sequenciality in conception. This is the basic "work horse" of analytic reason that postmodernist critique's concern with simultaneity wants to address.

Instead of actors who respond to what has been done to them by knowable others – the basis of a relationship – let us suppose that actors are acting (maybe even responding) to what is being done by unknowable others as they act (the play with synchronicity in experimental film and fiction – Joyce's *Ulysses* being a prime example – or the idea of "utterance" in Bakhtin are good examples from very well established modernisms). The imaginary/discourse of simultaneity is quite different to anything that has been explored in the dominant analytic realisms in play in most contemporary power/knowledges. It is precisely this alternative imaginary/discourse that postmodernist critique within the academy – and centrally in the realm of the analytic real as the common sense of most power/knowledges – wants to explore. Observations about defining aspects of contemporary societies as postmodern (for example, the centrality of time–space compression as reviewed by Harvey, or of speed as focused upon by Paul Virilio), enhance the fascination of current critical thought with simultaneity and its potential as a condition through which to evoke an alternative vision of contemporary life. Thus, the unrelenting concern with simultaneity is one of the most distinctive, and certainly one of the most subversive, provocative, and irritating characteristics of many forms of thought called postmodern. It is something that realist genres have not been able to abide, dependent as they are on linearity and the construct of transparent reciprocity which simultaneity undermines.[4]

A case in point: game theory and the prisoner's dilemma

Of all the varieties of contemporary discourses of analytic realism, game theory, and specifically, its most central and influential puzzle, the prisoner's dilemma (hereafter, PD), is the only one that foregrounds in its construction the problem of simultaneity, thus sharing an affinity with this key provocation of (post)modernist critique. The other main postwar paradigm of analytic realism was cybernetics and systems theory, but it was fully constructed on the imagery of linear relationships and continuous interconnection (see Heims, 1993). The PD was thus an attempt of rationality to find a perfect solution in the environment of a key problem of modernity – the condition of simultaneity – while avoiding the assumptions of systems/cybernetics theory, which posited linear relationships and direct connections. While by no means equally sharing the spirit or ethos of avant-garde critique – in fact the condition of simultaneity is constructed for rationalist manipulation by the metaphoric notion of game itself – PD does come a cropper as a puzzle for elegant solution for reasons that are not unrelated to the fascination that simultaneity has for postmodernist critical thought.

The history of game theory itself is intimately linked to cold war history and the policy management of nuclear weapons, especially in its early years (see Poundstone, 1992). Game theory begins with the 1944 publication of *Theory of Games and Economic Behavior* by John von Neumann and Oskar Morgenstern. It concerns conflict between thoughtful and potentially deceitful opponents in which players are assumed to be perfectly rational. Thus, it is a branch not of psychology but of mathematical logic that underlies real conflicts among not always rational humans. A "game" is a conflict situation where one must make a choice knowing that others are making choices too, and the outcome of the conflict will be determined in some prescribed way by all the choices made. This is the (post)modernist's problem of simultaneity under the logician's control.

Game theory found its most important application at the RAND Corporation, which was the prototypical think-tank founded at the behest of the Air Force shortly after World War II. RAND's original purpose was to perform strategic studies on intercontinental nuclear war. The need for RAND's "operations research" was indeed stimulated by a sort of "crisis of representation" in military matters brought on by the appearance of nuclear weapons: generals and scientists became wedded in new ways.

In 1950, two RAND scientists devised the most provocative version of game theory. Merrill Flood and Melvin Dresher devised a simple "game" that challenged part of the theoretical basis of game theory. RAND consultant Albert W. Tucker dubbed this game the prisoner's dilemma, so called because of a story Tucker told to illustrate it. Not published as such until years after its invention, the prisoner's dilemma – a story that is both a precise mathematical construct and also a real-life problem – spread through the scientific community of the 1950s by oral transmission. From the 1960s, this dilemma paradigm became part of a much broader intellectual culture and even a marker of "cultural literacy." It has come to stand for game theory, its ethical ambiguities, and the tensions of the early nuclear era.

Flood and Dresher, the inventors of PD, were trying to take account of the fact that people are irrational within the realm of game theory. They thus dispensed to some degree with the narrow "game" assumptions of the original theory to make it relevant to everyday life situations of dilemma, choice, and calculation. Albert Tucker, a Princeton mathematician, gave the tale its classic formulation, of which Poundstone (1992: 118–19) presents a typical contemporary version:

> Two members of a criminal gang are arrested and imprisoned. Each prisoner is in solitary confinement with no means of speaking to or exchanging messages with the other. The police admit they don't have enough evidence to convict the pair on the principal charge. They plan to sentence both to a year in prison on a lesser charge. Simultaneously, the police offer each prisoner a Faustian bargain. If he testifies against his partner, he will go free while the partner will get three years in prison on the main charge. Oh, yes, there is a catch . . . if both prisoners testify against each other, both will be sentenced to two years in jail.
>
> The prisoners are given a little time to think this over, but in no case may either learn what the other has decided until he has irrevocably made his decision. Each is informed that the other prisoner is being offered the very same deal. Each prisoner is concerned only with his own welfare – with minimizing his own prison sentence.
>
> The prisoners can reason as follows. "Suppose I testify and the other prisoner doesn't. Then I get off scot-free (rather than spending a year in jail). Suppose I testify and the other prisoner does too. Then I get two years (rather than three). Either way I'm better off turning state's evidence. Testifying takes a year off my sentence, no matter what the other guy does."
>
> The trouble is, the other prisoner can and will come to the very same conclusion. If both parties are rational, both will testify and both will get two years in jail. If only they had both refused to testify, they would have got just a year each!

This story was not intended to be a realistic picture of criminology, but to serve the logician's challenge to game theory, by posing a puzzle without a perfect solution. In fact, an expected solution never came to the PD, and it remains a limiting case for the ambition of a theory which would impose perfect rationality on the (post)modern condition of simultaneity – the nonlinear nature of relationship as a *usual* circumstance of social and cultural life, and not just of dilemma situations.

So much for the disappointments of theory. In practice, no example of a prisoner's dilemma has been more popular, both in technical articles and the popular press, than nuclear arms rivalry. The "prisoner's dilemma" is sometimes taken to be part of the jargon of nuclear strategy, along with "mutually assured destruction" and "MIRV." At the time the PD was invented, the US and the Soviets had embarked on an expensive nuclear arms race. The situation could be seen as a PD (and was seen as such at RAND, whose "thinking about the unthinkable" was of maximum strategic influence at the time), in which building the bombs could be identified with defection, and holding off could be identified with cooperation. Each side would prefer that no one build the bomb (reward payoff for mutual cooperation), rather than both build it for no net gain of power (punishment payoff for mutual defection). But each side may well elect to build the bomb either out of hope of gaining the upper hand militarily (temptation payoff) or out of fear of being the one without it (sucker payoff).

As the cold war wore on and the US and the Soviet Union became implacable foes, whose relations remained focused on the politics of nuclear arms competition and then control, the relevance of exercises in perfect rationality as embedded in the project of game theory (and within it, its internal critique and limiting case in the form of the PD) clearly lessened. Yet the problematic around which the PD developed and which it shared with avant-garde modernisms – the fascination with relations of simultaneity – seems to be of crucial relevance in understanding the development of high-level nuclear diplomacy in terms of which cold war reality was articulated and managed. It is just that avant-garde modernisms have nothing as elegant as the PD to offer with which to understand the actual course of cold war nuclear diplomacy.

This is where the ethnographically sensitive translation between power/ knowledges and the probing for the PD in action, so to speak, come in. The basic setup of the PD – the condition of nonlinear relations of simultaneity – is probably useful to retain and quite ironic as a perspective on the actual playing out of US–Soviet relations at the end of the cold war. But a richer set of theories and concepts is needed to describe the human experience of operating in conditions of simultaneous processes, where one's relations are with unseen, or only partly perceived, others. Classic social theory and analytic realism, as noted, offer very few resources for this re-imagining of the PD in messy, human terms.[5]

Let's move to a set of exhibits/artifacts from the late cold war history of nuclear diplomacy that detect something of the dynamic in practice of the mixed PD/postmodernist problematic of simultaneity. When *do* we reach the point in "real" life when the utility of maintaining the fiction that what we are doing above is a game at all is exhausted, and we look for other terms and descriptive frames to deal with "provisionary strategies?" This would be, for nuclear diplomacy, a parallel to the crisis of representation that pervaded academic disciplines. No such dramatic breaking of frame in nuclear diplomacy at the end of the cold war is apparent, but certainly the game metaphor, implied or explicit, wavered at various points in the events of the 1980s.

Finally, it seems to me that revisions in systems theories to encompass discontinuity, contingency, nonlinearity, and apparent simultaneity – or to put it simply, complexity – have generated theoretical paradigms, such as chaos, that have thoroughly displaced game theory in terms of prestige and also popularity. The new systems theories retain the goal of establishing principles of embedded or underlying order in accounts of much more complex phenomena. This is a heady brew that both promises order and yet recognizes in phenomena the contradictions, paradoxes, and processes of disorder, so focused upon by (post)modernist critical thought. It is no wonder, then, that the longstanding practice of the borrowing of theoretical metaphors and analogies from the natural sciences to enhance the rhetoric of new ideas in the human sciences continues, with frequent references to chaos, complexity theory, fractals, and the like in contemporary discussions of global cultures, new social formations, etc. Game theory, although at one time addressing within its dilemma stories (like the PD) key aspects of the problematics of avant-garde modernisms that systems theory ignored, now pales against the ability of revised systems theory (theories of chaos and complexity) to excite, contribute to, and legitimize developing imaginaries within the human sciences.

Nuclear diplomacy

Game theory turns out to be a very formalized portrait or calculus of the way that social actors think about interests in its *own* interest of pure rationality. However, because of its very specific intellectual and cultural history just outlined, it has a very close relationship to the mode of thought with which the cold war was identified and, in fact, produced as a practice of power/knowledge – the discourse of nuclear arms production, competition, and control. The purveyors of this discourse were not scientists, but establishment, or establishment-style, lawyers like Paul Nitze and Paul Warnke, who were brought into various administrations through political influence and alliance. Such nuclear arms negotiators presented a strange combination of the cultivated generalist/amateur posture of the establishment elite, and intricate, technical expertise about the character of nuclear weapon systems.

As noted, it is doubtful that game theory (the PD) itself had much presence in the actual "great game" after the early years of the cold war as it was articulated within the complex arena of those concerned with nuclear diplomacy. In practice, the "great game" has had all the characteristics of (post)modernist simultaneity and not "game" theory. Still, the PD is part of the elite lore of those charged with nuclear arms control. It is, therefore, I would argue, one prospective "mole" for probing affinities with postmodernist critique within the terms of this power/knowledge at the vortex of global change during the same period the critique emerged in US academia. As I argued, there are aspects of the way that the PD is constructed – having to do with relations defined by conditions of simultaneity – which are at the heart of a perception of a condition of (post)modernity in avant-garde thought. Could these aspects be reconfigured for probing within the characteristics of "nuclear diplomacy" discourse in which the "PD" has a chimerical, marginalized standing, as a once-important constituting paradigm of nuclear diplomacy, but is now an artifact of elite folklore? It is precisely in this latter capacity that it might serve as the bridge for a project of ethnographic translation between power/knowledges.

The insularity of actual nuclear diplomacy discourse is striking. With few exceptions (the Cuban missile crisis, Paul Nitze's "Walk in the Woods"), actual contacts and exchanges with the Soviet "other" are highly ritualized and technical. The dynamics are generated by politics among those in an administration charged with nuclear diplomacy – the president, the national security advisor, the secretary of state, those positions within the state department charged with arms control negotiation, and the community of various expertises – journalistic, academic, scientific, intelligence – oriented toward these "agent" positions in nuclear diplomacy. Only former cold warriors on the outside – epitomized by George Kennan – could articulate the contrary wisdom that argued for the recognition of the substantive alterity of the Soviets which would have expanded or transcended the discourse of nuclear diplomacy and conventionalized the relationship between the two powers at the highest levels.

The stylized manner of US–Soviet relations that was constituted by nuclear diplomacy was disrupted by two events in the 1980s – Reagan's SDI initiative unveiled in a speech on March 23, 1983, and Gorbachev's accession to power in 1985. As nuclear diplomats struggled to deal with the momentous consequences of both, to what degree did they self-consciously, or even ambivalently – in subtly marked ways – come to terms with the (post)modernist conditions of their power/knowledge, embedded within their own history and folklore in the PD story?

Reagan's SDI: a rupture in the discourse of arms control

Reagan's announcement of the Strategic Defense Initiative ("Star Wars") in 1983 took the nuclear diplomatic community by total surprise, and the rest of the decade was in part a struggle on the part of various factions to reassert their versions of the verities of arms control while seeming to pursue the president's unconventional initiative (Talbott, 1988). This idiosyncratic, radical, and highly futuristic move by the president to make nuclear weapons outmoded through space defenses, totally undermined the arms control efforts which were the form that nuclear diplomacy had taken through the period of detente. While the idea was to make the whole basis of the US–Soviet relationship irrelevant, the SDI was in fact a keenly aggressive move, since it would match the economic power of the two states in a way that had not been done since the arms buildups of the early cold war, and both sides knew that the Soviet Union was not up to this strain.

Reagan's attempt to dispense with the great game could not be attributed to such easy-to-perceive cunning in retrospect (i.e. the move was designed to break the Soviet economy). It had its roots in a kind of idealism, surrealism, and American exceptionalism (the latter treated as a major theme of US foreign policy in Henry Kissinger's (1994) retrospective *Diplomacy*) characteristic of Reagan's style of thinking. The byzantine efforts of nuclear diplomats like Paul Nitze and Richard Perle to continue to pursue their agendas through the new challenges that SDI imposed was the true game of nuclear diplomacy during the 1980s, as the Soviet Union continued to fall apart. These agendas, of course, had to do with the assumption of the possibility of nuclear war on which the simultaneously real and imaginary relationship of the US and the Soviet Union had been based.

Reagan's initiative, in its dreamy unreality, can be understood as an effort that would end the prisoner's dilemma of US–Soviet relations, in its (post)modernist inflection/affinity given here. The contemporary masters of the PD-in-practice embodied in nuclear diplomacy succeeded in sustaining this imaginary on which the focal cold war relationship of simultaneity was constructed (with all its psychological possibilities of paranoia and indulgent self-construction in the absence of any rich and broadly monitored contact with an "other").

What was not registered sufficiently in this insular, baroque game that guaranteed order in the world of the cold war was the appearance of real alterity for the first time in the person of Gorbachev. This event proved to be far more endangering to the assumptions of nuclear diplomacy than SDI.

George Schultz lectures Gorbachev on the information revolution, 1987

In his memoirs, George Schultz records a meeting in the Kremlin with Gorbachev in April 1987. The text is remarkable. Schultz takes advantage of a short break in the discussion about nuclear weapons control for a long lecture (complete with "brightly colored pie charts") about changes in the contemporary world that reads much like the kind of understanding of political economy that inspired thinking in academia about conditions of postmodernity. For example, compare Schultz (1993: 891–2) with David Harvey (1989). In this interlude, Schultz was trying to break the frame of faceless "rational" nuclear contestation in the spirit of the prisoner's dilemma. The lecture apparently engaged Gorbachev's whole attention, and only came to a close when, "after about twenty-five minutes, Marshal Akhromeyev walked in with a jaunty step and upbeat, confident manner. We turned to START and SDI. Gorbachev said that the idea of a 50 percent cut in strategic forces, first agreed on at the Geneva summit, could now be described in numerical terms: 1,600 launchers and 6,000 warheads" (Schultz, 1993: 892).

Schultz, the Stanford economics professor, was trying to give Gorbachev the bigger picture – the sense of the dramatically changing "real" on which the cogency of developing postmodernist cultural critique of the 1980s was most directly based – the changed conditions of capitalist political economy. But this was a mere interruption in the insular narrow frame to which Schultz's face-to-face meetings with Gorbachev and other high-level Soviets was restricted. The relationship of the US and the Soviets in simultaneity had been sustained in practice by the discipline of the discourse of arms control negotiation. Gorbachev was the first Soviet leader with the hint of a "face" that might be recognized in a normal face-to-face relationship. Schultz was trying to break through the rigid frame of the old world of US–Soviet relations to an account of a new world in which, apparently through the information revolution, simultaneity would continue to be the medium of relationship, but through speed and time–space compression in the global economy, rather than through the mannered relations in the blind of the cold war leviathans, who were, true to the PD, prisoners rather than gamesters of the nuclear world that they had created.

After 1988, the unravelling of the Soviet Union had unexpectedly displaced the centrality of the (post)modernist, PD basis of Soviet–US relations in high-level US diplomacy. Definitely for Reagan and even more so for Bush, the arrival of Gorbachev meant for the first time a complex, actual interlocutor "other" to be imagined as counterpart by the US president.

This gave a literalness, an intersubjectivity, a linearity of back-and-forth interaction – in essence, an illusion of presence – to US–Soviet relations that belied the conduct of their relationship in simultaneity, along with whatever insight into the nature of sociality in the (post)modern world that this previous condition offered.

The illusion of a relationship in the most conventional terms – an "affair," or partnership, as it were – impeded management at the highest levels of the speed of change in the late 1980s for which Schultz's lecture on the (post)modernist political economy was apposite and the conduct of US–Soviet relations in the simultaneity of nuclear diplomacy was perhaps more relevant (see Beschloss and Talbott, 1993, for the most detailed account of the end of the cold war). The Bush–Gorbachev affair was the ultimate limiting case (and failure) of the conventional idea of a relationship in the (post)modernist world in which Soviet–US relations, centered on nuclear diplomacy, had been conducted through much of the cold war, and with special intensity during the 1980s.

Yet, within a US context, the 1980s were a remarkable decade of new unconventional thinking (the exotic foray of avant-garde idioms into the human sciences with mixed results, thus far) and the struggle of old forms of unconventional thinking (nuclear diplomacy at the end of the cold war) with affinities and contradictory parallels between them (the (post)modernist fascination with simultaneity through the PD, for example). Critical work in the fin-de-siècle 1990s, I would argue, depends more upon the speculations of translating across the power/knowledges of this period, than on any self-conscious return to the eternal verities of existing metahistories (see Kissinger, 1994, for example), whose frames are likely to miss what is acknowledged by them as unprecedented, really different, and distinctively definitive about *these* times as they unfold.

Envoi

With a strong sense that the 1980s' intellectual ferment at the level of metatheoretical discussion is over and an equally strong sense of unrealized potential and irresolution of many of these "high" theoretical ideas in enactments of very specific genres of research and scholarship, what remains for critical cultural studies and its derivations is to seek not always comfortable engagements in arenas that it has been hesitant to enter, or frankly, has defined itself in opposition to. This would address unfinished aspects of the practice of reflexivity that has been such a major emblem and strategy of critical research in recent years. Critical cultural studies has produced impressive work on popular culture and the contemporary predicaments of those social actors conceived in subaltern positionings.

Reflexivity in such work has aided the construction of these valuable research genres. What has not been done within the framework of these very same critical cultural studies is to incorporate the reflexive dimension that makes visible the established and *potential* relationships of critical cultural studies to forms of institutional power. This essay, with some tentative exercises in this direction, has sought to argue strongly for not only making these connections, but also for *developing* them.

The point is not merely to suggest this kind of provocative reflexivity (as others, like Bourdieu, have done) for theoretical purpose and advantage. It is to consider the radical implications of performing it in all aspects of the research process, for the standard ways that critical cultural studies scholars position themselves in relation to subjects of study and presumed audiences, how they materialize objects of study, and how they create rhetorics of political purpose, affiliation, and virtue for their projects. For example, from the standpoint of critical ethnographic work in cultural studies, the most radical move required of scholars who have repositioned themselves by establishing affinities between themselves and those operating in other power/knowledges is overcoming typical distinctions between elites (and institutional orders) as "others" that anthropologists largely do not study, subalterns as "others" who anthropologists do study, and anthropologists themselves in the position of ethnographers as "other" to either of these. The self-perception of the practice of ethnography as a power/knowledge like, among, and with specific kinds of connections to others, based on certain ethical commitments and identifications, forces the refiguration of the terrain of research – unfixes standard positionings – in which the concepts of elites, anthropologists, and subalterns get rearranged. Leaving aside power structures and conspiratorial groups as the defining features of elites, what we have attributed to elites is not "other" to us as scholars at all, but rather the play of institutional orders, which incorporates "us" as merely a different institutional interest.

Operating within reconfigured spaces of research has implications for the traditional sympathetic involvements of researchers with their subjects. Now these involvements are multiple, conflicting, and much more ambiguous. The nature and quality of field work in one site can be very different from others. This requires a different kind of resolution of a research persona than that which had normally constituted the anthropologist in field work, and which was a major component of the much-critiqued traditional conventions of authority in ethnographic writing (I know because "I was there" – I saw, I sympathized, etc. – see Clifford and Marcus, 1986). The construction of new personae and identities, both in field work and in writing, creates what I have called elsewhere a kind of circumstantial activism (Marcus, 1995) in these reconfigured projects, stimulated by a style of reflexivity that places critical cultural studies much more complicitly in fields of power that it might have preferred to just as well leave as elite hegemonic "other."

But, finally, the stakes for critical cultural studies of cultivating a serious, performed view of itself as one power/knowledge among others are greater than just a revision of the research process and its habitual modes of preferred representation. It seems to me that to prevent cultural studies scholars from speaking only to themselves, and sometimes to those they presume to speak for as well – in other words, from occupying a place of "reservation" filled with both complacency and anxiety about "relevance" – the possibilities of relationship and discussion across the frontiers of standard positioning moves must be attempted. The process of trying to do so may not be any more satisfying. In fact, the risks for ethics, integrity, and confusion are much greater. But at the current juncture, there is little other choice. At least it gives a radically reflexive cultural studies the kind of activist engagement that it has in fact imagined for itself, but through strategems that it might never have thought it would undertake.

NOTES

1   Indeed, there has always been a legitimate "reservation" or "ghetto" for work critical of mainstream neoclassical economics, and such spaces have even found important patrons among revered figures of the discipline who in their seniority have had the license to cultivate a certain maverick position against the very mainstream that reveres them. In the past, such marginal domains have operated under the labels Marxist or institutional economics; at present, the designation "feminist" or "postmodern" more prominently labels this "reserved" space.

2   Engaged debate (dialogue? confrontation?) with the mainstream could, and often is, discussed in terms of metaphors of missionizing, warfare, or political struggle. And, indeed, a certain will to power always figures in projects of critique, such that images of wanting to overcome and replace dominant forms with something better are irresistible in characterizing the confrontational setting of critique. Critique is often powered by either the desire to convert (or merely convince), or the desire to subvert (calling up images of revolutionary action). Still, in trying to suggest here a somewhat hopeful strategy for a practice of critique that seeks engaged response from a glacial mainstream, at worst unlikely to listen to it, or at best, likely to marginalize it, I prefer to give it an anthropological expression, even though I am keenly aware of how anthropology itself has historically wrestled with missionizing and subverting, both as metaphorical and literal aspects of its own endeavors (Clifford and Marcus, 1986; and especially Clifford's (1988) essay on Marcel Griaule). But at least anthropology has squarely confronted, and in a reflexively active way, now deals with this past will to power, however ethically sensitive, in its new projects of critique (Marcus and Fischer, 1986).

3   The main channel of reference was through geographers who, among the theorists of changes in political economy, were most deeply and explicitly engaged with postmodernist critical thought, the most important statement being that of David Harvey (1989). See also the work of Scott Lash, James Urry, and the interesting "Theory, Culture, and Society" group for whom Zygmunt Bauman eventually became a key figure.

4   For example, it is a nub of the complaint of Habermas, who builds his system on conventional notions of intersubjectivity, against most of the poststructuralists, who in their concern with self, being, and presence, tie into the modernist avant-garde legacy of posing issues of simultaneity against realist visions of society and culture.

5   Some of the recent forays into culture theory within the (post)modernist trend of critique might be promising. For example, it would be an interesting exercise to rethink the PD paradigm in terms of Mick Taussig's mimesis/alterity perspective derived from Walter Benjamin; alterity/otherness is a vital concept missing from the PD paradigm, necessary if one wants to follow it into the real life of nuclear diplomacy; and Taussig's/Benjamin's notion of the mimetic is suggestive of how involvements and relationships with others through conditions of simultaneity might be materialized for study.

REFERENCES

Bauman, Zygmunt 1991: *Modernity and Ambivalence.* Cambridge: Polity Press.

Beck, Ulrich 1992: *The Risk Society: Towards Another Modernity.* London: Sage.

Beck, Ulrich, Giddens, Anthony, and Lash, Scott 1994: *Reflexive Modernization: Politics, Tradition and Aesthetics in the Modern Social Order.* Stanford: Stanford University Press.

Beschloss, Michael R. and Talbott, Strobe 1993: *At the Highest Levels: The Inside Story of the End of the Cold War.* Boston: Little Brown.

Bourdieu, Pierre 1984: *Distinction.* Cambridge, MA: Harvard University Press.

—— 1990: The Scholastic Point of View. *Cultural Anthropology,* 5 (4), 380–91.

de Certeau, Michel 1984: *The Practice of Everyday Life.* Berkeley: University of California Press.

Clifford, James 1988: Power and Dialogue in Ethnography: Marcel Griaule's Initiation. In *The Predicament of Culture,* Cambridge, MA: Harvard University Press.

Clifford, James and Marcus, George E. (eds) 1986: *Writing Culture: The Poetics and Politics of Ethnography.* Berkeley: University of California Press.

Fukuyama, Frances 1991: *The End of History and the Last Man.* New York: Vintage Books.

Geertz, Clifford 1988: *Works and Lives: The Anthropologist as Author.* Stanford: Stanford University Press.

Halberstam, David 1994: The Decline and Fall of the Eastern Empire. *Vanity Fair,* October, 246–64.

Harding, Sandra 1995: Can Feminist Thought Make Economics More Objective? *Feminist Economics,* 1 (1), 7–32.

Harvey, David 1989: *The Condition of Postmodernity*. Oxford: Basil Blackwell.

Heims, Steve Joshua 1993: *Constructing a Social Science for Postwar America: The Cybernetics Group, 1946–1953*. Cambridge, MA: MIT Press.

Kissinger, Henry 1994: *Diplomacy*. New York: Simon and Schuster.

Lash, Scott 1993: Reflexive Modernization: The Aesthetic Dimension. *Theory, Culture & Society*, 10, 1–23.

McCloskey, Donald 1995: Comment. *Feminist Economics*, 1 (2).

Marcus, George E. 1992: Review of Writing Worlds: Discourse, Text and Metaphor in the Representation of Landscape, edited by T. J. Barnes and J. S. Duncan. *Society & Space*, 10 (3), 361–3.

—— 1995: Ethnography In/Of the World System: The Emergence of Multi-sited Ethnography. *Annual Review of Anthropology*, 24, 95–117.

—— (ed.) n.d.: *Critical Anthropology in Fin-de-Siecle America: New Locations, Non-standard Fieldwork*. Santa Fe: School of American Research Press.

Marcus, George E. and Cushman, Dick 1982: Ethnographies as Texts. *Annual Review of Anthropology*, 11, 25–69. Stanford: Annual Review Press.

Marcus, George E. and Fischer, Michael M. J. 1986: *Anthropology as Cultural Critique: An Experimental Moment in the Human Sciences*. Chicago: University of Chicago Press.

Piore, Michael and Sabel, Charles 1984: *The Second Industrial Divide*. New York: Basic Books.

Poundstone, William 1992: *Prisoner's Dilemma: John von Neumann, Game Theory, and the Puzzle of the Bomb*. New York: Doubleday.

Schultz, George P. 1993: *Turmoil and Triumph: My Years as Secretary of State*. New York: Scribners.

Strassman, Diana 1995: Editorial: Creating a Form for Feminist Economic Inquiry. *Feminist Economics*, 1 (1), 1–6.

Talbott, Strobe 1988: *The Master of the Game: Paul Nitze and the Nuclear Peace*. New York: Knopf.

Taussig, Michael 1992: *Mimesis and Alterity*. New York: Routledge.

Von Neumann, John and Morgenstern, Oscar 1944: *The Theory of Games and Economic Behavior*. Princeton: Princeton University Press.

15

The Men We Left Behind Us: Narratives Around and About Feminism from White, Leftwing, Academic Men

JUDITH NEWTON AND JUDITH STACEY

> And maybe if you're a man of a generation younger than mine, you can be a feminist. But if you're a heterosexual white male of the generation that went through the beginnings of the feminist move- ment, with some sympathetic but complicated and vexed relationship to feminism and to women who were becoming feminist, it's very hard to feel, to declare oneself, myself, a feminist. I cringe at the thought of it. You become hypersensitized to all of the contradictions and the possibly self-serving motivations of arrogating such a title to myself.
>   (*Forty-something Academic Man, September 1992*)

Times They Are a Changing, or How We Came to Write on Men

In the fall of 1991 we began to conduct oral histories and field work among leftist, academic men, men who, like ourselves, had been engaged in 1960s politics and had transferred some of that political commitment into academic careers. Our goal was to understand how male peers might narrate the stories of their intellectual and political journeys over the last 30 years, and most particularly, how they would construct their relation to gender and race politics. In the course of eliciting their narratives we found it necessary to construct and analyze our own and to reflect upon how we came to write on white, leftwing, academic men, the men we did and did not leave behind. What follows is one version of that story.

When Bob Dylan's "Times, They are a Changin'" first hit the airwaves around 1963 – to become an unofficial anthem of the decade – the authors of this essay, then students, were barely launched on their involvement in the political and cultural movements of that era. 1963 was the beginning for us, as for many feminists, of three decades of political engagement, starting with civil rights, continuing in the student and anti-war movements, and reaching an emotional culmination in the revolutionary feminisms of the early 1970s.

1963, of course, takes us back to a time in which our politics appeared to have nothing whatsoever to do with our gendered identities. We were beginning to see ourselves as part of a community of those who took the "right" (that is, the left) side. As white girls raised in racially mixed, but unintegrated, communities, we assumed the inevitability of male leadership and too readily conjured blacks as our racial others – at once unknown, the objects of our somewhat patronizing empathies, and of our secret, often eroticized, cross-race identifications.

Ten years later our sense of political community had undergone profound change, for the draft and the Vietnam war had officially ended, black nationalism had displaced the integrationist framework of the civil rights movement, and a dynamic, grassroots movement for women's liberation was spreading "all over this land." *Sisterhood is Powerful*, one of the most influential anthologies of the period, captured the spirit of the times, as for many white feminists, ourselves included, a militant sisterhood rapidly displaced the passionate "brotherhoods" of the 1960s.[1]

The 1970s also marked our entry, and the entry of many second-wave feminists, into the academy and the merging of our politics with our careers. White, male-authored accounts of this period often characterize the 1970s as a time of political withdrawal and decline and, for academic men, a time of retreat into the politics of theory.[2] But for us and many feminists, entry into the academy, far from signalling a retreat from politics, represented an extension of the battle, because feminist politics at that time often worked against a smooth trajectory to success.[3]

Throughout the 1970s, both authors enthusiastically participated in the creation of academic feminist communities which collectively produced women's studies programs, feminist curricula, women's caucuses within the disciplines, feminist journals, conferences, and the first streams of feminist scholarly publication, which ultimately led to the deluge of literature in which we currently attempt to keep afloat. As ardent members of early consciousness-raising groups, as participants in reading groups and conferences, as editors of feminist journals like *Feminist Studies* (where we first met), as members of women's caucuses, as often-embattled faculty in our universities, we moved primarily in an intellectual and political world of feminist women. We remember the years between 1970 and the mid-1980s primarily as a time of passionate alliance with sisters, rather than one of radical devotion to a "band of brothers standing in a circle of love" (Gitlin, 1987: 106).

At the same time, of course, "sisterhood" was scarcely an untroubled concept, and as a practice it was often fraught. For if the early 1970s were characterized by the forging of feminist communities, they also were marked by fractious splits between lesbians and heterosexuals, as well as between liberal, radical, and socialist feminists, and by the proliferation of lifestyle litmus tests for true sisterliness and authentic "woman-identified" politics.[4] By the end of the 1970s the concept "woman" itself had become an embattled term. The outpouring of literature and scholarship by feminists of color in the 1970s and early 1980s had successfully exposed the ethnocentricism of white feminist pretensions to universal sisterhood.

Meanwhile, rightwing women like Phyllis Schafley, who played substantial roles in the defeat of the ERA, were putting feminists on far less sisterly notice that we did not speak for them. The rise of an explicitly antifeminist, antigay New Right during the late 1970s and early 1980s did at least as much as intrafeminist conflicts to disabuse us of our earlier utopian illusions. By then, too, political and economic winds "outside" the academy had begun to blow in increasingly unfavorable directions. The oil crisis of 1973 marked the onset of an enduring downward turn in real income for working people in the US. Abetted by the political cynicism that had been bred by Watergate at home and by the increasingly visible crises of dictatorial, socialist societies abroad, these chastening developments set the stage for tax revolts and social backlash movements that propelled the Reagan counter-revolution of 1980.

During the same years, a "theory revolution" that would later become identified with the debated category of "postmodernity" was gradually entering into and being produced from within feminist scholarship in the US. This provided another language for deconstructing the notion of unified sisterhood, and, indeed, of unified, internally coherent sisters. Less constructively, the increasingly professionalized and competitive academy fomented fractious feminist theory wars – often conducted in distinctly nonsisterly tones.[5] At the same time, finally, the theory revolution provided a basis on which some white feminists in particular might meet progressive men on newly common ground.

For although white academic men sometimes took up feminist challenges to a specifically masculine objectivity and authority in the more abstract and arguably more ego-enhancing forms of poststructuralist critique, the latter, nonetheless, often resonated with feminist analyses. Male colleagues with compatible theoretical orientations, indeed, began, at times, to appear more congenial and receptive, despite gender limitations in their work, than did feminist "sisters" identified with competing theoretical stances. By the end of the 1980s, it was clear that theoretical and political stakes in deconstruction, reflexivity, multiculturalism, cultural studies, queer studies, not to mention affirmative action and canon wars, did not divide neatly along gender lines.

Meanwhile, the long siege of the Reagan–Bush era wore on, producing in its wake a rightwing smear campaign against "political correctness" on our nation's campuses that twisted internal, self-criticism of ideological purity into backlash propaganda against all progressive intellectual and institutional reforms (Messer Davidow, 1993). By the early 1990s, both mainstream political parties were displacing the assault on political correctness with a campaign for "family values," whose demonology centered on "broken" (often black and lower-class) families and on the cultural legacy of 1960s and 1970s-style radicalism and the "misguided" welfare and gender equity policies these permissive values purportedly helped to generate.[6]

As the bleak dawn of this century's last decade appeared, the authors of this essay had come to view ideological purity as a youthful luxury which harsher times could not support. Broader coalitions had become a political necessity, and oversimplifying rhetorics of male/female struggle seemed decidedly inadequate to the political tasks at hand. Our distance from those rhetorics and early struggles, a distance at once curious and engaged, permitted us to make research subjects of our male academic peers.

Age, moreover, fuels a desire to gain historical perspective on ourselves. Feminists of our generation have been engaged, of late, by what seems a historical imperative to tell the story of our journeys through the second wave and to try to come to terms with what 30 years of collective struggle have, in fact, "meant."[7] To some degree, our desire to elicit unspoken histories of progressive academic men is a desire to know still more about ourselves and the history we have shared. (Indeed, we began this project on academic men by interviewing one another, which provides the basis for our historical narrative above.)

Our project, however, is not merely an expression of feminist narcissism once-removed, as one of us has joked. It is equally a product of a political humility born of the Reagan–Bush and the Clinton–Gingrich eras, and of the critique of white feminism by women of color over the last 20 years. It reflects our understanding that the meaning of any politics is partly shaped by the character of its reception, its impact not only upon institutions and ideologies, but also upon the minds and hearts of those with whom a movement has engaged. It is informed by our conviction that broader alliances demand a capacity for flexibility and compassion we have not always exhibited, and it expresses, finally, an "optimism of the will" born of the 1960s, that has never left us, a sense that the "times," whatever unanticipated horrors they seem to present, also offer space for further struggles and for dreams.

Notes from the field

1　When men and women are sitting on two sides of the room there's gender tension. Even though we're friends I'm worried about what you'll think of me. Nothing can take that worry away.
2　I had trepidations about the interview, about being distrusted and disapproved of . . . but it was important for me to do it. Feminists have been brave and generous. I wanted to do it back.

Conversations Among Others

Although we lightly refer to the subjects of our study as "the men we left behind us," and although there are historical and structural ways in which that jest rings true, our interest in this project centers on men who might also be constructed as our peers. The stories of such men, we feel, are the object of some historical curiosity, for few progressive white men, however voluble their published scholarship, have come forward with personal histories of their own.[8] This reticence may be a legacy of the role played by the category "white straight men," as generalized object of suspicion in recent histories by their many "others." Under the critical scrutiny of so many nonwhite, nonmale, non-Western eyes, it is not surprising that strategic silence, evasion and play, or defensive self-critique might characterize such autobiographical writing by white academic men as has surfaced. In an age when identity politics had valorized the story of oneself as victim or as resistor to oppression, in what voice, we wondered, would leftwing white men tell their stories?

Although our larger project elicits stories from men of diverse races, ages, ethnicities, and sexualities, as well as from women of multiple identities, this essay concentrates upon white, heterosexually identified, now middle-class, men between the ages of 45 and 55, those most like ourselves, the familiar often proving quite unfamiliar when looked upon afresh. Because we wished to focus upon men who seemed open to alliance politics across race and gender, our subject population consists largely of men self-identified with critical forms of cultural studies or allied with some of its central projects, such as the production of scholarship across disciplinary and cultural lines.[9] Between 1991 and 1994 we conducted oral histories with 27 white academic men between the ages of 45 and 55 whose published work is marked by some visible identification with the politics of leftwing cultural criticism.[10] Seventeen of the oral histories were in-depth and comprehensive, involving one or two sessions, of two to four hours each, often extending into shared meals and informal relating. At conferences and professional meetings, we also gathered shorter, more opportunistic interviews, typically one-hour long, with men from this same group.

To contextualize narratives elicited in formal interviews, we conducted field research in many of the conferences, meetings, seminars, and corridors in which our subjects and ourselves are prone to appear. Among our field sites have been meetings of the Modern Language Association, the American Anthropological Association, the American Sociological Association, the Society for the Study of Social Problems, the World Congress of Sociology, the American Studies Association, and the Marxist Literary Group, as well as conferences and meetings convened by Teachers for a Democratic Society and the Union of Democratic Intellectuals. Additionally, we have attended multiple conferences, seminars, and symposia in cultural studies and radical multiculturalism and on masculinities. Our ethnographic practice has often included presenting papers or commentary ourselves, but always we attended the most overtly relevant sessions, observed and engaged in the raced, gendered, and sexed dynamics and personal interactions, and generally hung out, pens and paper close at hand.

The remainder of this essay draws most directly on transcripts of the 17 comprehensive oral histories narrated by white men between the ages of 45 and 55, and we base all enumerations of their features on this "n" of 17. Eleven of these men teach on the West coast, all but one were US born, and nine are Jewish. Only two identify their family backgrounds as working class, while seven claim lower middle class, and eight professional, middle-class origins. All 17 men define themselves as heterosexual.[11] Their disciplinary credentials divide between literature (nine), history (three), anthropology (four), and political science (one), but six currently teach in interdisciplinary programs, and four of the shorter interviews, as well as a significant portion of the field work, involved sociologists. Eight currently work on journals which publish cultural criticism, including *Cultural Studies, Cultural Critique, Cultural Anthropology, Social Text, American Quarterly*, and *Representations*. Thirteen have incorporated feminist analysis in their published work, six of those since at least the early 1980s. (We consider the work of at least four to provide feminist critique as trenchant as that by feminist women.)

Sharing with our subjects a view of knowledge as partial, situated, and a site of power, we do not regard the narratives our interviews elicited as empirical records of the ways in which the men actually lived their intellectual, political, and personal lives. We regard these, rather, as stories conceived from within specific historical positions and discourses, and narrated within the complicated web of social, emotional, and power relations of specific interview situations.

We have written elsewhere of the contradictory dynamics entailed in interviews conducted by "us," as embodiments of institutionalized feminism, of "them" – remarkably successful academic men (Newton and Stacey, 1995). We have discussed the ways in which heterosexual dating codes and our unconscious immersion in white feminist discourses about "the enemy" and about the suspect character of heterosexual desire,[12] initially predisposed us to guilty apology for consorting with this other, and impeded us from giving public voice to feelings of collegiality, friendship, and alliance-building in which we were also engaged. Having uncomfortably encountered some of the limitations in our scrutiny of these male "others," we offer this reading of their stories with less rectitude and more humility than when we began.

Notes from the field

1   In January 1992, a Judy recalls her first C-R meeting: "The first meeting, it was like the scales fell off my eyes. I went thinking, gee, what's wrong with me? There's something really wrong with me, I feel so terrible about myself, my terrible insecurities. I don't remember what we discussed, except that they were all feeling the same thing. And I don't even remember how the feminist discourse entered the room. It must have been in some of these women somehow. But by the time I left, I was a feminist. I suddenly saw the world complete. It was like another conversion experience. I saw the world completely differently. Everything I had put down to a kind of personal failing seemed far more complicated. That was it. I was in another movement. It was another narrative."

2   From an exploratory interview, 1991:

> *Judy:* What impact did feminism first have on you?
> *Ted:*   Ahh, I don't think I like your word.
> *Judy:* You don't like my word?
> *Ted:*   "Impact" doesn't get at the experience.
> *Judy:* What would get at the experience?
> *Ted:*   Something more, ahh, something more like . . . being annoyed.

Feminist Interruptus

The illuminating exchange quoted immediately above occurred during an exploratory conversation one of us had with a friendly male colleague when we were first formulating our project. His attempt to be honest and helpful, also refreshingly direct, was an early indication that the dramatic nature of our own narratives about first encounters with feminism would not be mirrored in the histories of our male comrades. While we had few illusions that men would echo feminist hymns of revolutionary awakening, we had imagined that a few might recall some sense of excitement and liberation, and that most would report the "impact," threat, hostility, resistance, or conscious defensiveness which we had taken for granted they had experienced.

One of the men did vividly remember reading Pat Mainardi's "The Politics of Housework" in the early 1970s and feeling that (1) it was one of the best pieces of political writing he had read and (2) "I am in shit. My life is going to change, and I am going to hate it." Far more commonly, however, early memories of feminism were muted at best:

I can't remember when feminism had a name. . . . I have no memories of its meaning anything to me until the late 70s.

I don't remember going through a strong set of reactions to . . . Somehow, I think I assimilated it. That may be a very naive perception, but I assimilated it somewhat. I don't have any kind of conscious reaction or sense of threat to it.

Feminism was a minimal kind of thing. . . . What I'm saying is that without anything coming to mind, I would have to think about it, and that tells you something.

Maybe it was around and I don't remember it. That would be interesting in itself. But I don't remember . . . I don't remember talking about – did we, and I not remember?

I was wondering about this whole question of how I could either get away with or justify to myself this kind of sense of, yes I know that this feminist sort of stuff is going on over there, yes I'm for it, feeling that it affected my way of dealing with women and so forth, but not really feeling impinged on. How could I do that? I'm not quite sure. So that's all I remember. It's a blank. An interesting blank.

The men who had been married to, or involved with, feminist women recalled far more, although most of their narratives still conveyed a sense of distance:

I don't remember what feminist issues might have arisen . . . that would prompt [her] to want to organize a woman's group.

[She] did a series on feminism, and I went, but it took a long time to take this in.[13]

Generally, the most detailed accounts of gender struggles came from the six men who continued to work in activist groups in the early 1970s. For example, one who worked on an underground newspaper in 1970 recalled efforts to structure in the rotation of women as chairs, and to require that women spoke first and had editorial bylines:

> By 70 it had to be done. I mean, there were people pointing out it should be, and if you didn't do it, there was no meeting and no unity. And if you did it you felt it was a necessary sphere to work at. You know, obviously there were a lot of things, for those of us who were male, that we didn't see at first. . . . And it was hard for us sometimes to see what they were talking about, the urgency that they were talking about on some of these things. . . . Sometimes you've got to be forced to bring those changes, and you have to structure things in so they'll be brought about.

The muted nature of most men's narratives about early encounters with feminism generally contrasted sharply with their narratives about the civil rights and antiwar movements. Like ourselves, they could vividly construct their first awareness of race struggles in the 1960s. Fourteen portrayed civil rights as the beginning of their political engagement, just as we did. As one of our Jewish subjects put it, civil rights "was the main source of both my beginning of an adult understanding of what forces were in play in America and again articulated at a level that connected to my life in a direct way."[14] A movement characterized by dramatic encounters and mass demonstrations and situated within the context of a long legacy of national shame and organized protest, the civil rights movement initially offered white men and women alike a historically legitimated subject position for cross-racial activism. These 14 men recorded participation in the civil rights struggle, ranging from attending demonstrations, registering voters, organizing community protests, to working with CORE or SNNC. Two of these reported participating in freedom rides or working in the South as well. Five moved from an identification with civil rights to a modest cathexis to black nationalism, even though after 1967 whites were not particularly welcomed in nationalist circles.

Unsurprisingly, cathexis to black nationalism did not foreshadow similar emotional ties to feminism, another movement from which white men were initially excluded. Five of the 14 men acknowledged that feminism was too close to home: "Civil rights didn't challenge whites in the same ways; it wasn't in bed for the most part." White men could deal with black hostility by "feeling they deserved it," by evading direct engagement with it, or by vicarious identification. In the words of one subject:

> Yeah, the interesting thing is the civil rights movement, which is also not about me, I'm all involved in. But the women's movement which is, I'm not.

I mean it's interesting, white men's relation to black men, and women, but especially men I think . . . the whole white fascination with, fantasies about, black people, which includes a lot of support, but also a lot of vicarious identification and domination. . . . Justice for black people, that was far enough away that it wasn't threatening in this period. Although I was generally a Panther supporter, you know, there's a whole romance that's further away from home than the question of feminism for men. So I think it's more, it's easier for white men to be better on civil rights and the race question than on, it costs them less, than it does on the woman question.

White race privilege, therefore, appears to have allowed white men, as it allowed us too, to passionately support race struggles and to feel both guilt and responsibility, while remaining generally secure in the feeling that neither public nor personal power was much at risk.

As might be expected, the political activism which our subjects narrated most vividly concerned the antiwar movement.[15] The antiwar movement was the closest that young, white, radical men could come to a politics of interest or identity, in that *they* were potential and actual victims of the draft, of the longstanding imperialist relations which Vietnam represented, and of a ruling-class masculinity which they regarded as evil. One subject described his gradual withdrawal from activism once he had been declared 4-F: "Then, when I was off the hook, a certain kind of politics that would have seriously pulled me away from my studies waned. I became an academic politician at that point. So I would say in all honesty that my radical moment in the GI movement reflected my own exposed position and a radicalization around that time."

Five men portrayed the antiwar movement as the high point of their political past: "thrilling and scary," it was a "high adventure," a "revolutionary moment" that justified "sacrifice," a time that exposed them to "danger," changed their and other people's lives, and involved them in struggle with the "evil" and "horror" of the war. These descriptions often evoked for us the genre of action–adventure drama, or revolutionary autobiography, in which the narrators had been cast in heroic, leading roles. A tie between masculine mythologies and the war was also suggested in fond, if ironic, memories of revolutionary fervor. One subject recalls sleeping under a poster of Malcolm X. Another remembers taking Ph.D. orals at an ivy university dressed in a work shirt and red arm band. For some, however, a sense of failure attended this link. One man felt his decision not to renounce citizenship was a "lost moment"; another who had a medical deferment linked this to his "vulnerability in terms of manhood."

Feminism, in contrast, did not offer many opportunities for a man "to put your body on the line," as one subject put it. The absence both of a personal sense of interest and of an opportunity for heroic engagement dampens the dramatic tension in most men's narratives of feminist engagement. Indeed, the tales of antiwar activism that our interviews elicited were marked by such clarity of detail and ease of recall that they suggested the rehearsed quality of stories long familiar to the storytellers (much like our own less heroic stories of civil rights and the antiwar movement.) Antiwar stories, that is, seemed to belong to the realm of official autobiography. Men spontaneously produced these stories when asked to relate their intellectual and political trajectories. Their narratives of their first encounters with feminism, however, often marked a shift in style.

Our processed narratives, like those of many second-wave feminists, convey a sense of historical continuity – first civil rights, then the student and antiwar movements, culminating in feminist revolution. Indeed, they assume the shape of a feminist *Bildungsroman* in which feminist awakening gives narrative resolution to a life journey. In sharp contrast, the topic of first encounters with feminism generally marked an interruption in the narrative flow for men. The tales of antiwar activism that our interviews elicited were marked by such clarity of detail and ease of recall that they seemed to belong to the realm of official autobiography, spontaneously produced upon cue. When it came to feminism, however, we found it necessary, in 11 of the 17 oral histories, to introduce the topic ourselves. "We're in the seventies now. Could you tell us about your first encounters with feminist politics?" Typically, awkward silences ensued as men struggled to recall their earliest memories, and what their thoughts, and especially their feelings, had been. Most men then shifted into a kind of "feminist interruptus" style as they attempted, sometimes with prompting and sometimes without, to integrate feminism into the narratives of their work and lives.

Just as the men's stories challenged and recast our own self-congratulatory, feminist narrative, with its presumption of dramatic impact and threat, similarly, our interventions provided male peers an opportunity to reconstruct the official stories of their lives. "It's interesting to be made to rethink some of those periods around these issues," one reported, while two others volunteered that "this is like therapy." Another, who readily offered to subject himself to our feminist inquisition, warned us that "you risk drawing to you all the sympathy-with-a-gentle-whipping seekers on the male left," because, like him, they might view our project as an opportunity to indulge "in a childish quest for even very partial approval from feminists."

A halting discourse also marked men's discussion of domestic histories. Only 6 of the 17 spontaneously incorporated mention of marriages and intimate relationships into official narratives of their intellectual and political history. The 11 others did not spontaneously include personal life as integral to the trajectories we had asked them to recount. Narratives produced by feminists, like ourselves, in contrast, typically braid discussions of sexuality, lovers, husbands, and children into the most visible fabric of our politics and work.[16]

Through direct questioning, we learned that only four of the men were initially married to, or coupled with, women whose career status had been as established as their own. Only three men sacrificed a career move to accommodate a feminist mate, while 14 were in relationships with women who moved or stayed with them in institutions where the woman's status was secondary. Indeed, one of the more deflating discoveries of our interviews was realizing that the success of even some of the men most visibly committed to feminism depended partly on the personal dominance or autonomy they enjoyed in making decisions about careers. That the significance of this privilege was rarely apparent to the men was another indication that they regarded intimate relations as distinct from their political and intellectual stories. (It was visible to us, perhaps, because we had each accommodated male priorities in our own career decisions.) As one of us recorded in an early set of fieldnotes:

> It seems striking to me how little feminism seems to have cost [them], how little personal sacrifice or transformation women seem to have expected from them. . . . The majority seem to have had women/wives following them in lesser and even negative career situations, and this seems true for even the most feminist men, and even those mated to powerful intellectuals. . . . Of course some of this is skewed by the character of the sample we choose, i.e. very prominent accomplished types. Almost by definition most of the men who were most transformed by feminism sacrificed and/or subordinated career ambitions to their politics and/or personal lives in ways that would have inhibited their achieving the level of achievement and celebrity of the ones we've been interviewing.

It is not surprising that the personal and the domestic often surfaced as interruptions of our subjects' narratives and that feminism did as well, for feminism was initially linked to critique of the personal, the domestic, and the everyday – spheres which, historically, have hardly ever been defined as an important part of the story of elite men's work or even lives. Seventies feminisms also offered a political practice which relied upon a mode of organization – intimate, emotionally revealing, consciousness-raising groups – that was decidedly incompatible with conventional cultures of masculinity. The marginal place of feminist personal politics in the men's narratives was in keeping with the traditions of masculine life stories in which work is the central focus and is linked with achievement in the public sphere.

Two men, for example, recalled feeling support for women's equality in the early 1970s because it was consistent with the enlightenment politics of equality that had initiated their participation in civil rights, but they found feminist critique of daily behaviors hard to take, or hard even to see as "politics." One claimed that from his first encounter with feminism in the late 1960s he agree that women should have the same rights as men, that he defended the women's movement, gave support to women colleagues and opposed stereotypes, but he had difficulty seeing himself as "an oppressive male," finding it particularly difficult to adjust his speaking style or to self-consciously make room for women to speak in meetings. Another reported that

> the political stuff always, the things that were positions, things that could be remedied by public policy in some way, always made sense to me; they weren't a problem. The more difficult things were the politics of everyday life. The assumptions of what is erotic, the assumptions of what's humorous. . . . We were very influenced then by . . . Pat Mainardi's article on "Politics of Housework." But that fit perfectly with what we thought of as socialism, and in a certain way that critique was easier to take than questions of, what kind of joking do you do.

Now, with belated appreciation, he defined this critique as the difference between feminism and other politics. In the words of another, "no other theory forces you to look at daily life. Marxism could do this, but doesn't." Past forms of liberation, he continued, were "articulated in sexism."

When the antiwar movement declined in the early 1970s, most of our male peers were, like ourselves, already at work in academic jobs. In the 1970s, however, as we have suggested, an academic career could seem political in itself for most female feminists, because the academy was a distinct site of political struggle. For our male peers, however, entry into faculty status frequently signalled a break with political activism, even if it was accompanied by a translation of political concerns into their scholarship.[17] As one subject phrased it:

> I realize that my story may be part of what I think is, you can tell me, a somewhat common story, of men involved in the '60s anti-war movement, but who then when that ends would go into some sort of more abstract political space and are not immediately involved in what's happening, the sort of political stands that spin out of that, feminism, and black power, or various other ethnic movements. You know about, you read about, you have opinions about it, but you're not, it's not engaging you.

Thus, if feminism seemed to decenter radical white men from the heroic roles some had played in the antiwar movement, it also emerged at a moment when many were ready to relinquish that role for traditional career-building activities, activities in which public performances were to yield considerably more privilege and power.

Notes from the field

HIM: I think that as a graduate student and an assistant professor
         I was very much focused on my career. And even though
         increasingly, certainly as an assistant professor, I became
         personally interested in feminist issues and feminist theory,
         that doesn't necessarily translate immediately into my prac-
         tices, domestic environment.

J: So the Intellectual stuff actually came first.

HIM: Yeah, I think it did. It's hard for me to reconstruct now, but
         I think that it was a combination of an intellectual interest and
         I think a very powerful desire to be approved of by women
         whom I liked and respected.

Feminism, In Theory

Although several of the men we studied had not yet incorporated feminist analyses into their published work, nearly all the men volunteered
celebratory appraisals of feminism as an intellectual force, such as the
following:

> The only thing in my generation to have had this identity and strength as
> a kind of intellectual movement has been feminism. . . . It's feminism in my
> generation. There's nothing comparable to it. Poststructuralism, all this stuff
> in American cultural studies, forget it. It's feminism.

The institutionalization of feminist scholarship, its entry into the world of
work, the "public" sphere, seems to be where feminism has achieved its
greatest "impact" on our male peers. By their own assessments, however,
most men engaged with feminist scholarship in their teaching earlier than
in their writing. Even men who described their work as still focused on
"dead white males" reported that they had been teaching gender and
domestic race issues for many years. Their course syllabuses and descriptions, moreover, tend to tell the same story. Several men explained this
division between classroom and publication by acknowledging that the
classroom seemed a less public space, a sphere in which they retained
relative authority and felt free, as well as challenged, often by feminist
graduate students, to take more risks. Indeed, several subjects directly
credited women graduate students with getting gender and race to the
seminar table.

Published work, in contrast, the area of our subjects' lives most open
to public, particularly male, scrutiny and most crucial to career advance,

tended to be less (or last) informed by gender critique. Only 8 of the 17 men we interviewed at length had engaged in scholarly work on gender before the late 1980s. Dominant academic discourses in the 1970s, of course, hardly encouraged young scholars, female or male, to make feminist analysis an important feature of their work, while the tightening job market in academe generated cross-gender anxiety about building a career. The balance sheet, however, could look different to women than to men. Since publishing in respectable, established slots offered fewer secure rewards to women than it did to men, publishing feminist work in the 1970s could seem worth the risk. For men, in contrast, the rewards for publishing respectably and thus the risks of failing to do so might seem more substantial.

For many academic men, moreover, gender disloyalty, as opposed to race disloyalty or anti-imperialist and anticapitalist discourse, seemed to lack historical precedent. One man acknowledged, for example, that he had asked himself what had inhibited him from

> actually engaging in feminist analysis up until recently, very recently. One thing, and I don't think this is entirely a cop-out – although it has elements of it, is this: it seems to me that, in terms of discursive positions, there is a slot well established for being anti-white, or . . . anti-Western; there's long tradition. But to be anti-masculinist, the positions, they just don't come to mind. And in fact, in terms of a masculinist definition, that we are all prey to, being disloyal to manhood, construing it that way, leads into, either you're tagged as homosexual, or there are lots of slots for you that have negative valences. . . . It is just a lot easier again to be enthused about the black movement, or to be anti-colonial, or any of those, than to be a feminist man.

As feminist analysis became more respectable in the 1980s, men also worried that they might not do feminist analysis well enough and so would forfeit a sense of mastery which they, as now well-established male scholars, ought to maintain. Reflecting the keenly competitive, hierarchical realm of academic scholarship, the norms of which are still largely set by men,[18] some subjects recorded anxieties about "fucking up," of not being "expert," of "losing one's edge," if they attempted gender critique, while others expressed fear of not being seen as serious by other men, or of being perceived as "soft" on feminism. As one man succinctly put it, "writing is there to shoot."

Gender analysis, moreover, often retained an association with women's insights and perspectives:

> I'm very comfortable writing in an anti-anti-feminist voice, if that's what you mean, anti-chauvinist voice. That's easy to do. But I don't think I could

write – to write as a feminist, to me is a little bit like trying to write as a Native American, though I know that isn't quite right either. But I can't put it much more clearly than that, but it just feels like assuming a voice that I don't have a right to have.

This association of feminist analysis with a female voice, of course, was by no means solely a figment of masculine imaginaries. Almost every man we interviewed testified to the fear of offending women both by saying the wrong thing and by venturing into gender domains at all:

If I'm wrong, the person who's upset is across the table.

I'm afraid to talk about gender; that's where the PC policing is done.

Even those whose work does seriously engage gender analysis expressed considerable anxiety:

I feel more on the line when I foreground gender than when I write in any other voice. From direct and indirect experience, I feel scrutinized, held accountable by feminists. I worry about becoming a target of their hostility or ridicule.

These anxieties, moreover, are scarcely misplaced. Feminists have often criticized male scholars for encroaching on feminist terrain, only to criticize them more harshly for avoiding it, producing the "damned if you do and damned if you don't" conundrum. It should not be surprising that until recently, so few male scholars have made the effort. As one man confessed, "it's easier to be damned if you don't."

The Personal Becomes the Political

What *did* prompt some of our male peers to take feminism into that most protected arena of published scholarship? While the reasons given for this move are various, the narratives of the six men who had published a significant degree of feminist-inscribed work before the mid-1980s share several features. All claimed that feminist critique of the everyday and of personal relations had touched them in a highly personal and ultimately enriching way. Three had been husbands or lovers in the early 1970s to women who became feminists from early on, and their mates' early engagement with feminist politics and scholarship drew these men in. These three published feminist-inspired scholarship in the 1970s and claimed to have assumed profeminist responsibilities in their institutions – criticizing the "cheerful sexism" of their universities and supporting feminists on the job.

The three other men who engaged seriously with critical gender analysis before the mid-1980s, all Jewish, narrated a heightened sense of
marginality to the hegemonic masculine scripts which feminism inter-
rogated. One reports that he was a small kid and a "nerd" in high school.
Another that,

> my close friends have always been women. I'd rather play with girls than
> boys. I've always been very woman-identified from the time I was a little
> boy. . . . I was terrible at sports. I had no male bonding. . . . By the mid-70s
> it was clear that my close friends were women. . . . So, me, resist women?
> On the contrary, I *am* a woman, a woman with a penis.

Similarly, the third remembers feminism as,

> the first critique of gender roles that I had come across . . . and instead of
> taking that as an attack on me, I thought, boy, this was – all this stuff
> in terms of physical strength, or in my high school, if you had glasses and
> were Jewish or read books, the worst thing you could be called would be
> a fag. And . . . you're expected to go and date and you don't know what to
> do on the date or something . . . you're supposed to dance with people; it
> makes you uncomfortable, and you can't control your body and everything.
> So there's a whole very oppressive narrative about what that role was, that
> when that was critiqued that seemed good to me.

While these were not the only men we interviewed who distanced themselves from hegemonic masculinities, they were the ones who claimed the
most personal satisfaction from feminist critiques of masculine gender constraints. Early, meaningful exposure to critical gender analysis seemed to
enhance their self-esteem and/or provide them, through intimate relationships, with an entry into feminist analysis as something they could "get,"
partially, at least, "right."

Around 1988

Jane Gallop chooses "around 1981" to mark the establishment of feminist
literary criticism in the US academy (Gallop, 1992). If we were to choose
a time by which feminism had entered into most of our subjects' published
work, "around 1988" would be about right – the year in which George
Bush was elected, the year of the Willy Horton campaign, of Operation
Rescue blockades, and just before communism collapsed in eastern Europe and the anti-political correctness campaign erupted in the US. By
around 1988, 14 of the 17 men had begun regularly to cite feminists in

their published work, and 12 had published or begun work that incorporated gender critique into its conceptual framework.

We initially took this "lag," between the emergence of feminism in the late 1960s and 1988, to be further evidence of male recalcitrance, and some of our interviews did indeed suggest that predictable elements of fear, need, and anxiety had motivated men to resist. Two men were unusually explicit and self-analytic about this reluctance. One reflected on his own amnesia about first encounters with feminism: "But you know, you don't remember something, you figure there might be a reason for that, that there's a lot of anxiety there." A second, noting that feminism had decentered white males, observed: "The ego doesn't like this. The kid in us wants to be attended to. It's hard to become an adult".

In the end, however, recalcitrance and anxiety no longer seemed appropriate explanations for the delay. Indeed, we came to suspect that the question "why so late?" might be a misguided one. It may simply require more than a decade for an identity politics formulated by one subject group to fully "hail" those located in different subject positions, particularly those occupying positions that appear to be structurally antagonistic. Certainly, the work of many white feminists evinced a long silence on race, despite the efflorescence of writing by black women in the 1970s and the critiques of white feminists by feminists of color that had become highly visible by the early 1980s.[19] To some extent, then, the "lag" may not be surprising. Indeed, given feminist unfriendliness to male forays into feminist terrain, it may be less surprising that our male subjects took so long to incorporate a feminist intellectual agenda than that they did so at all.

By around 1988, at any rate, the very factors that allowed us to conceive this formerly unimaginable project had become evident to men as well. A good deal of the sting in relations between at least white academic feminists and progressive academic men had been soothed. The partially shared theory revolution, as we have suggested, provided some white feminist women and progressive men with a more compatible set of epistemological and political concerns than in the recent past. Academic feminisms had become less heatedly politicized, more established, and thus partly establishment, while the meanings of academic careers for feminist women had come more closely to resemble those of their male peers.[20] Now, we too were sitting on tenure and grant-review panels, rather than sitting-in to demand women's studies programs and women's centers.

Mainstream feminisms, moreover, had themselves been under fire for almost 20 years. Sexuality debates, race critiques, as well as "postmodern" critiques of unified categories and identities had initiated a restructuring of feminist identity politics into a desire for alliance across suspect categories and had opened many feminist minds to a greater appreciation of the limitations of our own deeply held "truths." Under these conditions, critical gender critique had become both less fraught and less fashionable for men to engage. "I think that the intellectual climate had moved so that to speak about people of color is much more charged," reflected one man who had begun to shift some of his attention from gender to race. "Whereas five years ago, for a man to speak about a woman was much more charged, and that's kind of shifted."

Finally, by the late 1980s, 10 of the 17 men were doing work situated within postcolonial discourse, which served not only as a continuation of the anti-imperialism of their antiwar days, but also as a less exposed site on which to examine some of the very issues which feminist and domestic antiracist scholarship had raised.[21] When we began this project we were inclined to see this work on colonization as a displaced, and therefore suspect, way of engaging feminist or domestic racial concerns, and in hindsight several subjects seemed to share this assessment of their motives. But *displaced* response, we came to realize, is not lack of response. It is, in fact, partial response, and, more to the point, perhaps, not the response that we were looking for! In the end our implicit assumption, that if men were not responding on our terms, they were not responding at all, began to seem as tied to infantile emotion as we had interpreted male displacement to be. Something of the "kid," we began to feel, had entered into feminist insistence that when male feminism did not appear in the forms that we were looking for, it was illusory and that men were perpetually underdeveloped beings who could never "get it right." The seeming lag in male response to feminism began to seem at least a partial product of our own insistence on a (nonpostmodern) "fit" between our own languages and terms and those of progressive male others.

Gender progress, however, is never simple or in a straight line. If, by the late 1980s, most of the men we interviewed had begun to assimilate a critical gender perspective into their scholarship, just about that time we had also begun to observe numerous calls, within critical cultural studies, for restoring analytical centrality to social class and political economy.[22] In part, this was a salutary reaction to the ways in which an identity politics focused on race, gender, and sexuality, and abetted by postmodernist rejections of metanarratives, had marginalized materialist theory and succumbed to the "dominant fiction" of the United States as a classless society. At the same time, however, prominent versions of this return to political economy simultaneously return gender and sexual analyses to positions of structural subordination, if not to invisibility.

For example, four of the five papers delivered at a session on "culture at large" held at an annual meeting of the American Anthropological Association appeared to deem gender too "small" or local a concern to deserve specific analytical attention, despite the fact that all four authors had previously published feminist work. Thus, one presenter who urged anthropologists to embrace the challenge of an "ethnography of trans-national capitalism," offered a theoretical rubric for doing so in which attention to international capital, labor, and technological transfers took precedence over the gender-blind category, "culture of everyday life." Thus, the voguish, albeit legitimate, return to political economy too frequently locates itself within what Julie Graham describes as a hegemonic narrative on the left, a narrative which posits capitalism as the auto-nomous (implicitly masculine) hero of a story in which, inevitably dominant, it subsumes everything, including the feminized realm of household labor and relations.[23]

In foregrounding the public, the masculine, and the political, and in sub-ordinating the private, the feminine, and the emotional, this capitalism-as-hero narrative replicates the most dominant tradition of masculine life histories, a tradition which continues to govern the official life histories and scholarship of most of the men we interviewed. This hegemonic nar-rative, moreover, maintains the invisibility of the very elements which often secure popular consent for the ideologies, the cultural phenomena, and the political agendas which critical cultural studies scholarship seeks to disrupt.

Bringing It Back Home

The narratives around and about feminism of the men we interviewed need to be read, finally, in relation to a broad series of changes in the lives of white, middle-class US men over the last 30 years. Current work on the "crisis" of white masculinity underscores the erosion of hegemonic, bread-winner masculinity through the combined effects of global economic restructuring, with its attendant loss of well-paid, unionized jobs and a fall in real income for even white, middle-class men, the massive entry of women into the paid labor force, rising divorce rates, and growing rates of households headed by single mothers. Shifting racial demographics and affirmative action, of course, are also widely constructed as further threats to white male privilege, particularly when received in the wake of the vigorous, if over-generalized, critiques of "white, middle-class men" that have been central to feminist, antiracist, and gay politics for three decades. By the late 1980s, and most consequentially during the 1992 and 1994 electoral seasons, media constructions of a "crisis" in white mascu-linity and of "the angry white male" had become ubiquitous "social facts."

Most of the men we interviewed, of course, are tenured, primary bread-winners in two-career households, relatively insulated from the economic insecurities which underpin the crisis in white masculinity, although they too have had to adjust to dramatic shifts in gender and domestic relations which few of them had initiated. During the years, however, in which the men we studied moved toward incorporating critical gender analysis into their published work, nonacademic, white, middle-class men were also taking gender on and indeed launching efforts to restructure masculinity. From the profeminist men's movements to the groups for men's and fathers' rights, to the mytho-poetic and the evangelical Christian men's movements and the current national obsession with fatherless families, white, middle-class men have demonstrated their increasing preoccupation with masculinity.[24] These more popular developments, we believe, have intersected with male academic writing, and have helped to make masculinity, and therefore gender, a fashionable topic (such as in the flourishing literature of men's studies), and to further erode the analytic separation of public and private.[25]

Of course, many attempts to link the public and the private, in current political discourse, strike us as illusory and worse. Conservatives and centrists alike, for example, now represent fatherless families as the source of nearly all our social woes and resanctify heterosexual marriage as the only basis for legitimate "family values," which they regard as the cure for social malaise.[26] But even twisted couplings such as these open further space for critical analysis, by making it more difficult and dangerous to sustain the analytic separation of public and private, a separation which has impeded many left academics from integrating gender critique into their work, and by challenging progressives to take on the family, masculinity, and gender relations in all the complexity of their relations to sexuality, race, and class and to social analysis and public policy debate.

We welcome evidence, therefore, gleaned from our field work and recent literature, that leftwing male academics increasingly regard gender critique as their legitimate and necessary scholarly terrain, and we believe that female feminists, while engaging in critical and supportive dialogue with progressive male peers, should encourage this move rather than disparage it. To achieve this more nuanced stance, however, we must be prepared to forego some of the intensity of our desire that men's analyses of gender, or their reinventions of masculinities, will be on the terms we might prescribe and we must own up to the ways in which we, too, have been "part of the problem."

Perhaps it is only now, after the ideological clarity and narrative coherence of our own feminist *Bildungsromans* have been decentered by the cross-pressures of antiracist critiques, feminist professionalization, and political backlash, that white feminists like ourselves may begin to perceive the ways in which we have colluded with an intellectual division of labor which reserved feminism and gender critique for women, while blaming men for failing to take on the tasks which we have often implied that they were incapable of doing. Certainly, "the times" and political conditions have been "a changin'," disturbingly enough to give progressive academics of diverse genders, races, sexualities, and aesthetics compelling cause to overcome disabling divisions. In the process of eliciting and reading the "feminist interruptus" narratives of our male peers, we have dared to indulge this dream.

NOTES

1 The slogan "sisterhood is powerful" was first employed in 1968, at the New York Radical Women's "Burial of Traditional Womanhood." Modeled on "Black power," which had become the rallying cry of SNCC two years before, it was precursor to "pink power," a short-lived slogan coined on the occasion of the Stonewall uprising in 1969. See Gitlin (1987) on the employment of the brotherhood term in 1960s politics.

2 See, for example, Eagleton (1983: 142–50).

3 One of us, for example, shelved her dissertation on men instead of publishing it as the requisite, tenure-advancing, first book and then resigned her position at an ivy university because of the elitism and sexism in her department. The other dropped out of one doctoral degree program at the "ABD" stage to begin another in a totally new discipline, department, and community because they were reputed to provide hospitable conditions in which to pursue her budding, passionate interests in feminist theory and social transformation. See Greene and Kahn (1993) for similar stories.

4 Indeed, one of us dubbed a July 1982 journal entry that she composed just after the ERA had suffered its humiliating defeat, "Sisterhood: The Goddess That Failed?" There she ruminated over "an increasing sense of alienation from feminist ideology and culture, my impatience with new dogma and issues. . . . My particular intolerance seems to center on the moralism of constant internal purification movements." See also Echols (1989: 281–6).

5 For one account of intrafeminist conflict see Gallop, Hirsch, and Miller (1990).

6 See Stacey (1994a, 1994b, 1996).

7 See, for example, Miller (1991), Greene and Kahn (1993), Goetting and Fenstermaker (1995), and Scott (1994).

8 Among the white, leftist, academic men who have engaged in personal writing are Lentricchia (1994), Ryan (1989), MacLean (1989).

9 On the objectives of leftist cultural studies, see Nelson (1991: 31–5).

10 We also interviewed younger and older men for perspective, although data from these interviews are not included in the following figures.

11 This is by design, because we have excluded interviews conducted with self-identified homosexual men from this "sample."

12   For a nuanced discussion of this phenomenon, see Segal (1994).

13   Interestingly, and not surprisingly, some of the most vivid personal memor-
     ies of early feminism had, pleasurably, to do with sex. One man recalls that
     his feminist girlfriend liked to be on top, a position with which he had "no
     problem." Another recalls images of women without bras, different attitudes
     about sex, women coming on to him.

14   Several Jewish men, in particular, claimed that sensitivity to their own exclu-
     sion forged emotional identification with the struggle of blacks.

15   Most were in danger of being drafted, a few were prepared to leave the
     country, a few to go to jail. Several burned their draft cards (one subject
     twice). Others resisted induction, engaged in draft counseling, or at the least
     attended sit-ins and demonstrations against the war.

16   Each of us has published work that integrates accounts of her personal and
     domestic life into the text. See, for example, Newton (1996, 1995, 1994) and
     Stacey (1990).

17   Of course, some men dropped out on political grounds, but our ethno-
     graphic "sample" includes only those for whom a break with direct political
     activism was acceptable.

18   See, for example, Becher (1989) for a discussion of pecking orders, gate-
     keepers, and great men.

19   See Hall (1992) for an account of this lag.

20   At the same time that backlash forces began to counter grassroots feminist
     and antiracist struggles in the US as a whole, feminist and ethnic studies
     scholarship were achieving increasing institutional and intellectual success in
     the academy. What had once been oppositional and subversive was becom-
     ing respectable and professionalized. Theory and politics could not seem so
     neatly interwoven, nor so transparent, now that it had become possible to
     pursue feminism and ethnic studies as professional and even fashionable
     careers.

21   We discuss this sort of displacement in the work of Stephen Greenblatt and
     James Clifford, for example, in Newton and Stacey (1992). White feminists
     also seem to write far more frequently of women in the "Third World" than
     of "third world women" far closer to home.

22   See, for example, Williams (1995), Berube and Nelson (1995), and Berman
     (1992).

23   What might, in an alternative framework, be seen as noncapitalist forms of
     economy, labor, and social relations – most pointedly those of the household
     – are reduced within this narrative to feminized others, are constructed as
     precapitalist perhaps, or are seen as vulnerable to the penetration of capital-
     ism and to an existence that consists, by and large, of reproducing its forms.
     Within this narrative, Graham argues, capitalism becomes abstract, unified by
     the commonality of its manifestations, while concrete conditions such as, for
     example, gender and race, become add-ons rather than constituting elements.
        It might also be argued that the figure of capitalism as hero or heroic
     villain offers a recognizably masculine and heroic role to the critic him (or
     at times her)self. For within this narrative, leftist cultural criticism can function

as a form of identity politics, too, a politics in which a beleaguered and marginalized hero (marginalized by capitalism and by profession) contends with the authentic enemy, the primary cause of exploitation and oppression. Emotional investments in this narrative, which are particularly strong perhaps in an era that valorizes the marginalized and beleaguered, go unanalyzed, however – in part because gender and race retain add-on status with regard to the economic in all its manifestations, and in part because masculine subject positions, in contrast to feminine ones, remain under-examined in relation to both work and life.

24 Some 1990s publications from mytho-poetic, Christian, and social conservative positions are Bly (1990), Blankenhorn (1995), and Weber (1993).
25 See, for example, Aronowitz (1995).
26 Stacey (1994a, 1994b).

REFERENCES

Aronowitz, Stanley 1995: My Masculinity. In Maurice Berger, Brian Wallis, and Simon Watson (eds), *Constructing Masculinity*, New York: Routledge.

Becher, Tony 1989: *Academic Tribes and Territories: Intellectual Enquiry and The Cultures of Disciplines*. Stony Stratford: Open University Press.

Berman, Paul (ed.) 1992: *Debating P.C.: The Controversy Over Political Corretness on College Campuses*. New York: Bantam.

Berube, Michael and Nelson, Cary (eds) 1995: *Higher Education Under Fire: Politics, Economics, and the Crisis of the Humanities*. New York: Routledge.

Blankenhorn, David 1995: *Fatherless America: Confronting our Most Urgent Social Problem*. New York: Basic Books.

Bly, Robert 1990: *Iron John: A Book About Men*. Reading, MA: Addison-Wesley.

Bordo, Susan 1990: Feminism, Postmodernism, and Gender-scepticism. In Linda J. Nicholson (ed.), *Feminism/Postmodernism*, New York: Routledge, 133–56.

Braidotti, Rosa 1987: Envy: or With Your Brains and My Looks. In Alice Jardine and Paul Smith (eds), *Men in Feminism*, New York: Methuen, 233–41.

De Lauretis, Theresa 1987: *Technologies of Gender: Essays on Theory, Film, and Fiction*. Bloomington: Indiana University Press.

Eagleton, Terry 1983: *Literary Theory*. Minneapolis: University of Minnestoa Press.

Echols, Alice 1989: *Daring To Be Bad: Radical Feminism in America 1967–1975*. Minneapolis, University of Minnesota Press.

Gallop, Jane 1992: *Around 1981: Academic Feminist Literary Theory*. New York: Routledge.

Gallop, Jane, Hirsch, Marianne, and Miller, Nancy K. 1990: Criticizing Feminist Criticism. In Marianne Hirsch and Evelyn Fox Keller (eds), *Conflicts in Feminism*, New York: Routledge, 349–69.

Gitlin, Todd 1987: *The Sixties: Years of Hope, Days of Rage*. New York: Bantam.

Goetting, Ann and Fenstermaker, Sarah (eds) 1995: *Individual Voices, Collective Visions: Fifty Years of Women in Sociology*. Philadelphia: Temple University Press.

Greene, Gayle and Kahn, Coppelia (eds) 1993: *Changing Subjects: The Makings of Feminist Literary Criticism*. New York: Routledge.

Hall, Catharine 1992: *White, Male, and Middle Class: Explorations in Feminism and History*. New York: Routledge.

Hull, Gloria T., Bell Scott, Patricia and Smith, Barbara (eds) 1982: *All the Women are White, All the Blacks are Men, But Some of Us Are Brave*. Old Westbury: Feminist Press.

Jardine, Alice and Smith, Paul (eds) 1987: *Men in Feminism*. New York: Methuen.

Lentricchia, Frank 1994: *The Edge of Night*. New York: Random House.

MacLean, Gerald 1989: Citing the Subject. In Linda Kauffman (ed.), *Gender and Theory: Dialogues on Feminist Criticism*, Oxford: Basil Blackwell.

Meadow, Orlans, Wallace, Kathryn P., and Wallace, Ruth A. (eds) 1994: *Gender and the Academic Experience: Berkeley Women Sociologists*. Lincoln: University of Nebraska Press.

Messer-Davidow, Ellen 1993: Manufacturing the Attack on Liberalized Higher Education. *Social Text*, 36, 40–80.

Miller, Nancy 1991: *Getting Personal: Feminist Occasions and Other Autobiographical Acts*. New York: Routledge.

Moraga, Cherrie and Anzaldua, Gloria (eds) 1981: *This Bridge Called My Back: Writings By Radical Women of Color*. New York: Kitchen Table: Women of Color Press.

Morgan, Robin (ed.) 1970: *Sisterhood is Powerful: An Anthology of Writings From the Women's Liberation Movement*. New York: Random House.

Nelson, Cary 1991: Always, Already Cultural Studies: Two Conferences and a Manifesto. *The Journal of the Midwest Modern Language Association*, 24, 24–8.

Newton, Judith 1994: *Starting Over: Feminism and the Politics of Cultural Critique*, Ann Arbor: University of Michigan Press.

—— 1995: Why Am I Always the Bad Guy? A Reverie on the Virtues of Confession. In Harold Veeser (ed.), *Confessions of the Critics*, New York: Routledge.

—— 1996: Growing Old – and Growing Up with the Women's Movement. In E. Ann Kaplan and Devoney Looser (eds), *Feminisms and Generations*, Ann Arbor: University of Minnesota Press.

Newton, Judith and Stacey, Judith 1992: Learning Not to Curse, or Feminist Predicaments in Cultural Criticism by Men: Our Movie Date with James Clifford and Stephen Greenblatt. *Cultural Criticism*, 23, 51–82.

—— 1995: Ms. Representations: Feminist Dilemmas in Studying Academic Men. In Ruth Behar and Deborah Gordon (eds), *Women Writing Culture/Culture Writing Women*, Berkeley: University of California Press, 287–305.

Ryan, Michael 1989: *Politics and Culture: Working Hypotheses for a Post-revolutionary Society*. Baltimore: Johns Hopkins Press.

Scott, Patricia Bell 1994: *Life Notes: Personal Writings by Contemporary Black Women*. New York: W.W. Norton.

Segal, Lynne 1994: *Straight Sex: Rethinking the Politics of Pleasure*. Berkeley: University of California Press.

Stacey, Judith 1990: *Brave New Families: Stories of Domestic Upheaval in Late Twentieth Century America*. New York: Basic Books.

—— 1994a: The New Family-values Crusaders. *The Nation*, July 25/Aug 1, 119–21.

—— 1994b: Scents, Scholars and Stigma: The Revisionist Campaign for Family Values. *Social Text*, 40, 51–75.

—— 1996: *In the Name of the Family: Rethinking Family Values in the Postmodern Age*. Boston: Beacon Press.

Weber, Stu 1993: *Tender Warrior: God's Intention for a Man*. Sisters, Oregon: Multnomah Books.

Williams, Jefferey (ed.) 1995: *PC Wars: Politics and Theory in the Academy*. New York: Routledge.

16

Reinventing Cultural Studies: Remembering for the Best Version

RICHARD JOHNSON

Introduction

In this essay I want to argue for a version of cultural studies – a "best" version if you will.[1] In this version, cultural studies is not an academic discipline, but is a critical process that works in the spaces between academic disciplines, and on the *relations* between the academy and other political sites. From this point of view, something like cultural studies needed to be invented. Neither literary criticism, nor sociology, nor any other academic discipline would do. I agree with Andrew Goodwin and Janet Woolf (chapter four, this volume) who argue for measures of "conservation," but I don't think that conservation is enough. I'd rather say that cultural studies should be recurrently reinvented or, to borrow Stuart Hall's term, "renewed" (Hall, 1996: 398). I am reminded of the importance of other reinventions/renewals today – of socialism for example.

In my own case, the process of reinvention has to be closely associated with the process of remembering. I taught for nearly 20 years in the Centre for Contemporary Cultural Studies (CCCS) at the University of Birmingham, an institution often credited with a founding role. This was my main cultural studies experience and I cannot but refer to it here.[2] I hope I am not read, however, as reproducing a conventional story of origins, especially not an idealization.[3] What interests me most about CCCS, now, is that I found the whole experience perpetually perplexing, often impossibly contradictory. Ultimately, it was impossible to live with. My "best version" of cultural studies is necessarily formed in relation to this experience: remembering, revaluing, and forgetting no doubt, in different modalities. Sometimes I mourn the loss and the waste of my own hard-won skills and experience, especially as a teacher. Sometimes I'm critical of the project or my own part in it. Sometimes I wish we had done more of what we started well, or wished to do but never accomplished.

Sometimes I operate retrospectively the kind of "mid-course correction" so familiar in my teaching, though I'm not teaching any more.[4] Above all, I do not wish to try to reproduce an "impossible" project in a retrospective and highly imaginary form.

What about sociology in this? I do not have a disciplinary identity as a sociologist, though I worked for eight years in a faculty of social science, teaching social and economic history to social science and humanities students. I have a long-term interest in social and cultural theory. I am fascinated by the way questions posed in cultural studies are also posed, in a different idiom, in debates among sociologists and anthropologists. And, yes, some of my closest colleagues and co-workers are sociologists! I am not much interested, however, in the defense of any particular discipline. We do have to attend to the politics of the academic disciplines, but, most of the time, disciplinary boundary-drawing and rivalry is a particularly self-defeating aspect of academic competition. Yet I do join contributors to this volume in arguing for a thoroughly "social" version of cultural studies, while agreeing with others that there are different ways of theorizing the social, not all recognizably "sociological" (Seidman, this volume). I also want to argue that what is called the "textual" is equally central to any cultural study and that we need ways to describe cultural forms if we are not to fall back into reductions. In the end, there is something phony about the social/textual distinction and some of the fears of "textualization" which follow.

My current perspective is influenced by my partial withdrawal from the academy and a slow search for other forms of political–intellectual activity. I know my interest in reviewing the Birmingham experience derives, in part, from a sense of loss. But it is shaped, too, by new experiences and possibilities. I am now employed, part-time, in a "new university" in Britain (that is, an ex-polytechnic), where many familiar elements of cultural studies have taken root, but where I encounter different "cultural approaches," not previously within my own interdisciplinary range. I am a reader in a center particularly committed to internationalization.[5] This leaves me time to write, but also to consider other networks. This essay is about remembering Birmingham, certainly, but is also part of a search for something different.

Qualifying the Academy

The first thesis in my "best version" is that cultural studies is not an academic discipline. Cultural studies has had to live in the academy, but has never been quite at home there. It is, or ought to be, "marginal" in several senses of this fashionable term.[6] Insofar as cultural studies is an academic movement, it is about *qualifying* the academy in certain ways.

I think this can stand as a historical statement about cultural studies at Birmingham, as well as a more general prescription – or provocation. It is especially important to stress this marginality at a time of more thorough institutionalization (c.f. the warnings in Hall, 1992: 285–6). Ambivalence has had many different sources: historical layer upon layer, indeed. It is as good a starting point as any for thoughts about "best practices," especially with the complications left in.

In what is often taken to be its "first" formation and in much of its "prehistory," cultural studies, as noted by Goodwin and Woolf (chapter four, this volume) derived not from the academy but from adult working-class education, with its particular class (and gender) relationships, its links to organized labor and the left, and its particular (dissident) involvement in questions of "Englishness."[7] This is an important memory for cultural studies, rooting a different, less exclusively academic account of "origins." Even after its incorporation in polytechnic and university programs, however, working-class affinities (in recruitment and scholars' backgrounds, thence in topics of research and orientations towards study) continued to challenge and to skew more orthodox academic relations. This remains the case in England, where national cultural formations and their histories still draw a particularly brutal divide between working people and academic intellectuals, but where policies of "access" are now considerably developed. Anyway, suspicion of academic knowledges, including an "academic" cultural studies, runs deep and wide, always complicating teaching and all forms of publication. Every teacher and every student has to negotiate this difference, sooner or later, whether they see themselves as working class or not.

In its "second," 1970s, formation, cultural studies took many features from the student movement. For many activists, including myself, cultural studies was a way of continuing, on a narrower and apparently more manageable front, the struggle to change the universities as a whole. Again, cultural studies had an awkward sideways relation to the academy, partly as a critique or as an alternative, but now from within. In CCCS there were many continuing '68-ish features which were deliberately reproduced, rather raggedly by the later 1980s, as a kind of internal tradition: especially the commitment to relatively democratic or "participatory" ways of working, to "collective work," and to a particularly thorough-going collaboration between students and teachers.

These aims were expressed most solidly in the way CCCS was organized. When I arrived in the Centre in the mid 1970s, distinctive features were already in place.[8] Administration was conducted through staff/student groups;[9] policy was made in a Centre General Meeting (CGM) to which administrative groups and intellectual groupings reported, all members attending and voting. There was a General Theory Seminar, which was soon subsumed into the new Master's program and the CGM. Most distinctively, perhaps, there were a number of "subgroups," small self-governing groups of researchers and teachers, focused around a particular topic or social agenda. In 1974, for example, there were groups on Art and Politics, Cultural History, Media, Subcultures, Women's Studies, and Cultures of Work, as well as two Marx Reading Groups.[10] Groups began and sometimes ended as reading groups following a program negotiated between members, in support of thesis or course work. They could also become research and writing groups. Most CCCS books and journals were produced by subgroups and the "collective book" – something more than the "edited collection" – remained typical of work from Birmingham circles right into the 1990s.[11]

One of the strengths of subgroups was their self-governing nature. They did not have to take on a dominant staff agenda. They did not have to have a staff member at all. Because members were not subject to university assessments, except eventually through a thesis, hierarchical arrangements and academic control could be minimized. Subgroups could include people who were not centre or university members. They could meet off campus and work to intensive rhythms. None of these features were uncontradictory, but the subgroup device was remarkably adaptable to a range of intellectual, political, and support functions. I have only recently completed work with a book-writing group on the CCCS model (Steinberg, Epstein, and Johnson, 1997) and still attend a reading group with strong Birmingham cultural studies connections.

In retrospect, it was the *combination* of subgroup autonomy and a centre-wide discourse that was so generative. There never was a single centre to the Centre; there were points of dialogue and summary and a struggle for hegemony in which staff and directoral positions were pivotal but not always decisive. The group system allowed new intellectual agendas to emerge and could be used to organize more politically, both within and outside.[12] At the same time, the centre-wide discourse helped produce a common language and terms of dialogue. From the beginning this level was harder to sustain than the tougher but dispersed pluralism of the subgroups. It condensed internal conflicts, tended to lose credibility among students (who *really* made decisions?) and, later, succumbed to the encroachments of university managerialism. In the 1970s and early 1980s, however, there were specific institutions that supported general dialogue: a regular weekly newsletter of events, the annual journal,[13] a centre report,[14] general meetings of different kinds, end-of-year "presentations" by subgroups,[15] discussions of "Priorities for the Year",[16] lengthy inductions for new people, and end-of-year reviews. Later, as the whole academic and political context changed, these practices became harder to maintain.

What is important to stress here, however, is that CCCS was never completely comfortable in the academy because it was (re)invented as a practical critique of academic paternalism, hierarchy, and individualism.

Yet what was critiqued could never be expelled, rendered wholly Other or outside. Rather, academic social relations had to be lived, sometimes by transforming them, but most often perhaps by producing them in forms that made the contradictions especially sharp and visible.

One result of these arrangements was to create an academic *milieu* that was unusually responsive to new student demands, both at the level of individual projects and in terms of social movements (I want to qualify this "responsiveness" later). Individual or group projects that did not obtain academic recognition elsewhere often found some in cultural studies. Many CCCS members had a critical and often painful relation to dominant academic knowledges, a pattern repeated in different ways for very different positionalities and politics. Because of its academic location, and increasingly because of its academic success, CCCS wasn't immune from the suspicion of complicity with mainstream academic beliefs and practices. On the contrary, it was often seen, from inside and especially outside, as super-academic or at least super-intellectual, producing work that was seen as characteristically "difficult," sometimes "theoreticist." Yet, paradoxically, many forms of marginality entered "the Centre"; many forms of critique of the academy were uncomfortably housed there. Teachers had to manage (as in "he only just managed to") the inevitable tensions between an often justifiably obstreperous student body and the official university hierarchies and rules.

The marginalities of class, gender, sexuality, race, and nation have been central to cultural studies' successive reinventions. Academic institutions are exclusive and oppressive because they have institutionalized the agenda and preferences of particular social groups and have given them the force of universal or general knowledges and practices. They have privileged the public world and public knowledges over the private and domestic, for example. They have marginalized central experiences like mothering, caring, and domestic work which have usually been performed by women. Academic knowledges, including canons of literature and of theory, have been thoroughly white and Euro- or (in Britain) Anglo- or Anglo-American-centered. In Britain, in most institutions, black British students (including British students of South Asian heritage) are still a small minority. Most institutions, despite increases in a "mature student" intake, are also dominated by middle-class studentdom and by teachers who are middle class by occupational definition if not by self-identification. All this means that it is extra hard work, against the grain, to arrive, survive, and flourish in a British university if you are a woman, and/or of working-class heritage, and/or black. Academic discrimination requires no more than that the relevant differences are overlooked and that existing "general" rules are applied with an "impartiality" which, in context, is brutal. This kind of liberal or "unconscious" discrimination is often accompanied, of course, by more active and nastier kinds, especially when the "margins" make demands on the "centers."

Cultural Studies and "the Popular": An Imaginary Relation?

In CCCS, a distance from the academy was often linked with an affinity for other forms of knowledge and culture, especially with popular or "commonsense" forms. This issue of "the popular" or of "cultural populism" has been much discussed within and around cultural studies, whether the issue has taken political shape – the construction of and alignment with versions of popular identity or political interests – or found a more cultural register – a kind of fanship, perhaps, or perhaps a commitment to recover and develop what Gramsci called "the good sense" in "common sense" (Gramsci, 1971: 328).[17] In such dialogues, the popular has taken many different forms: "working-class culture," youth subcultures, "women's genres" and conventional femininities (sometimes defended against feminism), elements of black consciousness or of popular ethnic hybridity or syncretism, gay or lesbian identities or popular performances of "queer." I do not want to explore in full here the different discourses, personal ambivalences, more or less imaginary resolutions, and political traps and openings that constitute the field of "the popular" for cultural studies practitioners. At CCCS, discourses of the popular, particular forms of popular commercial culture and versions of the everyday life of particular social groups were sites where cultural studies persons themselves, over and again, worked out their own cultural identifications and political affiliations.

In the context of a critical cultural studies, these popular identifications could never be straightforward. On one hand, the visibility of popular forms within cultural studies, especially when associated with otherwise hidden spheres and marginalized groups, reinforced the distance from the usual (high-) cultural evaluations in the academy. On the other hand, the fact that these forms were the object of critical evaluations, in an academic context, meant that a wholehearted or fully "populist" identification with extra-academic groups was often difficult and always troubled (cf. McGuigan, 1992). Often, CCCS was positioned, from outside, as distinctly antipopular, apolitical, and intellectually elitist.[18] In my view, a key problem was the absence of political contexts – parties or movements – that would link academic radicals and popular experiences and develop what Gramsci called a "popular," "collective," or "national-popular collective will" (cf. Gramsci, 1971: 125–33). Latterly, the erosion of nonvocational forms of adult education – cultural studies' first popular formation – has been very important, though many cultural studies students continue to teach on

Open University courses and other adult education programs. Without conditions like these, the dream, the aspiration, among cultural studies intellectuals to be "organic" to the experience and everyday needs of popular groups was always to some degree unrequited (cf. Hall, 1992: 287–9; 1995: 670–1). At the same time, involvement in the dilemmas around the academic and the popular has often produced forms of splitting, projection, and negotiations between different selves which I have come to see as characteristic of the cultural studies teachers and students, including myself.

Perhaps the least invidious way of illustrating this is to take myself as an example, though this is a very particular, and perhaps extreme, case. Positioned on the "dominant" side in almost all of the key conflicts of the 1970s and 1980s, I found my own outlooks repeatedly transformed by attempting to ally with others more marginal in the academy, as students and in other ways, than myself. I rebelled in the late 1950s from my own commercial middle-class background through a sentimental affiliation to working-class culture and history. This was an affiliation later caught up and developed by assuming the identity of a "social" or "Marxist" historian. I was active in the movement for university reform, but as a young teacher, not as a student. I encountered feminism as a man, and black politics and black feminism in particular as a white Englishman, who was only quite recently conscious of the personal politics of nationality and hardly at all of being white. Later, I met lesbian, gay, and queer critiques of heterosexuality just at the time when Jill, my partner since the early 1960s, died suddenly in 1992.[19] During much of this period I was also a more or less (often less) active member of the Labour Party, and until quite late in the 1980s, in the absence of an alternative of a New Left kind, still saw Labour as the only hope on the formal political scene. At the same time, the gap between the party's policies and local culture and "the best" of what I felt I was learning elsewhere was so vast, that the split between my ("academic"?) politics and the political means available to realize some larger political change seemed quite unbridgable. Of course, there were always more particular campaigns and organizations, especially the movements for peace and the environment, campus trade unionism and struggles over public educational policy and over educational practice, but this most often involved working with people very like myself. Attempts to break out of these limits, noted later in this essay, could meet with painful rebuffs, in which theory, the academy, and cultural studies were all identified by others with the antipopular side.

During these decades, then, it was often the daily, absorbing practices of a cultural studies teacher that seemed the most solid political connection that I had. The classroom seemed the political space in which I could be most effective – and most recognized. Over and again, I experienced the key political conflicts of the 1970s and 1980s as conflicts that were mediated, perhaps directly expressed, in differences between myself, colleagues, and students. The "popular," or the to-be-allied-with, usually appeared in the shape of students with working-class or feminist or black or lesbian or gay identifications. As a teacher, I had to respond to their agenda, if only to help them with their work. I also had to make my own mind up about new intellectual challenges that were clearly related to the different forms of social politics, revising or extending my Marxism, for instance. These challenges were always more than theoretical. They affected everyday social practice at CCCS and outside. They were personal and professional, too.

I shall discuss later the limits of this kind of politics. Insofar as it succeeds within its own domain, however, insofar as cultural studies becomes a representational space for marginalized positions, it cannot be comfortable in the academy, old or new style.

Of course, marginality in such a case as mine is indirect, derivative, and, most importantly, voluntary or chosen (so it may be reversed or more easily compromised over). For many students (and teachers) in cultural studies, marginality is direct, personal, and imposed. It may be struggled against. It may be turned into a resource, but it can hardly be given up. In either case, marginality as a strategy may involve letting go some narrowly academic ambitions to make space for other purposes. For teachers it may involve us in defending and nurturing ways of working and particular projects, individual or collective, which the institutions may not recognize or approve of. It is not easy to sustain such tensions, especially if you are not yourself well established. Academic routines are supported, not only by rules and resources, but by personal needs and investments – including the need to make a living and gain respect. There are also good reasons, aside from personal ambition, to value the academy as a site of critical intellectual activity, where, in the West, puzzling over and pursuing social betterment is now itself so devalued and marginalized. Yet the more academic institutions are articulated to the market and existing forms of unequal power, the more academic activity becomes intellectual commodity production aimed to enhance the marketability or the cultural and economic capital of the individual or institution. This is far advanced in Britain, with coming consequences for older academic autonomies that are still scarcely imaginable, including the radical deskilling of academic labor. This means that the simple correspondence between critical intellectual work and academic institutions is an illusion hard to sustain here. Is it easier in the United States, where the academic community seems so large and apparently self-sustaining? In any case, it may be that a many-layered critical ambivalence towards the academy, uncomfortable though that is, is a necessary condition for the best practice of cultural studies within the academy itself, maybe also outside of it. Certainly, I always find it disturbing to meet colleagues who are "critical" in what they research and teach, but have no sense of the significance of the powers which they still wield within the ordinary academic routines. "Critical scholars" they may be, but very conventional academics nonetheless.

Insofar as academic spaces can be transformed in another direction – towards participatory and democratic forms and the recognition of power and difference – the tension between the academic and useful political–intellectual activity can be reduced. As I see it, the project of cultural studies has been to construct such spaces and, as important, to work productively within them. This strategy has certainly produced major changes in academic life. In the further stages of the struggle this means that cultural studies is already *of* the academy in the strongest way – it has already produced changes there and so has some things to defend.

In partially transformed spaces, however, the contradictions never go away. In any central intellectual activity it is hard to sort out what is oppressive and what is useful. I have written elsewhere (Canaan and Epstein, 1997) about the hard – and partially transformative – battles that were fought around the teaching of the MA course in cultural studies at Birmingham between 1975 and 1993. There is still more to say about how a practice like "mapping the field," so often associated with lecturing and with a "masterly performance," both performs intellectually indispensable functions and, in its untransformed and habitual academic guises, excludes, divides, oppresses, and also places intolerable burdens on the central "performer." The difficulty here, as so often, is that intellectually and politically useful practices are connected to and often confused with routinely oppressive features of an academic pedagogy. The extremity of contradictions – trying to produce "really useful knowledge" in this controlling academic space – has often made me wonder if cultural studies can be delivered in the academy at all!

Academic and Other Politics

Harry Court was my first head of department. A deeply liberal and scholarly professor of economic history, he died, quite suddenly and unexpectedly, on the eve of his retirement. He must have known he was dying and he asked his wife Audrey to give a message to each of the members of his department. His message to me was something like: "You are doing really well, Richard, but remember that scholarship is more important than politics." His comment was addressed to my involvement in post-'68 politics on the campus, during which he always defended me against pressure from higher up the academic hierarchy. Curiously, however, a similar split operates for students of cultural studies (and other subjects) who are or would be political activists in other sites. "It is all very well talking about 'theory'" they say, "but real politics is 'outside.'"

It's easy to understand this response, especially in the light of the kinds of marginality we have already discussed and the gross contradictoriness of the best practices. It's a relief to lighten the burden in this way, to project the problems and responsibilities to some other place. But in its liberal or its critical form, this splitting of the academic and the political is disastrous for the political–intellectual strategy which is cultural studies. Perhaps, because I am defending my own identifications as well, I have a tendency to deliver lectures on this topic. These are some of the things I say.

The academy, and more generally intellectual work, are sites of political struggle, as "real" as any other. Even the pursuit of knowledge, "for its own sake," has political significance, depending on the context. When, as today, knowledge is mainly judged in terms of a narrow capitalist utility, even "for its own sake" has an oppositional potential. Of course, there are many mystifying, blocking, and specific features of the academy as a political site. But this holds true for everywhere. Politics doesn't exist in a pure unproblematic form, anywhere – well, rarely perhaps, in moments of exceptional insurgency. "The point of production," big-P politics, or "the public sphere" (for each of which political priority is sometimes claimed) are equally specific sites, as constraining, though in different ways, as the academy is. There is nothing *uniquely* recuperable or corruptible about radical academic work. And any of these sites can become the subject of powerful imaginary wishes – where the real action happens, anywhere but here. In some circumstances, the academy offers political benefits: it can be a place where the short-termism of formal politics or its sectarian tendencies, or the trap of wish-fulfilling knowledges, can be countered by something more long term and thoughtful. Why else have activists from different movements sought refreshment there? Yes, the academy is an elite rather than a popular institution, and internally hierarchical too. So what's new? The feelings of marginality it produces (including the sense of "no real politics" not "in the real world") is one way it dominates. Deny on-site politics (anywhere) and you succumb to that power.

Teaching and learning are profoundly political practices. They are political at every moment of the circuit: in the conditions of production (who produces knowledge? for whom?), in the knowledges and knowledge forms themselves (knowledge according to what agenda? useful for what?), their publication, circulation, and accessibility, their professional and popular uses, and their impacts on daily life. There's enough "politics" here to keep anyone busy for a lifetime. And what about our daily practices? Everyday life in cultural studies involves the struggle with academic hierarchies and exclusions and many other social injustices. It matters very much what we do each day and how we treat each other round the seminar table, or in the group.

At the same time, the academy limits intellectual and political practice within definite social horizons, not least by pressuring us towards political self-abnegation. It encourages us to split-off professional knowledge production from other social practices including other professions. So political practice in the academy should not stand in for politics *per se*, politics, that is, in other sites and also as a practice of organizing across them. Professional intellectuals and students may have a political role, but especially in linkage with other struggles, both during and after the periods of intensive self-education. Skepticism about professional intellectuals (hardly avoidable in English culture) is important. It's equally important to pay regard to other versions of the intellectual – Gramsci's version of the "organic intellectual" as cultural – political organiser, for instance (Gramsci, 1971: 3–43).

Much more difficult than arguing this case is rendering it into practice on either side of the split, in some consistent and livable way. On one side, there is the work of creating and using academic spaces in transformative ways. On the other side, there is the making of links with other political sites and their critical activists.

In CCCS specifically, perhaps in cultural studies more generally, it seems to me we had most successes on the first side, especially if the growth of cultural studies nationally and internationally, but usually *within the academy*, is borne in mind. Although cultural studies in the CCCS version was much less of a narrowly academic practice than it is sometimes represented to be, I think we were less successful on the second side. The outcomes, however, have often been very paradoxical. Cultural studies has often seemed to do more to create new currencies for ordinary academic aggrandizement than to produce knowledges to renew movements and politics. But this has to do as much with larger determinations of a strongly structural kind – educational, political – than a simple lack of "will" or a mistaken position.

Working the Boundaries and the Social/Textual Split

Cultural studies has been a relatively successful project of academic transformation insofar as it has worked certain boundaries: boundaries between disciplines; boundaries between the academy and other sites.

This liminality is in part a version of the familiar strategy of "interdisciplinarity." Interdisciplinarity made initial sense in cultural studies – as it has in women's, black, or gay and lesbian studies – because the object of study could not be adequately grasped by any single discipline. Whether defined in terms of "whole ways of life or struggle" (Williams, 1958; Thompson, 1961) or "the historical forms of consciousness or subjectivity" (Johnson, 1983), the object of culture figured in many disciplines but was fully engaged with in none. The split between the humanities, where means existed for the analysis of cultural forms, and the social sciences concerned with social structure and processes was (and often remains) especially disabling.

One of the difficulties of critiques of the "textualization" of cultural studies is that it tends to preserve this split between disciplines, a split which cultural studies at best has worked across. The "social" versus "textual" distinction can be taken as corresponding to disciplinary emphases – broadly, the sociological versus the literary – but might more productively be viewed as a difference of paradigms or frameworks. This difference is sometimes internal to disciplines (more formal and more historical approaches to literature, for example) and can polarize approaches into clusters of disciplines and disciplinary fragments. Discipline is important here because it adds further political stakes to cross-paradigmatic wars: to uphold a social "cultural studies" can be to uphold the sociology of culture; to privilege work of a literary kind within cultural studies can promote the literary disciplines.

I have argued elsewhere that paradigmatic differences can be usefully understood as corresponding to different moments in the circuit of cultural production and consumption (Johnson, 1983). To simplify a more complex argument, there is a large and heterogeneous cluster of approaches which center on culture from the point of view of its production. These may focus on the specialized production of relatively abstracted cultural products (as in studies of media institutions and the political economy of culture) or on the dispersed forms of cultural production which occur in everyday life (as in much ethnographic research). Within more critical versions of this work, Marxist notions of production – of "sensuous human activity" in general or of capitalist commodity production specifically – remain major resources, even where class is not prioritized. These are indispensable versions of a "social" cultural studies – but by no means the only ones. It is here, too, that work in the sociology of culture and in a more sociological cultural studies (some forms of subcultural analysis and media audience study, for instance) tends to cluster. The characteristic weakness of the more institutional approaches, in particular, lies in the analysis of the forms of culture and representation themselves and the difference that they make – the basis of any nonreductive account of social–cultural process.

Those concerned with anatomizing cultural forms and their pressures on readers or "subjects" are often richly engaged with literary and linguistic traditions and the different ways in which still or moving images have been analyzed by the disciplines of the "visual." Although there have been more sociological receptions of structuralism, it is here that the main receptions of structuralist and poststructuralist work have occurred. There is some correspondence, therefore, between the advocacy of a more "social" cultural studies and materialist paradigms on the one side, and a concern with textual or cultural forms and the deployment of post-structuralist and postmodernist frameworks on the other.

Though the literary/sociology split was familiar enough at Birmingham, the reception of structuralist and poststructuralist theory was crucial for the analysis of forms as diverse as youth cultural styles, photographic images, and forms of self-narration. The reception of the work of Barthes, for example (on myth, on narrative, and on the image especially), was as formative for the second formation of cultural studies at Birmingham as the (rather structuralist) reading of Gramsci. Barthes's argument in *Mythologies* – that a level of formal (for him, semiological) analysis, even a certain formalism was crucial to historical interpretation – provided a powerful point of intersection with Marxist models (Barthes, 1973: 112). The reading of Foucault and of other ("post-Althusserian") discourse theorists was just as important for the middle stages of cultural studies in one Birmingham mode. This is one reason why, from an ex-CCCS point of view, it doesn't make sense to oppose a "social" cultural studies to a "textual" or text-based one. In much of Stuart Hall's work, for example, a version of discourse analysis has been appropriated within the framework of a Gramscian analysis of hegemony, mainly to try to specify the larger political effects of struggles over meaning and identity in the public sphere – the popular purchases and limits of Thatcherism for instance (Hall and Jacques, 1983; Hall, 1988). Though Stuart himself has recently criticized "literary textualism," he has also pointed out:

> In my own work, the textual is the moment when culture and the discursive is recovered; and that moment is absolutely decisive for me – endlessly displacing any kind of homogeneous return to the economic or the political, the material in some simple vulgar sense. To me, cultural studies is impossible without retaining the moment of the symbolic; with the textual, language, subjectivity and representation forming the key matrix. (Hall, 1996: 403)

One of the difficulties on the "social" side of this argument – and indeed, in general – is how "the textual" is understood. "The Text" still carries all its older pure-literary, not to say biblical, connotations. It is easy to underrate the shift in the definition of "the text" in literary and linguistic theory and practice, a shift itself linked to the influence of more "cultural" approaches – from Raymond Williams onwards. In Williams's own *The Country and the City* (1973) for instance, or, much later, in Edward Said's *Culture and Imperialism* (1993), generic analysis and even the reanalysis of classic literary texts are routes to a larger analysis of historical cultural formations. Another interesting recent example is the kind of literary–historical analysis, also influenced by psychoanalysis, which is one strand in contemporary "queer theory" (e.g. Sedgewick, 1985, 1990; Dollimore, 1991; cf. also, in method, Stallybrass and White, 1986). A social historian might be critical here of the combination of relatively "thin descriptions" and ambitious argumentation. Politically, too, these are not the most accessible of texts. A study like Graham Dawson's of the "military imaginary" in *Soldier Heroes* (1994) might be a better model. Here, cultural study, including analytically literate text-based methods, is accompanied by close historical case-study work. Nonetheless, a textually based method, even one that reads familiar literary sources, has proved enormously generative for new mappings of the sexual in Anglo-American cultures especially. Indeed, if we take account also of historical studies of sexuality influenced by Foucauldian theories of discourse (Foucault, 1979; Weeks, 1981; Mort, 1987), the contribution of a "textual" cultural studies in founding a new history of sexual formations is very significant indeed (for debates around this see Duberman, Vicinus, and Chauncey, 1989).

It is clear that in work of this kind it is not so much the literary text itself, but more the larger "social text" that becomes the main object of study. Even so, it can be argued that text-based studies only look at language, and not the real world of social action. In a parallel argument, R. W. Connell in his recent excellent book on masculinities, critiques the limits of what he calls "semiotic" accounts of masculinity. He writes:

> This definition of masculinity has been very effective in cultural analysis. It escapes the arbitrariness of essentialism and the paradoxes of positivist and normative definitions. It is, however, limited in its scope – unless one assumes as some postmodern theorists do, that discourse is all we can talk about in social analysis. To grapple with the full range of issues about masculinity we need ways of talking about relationships of other kinds too: about gender places in production or consumption, places in institutions and in natural environments, places in social and military struggles. (Connell, 1995: 70–1)

I certainly don't think discourse is "all we can talk about in social analysis," but is there enough attention in this and similar passages to the definition of discourse itself? There are, it is true, more narrowly linguistic versions, closer to "semiotics." Partly because of this, the term can never entirely lose its linguistic connotation. On the other hand, the notion of discourse in some Foucauldian accounts is very close indeed to the idea of structured and structuring social practice with the elements of knowledge and power in the foreground. "Discourse" in Foucault's own later work, for instance, clearly includes practices like regimes of imprisonment or schooling or forms of care of the self or self-production (e.g. therapies)

– classic objects of critical institutional study (Foucault, 1977, 1990). Of course, even in a more narrowly linguistic or epistemic sense closer to the earlier Foucault (Dreyfus and Rabinow, 1982), it would be hard to address "gender places in production" or even "military struggles" without a discursive dimension – military struggles, for example, without a knowledge of "military science" as well as the contingent chaos of the battlefield. In these, as in other ways, oppositions between social practice and "discourse," or between text and social practice, are themselves extremely risky.

Within such frameworks, the textual is a very wide category indeed – indeed, it is a way, one way, of looking at social practice as such, a way that is preoccupied with the production of meanings, feelings, knowledges, subjectivities, etc. If we understand "text" in this way – not in some narrowly literary or linguistic reduction – it is hard to avoid the conclusion that all research on human (and perhaps nonhuman) phenomena has in part to be textual. This, of course, goes for ethnography or studying "lived experience" too (cf. Schudson, chapter 13, this volume). Human social interactions of the most direct and personal kinds have themselves a textual patterning, a resource that was rather persistently pursued in Richard Hoggart's *The Uses of Literacy* and which figured in the later cultural studies ethnographies, too. Hoggart, for instance, reads "closely" not only the forms of 1950s mass consumption but also popular myth-making, the idiomatic phrases used in everyday conversations, the lay-out, contents, and use of working-class living rooms, the definition of a "good table," and even the lines on people's faces (1958: passim, esp. 49). Nor do I see how else we get to meaning in any full or complex way except through the understanding of "languages" of many different kinds. These are far from exhausted in the images and narratives of public media (including art and literature); they include the codes and conventions of everyday genre, right through to those of "inner speech" and secret imagining.

Another area of cross-disciplinary misrecognitions is the matter of "methodology." This has struck me especially forcefully in jointly teaching, at Trent, a course in research practice for beginning Ph.D. students.[20] The course covers both social science and humanities methods, with cultural studies seen as a bridge. One obvious conclusion, near the end of our first year, is the extraordinary contrast between disciplinary cultures on matters of method: the remarkable elaboration of technical methodology in the social sciences, the dependence on largely implicit but actually very specific methods (especially of reading) in the humanities. As to the "bridge," there is no available mapping of methods in cultural studies – virtually no "methodology" in that sense.[21]

It is easy to see how in this context, "textual" approaches seem, over and again, to transgress social scientific criteria (of "representativeness," for example) and therefore reliability in research. It is also easy to mistake the nature of truth claims in their more literary and humanities registers. Critical of science, cultural studies invariably occupies the humanities side of this division. Typically, the aspiration to "science" is absent (or it is disavowed): some of the best work is satisfied with interesting and suggestive theses for other scholars to discuss – and why not? At the same time, truth claims can simply be imprecise and therefore slippery, an indeterminacy which may be allied both to postmodern philosophy and to large intellectual ambitions, even an imperialism. Michael Schudson argues that cultural studies, "often lays claim to being 'the' approach to the study of just about *everything*" (chapter 13, this volume). From one point of view, it is just this ability to work across the usual boundaries that I value. Such freedom, however, can also connect with an older (English?) intellectual amateurism which "can turn its hand to anything" and which is "carried off" only with the help of cultural capital and social privilege (cf. Bourdieu, 1988). Where work in a literary or high-theoretical mode *is* more imperialistic – in some kinds of postmodern philosophical critique, for example – it is certainly right to resist. Sociologists and others, for example, should certainly resist the wholesale dismissal of the "sociological" or even "the social" which features in some critiques (e.g. in the debates around Baudrillard, 1983, interestingly reviewed in Chen, 1966). Even more worrying is the way in which cultural and media studies threaten to displace or compete with disciplines or cross-disciplinary areas – black studies, African-American studies, women's studies – with which it should ally, feed, and be fed by (cf. Hall, 1996: 397; Taylor, 1996; West, 1992).

Differences in the ways in which the objects of research are conceptualized also deeply affect questions of method. Much social science remains fixated on the figure of "population" and, therefore, in cultural research, continues to sample the "attitudes" of individuals rather than tapping into cultural structures, circuits, or repertoires. This is especially true for orthodox psychologies which often, despite their conceptual banality, exercise a disproportionate influence on research on issues of subjectivity and in the study of "communication."[22] Even where social research flies the "qualitative" banner, it often mimics in its epistemologies, justifications, and procedures, the other, dominant pair in this binary – the "quantitative."[23]

Cultural studies is usually characterized by small-scale studies, which are qualitative of course, but also intensive, at least in part. This model applies whether the materials are limited to already public texts or are directly produced (like interviews or textually recorded observations). Intensive study enables the complex layered analysis of contradictory forms of consciousness and of the sayable and unsayable in situations of unequal power. But such studies can also prove to have a wider scope of reference than the "size of the sample" might suggest. This is because the object here is not really individual attitudes at all. Rather, the researcher, through a particular instance or case study, is attempting to tap into cultural structures or formations, which are precisely social or shared. They are likely to have a larger range of occurrence than the single example suggests.

The idea of cultural structure or formation – present and fully historicized in Raymond Williams's early work as "structure of feeling" (Williams and Orrom, 1954; Williams, 1961), but further developed by drawing on structuralist and poststructuralist ideas – is indispensable here. Cultural studies uses different version of this idea, drawing on Gramsci, as Williams (1977) later does and on Foucault. Though important differences remain, there are indeed a number of convergences here. In his discussion of the relation between discourse and power in his later texts, Foucault writes of "strategy" in terms very similar to Gramsci's view of hegemony as "relations of force." For Foucault, it is a question of analyzing "a multiple and mobile field of force relations" (e.g. 1979: 102). Some such convergence is often implied in contemporary uses of terms like "discursive formation" – which at once indicate particular discourses and interdiscursive clusters (Foucault), hegemonic relations and alliances (Gramsci), and residual and emergent layers and moments (Williams). Cultural research seeks to tap into such structures, formations, or circuits which are systematically present over a wide social area. This can be done at different moments in the circulation of cultural forms: at their points of production, at the moment of their embodiment in publicly available texts, at the moment of reading or reception, or, "ethnographically," in the complex lived tissues of everyday life.

Such forms are more or less universal, more or less local, whether we think local/universal here in terms of the nation-state or globally. The elaboration of notions of structure and of process in structuralist and poststructuralist theory, especially the play around presence and absence, suggests, however, that we should always look for the effects of adjacent cultural forms on each other. Psychoanalytic insights, focusing on identity relations of Us/Others, activate the manifold connections of culture with a further psychic charge. Thus, contemporary homophobias in the public domain – of the kinds found in debates in the British parliament or daily press over the age of consent for gay men or the Aids epidemic, for instance – carry the traces of several decades of gay and lesbian theory and activism in the "monstrous" figure of the assertive, proselytizing "homosexual" (Johnson, 1996; Redman, 1997).

The relations between cultural formations operate interdiscursively and interpsychically. Spatially, they now often operate globally. This cross-cultural interpsychic global culture of communication can produce extraordinary condensations of meaning in a single image or phrase. In April 1996, for instance, the Saudi dissident Mohammed al-Masari, recently reprieved from banishment from Britain against the wishes of the Saudi authorities, was asked to comment by the *Guardian* newspaper on the unilateral shut-down of the BBC's World Service Arabic television channel by the Saudi authorities. He had also written a letter, printed in the same issue, defending press freedom, democracy, and women's rights in Saudi Arabia. The Saudis had objected to BBC coverage of human rights abuse in Saudi Arabia: Prof. al-Masari last night welcomed the fallout. "It is the best thing" he said. "The BBC should not submit to Saudi censorship. There is no way you can get into the same bed with someone who has Aids and get away safely" (The *Guardian*, 9 April 1996). Of course, such a comment is read in other parts of the world (in my own household, for instance) in the context of the desperate struggle to defeat the spread of the AIDS virus by safer sex practices.

In today's world, then, the object of cultural studies often becomes itself a kind of worldwide net with all kinds of unexpected linkages, vicinities, identities, though with differences and hidden elements, too. It is easy to see how in this world, standard criteria like "representativeness" may give way to a preference for reading from "the margins." Starting there, or with the traces, or with the supplements, often reveals more about central categories than the focus on "presence" which "representativeness" implies (Derrida, 1974). Within a national frame I am thinking concretely also of the way in which criticism influenced by black British intellectuals and artists has made visible many aspects of English national identity and history, forgotten in the extraordinary amnesias around empire (e.g. C. Hall, 1992; S. Hall, 1991). More generally, contemporary approaches to identity have shown how integral versions of the Other are to the production of centered or "pure" identities (e.g. Stallybrass and White, 1986).

The familiar issues of "representativeness," "reliability," and "validity" do not altogether disappear here, but they certainly have to be reformulated.

Limits of the Textual Turn

I do have some difficulties, however, with the "textual" turn in cultural and other studies.

I am concerned, first, with the kinds of texts that are privileged, bearing in mind that almost anything can be "read" as a text. In practice, the most publicly available forms of culture are most often read, from familiar literary or visual classics to mainstream media forms. In critical accounts of disciplines it is often the disciplinary canon that is re-read. Without some connection with hidden and subordinated cultural worlds, the study of public culture tends to recycle the dominant forms. It is one thing to produce a critical, even deconstructive, account of the world of the academics, the bourgeoisie, or the colonialist; another to show how this world is also made by the strategies of the subordinated majorities.

This old concern with culture "from below" (or from the so-called margins) is very relevant to the project of redefining "representativeness." Representativeness should primarily be judged in relation to spatially distributed relations of power, especially the exclusion of the points of views of subordinated majorities. These regular exclusions are the really gross distortions. Though globalization produces links and vicinities that have not existed before, cultural forms do have a more or less universal, or a more or less local, circulation. They are visible or invisible, present directly or in their effects, depending on the social and spatial locations of the researcher. Subordinated cultures do not disclose themselves, fortunately, to the universalizing or powerful gaze. Questions of "representativeness" reemerge, therefore, as questions of power, positionality, and epistemology. The personal positionalities of cultural researchers matter very much for the quality of work that they produce. So, too, do the alliances which they can make in the process of research and in their everyday lives. Working across major relations of power can challenge researchers' points of view and, where this is appropriate or possible, make available the points of view of others and even create new publics. All this depends, not only on positionalities and relationships, but also on the theoretical frameworks that are in play. These may reconfirm and even universalize a particular point of view – a Western cosmopolitan's take upon the global, for instance[24] – or reorder a taken-for-granted landscape.

A second difficulty is that some forms of textual analysis move in an opposite direction to the reconstruction of larger cultural formations. Rather, they abstract particular forms from the text and then look at their effectivities as relatively discrete cultural technologies. An example would be the famous debates around "the gaze" and spectatorship in the analysis of film (Mulvey, 1989). This approach is poor at grasping the concrete combinations of cultural and practical–social elements as they are lived in historical contexts and in individual and collective life histories. Yet if we are to understand the social life and relations of filmmakers and cinemagoers, let alone the place of cinema within a wider social history, this perspective is essential (for a useful version of these debates, see Stacey, 1993).

Initially, the take-up in cultural studies of the stress on text and language (at best on cultural forms/formations in a larger sense) was a reaction to the persistent reduction to economic and political power characteristic not only of older Marxisms but also of much orthodox social science. Perhaps it should still be judged in relation to the conventional "realism" (in the Hobbesian or Machiavellian sense) of Political Man. Within this larger move, one of the attractions of structuralist and poststructuralist models was the identification of specifically cultural pressures and forms of power. The tendency to overstate these or to make a linguistic or cultural reduction needs reading in this context. It may be that we have reached a stage today when the most productive way forward is to invest less in the old structuralist/humanist polemic and to seek to incorporate within our own frameworks the indispensable insights of each paradigm.

This can best be illustrated in terms of two main issues. I discuss the first – the question of political agency – here, as my third difficulty with the textual turn. Later, I shall consider the second – the relative social embeddedness or separation of cultural forms.

I agree with those many critics who argue that it is hard to develop an adequate account of political and personal agency from the whole structuralist/poststructuralist research program.[25] Poststructuralist critiques have loosened up the determinism and ahistoricism of classic structuralism and brought postmodern analysis nearer, in some ways, to a cultural materialism, but there are still key differences in the ways in which agency is understood. There is a real difficulty within poststructuralist paradigms of getting back to the agency of individuals or movements at all. Often this is an empty space in the theory, filled by fairly commonsense assumptions or by a universalizing version of the psychic. Theories are for ever speaking of cultural means and conditions, especially of language and the unconscious, but rarely of cultural production or acts. The current interest in "performativity" (e.g. Butler, 1993) is clearly an attempt to close this gap in theories of discourse. Yet who or what performs remains obscure, as does the relation between the general category – "performativity" – and specific actual "performances."

This is one instance, therefore, where it seems necessary to move outside a structuralist legacy and recover aspects of a materialism that focuses upon human practice. It is important to take the full weight of the postmodern critique of essential or centered selves and of "simple" psychologies, including those that over-value psychic unity or integration as a therapeutic goal. It seems to me quite possible to combine postmodern insights with the double stress on active self-production and on "conditions" which is characteristic of Marxism, but especially of the early Marx (of *The 1844 Manuscripts* (Marx, 1973), *The Theses on Feuerbach* (Marx, 1979), and *The German Ideology* (Marx and Engels, 1970) particularly). Of course, we must re-read "conditions" to include not only nature, technologies, and (all kinds of) social relations, but also bodily – psychic possibilities and limits and cultural structures and formations. Conditions include, indeed, the existing dynamics of subjectivity and consciousness, the immediate terms of self-production. The production of selves, individual and collective, is a real practice which involves particular forms of conscious activity, of cultural production. It always occurs, however, in relation to a historical repertoire of social identities and cultural forms, and is a necessarily decentered process, always in some sense out of control, deeply relational, ongoing, and always "impossible" or incomplete. This goes for the most powerful identities, too. Such a perspective, which must grasp both deconstructive and compositional moments, has important implications for politics and for education, in the academy and elsewhere. It does not displace everyday issues of responsibility, evaluation, and political choice, but deepens and complicates them. It implies, for instance, that education and, indeed, politics, must in some sense be "therapeutic" or have ways of working on the unconscious.

This is quite a long way away from academic business as usual, however. Investment in particular paradigms, and for the academic disciplines with which they have affinities, means that the study of culture is pulled back, time and again, to some restricted disciplinary definition. This may be the sociologist's stress on social structure and on scientificity, the philosopher's preoccupation with general categories, the literary pull to the discrete text or a narrowed textuality, or the out-of-control elaboration of formal disciplines like technical linguistics. Given the importance of "discipline" in the organization of the academy everywhere, the replaying of disciplinary limits on the new ground of cultural studies is to be expected. It is also one of the conditions of a transformative practice. We need to recognize how disciplines (with their strongly institutionalized bases of power) attempt to colonize or reappropriate any new approach. It is equally fascinating to see how the "cultural" agenda has rippled through the different disciplines – with cultural geography currently of particular interest.[26] Even the hardest targets – psychology for instance – have started to fray at the edges. Equally important are the returns, our own re-reappropriations: taking on board, for instance, the cultural geographer's concern with "spatialization."

If, in a dream of absolute power, I could legislate a new academic map, I shouldn't want to abolish existing disciplinary differences. I shouldn't want a cultural studies empire. I want a cultural studies that occupies thresholds, between disciplines and, as in the mapping exercise, between paradigms too, sometimes with tensions unresolved, sometimes with syncretic moves. Would thresholds be such exciting places without some well-inhabited houses too? And isn't it more productive to influence and be influenced by the whole disciplinary range rather than to reduce it in some image of your own?[27]

Inward and Outward: Cultural Studies and Other Sites

In the last two sections of this essay, I want to return to the question of the "responsiveness" of cultural studies to extra-academic agendas and needs. This is a more complicated matter than I have so far allowed, not exempt from the usual ambiguities. Responsiveness (or a real "organicity") involves both inward and outward movements, relations of appropriation and return. It is one thing to respond to political agenda by taking new questions on board as objects of study; it is another to return such know-ledges to source – or to some other agency – in the form of solidarity, really useful insights, or new resources. The failure to return, or worse to steal the knowledges away for self-aggrandizement, or worse still to return them in mystifying ways, are all familiar charges against cultural and other critical studies.

On the whole, I believe that CCCS – and cultural studies more generally perhaps – was relatively responsive in the first sense. But it is certainly arguable that the benefits of new agenda have much more often been cashed within the academy than outside. In other words, the cycle of return has been at worst appropriative or at best short-circuited and self-reproducing. Cultural studies has been most successful in producing and reproducing itself as a tendency – political in some sense maybe – but primarily as a politics of education, research, and academic publication, operating within a significant but limiting space.

Significantly, the picture is clearest to me on the "inward" side of this circuit. It is obvious that much of the energy of cultural studies has come from its connections with social movements. Especially important has been those reinventions of cultural studies that derived from feminist con-cerns: the explicit en-gendering of research and teaching agenda and the redrawing of the maps of theory and of methods in subfield after subfield (e.g. in media, see Van Zoonen, 1994; in subcultures and youth studies, MacRobbie, 1991). Slower and more discontinuous – interminable it must seem to black activists – has been the struggle over issues of race and nation, especially the critique of the nationalist origins of cultural studies in the light of contemporary racism and the persistence in a formally postcolonial world of relations of white supremacy in which nation-structures are crucial. Important, too, is the deeper questioning of "gender" in relation to heterosexuality, by lesbian, gay, and "queer" theory and re-search. It is clear that another reinvention is currently occurring as social relations of power and identity are stretched across the globe. Aside from reinforcing the deconstruction of the national and imperial frameworks of earlier phases of cultural studies, and rebuking the Anglo-American hegemony, this "globalization" of the study adds a host of new questions to the agenda, including the need to recognize that there are different national and regional traditions of cultural study itself (e.g. Hall, 1991; Schwarz, 1994; Stratton and Ang, 1996; Chambers and Curti, 1996). The whole character of cultural studies is inconceivable except as an intellectual extension of movements like these.

Movement agenda haven't been the only relays here. The idea of the "contemporary" (the often forgotten "C" in CCCS) has also been important. Coming from history, I found this "contemporary" troubling at first, partly because it seemed to mean abandoning my nineteenth-century research. Nowadays, I see a nicely paradoxical identity and role for myself as a kind of contemporary historian – working on the present but therefore necessarily concerned with memory and with pasts. For everyone there was a pressure at Birmingham to respond to immediate events – within intellectual fields and "theory" certainly, but also in everyday life, public politics, and popular media. The projects around "mugging" are a good example here. They were responses not only to press and judicial constructions of youthful criminality, but also to the rise of the New Right politically and to specific local happenings in which the researchers were involved (see Hall, 1996: 665–6). *Policing The Crisis*, researched before the electoral rise of Thatcherism, provides the first full analysis of this hegemonic formation: subsequent work, especially Stuart Hall's own essays and journalism, is a running, theorized commentary on its particular strengths and limits (e.g. Hall and Jacques, 1983). There is an allied strand of work on education policy, from studies of the vulnerabilities of Labourism and social democratic policies in the mid to later 1970s, to the later critiques of the New Right (CCCS, 1980; Education Group II, 1991).

It is much harder to assess the outward movements, the cycles of return, and perhaps too easy to minimize them. It is easy to overlook the conscious attempts to make popular connections, partly because of their limited success. There was always a strong current in CCCS preoccupied by questions of accessibility and returning work to the constituencies whose experiences we were often attempting to represent. This was in tension with the pressure to seek recognition of the work not only as academically creditable, but also really notable. This tension is visible within and between the different forms of publication from the home-produced journal *Working Papers in Cultural Studies* (nos 1–10, 1971–7) to the series of *Stencilled Occasional Papers* (over 80 items by 1985), a cheap and flexible mode of communication with the occasional attempt at "intervention," to the much fought-over book series. Another example, characteristic especially of the later 1970s and early 1980s, was something of a minor tradition of campaigns and what we called for a while "road shows." The authors of *Unpopular Education*, the critique of Labour traditions in education policy, sought dialogues with teachers, teacher educators, and labor and trade union activists on these themes, talking to

Labour Party, Socialist Teacher, and other meetings. The Popular Memory group was similarly in dialogue with teachers and students in the world of further education and radical history. It is true, however, that these activities were rarely sustained, except, perhaps, where they came to coincide with professional activity in some way. The most important connection of this kind was always with formal education: secondary schooling and especially adult, further, and higher education. Even here, however, where researchers were more often also teachers, ex-teachers, or intending teachers, there were (are) some familiar tensions between research in an academic setting and practice in a college or school. Intermediate organization is often needed: in Britain, for example, organizations like the National Association of Teachers of English and the Humanities Association – both organizations that have linked radical teachers and academics and, in recent years, resisted state control of the curriculum in their subject areas. Often, such connections have been most successful when they have been local, as in the many links that have been set up between cultural politics in the city of Birmingham and courses taught at CCCS and at its successor department on the subject of "The West Midlands." On the whole, however, CCCS did not produce the kind of theoretically informed action research or policy-oriented prescriptions that connect most directly with practice in other sites. Undoubtedly the most accomplished connection, the tighter circle again, was in the development of cultural studies itself, as a subject at all or most levels of the education system, but especially in universities.

It is even more difficult to assess the diffused cultural effects of cultural study – the connections that are not so much made as happen. When ideas, new forms of representation, and partially transformed practices are out in the world it is unpredictable how they will be read and used. My guess is that cultural studies research and teaching, where it has connected with or has been grounded in larger cultural and political movements, has had more effect on popular consciousness and practice than we usually allow ourselves to believe. This is not to say that such effects have always been positive in every way. This dispersed and combined influence is hard to assess because so mixed up with other currents and also often invisible to the more formal kinds of social monitoring. We might ask, for example, about the diffused influence of cultural and media studies on professional media practices and on the ways in which popular media, advertising, or publicity are viewed. We might investigate the links between professional media work, art centers, local "workshops," and other voluntary associations and the large numbers of students now coming out of cultural and media studies courses. It is worth considering the wider influence of cultural studies-influenced journalists and columnists (e.g. in Britain, Rosalind Coward, Suzanne Moore, or Beatrice Campbell). We might trace the influences of cultural studies' representations of subcultures on the self-reflexivity of subculturalists themselves, not only in Britain but at points of translation of British forms elsewhere, in Germany or the USA for example.[28] What effects has the questioning of gender in women's studies, in sociology, and cultural studies had on the crisis tendencies of patri-archal gender identities? What have been the impacts on black British and Asian British artistic practice, and on black activists and audiences, of cultural theories, the critical discourses on racial essentialism, marginality, and "hybridity" for instance? How have the same or similar intellectual currents influenced the ways in which Britishness is lived by young white people? How have theoretical debates and especially poststructuralist and queer theory shaped or converged with the increased visibility of lesbian, gay, and other marginalized sexualities?

Cultural Studies and Popular Politics

If cultural studies has been dependent for its intellectual innovations in part on the political programs of movements, how far has it made its own returns here? Again, a proper answer would require ways of tapping into networks and biographies and everyday life changes – many research projects in themselves. Here, since I am concerned with limits, I can only highlight what seems to me the greatest disappointments. These are in relation to popular representation in the largest sense, though the inter-twined relations of class and race seem to focus the problems most sharply. I found it disconcerting, for example, to read bell hooks' "Eating the Other: Desire and Resistance" as a commentary on cultural studies and, personally, on my part in it (hooks, 1992: 21–39; cf. Moore, 1988). Does cultural studies, located in the predominantly white academy, simply con-sume the Other, not sexually perhaps, but intellectually and always with a dimension of desire? And how often are (real) others (as students, yes, but also as the majority of not-students) "fed" (fed) in this process? If we ask what cultural studies does – directly or indirectly – to benefit the poorer people of the world, I think we put any achievements we might claim in the right perspective and set the most appropriate terms for reinventions.

The disappointments are most obvious in relation to formal politics and policies in most Western countries. After all, from the New Left onwards, we have always claimed an oppositional political role. The greatest roll-backs, which are also on a global scale, are in the broad domain of economic policy, the turning of social policies into "economics," the intensification of relations of exploitation, overwork, and underemployment, and the increase of social inequalities of obvious and primary kinds along class, gender, and racialized lines. Even in the most transformed view of politics – as everyday or diffused, the economic effect of rightwing politics and of capital's global recomposition – this has to be reckoned a grand and grievous political fact.

Contemporary reinventions of cultural studies have to take *this* contemporaneity on board. This is more than a question of debating whether we are postmodern, late-modern, late capitalist, postindustrial, or moving towards a "risk society." It includes reassessing the political value of the study of culture itself, including the models we use for this purpose. It may be that the priority of developing the study of culture as a *specific kind of analysis and activity* is now weaker than it was in the 1960s, 1970s, or even the 1980s.

In those decades there were important battles to be fought about supplying the cultural (including the common, ordinary, and everyday) as a dimension of politics. This included pointing up the political stakes in forms of public representation or recognition. It meant upholding the hidden cultural resourcefulness of oppressed or marginalized groups. It involved emphasizing how connected politics always is with everyday questions of identity and subjectivity, wishes and desires. It did involve redefining "politics" itself.

These remain key issues, of course, some of them even more urgent than before, but it may be that the priority today is somewhat different. Because of the neglect of cultural questions in previous left theories, especially in the dominant Marxisms, there was a pull to develop an understanding of cultural processes as relatively abstracted cultural forms, a tendency that was given paradigmatic momentum by the reception of structuralist and poststructuralist theory. Today, when material conditions are shifting so adversely for the worldwide majorities, we need especially to understand how forms of representation, social identities under pressure, and "the good sense in common sense" are imbricated in other forms of power, contradiction, and struggle. This is not to depart the field of cultural studies or cultural theory, nor to disengage from the struggle against reductions. It will not do simply to return to the frameworks which cultural studies has criticized. The reduction of questions of power to politics-and-economics retains after all a hegemonic position, especially in the academic disciplines that serve the most powerful – in orthodox international relations for instance. It does mean engaging more fully with approaches in political economy and economic geography, especially where they have been influenced by feminism and the concern with "the global," to see how cultural conditions and processes set the terms of economic ends, and are always actively present in relations which are usually read as "economic." No doubt this will involve inserting new "classic" texts in cultural studies programs and revising or pluralizing the canon; but it will involve new interdisciplinary connections as well.

A central question for me today is how hegemonic groups and institutions in the world – mainly male and white – are sustained in the impossible belief that the policies they pursue can ever create a viable, livable social and natural world. Even in today's brutalities, I don't think this question can be resolved by some simple appeal to "interests." Similarly, if we are speaking of a narrow "realism" here or a lack of imagination, these closures still have to be explained in more than conspiratorial or pathological terms. Another important question is how groups which do have a clearer interest in changing the relations of power and in creating new forms of sociality can organize in ways that span the earth and protect it. Again, questions of culture, identity, "consciousness," and now of "locality" are intimately involved.

It is important to stress that the disappointments about the work stem mainly from much broader political conditions. Even policy-oriented or practical cultural studies (both recognizable currents today) have difficulty in reconciling usefulness with a critical stance, especially a critical position with some popular potential. This may sometimes flow from the treason of the academics, but it certainly stems from the state of policy-making. The crucial question – often fudged in the pursuit of policy – is *whose policy, useful for whom?* The crucial difficulty is often the absence of appropriate political sites and organizations which are not simply agencies of domination or control, are in touch with commonsense conceptions and popular needs, and have a broad educational or educative perspective – that is, they do not know the answers already. Only such organizations can give critical intellectual work the political direction it needs, offsetting the pressure to split politics and scholarship, and holding an open space against pragmatic political closure, dogmatic rigidities, or wish-fulfillment. In many versions, in Gramsci's communist scenario for instance, this is the work of political parties, organizations which can prioritize issues of strategy but recognize the role of critical thinking. Such organizations must wish to make reinventions of their own. There have been moments in Clinton's campaigning in the USA and Blair's New Labour in Britain where this ideal role – agitating, educating, creating new social relations within the party first – have been promised but then mimicked or parodied. The contemporary Blairite shift, which splits (selected) experts and people and demobilizes independent activism within the party, is doing almost incalculable harm to the Labour Party as a site for the reinvented socialist project which is desperately needed by millions of people today.

One conclusion I draw is that educational–political connections need to be made elsewhere than in the academy or in formal political organizations. Circumstances can hardly be worse, in the managerialized academy and in managerialized politics, for realizing the kinds of transformations with which cultural studies has always been associated – by aspiration at least. In general, the project of a radical professional politics, within the public institutions themselves, seems more and more difficult to sustain. This is not to say that the remaining spaces should be given up, nor to underestimate the important work that can still be done in formal educational institutions, especially where the conditions of access have improved. But it may be that we need to reinvent other sites of activity too. Perhaps we need to remind ourselves, that though in their time, universities, adult education institutions, and even schools have been important points of political education and cultural mobilization, social movements have more commonly depended on informal networks and cultural and social inventions of their own. I am thinking of the long tradition in Britain of countereducational activity, from the Painites, Chartists, and Owenites of the early nineteenth century, to the interwar Plebs League and Labour Colleges; of the social and cultural politics of the women's movement in its first and second uprisings; of the forms of community education, religion, collective memory, and art associated with civil rights and other forms of black politics, and of lesbian, gay, and queer culture, campaigning, communal support, and commemoration.

In these contexts I wonder – it is not much more than a dream so far – about the possibility of helping to organize political–intellectual work outside the academy, in *relation to* critical academic work, and adult education, but also to informal community and local–global campaigns and links. Such a strategy needs to connect with increasingly common everyday experiences – of widespread unemployment and part-time casual work, of environmental loss and deterioration, of the closing down of emancipatory educational opportunities, and perhaps the desire to "downshift" among overemployed professionals and skilled workers. It would seek to be "organic" in this sense, drawing its agenda and method from popular contradictions and difficulties. At the same time, it would hope to continue to influence the forms of critical intellectual work, which nonetheless remain "traditional" or narrowly academic, not least in encouraging a more outward and popular turn, offering points of recognition and reward other than those of research gradings and professional appraisal and the sharper utilitarianisms of the future. Such connections are to be made, not only in terms of the content of campaigns and research questions, but also in the ways of organizing, especially along dimensions of space and time. To stand the chance of being popular (in the minimum sense of allowing participation) such organization would have to be local and appropriately "part-time" for instance, though it should also use the new media for its wider links.

It may be possible to adapt many of the organizational tools and educational strategies learned by teaching cultural studies (and other critical subjects) in universities to the organization of networks of teachers, learners, researchers, writers, artists, and political activists outside. This would, at least, be one form of palpable return to adult education, itself so generative a space for the critical academy. It may be that one of the most important legacies of CCCS has been the research subgroup, for instance. The potential of this form has many aspects, but I value it in this context as a way of handling productively major social differences and relations of power, including those that are carried in untransformed intellectual practices. Small-group work may often be a way of turning major contradictions and difficulties around discrepancies of power into resources for both individuals and for some common project. In my "good memory," CCCS was an arena where institutionalized and other powers were made visible and could be challenged and partially transformed. In the spaces so created, commitments which often had to go their own way outside, found ways to dialogue and engage with each other. Partly because of the site, partly because of the fissiparous tendencies of the times, partly because of our lack of skills, there is a "bad memory" of disorganization, impossible ambitions, and failure too – quite enough to learn from.

Institutional connections and access to resources remain important, of course; but so, too, do the more intimate dynamics of group work, collaboration, intellectual dialogue, personal friendships, new forms of sociability, and expanded domestic spaces. I am not at all sure that all political reinventions don't start – or continue – from some such matrix as this.

NOTES

1 A version of this essay was given to the staff–postgraduate seminar at the London University Institute of Education in March 1996. I am especially grateful to Debbie Epstein and Ken Jones for their comments. I have also had full and invaluable feedback from Elizabeth Long which encouraged me to be more specific about, among other things, aspects of the history of the Birmingham Centre and Department. I am grateful for her friendship and support. Thanks also to those members of CCCS who have replied to my requests for memories of their times there. Their letters are not directly quoted in this piece but have informed my approach. For more details, see Johnson (1997a).

2 "Cannot but" because having worked at CCCS can be a liability for fresh thinking and listening about cultural studies because of the ways "the Birmingham School" has figured in contemporary polemics. Also, there's a danger of being read as "speaking for Birmingham." This is something I don't have to do anymore and this is a great relief. I am speaking for myself in this essay. For the dilemmas of other participants in speaking and writing about CCCS, see Brunsdon (1996); Canaan and Epstein (1997), especially the chapters by McNeil and by Johnson; Green (1982); Grossberg (1989) and, especially, Hall (1992, 1996).

3 For sharp and pertinent comments on the problem of constructing Birmingham – and Britain more generally – as the point of origin of cultural studies, see Stratton and Ang (1996).

4 It's a paradox that I have only been able to have time to write about teaching cultural studies since I stopped teaching it so excessively! Although this piece takes pedagogy as one instance of transformation in the academy, the new edited volume on teaching cultural studies, with several ex-CCCS authors (including myself), opens up these questions more centrally. See Canaan and Epstein (1997).

5 The Centre for Research in International Communication and Culture (CRICC), Faculty of Humanities, Nottingham Trent University.

6 Contemporary debates about the creativity of marginality are closely linked to older discussions of the creativity of popular "resistance" and also to contemporary critical discourses of "the liminal," of "cultural hybridity," and "double consciousness" – though in each case there are significant theoretical and political shifts. Today, these debates are often most pointedly carried through around questions of "race." See, for example, hooks (1991, 1992), where discourses of marginality and of resistance are both powerfully present; Gilroy (1993a, 1993b); Hall (1990, 1991); Bhabha (1990, 1994).

7 I am grateful to Tom Steele of the Department of Continuing Education at the University of Leeds for discussions about the prehistory of cultural studies in explicitly left-wing and popular educational practices in the period from the 1930s to the 1950s. I look forward to the publication of his full account of this.

8 Most of these arrangements were in place when I arrived in 1974. CCCS Annual Reports start to stress "collective work" in 1969; in this year, too, "subgroups" are first listed (Centre for Contemporary Cultural Studies, *Report*, 1969–71, 10–13). In one useful unpublished account of the early years of CCCS, "the first properly collective project" took place in 1966–7, but collective work really developed in the years after 1968 and during Stuart Hall's Acting Directorship. See Hall, Green, and Johnson (1979).

9 In 1975–6, for instance, the groups were Admissions Advisory Group, Working Papers in Cultural Studies (the CCCS journal), Inter-faculty Studies (a jointly taught course), Administration (the weekly newsletter), Books (contacts with publishers), Conference Planning and Library and Equipment (see "Notes for New Members," unpublished departmental paper, 1975–6). There was no written constitution till 1985 – by which time any reasonably democratic system was hard to operate.

10 Subgroups reported regularly and at some length in the CCCS Annual Report. See, for example, Centre for Contemporary Cultural Studies, *Report*, 1975–6, 14–26.

11 The first collective books were in fact thematic issues of *Working Papers in Cultural Studies*, the Centre's journal. Two of these (WPCS 7/8, *Resistance Through Rituals* and WPCS 10, *On Ideology*) were later published in the Hutchinson series as Hall and Jefferson (1976) and CCCS (1977). Late examples of collective books with strong Birmingham connections include Education Group II (1991); Franklin, Lury, and Stacey (1991); Steinberg, Epstein, and Johnson (1997).

12 This occurred especially in relation to feminism and women's-movement politics and different forms of black politics. But at different times other groupings – working-class "mature" students, lesbian and gay students, "women thesis writers," and men interested in studying masculinities – also used the spaces which the subgroup and caucus tradition gave some legitimation to.

13 *Working Papers in Cultural Studies*, 1–10, published by CCCS from 1971 to 1977.

14 The first appeared in September 1964; the last in February 1987.

15 Presentations lasted till the mid 1980s. Even when not intended for publication they were usually written up and survive.

16 Such discussions occurred in 1976, 1977, 1979, 1980, and 1983.

17 For the cultural studies intellectual as "fan," see Ross (1992: 553) and Jameson (1995). For valuable discussions of "the popular" as a problematic term and project in cultural studies, see Hall (1981) and McGuigan (1992), which includes a "sympathetic critique" of "cultural populism," including Birmingham work. I am also grateful to Charlotte Brunsdon for discussions on these topics in their applications to the history of feminist work on "women's genre" and soap opera especially, I hope her important thesis on these issues will soon be published.

18 In, for example, debates about history and theory, and notably by E. P. Thompson. This feeling was quite strong, however, within the History Workshop movement. See, for example, Samuel (1981: xl–lvl, 376–417).

19 These events are remembered and reflected upon in the poem sequence "Grievous Recognitions" and in the autobiographical commentary "Sexual Identity and the Grieving Process," Johnson (1997b).

20 I am particularly grateful for active collaboration and long discussions with Parvati Raghuram about the methodological literatures of social sciences, and to Deborah Chambers for sharing dilemmas about cultural studies particularly. Also to the Ph.D. students of the Humanities Faculty at Nottingham Trent for making a resource (and much fun) out of our still-wildly different approaches.

21 See, however, Alasuutari (1996) which, nonetheless, we found disappointingly captive to social scientific discussions. We have used feminist discussions which have deeply influenced cultural studies practices (e.g. Lather, 1991). For qualitative sociological methods influenced by "cultural" debates, see Denzin and Lincoln (1994). Other points of overlap are with life history/

autobiography (where compare Stanley, 1993, and Probyn, 1993) and anthropology (e.g. Clifford and Marcus, 1986). I am grateful to Ann Gray for discussions and help on these issues, including a view of an outline of her planned book on ethnographic methods.

22 In Britain the opening up of psychology as a discipline to approaches out of contemporary cultural theory – especially to theories of discourse – has been one of the most welcome recent developments in an adjacent discipline. Psychology which takes a cultural turn is now among the most vibrant of the cluster of cultural approaches (e.g. Henriques *et al.*, 1984; Parker and Shotter, 1990; Walkerdine, 1990; Hollway, 1989).

23 E.g. Alasuutari (1996).

24 For a useful discussion of universalization, parochialism, and transnational positionalities in cultural studies, see Stratton and Ang (1996).

25 I use this term in the sense employed in Lakatos (1970).

26 Cultural geography is now a very well-established subfield, often closely allied to others – feminist geography, for example. Within this vigorous and growing field it is interesting to trace the changes of perspective of particular leading scholars. See, for example, the economic geographer Doreen Massey (1984, 1994). I am grateful to my Trent colleague Tracey Skelton for discussion on these themes.

27 In the real world, it may be more appropriate to anticipate the threat to the relative plurality of current academic maps from the newer imperialists, who, having intervened in schools and colleges, will seek to redesign the academy too, more radically than before, according to a capitalist utility. Will there be a place for "humanities" at all in this empire?

28 I am grateful to Rolf Lindner of the Institute for European Ethnology at the Humboldt University, Berlin, for discussions on the impacts of British theory and practice on the (West) German scene.

REFERENCES

Alasuutari, P. 1996: *Researching Culture: Qualitative Method and Cultural Studies*. London: Sage.

Barthes, R. 1973: *Mythologies*. London: Paladin.

Baudrillard, J. 1983: *In the Shadow of the Silent Majorities*. New York: Semiotext(e).

Bhabha, H. 1990: The Third Space: Interview. In J. Rutherford (ed.), *Identity, Community, Culture, Difference*, London: Lawrence and Wishart.

—— 1994: *The Location of Culture*. London: Routledge.

Bourdieu, P. 1988: *Homo Academicus*. Cambridge: Polity Press.

Brunsdon, C. 1996: A Thief in the Night: Stories of Feminism in the 1970s at CCCS. In D. Morley and Kuan-Hsing Chen (eds), *Stuart Hall: Critical Dialogues*, London: Routledge.

Butler, J. 1993: *Bodies That Matter*. London: Routledge.

Canaan, J. and Epstein, D. (eds) 1997: *A Question of Discipline: Teaching Cultural Studies*. Colorado: Westview Press.

Centre for Contemporary Cultural Studies 1969–71: *Annual Report.*
—— 1971–7: Working Papers in Cultural Studies, 1–10.
—— 1974–85: *Stencilled Occasional Papers,* nos 1–85.
—— 1975: Working Papers in Cultural Studies, 4.
—— 1975–6a: "Notes for New Members".
—— 1975–6b: *Annual Report.*
—— 1978: *On Ideology.* London: Hutchinson.
—— 1982: *Making Histories.* London: Hutchinson.
Centre for Contemporary Cultural Studies, Education Group 1980: *Unpopular Education.* London: Hutchinson.
Chambers, I. and Curti, L. (eds) 1996: *The Post-colonial Question: Common Skies, Divided Horizons.* London: Routledge.
Chen, Kuan-Hsing 1996: Post-Marxism: Between/Beyond Critical Postmodernism. In D. Morley and Kuan-Hsing Chen (eds), *Stuart Hall: Critical Dialogues,* London: Routledge.
Clarke, J. 1991: *New Times, Old Enemies: Essays on Cultural Studies and America.* London: HarperCollins.
Clifford, J. and Marcus, G. 1986: *Writing Culture: The Poetics and Politics of Ethnography.* Berkeley: University of California Press.
Connell, R. W. 1995: *Masculinities.* Cambridge: Polity Press.
Dawson, G. 1994: *Soldier Heroes: British Adventure, Empire and the Imagining of Masculinities.* London: Routledge.
Denzin, N. K. and Lincoln, Y. S. (eds) 1994: *A Handbook of Qualitative Research.* London: Sage.
Derrida, J. 1974: *Of Grammatology.* Baltimore: Johns Hopkins University Press.
Dollimore, J. 1991: *Sexual Dissidence: Augustine to Wilde, Freud to Foucault.* Oxford: Clarendon Press.
Dreyfus H. L. and Rabinow, P. 1982: *Michel Foucault: Beyond Structuralism and Hermeneutics.* Brighton: Harvest Press.
Duberman, M. B., Vicinus, M., and Chauncey, J. (eds) 1989: *Hidden From History: Reclaiming the Gay and Lesbian Past.* London: Penguin.
Education Group II, Cultural Studies, Birmingham 1991: *Education Limited.* London: Unwin Hyman.
Epstein, D. 1997: The Voice of Authority: On Lecturing in Cultural Studies. In J. Canaan and D. Epstein (eds), *A Question of Discipline: Teaching Cultural Studies,* Colorado: Westview Press.
Fanon, F. 1986: *Black Skin, White Masks.* London: Pluto Press.
Foucault, M. 1977: *Discipline and Punish: The Birth of the Prison.* London: Allen Lane.
—— 1979: *The History of Sexuality, Volume I.* London: Penguin.
—— 1990: *The Care of the Self: The History of Sexuality, Volume III.* London: Penguin.
Franklin, S., Lury, C., and Stacey, J. (eds) 1991: *Off-centre: Feminism and Cultural Studies.* London: HarperCollins.
Gilroy, P. 1987: *There Ain't No Black in the Union Jack.* London: Hutchinson.
—— 1993a: *Small Acts: Thoughts on the Politics of Black Cultures.* London: Serpent's Tail.

—— 1993b: *The Black Atlantic: Modernity and Double Consciousness*. London: Verso.

Gramsci, A. 1971: *Selections from the Prison Notebooks*. London: Lawrence and Wishart.

Green, M. 1982: The Centre for Contemporary Cultural Studies. In P. Widdowson (ed.), *Re-reading English*, London: Methuen.

Grossberg, L. 1989: The Formations of Cultural Studies: An American in Birmingham, *Strategies*, no. 2, 114–49.

Hall, C. 1992: Missionary Stories: Gender and Ethnicity in England in the 1830s and 1840s. In L. Grossberg, C. Nelson, and P. Treichler (eds), *Cultural Studies*, New York: Routledge.

Hall, S. 1975–6: *MA in Cultural Studies, Course I:* Problems of Theory and Methods in Cultural Studies: Aims, Outline and General Reading List. Birmingham: CCCS/DCS.

—— 1981: Notes on Deconstructing "the Popular." In R. Samuel (ed.), *People's History and Socialist Theory*, London: Routledge.

—— 1988: The Toad in the Garden: Thatcherism Among the Theorists. In Cary Nelson and Lawrence Grossberg (eds), *Marxism and the Interpretation of Culture*, London: Macmillan.

—— 1990: Cultural Identity and Diaspora. In J. Rutherford (ed.), *Identity, Culture, Community and Difference*, London: Lawrence and Wishart.

—— 1991: Old and New Identities, Old and New Ethnicities. In A. D. King (ed.), *Culture, Globalization and the World-system*, London: Macmillan.

—— 1992: Cultural Studies and its Theoretical Legacies. In L. Grossberg, C. Nelson, and P. Treichler (eds), *Cultural Studies*, New York: Routledge.

—— 1995: Interview with Roger Bromley. In J. Munns and G. Rajan (eds), *A Cultural Studies Reader: History, Theory, Practice*, London: Longmans.

—— 1996: Cultural Studies and the Politics of Internationalization: Interview with Kuan-Hsing Chen. In D. Morley and Kuan-Hsing Chen (eds), *Stuart Hall: Critical Dialogues*, London: Routledge.

Hall, S. and Jefferson, T. (eds) 1976: *Resistance Through Rituals: Youth Subcultures in Post War Britain*. London: Hutchinson.

Hall, S. et al. 1978: *Policing The Crisis: Mugging, the State and Law and Order*. London: Macmillan.

Hall, S. and Jacques, M. (eds) 1983: *The Politics of Thatcherism*. London: Lawrence and Wishart.

Hall, S., Green, M., and Johnson, R. 1979: On Contradictions. Unpublished CCCS/DCS paper, January.

Harding, S. 1986: *The Science Question in Feminism*. Milton Keynes: Open University Press.

Henriques, J. et al. 1984: *Changing the Subject: Psychology, Social Regulation and Subjectivity*. London: Methuen.

Hoggart, R. 1958: *The Uses of Literacy*. London: Penguin.

Hollway, W. 1989: *Subjectivity and Method in Psychology: Gender, Meaning and Science*. London: Sage.

hooks, b. 1991: *Yearning: Race, Gender and Cultural Politics*. London: Turnaround.

—— 1992: *Black Looks: Race and Representation*. London: Turnaround.

Jameson, F. 1995: On Cultural Studies. In J. Munns and G. Rajan (eds), *A Cultural Studies Reader: History, Theory, Practice*. London: Longmans.

Johnson, R. 1979: Three Problematics: Elements of a Theory of Working-class Culture. In J. Clarke, C. Critcher, and R. Johnson (eds), *Working-class Culture: Studies in History and Theory*, London: Hutchinson.

—— 1981: Against Absolutism. In R. Samuel (ed.), *People's History and Socialist Theory*, London: Routledge.

—— 1983: What is Cultural Studies Anyway? Birmingham: Centre for Contemporary Cultural Studies, stencilled occasional paper, no. 74.

—— 1992–3: *M. Soc. Sci. in Cultural Studies, Course CSG1 H*: Frameworks of Cultural Study: Aims, Ways of Working, Programme Birmingham: CCCS/DCS.

—— 1996: Sexual Dissonances: On the "Impossibility" of Sexuality Education. *Journal of Curriculum Studies*, special issue on sexuality education, summer.

—— 1997a: Teaching without Guarantees: Cultural Studies, Pedagogy and Identity. In J. Canaan and D. Epstein (eds), *A Question of Discipline: Teaching Cultural Studies*, Colorado: Westview Press.

—— 1997b: Grievous Recognitions: The Grieving Process and Sexual Boundaries. In D. Epstein, R. Johnson, and D. L. Steinberg (eds), *Border Patrols: Policing the Boundaries of Heterosexuality*, London: Cassell.

Lakatos, I. 1970: Falsification and the Methodology of Scientific Research Programmes. In I. Lakatos and A. Musgrove (eds), *Criticism and the Growth of Knowledge*, Cambridge: Cambridge University Press.

Lather, P. 1991: *Getting Smart: Feminist Research and Pedagogy within the Postmodern*. New York: Routledge.

McGuigan, J. 1992: *Cultural Populism*. London: Routledge.

MacKinnon, C. 1982: Feminism, Marxism, Method and the State: An Agenda for Theory. *Signs*, 7, 3, 515–44.

MacRobbie A. 1991: *Feminism and Youth Culture*. Basingstoke: Macmillan.

Marx, K. 1973: *Economic and Philosophical Manuscripts of 1944* (Ed. and intro. Dirk J. Struik.) London: Lawrence and Wishart.

—— 1979: *Theses on Feuerbach*. (Translated and interpreted by Wal Suchting, "Marx's Theses on Feuerbach.") In J. Mepham and D.-H. Ruben (eds), *Issues in Marxist Philosophy*, vol. II, Brighton: Harvester.

Marx, K. and Engels, F. 1970: *The German Ideology: Part I with selections from Parts II and III*. (Ed. and intro. C. J. Arthur.) London: Lawrence and Wishart.

Massey, D. 1984: *Spatial Dimensions of Labour: Social Structures and the Geography of Production*. Basingstoke: Macmillan.

—— 1994: *Space, Place and Gender*. Cambridge: Polity.

Moore, S. 1988: Getting a Bit of the Other: The Pimps of Postmodernism. In R. Chapman and J. Rutherford (eds), *Male Order: Unwrapping Masculinity*, London: Lawrence and Wishart.

Morley, D. and Chen, Kuan-Hsing (eds) 1996: *Stuart Hall: Critical Dialogues*. London: Routledge.

Mort, F. 1987: *Dangerous Sexualities: Medico-moral Politics in England since 1930*. London: Routledge.

Mulvey, L. 1989: *Visual and Other Pleasures*. London: Macmillan.

Parker, I. and Shotter, J. 1990: *Deconstructing Social Psychology*. London: Routledge.

Probyn, E. 1993: *Sexing the Self: Gendered Positions in Cultural Studies*. London: Routledge.

Redman, P. 1997: Invasion of the Monstrous Others: Heterosexual Masculinities, "the AIDS Carrier" and the Horror Genre. In D. Epstein, R. Johnson, and D. L. Steinberg (eds), *Border Patrols: Policing the Boundaries of Heterosexuality*. London: Cassell.

Redman, P. and Mac An Ghaill, M. 1997: Educating Peter: Heterosexual Masculinities, Schooling and the Unconscious. In D. Epstein, R. Johnson, and D. L. Steinberg (eds), *Border Patrols: Policing the Boundaries of Heterosexuality*, London: Cassell.

Ross, A. 1992: New Age Technoculture. In L. Grossberg, C. Nelson, and P. Threichler (eds), *Cultural Studies*, New York: Routledge.

Said, E. 1993: *Culture and Imperialism*. London: Verso.

Samuel, R. (ed.) 1981: *People's History and Socialist Theory*. London: Routledge.

Schwarz, B. 1994: Where is Cultural Studies? *Cultural Studies*, 8, 3, 377–93.

Sedgewick, E. K. 1985: *Between Men: English Literature and Male Homosocial Desire*. New York: Columbia University Press.

—— 1990: *The Epistemology of the Closet*. London: Penguin.

Stacey, J. 1993: *Star Gazing: Hollywood Cinema and Female Spectatorship*. London: Routledge.

Stallybrass, P. and White, A. 1986: *The Politics and Poetics of Transgression*. London: Methuen.

Stanley, L. 1993: On Auto/biography in Sociology. *Sociology*, 27, 1, 41–52.

Stanley, L. and Wise, S. 1993: *Breaking Out Again: Feminist Ontology and Epistemology*. London: Routledge.

Steinberg, D., Epstein, D., and Johnson, R. 1997: *Border Patrols: Policing the Boundaries of Heterosexuality*. London: Cassell.

Stratton, J. and Ang, I. 1996: On the Impossibility of a Global Cultural Studies: "British" Cultural Studies in an "International" Frame. In D. Morley and Kuan-Hsing Chen (eds), *Stuart Hall: Critical Dialogues*. London: Routledge.

Taylor L. 1996: Nothing Personal: The Place of Subjugation and Marginalisation within the Field of Cultural Studies. Unpublished paper given at the Conference on "Teaching Culture and the Cultures of Teaching," University of Sussex, 22–23 March.

Thompson, E. P. 1961: Review of The Long Revolution. *New Left Review*, nos 9 and 10.

Van Zoonen, L. 1994: *Feminist Media Studies*. London: Sage.

Walkerdine, V. 1990: *Schoolgirl Fictions*. London: Verso.

Weeks, J. 1981: *Sex, Politics and Society: The Regulation of Sexuality Since 1800*. London: Longmans.

West, C. (with Gilroy, P. and hooks, b.) 1992: The Postmodern Crisis of the Black Intellectuals – and Discussion. In L. Grossberg, C. Nelson, and P. Treichler (eds), *Cultural Studies*, New York: Routledge.

Williams, R. 1958: *Culture and Society 1780–1950*. London: Chatto and Windus.
—— 1961: *The Long Revolution*. London: Chatto and Windus.
—— 1973: *The Country and the City*. Oxford: Oxford University Press.
—— 1977: *Marxism and Literature*. Oxford: Oxford University Press.
Williams, R. and Orrom, M. 1954: *Preface to Film*. London: Film Drama.
Working Papers in Cultural Studies, no. 7/8, "Resistance Through Rituals".
Working Papers in Cultural Studies, no. 10, "On Ideology".

17

Whither Cultural Studies?

ELLEN MESSER-DAVIDOW

All along, practitioners of cultural studies have debated the question posed by my title, variously predicting that their field would (behind "would" lurks "should") investigate politics in their broader socioeconomic dimension or their narrower cultural one, forge linkages with communities or entrench itself in universities, remain antidisciplinary or become properly disciplined. So why ask yet again? I pose the question not to summarize what is "in" cultural studies (arguments about its purposes and practices), but to analyze what cultural studies is "in." It is in big trouble. That trouble, I intend to show, may well determine what happens to cultural studies and more.

Since the mid-1980s, accusations about academic and cultural politics have ricocheted across the surfaces of public discourse in the United States probably a hundred thousand times, having been blasted from the guns of warring scholars, newspaper columnists, talk-show hosts, legislators, and public figures.[1] The clamoring parties agree that academic and cultural institutions are politicized, though by whom and for what interests they continue to dispute. To sort out the confusion, let us look more closely at the discourse that has enabled them to make accusations. The discourse of politics that entered the US academy during the 1960s flowed from a marginalized scholarship long concerned with societal inequalities and from social movements – civil rights, New Left, and women's liberation – mobilized to change the institutions that perpetuated those inequalities. Using the discourse, scholars produced studies showing that the academy discriminated against certain populations – universities by denying them equal educational and employment opportunities and disciplines by ignoring their histories, contributions, and persons. Although committed to producing new knowledge, they debated its uses: correcting disciplines and reforming universities, or exposing social realities and fueling movement activism?

In the 1970s, the discourse took an intellectualizing turn when it was infused by esoteric theories about discourse and discipline themselves. As usually happens with insider knowledges, the scholars who applied these theories have had what I can only describe, from the vantage-point of the present moment, as an internalizing and isolating focus. Most concentrated on issues within a discipline, or debates about models within a cross-disciplinary approach (e.g. structuralism vs. humanism in Marxian thought, gender vs. multiple identities as analytical categories in feminist studies), or contests between academic discourses (e.g. modernism vs. postmodernism). By doing so, they recast knowledge politics as discursive practice situated within and across disciplines. More recently, other scholars have worked to link knowledge-production with societal practices; they study popular culture as constitutive of subjects, science as social practice, and the academy as a power/knowledge formation. Yet far too much of even this recent work shares the illusory presupposition that informs the rest. It construes the academy as if it were a bounded entity occasionally permeated by streams of discourse: forms of popular culture flowing in and analyses of them flowing out, or the contextual values of society influencing the constitutive practices of science, or the dispersal of observation, examination, and normalizing judgment throughout education.

When conservatives launched their war on progressive trends in the academy, they targeted critical approaches to knowledge, culture, and society – feminist, Marxist, multicultural, poststructuralist, social constructivist – that are included under the big tent of cultural studies. As an example, I quote from Lynne V. Cheney's speech to the 1988 meeting of the American Council of Learned Societies (ACLS):

> When I become most concerned about the state of the humanities in our colleges and universities is not when I see theories and ideas fiercely competing, but when I see them neatly converging, when I see feminist criticism, Marxism, various forms of poststructuralism, and other approaches all coming to bear on one concept and threatening to displace it. I think specifically of the concept of Western civilization, which has come under pressure on many fronts, political as well as theoretical. Attacked for being elitist, sexist, racist, and Eurocentric, this central and sustaining idea of our educational system and our intellectual heritage is being declared unworthy of study. (Cheney, 1988: 6)

Cheney's conceit that these critical approaches had declared war on the national cultural heritage was not idiosyncratic. She pronounced it at a time when her fellow conservatives were widely circulating a new discourse, political correctness (PC), that demonized progressive scholars as McCarthyites hunting down conservative colleagues and tenured radicals revolutionalizing their universities. Although her expression of concern was more subdued than their inflammatory accusations, its import was more devastating, for she spoke and acted as Chairman of the National Endowment for the Humanities, the government agency that supplied almost 75 percent of the total grants for humanities scholarship and programs.

To recap, when conservatives entered the arena of knowledge politics, they constituted a PC discourse that combined Manichean dualism of communism/democracy with the humanist notion of enduring values and truths to accuse progressive scholars of demolishing Western civilization and the academic institutions entrusted with preserving it. When progressives responded from within the confines of PC discourse, the result was a more sharply dualized politics, with one camp claiming that its scholarship discovered the true and valuable and the other camp claiming that its critique revealed the constructedness of truth and value. Only belatedly did progressive scholars recognize that the real action was not their debate with conservatives about intellectual issues, but conservatives' translation of PC discourse into public policies that would damage academic and cultural institutions. How did progressives come to mistake the denigrating talk for the destructive action? I would argue that their own intellectualizing of politics obscured the real politics of the conservative movement. By using the term "real politics," I wish to differentiate what progressive scholars are doing from what conservatives are doing, because, at first glance, both groups *seem* to be doing discourse. But, in fact, progressives are producing and circulating academic discourses, while conservatives are using anti-academic discourse to manipulate the resources, regulations, and constituency demands that enable and constrain the entire academic-knowledge enterprise.

If I have learned anything from my own research, it is that what we usually regard as extra-academic institutions, resources, and practices have always enabled and constrained the academic enterprise. Today, however, they are being deployed with a vengeance against it. The defunding of the National Endowments for the Humanities and Arts; a Congressional proposal to eliminate the social, behavioral, and economic sciences as funding categories of the National Science Foundation (NSF) that was defeated in this session but will return in future sessions; the Supreme Court's *Rosenberger* decision overturning the University of Virginia's refusal to fund a religious student newspaper; the California Civil Rights Initiative to curb affirmative action in state agencies and universities; the attack on regional accrediting agencies for their diversity standards; the founding of conservative alumni organizations to pressure university administrations on personnel and curricular matters – these are a few of the many examples I have analyzed in recent and forthcoming publications to show how a superbly organized and funded conservative movement is restructuring the higher-education system. My point is that if we consider politics to be power-imbued arrangements for ordering a system's affairs (whether that system is the academy or the nation), then we must see the politics actually performed by most cultural studies scholars as internal to academic discourse.

The question of where cultural studies is headed is worth pondering differently than it has been, because at present the conservative movement is far more likely than cultural studies scholars to determine not only its direction but its very existence. By way of situating cultural studies "in" (and maybe "out") of trouble, this essay will careen vertiginously through a number of questions that scholars have asked but not linked: What is cultural studies in the USA today? What trouble is it in, and how was that trouble produced? How might we reconceptualize discourse in order to link the cultural, social, and political? Should we instrumentalize academic knowledge-production? That these matters are linked will become evident as I proceed to recast academic cultural studies and/as its context.

What is Cultural Studies?

When most scholars define cultural studies in the United States, they implicitly cast it as an academic field by describing its precursors, strains, objects, methods, and relations. For instance, essays in this volume and others (e.g. Grossberg, Nelson, and Treichler, 1992) recount the contributions of scholars associated with the Frankfurt School, humanist and structural Marxism, and the Birmingham Centre for Contemporary Cultural Studies, showing how they constituted and complexified the emerging field. They map the intricated strains of cultural studies by ideology (Marxism, feminism, poststructuralism) and discipline. They detail the objects populating the field (elaborations of "cultural" not demarcated from the political and economic, into the elite and popular, across the public and private) and debate the methods of constru(ct)ing it (survey research, content analysis, ethnography, ethnomethodology, textual analysis, semiotics, and psychoanalysis). Finally, they focus on cultural studies' commerce with disciplines – the flow of discourse (or not) across borders that demarcate it from sociology, history, and literary studies – and its exchanges with the publics who are its audiences, allies, and adversaries. Although most scholars see cultural studies as antidisciplinary, they should not for a minute think it is nondisciplinary. Their own accounts rightly delineate it as a cross-discipline with permeable boundaries.

What do I mean by a discipline? Although the etymology of that term reveals the historical proliferation of its meaning, "discipline" has come down to us with the double sense of knowledge as system and power. It has been used since Chaucer's time to denote branches of knowledge, even though the branches themselves have changed, e.g. the classical divisions of philosophy, the medieval trivium and quadrivium, the Scholastic arts and sciences, and the modern disciplines emerging in the nineteenth century. The term also denotes methods of training organized by and productive of power, e.g. the discipline of the child, the military conscript, and the religious novitiate (Shumway and Messer-Davidow, 1991). Foucault was the first to explain how the techniques for producing knowledge and regulating subjects were intricated, and others have shown how discipline, through institutionalization, became the dominant form of academic knowledge production.

Today, academic knowledges and knowers are produced and regulated through the machineries of specialisms, disciplines, and cross-disciplines. As Timothy Lenoir put it, "Disciplines are dynamic structures for assembling, channeling, and replicating the social and technical practices essential to the functioning of the political economy [of knowledge production] and the system of power relations that actualize it" (Lenoir, 1993: 72). Each (cross-)discipline is organized and organizing through two intricated infrastructures: a localized one of university departments that socialize knowers through training, examination, and review and circulate knowledges through the curriculum, and an international one of associations, publications, and conferences that regulate knowledges through review processes and circulate them to the scholarly community. This model allows us to see disciplines and cross-disciplines differently from how other models do. The humanist model, which casts a discipline as an accumulation of knowledge about a particular subject, foregrounds its intellectual core of facts, theories, and methods. The discourse model, which construes a discipline as a system of statements and the rules for producing them, foregrounds its formation of objects, speaking subjects, concepts, and strategies. By contrast, this model casts disciplines as economies of practices, resources, and institutions that together organize the academic-knowledge enterprise.

The most significant ways that disciplines differ from each other are attributable to the permeability of their boundaries. As Tony Becher has observed, impermeable boundaries cause and result from "tightly knit, convergent disciplinary communities"; they allow practitioners to maintain a uniformity of ideas, methods, and standards, to monopolize a field of expertise, and to garner resources. Conversely, permeable boundaries cause and result from "loosely knit, divergent academic groups"; they allow practitioners to borrow ideas, methods, and authority from other fields, to expand their expertise, and to compete for resources they may have been denied (Becher, 1989: 37–8). Although a discipline can become multidisciplinary when it trades in knowledges, a cross-discipline emerges only when disciplinarily trained practitioners institutionalize a boundary space (e.g. a temporary problem-solving team, a center, or a program) and constitute an object (e.g. sex–gender systems) that does not confine itself to a single field. With its "big tent" inclusivity, varied forms of institutionalization (programs, centers, disciplinary subfields, and even ephemeral reading groups), and "culture" as object, US cultural studies is rightly described as a cross-discipline with permeable boundaries, divergent practitioners, and a nonuniform intellectual core.

Now, to recast this cross-discipline and/as its context, I shall describe not its intellectual core of ideas and methods, but the complex of practices in which it participates – specifically, what it is doing and what is being done to it. In the United States, cultural studies is an institutionalized enterprise for producing and circulating knowledges. Even though it is institutionalized in both the academy and other organizations (see below), it is but a small enterprise in a much larger economy. Academic cultural studies is part of the academic-knowledge enterprise, which itself participates in a larger economy of what might generically be termed "expert knowledges" that, in turn, are commonly marked off from "everyday knowledges" for several reasons. Expert knowledges are regarded as having an enhanced informational value because their producers have an institutional imprimatur: they are trained, credentialed, and employed by institutions, and they bolster the authority of their knowledges by using the legitimating rhetoric (about the pursuit of truth, beauty, and usefulness) that has long been circulated by institutions. Everyday knowledges, such as folk wisdom, street smarts, and family ways, also make claims, but they use a rhetoric that appeals to the legitimacy of the experiential, anecdotal, and affective rather than the institutional.

Moreover, the expert and the everyday are differently organized systems for producing knowledges and knowers – as Basil Bernstein has shown in *Class, Codes, and Control* by analyzing how children learn everyday and school knowledge codes. To master these codes, children must learn their contents, their ordering, and the procedures for attaining proficiency in that content and ordering. Even when an everyday discourse and a school discourse seem to afford an opportunity for dealing with the same type of knowledge (e.g. solving the same math problem), they entail different languages, structures of classification, learning procedures, modalities for socializing children into learning, and goals (Bernstein, 1975: 31). As an example, Johan Muller and Nick Taylor describe the mathematics performed by the Brazilian children who make a living by selling coconuts in street markets. The street method for calculating the price of seven coconuts is $(7 \times 30) + (7 \times 5)$, whereas the school method for the same calculation is $7 \times (30 + 5)$ (Muller and Taylor, 1995: 260). When the children migrate from street to school, they must transform coconuts to marks on paper, one method of calculating to another, the informal street modalities (peer-group interactions and seller–buyer trans-actions) to the formal school modality (the hierarchical students–teacher tutorial), and one goal (making a profitable deal) to another (producing a correct answer).

Expert and everyday knowledges are not merely discontinuous, but also asymmetrically so, because the former maintain themselves as such precisely by excluding the latter. For example, recent accounts show that the formation of sociology as a discipline was owing to such discontinuities. The early practitioners styled their work as academic to disassociate it from social projects, such as the reform crusades of improvement soci-eties, the political agendas of socialists, and social services. They styled it as scientific to separate from older traditions of social thought, notably history of civilization and moral philosophy. And they differentiated it from other disciplines scientifically studying the social, such as economics and political science, by producing a new object of study, "society." The result was that disciplinary practitioners performed convention-structured practices that reorganized the multivalent practices of everyday people who think, feel, and act into the discourse recognized as sociology (Bernard, 1987: 197–201; Bottomore and Nisbet, 1978: viii; Smith, 1989: 44–52). This discipline is no exception; the same point can be made about literary stud-ies, art history, economics, physics – or cultural studies, which reorganizes everyday cultural practices into academic discourse.

Having situated academic cultural studies in the expert-knowledge economy, I now turn to that knowledge's production and circulation. Expert knowledges are produced by diverse organizations located in dif-ferent sectors – academic, governmental (laboratories, bureaus, legislative committees), public (museums, libraries), community (chautaquas, fest-ivals), quasi-public (media, churches, unions), corporate (research and development units, advertising agencies), and private (think-tanks, founda-tions). Just so, cultural knowledge is produced and circulated not merely by academic cultural studies, but also by museums, libraries, chautaquas, festivals, television, radio, film, theater, government agencies, schools, churches, and, increasingly, partisan think-tanks that disguise their propa-ganda as research. For instance, the Free Congress Foundation's Institute for Cultural Conservatism promulgates "retroculture," a mix-and-match ensemble of Ralph Lauren chic, Victorian sexuality, and white Western values; the conservative Heritage Foundation's Cultural Policy Studies Working Group helped launch the drive to privatize public broadcasting by sponsoring so-called research papers and issuing press releases; and the right-wing Center for the Study of Popular Culture initiated the attack on Hollywood through the same means.

Once it is circulated in society, academic cultural knowledge competes with all of the other expert cultural knowledges. Or, to put it another way, when the average consumer is presented with a slice of Americana, s/he does not make fine discriminations about whether it was baked by a Penn State professor, the Philadelphia Library, or the Commonwealth Foundation, a right-wing think-tank in Harrisburg. How effectively the academic knowledge can compete depends upon its circumstances in the academy, such as the hiring of faculty and funding of programs. Those circumstances depend, in turn, on what enables and constrains the entire academic enterprise: "extra-academic" resources (e.g. federal funds, state allocations, contracts and consultancies, foundation grants, alumni giving), regulations (e.g. for curricular diversity, affirmative action, research on human subjects), constituency demands (e.g. parents, alumni, citizens), and media exposure (pun intended). At present, the two often function inversely; that is, a university that supports a cultural studies program may find itself attacked by conservative alumni, ridiculed in the media, and questioned by back-to-basics legislators.

While the academy is always intricated with extra-academic institutions, resources, and practices, disciplines themselves vary in terms of how they link up with extra-academic sectors. As one model, "big science" was formed after World War II by hybridizing the academic and military at laboratory sites and meshing the flow of human, financial, and technical resources across these sectors (Pickering, 1995). As another model, policy knowledge is produced by discrete organizations (universities, think-tanks, public-interest groups), but to be effective in policy formation and implementation it must circulate across sectors (media, voter constituencies, advocacy organizations, legislatures, government agencies) that themselves are both differently organized and inadequately meshed (Nelson, 1984; Scott and Meyer, 1991). In contrast, expert cultural knowledge is produced by the institutions mentioned previously, and that is to say nothing of the informal cultural knowledge transmitted by families, peer groups, and neighborhoods. Some meshing across sectors does occur when scholars serve as consultants for museum exhibitions, or think-tank fellows, or television commentators. But academic and nonacademic organizations generally do not coproduce and cocirculate cultural knowledges; they tend to confine their operations to their own sectors. What I show next is that conservatives, precisely by meshing organizations across sectors, have produced the big trouble that cultural studies is in.

Who and What Produced the Trouble?

The big trouble that cultural studies is in was produced through a complex process choreographed by the conservative movement. To summarize that process, conservatives mounted a wide-ranging attack on progressive higher education and culture, manipulated the National Endowments for the Humanities and Arts, translated their anti-PC discourse into policy discourse, and now are enacting legislation that will curb the production and circulation of some cultural knowledges. Although many conservative organizations have participated in the attack, I profile three – Madison Center for Educational Affairs, Intercollegiate Studies Institute, and National Association of Scholars – that have coordinated their operations to advance the agenda of cultural conservatism. What has made them such effective operators is the movement's own reticulation. Thus, in this section and the next, I trace a complex network of individuals who link up conservative organizations that in turn link up with governmental ones to leverage change.

The Madison Center for Educational Affairs (MCEA) was formed in 1990 by merging two predecessor organizations: the Institute for Educational Affairs, founded by Leslie Lenkowsky (now Hudson Institute President), William Simon (President, Olin Foundation), and Irving Kristol; and the Madison Center, founded by William Bennett (former NEH Chairman, now Heritage Foundation and Hudson Institute Fellow), and John Agresto (former NEH Acting Chairman, afterwards Madison Center President). MCEA's launching was supercharged by other conservative organizations. Its 1990 revenues of $1,162,367 and 1991 revenues of $929,038 were supplied by the Bradley, Coors, JM, Joyce, Olin, Sarah Scaife, and Smith Richardson Foundations, among others (Madison Center for Educational Affairs, 1991, 1992). Its 1990 and 1991 Board included Lenkowsky (NAS Board), Kristol (NAS Board), Agresto, John Bunzell (NAS Board, Hoover Institute Fellow), T. Kenneth Cribb (ISI President), Chester E. Finn, Jr (NAS Board), and Harvey Mansfield (member of NAS and NEH National Council). In addition, MCEA was linked with the Hudson Institute, a right-wing think-tank, where Lenkowsky was president, Bennett a fellow, and Finn an associate.

In 1990, Stephen Balch, President of the National Association of Scholars (NAS), said that MCEA and NAS were "closely allied with the conservative educational philosophy" (Innerst, 1990: A5) of Bennett and Allan Bloom and would carry out projects together (also Innerst, 1991; Delany and Lenkowsky, 1988). MCEA's highest-profile projects enact its top-priority agenda item – attacking and weakening progressive trends in the academy. The most ambitious project to date is the Collegiate Network, consisting of some 70 conservative student newspapers that MCEA supports with cash, technical advice, conferences, and summer internships for students. These campus-based newspapers have conducted vitriolic campaigns against feminism, multiculturalism, affirmative action, and anti-sexual harassment policies, to name a few. Another project, *The Commonsense Guide to American Colleges*, attempts to direct prospective students and

their parents away from these campuses by villifying them and to conservative colleges by praising them. Moreover, MCEA grants to such right-
wingers as Dinesh D'Souza have supported the writing and marketing of
a stream of anti-higher education books. Less known, however, are MCEA's
connections with Cheney during her tenure as NEH Chairman. In 1990
and 1991 alone, she spoke at the Collegiate Network conference and an
MCEA conference; wrote a feature story, "Depoliticizing the Academy,"
for *Newslink* (an MCEA newsletter); quoted Collegiate Network newspapers in her NEH annual reports; and provided summer internships at
NEH for Collegiate Network student journalists. Today, she is a member of
the MCEA board (see Madison Center for Educational Affairs, 1991, 1992;
Newslink, 1991; Horner, 1995: 16).

The Intercollegiate Studies Institute (ISI) was founded about 30 years
ago by Old Right leaders to promote traditional American education, free
enterprise, and individual responsibility. For 1992, it claimed impressive
numbers: 55,000 members, 20 conferences per year, magazine circulation
to 160,000 readers, and scholarships totaling $200,000. ISI sponsors
several publications: *Intercollegiate Studies Review, Modern Age*, and *The
Political Science Review*, journals for conservative faculty and intellectuals; *Campus*, a student magazine founded in 1989 to attack progressive
trends on campus; and *The Canon*, an organizational newsletter launched
in 1992. In 1995, it took over two MCEA projects, *The Commonsense
Guide to American Colleges* and the Collegiate Network. ISI also sponsors
lecture series, televised lectures, and a speakers bureau profusely staffed
by NAS members (Chairman Herbert I. London, former Vice President
Peter Shaw, Vice President Christina Hoff Sommers, Harvey Mansfield,
and Jeffrey Hart), government officials (Bennett, Agresto), and the usual
right-wingers (Russell Kirk, Hilton Kramer, Dinesh D'Souza, and David
Horowitz, Director of the Center for the Study of Popular Culture and
publisher of *Heterodoxy*, the right-wing academic scandal sheet) (Intercollegiate Studies Institute n.d. b and c; and Ritter, 1995).

ISI's networks of students, faculty, and alumni now pose the greatest
threat to the academy. The *I.S.I. Leadership Guide* is an eye-opening
manual that instructs students on how to organize conservative groups on
campus, apply for institutional funding, do donor fundraising, sponsor
campus and community activities, conduct literature blitzes, attract media
coverage, produce cable TV shows, run internship placement services,
hold demonstrations, distribute flyers at public-policy events, produce letter-
to-the-editor campaigns, and meet with elected officials. Ironically, a page
in this manual of conservative activism announces ISI's status as a nonpartisan educational and therefore tax-exempt organization (Intercollegiate
Studies Institute n.d. a: 13). ISI trains its faculty associates, all expenses
paid, at colloquia held throughout the year, and uses them to distribute

Campus and arrange conservative lectures. It has also been busy organizing conservative alumni groups now consolidated as the National Alumni Forum (NAF). Far from independent, NAF was jump-started in 1994 with revenues of $200,000 from Olin and Bradley and is led by Co-chairman Cheney, Co-chairman Richard Lamm (former Governor of Colorado and an habitué of the right-wing Heritage Foundation), and President Jerry L. Martin, formerly Cheney's NEH inner-staffer (*Campus* 1993; Messer-Davidow, 1994; Mercer, 1995a and b; Olin Foundation, 1995: 19; and Bradley Foundation, 1995: 33). NAF is now implementing a plan that was announced at an ISI Leadership Conference in 1992. Claiming that ISI had targeted the 20 most PC campuses in the country, an ISI staffer said that conservatives will use private foundation support to counter academic funding of multiculturalism, will tabulate academic funding of liberal vs. conservative speakers and student groups, and, for public universities, will make such funding into a taxpayers' issue (Messer-Davidow, 1992). My own research shows how ISI is proceeding. It uses *Campus* to publish articles attacking these campuses, mails the magazine to thousands of alumni, and organizes conservative alumni as activist groups. The alumni groups then act (e.g. through letter-writing campaigns and threats to withhold donations) to pressure administrators and trustees on personnel and curricular matters, thereby making vulnerable to social force what traditionally has been decided by academics on intellectual and educational merits (Messer-Davidow, 1994; Mercer, 1995b).

It was no coincidence that ISI's *Campus* printed the following recruitment ad: "Faculty concerned with . . . the deterioration of academic standards at America's colleges and universities can benefit from the National Association of Scholars (NAS). NAS confronts issues such as the politicization of the academy and the rise of political correctness. For an informational packet, contact . . ." (*Campus*, 1991: 24). NAS is not merely the largest organization of conservative academics, with some 3,000 members, 37 state and campus chapters, caucuses within the disciplines, and international affiliates. It has also spawned other academic and political organizations. For instance, NAS has formed disciplinary caucuses in many disciplinary associations and launched a competitor to the Modern Language Association, the Association of Literary Scholars and Critics, which claims to have 1,300 members and held its first annual meeting in fall 1995 (Ellis, 1995). Objecting to the diversity standards maintained by the six regional agencies that accredit universities and colleges, NAS founded the American Academy for Liberal Education (AALE), which recently obtained the Department of Education's approval to accredit (DePalma, 1993; National Association of Scholars, 1993a: 1; In Box, 1995: A15). Since universities and colleges must be accredited to receive federal funds, those that do not wish to comply with diversity standards can now obtain AALE accreditation without meeting those standards and still receive federal funds. Finally, two officers of NAS's California chapter, Executive Director Thomas E. Wood and Vice President Glynn Custred, serve as chairs of the California Civil Rights Initiative, a statewide ballot initiative to curb affirmative action in state agencies and universities (California Civil Rights Initiative, n.d.; Raza, n.d. a and b, 1994; *The California Association of Scholars*, 1992–93; and *The CAS Bulletin*, 1994: 1–2).

To recap, MCEA, ISI, and NAS used the media to circulate a discourse demonizing progressive higher education; with the discourse, they mobilized constituencies to pressure academic institutions from within and without. In addition, they began operating on the academic sector by setting up operations in the governmental sector. My case study of governmental operations is the conservative manipulation of the National Endowment for the Humanities (NEH), where many who do cultural studies work seek funding.

A Case of Trouble: The National Endowment for the Humanities

While Lynne V. Cheney was NEH Chairman from 1986 to 1993, rumors circulated that she was using NEH to advance cultural conservatism. Critics alleged that to filter out nontraditional projects she stacked the staff, packed the NEH National Council, and manipulated the application and peer-review processes. In what follows, I examine the evidence for each of these allegations.

According to a 1992 article by David Segal, who interviewed then current and former NEH staffers, Cheney appointed

> a trusted and insular circle of six people: Deputy Chairman Celeste Colgan, Special Assistants to the Chairman Susan Prado and Lynne Munson, General Counsel Anne Neal, Director of Public Affairs Claire del Real, and Assistant Chairman for Programs and Policy Jerry Martin. It is through this "fifth-floor mafia," as they are known in the agency, that Cheney conducts virtually all of her dealings with the staff. They met up to three times a week at 4 P.M. in the chairman's office to strategize about policy. . . . "The rest of the staff are then treated as functionaries who carry out these decisions." (Segal, 1992: 60)

My research on Colgan, Munson, Martin, and John T. Agresto (unmentioned by Segal) reveals their organizational affiliations and opposition to progressive humanities approaches.

Celeste Colgan, who earned a Ph.D. in British literature but never held an academic position, was appointed Deputy to the Chairman in 1986 and was quickly elevated to Deputy Chairman of Programs and Administration in 1988 and Deputy Chairman in 1989. While serving as Deputy Chairman, with responsibility for NEH's day-to-day operations, she attended the 1991 NAS national conference to recruit NEH grant applicants and peer panelists (see below) and the 1993 conference to speak at a plenary on the decaying curriculum (National Association of Scholars, 1993b; National Association of Scholars, 1993c: 1, 4–5; Hammer, 1989: 5; and National Endowment for the Humanities, 1987–95). *Lynne Munson* was appointed Special Assistant to the Chairman soon after earning a BA degree in 1990 from Northwestern University, where she was editor of the *Northwestern Review*, an MCEA newspaper attacking progressive trends on campuses. In 1991, she participated in recruiting NAS members (see below) and published an article in NAS's *Academic Questions* attacking "the new moral educators" at Northwestern, who sought to "overhaul the supposedly racist, sexist, and homophobic sensibilities of incoming students" by including cultural diversity programming in freshman orientation and permitting students from women's, gay/lesbian, and African-American groups to help in the planning (see Segal, 1992: 61; Munson, 1991: quotations 65).

While serving as Director of the NEH Division on Education Programs and later Assistant Chairman for Programs and Policy, *Jerry L. Martin* published an article in *Academic Questions* attacking a range of approaches – feminist, Marxist, multiculturalist, Foucauldian, pragmatic, pedagogic, postmodern – in as broad a range of humanities disciplines (Hammer, 1989: 6; National Endowment for the Humanities, 1987–95; Martin, 1993). Martin now serves as President of the National Alumni Forum. *John Agresto*, NEH Acting Chairman (1985–86) after Bennett's resignation, was Cheney's Deputy Chairman (1986–87) and Deputy Chairman of Policy (1988). During and after his NEH tenure, he was MCEA president, an MCEA board member, an NAS board member, and a member of ISI's speakers bureau (Agresto, 1992: 2; Hammer, 1989: 5; Madison Center for Educational Affairs, 1991, 1992; National Association of Scholars, various). At the 1990 NAS conference, he praised St John's College, where he served as president, for having a compulsory Great Books curriculum and for not having affirmative action or unrest because the number of "minorities are . . . too few to form an insular group" (Agresto, 1990–91: 24).

During Cheney's chairmanship, a large number of appointees to the NEH National Council (term in parenthesis) were also self-declared opponents of nontraditional humanities approaches and leading members of conservative organizations that attacked these approaches. *Hillel Fradkin* (1988–94), former Program Officer at the Olin Foundation, was then Vice President of the Bradley Foundation; these foundations were the leading funders of conservative professorships, academic programs, and, not coincidentally, the NAS, MCEA, and ISI.[2] *Edwin J. Delattre* (1988–94), Olin

Professor of Education at Boston University, was a longtime NAS board member, former Bradley Fellow at the right-wing American Enterprise Institute, recipient of Olin grants, and participant at the right-wing Hudson Institute, whose President Leslie Lenkowsky and associates Bennett and Chester E. Finn, Jr, were also leaders of MCEA. *Donald Kagan* (1988–94), Professor of History and Classics at Yale University, was an NAS member; as Dean of Yale College, he tried to implement a $20 million gift from Lee M. Bass that would tie Western civilization professorships to an ideological agenda promoted by the ISI (Kagan, 1990–91; Flint, 1991; Felton, 1995; ISI, 1995: 1, 4). *Paul A. Cantor* (1992–98), Professor of English at the University of Virginia, was an NAS member who had published in *Academic Questions*, lectured at right-wing Olin Centers and the American Enterprise Institute, and received grants from the Bradley Foundation (Cantor, n.d., 1993). *Bruce Cole* (1992–98), Professor of Fine Arts at Indiana University, was an NAS member (Cole, 1992). *Theodore Hamerow* (1992–98), Emeritus Professor of History at the University of Wisconsin, was a longtime NAS member, President of the Wisconsin Association of Scholars from 1989 to 1991, and contributor to *Academic Questions* (Hamerow, 1991, 1992). *John R. Searle* (1992–98), Professor of Philosophy at UC Berkeley, spoke at the 1993 NAS conference; his article for *Academic Questions* censured academic postmodernism for (among other things) blurring the distinction between high and popular culture and argued that women's studies should be appropriated by existing departments and taught by antifeminist males as well as feminists (Searle, n.d., 1993–94; National Association of Scholars, 1993b). The fullest inventory of despised approaches was provided by *Peter Shaw* (1990–96), Professor of Humanities at St Peter's College (NJ), NAS Vice president, and editor of *Academic Questions*. He denigrated reader-response criticism, New Historicism, semiotics, deconstruction, Lacanian psychoanalysis, feminist criticism, film studies, cultural studies, and several others (National Association of Scholars, various; Shaw, 1990: 28; 1991).

Three appointees made the most stupifying comments. When *Kenny J. Williams* (1991–97), a Professor of English at Duke University who co-founded NAS's Duke chapter in 1990 and launched its anti-MLA literature organization (Williams, n.d.; Messer-Davidow, 1991; Iannone, 1991; Trueheart, 1991), styled affirmative action as imposing quotas, multiculturalism as gushing over primitive cultures, and the humanities as overrun by political concerns, she was asked if academia was obsessed with race and gender. "Well, yes," she replied, "there certainly seems to be that kind of an obsession in literary studies, but in certain approaches to history, too, everything is reinterpreted in terms of race, gender, and class. I don't teach race, gender, and class issues, so I'm not quite sure what the terms mean" (Hamilton, 1992: 6). *Alan C. Kors* (1992–98), Professor of History at the University of

Pennsylvania, an NAS member since 1988, and an MCEA associate since 1989, was the most vitriolic (Kors, n.d.; National Association of Scholars, various; Madison Center for Educational Affairs, 1991, 1992). In 1988, he attacked his university's anti-harassment policy as "thought reform" and opined, "The barbarians are in our midst. . . . We need to fight them for a good long time" (Collins, 1988). In 1989, he asserted that "Students find themselves in an Orwellian and profoundly politicized world of ideological, privileged power structures" (Innerst, 1989). Repeatedly arguing that the study of women and minorities should not be incorporated into the curriculum, he was the only faculty member on his campus to vote against establishing a women's studies program (see also Berger, 1988; Collins, 1988; Iannone, 1988; Vobejda, 1988; Innerst, 1989; Charon, 1990; Kors, 1990, 1991). *Harvey Mansfield* (1991–97), Professor of Government at Harvard University, an NAS member, an MCEA board member, and a funder of *Peninsula*, an MCEA student magazine at Harvard (MesserDavidow, 1993: 47–9; Reidy, 1992; Intercollegiate Studies Institute, 1992: 13), was the most direct about conservative politics. After denouncing multicultural, women's, and African-American studies, he said, "That kind of politicization of the campus is particularly extensive in the humanities . . . . That's why I'm delighted to be going to Washington to serve on the NEH advisory council – I think the council can and should take a stand against what is happening to the American academy." He added, "It's ironic that conservatives have to use politics to rid the campus of politics, but we do" (Winkler, 1991).

By 1992, these appointments had dramatically altered the composition of the NEH National Council. At least 11 of its 26 members were active NAS members (and\or financial supporters) and self-declared opponents of nontraditional humanities approaches. Other members were key supporters of Republican politics: Michael Bass (1988–94), Republican alderman; Michael Malbin (1988–94), speech writer for Defense Secretary Dick Cheney; Bruce Benson (1990–96), head of the Colorado Republican Party; Helen Crawford (1990–96) and Margaret Duckett (1990–96), contributors to national Republican funds; and Joseph Hagan (1992–98), contributor to the Bush re-election campaign (Lukasik, 1991: 16; Burd, 1992a: A21).[3] Although enjoined by NEH authorizing legislation to encourage the humanities and their reflection of cultural diversity, Cheney, her staff minions, and her National Council appointees were opposing, in word and deed, *almost all nontraditional* humanities approaches and especially castigating those that promoted cultural diversity. To Segal's claim that NEH operations were driven by the ideological commitments of the Cheney circle, I would add that their ideology-driven control was made possible by meshing NEH operations with MCEA, ISI, and NAS operations. MCEA, ISI, and NAS publications and conferences mounted an attack on the humanities that legitimated Cheney's NEH reports and actions, NAS supplied NEH with Council members, peer panelists, and outside reviewers, and ISI added the pressure for change through its alumni groups. I turn next to allegations that Cheney's NEH manipulated the application and peer-review processes.

From a population of probably 100,000 humanities scholars, NEH received more than 8,000 grant applications per year in the early 1990s and funded under 2,000 (Innerst, 1992: A1). To win funding, projects had to flow through several decision-points: submission of applications by scholars; evaluation by external reviewers; evaluation by peer panels; recommendation by program officers on whether and how much to fund; recommendation by the National Council; and approval by the chairman. Along the way, many projects dropped out for legitimate reasons. Scholars failed to complete applications, applications lacked merit, and available funding did not cover all meritorious applications. But critics charged that Cheney's NEH filtered the so-called PC scholarship out of the process at three stages: in the pre-application stage, staffers discouraged some and encouraged other potential applicants; in the pre-evaluation stage, they selected conservative reviewers and panelists who would give low ratings to offending scholarship; and in the evaluation stage, conservative reviewers and panelists did assign low ratings.

In 1992, NEH sources told David Segal that staffers eliminated the so-called PC scholarship by informing "prospective applicants who actually have disagreed with Mrs. Cheney – or who are merely likely to – that their names are a proposal's kiss of death" (Segal, 1992: 59), but Cheney mentioned only that "In her travels around the country . . . she collects names of people she thinks would make good panelists and passes them on to her staff" (ibid). Through my field work, however, I can confirm that Cheney's inner-circle staffers did recruit applicants and peer panelists – conservative ones. At the NAS national conference in 1991, Celeste Colgan (Deputy Chairman) and Lynne Munson (Special Assistant to the Chairman) were inviting NAS members to submit grant applications and serve as peer panelists. Ironically, one morning Colgan approached me to ask if I had ever served on a peer panel. When I replied "no," she offered to send me an NEH panel application and subsequently did so (Messer-Davidow, 1991).[4] Although one might argue that they were appropriately scouting talent at scholarly conferences, no NEH staffers showed up to scout the talent at the progressive conferences I attended during Cheney's years. Nor was the NAS conference scholarly. One speaker after another – John Bunzell and Robert Conquest of the right-wing Hoover Institution, Roger Kimball who authored *Tenured Radicals*, Joshua Muravchik of the right-wing American Enterprise Institute, and a host of NAS officials – viciously attacked feminists, Marxists, multiculturalists, theorists, and affirmative-action supporters. The audience laughed at insults and heckled non-NAS speakers who supported affirmative action, multiculturalism, and teaching the conflicts. In a session attacking multiculturalism, Barry Gross, an NAS founder and leader, steered the discussion to activist strategies against universities, and Kimball recommended working the pressure points, public funding and university trustees. Indeed, NEH funders were there listening, as were private funders from the Bradley Foundation, Olin Foundation, MCEA, and think-tanks.

Once applications were submitted, Cheney's critics allege that the so-called PC projects were eliminated by two means. Cheney unilaterally vetoed some that received high peer-review ratings (e.g. 10 vetoes in one 1992 quarter) and ensured that others would receive low marks by vetting the peer panels. A staffer who served under Cheney reported that "Before panels are composed, a list is sent to the chair and she makes it clear if any are acceptable" (Segal, 1992: 59). Cheney's conservative supporters, however, alleged that her agency disproportionately funded the so-called PC projects. David Horowitz complained that even under Republican leadership NEH somehow "managed to fund whole libraries of Marxist *cum* radical *kitsch*" (Horowitz, 1995: 49), and Heather MacDonald, former associate of the right-wing Manhatten Institute, denounced NEH for sponsoring an "orgy of poststructural and postmodernist scholarship. It has awarded numerous research fellowships on gender and race; it has funded that engine of multiculturalism: curricular transformation projects" (MacDonald, 1995: 19). Which claim, that peer review filtered out or funded the new scholarship, can be substantiated?

Evidence about peer review began to appear in 1992 when Stephen Burd published a feature story in the *Chronicle of Higher Education* based on interviews and application evaluations. Evaluations that applicants obtained from the endowment, Burd wrote, "indicate a pattern in which a single reviewer makes critical remarks – generally based on the applicant's differences with the traditional approach to scholarship advocated by Mrs. Cheney – and that opposition is used to reject the grant" (Burd, 1992b: A1). A former staffer confirmed that Cheney furnished NEH program officers with a list of scholars, some reputable and some with a definite conservative tilt, from which they were required to choose panelists. Other staffers added that the strategy of selecting peer panelists who would downgrade applications that did not use the approaches espoused by Cheney "shields the chairman from criticism because 'undesirable' grants are rejected before they reach her" (ibid: A32). Another former staffer said, "Projects dealing with Latin America, the Caribbean, some women's studies, and anything appearing as vaguely left wing are seen as suspect. Controversy is a central issue: Will this cause a headline and get us in hot water with our conservative constituency?" (ibid). Other staffers disagreed, pointing out that with thousands of applications NEH had to reject many that had some merit. But Burd's data on four applications show that each one, after receiving excellent rating from outside reviewers and panelists, was shot down by a conservative panelist who gave it a low rating. Confirmation of this maneuver came, ironically, from David Horowitz, Director of the right-wing Center for the Study of Popular Culture. As a peer panelist in 1992, he had argued that 12 of the 30 projects he reviewed were political and had marked them "ineligible," a rating that did not exist. A project on the women of Juchitan (Mexico), he described as ridiculous and ideological. A project on the homeless that questioned the American Dream, he dismissed with "Right." And the producers of a film on Jim Crow in the South, he derogated as an "outfit that made promotional films for the Black Panthers in the days when they were murdering blacks in the East Oakland ghetto" (Horowitz, 1995: 50–2; also National Endowment for the Humanities, 1992: 176).

The best findings appear in *Peer Review: Reforms Needed to Ensure Fairness in Federal Agency Grant Selection* (1994), the General Accounting Office (GAO) study of evaluation processes at the National Institutes of Health, National Science Foundation, and NEH. At NEH peer-panel meetings, GAO investigators witnessed several "intellectual camp" conflicts that went unchallenged by program officers and panelists and provided these examples:

> "I have philosophical problems with that whole project."
> "I do not like the post-structuralist approach."
> "I am trying to overcome my prejudice against Midwestern literature."
> "He's a lefty trendy."
> "My three equals taste; this is a loser strategy and a bad line of research, although he is in the top four of this dubious field of research." (General Accounting Office, 1994: 30)

While the first and third comments could be made about traditional work, the others target nontraditional work. Since no comments specifically targeting traditional work were provided by GAO, presumably none were made at the panels GAO observed.

In addition, the GAO study documented biases of gender, race, rank, and reputation in NEH peer review, but its investigators were constrained because NEH (unlike NIH and NSF) did not gather data on race. GAO reported that women were underrepresented among external reviewers, that men's applications received better scores than women's, that a far greater percentage of applications funded were those submitted by men than by women (ibid: 37, 3, 74–5), and also that younger and junior scholars were greatly underrepresented among applicants, external reviewers, and peer panelists (ibid: 43–4, 46). On reputation, it noted that scores were better for applicants known to reviewers, or hailing from prestigious institutions, or perceived to be major contributors rather than competent or unknown scholars (ibid: 63, 74–5). These findings show that biased peer-reviewing can be attributed to two groups of people: the under-representation of women and younger/junior scholars to the NEH staffers who made the selections, and the perceptions favoring certain groups of applicants to the panelists, outside reviewers, and staffers involved in peer review.

Despite findings of bias, the NEH rejected three GAO recommendations for improving peer review. It balked at the recommendation to use comparative samples of blind and nonblind applications to test for discrimination in the review process (ibid: 85). It disagreed with the recommendation to collect data on the race of applicants, arguing "that GAO had not found evidence of discrimination at NEH." GAO replied that the disagreement "is specious: the basis of the recommendation is not that GAO *found* discrimination but, rather, that there were no data to *evaluate* whether there was discrimination or not. Unless the data are made available, neither the agency nor the Congress can know whether such discrimination is occurring" (ibid: 5, 94). To deal with "intellectual camp" conflicts, GAO recommended improving "the calibration of ratings among reviewers. NEH argued that it already makes such efforts, but GAO did not observe them when attending NEH panels" (ibid: 5; also 114–28).

While the GAO study documented several of the biases alleged by NEH critics, it did not profile the outcome: NEH's awards patterns. Elsewhere, I reviewed awards for the years 1986–90 in four NEH programs that support scholars' research: (1) Fellowships for University Teachers of $27,500 (or less) to support faculty of Ph.D.-granting universities in full-time research; (2) Fellowships for College Teachers (and Independent Scholars), the same; (3) Summer Stipends of $3,500 to support university and college teachers in two months of research; and (4) Interpretive Research-Collaborative Projects, support of $150,000 and less for large projects (i.e. often archaeological and historical). For each program and year, I contrasted total awards with WGF awards (i.e. projects on women, gender, and feminism, whether traditional or feminist in approach). For the total awards and WGF awards in each program, I tabulated the number of projects and dollar amount, as well as the WGF dollars as a percentage of the total dollars. My findings were that WGF projects averaged less than 8 percent of the dollars awarded, with a low of 0 percent in the Interpretive Research Program for 1987 to an atypical high of 20.5 percent in the Fellowships for University Teachers Program for 1988; and that the awards to projects indicating Marxist, poststructuralist, and multicultural content or viewpoint were trifling in numbers and dollars (for details, see Messer-Davidow, forthcoming a). Thus, conservative claims that NEH funded a great deal of feminist, Marxist, poststructuralist, and multicultural scholarship are false. Cheney's NEH funded very little of such work and even less if one subtracts projects using traditional approaches to the topics of women, Marxism, and poststructuralism.

What Do We Do When We Do Discourse?

Although conservatives managed to roil a number of legislators, still erudite academic knowledge was not exactly a matter for legislative action, as conservatives themselves knew. When they moved into the policy-making arena, they translated their attack on progressive academic and cultural institutions into a legislatively actionable discourse that put the question of NEH–NEA funding in the same moralistic and economistic terms long used by advocates of conservative policies on crime, single motherhood, and racial unrest. To explain how that translation works, I turn to a conservative symposium on the NEH and NEA, held at New York University in 1993 and supported by Bradley, Olin, and other conservative foundations. Symposium presentations appeared in *The National Endowments: A Critical Symposium* (1995), published by Second Thought Books, the imprint of Horowitz's right-wing Center for the Study of Popular Culture.

Conservative leaders portrayed the NEH and NEA as corrupt and inefficient government agencies. Charles Horner, MCEA President, sketched the "decade of greed" when universities became "bloated with money," companies "delivering art and entertainment and cultural artifacts became even richer," and the endowments became "revolving slush funds for those with the right kinds of connections" (Horner, 1995: 18). Herbert London, NAS Chairman, invoked the specter of government abuse of tax revenues. When the endowments were established in 1965, he explained, President Lyndon Johnson "made the point that the Great Society would now use taxpayer money to promote the arts and humanities . . . it was assumed that spending money would inexorably lead to fine art and notable scholarship." But today, when it is clear that Johnson was wrong, "the money mill is still in service, and those who reap its rewards refuse to examine the abuses in this government system" (London, 1995: 3). Anne-Imelda Radice, Acting Chairman of NEA before Jane Alexander, emphasized NEA's wastefulness: "It costs between $14,000 and $18,000 to bring a panel together – a panel that may give out $40,000 in grants. That is inefficient, and it is unfair to the arts as well as unfair to the taxpayer" (Radice, 1995: 67). As London and others saw it, "government-sponsored programs are insulated from the market" and should be made responsive to consumer demand (London, 1995: 3).

To summarize the translation, symposium participants modulated the NEH–NEA corruption argument into an NEH–NEA abuse of taxpayer rights argument by implicitly invoking principles that make sense in three other discourses: the political–individualist principle that taxpayers have a right to responsible and fair governance, the business principle that government agencies should use tax dollars cost-effectively, and the free-market principle that consumer demand should calibrate NEH–NEA supply. Peter Shaw, NAS Vice president, went a step further: "With the National Endowment for the Humanities, the congressional authorization begs the question. The agency is charged with advancing humanities, but we are not told which humanities, whose humanities, are meant. Is it the tradition deriving from the humanists of the Renaissance? Or is it the postmodern repudiation of the human subject, as the current jargon has it, and the rejection of European and Western humanism?" (Shaw, 1995: 9). By implying that authorizing legislation should specify which types of humanities and arts a federal agency can use tax dollars to support, he stepped away from the principle of responsible governance and into the proposition that government should regulate the content and viewpoint of scholarship and art. Note what his discourse *does*: by puffing responsible governance, it completely eclipses the traditional principles guiding academic and cultural production – freedom of research and teaching, artistic expression, and speech.

Symposium participants proposed four solutions: terminating the endowments, restricting the use of endowment funds, replacing peer review with patronage, and privatizing humanities and arts funding. Weighing in for termination, Shaw (and others) argued that conservatives could most effectively stem the tide of "politically correct anti-humanism . . . by giving away no money at all. That is, by not having an NEH. As for helping the few deserving scholars, this, I should say, is not worth maintaining a $180-million agency for. Anyone who wouldn't write a book without financial support perhaps shouldn't be writing that book" (ibid: 12–13). Funding-restriction advocates were hard pressed to come up with criteria that would do the job. When Richard Brookhiser, senior editor of the *National Review*, proposed restricting endowment "money to preserving or performing the work of scholars or artists who are dead," he noted that the criterion "dead" would still permit NEA to fund exhibitions of such artists as Robert Mapplethorpe (Brookhiser, 1995: 36). Frederick Turner, a co-founder of the new formalism movement, suggested replacing peer panels with panels of leading citizens in business, law, sciences, religion, and philanthropy, whom NEA would tithe for financial contributions, matching each of their dollars with a hundred agency dollars (Turner, 1995: 80).

His model recast the NEA as a church and peer review as Renaissance patronage. Finally, privatization, the remedy proposed by conservatives for every public service from broadcasting to garbage collection, was also ballyhooed here in free-market rhetoric. Turner imagined that funding could be taken over by a quasi-public corporation, like Fannie Mae, but neglected to mention that the humanities and arts would not have income-producing activities sufficient to maintain a reasonable level of awards. Samuel Lipman, publisher of the right-wing *New Criterion*, visualized supporting the arts with a $200 million donor-controlled trust, but did not consider that the principal would generate only a fraction of the NEA's then current $160 million budget (Lipman, 1995: 89).

I do not want to give the impression that conservative discourse consisted of PC talk and translation, but no other action. Also speaking at the symposium was William Kristol, *enfant terrible* of the troika that strategized the right-wing electoral sweep in 1994. Predicting that the dynamics on the Hill would change "over the next three years towards fairly radical cuts in some of the programs of the NEA and NEH," he declared, "We may decide simply to fund the preservation of old manuscripts, old books, nice editions, new editions of older books, reprinting of translations, etc., but not the kind of 'cutting edge' scholarship that, of course, is what the arts community and the professors and the educational establishment really wants from the NEA and NEH" (Kristol, 1995: 39–40). It was no coincidence, then, that the symposium discourse reappeared two years later as two forms of Congressional activity – proposed bills and debates on the endowments.

During the summer of 1995, the House of Representatives and the Senate considered various proposals to slash NEH and NEA appropriations and prohibit the funding of certain kinds of projects. In July, the House passed a bill that would reduce endowment appropriations by about 40 percent and terminate the agencies in, respectively, two and three years, but, at the same time, defeated the more drastic amendment to eliminate NEH this year (Burd, 1995a). In August, the Senate approved a bill cutting NEA and NEH appropriations by over 30 percent and adopted language, championed by Senator Jesse A. Helms (Republican, North Carolina), that prohibits NEA awards to most individual artists, to projects that "depict or describe, in a patently offensive way, sexual or excretory activities or organs," and to works that "denigrate the objects or beliefs of the adherents of a particular religion" (thus neatly resolving Brookhiser's dilemma that support for exhibitions of dead artists would be support for Mapplethorpe's work) (Burd, 1995b). The conservatives who were invited to speak at NEH and NEA hearings (Bennett, Cheney, NAS members Delattre and Gross, and American Enterprise Institute associates) "delivered an almost unrelenting stream of anti-NEH, anti-higher education testimony" (Hammer,

1995: 3). Republican legislators reiterated their PC complaints, argued that the federal government should defund the humanities and arts, and proposed the same options discussed at the 1993 symposium.

Some humanities and arts lobbyists were heartened that Congress did not immediately terminate the endowments and were hopeful that they had time to recoup losses. But their hopefulness is unrealistic for several reasons. First, whatever budget-cutting option Congress enacts, the humanities will be severely curtailed. Close to 75 percent of the support for humanities research and programs has come from the NEH, and the remainder from private foundations and universities/colleges that can provide awards. These sources are in no position to compensate for reductions in federal revenues. Private foundations, now funding other initiatives that lost federal support, will not cover the funding deficit. Independent and campus-based humanities centers, always precariously funded, will scuttle for endowments; if unsuccessful, they will scale back or shut down. Universities and colleges, downsizing with recessionary budgets, will be unable to divert funds to humanities research. With NEH's demise, the humanities will effectively be defunded.

Second, another proposed bill, the Istook Amendment to the Labor, Health and Human Services, and Education appropriations bill, would curtail even more drastically an enormous range of institutions and organizations. Originating at the Heritage Foundation and sponsored by Representatives Ernest Istook (Republican, Oklahoma), Robert Erlich (Republican, Maryland), and David McIntosh (Republican, Indiana), this bill was passed by the House on August 4 and is pending before the Senate. If approved, it will gag organizations and citizens that receive federal funds or funds from other entities that can be traced to federal sources. It prevents them from engaging in virtually all communicative activities (however financed) with any level (municipal, state, federal) and sector (legislatures, agencies, courts) of government. Prohibited activities include even distributing publicity on issues before a legislature and filing an *amicus curia* in lawsuits to which any government entity is a party. The few exempt activities are distributing nonpartisan polls and giving invited legislative testimony. The Istook Amendment will not neutrally limit advocacy. It will prevent associates of nonprofit organizations – higher-education and disciplinary associations, universities and colleges, philanthropies, cultural organizations (e.g. museums), community organizations (e.g. battered women's shelters), charities (e.g. Red Cross), and interest organizations (e.g. National Geographic Society) – from speaking on issues that concern them. But it will not affect the very people who did speak at NEH–NEA hearings – associates of conservative think-tanks and advocacy organizations. Their invitation to testify and their organizations' private funding exempt them from the Istook prohibition (see OMB Watch, 1995a;

OMB Watch, 1995b; National Committee for Responsive Philanthropy, 1995a: 10–14, 1995b; Murawski and Stehle, 1995).

One might be tempted to assert that Congressional legislation is merely textualized language, but that would be to miss the crucial point that it will reorganize the functioning of the academic, cultural, philanthropic, and service enterprises. I have presented the NEH case at length because it offers us several lessons about the trouble cultural studies is in and the trouble in cultural studies. First, it suggests that we must gauge the status of cultural studies in relation to the expert knowledge economy and the forces restructuring it. The fate of our field depends upon what happens to the academic and cultural institutions that house it, and what happens to these institutions, in turn, depends upon the political forces manipulating their lifelines: the resource flows that enable and the regulations that organize their functioning. Second, we have been slow to understand the trouble cultural studies is in because our core concepts and methods reiterate divisions – cultural/social/political/economic – that are not observed in actual practice. We did not see that to re-form the nation conservatives use any particular set of practices as the matrix for producing what restructures other sets – cultural practices as a matrix for restructuring social, political, and economic practices; political practices as a matrix for restructuring cultural, social, and economic practices; and so on – in effect orchestrating activities across social, political, and economic sectors. Their successes should tell us that the sectors can be reciprocally meshed and that their divisions are artifacts of disciplinary discourses. While we cannot speak about processes without using terms that divide, because they are the ones furnished by the discourses available to us (as my own writing in this paragraph shows), we can begin to erode the divisions by focusing on linkage points and meshing operations. Or, as Richard Johnson puts it at the beginning of his essay for this volume, cultural studies "works *in* the spaces between academic disciplines and *on* the *relations* between the academy and other political sites." Finally, the NEH case suggests that discourse, as one of the objects cultural studies investigates, is something more than language. Rather, discourse is constituted through and as flows of (people's) linguistic practices, nonlinguistic activities, resource allocations, and rules (policies, regulations, etc.) that are regularized, distanciated (spread in space and time), and institutionalized.

How Do We (Re-)Articulate "Discourse?"

Cultural studies in the United States, as many contributors to this volume point out, has been multiply disciplined. It is institutionalized in the academy, practiced by scholars already trained by particular disciplines, and, through demographic happenstance, weighted heavily with the conceptual and methodological cargo of textually oriented disciplines. No surprise, then, that we too often equate discourse with language and read all sorts of phenomena – paintings, rap music, people queueing, shopping malls, and factory corridors on the Mexican side of the border – as instantiations of linguistic, or linguistically analogous, practice.

The limitations of such notions of discourse are clear from the work of Ernesto Laclau, Chantal Mouffe, and Foucault. "Let us suppose," Laclau and Mouffe write, "that I am building a wall with another bricklayer. At a certain moment I ask my workmate to pass me a brick and then I add it to the wall. The first act – asking for the brick – is linguistic; the second – adding the brick to the wall – is extralinguistic." The two acts, they add, "are both part of a total operation which is the building of the wall" (Laclau and Mouffe, 1987: 82). This total operation, which they call discourse, consists of actors (bricklayers), linguistic and nonlinguistic practices, and resources (bricks, tools, spaces) bound by rules that both configure the elements and make them meaningful in a particular way. Whereas this example foregrounds constructedness, discourse as an organized and organizing configuration of material entities and practices, Laclau and Mouffe's second example emphasizes construal, discourse as bestowing and inviting meanings. When a person kicks a spherical object in the street rather than in a football match, they explain, "the *physical* fact [the person, the act of kicking, and the spherical object] is the same, but *its meaning* is different. The object is a football only to the extent that it establishes a system of relations with other objects, and these relations are not given by the mere referential materiality of the objects, but are, rather, socially constructed" (ibid: 82). The two dimensions of discourse, construction and construal, are intricated, because without some meaning construed we don't even have distinguishable actors, objects, and practices. Foucault's work amplifies these micro-examples. His theoretical writings tell us how to analyze a discourse at the macro-level as a rule-bound system for the production and dispersion of not merely a population of énoncés but their speaking subjects, objects, concepts, and strategies. His applied studies of medicine and penality join macro-analysis of discursive formations and micro-analysis of actors' practices to mid-range analysis of institutions that, by functioning as operators of discursive economies, mesh the formations and practices. When he analyzes discipline, he details how educational institutions, for example, instantiated its logic in the regulated gestures of students praying, the instrument–body articulation of handwriting, the architecture of classrooms, and the organization of a national educational system.

Scholars who treat culture as structure or as signification are acting as properly socialized disciplinary practitioners. When a discipline socializes its novices, it does not simply instruct them in its core of knowledge. By exercising them in its particular ways of perceiving, thinking, valuing, relating, and acting, it inserts them into its schemes of practice (Lenoir, 1993: 72); and by examining their work in tenure, promotion, article, and grant reviews, it ensures that they continue to observe its schemes of practice. It is no surprise, then, that when textually trained scholars read cultural conservatism as the formation of a contentious debate and structurally trained scholars read it as the emergence of a protest movement, they have uncoupled the two dimensions, construal and construction, of cultural discourse.

What I have tried to show in this essay is that since the two are meshed in practice, they could be linked in our analyses of them if we redefined articulation itself. Now defined as the construction of nodal points to temporarily fix meaning (Laclau and Mouffe, 1985: 113), articulation should be reconceptualized as a larger variety of linking and meshing practices. My analysis of the conservative movement shows that it did construct nodal points to stabilize meanings about cultural knowledges (e.g. by linking of PC discourse to legislatively actionable discourse), but it also performed macro-level linking practices: the horizontal meshing of MCEA, ISI, and NAS activities; and the vertical linking that occurred when the movement used these organizations to leverage change on federal agencies and Congress that, in turn, are now leveraging change on the higher-education system. To summarize, the conservative movement has articulated horizontally through the grassroots in order to be able to articulate vertically from government institutions down to everyday academic practice and back up to the restructuring of higher education, hoping that a re-formed higher education will radically change the sociocultural order. Thus, the final lesson I draw from my case study of conservative discourse is that to change the sociocultural order, actors must act through the instrumentalized mediation of institutionalized practices.

(How) Should We Instrumentalize Academic Knowledge?

In scholarly circles, instrumentalism is a discredited notion. Most scholars believe that instrumentalism would violate the very conditions of possibility for a truly academic knowledge: the objectivity needed to discover truths, the disinterestedness needed to recognize enduring values, and the institutional autonomy needed to safeguard freedom of research and teaching. Moreover, some object that instrumentalism is deeply implicated with the coercive power that characterizes female domination in the sex-gender system and the social engineering that characterizes capitalism, militarism, and technologism. While such critiques of instrumentalism make sense in the discourses where they are situated, they do not make sense in the discourse I have been examining, where conservatives have instrumentalized cultural knowledge and policy formation to achieve their goal of imposing a conservative America on all of us. The critiques don't make sense because they don't change the actuality; they don't prevent conservatives from instrumentalizing, and they don't give us the wherewithal to act against their instrumentalizing.

As I see it, the issue turns on how we have been constru(ct)ing academic responsibility. For some, producing, publishing, and teaching scholarly knowledge mark the limits of responsibility; for me, the point of engaging in these activities is to enhance the lives that people live individually and together. Determining whether the activities enhance lives, let alone what constitutes good lives, is a complex matter that suggests further responsibilities. At a minimum, complex knowledge activities should be sorted out not by legislative fiats that defund and prohibit them, but by careful evaluation of their diverse effects. Such evaluation requires scholars to consider what our knowledge activities do for society and what societal forces do to them. Detachment from that social world is not even a choice we have when it, willy-nilly, impacts on us. Our choice is only whether, how, and to what extent we will attempt to act effectively in that world.

To act, scholars need to move beyond the (undeniably real) knowledge-politics of the academy to build coalitions that will counter the conservative politics of denigration and destruction all over the societal terrain: in legislatures and courts, through the media, and with people. What coalition-building means is that scholars will have to address at least some of their work to nonscholarly communities that increasingly turn to think-tanks, government agencies, and advocacy groups for research with immediate applications. It also means that we will have to work with people, including academic colleagues, who may be more leftist, centrist, or conservative than we would like them to be. Long habituated to our own balkanization by discipline and specialism, by ideology and activity, we need to remind ourselves that a coalition is not a union of groups that have identical beliefs, agendas, and priorities. Rather, it is the commitment of differing groups to join together – across sectors, in varying combinations, on some but not all issues, leading or assisting others. If we intend to use cultural studies to help the academy and society get out of the trouble they are in, then we as scholars must recognize that we as actors will enter a world that operates through shifting points of alliance and complexly meshed practices all across the cultural, social, political, and economic spectrum.

NOTES

Many thanks are owing to Elizabeth Long for her thoughtful comments on this essay. Portions of it are taken from my "Dollars for Scholars: The Real Politics of Humanities Scholarship and Programs," with kind permission from Rutgers University Press, and *Disciplining Feminism: Episodes in the Discursive Production of Social Change.*

1 The conservative circulation of PC was so astonishingly successful that it gave new meaning to the phrase "exponential growth." A NEXUS search showed no news articles mentioning PC in 1985, 7 in 1986, 66 in 1990, 2,672 in 1992, and 1,427 in the first three months of 1994 (Booth, 1994). If we add similar phrases uttered in all publications and electronic media, then my estimate would have to be low.

2 For FY 1990–91, the NAS received $105,400 from the Bradley Foundation and $125,000 from the Olin Foundation (National Association of Scholars, 1991a). For FY 1991–92, the NAS estimated receiving $155,000 from Bradley and $125,000 from Olin (National Association of Scholars, 1991b). Bradley's annual report shows $86,788 paid to NAS in 1990 and $90,400 authorized to be paid later (Bradley Foundation, 1990: 34), and Olin's annual report confirms $125,000 paid to NAS in 1990 (Olin Foundation, 1991: 21). For FY 1990, ISI received $35,000 and was authorized to receive $40,000 more from Bradley (Bradley Foundation, 1990: 27); it received $86,200 and was authorized to receive $20,000 more from Olin (Olin Foundation, 1991: 19). For FY 1990, MCEA received $205,000 from Bradley (Bradley Foundation, 1990: 30); it received $35,000 and was authorized to receive $118,000 more from Olin (Olin Foundation, 1991: 19). Unfortunately, the dollar amounts that organizations list in their reports as having been received from these foundations do not always match the dollar amounts that the foundations list in their reports as having given to the organizations.

3 The issue of political appointments needs to be clarified. While it has been traditional for both Democratic and Republican presidents to appoint their political supporters to seats on the NEH National Council that are reserved for representatives of the public sector, I object to this practice. Not only does it smack of political pay-off, but it also demotes what should be the most important consideration in any appointment – the merits of the candidates relevant to the job.

4 I determined the affiliations of conference participants by crosschecking name tags against several documents: the "1991 Conference Registrants" list distributed by the NAS, NAS stationery, listings in *Academic Questions*, materials from other conservative organizations, and my field notes from conservative organizations and events. The Colgan solicitations I witnessed occurred on October 18 and her conversation with me occurred on October 19.

REFERENCES

Agresto, John 1990–91: St. John's College: Preserving a World Apart. *Academic Questions* 4, 1 (winter), 23–6.

—— 1992: Statement for Completion by Presidential Nominee, January. 2-page, unpublished document supplied by an anonymous source.

Becher, Tony 1989: *Academic Tribes and Territories: Intellectual Enquiry and the Culture of Disciplines.* Milton Keynes: Society for Research into Higher Education/Open University Press.

Berger, Joseph 1988: Scholars Attack Campus "Radicals." *New York Times,* 15 November, A22.

Bernard, Jessie 1987: Re-viewing the Impact of Women's Studies on Sociology. In Christie Farnham (ed.), *The Impact of Feminist Research in the Academy,* Bloomington: Indiana University Press, 193–216.

Bernstein, Basil 1975: *Class, Codes and Control, Volume III: Towards a Theory of Educational Transmission.* London: Routledge & Kegan Paul.

Booth, Wayne 1994: A Politically Correct Letter to the Newspaper. *Democratic Culture,* 3 (spring), 2.

Bottomore, Tom and Nisbet, Robert 1978: Introduction. In Tom Bottomore and Robert Nisbet (eds), *A History of Sociological Analysis.* New York: Basic Books, vii–xvi.

Bradley Foundation 1990: *Report of the Lynde and Harry Bradley Foundation August 1988–July 1990.* Milwaukee: Bradley.

—— 1995: *Report of the Lynde and Harry Bradley Foundation 1994.* Milwaukee: Bradley.

Brookhiser, Richard 1995: Fund the Dead. In Lawrence Jarvik, Herbert I. London, and James F. Cooper (eds), *The National Endowments: A Critical Symposium,* Los Angeles: Second Thought Books, 33–6.

Burd, Stephen 1992a: New Fight May Be Imminent Over Nominations by Bush to National Humanities Council. *Chronicle of Higher Education,* February 19, A21.

—— 1992b: Chairman of Humanities Fund Has Politicized Grants Process, Critics Charge. *Chronicle of Higher Education,* April 22, A1, A32–3.

—— 1995a: House Votes to End Funds for Arts in 2 Years, Humanities in 3. *Chronicle of Higher Education,* July 28, A31.

—— 1995b: Senate Approves 30% Cut for Arts and Humanities, but Votes to Keep Both National Endowments Alive. *Chronicle of Higher Education,* August 18, A28.

The California Association of Scholars 1992–93: 2 (winter).

California Civil Rights Initiative n.d.: California Civil Rights Initiative: Prohibition Against State Discrimination or Preferential Treatment, Initiative Constitutional Amendment, Proposal for the Statewide Ballot, 1996. 2-pages unpublished. Los Angeles: California Civil Rights Initiative.

Campus 1991: 2, 3 (spring).

—— 1993: 5, 1 (fall).

—— 1995: 7, 1 (fall).

Cantor, Paul A. n.d.: *Curriculum vitae.* 6-page, unpublished document supplied by an anonymous source.

—— 1993: Stephen Greenblatt's New Historicist Vision. *Academic Questions,* 6, 4 (fall), 20–36.

The CAS Bulletin 1994: 2, 2 (January 26).

Charon, Mona 1990: A Losing Battle vs. Campus Thought Police. *Newsday,* December 5, 132.

Cheney, Lynne V. 1988: Scholars and Society. *ACLS Newsletter*, 1 (summer), 5–7.

Cole, Bruce 1992: *Curriculum vitae*. 9-page, unpublished document supplied by an anonymous source.

Collins, Huntly 1988: Campus War Pits "Classics" against Cultural Diversity. *Philadelphia Inquirer*, June 27, B1.

Delany, Lawrence J., Jr and Lenkowsky, Leslie 1988: The New Voice on Campus: "Alternative Student Journalism." *Academic Questions*, 1 (spring), 32–8.

DePalma, Anthony 1993: Traditionalist Scholars Plan to Rate Liberal Arts Colleges. *New York Times*, March 3, B13.

Ellis, John M. 1995: Secretary/Treasurer's Letter to Members with 1995 Conference program. Santa Cruz, CA: Association of Literary Scholars and Critics, August 9.

Felton, Nick 1995: Yale's $20 Million Deception. *Campus*, 6, 3 (spring), 3, 15.

Flint, Anthony 1991: Controversial Dean at Yale Says He Will Take Sabbatical. *Boston Globe*, October 8, 22.

General Accounting Office 1994: *Peer Review: Reforms Needed to Ensure Fairness in Federal Agency Grant Selection*. Washington, DC: General Accounting Office.

Grossberg, Lawrence, Nelson, Cary, and Treichler, Paula A. (eds) 1992: *Cultural Studies*. New York: Routledge.

Hamerow, Theodore S. 1991: Historical Scholarship and Practical Judgment. *Academic Questions*, 4, 4 (fall), 26–31.

—— 1992: *Curriculum vitae*. 4-page, unpublished document supplied by an anonymous source.

Hamilton, Wendy 1992: A Lone Duke English Professor Takes Her Stand (interview of Kenny J. Williams). *Campus*, 3, 3 (spring), 6–7.

Hammer, John 1989: Executive Director's Memorandum to Members, Washington DC: National Humanities Alliance, May 22. 10-page, unpublished document.

—— 1995: Executive Director's Memorandum to Members, Washington DC: National Humanities Alliance, April 25. 7-page, unpublished document.

Horner, Charles 1995: The People Are With Us. In Lawrence Jarvik, Herbert I. London, and James F. Cooper (eds), *The National Endowments: A Critical Symposium*, Los Angeles: Second Thought Books, 16–18.

Horowitz, David 1995: Funding the Left. In Lawrence Jarvik, Herbert I. London, and James F. Cooper (eds), *The National Endowments: A Critical Symposium*, Los Angeles: Second Thought Books, 47–52.

Iannone, Carol 1988: Thought Reform and Education: A View from the University of Pennsylvania (interview of Alan C. Kors). *Academic Questions*, 1, 4 (fall), 75–89.

—— 1991: Caste and Class in a University Town (interview of Kenny J. Williams). *Academic Questions*, 4, 2 (spring), 40–61.

In Box 1995: *Chronicle of Higher Education*, August 18, A15.

Innerst, Carol 1989: Conservative Professors Bash Academic Liberalism. *Washington Times*, October 30, A7.

—— 1990: College Guide to Rate Teaching, Ethics, Value. *Washington Times*, January 22, A5.

—— 1991: New Guide Rates GU, GWU as Free from "PC." *Washington Times*, July 15, A3.

—— 1992: NEH Chief Chides Activist Academics. *Washington Times*, September 28, A1, A8.

Intercollegiate Studies Institute n.d. a: *I. S. I. Leadership Guide*. Bryn Mawr, PA: Intercollegiate Studies Institute.

—— n.d. b: *Join the Battle of Ideas*. Bryn Mawr, PA: Intercollegiate Studies Institute.

—— n.d. c: *Speakers Guide*. Bryn Mawr, PA: Intercollegiate Studies Institute.

—— 1992: P. C. Foe Appointed to Humanities Post. *Campus*, 3, 2 (winter), 13.

—— 1995: Students Expose Yale's $20 Million Deception. *The Canon*, 2 (spring), 1, 4.

Jarvik, Lawrence, London, Herbert I., and Cooper, James F. (eds) 1995: *The National Endowments: A Critical Symposium*. Los Angeles: Second Thought Books.

Kagan, Donald 1990–91: Yale University: Testing the Limits. *Academic Questions*, 4, 1 (winter), 31–7.

Kors, Alan C. n.d.: *Curriculum vitae*. 6-page, unpublished document supplied by an anonymous source.

—— 1990: The Politicization of Extracurricular Life. *Academic Questions*, 3, 2 (spring), 36–40.

—— 1991: On Liberty and Learning. *Academic Questions*, 4, 3 (summer), 60–3.

Kristol, William 1995: Drive-by Debates. In Lawrence Jarvik, Herbert I. London, and James F. Cooper (eds), *The National Endowments: A Critical Symposium*, Los Angeles: Second Thought Books, 37–40.

Laclau, Ernesto and Mouffe, Chantal 1985: *Hegemony and Socialist Strategy*. London: Verso.

—— 1987: Post-Marxism without Apologies. *New Left Review*, 166 (November–December), 79–106.

Lenoir, Timothy 1993: The Discipline of Nature and the Nature of Disciplines. In Ellen Messer-Davidow, David R. Shumway, and David J. Sylvan (eds), *Knowledges: Historical and Critical Studies in Disciplinarity*, Charlottesville: University Press of Virginia, 70–102.

Lipman, Samuel 1995: The Real Problem is Private Patronage. In Lawrence Jarvik, Herbert I. London, and James F. Cooper (eds), *The National Endowments: A Critical Symposium*, Los Angeles: Second Thought Books, 88–90.

London, Herbert I. 1995: Introduction to the NEH. In Lawrence Jarvik, Herbert I. London, and James F. Cooper (eds), *The National Endowments: A Critical Symposium*, Los Angeles: Second Thought Books, 3–5.

Lukasik, Christopher 1991: Humanities Council Tilting Dangerously to the Right. *In These Times*, November 20–6, 16.

MacDonald, Heather 1995: Certain Paradoxes. In Lawrence Jarvik, Herbert I. London, and James F. Cooper (eds), *The National Endowments: A Critical Symposium*, Los Angeles: Second Thought Books, 19–22.

Madison Center for Educational Affairs 1991: *Annual Report of the Madison Center for Educational Affairs 1990*. Washington, DC: Madison Center for Educational Affairs.

—— 1992: *Annual Report of the Madison Center for Educational Affairs 1991*. Washington, DC: Madison Center for Educational Affairs.

Martin, Jerry L. 1993: The University as Agent of Social Transformation: The Postmodern Argument Considered. *Academic Questions*, 6, 3 (summer), 54–72.

Mercer, Joye 1995a: Lynne Cheney to Head New Alumni Group. *Chronicle of Higher Education*, March 24, A38.

—— 1995b: Alumni Activism. *Chronicle of Higher Education*, March 31, A29–30.

Messer-Davidow, Ellen 1991: Author's Fieldnotes at "On the State of Academic Discourse," Third General Conference, National Association of Scholars, Minneapolis, Minnesota, October 18–20.

—— 1992: Author's Fieldnotes at "Upper Midwest Leadership Conference," Intercollegiate Studies Institute, Minneapolis, Minnesota, October 10.

—— 1993: Manufacturing the Attack on Liberalized Higher Education. *Social Text*, 36 (fall), 40–80.

—— 1994: Who (Ac)Counts and How. *MMLA Journal*, 27, 1 (spring), 26–41.

—— forthcoming a: Dollars for Scholars: The Real Politics of Humanities Scholarship and Programs. In George Levine and E. Ann Kaplan (eds), *The Politics of Research*, New Brunswick: Rutgers University Press.

—— forthcoming b: *Disciplining Feminism: Episodes in the Discursive Production of Social Change*. Durham, NC: Duke University Press.

Muller, Johan and Taylor, Nick 1995: Schooling and Everyday Life: Knowledges Sacred and Profane. In Ellen Messer-Davidow and David R. Shumway (eds), "Knowledge (Ex)Change," special issue of *Social Epistemology*, 9 (July–September), 257–75.

Munson, Lynne A. 1991: The New Moral Education: A Northwestern Perspective. *Academic Questions* 4, 3 (summer), 64–7.

Murawski, John and Stehle, Vince 1995: House Panel Approves Bill to Tighten Limits on Lobbying and Litigation by Charities. *The Chronicle of Philanthropy*, August 10, 33, 36–7.

National Association of Scholars various: Names listed on letterhead, stationery from various times.

—— 1991a: N. A. S. Revenues – July 1–June 30, 1991. 1-page, unpublished document distributed by NAS at the 1991 conference.

—— 1991b: N. A. S. Revenues – July 1–June 30, 1992. 1-page, unpublished document distributed by NAS at the 1991 conference.

—— 1991c: 1991 Conference Registrants. List available at 1991 conference.

—— 1993a: The Nation's First Liberal Arts Accrediting Agency is Formed. *NAS Update*, 4, 1 (spring), 1.

—— 1993b: What Should a University Be? Fourth General Conference, San Francisco, April 16–18.

—— 1993c: Fourth General Conference Meets in San Francisco. *NAS Update*, 4, 2 (summer), 1, 4–5.

National Committee for Responsive Philanthropy 1995a: *Foundations in the Newt Era*. Washington, DC: National Committee for Responsive Philanthropy, September.

—— 1995b: Oppose the "Silence America Amendment," October.

National Endowment for the Humanities 1987–95: *Annual Report*. Washington, DC: National Endowment for the Humanities.

Nelson, Barbara J. 1984: *Making an Issue of Child Abuse*. Chicago: University of Chicago Press.

Newslink 1991: 6, 6 (February).

OMB Watch 1995a: Analysis of the Istook Nonprofit Gag Order. Circulated on the Internet, August 10.

—— 1995b: Title VI – Political Advocacy, Prohibition on the Use of Federal Funds for Political Advocacy. Text of the proposed Istook Amendment to the Labor, Health and Human Services, and Education Appropriations Bill, circulated on the Internet, August 14.

Olin Foundation 1991: *John M. Olin Foundation, Inc. 1990 Annual Report*. New York: Olin.

—— 1995: *John M. Olin Foundation, Inc. 1994 Annual Report*. New York: Olin.

Pickering, Andrew 1995: Cyborg History and the World War II Regime. *Perspectives on Science*, 3, 1–48.

Radice, Anne-Imelda 1995: What Can Be Done. In Lawrence Jarvik, Herbert I. London, and James F. Cooper (eds), *The National Endowments: A Critical Symposium*, Los Angeles: Second Thought Books, 66–70.

Raza, M. Ali n.d. a: Chronology of Events: Opposition to Race, Ethnicity, and Gender-based Preferences in Higher Education in California. 4-page, unpublished document; covers period 9/88 to 4/91.

—— n.d. b: Intellectual Evolution of the Policy Proposed to Challenge Race, Gender, and Ethnicity-based Preferences in California Higher Education System: Key Events. 3-page, unpublished document; covers period 7/91 to 9/94.

—— 1994: Letter to Colleagues. Sacramento, CA, January 24. With enclosure: Documents Submitted to the Attorney General in Support of our Position and the Principle of Non-discrimination (listing how California Association of Scholars leaders, State Senator Quentin L. Kopp, and the Pacific Legal Foundation were involved in anti-affirmative action lobbying).

Reidy, Chris 1992: Gay vs. Antigay: A Harvard Debate. *Boston Globe*, January 28, C25.

Ritter, Ann M. 1995: Membership Director's Letter to Faculty Associates. Bryn Mawr, PA: Intercollegiate Studies Institute, September 7.

Scott, W. Richard and Meyer, John W. 1991: The Organization of Societal Sectors: Propositions and Early Evidence. In Walter W. Powell and Paul J. DiMaggio (eds), *The New Institutionalism in Organizational Analysis*, Chicago: University of Chicago Press, 108–40.

Searle, John R. n.d.: *Curriculum vitae*. 22-page, unpublished document supplied by an anonymous source.

—— 1993–94: The Mission of the University: Intellectual Discovery or Social Transformation? *Academic Questions*, 7, 1 (winter), 80–5.

Segal, David 1992: Cheney's Command: A Report from the NEH Trenches. *Lingua Franca*, September–October, 58–63.

Shaw, Peter 1990: Making Sense of New Academic Disciplines. *Academic Questions*, 3, 3 (summer), 23–8.

—— 1991: Academic Marxism and Communism's Fall. *Academic Questions*, 4, 3 (summer), 48–53.

—— 1995: The Way the NEH Works. In Lawrence Jarvik, Herbert I. London, and James F. Cooper (eds), *The National Endowments: A Critical Symposium*, Los Angeles: Second Thought Books, 9–13.

Shumway, David R. and Messer-Davidow, Ellen 1991: Disciplinarity: An Introduction. *Poetics Today*, 12 (summer), 201–25.

Smith, Dorothy E. 1989: Sociological Theory: Methods of Writing Patriarchy. In Ruth A. Wallace (ed.), *Feminism and Sociological Theory*, Newbury Park, CA: Sage, 34–64.

Trueheart, Charles 1991: New Nominee for Humanities Panel Duke U's Kenny J. Williams Critical of Ethnic "Pork Barrel." *Washington Post*, November 15, Fl.

Turner, Frederick 1995: An Embattled Establishment. In Lawrence Jarvik, Herbert I. London, and James F. Cooper (eds), *The National Endowments: A Critical Symposium*, Los Angeles: Second Thought Books, 75–80.

Vobejda, Barbara 1988: "New Orthodoxy" on Campus Assailed; Conservative Academicians Fault Studies of Pop Culture. *Washington Post*, November 14, A3.

Williams, Kenny J. n.d.: *Curriculum vitae.* 6-page, unpublished document supplied by an anonymous source.

Winkler, Karen 1991: A Conservative Plans to "Sound the Guns" at NEH. *Chronicle of Higher Education*, October 16, A5.

Index

AEG -1960